1000 Recipe COOKBOOK

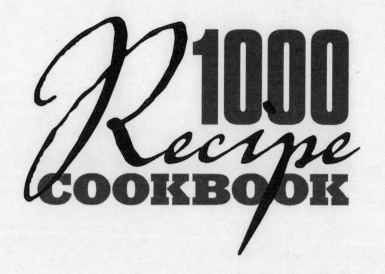

Capella

This edition published in 2008 by Arcturus Publishing Limited
26/27 Bickels Yard, 151–153 Bermondsey Street,
London SE1 3HA

In Canada published for Indigo Books
468 King St W, Suite 500,
Toronto, Ontario M5V 1L8

ISBN: 978-1-84193-998-8

Printed in the UK

Contents

Introduction 6

Soups 9
Starters and canapés 47
Salads 93
Eggs and cheese 121
Pasta, grains and pulses 133
Savoury pies and tarts 159
Casseroles and stews 181
Meat and game 257
Chicken and other poultry 331
Fish and seafood 405
Vegetables and vegetarian 479
Hot desserts and puddings 553
Cold desserts 601
Fruit desserts 641
Cakes and pastries 659
Biscuits and sweet treats 697
Dips, dressings, sauces and stocks 717

Conversion tables 733
Index 736

Introduction

Whatever type of food you are passionate about, whether you need to plan menus for feeding a large family, three courses for an elegant dinner party or a romantic meal for two, this selection of 1000 fabulous recipes is sure to inspire you for each and every occasion.

Many of the recipes included in the book are considered classics, and theyt have become so partly because they have proven so popular over the years. Often when we go to a restaurant, we instinctively order those dishes that we know we have enjoyed time and again. But likely as not, going out to a restaurant to treat yourself to these favourites is not something you can either afford or want to do every day. So this book contains dozens of these classic recipes for you to make and enjoy at home.

The 1000 recipes featured here offer you a veritable treasure trove of dishes from which to choose, representing cuisines from all around the world. You will find traditional British, French, Italian, Spanish, Mexican, Caribbean, Moroccan, Indian, Chinese, Thai and Japanese recipes, to name but a few. All the essentials are there: roast beef and Yorkshire pudding from Britain, coq au vin from France, paella and gazpacho from Spain, lasagne and spaghetti bolognese from Italy, chicken chow mein from China and chicken korma from India.

But you will also find hundreds of more unusual recipes. They might be innovative variations on a familiar dish, such as turkey and spinach Lasagna; use ingredients that you have not used before, such as quail's eggs, guinea fowl or okra; or may offer a really surprising combination of ingredients, such as cod with mango.

Virtually every cooking method ever invented is utilized in these 1000 recipes. There are the ones we use every day, such as grilling, frying and baking, but you will find also poaching, braising and stewing. Even those techniques traditionally regarded as a bit trickier, such as those required to make pastries, soufflés and mousses, have been made straightforward and accessible by the simple and easy-to-follow recipe instructions, and the majority of recipes in the book require minimal preparation.

Nowadays more and more of us are concerned about eating a healthy and balanced diet, and for this reason we have included a wide range of specifically lower-calorie recipes throughout all the chapters in the book.

The recipes as a whole have been organized into 17 chapters to help you find exactly what you are looking for. The Soups chapter will impress you with the range and variety of recipes. There are hearty soups such as minestrone and Scotch broth, which, when served with warm crusty bread, can be a main meal in their own right. There are chilled soups perfect for a summer afternoon, and numerous others using meat, fish and vegetable ingredients that make ideal starters for dinner parties.

The Starters and Canapés chapter offers everything from salads, tarts and breads to fritters and pâtés, offering a range of options for meat eaters, fish lovers and vegetarians alike. The Salads chapter that follows shows that a salad is a lot more than just a bunch of green leaves! Here you will find light, refreshing salads, salads that make ideal accompaniments to main courses, or even salads that are substantial enough to form a complete meal.

The two chapters on Eggs and Cheese and Pasta, Grains and Pulses demonstrate the variety of taste sensations that can be achieved using these apparently simple ingredients. And of course, eggs, cheese, pasta and rice are used in recipes in other chapters as well. Savoury Pies and Tarts are given a chapter all to themselves so that you can feel confident working with pastry, to make pies, flans and quiches. The recipes chosen in these chapters offer you great versatility, as many can be used as either starters or main courses, depending on your needs.

There are no fewer than five chapters devoted to main courses, and the first of these offers you mouth-watering stews and casseroles. Casseroles are enjoying a great resurgence in popularity as we rediscover the virtues of slow cooking and of cooking a complete meal in one pot. They require minimal preparation and you simply cook them in the oven or on the hob. Perfect for family and everyday meals, some are also sophisticated enough to serve at dinner parties or more formal occasions.

More often than not meat is the choice for any main course, whether intended for a weekday dinner or special occasion. When planning a dinner menu, you need to choose the right meat to complement the other courses and the wine, if any, you intend to serve. All the beef recipes are therefore grouped together, as are all the pork recipes, lamb recipes and so on. There are also some tasty recipes to make with venison and other game meat if you are feeling more adventurous.

The Chicken and Other Poultry chapter offers numerous imaginative ways to serve chicken – it is such a versatile meat which can be combined with any number of other ingredients. 'Poultry' does not simply mean chicken, however, as all the recipes using turkey, duck, poussin, guinea fowl and goose testify.

There are more types of fish than there are meat and poultry put together, so the chapter on Fish and Seafood will open your eyes to this great diversity and help you to expand your recipe repertoire. Similarly the Vegetables and Vegetarian chapter will surprise you with the huge range of delicious meals that are nourishing enough to appeal to the taste buds of even the most die-hard meat lover, while delighting all your vegetarian guests.

Dessert is often the course of a meal to which people look forward most. To help you plan your menus, we have dedicated three chapters to this finale: Hot Desserts and Puddings, Cold Desserts and Fruit Desserts. Choose from substantial hot sponge puddings, refreshing ice creams, sorbets, rich and creamy mousses and succulent fruit tarts and jellies. And not to forget all those other times when you want a snack or treat, we've included a chapter dedicated to biscuits and other sweet nibbles.

To supplement all the other recipes in the book, the last chapter offers you recipes for dips which can be served with crudités at parties; basic stocks and sauces, which you will find useful for all sorts of soups, casseroles and main courses; and dressings to accompany the salads.

Whatever the occasion and the taste preferences of your family and guests, you are bound to find recipes here to set your taste buds alight and your mouth watering for many years to come.

Soups

Soups are wonderfully versatile and can be made to appeal to a wide range of tastes and occasions. Vegetables, meat, poultry and seafood – all are used as ingredients for both light and heartier soups, which can be served either as starters or as meals in their own right. This chapter contains chilled soups such as vichysoisse and the Spanish classic gazpacho, traditional soups such as French onion and mulligatawny, and more unusual offerings such as Red Onion and Beetroot, and Curried Carrot and Apple.

Almond soup

serves 4

ingredients

225g/8oz blanched almonds,
    minced
3 egg yolks, hard-boiled
1.2 litres/2pt chicken stock
25g/1oz butter, softened
25g/1oz plain flour
125ml/4fl oz single cream
salt and freshly ground
    black pepper

- Using a mortar and pestle, reduce the almonds to a paste with the egg yolks and 1 tablespoon of the stock. Set aside.
- Make a beurre manié by working the butter and flour together into a smooth paste using a fork. Bring the remaining stock to a simmer in a heavy saucepan. Add the beurre manié in small knobs, whisking vigorously after each addition until completely dissolved. Whisk in the almond paste until smooth, then cook gently for 30 minutes.
- Strain the soup through a sieve into a clean pan. Add the cream, and season with salt and pepper. Reheat gently and serve.

● ●

Jerusalem artichoke soup

serves 4

ingredients

1 onion, sliced
50g/2oz butter
700g/1½lb Jerusalem artichokes,
    peeled and sliced
600ml/1pt milk
salt and ground white pepper

- In a heavy saucepan over a low heat, gently sweat the onion in the butter until soft and translucent.
- Add the artichokes to the onion. Cook, covered, for 10 minutes, stirring a few times.
- Add 600ml/1pint water and the milk. Season with salt and pepper to taste, and simmer slowly – do not boil or the milk may curdle.
- Purée the soup using a blender or food processor. Taste and add more seasoning if needed. Reheat gently and serve.

Chilled avocado soup

serves 4

ingredients

2 ripe avocados
600ml/1pt chicken stock
2 tablespoons lemon juice
2 tablespoons chopped fresh chives
½ teaspoon chilli powder
salt
2 tablespoons sour cream, to serve

- Peel and stone the avocado. Blend or process the flesh into a purée. Add the remaining ingredients, except the sour cream, and blend until smooth. Allow to chill for a few hours before serving.
- To serve, add the sour cream, stir through and serve the soup chilled.

Bacon & split pea soup

serves 4

ingredients

50g/2oz dried split peas
25g/1oz butter
1 garlic clove, finely chopped
1 onion, thinly sliced
175g/6oz long-grain rice
2 tablespoons tomato purée

1.2 litres/2pt vegetable stock
175g/6oz carrots, diced
2 tablespoons chopped fresh
   flat-leaf parsley
4 tablespoons single cream
100g/4oz streaky bacon rashers
salt and ground black pepper

- Cover the split peas with plenty of cold water, cover loosely and leave to soak for at least 12 hours.
- Melt the butter in a heavy saucepan over a medium heat, add the garlic and onion, and cook for 2–3 minutes until soft but not coloured. Add the rice, drained soaked split peas and tomato purée, and cook for a further 2–3 minutes, stirring constantly to prevent sticking. Add the stock, bring to the boil, then reduce the heat and simmer for 20–25 minutes until the rice and peas are tender. Remove from the heat and allow to cool.
- Blend three-quarters of the soup in a blender or food processor to form a smooth purée. Pour into the remaining soup in the saucepan. Add the carrots and cook for a further 10–12 minutes until the carrots are tender.
- Stir in the parsley and single cream. Keep warm.
- Finely chop the bacon and put in a frying pan over a gentle heat. Sauté until the bacon is crisp. Remove and drain on kitchen paper. Sprinkle over the soup, and season well with salt and pepper. Serve immediately.

Borscht

serves 6

ingredients

900g/2lb large raw beetroot
225g/8oz onion, diced
225g/8oz leeks, sliced
2 celery sticks, chopped
50g/2oz butter
600ml/1pt chicken stock
1 bay leaf
150ml/5fl oz soured cream
salt and freshly ground
    black pepper

- Boil the beetroot whole in salted water for 15 minutes. Drain and refresh in cold water. Peel and cut into 2.5cm/1in chunks.
- In a frying pan, gently sweat the onion, leek and celery in the butter until softened. Add the beetroot, stock and bay leaf. Bring to the boil, skim the surface, reduce the heat and simmer for 45 minutes.
- Discard the bay leaf, and purée the soup in a blender or food processor. Return to a clean pan, season and bring back to the simmer. Remove from the heat, stir in the sour cream and serve.

Boston bean soup

serves 4

ingredients

850g/1¾lb canned cooked pinto
    beans, drained
2 tomatoes, chopped
1 celery stick, sliced
1 medium onion, chopped
1 bay leaf
450ml/¾pt beef stock
salt and freshly ground
    black pepper

- Put the beans, tomatoes, celery, onion, bay leaf and stock in a medium saucepan. Cover the pan, and bring the mixture to the boil over a medium-high heat.
- Reduce the heat and simmer for about 20 minutes until the vegetables are quite soft. Leave the soup to sit, uncovered, for a further 20 minutes. Remove the bay leaf.
- Pureé half the soup in a blender or food processor. Mix into the remaining soup. Season to taste with salt and pepper, and serve.

Carrot & coriander soup

serves 6

ingredients

175g/6oz onion, diced
50g/2oz butter
500g/1lb 2oz carrots, sliced
1 garlic clove, finely chopped
1.2 litres/2pt vegetable stock
2 teaspoons caster sugar
150ml/5fl oz whipping cream
2 tablespoons chopped fresh
   coriander leaves
salt and freshly ground
   black pepper

• In a heavy saucepan, gently sweat the onion in the butter until soft and translucent. Add the carrots to the pan, and cook, stirring from time to time, for a further 5 minutes.

• Add the garlic and stock. Season with salt and pepper and the sugar. Bring to the boil, reduce the heat and simmer for 30 minutes.

• Pour the contents of the pan into a blender or food processor, and blitz to a purée. Pour back into a clean pan, and add the cream and coriander. Taste and adjust the seasoning, then heat the soup through gently, stirring. Serve hot.

Catalan soup

serves 6

ingredients

1 tablespoon vegetable oil
900g/2lb beef mince
2 carrots, chopped
2 onions, chopped
2 tomatoes, chopped
25g/1oz plain flour
1.2 litres/2pt hot vegetable stock

• Heat the oil in a flameproof casserole dish over a medium heat. Sauté the beef until it is just cooked, then remove and keep to one side. Sauté the carrots, onions and tomatoes in the same pan for a few minutes, stirring continuously to prevent sticking.

• Blend in the flour using a wooden spoon, and cook for a few more minutes. Return the cooked mince to the casserole.

• Cover the mixture with the hot stock, and simmer the soup gently for about 45 minutes. Serve hot.

Cauliflower & walnut soup

serves 4

ingredients

1 medium cauliflower, broken
   into florets
1 onion, roughly chopped
450ml/¾pt vegetable stock
450ml/¾pt milk
25g/1oz walnut pieces
salt and freshly ground
   black pepper

- Put the cauliflower, onion and stock in a large heavy saucepan. Bring to the boil, cover and simmer for about 15 minutes until soft.
- Add the milk and walnuts, and stir through. Purée in a blender or food processor until smooth.
- Return the soup to the pan. Season to taste with salt and pepper, then bring to the boil – be careful not to scorch. Serve hot.

Celery & Stilton soup

serves 4

ingredients

4 celery sticks, finely chopped
1 onion, finely chopped
50g/2oz butter
45g/1½oz plain flour
½ glass white wine
900ml/1½pt chicken stock
300ml/10fl oz milk
225g/8oz crumbled Stilton
   cheese
salt and freshly ground
   black pepper

- In a heavy saucepan over a low heat, gently sweat the celery and onion in butter until soft. Add the flour and remove from the heat.
- Pour in the wine and stock, stirring continuously. Return to the heat and slowly bring to the boil, stirring until the mixture thickens. Simmer for 25 minutes.
- Add the milk, simmer for a further 2 minutes and remove from the heat. Whisk in the Stilton.
- Purée the soup in a blender or food processor, then push through a sieve into a clean pan. Season with salt and pepper.
- Reheat gently and serve.

Chicken soup

serves 4

ingredients

1 roast chicken carcass with
  meat left on
225g/8oz chicken wings
1 onion, diced
1 leek, diced
1 parsnip, diced
6 whole black peppercorns

- Preheat the oven to 150°C/300°F/ Gas mark 2. Put in a large heavy saucepan with the chicken wings.
- Add the onion, leek and parsnip, and bring to the boil. While the water is heating, add the whole peppercorns.
- Once the stock has boiled, transfer to an ovenproof dish and cook in the oven for 2 hours. Skim off any scum from the surface using a slotted spoon, and strain the stock you have created. Discard everything except for the chicken.
- When cool enough to handle, take out the carcass and shred the chicken before returning it to the stock. Serve hot.

Chicken noodle soup

serves 6

ingredients

900ml/1½pt chicken stock
1 bay leaf
4 spring onions, sliced
225g/8oz button mushrooms,
  sliced
100g/4oz cooked skinless
  chicken breast, thinly sliced
50g/2oz soup pasta such as
  orzo or ditalini
150ml/5fl oz dry white wine
1 tablespoon chopped fresh
  flat-leaf parsley
salt and ground black pepper

- Put the stock and bay leaf into a heavy pan, and bring to the boil. Add the spring onions and mushrooms to the simmering stock.
- Add the chicken to the soup, and season with salt and pepper. Heat through for 2–3 minutes.
- Add the pasta, cover and simmer for 7–8 minutes.
- Just before serving, add the wine and parsley, heat the soup through for 2–3 minutes, then check the seasoning and adjust if necessary. Serve hot.

Clam chowder

serves 6

ingredients

8 celery sticks, chopped
700g/1½lb onions, chopped
1.8kg/4lb red potatoes, diced
900g/2lb canned clams
with juice
3 teaspoons dried thyme
1 teaspoon dried oregano
2 teaspoons dried basil
225ml/8fl oz fish bouillon
2 teaspoons ground white pepper
225g/8oz butter
250g/9oz plain flour
3 garlic cloves, finely chopped
1.2 litres/2pt milk

- Put the celery, onions, potatoes, clams, thyme, oregano, basil, bouillon and pepper in a large heavy saucepan. Gently cook for 30–45 minutes until the vegetables and potatoes are soft.
- To make a roux, melt the butter in a small heavy pan, add the flour and garlic, and stir constantly with a wooden spoon for a few minutes until slightly brown.
- Combine the roux with the vegetable mixture and add the milk. Stir well and cook for 10 minutes. Serve hot.

Cock-a-leekie

serves 6

ingredients

450g/1lb prunes, stoned
1.3kg/3lb boiling chicken
2.4 litres/4pt chicken stock

900g/2lb leeks, well rinsed
1 bouquet garni
salt and ground black pepper

- Put the prunes in a bowl, cover with cold water and soak overnight.
- Set the chicken, breast-side down, in a large casserole dish. Pour in the stock and bring to the boil, skimming off any scum from the surface.
- Using string, tie half the leeks in a bundle; thinly slice the remainder. Add the bundle of leeks to the casserole dish with the bouquet garni and a pinch of salt. Reduce the heat, part-cover and simmer for 2 hours.
- Lift out the chicken and keep to one side to cool slightly. Remove and discard the bundle of leeks and bouquet garni. Drain the prunes, add them to the casserole dish and simmer for 20 minutes.
- Shred the meat from the cooled chicken, discarding any skin and bones, and add the meat to the soup. Season to taste with salt and pepper, then add the sliced leeks. Simmer for a further 10 minutes, then serve.

Courgette & spinach soup

serves 4

ingredients

2 tablespoons vegetable oil
1 onion, chopped
2 courgettes, chopped
1 potato, chopped
100g/4oz spinach, chopped
3 sprigs of fresh flat-leaf parsley
1.2 litres/2pt vegetable stock
150ml/5fl oz double cream
salt and freshly ground
    black pepper

- Heat the oil in a saucepan, and sweat the onion and courgette until the onion is transparent.
- Add the potato, spinach, parsley and stock. Bring to the boil, reduce the heat and simmer the soup for 20 minutes. Allow to cool before blending or processing to a purée.
- Return the soup to a clean pan, stir in the cream and season with salt and pepper. Reheat gently without boiling and serve.

Hot & sour soup

serves 4–6

ingredients

8 dried shiitake mushrooms
25g/1oz cornflour
3 tablespoons dry sherry
100g/4oz pork loin
1.2 litres/2pt chicken stock
50g/2oz bamboo shoots, sliced

1 tablespoon light soy sauce
2 tablespoons red wine vinegar
1 egg, lightly beaten
225g/8oz tofu, diced
salt and freshly ground
    black pepper

- In a medium bowl, soak the mushrooms in warm water for 20 minutes, then drain, squeeze out any excess moisture and cut into 1cm/½in slices.
- In a small dish, stir the cornflour into the sherry and set aside.
- Put the pork loin in a large heavy pan and completely cover with water. Simmer until tender, then cool and shred.
- Bring the stock to the boil. Stir in the pork, mushrooms and bamboo shoots. Simmer for 10 minutes, then stir in the soy sauce and red wine vinegar. Season with salt and pepper, then stir in the reserved cornflour mixture. Keep stirring until the soup has thickened.
- Remove from the heat and whisk in the egg. Mix in the tofu and heat through. Serve the soup hot.

Fish chowder

serves 10

ingredients

3 tablespoons olive oil
200g/7oz onion, finely chopped
200g/7oz celery, finely chopped
150g/5oz carrot, finely chopped
400g/14oz canned chopped
   tomatoes
1 teaspoon finely chopped garlic
100g/4oz plain flour
½ teaspoon ground cinnamon

½ teaspoon dried marjoram
½ teaspoon dried oregano
2.4 litres/4pt fish stock
200g/7oz cooked boneless cod
   fillets, flaked
25ml/1fl oz dark rum
25ml/1fl oz Worcestershire sauce
1 tablespoon Tabasco sauce
salt and ground black pepper

- Heat the olive oil in a heavy saucepan over a medium heat. Sweat the vegetables, tomatoes and garlic for 5 minutes, stirring continuously.
- Add the flour, cinnamon and herbs, and continue to cook for a further 2 minutes. Add the stock and bring to the boil, then crumble the fish into the pan with the rum, Worcestershire sauce and Tabasco. Simmer for 1 hour, stirring occasionally.
- Season with salt and pepper, and serve hot.

• •

French bean soup

serves 4

ingredients

1 tablespoon olive oil
1 onion, chopped
2 celery sticks, thinly sliced
3 garlic cloves, minced
550g/1lb 4oz canned cooked
   cannellini beans, drained
400ml/14fl oz vegetable stock
125ml/4fl oz white wine
3 sprigs of fresh rosemary
¼ teaspoon ground white pepper
100g/4oz mozzarella cheese,
   grated

- Heat the oil in a large saucepan over a medium-high heat. Add the onion, celery and garlic, and sweat for 5 minutes until soft, stirring frequently.
- Add the remaining ingredients except the cheese, and bring the mixture to the boil. Reduce the heat and cover the pan, then simmer for 10–15 minutes.
- To serve, remove and discard the rosemary sprigs. Ladle the soup into warm bowls, and top each serving with a little of the cheese.

French onion soup

serves 6

ingredients

900g/2lb onions, thinly sliced
50g/2oz butter
900ml/1½pt vegetable stock
salt and freshly ground
     black pepper

- Fry the onions very gently in the butter in a covered saucepan for 15 minutes until soft and starting to caramelize. Remove the lid, increase the heat and fry, stirring, for about 20 minutes until the onions are a rich golden brown.
- Add the stock and bring to the boil. Reduce the heat, part-cover and simmer for 15 minutes. Season with salt and pepper, and serve.

Gazpacho

serves 6

ingredients

2 large garlic cloves
1 egg yolk
1 thick slice bread, crust
     removed
90ml/3fl oz olive oil
450g/1lb canned whole peeled
     plum tomatoes
900g/2lb ripe tomatoes,
     deseeded and chopped
1 large onion, choped
1 cucumber, peeled and
     chopped
2 red peppers, seeded and
     chopped
1 tablespoon tomato purée
sea salt and freshly ground
     black pepper
2 lemons, cut into wedges,
     to serve

- Put the garlic, egg yolk and bread in a blender or food processor. With the motor running, slowly add the oil in a thin steady stream until the mixture turns to mayonnaise.
- Add the chopped tomatoes, onion, cucumber, peppers and tomato purée in batches, and continue blending until smooth.
- Season with salt and pepper to taste, and chill in the refrigerator until ready to serve.
- Just before serving, check the seasoning and adjust if necessary. Serve cold with lemon wedges for squeezing over.

Chilled cucumber soup
serves 6–8

ingredients

1 onion, diced
50g/2oz butter
550g/1lb 4oz cucumber, diced
1.8 litres/3pt vegetable stock
2 tablespoons chopped fresh
 parsley
juice of ½ lemon
600ml/1pt single cream
salt and freshly ground
 black pepper

- In a heavy saucepan, gently sweat the onion in the butter until soft and translucent, but not coloured. Add the cucumber and continue to cook gently for a further 5 minutes.
- Pour in the stock and bring to the boil. Reduce the heat, season with salt and pepper, and simmer for 5 minutes. Add the parsley and lemon juice, and continue to cook for a further 5 minutes.
- Blend or process the soup to a purée. Allow to cool, then transfer to the refrigerator to chill.
- When ready to serve, whisk in the single cream. Serve chilled.

Leek & potato soup
serves 4

ingredients

50g/2oz butter
450g/1lb leeks, trimmed and
 finely sliced
700g/1½lb potatoes, roughly
 chopped
900ml/1½pt vegetable stock

4 sprigs of fresh rosemary
450ml/¾pt milk
2 tablespoons chopped fresh
 flat-leaf parsley
2 tablespoons crème fraîche
salt and ground black pepper

- Melt the butter in a large saucepan, add the leeks and sweat gently for 5 minutes, stirring frequently. Add the potatoes, stock, rosemary and milk. Bring to the boil, then reduce the heat, cover and simmer gently for 20–25 minutes until the vegetables are tender. Remove from the heat.
- Cool for 10 minutes. Discard the rosemary, then pour into a blender or food processor, and purée until smooth. Return to a clean pan, and stir in the parsley and crème fraîche. Season to taste. Reheat gently and serve.

Beef & lentil soup
serves 8

ingredients

300g/11oz dried red lentils,
  picked and rinsed
225g/8oz stewing beef, cubed
1 leek, finely chopped
3 large carrots, finely chopped

2 celery sticks, finely chopped
1 tablespoon vegetable oil
2 onions, finely chopped
2 tablespoons plain flour
50ml/2fl oz dry white wine

- Bring 1.8 litres/3pt water to the boil in a large heavy saucepan. Add the lentils, beef, leek, carrots and celery. Return to the boil, then reduce the heat, cover the pan and simmer for 40 minutes.
- Remove the beef, drain on kitchen paper and brown in the oil in a frying pan over a high heat. When the pan is very hot, add the onions and sauté for 15 minutes, stirring frequently. Sprinkle the flour over the onions and stir with a wooden spoon until the flour browns.
- Pour 225ml/8fl oz of the lentil mixture over the onions and stir vigorously. Add the white wine; cook for a further 1 minute. Tip the contents of the frying pan into the lentil mixture. Simmer for 30 minutes before serving.

Lettuce soup
serves 6

ingredients

600ml/1pt chicken stock
1 round lettuce, shredded
1 small onion, chopped
25g/1oz butter
½ teaspoon freshly grated nutmeg

300ml/10fl oz milk
1 egg yolk
2 tablespoons single cream
salt and freshly ground
  black pepper

- Bring the stock to the boil, add the lettuce and boil for 5 minutes. In a separate pan, sweat the onion in the butter for 3 minutes until soft.
- Pour in the lettuce and stock, and season with the nutmeg, salt and pepper. Simmer for 5 minutes until the onion is very soft. Purée in a blender or food processor, and return to the saucepan. Stir in the milk.
- Whisk the egg yolk and cream together. Whisk in a little of the soup, then pour back into the remaining soup and heat through, stirring all the while. Do not allow to boil or the egg will curdle. Serve hot.

Lobster bisque
serves 4

ingredients
700g/1½lb lobster
100g/4oz butter
50g/2oz carrots, diced
1 small onion, chopped
½ bay leaf
pinch of thyme
2 sprigs of fresh flat-leaf parsley
3 tablespoons Cognac
75ml/3fl oz dry white wine
125ml/4fl oz fish stock
50g/2oz plain flour
350ml/12fl oz boiling milk
3 tablespoons double cream
salt and freshly ground black pepper

- Crack the lobster claws and cut the body and tail into four or five pieces. Set aside.
- Sauté the carrots and onion in 25g/1oz of the butter for 5 minutes. Add the bay leaf, thyme, parsley and lobster, and cook for about 5 minutes until the lobster turns red. Add 2 tablespoons of the Cognac and ignite.
- When the flames die down, add the wine and stock, and simmer for 20 minutes.
- Remove the meat from the lobster, reserving the shells and broth.
- Melt the remaining butter in a saucepan. Add the flour and cook, stirring constantly, for 2 minutes to make a roux. Gradually add the boiling milk, whisking or stirring with a wooden spoon until smooth.
- Crush the lobster shells and add to the sauce. Add the reserved broth with the vegetables and simmer, covered, for 1 hour. Strain through a sieve into a clean pan. Bring to the boil and stir in the cream.
- To serve, add the lobster meat and the remaining Cognac. Season with salt and pepper, and serve hot.

Minestrone
serves 4–6

ingredients

100g/4oz carrot, chopped
100g/4oz celery, chopped
100g/4oz onion, chopped
2 garlic cloves, minced
1 tablespoon chopped
    fresh basil
1 tablespoon chopped
    fresh oregano
½ teaspoon ground pepper
425g/15oz canned cooked red
    kidney beans, drained
400g/14oz canned chopped
    tomatoes
150g/5oz cabbage, coarsely
    chopped
1 courgette, chopped
75g/3oz soup pasta such as
    orzo or ditalini

- Pour 900ml/1½pt water into a large heavy saucepan. Add the carrot, celery, onion, garlic, basil, oregano and pepper.
- Bring to the boil, then reduce the heat. Cover the pan, and simmer the mixture for 15 minutes.
- Add the kidney beans to the pan with the tomatoes, cabbage, courgette and pasta. Return to the boil and reduce the heat. Cover the pan and simmer for 5–10 minutes until the pasta is cooked until al dente. Serve hot.

Mushroom soup
serves 4

ingredients

350g/12oz mushrooms, finely
    chopped
50g/2oz butter
3 tablespoons chopped fresh
    flat-leaf parsley
2 tablespoons fresh breadcrumbs
    (without any crust)
½ garlic clove
900ml /1½ pt chicken stock
pinch of freshly grated nutmeg
2 tablespoons double cream
salt and ground black pepper

- Sauté the mushroom with the butter in a heavy saucepan for a few minutes. Add the parsley and cook, stirring, until soft.
- Add the breadcrumbs and garlic, stir and pour in the chicken stock with a pinch of nutmeg. Season with salt and pepper. Bring to the boil and simmer for 15 minutes.
- Purée the soup in a food processor or blender until smooth. Return to a clean pan, stir in the cream and reheat gently. Serve hot.

23

Mulligatawny
serves 12

ingredients

1 garlic clove, minced
¼ teaspoon ground cumin
6 cloves, finely crushed
1 tablespoon curry powder
¼ teaspoon ground ginger
50g/2oz butter
1 roasting chicken, cut into serving pieces
3 celery sticks, thinly sliced
2 large onions, chopped
2 carrots, diced
1 leek, white part only, thinly sliced
2.4 litres/4pt chicken stock
salt and freshly ground black pepper
200g/7oz long-grain rice
2 dessert apples, peeled, cored and diced
225ml/8fl oz plain yogurt
2 tablespoons lemon juice
150ml/5fl oz whipping cream, gently warmed

- Combine the garlic and spices. Melt the butter in a large heavy frying pan over a medium-high heat. Add the chicken and sauté until lightly browned on all sides. Transfer the chicken to a casserole dish.
- Drain all but 1 tablespoon of the fat from the frying pan. Add the celery, onion, carrot, leek and spice mixture, and blend well until the spices are aromatic. Add a small ladle of stock and cook over a low heat, stirring constantly, until the vegetables are tender. Add to the chicken.
- Stir the remaining stock into the casserole dish, and season with salt and pepper. Cover and simmer for 30 minutes.
- Remove the chicken with a slotted spoon and set aside. Add the rice to the soup and continue cooking for a further 15 minutes.
- When the chicken is cool enough to handle, cut into bite-sized pieces, discarding the skin and bones. Return the chicken to the soup. Peel, core and dice the apples, and blend into the soup with the yogurt. Simmer for 10 minutes.
- Stir in the lemon juice, then blend in the cream. Taste and adjust the seasoning if necessary. Serve hot.

Oxtail soup

serves 2

ingredients

25g/1oz beef dripping
2 oxtails
1 large onion, diced
1 carrot, diced
2 celery sticks
2 sprigs of fresh flat-leaf parsley
1 bay leaf
2 tablespoons pearl barley
1 tablespoon plain flour mixed
   with 2 tablespoons water
salt and freshly ground
   black pepper

- Melt the dripping in a heavy saucepan. Fry the oxtails, onion and carrot until brown, then add 1.2 litres/2pt water.
- Tie the celery, parsley and bay leaf together, and add to the soup.
- Bring to the boil, add the pearl barley and simmer for 4 hours, skimming off any scum that rises to the surface.
- Remove the large bones and celery, parsley and bay leaf, then thicken the soup with the flour paste, stirring all the while.
- Season with salt and pepper, and serve hot.

Oyster soup

serves 4

ingredients

50g/2oz butter
50g/2oz plain flour
900ml/1½pt fish stock
12 large oysters, shucked and
   quartered
2 tablespoons finely chopped
   fresh flat-leaf parsley
1 lemon, cut into wedges,
   to serve

- Heat the butter and, using a wooden spoon, stir in the flour and cook for 2 minutes. Stir in the stock slowly, until smooth and thick.
- Put the oysters in the stock and simmer for no more than 3 minutes.
- Sprinkle the soup with the parsley and serve with lemon wedges.

Chilled pea soup
serves 5

ingredients

1 large fennel bulb, coarsely
  chopped
275g/10oz frozen peas, thawed
75ml/3fl oz double cream
1 teaspoon lemon liqueur such as
  lemon schnapps or limoncello
1 teaspoon chopped spring onion
salt and freshly ground
  black pepper
1 tablespoon chopped fresh mint,
  to garnish

- Put the fennel and 1.2 litres/2pt water in a large pan over a medium-high heat, and simmer for 10 minutes. Strain the fennel broth and discard the solids.
- Purée the peas, cream, liqueur and spring onions in a blender or food processor. Season with salt and pepper, then add the broth and blend until smooth.
- Strain the soup through a sieve into a metal bowl. Set in a larger bowl, and fill the outer bowl with iced water to reach halfway up side of the inner bowl. Stir until the soup is cold. Serve garnished with mint.

Pea & mint soup
serves 6

ingredients

450g/1lb frozen peas
900ml/1½pt vegetable stock
pinch of granulated sugar
1 large sprig of fresh mint
1 egg yolk
50ml/2fl oz single cream
salt and freshly ground
  black pepper

- Put the peas in a large pan with the stock, sugar, mint and a little salt and pepper. Bring to the boil, reduce the heat, cover and simmer for 15 minutes.
- Discard the mint, then purée the mixture in a blender or food processor. Return to the heat.
- Blend the egg yolk with half the cream and stir into the soup. Return the soup to a clean pan and reheat, but do not allow to boil.
- Taste and adjust the seasoning if necessary. Serve garnished with the remaining cream.

Potato soup
serves 6

ingredients
8 rashers back bacon
200g/7oz onion, chopped
450g/1lb potatoes, cubed
275g/10oz canned condensed
  chicken soup
600ml/1pt milk
1 teaspoon dried dill
salt and freshly ground
  black pepper

- In a large saucepan, sauté the bacon until crisp. Remove and drain on kitchen paper. Sauté the onions in the bacon fat over a medium heat until soft and golden.
- Add the potatoes and enough water to cover. Cover the pan, and cook for 15–20 minutes until the potatoes are tender.
- Stir together the condensed soup and milk until smooth, and add to potato mixture. Heat but do not allow to boil. Season with salt and pepper to taste, and stir in the dill.
- Crumble the bacon and sprinkle on top to garnish. Serve hot.

• •

Pumpkin soup
serves 4

ingredients
900ml/1½pt milk
500g/1lb 2oz pumpkin, peeled,
  deseeded and cubed
1 teaspoon ground nutmeg
300ml/10fl oz single cream
salt and freshly ground
  black pepper
extra virgin olive oil for drizzling

- Put milk and pumpkin in a heavy saucepan. Add the nutmeg, and season with salt and pepper. Bring to the boil. Reduce the heat and simmer until the pumpkin is tender.
- Using a food processor or hand-held blender, purée until smooth.
- Return to a clean pan, and stir in the cream. Check the seasoning and adjust if necessary, then gently reheat the soup.
- Serve hot, garnished with a drizzle of extra virgin olive oil.

Red pepper soup
serves 6

ingredients

4 red peppers
4 tomatoes
50ml/2fl oz vegetable oil
½ teaspoon dried marjoram
½ teaspoon dried mixed herbs
2 garlic cloves, crushed
1 teaspoon mild curry paste
1 red onion, sliced
1 leek, white part only, sliced
1 teaspoon sweet chilli sauce
salt and freshly ground
   black pepper

- Cut the peppers into quarters. Remove the seeds and membrane. Grill until the skin blackens and blisters. Place on a cutting board, cover with a tea towel and allow to cool before removing and discarding the skin.
- Mark a small cross on the top of each tomato. Put in a bowl and cover with boiling water for about 2 minutes. Drain and cool. Skin, halve and remove the seeds.
- Heat the oil in a large heavy pan over a low heat, and add the marjoram, mixed herbs, garlic and curry paste. Stir for 1 minute until aromatic, then add the onion and leek. Cook for a further 3 minutes. Add the cabbage, tomatoes, peppers and 1.2 litres/2pt water. Bring to the boil, reduce the heat and simmer for 20 minutes.
- Allow the soup to cool slightly, then purée in a blender or food processor for 30 seconds or until smooth. Return to the pan and reheat gently. Stir in the chilli sauce, and season with salt and pepper. Serve hot.

Scotch broth
serves 6–8

ingredients

900g/2lb neck of lamb, cubed
1 large onion, chopped
50g/2oz pearl barley
1 bouquet garni
1 large carrot, chopped

1 turnip, chopped
3 leeks, chopped
½ small white cabbage, shredded
salt and freshly ground
    black pepper

- Put the lamb and 1.8 litres/3pt water in a large heavy saucepan, and bring to the boil. Skim off any scum from the surface, then stir in the onion, pearl barley and bouquet garni. Bring the soup back to the boil, part-cover the pan and simmer gently for 1 hour.
- Add the remaining vegetables, and season with salt and pepper. Bring to the boil again, part-cover and simmer for 35 minutes.
- Use kitchen paper to skim surplus fat from the top of the soup. Discard the bouquet garni and serve hot.

Tomato soup
serves 6

ingredients

25g/1oz butter
1 large onion, sliced
1 garlic clove, crushed
2 rashers rindless streaky bacon,
    chopped
700g/1½lb tomatoes, peeled and
    chopped
1 tablespoon chopped fresh
    flat-leaf parsley

½ teaspoon chopped fresh thyme
½ teaspoon grated lemon zest
1 teaspoon soft brown sugar
900ml/1½pt vegetable stock
1 tablespoon double cream
salt and freshly ground
    black pepper
1 tablespoon chopped fresh chives,
    to serve

- Heat the butter in a heavy pan. Sweat the onion for a few minutes until soft. Add the garlic and bacon. Fry for 2 minutes without browning the bacon. Add the tomatoes and fry for a further 2 minutes. Add the other ingredients except the cream and chives. Cook, covered, for 25 minutes.
- Blend or process the soup into a purée, and adjust the seasoning if necessary. Add a dollop of cream and the chives to each bowl to serve.

Vegetable minestrone
serves 6

ingredients

pinch of saffron strands
1 onion, chopped
1 leek, sliced
1 celery stick, sliced
2 carrots, diced
3 garlic cloves, crushed
600ml/1pt chicken stock
850g/1¾lb canned chopped
    tomatoes
50g/2oz frozen peas
50g/2oz soup pasta
1 teaspoon caster sugar
salt and freshly ground
    black pepper

- Soak the saffron strands in 1 tablespoon boiling water. Leave to stand for 10 minutes.
- Put the onion, leek, celery, carrots and garlic in a large pan. Add the stock, bring to the boil, cover and simmer for about 10 minutes.
- Add the tomatoes, the saffron and its soaking liquid and the peas. Bring back to the boil and add the pasta. Simmer for 10 minutes until the pasta is al dente.
- Sprinkle in the sugar, and season with salt and pepper. Stir through and serve hot.

Vegetable soup
serves 4

ingredients

1 onion, diced
3 garlic cloves, finely chopped
1 tablespoon olive oil
175g/6oz carrots, chopped
175g/6oz celery, chopped
1 small courgette, chopped
1 small yellow squash, chopped,
200g/7oz fresh broccoli, broken
    into florets

200g/7oz fresh cauliflower,
    chopped
100g/4oz mushrooms, sliced
400g/14oz canned chopped
    tomatoes
200ml/7fl oz tomato sauce
1 teaspoon dried basil
1 teaspoon dried oregano
3 chicken stock cubes, crumbled

- Lightly sauté the garlic and onions in the oil. Add the carrots and celery, and sweat for 3–5 minutes.
- Add the courgette and squash. Cook for a further 3–5 minutes, then add the remaining ingredients and 1.8 litres/3pt water. Bring to the boil and simmer for 15 minutes. Serve hot.

Vichyssoise
serves 6

ingredients

50g/2oz butter
3 large leeks, trimmed and
   thinly sliced
1 onion, thinly sliced
500g/1lb 2oz potatoes, chopped)
900ml/1½pt vegetable stock
2 teaspoons lemon juice

pinch of ground nutmeg
¼ teaspoon ground coriander
1 bay leaf
1 egg yolk
150ml/5fl oz single cream
salt and freshly ground
   black pepper

- Melt the butter in a saucepan, and sweat the leeks and onion, stirring
  occasionally, for about 5 minutes. Add the potatoes, stock, lemon juice,
  nutmeg, coriander and bay leaf. Season with salt and pepper. Bring to
  the boil, cover and simmer for 30 minutes until the vegetables are soft.
- Cool the soup a little, remove the bay leaf and purée the soup in a
  blender or food processor until smooth. Pour into a clean pan.
- Blend the egg yolk into the cream, add a little of the soup to the mixture,
  then whisk it all back into the soup and reheat gently. Cool and chill
  before serving.

Watercress soup
serves 6

ingredients

1 onion, chopped
15g/½oz butter
350g/12oz watercress, roughly
   chopped
1 tablespoon plain flour
1.2 litres/2pt vegetable stock
¼ teaspoon grated nutmeg
50ml/2fl oz single cream
2 eggs, hard-boiled and finely
   chopped
salt and freshly ground
   black pepper

- Sweat the onion in the butter for
  2 minutes, add the watercress and
  cook, stirring with a wooden
  spoon, for a further 2 minutes. Stir
  in the flour. Remove from the heat
  and gradually blend in the stock.
- Return to the heat, and bring to the
  boil, stirring. Season with salt,
  pepper and nutmeg. Reduce the
  heat and simmer for 20 minutes.
- Blend or process to a purée, and
  return to a clean pan. Stir in the
  cream and reheat gently. Sprinkle
  the chopped eggs on top and serve.

Consommé

serves 6

ingredients
1.25 litres/2¼pt beef stock
225g/8oz extra lean beef mince
2 tomatoes, chopped
2 large carrots, chopped
1 large onion, chopped
2 celery sticks, chopped
1 turnip, chopped
1 bouquet garni
2 egg whites
shells of 2 eggs, crushed
1 tablespoon sherry
salt and freshly ground
     black pepper

- Put the stock and beef mince in a heavy saucepan. Add the tomatoes, carrots, onion, celery, turnip, bouquet garni, egg whites, egg shells and plenty of seasoning.
- Bring almost to the boiling point, whisking all the time with a flat whisk.
- Cover and simmer for 1 hour, taking care not to allow the layer of froth on top of the soup to break.
- Carefully pour the soup through a scalded fine cloth such as muslin, keeping the froth back. Repeat if necessary until the liquid is clear. Add the sherry and reheat. Serve hot.

Potato & pork soup
serves 4

ingredients
1 litre/1¾pt chicken stock
2 large potatoes, diced
2 tablespoons rice wine vinegar
25g/1oz cornflour
100g/4oz pork fillet, sliced
1 tablespoon light soy sauce
1 teaspoon sesame oil
1 carrot, cut into matchsticks
1 teaspoon chopped fresh
  root ginger
3 spring onions, thinly sliced
1 red pepper, deseeded and sliced
225g/8oz canned bamboo shoots,
  drained

- Put the chicken stock, potatoes and 1 tablespoon of the vinegar in a heavy saucepan and bring to the boil. Reduce the heat until the stock is just simmering.
- Mix the cornflour with 4 tablespoons water to make a paste, then stir into the hot stock.
- Bring the stock back to the boil, stirring until thickened, then reduce the heat until it is just simmering again.
- Put the pork in a glass or ceramic dish, and season with the remaining vinegar, the soy sauce and the sesame oil.
- Add the pork, carrot and ginger to the stock and cook for 10 minutes. Stir in the spring onions, pepper and bamboo shoots. Cook for a further 5 minutes. Pour into warm serving bowls and serve immediately.

Onion avgolemono soup

serves 6

ingredients

4 large onions, thinly sliced
50g/2oz low-fat spread or butter
450ml/¾pt vegetable stock
450ml/¾pt skimmed milk
2 egg yolks
½ teaspoon freshly squeezed
  lemon juice
2 thick slices wholemeal bread,
  cubed
salt and freshly ground black pepper

- Preheat the oven to 200°C/400°F/Gas mark 6.
- Melt the low-fat spread or butter in a heavy saucepan, add the onions and cook gently, covered, for 10 minutes, stirring from time to time, until soft. Add the stock, and season with a little salt and pepper. Bring to the boil, reduce the heat and simmer gently for 30 minutes.
- Stir in the milk and heat through.
- Whisk the egg yolks with the lemon juice. Add 2 ladlefuls of the hot soup and whisk well. Stir the egg and lemon mixture into the soup, and heat through gently, still stirring, until slightly thickened. Do not allow the soup to boil or the egg will curdle.
- To make the croûtons, spread out the bread cubes on a baking tray, and bake in the oven for 10 minutes until a deep golden brown.
- Ladle the soup into warm individual bowls, and sprinkle with the croûtons just before serving.

Chinese cabbage soup

serves 4

ingredients

450g/1lb pak choi
600ml/1pt vegetable stock
1 tablespoon rice wine vinegar
1 tablespoon light soy sauce
1 tablespoon caster sugar
1 tablespoon dry sherry
1 fresh red chilli, seeded and
   thinly sliced
1 tablespoon cornflour

- Wash the pak choi thoroughly under cold running water, rinse and drain. Pat dry with kitchen paper. Trim the stems from the pak choi, and shred the leaves.
- Heat the stock in a large heavy saucepan. Add the pak choi and cook for 10–15 minutes.
- Mix together the vinegar, soy sauce, sugar and sherry in a small bowl. Add this mixture to the stock, together with the chilli. Bring to the boil, reduce the heat and cook for 2–3 minutes.
- Blend the cornflour with 2 tablespoons water to form a paste, and gradually stir into the soup. Cook, stirring constantly, until it thickens. Cook for a further 4–5 minutes, then ladle the soup into warm individual serving bowls and serve immediately.

Red onion & beetroot soup

serves 6

ingredients

2 teaspoons olive oil
350g/12oz red onions, sliced
2 garlic cloves, crushed
275g/10oz cooked beetroot, cut
  into matchsticks
1.2 litres/2pt vegetable stock
50g/2oz soup pasta, cooked
  until al dente
2 tablespoons raspberry vinegar
salt and freshly ground
  black pepper

- Heat the oil in a casserole dish over a low heat, and add the onion and garlic. Sweat gently for 20 minutes or until soft and tender.
- Add the beetroot, stock, pasta and vinegar, and heat through. Season with salt and pepper to taste, and serve hot.

Smooth cheese soup

serves 4

ingredients

1 large potato, diced
1 large carrot, diced
1 small onion, diced
1 celery stick, diced
600ml/1pt vegetable stock
½ teaspoon dried mixed herbs
100g/4oz low-fat Cheddar
  cheese, grated
150ml/5fl oz skimmed milk

- Put the vegetables in a saucepan with the stock and herbs. Bring to the boil, reduce the heat, part-cover and simmer gently for 15 minutes until the vegetables are soft.
- Purée in a blender or food processor, and return to the pan. Add the cheese and milk, and heat gently until the cheese melts. Ladle into bowls and serve hot.

Mushroom & corn soup
serves 4

ingredients

25g/1oz low-fat spread
25g/1oz plain flour
100g/4oz button mushrooms,
  sliced
1 onion, finely chopped
300ml/10fl oz vegetable stock
300ml/10fl oz skimmed milk
350g/12oz canned sweetcorn
  kernels, drained
salt and freshly ground
  black pepper
4 teaspoons low-fat single
  cream, to garnish

- Heat the low-fat spread in a heavy saucepan. Add the mushrooms and onion. Cook, stirring constantly with a wooden spoon, for 3 minutes. Add the flour and cook, stirring, for 1 minute.
- Remove from the heat. Gradually blend in the stock, then the milk and sweetcorn. Return to the heat, bring to the boil, reduce the heat and simmer the soup gently for 10 minutes, stirring occasionally. Season with salt and pepper.
- Ladle into warm bowls and garnish each serving with a swirl of cream.

Tomato & carrot soup
serves 4

ingredients

400g/14oz canned chopped
  tomatoes
2 large carrots, grated
1 small onion, finely chopped
300ml/10fl oz vegetable stock
  (made with 1 stock cube)
1 teaspoon dried oregano
pinch of grated nutmeg
pinch of salt
1 bay leaf
1 tablespoon chopped fresh
  flat-leaf parsley

- Put all the ingredients except the parsley in a heavy saucepan and bring to the boil, stirring. Reduce the heat, part-cover and simmer for 30 minutes.
- Discard the bay leaf, ladle the soup into bowls and serve hot, garnished with the parsley.

Curried carrot & apple soup

serves 4

ingredients

2 teaspoons sunflower oil
1 tablespoon mild korma curry
  powder
500g/1lb 2oz carrots, chopped

1 large onion, chopped
1 cooking apple, chopped
900ml/1½pt chicken stock
salt and ground black pepper

- Heat the oil in a saucepan over a low heat, and gently fry the curry powder for 2–3 minutes until fragrant.
- Add the carrots, onion and apple, stir well, then cover the pan. Cook over a very low heat for about 15 minutes, shaking the pan from time to time, until the vegetables are softened.
- Spoon the vegetable mixture into a blender or food processor, then add half the stock and blend until smooth.
- Return the mixture to the pan, and pour in the remaining stock. Bring the soup to the boil, and season with salt and pepper. Serve hot.

• •

Green soup

serves 4

ingredients

1 tablespoon olive oil
1 onion, chopped
1 garlic clove, chopped
200g/7oz potato, cut into
  2.5cm/1in cubes
700ml/1¼pt vegetable stock

1 small cucumber, cut into chunks
75g/3oz watercress
100g/4oz green beans, trimmed
  and halved
salt and freshly ground
  black pepper

- Heat the oil in a large saucepan. Sweat the onion and garlic for 3–4 minutes until softened. Add the potato and cook for a further 2–3 minutes.
- Stir in the stock, bring to the boil and leave to simmer for 5 minutes.
- Add the cucumber to the saucepan, and cook for a further 3 minutes or until the potatoes are tender.
- Add the watercress and allow to wilt, then transfer the mixture to a blender or food processor and purée until smooth.
- Bring a small saucepan of water to the boil. Cook the beans for 3–4 minutes until tender. Add the beans to the soup, season and warm through.

Oriental noodle soup

serves 6

ingredients

1.8 litres/3pt beef stock
1 teaspoon finely chopped
  lemon grass
2 teaspoons light soy sauce
175g/6oz vermicelli, broken
  into small pieces

- Bring the stock to the boil with the lemon grass and soy sauce.
- Add the vermicelli and simmer for 6 minutes or until the noodles are just tender. Serve hot.

Greek lemon soup

serves 4

ingredients

1 tablespoon cornflour
1 litre/1¾pt chicken stock
50g/2oz long-grain rice
4 tablespoons freshly squeezed
  lemon juice
3 eggs

- Stir the cornflour into 225ml/8fl oz chicken stock of the until it has dissolved. Pour into a saucepan over a medium heat, and add the remaining stock.
- Bring to the boil. Add the rice, reduce the heat and simmer for about 20 minutes until tender. Remove from the heat.
- Beat the lemon juice and eggs together. Whisk half the stock, a little at a time, into the egg mixture. Pour the egg mixture into pan with the remaining stock, mixing well.
- Return to a low heat and cook, stirring constantly, until the soup is just thickened. Serve immediately.

Rich kidney soup
serves 4

ingredients
25g/1oz low-fat spread
225g/8oz lamb's kidneys, finely
   chopped
1 small onion, finely chopped
25g/1oz plain flour
750ml/1¼pt lamb stock
1 small bay leaf
2 tablespoons port
salt and freshly ground black pepper

- Melt the low-fat spread in a heavy saucepan over a gentle heat, and add the kidneys and onion. Gently sauté for 1 minute, stirring, so that the kidneys do not toughen. Add the flour and cook for 1 minute.
- Remove from the heat and blend in the stock. Add the bay leaf, and season with salt and pepper.
- Return the pan to the heat and bring the soup to the boil, stirring, until thickened. Reduce the heat, part-cover and simmer gently for 30 minutes.
- Remove and discard the bay leaf. Purée the soup in a blender or food processor, and return to the clean pan. Stir in the port, heat through gently and serve.

Prawn wonton soup

serves 4

ingredients

For the wontons

175g/6oz cooked prawns, peeled
   and deveined
1 garlic clove, crushed
1 spring onion, finely chopped)
1 tablespoon light soy sauce
1 tablespoon Thai fish sauce
1 tablespoon chopped fresh
   coriander leaves
1 small egg, separated
12 wonton wrappers

For the soup

1 litre/1¾pt beef stock
1 tablespoon Thai fish sauce
1 tablespoon light soy sauce
1 tablespoon Chinese rice wine
2 small fresh red chillies, seeded
   and sliced
2 spring onions, sliced

- To make the wonton filling, finely chop the prawns. Transfer to a glass or ceramic bowl, and stir in the garlic, spring onion, soy sauce, fish sauce, coriander and egg yolk.
- Lay the wonton wrappers on a work surface in a single layer, and put about 1 tablespoon of the filling mixture in the centre of each. Brush the edges with egg white and fold each one into a triangle, pressing lightly to seal. Bring the two bottom corners of the triangle around to meet in the centre, securing with a little egg white to hold in place. Cover with a damp tea towel or cloth until needed.
- To make the soup, put the stock, fish sauce, soy sauce and rice wine in a large heavy saucepan, and bring to the boil over a medium heat. Add the chillies and spring onions. Drop the wontons into the pan and simmer for 4–5 minutes, until thoroughly heated. Serve immediately.

Cream of artichoke soup

serves 6

ingredients

750g/1lb 11oz Jerusalem
   artichokes, peeled and sliced
1 lemon, thickly sliced
50g/2oz butter
2 onions, chopped
1 garlic clove, crushed
1.5 litres/2¼pt vegetable stock
2 bay leaves
¼ teaspoon ground nutmeg
1 tablespoon freshly squeezed
   lemon juice
150ml/5fl oz single cream
salt and freshly ground
   black pepper

- Put the artichokes in a bowl with the lemon slices, and cover with water.
- Melt the butter in a large saucepan over a low heat. Add the onions and garlic, and sweat gently for 3–4 minutes until soft.
- Drain the artichokes, discarding the lemon, and add to the pan. Mix well and sweat gently for 2–3 minutes without allowing to colour.
- Add the stock, bay leaves, nutmeg and lemon juice. Season with salt and pepper. Bring slowly to the boil, then cover and simmer gently for about 30 minutes.
- Discard the bay leaves. Cool the soup slightly, then purée in a blender or food processor until smooth.
- Pour the soup into a clean pan and bring to the boil. Reduce the heat, stir in the cream and cook gently, without boiling, for 2 minutes. Serve immediately.

Sweetcorn chowder
serves 4

ingredients

25g/1oz low-fat spread
25g/1oz plain flour
1 bunch of spring onions, finely
  chopped
1 large potato, diced
300ml/10fl oz vegetable stock
300ml/10fl oz skimmed milk
200g/7oz canned sweetcorn
  kernels, drained
salt and freshly ground
  black pepper
50g/2oz low-fat Cheddar
  cheese, grated

- Melt the low-fat spread in a heavy saucepan, and add the spring onions and potato.
- Gently sweat for 5 minutes, then add the flour and cook for a further 1 minute, stirring.
- Remove from the heat and gradually blend in the stock, then add the milk and sweetcorn.
- Return to the heat, and bring to the boil, stirring. Reduce the heat and simmer very gently for 15 minutes. Season with salt and pepper.
- Stir in the cheese and ladle into individual bowls to serve.

Chinese egg flower soup
serves 4

ingredients

900ml/1½pt chicken stock
1 tablespoon light soy sauce
2 tablespoons dry sherry
pinch of ground ginger
25g/1oz frozen peas
½ red pepper, seeded and diced
1 egg, beaten

- Put all the ingredients except the egg in a heavy saucepan, and bring to the boil.
- Simmer for 5 minutes until the peas are tender. Remove from the heat, and pour the egg in a thin stream through the prongs of a fork so that it 'flowers'.
- Let the soup stand for 20 seconds to allow the egg to set, then serve immediately.

Spicy oatmeal soup
serves 8

ingredients
15g/1/2oz margarine
1 tablespoon groundnut oil
2 large leeks, thinly sliced
4 carrots, sliced
2 potatoes, diced
2 celery sticks, sliced
1.2 litres/2pt chicken stock
1 tablespoon dried chives
1 tablespoon dried shallots
½ tablespoon dried tarragon
½ tablespoon dried basil
1 teaspoon salt
100g/4oz oatmeal
225ml/8fl oz white wine

- Heat the margarine and groundnut oil in a large saucepan over a medium-high heat. Add the leeks and sweat for 2–3 minutes.
- Add the carrots, potatoes, celery and chicken stock. Bring to the boil.
- Sprinkle in the chives, shallots, tarragon, basil and salt. Boil gently for 20 minutes. Add the oatmeal and cook for a further 5 minutes. Add the wine, cook for 15 minutes more and serve hot.

Cabbage soup
serves 6

ingredients

1 cabbage head, shredded
2 large onions, thinly sliced
2 carrots, thinly sliced
1 large potato, diced
700ml/1¼pt skimmed milk

2 tablespoons low-fat yogurt
1 bay leaf
½ teaspoon dried dill
½ teaspoon dried rosemary

- Put the cabbage, onions, carrots and potato in a heavy saucepan with a little water. Cover and cook slowly until tender.
- Add the milk, yogurt, bay leaf, dill and rosemary. Continue to cook for a further 15 minutes. Serve hot.

• •

Cullen skink
serves 4

ingredients

225g/8oz smoked haddock fillet
25g/1oz butter
1 onion, finely chopped
600ml/1pt milk
350g/12oz potatoes, diced
350g/12oz cod, boned, skinned
   and cubed

150ml/5fl oz double cream
2 tablespoons chopped fresh
   flat-leaf parsley
salt and freshly ground
   black pepper

- Put the haddock fillet in a large frying pan and cover with boiling water. Let stand for 10 minutes, then drain, reserving 300ml/10fl oz of the soaking water. Flake the fish, taking care to remove all the bones.
- Melt the butter in a large saucepan over a low heat. Add the onion and sweat gently for 10 minutes until softened. Add the milk and bring to a gentle simmer before adding the potatoes. Cook for 10 minutes.
- Add the reserved haddock flakes and the cod. Simmer for a further 10 minutes until the cod is tender.
- Remove about one-third of the fish and potatoes, put in a blender or food processor and purée until smooth. Return to the soup with the cream, parsley and salt and pepper to taste. Add a little of the reserved soaking water if the soup seems too thick. Reheat gently and serve hot.

Crab & ginger soup

serves 4

ingredients

1 carrot, chopped
1 leek, chopped
1 bay leaf
900ml/1½pt fish stock
2 medium cooked crabs
2.5cm/1in piece of fresh root ginger,
  peeled and grated
1 teaspoon light soy sauce
½ teaspoon ground star anise
salt and freshly ground black pepper

- Put the carrot and leek in a large heavy saucepan with the bay leaf and the fish stock. Bring to the boil, reduce the heat, cover and leave to simmer for 10 minutes or until the vegetables are nearly tender.
- Remove all of the meat from the crabs. Break off and reserve the claws; break the joints and remove the meat using a fork.
- Add the crabmeat to the pan together with the ginger, soy sauce and star anise, and bring to the boil. Leave to simmer for about 10 minutes until the vegetables are tender and the crab is heated through.
- Season the soup with salt and pepper, then ladle into warm individual serving bowls and garnish with the crab claws. Serve immediately.

Starters & Canapés

At the beginning of a meal, appetites tend to be
at their height, so it is important to choose your starter
carefully. This chapter contains a huge variety of recipes to fit
in with any dinner menu, and includes hot and cold dishes
chosen from cuisines from all around the world. There is also
plenty to choose from when it comes to canapés for evening
drinks or finger food for more informal get-togethers.
Whatever the occasion, you will find recipes here to whet the
appetite of even the most discerning dinner and party guests.

Baked mushrooms

serves 4

ingredients

8 large flat mushrooms, wiped
  with damp kitchen paper
2 tablespoons olive oil
250g/9oz Taleggio or Brie
  cheese, thickly sliced
1 bunch of fresh lemon thyme,
  leaves only
salt and freshly ground
  black pepper

- Preheat the oven to 200°C/
  400°F/Gas mark 6.
- Trim the stalks from the mushrooms.
  Put the mushrooms, rounded cap
  side down, in a medium roasting
  dish. Season with salt and pepper.
- Pour the olive oil over the
  mushrooms. Place the cheese slices
  on top, and finally sprinkle with the
  lemon thyme. Bake in the oven for
  20–25 minutes until the cheese has
  melted. Serve hot.

Grilled asparagus & leeks

serves 4

ingredients

12 small leeks, trimmed, with
  ends removed
12 fresh asparagus spears
olive oil for brushing
50g/2oz pecorino or Parmesan
  cheese, freshly grated
2 tablespoons freshly squeezed
  lemon juice

- Preheat the grill to high.
- Arrange the leeks and asparagus
  in a single layer in a shallow
  baking dish.
- Brush the vegetables with the olive
  oil, and place under the grill.
  Cook for 5–8 minutes, turning
  occasionally and brushing with
  more oil as needed.
- When almost done, sprinkle with
  two-thirds of the grated cheese and
  all of the lemon juice. Grill for a
  further minute.
- Finally, sprinkle the remaining
  cheese on top, and serve hot in the
  baking dish.

Beetroot & yogurt salad
serves 4

ingredients

350g/12oz cooked beetroot, chopped into bite-sized cubes

2 large gherkins, chopped into large chunks

4 tablespoons Greek-style yogurt

2 tablespoons white wine vinegar

salt and freshly ground black pepper

1 tablespoon finely chopped fresh dill, to garnish

• Put the beetroot and gherkins in a large serving bowl.

• In a separate bowl, mix together the yogurt and vinegar, and season with salt and pepper.

• Pour this mixture over the beetroot and gherkins, and stir. Sprinkle with fresh dill and serve.

Leek kuftadas
serves 4–6

ingredients

700g/1½lb leeks, trimmed and thinly sliced

175g/6oz feta cheese, crumbled

3 eggs, beaten

50g/2oz fresh breadcrumbs

4 tablespoons vegetable oil

• Steam the leeks for 4 minutes in a colander or steamer over a pan of boiling water. Remove from the heat and leave to cool.

• In a large bowl, combine the cooled leeks, feta cheese, eggs and breadcrumbs.

• Using a tablespoon of the mixture at a time, mould it into round patties with your hands.

• Heat the oil in a shallow heavy frying pan over a high heat. Shallow-fry the paties for about 5 minutes on each side or until golden brown, cooking in batches if necessary. Drain on kitchen paper, and serve warm.

Tomatoes on toast

serves 4

ingredients

olive oil for brushing and
   drizzling
6 large tomatoes, thickly sliced
4 thick slices of brown bread
balsamic vinegar for drizzling
50g/2oz Parmesan cheese,
   shaved
salt and freshly ground
   black pepper

- Brush a heavy frying pan with oil, and place over a high heat.
- Add the tomato slices and fry them for 3 minutes, turning once until soft and slightly blackened.
- Meanwhile, lightly toast the bread under a grill or in a toaster.
- Put the tomatoes on the warm toast. Drizzle each portion with a little olive oil and balsamic vinegar. Sprinkle with the Parmesan cheese shavings, season with salt and pepper, and serve immediately.

Roast garlic toast

serves 6

ingredients

1 ciabatta loaf
2 whole garlic bulbs
2 tablespoons extra virgin
   olive oil
5 sprigs of fresh rosemary
salt and freshly ground
   black pepper

- Preheat grill to high.
- Slice off the tops of the garlic bulbs. Leave the cloves whole with their skins on.
- Brush with some of the olive oil. Wrap the garlic bulbs in foil with 3 sprigs of the rosemary. Grill for 25 minutes, turning occasionally.
- Slice the bread and brush each slice with olive oil, then lightly toast both sides under the hot grill.
- Squeeze the garlic cloves from their skins onto the toast.
- Chop the leaves of the remaining rosemary sprigs, and sprinkle over the toast. Season with salt and pepper. Drizzle with the remaining olive oil, and serve warm or hot.

Sweet potato salad

serves 4

ingredients

4 sweet potatoes, peeled and
chopped into cubes
3 tablespoons vinaigrette (see
page 727)
salt and freshly ground
black pepper
2 spring onions, finely chopped
1 small bunch of fresh chives,
chopped
pinch of cayenne pepper
2 tablespoons chopped fresh
flat-leaf parsley

- Put the sweet potatoes in a heavy saucepan of boiling water. Cook for 10 minutes or until tender, taking care not to overcook. Drain.
- Transfer the warm sweet potatoes to a large bowl, and pour the vinaigrette over the top. Season with salt and pepper, and leave to cool.
- Once the sweet potatoes have cooled, mix in the spring onions and chives. Sprinkle with the pinch of cayenne and the parsley. Serve at room temperature.

Jerusalem artichokes

serves 4

ingredients

908g/2lb round Jerusalem
artichokes
3 garlic cloves, crushed
2 tablespoons chopped fresh
flat-leaf parsley
2 tablespoons olive oil
squeeze of lemon juice
salt

- Peel the artichokes, and boil for 8–10 minutes in slightly salted water. Drain in a colander, and place on serving dishes.
- Meanwhile, mix together the garlic, parsley, olive oil and lemon juice. Season with salt. Drizzle the dressing over the warm artichokes, and serve immediately.

Melon & strawberries
serves 4

ingredients
¼ honeydew melon
½ cantaloupe melon
150ml/5fl oz rosé wine
3 teaspoons rose water
175g/6oz small strawberries,
  rinsed and hulled

- Halve the melons. Scoop out the seeds from both melons using a spoon. Carefully remove the peel.
- Cut the melon flesh into thin strips, and put in a bowl. Pour over the wine and rose water. Mix together, cover and leave to chill in the refrigerator for at least 2 hours.
- Halve the strawberries and mix in with the melon. Allow to stand at room temperature for about 15 minutes before serving.

Onion rings
serves 4–6

ingredients
350ml/12fl oz plain flour
4 tablespoons cornmeal
4 tablespoons onion powder
2 teaspoons salt
350ml/12fl oz milk
1 large egg
8 large onions
vegetable oil for deep-frying

- Combine the flour, cornmeal, onion powder, salt, milk, egg and 125ml/4fl oz water in a large bowl. Stir well until there are no lumps and the batter is smooth.
- Slice the onions across to make rings about 1cm/½in thick.
- Heat the oil in a large saucepan until hot. Test to see whether the oil is hot enough by dropping a little of the batter into the oil – it should sizzle straight away.
- Dip the separated rings into the batter. Drop the coated rings into the oil and fry until golden brown. Cook in batches if necessary.
- Remove the onion rings with a slotted spoon, and drain on kitchen paper. Serve hot.

Mozzarella sticks

serves 4

ingredients

2 eggs, beaten
50ml/2fl oz water
350ml/12fl oz coarse dried
   white breadcrumbs
½ teaspoon garlic salt
1 teaspoon mixed spice
150ml/5fl oz flour
75ml/3fl oz cornflour
vegetable oil for deep-frying
450g/1lb mozzarella cheese,
   cut into finger-size sticks

- Whisk the eggs with 50ml/2fl oz water and set aside. Mix the breadcrumbs, garlic salt and mixed spice together, and set aside. Blend the flour with the cornflour.
- Heat enough vegetable oil for deep-frying in a heavy saucepan. Dredge the cheese sticks in the flour mixture, then dip in the egg. Lastly, coat in the breadcrumb mixture.
- Lower carefully into the hot oil, and fry for a few seconds until golden. Remove from the hot oil, and drain on kitchen paper. Serve hot.

Courgette fritters

serves 6

ingredients

100g/4oz self-raising flour
2 eggs, beaten
50ml/2fl oz milk
300g/11oz courgettes, grated
2 tablespoons chopped fresh
   thyme leaves
salt and freshly ground
   black pepper
1 tablespoon vegetable oil

- Sift the flour into a large bowl, and make a well in the centre. Add the eggs to the well, and gradually draw in the flour from the sides using a wooden spoon.
- Slowly add the milk to the mixture, stirring constantly to form a thick batter. Add the courgettes and thyme, season with salt and pepper, and mix thoroughly.
- Heat the oil in a large heavy frying pan until hot. Cooking in batches, carefully drop in tablespoons of the batter to make the fritters. Shallow-fry for 3 minutes on each side.
- Remove the fritters with a slotted spoon, and drain on kitchen paper. Serve hot.

Soft pretzels
serves 8

ingredients

700g/1½lb plain flour
1 tablespoon sugar
2 teaspoons salt
2 teaspoons baking powder

2 teaspoons active dry yeast
2 tablespoons softened butter, plus
   a little extra, melted
225ml/8fl oz warm milk

- Put a large pot of water on to boil. Preheat the oven to 200°C/400°F/ Gas mark 6. Lightly grease a baking sheet.
- Put about 125g/4oz of the flour, the sugar, salt, baking powder, yeast and the 2 tablspoons softened butter in a large bowl. Mix until smooth and the yeast starts to froth.
- Sift in the remaining flour, and continue mixing until a stiff dough forms. Knead the dough until it is smooth and elastic. Form into a ball and allow to rise in a warm place until doubled in size.
- Punch down the dough and knead for a minute or so. Divide into eight equal pieces. Roll or cut each piece into a rope 45cm/18in long and 1cm/½in in diameter, and twist each rope into a pretzel shape. Allow to rest for a couple of minutes.
- Using a slotted spoon or broad spatula, slide the pretzels into the boiling water one at a time, and boil each one until they float to the top. Remove immediately, drain off and transfer to the greased baking sheet.
- Bake in the oven for 15 minutes or until golden. Brush the pretzels very lightly with melted butter as they emerge from the oven. Serve warm.

Bruschetta
serves 4

ingredients

8 slices ciabatta bread
2 garlic cloves, halved
extra virgin olive oil for drizzling
8 ripe tomatoes, sliced
8 fresh basil leaves
salt and freshly ground
   black pepper

- Toast the bread lightly. Rub with the garlic, cut side down, while still hot. Season with salt and lots of pepper, and drizzle enough oil on each slice to soak thoroughly.
- Divide the tomato slices evenly between the slices of bread.
- Top each bruschetta with a fresh basil leaf. Serve immediately

Cheesy stuffed peppers
serves 2–4

ingredients

2 green peppers
1 egg, hard-boiled and finely chopped
75g/3oz Cheddar cheese, grated
2 ripe tomatoes
3 tablespoons mayonnaise
2 slices of bread, toasted

- Gently simmer the peppers in a saucepan of water for 20 minutes or until tender. Drain the peppers, cool slightly, halve and deseed.
- Preheat the grill until hot. Mix the chopped eggs, cheese and tomatoes in a small bowl. Add the mayonnaise and stir well.
- Fill the pepper halves with the egg mixture, and place on the slices of toast. Cook under the hot grill until lightly browned. Serve hot.

Greek spinach & cheese pie
serves 8

ingredients

150ml/5fl oz olive oil
1 onion, finely chopped
2 teaspoons ground cumin
2 garlic cloves, crushed

450g/1lb chopped spinach
100g/4oz feta cheese, crumbled
100g/4oz cream cheese
400g/14oz filo pastry

- Preheat the oven to 190°C/375°F/Gas mark 5.
- Heat 2 tablespoons of the olive oil in a frying pan over a low heat. Add the onion and cook gently, stirring frequently, for about 10 minutes until softened. Sprinkle in the cumin and stir for 2 minutes, then stir in the garlic and spinach. Remove the pan from the heat, and stir in the cheeses until evenly mixed.
- Brush the inside of a 30 x 23cm/12 x 9in baking dish with olive oil. Put a sheet of pastry in the dish, letting the edges hang over the side. Brush the pastry in the dish with oil, and continue until half the pastry is used.
- Spread the cheese mixture over the pastry. Use the remaining pastry to cover the mixture, spreading oil over individual sheets as before. Trim and seal the edges. Cut through the layers with a sharp knife to divide the pie into 16 segments.
- Bake in the oven for 30 minutes. Leave to cool for 10 minutes before serving.

Mini mushroom quiches

serves 6

ingredients

4 slices wholewheat bread, crusts
  removed
2 teaspoons butter
225g/8oz mushrooms, wiped
  with damp kitchen paper and
  finely chopped

1 garlic clove, minced
4 eggs
100g/4oz Emmental cheese,
  grated
salt and freshly ground
  black pepper

- Preheat the oven to 190°C/375°F/Gas mark 5.
- Roll each slice of bread with a rolling pin until flat, halve each slice and arrange in a greased muffin tray, pressing each slice into the cake mould. While the oven warms, bake the bread cups at a low heat until crisp and dry. Remove from the oven and set aside.
- In a small frying pan, melt the butter over a medium heat. Add the mushrooms and garlic. Sauté, stirring regularly, for 3–5 minutes until tender. Season with salt and pepper.
- Break the eggs in a bowl, piercing the yolks with a small sharp knife. Pour the eggs over the bread cups, dividing the mixture evenly. Top with the mushroom mixture, and sprinkle with the cheese.
- Bake in the oven for 15 minutes, or until the eggs are just set.

Olive cheese balls

serves 6

ingredients

225g/8oz Cheddar cheese,
  finely grated
300g/11oz plain flour
75g/3oz butter, melted
36 good-quality stuffed olives

- Mix together the grated cheese and flour, add the butter and mix thoroughly to form a dough. Mould 1 teaspoon of dough around each olive, and shape into a ball.
- Put the balls on a greased baking sheet. Cover and chill for 1 hour.
- Preheat the oven to 200°C/400°F/Gas mark 6.
- Once the balls are chilled, bake in the oven for 15–20 minutes. Serve warm.

Naan bread
serves 8

ingredients

1 teaspoon sugar
1 teaspoon fresh yeast
150ml/5fl oz warm water
200g/7oz plain flour

1 tablespoon ghee or butter
1 teaspoon salt
50g/2oz unsalted butter
1 teaspoon poppy seeds

- Put the sugar and yeast in a small bowl or jug together with the warm water, and mix thoroughly until the yeast has completely dissolved. Set aside for 10 minutes.
- Sift the flour into a large mixing bowl, making a well in the centre. Add the ghee or butter and the salt, and pour in the yeast mixture. Mix thoroughly to form a dough, adding more water if required.
- Place the dough on a floured work surface and knead until smooth. Return to the bowl, cover and set aside to rise for 1½ hours.
- Preheat the grill to very hot. Turn the dough out on to a floured surface and knead for a further 2 minutes. Break off small balls and pat them into rounds about 12.5cm/5in in diameter and 1cm/½in thick.
- Place the rounds on a greased sheet of foil, and grill for 7–10 minutes, turning twice and brushing with butter and sprinkling with poppy seeds. Serve immediately.

Garlic breadsticks
serves 4

ingredients

2 baguettes
2 garlic cloves, crushed
150ml/5 fl oz olive oil

- Preheat the oven to 200°C/400°F/Gas mark 6. Cut the baguettes into three lengthways, then halve each segment, creating 12 breadsticks. Place the sticks on a baking tray.
- Mix the garlic and oil in a small bowl, then spread over the breadsticks using a pastry brush. Bake for 15–20 minutes until golden brown. Serve either hot or at room temperature.

Crispy seaweed
serves 4

ingredients

1.1kg/21/2lb pak choi
groundnut oil for deep-frying

1 teaspoon salt
1 tablespoon caster sugar

- Rinse the pak choi leaves under cold running water, then dry thoroughly with kitchen paper. Roll each pak choi leaf up and slice through thinly with a small, sharp knife, or chop using a food processor. Make sure that the leaves are finely shredded.
- Heat the groundnut oil in a large wok or frying pan until hot. Carefully add the shredded pak choi to the wok, and fry for about 30 seconds until it shrivels and becomes crispy. You may need to do this in batches.
- Remove the crispy 'seaweed' from the wok with a slotted spoon, and drain on kitchen paper. Transfer to a large bowl, toss with the salt and sugar, and serve immediately.

King prawns in sherry
serves 4

ingredients

2 tablespoons olive oil
12 raw king prawns, peeled
  and deveined
2 tablespoons dry sherry
a few drops of Tabasco sauce
salt and freshly ground
  black pepper
crisp lettuce leaves such as Little
  Gem, to serve

- Heat the oil in a heavy frying pan over medium-high heat, and sauté the prawns for 2–3 minutes until pink in colour.
- Pour on the sherry and Tabasco, and season with salt and pepper.
- Give the prawns a quick stir, and serve immediately on a bed of crisp lettuce leaves.

Vegetable fritters

serves 4

ingredients

100g/4oz wholemeal flour
pinch of salt
pinch of cayenne pepper
4 teaspoons olive oil
100g/4oz broccoli florets
100g/4oz cauliflower florets
50g/2oz mangetout
1 large carrot, cut into
   matchsticks
1 red pepper, seeded and sliced
2 egg whites
vegetable oil for deep-frying

For the sauce
150ml/5fl oz pineapple juice
150ml/5fl oz vegetable stock (see
   page 730)
2 tablespoons white wine vinegar
2 tablespoons soft brown sugar
2 teaspoons cornflour
2 spring onions, chopped

- Sift the flour and salt into a large bowl, and add the cayenne. Make a well in the flour, and gradually beat in the oil and 175ml/6fl oz cold water to make a smooth batter.
- Put the vegetables in a pan of boiling water, and simmer for 5 minutes, then drain well.
- Whisk the egg whites until they form peaks, and gently fold them into the flour batter.
- Heat the vegetable oil to 170°–180°C/325°–350°F in a deep-fryer (a cube of bread should brown in 30 seconds).
- Dip the vegetables into the batter, turning to coat them well. Drain off any excess batter. Fry in batches until golden. Remove with a slotted spoon and drain on kitchen paper.
- Meanwhile, put all of the sauce ingredients in a heavy saucepan, and bring to the boil, stirring, until thickened and clear. Serve with the piping-hot fritters.

Breaded mushrooms

serves 4

ingredients

225g/8oz mushrooms, stalks removed

3 tablespoons freshly grated Parmesan cheese

4 tablespoons coarse dried white breadcrumbs

pinch of garlic salt

pinch of ground black pepper

1 tablespoon chopped fresh flat-leaf parsley

- Preheat the oven to 240°C/ 475°F/Gas mark 9. Lightly grease a non-stick baking tray.
- Gently wipe the mushrooms with damp kitchen paper. Set aside.
- Combine the cheese with the breadcrumbs. Add the garlic salt and black pepper.
- Roll the mushrooms in the cheese mixture, and set on the greased baking tray.
- Bake in the oven for 8–10 minutes until browned. Serve hot or warm.

Beef carpaccio

serves 6

ingredients

350g/12oz filet mignon or similar tender cut of beef

3 tablespoons freshly squeezed lemon juice

1 tablespoon red wine vinegar

75ml/3fl oz extra virgin olive oil

2 tablespoons capers, rinsed and gently squeezed dry

sea salt

200g/7oz rocket leaves, rinsed and thinly sliced, to serve

75g/3oz Parmesan cheese, freshly grated or shaved, to serve

- Wrap the beef in cling film; freeze for about 1 hour until firm. Cut the beef across the grain into 5mm/⅛in slices. Put the slices between two sheets of cling film, and pound with a mallet or rolling pin until paper thin. Roll the beef up in cling film once again, and chill for 1 hour.
- To make the vinaigrette, whiz the lemon juice, vinegar, oil and salt in a blender until smooth. Pour into a small bowl, and stir in the capers.
- Arrange the beef slices in a single layer on one large serving plate or six individual plates. Toss the rocket with half the dressing. Pile the rocket on top of the beef. Top with the Parmesan, and serve accompanied by the remaining dressing.

Melon in wine

serves 4

ingredients

2 small cantaloupe melons
175ml/6fl oz dry sparkling wine
3 tablespoons orange
   marmalade
½ bunch of fresh mint leaves,
   chopped

- Halve the melons lengthways and scoop out the seeds. Remove the flesh and cut into small cubes. Put the cubes in a bowl. Reserve the melon shells.
- In a separate small bowl, whisk together the wine, marmalade and mint. Pour the mixture over the melon flesh, and stir gently.
- Divide the mixture between the melon shells. Cover with cling film, and marinate in the refrigerator for 4–6 hours. Serve cold.

Chicken & bacon kebabs

serves 4

ingredients

2 corn on the cob
8 thick rashers back bacon
6 brown cap mushrooms, wiped
   with damp kitchen paper and
   halved
2 small chicken fillets
2 tablespoons sunflower oil
1 tablespoon freshly squeezed
   lemon juice
1 tablespoon maple syrup
salt and freshly ground
   black pepper

- Cook the corn in a saucepan of boiling water until tender, then drain and cool.
- Stretch the bacon rashers using the back of a knife. Cut each rasher in half, and wrap a piece around each mushroom.
- Cut both the corn and chicken into eight equal pieces. Mix together the oil, lemon juice and syrup. Season with salt and pepper, and brush over the chicken.
- Thread the corn, bacon-wrapped mushrooms and chicken pieces alternately on skewers, and brush all over with the lemon dressing.
- Grill for 8–10 minutes, turning once and basting occasionally with any extra dressing. Serve hot.

Cauliflower fritters

serves 8

ingredients

600g/1¼lb cauliflower, cut into bite-size florets
50g/2oz chickpea flour
2 teaspoons ground cumin
1 teaspoon ground coriander
1 teaspoon ground turmeric
pinch of cayenne pepper
½ teaspoon salt
50ml/2fl oz water
1 egg plus 1 egg yolk, lightly beaten
vegetable oil for deep-frying

• Cut the cauliflower into bite-size florets. Set aside.
• Sift the flour and spices into a bowl, then stir in the ½ teaspoon salt and make a well in the centre.
• Combine 50ml/2fl oz water with the beaten egg, and gradually pour into the well, whisking to make a smooth batter. Cover and leave to rest for 30 minutes.
• Fill a deep heavy pan a third full with oil, and heat until a cube of bread browns in 15 seconds.
• Holding the florets by the stem, dip into the batter. Deep-fry in batches for 3–4 minutes until golden. Remove with a slotted spoon, and drain on kitchen paper. Serve hot.

Stuffed mushrooms

serves 4

ingredients

3 large tomatoes
8 large mushrooms with stalks, wiped with damp kitchen paper
1 small onion, grated
25g/1oz butter
1 tablespoon chopped fresh flat-leaf parsley
salt and freshly ground black pepper

• Preheat the oven to 190°C/ 375°F/Gas mark 5.
• Put the tomatoes in a bowl of just-boiled water for 30 seconds. Peel off the skins and chop the flesh.
• Remove the mushroom stalks. Chop the stalks; mix with the tomatoes, grated onion, butter and parsley. Season with salt and pepper.
• Put the mushrooms cap side down in a large greased ovenproof dish. Fill each one with the stuffing.
• Cover with foil, and bake in the oven for about 30 minutes.

Feta cheese tartlets

serves 4

ingredients

8 slices white bread
100g/4oz butter, melted
100g/4oz feta cheese, cut into
  small cubes
4 cherry tomatoes, cut into wedges
8 black olives, pitted and halved

8 quail's eggs, hard-boiled
2 tablespoons olive oil
1 tablespoon wine vinegar
1 teaspoon wholegrain mustard
pinch of caster sugar
salt and ground black pepper

- Preheat the oven to 190°C/375°F/Gas mark 5.
- Remove the crusts from the bread. Trim the bread into squares, and flatten each slice with a rolling pin. Brush with melted butter, then arrange in bun or muffin trays. Press a piece of foil into each slice to secure in place. Bake for 10 minutes or until crisp and golden.
- Mix together the feta cheese, tomatoes and olives. Shell the eggs and quarter them. Mix together the olive oil, vinegar, mustard and sugar. Season with salt and pepper.
- Remove the bread cases from the oven, discard the foil and leave to cool.
- Just before serving, fill the bread cases with the cheese and tomato mixture. Arrange the quartered eggs on the top, and spoon over the dressing. Serve immediately.

Lobster rolls

serves 6

ingredients

450g/1lb lobster meat (fresh or
  canned)
2 celery sticks
250ml/9fl oz lemon mayonnaise
1 tablespoon chopped fresh
  tarragon
6 small flatbreads such as pitta
extra virgin olive oil for drizzling

- Cube the lobster meat and the celery, and put in a bowl. Stir in three-quarters of the mayonnaise and all of the tarragon.
- Warm the flatbreads under the grill. When warm but not toasted, spread with the extra mayonnaise, and scoop in the lobster mixture.
- Drizzle with extra virgin olive oil, and serve straight away.

Deep-fried fish
serves 6

ingredients

vegetable oil for deep-frying
300g/11oz plain flour
3 teaspoons salt
2 teaspoons baking powder
900g/2lb cod fillets
2 eggs
250ml/9fl oz milk
2 tablespoons olive oil

- Preheat the oil in a deep-fryer or wok to 180°C/350°F (test by frying a small cube of bread; it should brown in 30 seconds).
- In a bowl, mix together the flour, salt and baking powder. Dredge the cod fillets in the flour mixture, shaking off any excess. Reserve the remaining mixture.
- Lightly beat the eggs with the milk and olive oil. Mix in the reserved flour mixture and beat until smooth.
- Dip the cod fillets into the batter, and deep-fry until crunchy and golden brown. Drain on kitchen paper, and serve straight away.

• •

Devilled prawns
serves 6

ingredients

2 garlic cloves, crushed
125g/4oz onions, finely
 chopped
1 tablespoon olive oil
4 tablespoons dry sherry
½ tablespoon fresh thyme and
 oregano leaves
400g/14oz cooked peeled and
 deveined prawns
150ml/5fl oz double cream
1 tablespoon smoked paprika
salt and freshly ground
 black pepper
½ tablespoon finely chopped
 fresh parsley, to garnish

- In a heavy saucepan or frying pan over a medium heat, sweat the garlic and onions in the oil until softened. Add the sherry, thyme and oregano, and season with salt and pepper. Cook for 2 minutes.
- Stir in the cream and let the liquid reduce a bit. Add the prawns and cook for 2 minutes, but no longer.
- Remove from the heat and serve immediately, sprinkled with the paprika and parsley.

Calamari

serves 4

ingredients

100g/4oz plain flour
1 teaspoon salt
2 eggs, beaten
175ml/6fl oz soda or sparkling
  mineral water
600ml/1pt vegetable oil for
  deep-frying
450g/1lb cleaned and prepared
  squid, cut into rings

- Sift the flour and salt together into a bowl. Add the eggs and half the soda or mineral water, and whisk together until smooth. Gradually whisk in the remaining soda water until the batter is smooth.
- Fill a deep heavy saucepan about one-third full with oil. Heat the oil until a cube of bread browns in 30 seconds.
- Dip the squid rings into the batter, a few at a time. Carefully drop into the hot oil. Fry for 1–2 minutes until crisp and golden. Drain on kitchen paper, and serve immediately.

Prawn kebabs

serves 4–6

ingredients

1 clove garlic
1 small fresh red chilli
1 teaspoon crushed fresh
  root ginger
1 teaspoon granulated sugar
1 tablespoon olive oil
1 teaspoon sesame oil
1 tablespoon light soy sauce
juice of 1 lime
700g/1½lb raw prawns, peeled
  and deveined
175g/6oz cherry tomatoes
½ cucumber, cut into thick slices
  or chunks
1 bunch of fresh coriander
  leaves, to garnish

- Blend or process the garlic, chilli, ginger and sugar into a paste. Add the olive and sesame oils, soy sauce and lime juice. Put the prawns in a shallow glass or ceramic dish. Pour the marinade over the top. Cover and marinate in the refrigerator overnight.
- Soak bamboo skewers in cold water for at least 30 minutes to prevent them burning. Thread the skewers with the prawns, tomatoes and cucumber. Grill or barbecue for a few minutes until the prawns are pink and cooked through.
- Arrange on a platter, and garnish with coriander leaves. Serve hot.

Stilton & pear bruschetta
serves 6

ingredients

1 ciabatta loaf or ½ loaf
  country-style wholemeal
  bread, cut into at least
  6 thick slices
1 bunch of fresh watercress
75g/3oz butter, softened
2 small ripe pears such as Beurre
  Bosc or Comice
juice of ½ lemon
200g/7oz Stilton cheese, thinly
  sliced
freshly ground black pepper

- Preheat the oven to 200°C/ 400°F/Gas mark 6. Arrange the bread slices on a baking sheet. Toast in the oven for 10 minutes, turning halfway through the cooking time. Leave to cool.
- Strip the leaves from the watercress and chop finely, reserving a few whole leaves to garnish. Mix the chopped leaves together with the butter, and season with pepper.
- Halve the pears and remove the cores. Slice the pears thinly. Put in a bowl and add the lemon juice.
- Spread the watercress butter over the toast, then put 2 or 3 pear slices on top of each onem together with a slice of Stilton.
- Bake in the oven for about 15 minutes until the Stilton is golden brown. Cut the bruschetta into quarters, and serve on a large serving plate garnished with the reserved watercress leaves.

Grilled sardines
serves 3

ingredients

12 large fresh sardines
1 tablespoon freshly squeezed
  lemon juice
6 slices white bread, toasted

- Grill the sardines for a few minutes under a hot grill until tender, turning frequently.
- Trickle the lemon juice over the top of the sardines, and serve on toast while still warm.

Thai-style fish cakes
serves 4

ingredients

350g/12oz cod fillet, skinned
1 tablespoon Thai fish sauce
2 teaspoons Thai red curry paste
1 tablespoon freshly squeezed
   lime juice
1 garlic clove, crushed
4 fresh or dried kaffir lime
   leaves, crumbled
1 egg white
3 tablespoons chopped fresh
   coriander
125ml/4fl oz vegetable oil

- Put the cod into a blender or food processor with the fish sauce, curry paste, lime juice, garlic, lime leaves and egg white, and process until a smooth paste forms. Add the coriander and process again until mixed thoroughly.
- Divide the fish cake mixture into eight. Roll into balls, then flatten to make small round patties. (If you like, make smaller patties for canapés, but don't cook as long.)
- Heat the oil in a frying pan over a medium heat. Add the fish cakes in batches, frying for 3–4 minutes on each side until golden brown.
- Remove from the pan using a spatula, drain on kitchen paper, and serve hot.

Seared squid
serves 4

ingredients

450g/1lb shallots, thinly sliced
3 tablespoons groundnut oil
1 garlic clove, finely chopped
1 fresh red chilli, seeded
   and diced
900g/2lb cleaned and prepared
   squid, cut into rings
salt and freshly ground
   black pepper
1 tablespoon chopped fresh
   coriander leaves, to garnish

- In a heavy frying pan over a low heat, sweat the shallots in the oil for a few minutes until soft. Increase the heat and sauté, stirring, until golden and starting to crisp. Stir in the garlic and chilli. Sauté for a further 30 seconds, stirring constantly.
- Season the squid with salt and pepper. Toss into the frying pan, and sauté for 30–45 seconds until the squid curls.
- Serve immediately, garnished with the coriander leaves.

Smoked trout with cucumber & cumin

serves 4

ingredients

½ large cucumber
salt
1 tablespoon cumin seeds
250g/9oz smoked trout fillets,
    flaked into large pieces
150g/5oz crème fraîche

- Peel the cucumber, cut it in half lengthways and scoop out the seeds using a teaspoon. Cut the flesh into thin strips, put in a colander and sprinkle with salt. Leave for 30 minutes.
- Dry-fry the cumin seeds in a frying pan over a medium-high heat until toasted and aromatic.
- Rinse the cucumber under cold running water, drain and pat dry with kitchen paper. Put in a bowl, and sprinkle with the toasted cumin seeds. Mix in the crème fraîche.
- Serve at room temperature, with the pieces of flaked trout on top of the cucumber mixture.

Prawn cocktail

serves 4

ingredients

4 tablespoons mayonnaise
4 tablespoons single cream
2 teaspoons tomato purée
2 teaspoons lemon juice
dash of Worcestershire sauce
dash of dry sherry
salt and ground black pepper
225g/8oz peeled and deveined
    cooked prawns
a few lettuce leaves, shredded
lemon slices, to garnish

- Put the mayonnaise, cream, tomato purée, lemon juice, Worcestershire sauce and sherry in a small bowl, and mix together. Season with salt and pepper.
- Add the prawns and stir well until the prawns are coated.
- To serve, put the shredded lettuce in the bottom of four glasses, and top with the prawn mixture. Garnish each prawn cocktail with lemon slices, and serve cold.

Chilli-garlic crab sticks
serves 2–4

ingredients

2 tablespoons vegetable oil
1 onion, finely chopped
2 fresh red chillies, seeded and
  finely chopped
2 garlic cloves, crushed
250g/9oz crab sticks
2 teaspoons light soy sauce
1 teaspoon sesame oil

- In a frying pan, a wok or a saucepan, heat the oil over a medium heat. Sauté the onion for a few minutes. Add the chillies and garlic, and continue to sauté, stirring, for a further 1 minute.
- Tip in the crab sticks and cook for 2 minutes, until they have broken up, then fold in the soy sauce and sesame oil. Serve immediately.

Prawn crackers
serves 4

ingredients

250g/9oz raw prawns, peeled
  and deveined
250g/9oz tapioca flour
salt and freshly ground
  black pepper
vegetable oil for deep-frying

- Using a blender, purée the prawns into a smooth paste. Transfer to a bowl, and mix in the tapioca flour. Season with salt and pepper. Mix well to form a stiff dough.
- Divide the dough into three equal portions. Roll each portion into a thick sausage shape (like a Swiss roll), then set the rolls on a greased plate. Using either a stand in a pan of boiling water or a steamer, steam the rolls for 40–45 minutes over a high heat.
- Leave the rolls to cool, then wrap in a clean tea towel and chill well in the refrigerator. Using a very sharp knife, slice the rolls thinly, then allow to dry out slightly.
- Heat the oil in a deep wok, and deep-fry the crackers in batches until crisp. Remove and drain on kitchen paper. Serve hot or cold.

Butterfly prawns
serves 2–4

ingredients

16 raw tiger prawns, peeled and
    deveined, with tails intact
juice of 2 limes
1 teaspoon cardamom seeds
2 teaspoons ground cumin
2 teaspoons ground coriander
½ teaspoon ground cinnamon
1 teaspoon ground turmeric
1 garlic clove, crushed
1 teaspoon cayenne pepper
2 tablespoons vegetable oil

- If using bamboo skewers, soak in cold water for at least 30 minutes.
- Cut the prawns in half lengthways down to the tail, and flatten out to form a symmetrical shape.
- Thread a prawn onto two skewers, with the tail in the middle. Thread another 3 prawns onto the same two skewers in the same way. Repeat until you have four sets of 4 prawns on each two skewers.
- Lay the skewered prawns in a glass or ceramic dish. Sprinkle the lime juice over them. Combine the spices and oil in a small bowl, and use to coat the prawns well. Cover and chill for 2 hours.
- Cook the prawns on a foil-lined grill pan under a hot grill for 6 minutes, turning halfway through cooking. Serve immediately.

Devilled eggs with caviar
serves 4

ingredients

20 eggs, hard-boiled
6 tablespoons mayonnaise
2 tablespoons finely chopped
    fresh dill
100g/4oz caviar
salt and freshly ground
    black pepper

- Peel the hard-boiled eggs and cut in half lengthways.
- Carefully remove the yolks, and chop them finely. Put in a bowl, and add the mayonnaise and dill. Season with salt and pepper. Blend until smooth.
- Fill each half-egg with the devilled yolk mixture, and serve garnished with grains of caviar.

Bacon-wrapped prawns
serves 6

ingredients

24 large raw prawns, peeled and
  deveined
24 canned whole water chestnuts,
  drained
12 smoked bacon slices, halved
75g/3oz butter

250g/9oz cream cheese
125ml/4fl oz mayonnaise
125ml/4fl oz sour cream
3 tablespoons horseradish sauce
1 tablespoon freshly squeezed
  lemon juice

- Wrap a prawn around a water chestnut, then wrap both in a half-rasher of bacon and secure with a toothpick. Repeat the process until all the prawns, water chestnuts and bacon have been used.
- Melt 40g/½oz of the butter in a large heavy frying pan over a high heat. Add half of the prawn wraps and cook until the bacon browns. Transfer to a large dish. Repeat with the remaining butter and prawns.
- Beat the cream cheese in a medium bowl until smooth. Add the mayonnaise, sour cream, horseradish sauce and lemon juice, and blend thoroughly. Spoon the sauce over the prawn wraps.
- Grill under a medium heat until golden brown. Serve immediately.

• •

Smoked salmon rolls
serves 6

ingredients

200g/7oz ricotta cheese
50g/2oz crème fraîche
2 teaspoon wasabi paste
1 tablespoon freshly squeezed
  lime juice

12 slices brown bread, crusts
  removed
300g/11oz smoked salmon
100g/4oz baby rocket leaves,
  stalks removed

- Mix together the ricotta, crème fraîche, wasabi and lime juice. Use a rolling pin to flatten the bread slices slightly.
- Spread the ricotta mixture over the bread, then top with the smoked salmon and rocket leaves, leaving a border around the edges.
- Roll each piece of bread up lengthways like a Swiss roll. Wrap the rolls tightly in cling film, and chill in the refrigerator for 30 minutes.
- Unwrap the rolls and cut into 2.5cm/1in slices to serve.

Asparagus & chorizo salad

serves 4

ingredients
250g/9oz asparagus
2 chorizo sausages, sliced into
   bite-size pieces
3 tablespoons olive oil
½ tablespoon sherry vinegar
1 tablespoon wholegrain mustard
salt and freshly ground
   black pepper
2 slices white bread,
   crusts removed, cut into
   1cm/½in cubes
handful of rocket leaves

- Cook the asparagus in salted boiling water for about 10 minutes until tender. Drain, then refresh in cold water. Leave to cool.
- Grill the chorizo for 5 minutes under a hot grill. Leave to cool on kitchen paper.
- Combine 2 tablespoons of the olive oil with the sherry vinegar, mustard, salt and pepper.
- Heat the remaining olive oil in a pan and add the bread cubes. Fry until crisp and golden.
- Serve the asparagus on top of the rocket salad. Scatter with the chorizo and croûtons, and pour the dressing over the top.

Courgettes stuffed with mince

serves 4

ingredients
8 medium courgettes
450g/1lb minced beef
1 egg
2 garlic cloves, crushed
½ teaspoon dried mixed herbs
4 tablespoons fresh breadcrumbs
2 tablespoons water

- Pre-heat the oven to 180°C/ 350°F/Gas mark 4.
- Cut each of the courgettes in half lengthways. Using a sharp knife or teaspoon, scoop out the courgette flesh to make shells, taking care not to pierce the skin.
- Mix together all the remaining ingredients in a bowl. Spoon the mixture into the courgette halves and rejoin each half to another to form whole courgettes again.
- Put the filled courgettes in a lightly oiled baking dish, and roast in the oven for 30 minutes. Serve hot.

Beef satay
serves 4

ingredients
900g/2lb rump steak, cut into
  cubes
75ml/3fl oz black bean sauce
2 tablespoons vegetable oil

- Soak 4 bamboo skewers for at least 30 minutes.
- Thread the steak cubes onto the skewers, and brush with the black bean sauce.
- Heat the oil in a ridged grill pan over a medium-high heat. Grill the satay for 2–3 minutes on each side, brushing with any leftover black bean sauce. Serve hot.

• •

Moroccan lamb koftas
serves 4

ingredients
450g/1lb minced lamb
2 eggs, lightly beaten
200g/7oz stale coarse fresh
  breadcrumbs
2 onions, grated
2 tablespoons chopped fresh
  flat-leaf parsley
½ teaspoon ground cinnamon
1 teaspoon ground cumin
½ teaspoon chilli powder

2 teaspoons ground turmeric
1 teaspoon ground allspice

For the yogurt sauce
50ml/2fl oz Greek-style yogurt
2 teaspoons freshly squeezed
  lemon juice
2 tablespoons tahini paste
1 garlic clove, crushed

- In a blender or food processor, purée all the ingredients until smooth and paste-like. Divide the lamb mixture into two portions, and mould each half around a separate metal skewer to form two long sausage shapes.
- Just before serving, grill or barbecue both of the koftas until browned and cooked through, turning from time to time while cooking.
- Combine all the ingredients for the yogurt sauce in a small bowl. Add 2 tablespoons water, mix well and serve with the hot or warm koftas.

Devils on horseback

serves 3

ingredients

3 bacon rashers, cut into thin strips
12 pitted prunes
1½ teaspoons Tabasco sauce

- Soak 12 toothpicks in cold water for 30 minutes to prevent them burning. Wrap a piece of bacon around each prune, and secure with a toothpick.
- Preheat the grill until hot. Grill the prunes, turning occasionally, until the bacon is crisp.
- Serve hot, sprinkled with the Tabasco sauce.

• •

Mixed bhajias

serves 4

ingredients

175g/6oz gram flour
1 teaspoon bicarbonate of soda
2 teaspoons ground coriander
1 teaspoon garam masala
1½ teaspoons ground turmeric
1½ teaspoons chilli powder
2 tablespoons chopped fresh coriander
1 small onion, halved and sliced

1 small leek, sliced
100g/4oz cauliflower, blanched
vegetable oil for deep-frying

For the sauce
150ml/5fl oz Greek-style yogurt
2 tablespoons chopped fresh mint
½ teaspoon ground turmeric
1 garlic clove, crushed

- Sift the flour and bicarbonate of soda into a mixing bowl, add the spices and fresh coriander, and mix thoroughly. Divide the mixture between three separate small bowls. Stir the onion into one bowl, the leek into another and the cauliflower into the third. Add 4 tablespoons cold water to each bowl, and mix each one to form a smooth paste.
- Heat enough oil for deep-frying in a wok or heavy pan. Using two tablespoons, form the mixture into rounds. Cooking in batches, fry the bhajias in the oil until golden brown. Remove with a slotted spoon and drain on kitchen paper.
- Mix all the sauce ingredients together, and pour into a small serving bowl. Serve with the warm bhajias.

Minced beef with eggs
serves 6

ingredients

1 onion, finely chopped
40g/1½oz butter
450g/1lb minced beef
1 green pepper, sliced
2 tomatoes, peeled, seeded and
    diced
2 tablespoons chopped fresh
    flat-leaf parsley
6 eggs
salt and freshly ground
    black pepper

- Sweat the onion in the butter for about 10 minutes until starting to caramelize. Add the minced beef, and continue to cook, stirring, until the meat browns.
- Stir in the green pepper and diced tomato. Cook for 2 minutes. Mix in the parsley, and season with salt and pepper. Cover the pan, and simmer for about 8 minutes.
- Make six holes in the meat in the pan, and break an egg into each space. Cover and cook for about 5 minutes until the egg whites are cooked through. Serve hot.

Chicken saltimbocca
serves 6

ingredients

3 skinless chicken breast fillets,
    halved lengthways
6 thin slices boiled ham
6 slices Emmenthal cheese
1 tomato, thinly sliced
1 teaspoon crushed dried sage
75g/3oz fine dried breadcrumbs
2 tablespoons freshly grated
    Parmesan cheese
2 tablespoons chopped fresh
    flat-leaf parsley
50g/2oz butter, melted

- Preheat the oven to 180°C/ 350°F/Gas mark 4.
- Put the chicken fillets, bottom side up, between two pieces of cling film. Working out from the centre, pound each piece lightly with a meat mallet. Remove the cling film. Put a ham slice, a cheese slice and a few tomato slices on each piece.
- Sprinkle each fillet lightly with the sage, and roll up Swiss-roll style. Press to seal well.
- Combine the breadcrumbs, Parmesan and parsley. Dip the chicken in the butter, then roll in the breadcrumbs. Bake in a lightly oiled dish for 40–45 minutes.

Chicken liver pâté

serves 4

ingredients

450g/1lb chicken livers
50g/2oz butter
1 teaspoon brandy
2 eggs, hard-boiled
1 onion, roughly chopped

• Clean the livers thoroughly. Fry in a large frying pan over a medium-high heat with the butter and brandy.
• In a blender or food processor, purée the livers, eggs, onion and any cooking juices in the pan. Transfer the mixture to a serving dish. Cover with foil, then put a weight such as a plate on top. Chill overnight.
• Serve at room temperature.

Crab pâté

serves 10

ingredients

275g/10oz canned cream of mushroom soup
1 tablespoon powdered gelatine
100g/4oz mayonnaise
225g/8oz cream cheese, softened
350g/12oz cooked crabmeat
1 small onion, finely chopped
100g/4oz celery, finely chopped
½ teaspoon dried dill

• Heat the soup in a medium heavy saucepan over a low heat. Remove from the heat.
• In a small bowl, dissolve the gelatine in 3 tablespoons cold water. Add to the soup, stirring well until completely combined. Add the remaining ingredients and mix thoroughly.
• Spoon into an oiled 1.2-litre/2pt mould, and chill until firm.

Smoked mackerel pâté
serves 4

ingredients

1 smoked mackerel fillet, skinned
50g/2oz cottage cheese
60ml/2½ fl oz sour cream
½ teaspoon dried fennel
½ teaspoon dried dill
juice of 1 lemon
salt and freshly ground
    black pepper
freshly grated nutmeg

- Purée the mackerel in a food processor or blender.
- Add the cottage cheese, sour cream, lemon juice, fennel and dill. Continue blending until smooth, stirring occasionally.
- Spoon the mixture into a bowl. Season with salt, pepper and nutmeg to taste.
- Divide the mixture among four individual pots or dishes, cover and chill for 24 hours.

Pork & liver pâté
serves 8

ingredients

350g/12oz streaky bacon rashers
225g/8oz pork shoulder, roughly
    chopped
225g/8oz pork sausagemeat
225g/8oz pig's liver, chopped
1 small onion

2 garlic cloves
1 tablespoon chopped fresh
    oregano
1 tablespoon chopped fresh thyme
3 tablespoons marsala
salt and ground black pepper

- Preheat the oven to 170°C/325°F/Gas mark 3.
- Grease a 450g/1lb loaf tin. Line with the bacon rashers, reserving a few for the top.
- Put the pork shoulder in a food processor and chop until fine. Add the remaining ingredients, and blend for 30 seconds until smooth.
- Add the mixture to the loaf tin, smooth the top and cover with the reserved bacon rashers. Cover with foil.
- Put the loaf tin in a larger baking tray half-filled with boiling water. Carefully transfer to the oven, and bake for 1½ hours or until firm. Remove from the oven and take off the foil. Cover the pâté with greaseproof paper, and set a heavy weight on top such as a plate. Chill overnight in the refrigerator. Serve in slices at room temperature.

Pâté en croûte
serves 8

ingredients
450g/1lb streaky bacon rashers
250g/9oz chicken livers, cleaned
  and finely minced
1 onion, finely chopped
1 garlic clove, crushed
2 tablespoons fresh white
  breadcrumbs

3 tablespoons sherry
1 teaspoon freshly grated nutmeg
200g/7oz ready-made puff pastry
1 egg, beaten
freshly ground black pepper

- Preheat the oven to 180°C/350°F/Gas mark 4.
- Set aside 6 rashers of the bacon to line the pâté tin. Remove and discard the rinds from the remaining bacon rashers, and chop finely.
- Mix the rindless rashers with the chicken liver in a large bowl. Stir in the onion, garlic, breadcrumbs, sherry, nutmeg and black pepper to taste.
- Stretch the remaining rashers of bacon across the bottom and sides of a 1.1kg/2lb loaf tin, reserving 2 for the top. Spoon in the pâté mixture, and place 2 rashers on top.
- Cover with foil, and stand the pâté tin in a shallow roasting tin half-filled with hot water. Bake in the oven for 30 minutes until the pâté has shrunk away from the sides of the tin.
- Remove the pâté tin from the hot water, and pour off the excess fat. Leave to stand for 15 minutes.
- Increase the oven temperature to 200°C/400°F/Gas mark 6.
- Roll out the pastry thinly. Turn the pâté out of its tin, and brush with some of the beaten egg. Cover with the pastry, using the beaten egg to seal the edges and to brush the outside of the pastry case.
- Carefully place on an oiled baking sheet, and cook in the oven for a further 30 minutes until the pastry is golden brown. Remove from the oven, and allow to cool before serving.

Dolmades
serves 4

ingredients

1 tablespoon olive oil
100g/4oz minced beef
2 tablespoons pine nuts
1 onion, chopped
1 tablespoon chopped fresh
   coriander leaves
1 teaspoon ground cumin
1 tablespoon tomato purée

8 preserved vine leaves
salt and freshly ground
   black pepper

For the tomato sauce:
150ml/5fl oz passata
150ml/5fl oz beef stock
2 teaspoons caster sugar

- To make the filling, heat the oil in a pan over a medium heat. Add the minced beef, pine nuts and onion. Cook, stirring, for 5 minutes until the meat has browned and sealed.
- Stir in the fresh coriander, cumin and tomato purée. Cook for a further 3 minutes, then season well with salt and pepper. Remove from the heat and set aside.
- Rinse the vine leaves, and lay them shiny side down on a work surface. Put some of the filling in the centre of each leaf, and fold the stalk end over the filling. Roll up each parcel towards the tip of the leaf, and put in a lightly greased flameproof casserole dish, seam side down.
- To make the tomato sauce, mix together the passata, stock and sugar, and pour over the vine leaves, making sure that each one is covered. Cover the casserole, and cook over a medium heat for a few minutes. Reduce the heat, and cook gently for a further 30 minutes. Serve hot.

Cheesy potato skins
serves 4

ingredients

3 baking potatoes, scored into
  quarters
1 teaspoon vegetable oil
50g/2oz lean smoked back
  bacon, roughly chopped
175g/6oz brown cap mushrooms,
  roughly chopped

100g/4oz cream cheese, softened
2 tablespoons milk
1½ teaspoons wholegrain mustard
50g/2oz Cheddar cheese,
  grated

- Preheat the oven to 200°C/400°F/Gas mark 6. Put the potatoes in a baking dish, and bake in the oven for 1 hour or until cooked.
- Meanwhile, heat the oil in a frying pan over a medium heat, and sauté the bacon until cooked. Add the mushrooms and continue to sauté until any excess moisture has evaporated. Remove from the heat. Blend the cream cheese, milk, mustard and half of the Cheddar cheese in a bowl.
- When the potatoes are cooked, quarter them and scrape out the inside, leaving a thin layer of potato on the skin. Put the potato flesh to one side. Put the skins on a baking tray, and return to the oven for 5 minutes.
- Mash the potato flesh, and stir into the cheese mixture with the cooked bacon and mushrooms. Pile the mixture into the potato skins, and sprinkle the remaining cheese over the top.
- Return the potato skins to the oven for 10 minutes or until golden brown. Serve hot.

Cheesy garlic bread
serves 4–6

ingredients

100g/4oz butter, melted
4 garlic cloves, crushed
¼ teaspoon dried oregano
1 baguette, halved lengthways
3 tablespoons freshly grated
  Parmesan cheese

- In a small bowl, combine the butter, garlic and oregano. Spread the mixture over the cut sides of the baguette.
- Sprinkle the bread with Parmesan, and place on an ungreased baking sheet. Grill under a high heat for 3 minutes or until golden brown. Slice and serve hot.

Salmon-filled mushroom caps
serves 6

ingredients

200g/7oz canned salmon
25g/1oz fine dried breadcrumbs
2 tablespoons chopped onion
2 tablespoons chopped fresh
  flat-leaf parsley

18 large fresh mushrooms, caps
  about 4cm/1½in diameter
2 tablespoons red pepper, diced
pinch of salt and freshly ground
  black pepper

- Preheat the oven to 180°C/350°F/Gas mark 4.
- In a small mixing bowl, combine the salmon, breadcrumbs, onion and parsley. Season with a pinch of salt and pepper.
- Remove the stalks from the mushrooms, and wipe the mushroom caps with damp kitchen paper. Put in a baking tray, crown side down. Mould the salmon mixture into the caps. Put a little red pepper on top of each cap.
- Bake for 15–20 minutes until tender. Serve hot.

● ●

Salmon yakitori
serves 4

ingredients

350g/12oz salmon fillet, skinned
  and cut into 5cm/2in chunks
8 baby leeks, trimmed and cut into
  5cm/2in lengths

For the sauce

75ml/3fl oz light soy sauce
75ml/3fl oz fish stock
25g/1oz caster sugar
75ml/3fl oz dry white wine
50ml/2fl oz sweet sherry
1 garlic clove, crushed

- Soak 8 bamboo skewers in cold water for at least 30 minutes. Thread the salmon and leeks alternately onto the soaked skewers. Leave in the refrigerator until needed.
- To make the sauce, put all the ingredients in a small saucepan, and heat gently over a low heat, stirring, until the sugar dissolves. Bring to the boil, then reduce the heat and simmer for 2 minutes. Strain the sauce and leave to cool. Pour about one-third of the sauce into a small dish.
- Heat a barbecue or grill until medium-hot. Brush plenty of the remaining sauce over the kebabs, and cook for 10 minutes, basting frequently with the sauce. Serve hot with the reserved sauce for dipping.

Melon with Parma ham

serves 6

ingredients

1 honeydew melon, cut into
6 wedges and seeds removed
6 slices wafer-thin Parma ham
6 cherry tomatoes

- Remove the peel from the melon, and cut each wedge into two thin wedges. Halve the ham slices widthways.
- Wrap a piece of ham round the centre of each piece of melon, and arrange the wedges on serving plates. Garnish each serving with a cherry tomato. Serve.

Prawn & sesame seed toast

serves 4

ingredients

225g/8oz peeled and deveined
cooked prawns
1 spring onion
¼ teaspoon salt
1 teaspoon light soy sauce
1 tablespoon cornflour
1 egg white, beaten
3 thin slices white bread, crusts
removed
4 tablespoons sesame seeds
600ml/1pt vegetable oil for
deep-frying

- Put the prawns and spring onion in a blender or food processor, and whiz until finely chopped. Transfer to a bowl, and stir in the salt, soy sauce, cornflour and egg white.
- Spread the mixture on to one side of each slice of bread. Spread the sesame seeds on top of the mixture, pressing down well. Cut each slice into four equal triangles.
- Heat the vegetable oil in a wok over a medium-high heat.
- Carefully lower the triangles into the oil, coated side down, and fry for 2–3 minutes until golden brown. Remove with a slotted spoon, and drain on kitchen paper. Serve immediately.

Cheese & spinach puffs
serves 6

ingredients

150g/5oz cooked spinach, chopped
175g/6oz cottage cheese
1 teaspoon freshly grated nutmeg
2 egg whites

25g/1oz Parmesan cheese, freshly grated
salt and freshly ground black pepper

- Preheat the oven to 220°C/425°F/Gas mark 7, and lightly oil six individual ramekins.
- In a small bowl, mix together the spinach and cottage cheese. Sprinkle in the nutmeg, and season with salt and pepper. Stir through.
- Whisk the egg whites in a separate bowl until stiff enough to hold soft peaks. Fold the egg whites evenly into the spinach mixture using a large metal spoon, then spoon the mixture into the prepared ramekins. Smooth the tops using the back of the spoon.
- Sprinkle with the Parmesan, and place the ramekins on a baking tray. Bake for 15–20 minutes until well risen. Serve immediately.

Baked mozzarella & tomatoes
serves 5

ingredients

6 beefsteak tomatoes, sliced
100g/4oz mozzarella cheese, grated
6 black olives, stoned and sliced
12 fresh basil leaves
1 tablespoon extra virgin olive oil
1 tablespoon freshly squeezed lemon juice
2 slices white bread, diced

- Preheat the oven to 200°C/400°F/Gas mark 6.
- Lay the tomato slices, overlapping them slightly, in six individual shallow ovenproof dishes.
- Sprinkle the cheese, olives and basil leaves over the top. Add a few drops of olive oil to each, then a small splash of lemon juice.
- Put the bread on a baking tray, and place both the bread and the individual dishes in the oven. Bake for 8–10 minutes. Sprinkle the croûtons over the cheese, and serve hot.

Baked fennel

serves 4

ingredients

2 fennel bulbs

2 celery sticks, cut into
  7.5cm/3in lengths

6 sun-dried tomatoes, halved

200g/7oz passata

2 teaspoons dried oregano

50g/2oz Parmesan cheese,
  freshly grated

- Preheat the oven to 190°C/
  375°F/Gas mark 5.
- Using a sharp knife, trim the
  fennel, discarding any tough outer
  leaves, and cut the bulb into
  quarters.
- Bring a large saucepan of water to
  the boil, add the fennel and celery,
  and simmer for 8–10 minutes until
  just tender. Remove with a slotted
  spoon, and leave to drain.
- Put the fennel, celery and sun-dried
  tomatoes in a large ovenproof
  dish. Mix the passata and oregano
  together, and pour the mixture over
  the fennel in the dish.
- Sprinkle the Parmesan over the
  top, and bake in the oven for
  20 minutes. Serve hot.

Greek-style tomato platter

serves 6

ingredients

8 tomatoes, sliced

100g/4oz feta cheese, crumbled

8 black olives, stoned and sliced

1 tablespoon chopped fresh
  oregano

1 tablespoon white wine vinegar

1 tablespoon olive oil

- Arrange the tomato slices on
  six small serving plates or one
  large serving platter. Scatter the
  cheese, olives and oregano on top.
- Whisk together the vinegar and oil
  and drizzle over the top of the
  salad. Serve immediately.

Fruit cocktail

serves 6

ingredients

½ honeydew melon

225g/8oz canned pineapple
chunks in juice

225g/8oz seedless white
grapes, halved

125ml/4fl oz white grape juice

- Remove the seeds from the melon half, and use a melon baller to scoop out even-sized balls.
- Combine all the fruits in a glass bowl, and pour the pineapple and grape juices over the top.
- Cover and chill until required.

●●●●●●●●●●●●●●●●●●●●●●●●●●●●●●●●●●●●●

Griddled smoked salmon

serves 4

ingredients

350g/12oz sliced smoked
salmon

1 teaspoon Dijon mustard

1 garlic clove, crushed

2 teaspoons chopped fresh dill

2 teaspoons sherry vinegar

4 tablespoons olive oil

salt and freshly ground
black pepper

100g/4oz mixed salad leaves

- Fold the slices of smoked salmon, making two folds, accordion-style, so that they form little parcels.
- To make the vinaigrette, whisk the mustard, garlic, dill, vinegar and oil together in a small bowl. Season with salt and pepper.
- Heat a ridged grill pan over a medium heat until smoking. Add the salmon parcels, and cook on one side only for 2–3 minutes until heated through.
- Meanwhile, dress the salad leaves with some of the vinaigrette, and divide between four serving plates.
- Top the salad with the smoked salmon, cooked side up. Drizzle with the remaining vinaigrette, and serve immediately.

Chicken tikka

serves 6

ingredients

450g/1lb skinless chicken breast
  or thigh fillet, cubed
1 teaspoon grated fresh root
  ginger
1 garlic clove, crushed
1 teaspoon chilli powder
¼ teaspoon ground turmeric
1 teaspoon salt
150ml/5fl oz low-fat Greek-style
  yogurt
50ml/2fl oz freshly squeezed
  lemon juice
1 tablespoon chopped fresh
  coriander leaves
1 tablespoon sunflower oil

• In a medium bowl, mix together all
  the ingredients except the
  sunflower oil. Leave to marinate in
  the refrigerator for at least 2 hours.
• Preheat the grill to medium. Lay
  the marinated chicken on a grill
  tray in a flameproof dish lined with
  foil, and baste with the oil.
• Once the grill is hot enough, grill
  the chicken for 15–20 minutes
  until cooked, turning and basting
  three times during the cooking
  process. Serve hot.

Artichoke & prawn cocktail

serves 6

ingredients

900g/2lb canned artichoke
  hearts, drained and quartered
225g/8oz peeled and deveined
  cooked prawns
3 tablespoons olive oil
2 tablespoons freshly squeezed
  lemon juice
150ml/5fl oz sour cream
salt and freshly ground
  black pepper

• Put the artichokes in a bowl, and
  add the prawns. Drizzle the oil
  and lemon juice over the top, and
  season with a little salt and lots of
  pepper. Toss gently and chill until
  ready to serve.
• Just before serving, spoon the
  mixture into six wine goblets. Top
  each one with a spoonful of sour
  cream, and serve.

Sweetcorn pancakes
serves 4

ingredients

100g/4oz self-raising flour
1 egg white
150ml/5fl oz skimmed milk
200g/7oz canned sweetcorn
  kernels, drained
vegetable oil for brushing
salt and freshly ground
  black pepper

- Put the flour, egg white and milk in a blender or food processor with half the sweetcorn, and purée until a smooth paste forms.
- Season well with salt and pepper, and add the remaining sweetcorn.
- Heat a heavy frying pan over a medium heat, and brush with oil. Drop in tablespoons of the batter, and cook until set and the bottom is golden. Turn over and cook on the other side. Serve hot.

● ●

Avocado cream
serves 4

ingredients

1 tablespoon powdered gelatine
150ml/5fl oz vegetable stock
1 large avocado
2 teaspoons freshly squeezed
  lemon juice
4 tablespoons low-calorie
  mayonnaise
1 teaspoon Worcestershire sauce
1 teaspoon Tabasco sauce
2 tablespoons snipped
  fresh chives

- In a small bowl, mix the gelatine with 50ml/2fl oz cold water, and leave to soften for a few minutes. Stand the bowl in a pan of gently simmering water, and stir until the gelatine completely dissolves. Stir in the stock and leave to cool.
- Halve the avocado, remove the stone and scoop the flesh into a bowl. Mash well with the lemon juice. Beat in the mayonnaise, and flavour with the Worcestershire and Tabasco sauces. Stir in the chives. Stir the cooled stock into the avocado mixture.
- Divide between four small dishes and chill until set. Serve cold.

Sweet & sour baby onions
serves 4

ingredients

350g/12oz baby onions
2 tablespoons olive oil
2 fresh bay leaves, torn into strips
thinly pared zest of 1 lemon
1 tablespoon Demerara sugar
1 tablespoon clear honey
4 tablespoons red wine vinegar

- Soak the onions in a bowl of boiling water for 15 minutes. Using a sharp knife, peel and halve the onions.
- Heat the oil in a large frying pan over medium-high heat. Add the onions and bay leaves to the pan, and cook for 5–6 minutes until golden brown all over.
- Slice the lemon zest into thin matchsticks. Add to the frying pan with the sugar and honey. Cook for 2–3 minutes, stirring occasionally, until the onions are lightly caramelized.
- Add the vinegar to the frying pan. Continue to cook for 5 minutes or so, stirring, until the onions are tender. Transfer to a dish, and serve immediately.

Stuffed celery
serves 6

ingredients

225g/8oz low-fat cottage cheese
2 teaspoons freshly squeezed lemon juice
½ teaspoon light soy sauce
1 teaspoon prepared mustard
50g/2oz seeded red pepper, chopped
50g/2oz chives, chopped
1 garlic clove, crushed
6 celery sticks, leaves removed

- Put all the ingredients except the celery into a blender or food processor, and purée until smooth.
- Stuff the celery sticks with the cheese mixture. Refrigerate for at least 30 minutes before serving.

Parma ham & pepper pizzas
serves 4

ingredients
1 red pepper
1 yellow pepper
½ loaf ciabatta bread
4 slices Parma ham, cut into
   thick strips
50g/2oz reduced-fat mozzarella
   cheese, thinly sliced

- Grill the peppers for 5 minutes or so until their skins are charred. When cool enough to handle, peel off and discard the skin and seeds.
- Cut the bread into 4 thick slices, and toast until golden.
- Cut the peppers into thick strips, and arrange on the bread with the Parma ham.
- Preheat the grill until medium-hot.
- Arrange the mozzarella on top of the pizzas. Grill for 2–3 minutes until the cheese is melted and bubbling. Serve hot.

Crab & cucumber savouries
serves 6

ingredients
1 large cucumber, seeded if
   necessary and diced
50g/2oz low-fat spread
225g/8oz button mushrooms,
   sliced
2 teaspoons plain flour
150ml/5fl oz fish stock, made
   with ½ stock cube
1 tablespoon dry sherry
75ml/3fl oz low-fat single cream
175g/6oz canned cooked white
   crabmeat
salt and freshly ground
   black pepper

- Boil the cucumber in lightly salted water for 3 minutes, then drain well. In the same pan, melt the low-fat spread. Cook the mushrooms, stirring, for 2 minutes.
- Add the cucumber, cover and cook over a gentle heat for 2 minutes.
- Stir in the flour, remove from the heat and, while still stiriring, add the stock, sherry and cream.
- Return to the heat, bring to the boil and cook for 2 minutes, stirring.
- Add the crabmeat, and season with salt and pepper.
- Heat through, then spoon into six serving dishes. Serve hot.

Devilled eggs
serves 4

ingredients
100g/4oz low-fat cottage cheese
50g/2oz low-fat mayonnaise
50g/2oz onion, finely diced
50g/2oz celery, finely diced)
¼ teaspoon celery seed
¼ teaspoon salt
1 teaspoon Dijon mustard
8 eggs, hard-boiled, halved with yolks removed
2 tablespoons chopped fresh flat-leaf parsley

- In a medium bowl, beat the cottage cheese and mayonnaise until fluffy. Add all the remaining ingredients, except for the egg white halves and the parsley, and beat well once again.
- Stuff the eggs with the devilled mixture, and chill until needed.
- Just before serving, scatter the eggs with the parsley.

Note If you like, you can use the egg yolks in the devilled mixture. Simply chop finely and add with the other ingredients – although this will increase the calories.

Pineapple boats
serves 6

ingredients
1 pineapple
225g/8oz low-fat cottage cheese
1 red pepper, seeded and chopped
1 fresh green chilli, seeded and chopped
salt and freshly ground black pepper

- Cut the pineapple into six wedges, then cut most of the flesh from the skin and roughly chop, discarding any tough central core. Reserve the wedges of skin.
- Put the pineapple flesh in a bowl with the cottage cheese, red pepper and chilli. Mix well and season with salt and black pepper.
- Lay the wedges of pineapple skin flesh-side down on a work surface. Spoon the cheese mixture onto the skins, and chill for at least 1 hour before serving.

Tomato & cheese tarts

serves 4

ingredients
2 sheets filo pastry
1 egg white
100g/4oz low-fat soft cheese
handful of fresh basil leaves
3 small tomatoes, sliced
salt and freshly ground
   black pepper

- Preheat the oven to 200°C/400°F/ Gas mark 6.
- Brush the sheets of filo pastry lightly with the egg white, and cut into 16 squares, each measuring about 10cm/4in.
- Layer the squares in twos, in eight patty tins. Spoon the cheese into the pastry cases.
- Season with salt and pepper, and top with the basil leaves.
- Arrange the tomatoes on the tarts, and season again with salt and pepper. Bake for 10–12 minutes until golden. Serve warm.

Succotash

serves 4–6

ingredients
4 tablespoons vegetable oil
500g/1lb 2oz lean smoked
   bacon rashers, cut into
   squares
1 large onion, finely sliced
3 garlic cloves, finely chopped
1 red pepper, seeded and
   chopped
1 green pepper, seeded and
   chopped
900g/2lb canned red kidney
   beans, drained
1.4kg/3lb sweetcorn kernels
3 tomatoes, diced
150g/5oz Parmesan cheese,
   freshly grated

- Heat the oil in a heavy saucepan over a high heat, and sauté the bacon until browned.
- Reduce the heat and add the onion, garlic, peppers, kidney beans and sweetcorn. Pour in 350ml/12fl oz water. Stir well.
- Simmer the succotash over a low heat for 15 minutes, then add the tomatoes. Continue to simmer for a further 20 minutes or until the sauce has reduced.
- Sprinkle the succotash with the cheese, and serve hot.

Szechuan beaten chicken
serves 4

ingredients
2 chicken quarters
1 cucumber, seeded if necessary
 and cut into matchsticks

For the sauce
2 tablespoons light soy sauce
1 teaspoon granulated sugar
1 tablespoon finely chopped
 spring onions
1 teaspoon red chilli oil
½ teaspoon ground black pepper
1 teaspoon sesame seeds
2 tablespoons smooth peanut
 butter, creamed with a little
 sesame oil (see note)

- Bring 1 litre/1¾pt water to a rolling boil in a wok or a large heavy saucepan. Add the chicken quarters, reduce the heat, cover and poach for 30–35 minutes.
- Remove the chicken from the wok or pan, and immerse in a bowl of cold water for at least 1 hour to cool, ready for shredding.
- Remove the chicken pieces from the bowl, drain and pat dry with kitchen paper. Take the meat off the bones. On a flat work surface, pound the chicken with a rolling pin, then tear the meat into shreds using two forks. Mix the chicken with the cucumber, and arrange in a serving dish.
- To serve, mix together all the sauce ingredients until thoroughly combined, and pour over the chicken and cucumber in the serving dish.

Note Sesame oil is very pungent and strong-tasting, so a little of it goes a long way. Use sparingly, adding just a very little at a time, when creaming with the peanut butter, so that it does not overpower the other flavours. You should not need more than a teaspoon or so.

Salads

Although salads are traditionally associated with the summer months, there are many salad recipes that can be just as tempting at chillier times of year. While salads can sometimes provide a meal in themselves, many of these salads are suitable to serve as starters to a three-course dinner or as accompaniments to main courses. This chapter contains such classics as Caesar salad and salade niçoise, as well as recipes using a diverse range of ingredients, such as Spicy Noodle Salad and Tuscan Bean and Tuna Salad. Refer to pages 725–727 for ideas for mayonnaises and dressings to serve with your salads.

Spinach, feta & pear salad

serves 4

ingredients

2 dessert pears such as Comice,
   peeled, cored and sliced
4 tablespoons walnut oil
100g/4oz baby spinach leaves
175g/6oz feta cheese, diced
75g/3oz walnut pieces
1 teaspoon freshly squeezed
   lemon juice
freshly ground black pepper

- Toss the pears in a little of the oil.
- In a large salad bowl, combine the spinach, feta cheese and walnut pieces. Gently stir in the pears.
- Whisk together the lemon juice and remaining oil, and season with pepper. Drizzle over the salad.
- Refrigerate, covered, until required.

Grilled artichoke salad

serves 4

ingredients

400g/14oz canned artichoke
   hearts, drained and halved
olive oil for brushing
3 Little Gem lettuces
salt and freshly ground
   black pepper

For the dressing
200ml/7fl oz extra virgin
   olive oil
200ml/7fl oz grapeseed oil
125ml/4fl oz white wine vinegar
pinch of granulated sugar
pinch of mustard powder
2 garlic cloves, crushed

- Preheat the grill until hot. Season the artichoke hearts with salt and pepper, and brush with olive oil. Grill until charred round the edges.
- To make the dressing, put the oils, vinegar, sugar, mustard powder and garlic into a large screwtop glass jar. Seal the jar and shake well. Season with salt and pepper.
- Toss the lettuces in the dressing with the artichokes, and serve.

Tuscan bean & tuna salad
serves 4

ingredients

1 small onion, finely chopped
2 x 400g/14oz cans butter
  beans, drained
2 tomatoes, cut into wedges
175g/6oz canned tuna in oil,
  drained
2 tablespoons chopped fresh
  flat-leaf parsley

For the dressing
2 tablespoons olive oil
1 tablespoon freshly squeezed
  lemon juice
2 teaspoons clear honey
1 garlic clove, crushed

- Put the onion and butter beans in a bowl, and mix well. Add the tomatoes. Flake the tuna with a fork, and add it to the mixture together with the parsley.
- To make the dressing, mix together the oil, lemon juice, honey and garlic in a screwtop glass jar. Seal the jar tightly, and shake until the dressing thickens.
- Pour the dressing over the salad. Toss the ingredients together, and serve straight away.

Prawn salad
serves 3–4

ingredients

900g/2lb raw prawns
100g/4oz celery, finely
  chopped
450g/1lb canned pineapple
  chunks, drained
75g/3oz raisins
125ml/4fl oz mayonnaise
2 teaspoons curry powder
4 pitta breads
4 leaves of lettuce

- Bring a saucepan of water to the boil, add the prawns and cook for 3–5 minutes until the prawns turn pink. Drain and rinse with cold water. Peel and devein the prawns.
- In a bowl, combine the prawns and the remaining ingredients, except the pitta bread and lettuce. Refrigerate for at least 1 hour before serving.
- Serve the prawn salad in the pitta bread with the lettuce leaves.

Classic Caesar salad
serves 6

ingredients

1 small baguette
2 tablespoons olive oil
2 garlic cloves, halved
4 back bacon rashers, trimmed
   of fat
2 Cos lettuces
10 anchovy fillets in oil, drained
   and halved lengthways
100g/4oz Parmesan cheese,
   freghly grated

For the dressing
1 egg yolk
2 garlic cloves, crushed
2 teaspoons Dijon mustard
2 anchovy fillets in oil, drained
2 tablespoons white wine vinegar
1 tablespoon Worcestershire sauce
175ml/6fl oz olive oil
salt and freshly ground
   black pepper

- Preheat the oven to 180°C/350°F/Gas mark 4.
- To make the croûtons, cut the baguette into 15 thin slices, and brush both sides of each slice with the oil. Spread the slices out on a baking tray, and bake for 10–5 minutes until golden brown. Leave to cool slightly, then rub each side of each slice of bread with the cut edge of a garlic clove. Cut each slice into small cubes.
- Cook the bacon under a hot grill until crisp. Drain on kitchen paper until cooled, then break into chunky pieces.
- Tear the lettuce leaves into pieces, and put in a large serving bowl with the bacon, anchovies, croûtons and Parmesan.
- For the dressing, put the egg yolks, garlic, mustard, anchovies, vinegar and Worcestershire sauce in a blender or food processor. Season with salt and pepper, and process for 20 seconds or until smooth. With the motor running, gradually add the oil in a thin stream until the dressing is thick and creamy.
- Drizzle the dressing over the salad, and toss very gently until well distributed. Serve immediately.

Mussel salad

serves 4–6

ingredients
450g/1lb new potatoes
900g/2lb black mussels
175ml/6fl oz dry white wine
1 small onion, sliced
2 sprigs of fresh thyme

2 bay leaves
pinch of saffron threads
4 tablespoons sour cream
2 teaspoons chopped fresh parsley
salt and ground black pepper

- Put the potatoes in a pan of cold, lightly salted water. Bring to the boil, then reduce the heat and simmer for 20 minutes or until tender. Drain and leave to cool.
- Scrub the mussels with a stiff brush and pull out the hairy beards. Discard any broken mussels, or open ones that don't close when tapped on the work surface. Rinse well. Put the wine, onion, thyme, bay leaves and half the mussels in a saucepan with a tight-fitting lid. Cover and cook over a high heat, stirring once, for 4–5 minutes until the mussels start to open. Remove the mussels as they open (discard any that remain closed). Cook the remaining mussels the same way and leave to cool.
- Reserve 125ml/4fl oz of the mussel cooking liquid and strain. While it is still warm, stir in the saffron. Whisk in the sour cream and season well.
- Cut the potatoes into quarters. Remove the mussels and discard the shells. Combine the potatoes and mussels in a bowl, and add the saffron dressing. Sprinkle with the parsley, and serve immediately.

• •

Spicy noodle salad

serves 4

ingredients
250g/9oz cooked rice noodles
175g/6oz broccoli, blanched
175g/6oz mangetout, blanched
2 teaspoons sesame oil
2 tablespoons plum sauce
4 tablespoons soy sauce
sliced spring onions, to serve
chopped fresh red chillies,
    to serve

- In a large bowl, mix the noodles with the broccoli and mangetout, and toss with the sesame oil, plum sauce and soy sauce.
- Sprinkle with the spring onions and chillies, and serve.

Waldorf chicken salad
serves 4

ingredients

500g/1lb 2oz red apples
3 tablespoons freshly squeezed
   lemon juice
150ml/5fl oz mayonnaise
1 bunch of celery, thinly sliced
4 shallots, sliced
1 garlic clove, crushed
75g/3oz walnuts, chopped
500g/1lb 2oz skinless lean
   cooked chicken, cubed
1 Cos lettuce
salt and ground black pepper

- Quarter, core and dice the apples. Put the diced apple in a bowl with the lemon juice and 1 tablespoon of the mayonnaise. Cover with cling film; leave for 40 minutes.
- Add the celery, shallots, garlic and walnuts to the apple, mix then add the remaining mayonnaise and blend thoroughly. Add the chicken and mix well.
- Line a salad bowl with the lettuce leaves. Pile the chicken salad into the centre, season and serve.

Asparagus & potato salad
serves 6

ingredients

450g/1lb small waxy potatoes
125ml/4fl oz extra virgin olive oil
2 shallots, finely chopped)
4 tablespoons white wine vinegar
900g/2lb fresh asparagus tips or
   young asparagus, trimmed

225g/8oz young spinach leaves,
   rinsed and drained
salt and freshly ground
   black pepper

- Preheat the oven to 220°C/425°F/Gas mark 7.
- Put the potatoes in a roasting tin, drizzle with 1 tablespoon of the oil and season with salt and pepper. Roast for 20–30 minutes until just soft to the centre, then cool.
- Meanwhile, in a small bowl, whisk together some salt, pepper, the shallots, vinegar and the remaining oil. Slice the potatoes thickly, put into a large bowl, pour the dressing over and marinate for 10 minutes.
- Cook the asparagus in lightly salted boiling water for 3–4 minutes. Drain carefully, and put into a bowl of ice-cold water to retain the colour and stop the spears cooking further. Drain again, then add to the potatoes with the spinach. Toss together carefully, and serve.

Crab & crispy noodles

serves 4–6

ingredients

vegetable oil for deep-frying
50g/2oz Chinese rice noodles
2 cooked crabs
100g/4oz alfalfa sprouts
1 small iceberg lettuce
4 sprigs of fresh coriander,
   chopped
1 tomato, peeled and diced
4 sprigs of fresh mint, roughly
   chopped

For the dressing
50ml/2fl oz vegetable oil
1 tablespoon sesame oil
½ fresh red chilli, seeded and
   finely chopped
1 piece preserved stem ginger in
   syrup, cut into strips, drained,
   and 2 teaspoons syrup reserved
2 teaspoons light soy sauce
juice of ½ lime

- To make the dressing, combine the vegetable and sesame oils in a bowl.
  Add the chilli, ginger and syrup, soy sauce and lime juice.
- Heat the oil in a wok over a high heat. Fry the noodles, one handful at
  a time, until crisp. Lift out and drain on kitchen paper.
- Flake the white crabmeat into a bowl, and mix well with the alfalfa
  sprouts. Put the lettuce, coriander, tomato and mint in a serving bowl,
  pour the dressing over and toss lightly. Place a nest of noodles on top,
  then add the crabmeat and alfalfa sprouts. Serve.

Simple bean salad

serves 6

ingredients

2 tablespoons olive oil
2 garlic cloves, sliced
2 x 400g/14oz cans flageolet
   beans, drained and rinsed
extra virgin olive oil for drizzling
2 tablespoons basil pesto
freshly squeezed lemon juice
salt and freshly ground
   black pepper
small handful of fresh basil
   leaves

- Heat the oil in a small heavy pan.
  Sauté the garlic until golden but
  not scorched. Stir in the beans,
  then leave to marinate in the oil for
  10–15 minutes.
- When ready to serve, drizzle a
  little oil over until the beans are
  generously coated, then add the
  pesto sauce and lemon juice to
  taste. Season with salt and pepper,
  then stir in the basil leaves. Serve
  straight away.

Tomato & bean salad

serves 10

ingredients

225g/8oz broad beans
225g/8oz French beans, topped
and tailed
150ml/5fl oz olive oil
1 garlic clove, crushed
2 tablespoons lemon juice
3 tablespoons chopped
fresh basil leaves
100g/4oz mozzarella cheese,
diced
700g/1½lb cherry tomatoes,
halved
salt and freshly ground
black pepper

- Cook the broad beans in lightly salted boiling water for about 3 minutes, then drain.
- Cook the French beans in lightly salted boiling salted water for 7–10 minutes, then drain.
- Put the oil, garlic and lemon juice in a blender or food processor, and whiz to combine. Stir in the chopped basil and seasoning.
- Mix together the beans, mozzarella and tomatoes. Pour the dressing over and stir to coat completely. Cover and marinate for at least 1 hour before serving.

● ●

Crab, melon & cucumber

serves 4

ingredients

2 tablespoons white wine
vinegar
150ml/5 fl oz olive oil
salt and ground black pepper
2 tablespoons pickled ginger,
chopped
2.5cm/1in piece of fresh root
ginger, peeled and grated
225g/8oz fresh cooked white
crabmeat, flaked
1 large head chicory, trimmed
and leaves separated
½ cucumber, seeded and pared
into ribbons
1 charentais melon, peeled,
seeded and cut into quarters

- Whisk together the vinegar and oil, and season with salt and pepper. In a bowl, toss the crabmeat in half the dressing. Add the pickled ginger and root ginger.
- Arrange a few chicory leaves, cucumber ribbons and a melon quarter on each of four serving plates. Spoon the crabmeat and remaining dressing over the top, and serve.

Black bean & salsa salad
serves 4

ingredients

425g/15oz canned sweetcorn kernels, drained

425g/15oz canned black beans, drained

200g/7oz celery, chopped

100g/4oz onion, chopped

50g/2oz fresh coriander, chopped

175g/6oz ready-prepared salsa

25ml/1fl oz red wine vinegar

- Put the sweetcorn, beans, celery, onion and coriander in a large bowl, and mix well. Blend the salsa and vinegar together. Pour over the salad, and toss well.
- Cover and refrigerate for at least 1 hour before serving.

Tofu salad
serves 4

ingredients

225g/8oz firm tofu, cut into 2cm/¾in cubes

100g/4oz mangetout, cut into 3cm/1¼in lengths

2 small carrots, cut into matchsticks

100g/4oz red cabbage, finely shredded

2 tablespoons chopped peanuts

For the marinade

2 teaspoons sweet chilli sauce

½ teaspoon grated fresh root ginger

1 garlic clove, crushed

2 teaspoons light soy sauce

2 tablespoons olive oil

- To make the marinade, put the chilli sauce, ginger, garlic, soy sauce and oil in a screwtop glass jar, and shake well.
- Put the tofu in a medium bowl, pour the marinade over and stir. Cover with cling film and refrigerate for 1 hour.
- Put the mangetout in a small pan, pour boiling water over and leave to stand for 1 minute, then drain and plunge into ice-cold water. Drain well.
- Add the mangetout, carrots and cabbage to the tofu, and toss together lightly. Transfer the salad to a serving bowl, sprinkle with the peanuts and serve immediately.

Saffron rice salad
serves 8

ingredients

1 teaspoon saffron threads
6 green cardamom pods
6 cloves
1 cinnamon stick
450g/1lb basmati rice

2 tablespoons olive oil
squeeze of lemon juice
50g/2oz flaked almonds, toasted
salt and freshly ground
    black pepper

- Put the saffron in a small bowl with 3 tablespoons boiling water, and leave to infuse while the rice is cooking.
- Pour 1 litre/1¾pt cold water into a pan, season with salt and bring to the boil. Add the spices and rice. Return to the boil, stir with a fork, reduce the heat, cover and simmer for 10 minutes. Stir the rice again, then pour in the saffron liquid without stirring. Cook for a further 5–10 minutes until all of the liquid is absorbed and the rice is tender.
- Put the rice in a bowl and fluff up the grains with a fork. Stir in the oil and lemon juice, and leave to cool. Transfer to a large serving plate, season with salt and pepper, and sprinkle with the almonds.

• •

Borlotti bean salad
serves 4

ingredients

700g/1½lb canned cooked
    borlotti beans, drained
2 garlic cloves
2 tablespoons fresh sage leaves
1 tablespoon red wine vinegar
2 tablespoons French mustard
5 tablespoons extra virgin
    olive oil
250g/9oz rocket leaves
salt and freshly ground
    black pepper

- Put the beans in a saucepan; cover with cold water. Add the garlic and sage leaves. Bring to the boil, and simmer for 5 minutes. Drain, then season with salt and pepper.
- Combine the vinegar and mustard, and season. Slowly whisk in the olive oil.
- Toss the beans with two-thirds of the dressing. Toss the rocket leaves in the remainder of the dressing.
- Divide the dressed leaves between four serving plates. Spoon the beans over the leaves, and serve with the bean juices over the top.

Greek salad
serves 8

ingredients

4 large beefsteak tomatoes,
  about 700g/1½lb in total
1 large cucumber
2 red onions
1 Cos lettuce
100g/4oz pitted black olives
225g/8oz feta cheese

For the dressing
125ml/4fl oz olive oil
50ml/2fl oz lemon juice
3 tablespoons chopped fresh
  coriander leaves
pinch of granulated sugar
salt and ground black pepper

- Cut the tomatoes into bite-size chunks, discarding the cores. Cut the cucumber in half crossways, then cut a cross in the end of each piece and cut into quarters. Cut the quarters crossways into bite-size pieces. Peel the onions and cut into thin wedges. Shred the lettuce.
- Whisk the dressing ingredients together in a jug. Put all the salad vegetables in a large bowl, add the olives and toss the ingredients together using your hands.
- Pour the dressing over, and toss gently to mix, then crumble over the feta cheese. Serve immediately.

Warm pasta & crab
serves 6

ingredients

200g/7oz spaghetti
2 tablespoons olive oil
25g/1oz butter
3 x 200g/7oz canned cooked
  crabmeat, drained
1 red pepper, cut into thin strips
2 teaspoons finely grated
  lemon zest
3 tablespoons freshly grated
  Parmesan cheese
2 tablespoons chopped fresh
  chives
3 tablespoons chopped fresh
  flat-leaf parsley
salt and ground black pepper

- Break the spaghetti in half, and cook in a large pan of lightly salted rapidly boiling water until al dente. Drain.
- Put the spaghetti in a large serving bowl, and toss with the oil and butter. Add the remaining ingredients, and toss to combine.
- Season with salt and pepper, and serve warm.

Tuna & bean salad
serves 4

ingredients

200g/7oz canned tuna in oil
4 spring onions, sliced
2 celery sticks, chopped
400g/14oz canned cannellini
  beans, drained and rinsed
1 tablespoon drained capers
2 tablespoons chopped fresh
  flat-leaf parsley

For the vinaigrette
2 tablespoons balsamic vinegar
3 tablespoons orange juice
juice of 2 limes
several dashes of Tabasco sauce
2 garlic cloves, crushed
1 tablespoon caster sugar

- To make the vinaigrette, put all the ingredients in a screwtop glass jar, seal tightly and shake well.
- To make the salad, put the tuna in a bowl and flake with a fork. Toss in the spring onions and celery, then stir in the beans and capers.
- Pour the vinaigrette over, add the parsley and toss to distribute the dressing evenly. Cover and chill until ready to serve.

Greek cucumber salad
serves 4

ingredients

1 cucumber
1 teaspoon salt
3 tablespoons finely chopped
  fresh mint
1 garlic clove, crushed
1 teaspoon caster sugar
200ml/7fl oz Greek-style yogurt

- Peel the cucumber and cut in half lengthways. Remove the seeds with a teaspoon and discard. Slice the cucumber thinly. Put in a bowl, and sprinkle with the salt. Toss through, and leave for at least 15 minutes.
- Combine the mint, garlic, sugar and yogurt in another bowl.
- Rinse the cucumber in a sieve under cold running water to flush away the salt.
- Drain well and combine with the yogurt mixture. Chill for 15 minutes and serve.

Salad niçoise

serves 4

ingredients

3 eggs

2 vine-ripened tomatoes

175g/6oz baby green beans, trimmed

125ml/4fl oz olive oil

2 tablespoons white wine vinegar

1 garlic clove, halved

350g/12oz iceberg lettuce heart, cut into 8 wedges

1 red pepper, seeded and thinly sliced

1 cucumber, cut into 5cm/2in lengths

1 celery stick, cut into 5cm/2in lengths

¼ large red onion, thinly sliced

350g/12oz canned tuna, drained

12 pitted black olives

2 x 175g/6oz cans anchovy fillets in oil, drained

2 teaspoons baby capers, drained

12 small fresh basil leaves

- Put the eggs in a saucepan of cold water. Bring to the boil, then reduce the heat and simmer for 10 minutes. Stir during the first few minutes to centre the yolks. Cool under cold water, then peel and cut into quarters. Meanwhile, score a cross in the base of each tomato, and put in a bowl of boiling water for 10 seconds. Plunge into cold water and peel away from the cross. Cut each tomato into eight sections.

- Cook the beans in a saucepan of boiling water for 2 minutes, rinse under cold water, then drain.

- For the dressing, put the oil and vinegar in a screwtop glass jar, seal tightly and shake to combine.

- Rub the garlic over the bottom and sides of a platter. Arrange the lettuce over the bottom. Layer the egg, tomato, beans, red pepper, cucumber and celery over the lettuce. Scatter the onion and tuna over them, then the olives, anchovies, capers and basil. Drizzle the salad with the dressing, and serve.

Thai noodle salad

serves 4

ingredients

250g/9oz thin instant noodles
450g/1lb cooked large prawns,
   peeled, deveined and halved
   lengthways
5 spring onions, sliced
2 tablespoons chopped fresh
   coriander leaves
1 red pepper, chopped
100g/4oz mangetout, sliced

For the dressing
2 tablespoons grated fresh
   root ginger
2 tablespoons light soy sauce
2 tablespoons sesame oil
75ml/3fl oz red wine vinegar
1 tablespoon sweet chilli sauce
2 garlic cloves (crushed)
75ml/3fl oz kecap manis

- To make the dressing, put the ingredients in a large bowl, and whisk together with a fork.
- Cook the noodles in a large pan of boiling water for 2 minutes, then drain well. Add to the dressing and mix well. Leave to cool.
- Add the prawns and remaining ingredients to the noodles, and toss through gently. Serve at room temperature.

• •

Couscous & haddock salad

serves 2

ingredients

175g/6oz couscous
100g/4oz cooked, flaked
   smoked haddock
50g/2oz cooked green peas
pinch of curry powder
2 spring onions, sliced
1 small egg, hard-boiled and
   chopped
2 tablespoons olive oil
2 tablespoons freshly squeezed
   lemon juice
salt and freshly ground
   black pepper

- Cook the couscous according to the packet instructions.
- Mix the couscous with the haddock, peas, curry powder, spring onions and chopped egg.
- Toss with the olive oil and lemon juice, and season with plenty of salt and pepper. Serve.

Thai beef salad
serves 4–6

ingredients

vegetable oil for frying

450g/1lb lean rump steak

3 tablespoons freshly squeezed
  lime juice

3 tablespoons Thai fish sauce

1 tablespoon granulated sugar

4 shallots, thinly sliced

2 garlic cloves, crushed

2 fresh red chillies, seeded and
  finely sliced

6–8 lettuce leaves

1 tablespoon chopped fresh
  coriander leaves

1 tablespoon chopped fresh
  chives

½ cucumber, peeled and cut into
  slices 5mm/¼in thick

2 tomatoes, cut into eighths

- Preheat the oven to 240°C/
  450°F/Gas mark 8.
- Heat a little oil in a flameproof dish
  until it is very hot. Add the meat
  and brown it quickly over a fierce
  heat. Transfer to the oven, and
  roast for 10–15 minutes.
- Leave to rest for at least 5 minutes,
  then slice thinly.
- Mix together the lime juice, fish
  sauce and sugar, stirring until the
  sugar has dissolved. Add the
  shallots, garlic and chillies.
- Make a bed of lettuce on a serving
  dish, and pile the beef in the
  centre. Spoon the dressing over
  and scatter with coriander and
  chives. Arrange the cucumber and
  tomato wedges around the edge of
  the salad, and serve.

● ●

Curly endive salad
serves 4

ingredients

½ curly endive

½ small onion, very thinly sliced

grated zest and juice of ½ lemon

1 teaspoon clear honey

2 teaspoons walnut oil

salt and freshly ground
  black pepper

- Tear the curly endive into neat
  pieces, and put in a large salad
  bowl. Scatter the onion over.
- Whisk together the lemon zest,
  juice, honey, oil and 2 teaspoons
  water. Season with salt and
  pepper, and whisk again.
- Drizzle the dressing over the
  endive, and serve.

Smoked mackerel salad

serves 6

ingredients

450g/1lb new potatoes, halved
lengthways
4 tablespoons extra virgin olive oil
3 smoked mackerel fillets, skinned
and broken into strips
250g/9oz cherry tomatoes, halved

½ cucumber, seeded and diced
75g/3oz watercress
2 teaspoons horseradish sauce
2 tablespoons white wine vinegar
salt and freshly ground
black pepper

- Put the potatoes in a pan of cold water, cover and bring to the boil. Cook for 10 minutes or until tender. Drain well, tip back into the pan and add 1 tablespoon of the oil. Season well with salt and pepper. Cover the pan and shake well to mix. Spoon the potatoes into a large bowl.
- Add the mackerel, tomatoes and cucumber, and top with the watercress and a pinch of salt and pepper.
- Mix together the horseradish, remaining oil and the vinegar in a bowl, and season well with salt and pepper.
- Pour the dressing over the salad. Toss gently, and serve.

Chinese prawn salad

serves 6

ingredients

175g/6oz beansprouts
1 small red pepper, chopped
100g/4oz peeled and deveined
cooked prawns
2 teaspoons light soy sauce
2 teaspoons white wine vinegar
½ teaspoon granulated sugar
2 tablespoons sesame oil
salt and freshly ground
black pepper
6 large lettuce leaves
1 spring onion, chopped

- Put the beansprouts in a bowl with the pepper and prawns.
- Mix together the remaining ingredients except the lettuce and spring onion, and pour over the prawn mixture. Toss well.
- Put a lettuce leaf in the bottom of each of six individual bowls. Spoon some prawn mixture on to each lettuce leaf, and scatter the spring onion over the top. Serve.

Tomato & spring onion salad
serves 4

ingredients

8 ripe tomatoes
3 spring onions, finely sliced
1 tablespoon olive oil
1 tablespoon white wine vinegar
½ teaspoon granulated sugar
salt and freshly ground
   black pepper

- Put the tomatoes in a bowl of just-boiled water for 30 seconds. Remove with a slotted spoon, then peel off and discard the skin. Cut the flesh into wedges.
- Put the tomatoes in a dish, and sprinkle with the spring onions.
- Whisk together the remaining ingredients and drizzle over the top. Leave to stand for 30 minutes before serving.

Pear & grape salad
serves 4

ingredients

2 teaspoons skimmed milk
225g/8oz low-fat cottage
   cheese, whipped
1 teaspoon granulated sugar
2 large pears, halved, peeled
   and cored
8 iceberg lettuce leaves
20 seedless white grapes, halved

- Mix the milk with the cottage cheese and sugar, and blend until of a spreading consistency.
- Put the pear halves on the lettuce leaves, cut side down, and frost generously with the cottage cheese.
- Press the grapes, cut side down, into the cottage cheese.
- Chill the salad for at least 20 minutes before serving.

Baked seafood salad

serves 6

ingredients

1 small green pepper, seeded
  and chopped
1 small onion, chopped
225g/8oz celery, chopped
450g/1lb cooked crabmeat
450g/1lb small cooked scallops
225g/8oz low-fat sour cream
1 teaspoon salt
1 teaspoon Worcestershire sauce
225g/8oz coarse breadcrumbs
25g/1oz margarine

- Preheat the oven to 180°C/
  350°F/Gas mark 4.
- Mix all the ingredients except the
  breadcrumbs and margarine in a
  casserole dish. Sprinkle the
  breadcrumbs over the top, and dot
  with the margarine. Bake for
  30 minutes, and serve warm.

Brown rice & chicken salad

serves 8

ingredients

450g/1lb brown rice
450g/1lb lean skinless cooked
  chicken, diced
12 spring onions, sliced
2 celery sticks, chopped
2 green peppers, seeded and
  chopped
100g/4oz black olives, pitted
  and halved
50g/2oz pimiento, minced
100g/4oz cherry tomatoes,
  halved
100g/4oz fresh flat-leaf parsley,
  chopped
100g/4oz radishes, sliced
50ml/2fl oz olive oil
50ml/2fl oz white wine vinegar

- In a covered saucepan, cook the
  rice in 450ml/¾pt water over a
  medium heat for about 25 minutes
  or until the liquid is absorbed and
  the rice is fluffy. Remove from the
  heat and leave to cool.
- Add all the remaining ingredients
  and toss well. Serve.

Nutty rice salad
serves 4

ingredients

175g/6oz long-grain rice
50g/2oz frozen peas
50g/2oz raisins
50g/2oz toasted flaked almonds
2 tablespoons sunflower oil
1 tablespoon white wine vinegar
salt and freshly ground
   black pepper

- In a covered saucepan, cook the rice in 175ml/6fl oz water over a medium-high heat for about 20 minutes. Add the peas and cook for a further 5 minutes. Drain, rinse with cold water, and drain again. Empty into a salad bowl.
- Add the raisins, almonds, oil and vinegar. Season with salt and pepper. Toss well and serve.

Rocket salad
serves 4

ingredients

1 slice white bread, cubed
1 garlic clove, quartered
1 tablespoon low-fat spread
100g/4oz rocket leaves
1 sprig of fresh coriander, leaves
   picked
1 sprig of fresh flat leaf parsley,
   leaves picked
1 red onion, sliced
1 tablespoon tarragon vinegar
salt and freshly ground
   black pepper

- Put the bread, garlic and low-fat spread in a small heavy frying pan over a gentle heat, and toss until golden. Remove from the heat, discard the garlic and drain the croûtons on kitchen paper.
- Put the rocket, coriander and parsley in a small salad bowl. Scatter the onion and croûtons over the top of the greens. Sprinkle with the vinegar, and season well with salt and pepper. Serve.

Beetroot & orange salad
serves 4

ingredients

1 Little Gem lettuce, leaves
   separated
2 oranges
2 large cooked beetroot, diced
1 tablespoon orange juice
1 teaspoon balsamic vinegar
salt and freshly ground
   black pepper

- Divide the lettuce leaves evenly among four small serving plates.
- Holding the oranges over a bowl, remove all the pith and zest. Cut the flesh into segments. Squeeze any juice from the membranes into the bowl, then discard them.
- Pile the beetroot in the centre of the lettuce leaves with the orange segments surrounding them.
- Add the orange juice to the bowl with the vinegar. Season with salt and pepper. Spoon the dressing over the beetroot, and serve.

Hot potato & bean salad
serves 4

ingredients

450g/1lb potatoes, scrubbed
   and diced
100g/4oz French beans,
   topped and tailed, cut into
   short lengths
75ml/3fl oz low-fat crème
   fraîche
2 teaspoons chopped fresh mint
salt and freshly ground
   black pepper

- Cook the potatoes in lightly salted boiling water for 5 minutes.
- Add the beans to the potatoes, and cook for a further 5–10 minutes until the potatoes are tender. Drain and return to the pan.
- Add the crème fraîche and mint, and season with salt and pepper. Toss gently, and serve warm.

Fresh salad with raspberry vinaigrette

serves 10

ingredients

1 bunch watercress, torn
2 heads Bibb lettuce, torn into
   bite-size pieces
450g/1lb mushrooms, sliced
425g/15oz canned artichoke
   hearts, drained
1 bunch white radishes, sliced
225g/8oz fresh raspberries

For the vinaigrette
125ml/4fl oz raspberry vinegar
½ teaspoon salt
225g/8oz olive oil
½ teaspoon Dijon mustard
½ teaspoon freshly ground
   black pepper

- Put the watercress, lettuce, mushrooms, artichoke hearts and radishes in a large bowl.
- Shake the vinaigrette ingredients together in a screwtop glass jar, and drizzle over the salad. Toss well. Serve with the raspberries scattered over the top.

Beetroot & chive salad

serves 4

ingredients

4 cooked beetroot, chopped
2 tablespoons low-fat crème
   fraîche
1 tablespoon snipped fresh
   chives
salt and freshly ground
   black pepper

- Put the beetroot in a bowl. Add the crème fraîche, and season with salt and pepper.
- Sprinkle over the chives, toss and serve immediately.

Mustard carrot salad

serves 4

ingredients

450g/1lb carrots, coarsely
   grated
25g/1oz low-fat spread
1 tablespoon mustard seeds
1 tablespoon freshly squeezed
   lemon juice
salt and freshly ground
   black pepper

- Put the carrots in a salad bowl, and season with salt and pepper.
- Melt the low-fat spread in a frying pan over a medium heat, and add the mustard seeds.
- When they start to pop, add the lemon juice, stir and pour over the salad. Toss well and serve straight away, while still warm.

Banana & pecan salad

serves 6

ingredients

50g/2oz finely chopped lean
   back bacon
50g/2oz pecan nuts, chopped
200g/7oz banana, sliced
300g/11oz celery, sliced
½ lime, thinly sliced
250g/9oz low-fat Greek-style
   yogurt
6 lettuce leaves

- Grill the bacon until crisp, then cut into small pieces.
- Mix together the bacon, pecan nuts, banana, celery, lime and yogurt in a bowl.
- Put a lettuce leaf on the bottom of each of six individual bowls, and divide the mixture between each bowl. Serve.

Turnip salad
serves 4

ingredients

350g/12oz turnips
2 spring onions, white part only,
  chopped
1 tablespoon caster sugar
pinch of salt
2 tablespoons horseradish cream
2 teaspoons caraway seeds

- Peel, slice and shred the turnips.
  Add the spring onions, sugar and
  salt, then rub together with your
  hands to soften the turnip.
- Fold in the horseradish cream and
  caraway seeds, and serve.

• •

Cranberry cream salad
serves 6

ingredients

75g/3oz cherry elatine
225ml/8fl oz hot water
450g/1lb cranberry sauce
100g/4oz celery, diced
50g/2oz raisins
225g/8oz low-fat sour cream

- Dissolve the gelatine in the hot
  water, and chill until slightly
  thickened. Fold the cranberry
  sauce into the gelatine, and add
  the celery and raisins.
- Fold in the sour cream, and pour
  the mixture into a mould. Chill until
  firm, then turn out and serve.

Basque tomatoes

serves 8

ingredients

8 firm ripe tomatoes
100g/4oz fresh flat-leaf parsley, chopped
1 garlic clove, crushed
1 teaspoon salt
1 teaspoon granulated sugar
¼ teaspoon coarse-ground black pepper
100g/4oz black olives
50ml/2fl oz olive oil
2 tablespoons tarragon vinegar
1 teaspoon Dijon mustard

- Slice the tomatoes, spread them in a shallow dish and sprinkle with the parsley.
- Combine the remaining ingredients in a bowl, mix well and pour over the tomatoes. Cover with cling film, and refrigerate for at least 2 hours before serving.

Spinach & bacon salad

serves 4

ingredients

1 slice white bread, crusts removed
1 tablespoon low-fat spread
3 rashers rindless streaky back bacon, diced
175g/6oz spinach leaves, torn into pieces
1 small onion, thinly sliced and separated into rings
1 tablespoon olive oil
2 teaspoons red wine vinegar
1 teaspoon Worcestershire sauce
freshly ground black pepper

- Spread the bread with the low-fat spread on both sides, and cut into small dice.
- Sauté the bread cubes in a frying pan until golden. Remove from the pan, and drain on kitchen paper.
- Wipe out the pan, add the bacon and fry until crisp. Remove from the pan. Drain on kitchen paper.
- Put the spinach in a salad bowl with the onion. Whisk together the oil, vinegar, Worcestershire sauce and some pepper.
- Drizzle the dressing over the salad, and top with the croûtons.

Bamboo shoot salad

serves 4

ingredients
400g/14oz canned whole
    bamboo shoots
25g/1oz long-grain rice
2 tablespoons chopped shallots
1 tablespoon chopped garlic
3 tablespoons chopped spring
    onion
2 tablespoons Thai fish sauce
2 tablespoons lime juice
1 teaspoon granulated sugar
½ teaspoon dried red chilli flakes
20 small fresh mint leaves
1 tablespoon sesame seeds,
    toasted

- Rinse and drain the bamboo shoots, then slice and set aside in a serving bowl.
- Dry-roast the rice in a heavy frying pan until it is golden brown. Remove and grind to fine crumbs using a mortar and pestle.
- Tip the ground rice into a bowl. Add the shallots, garlic, spring onions, fish sauce, lime juice, sugar, chilli flakes and half of the mint leaves. Mix thoroughly.
- Pour over the bamboo shoots, and toss together. Serve the salad sprinkled with the sesame seeds and the remaining mint leaves.

Beansprout & pepper salad

serves 4

ingredients
175g/6oz beansprouts
1 red pepper, seeded and cut
    into thin rings
1 green pepper, seeded and cut
    into thin rings
1 onion, thinly sliced and
    separated into rings

For the dressing
2 tablespoons light soy sauce
1 tablespoon sherry
salt and freshly ground
    black pepper

- To make the dressing, put all the ingredients in a screwtop glass jar, add 2 tablespoons water, seal tightly and shake well.
- Mix together the beansprouts, peppers and onion in a large salad bowl. Pour over the dressing, toss gently and serve.

Fruity pasta & prawn salad
serves 6

ingredients
175g/6oz pasta shells
225g/8oz frozen prawns, thawed and drained
1 large cantaloupe melon
2 tablespoons olive oil
1 tablespoon tarragon vinegar
2 tablespoons snipped fresh chives
200g/7oz Chinese leaves, shredded

- Cook the pasta in lightly salted boiling water until al dente. Drain well and allow to cool.
- Peel the prawns, and discard the shells.
- Halve the melon, and remove the seeds with a teaspoon. Scoop the flesh into balls with a melon baller, and mix with the prawns and pasta.
- Whisk the oil, vinegar and chives together. Pour over the prawn mixture, and toss to coat. Cover and chill for at least 30 minutes.
- Use the Chinese leaves to line a shallow bowl. Pile the prawn mixture onto the leaves, and serve.

Cucumber salad
serves 6

ingredients
3 large cucumbers, peeled and thinly sliced
1 large red onion, sliced and separated into rings
125ml/4fl oz white vinegar
3 tablespoons granulated sugar
1 teaspoon salt
¼ teaspoon pepper
¼ teaspoon ground ginger
1 tablespoon snipped fresh chives

- Layer the cucumbers in a bowl. Add the onion.
- Put the vinegar, sugar, salt, pepper, ginger and chives in a screwtop glass jar. Seal tightly and shake well to combine.
- Pour the dressing over the cucumbers, and refrigerate for at least 1 hour before serving.

Hot bulgur salad
serves 4

ingredients
100g/4oz bulgur wheat
1 teaspoon salt
2 tablespoons olive oil
2 tablespoons freshly squeezed
  lemon juice
1 garlic clove, finely chopped
2 tablespoons chopped fresh
  flat-leaf parsley
1 tablespoon chopped fresh mint
1 teaspoon chopped fresh
  coriander leaves
3 ripe tomatoes, chopped
5cm/2in piece of cucumber,
  chopped
1 green pepper, seeded and
  chopped
4 black olives, pitted and halved

• Put the bulgur in a pan. Add
  250ml/9fl oz boiling water and
  sprinkle with the salt. Stir and leave
  to stand for 20 minutes until the
  bulgur has absorbed all the water.
• Add the oil, lemon juice, garlic,
  herbs, tomatoes, cucumber and
  green pepper. Toss over a gentle
  heat for 1 minute.
• Pile the salad onto individual
  serving plates, and garnish with
  the olives before serving.

Banana & chicory salad
serves 4

ingredients
2 bananas, thickly sliced
grated zest and juice of 1 lemon
2 heads chicory
1 tablespoon sunflower oil
1 teaspoon granulated sugar
1 tablespoon chopped fresh
  coriander leaves
1 tablespoon desiccated
  coconut, toasted
salt and freshly ground
  black pepper

• Toss the bananas in a little of the
  lemon juice to prevent browning.
• Cut a cone-shaped core out of the
  base of each chicory head, then
  separate into leaves. Arrange the
  leaves on a serving plate, and pile
  the bananas in the centre.
• Whisk together the remaining
  lemon juice, zest, oil and sugar.
  Season with salt and pepper, and
  whisk again.
• Pour the dressing over the salad.
  Sprinkle with the coriander and
  coconut. Serve straight away.

Orange & chicory salad

serves 4

ingredients

1 head radicchio
1 head chicory
2 oranges
75g/3oz raspberries

1 tablespoon raspberry vinegar
1 tablespoon freshly squeezed
   orange juice
freshly ground black pepper

- Separate the radicchio into leaves, and tear into small pieces. Cut a cone-shaped core out of the base of the chicory, cut the head into chunks, then separate the layers.
- Cut off all the zest and pith from the oranges. Cut the fruit into thin rounds, then slice each round into quarters. Mix together with the salad leaves, and spoon on to four individual serving plates.
- Scatter over the raspberries, and add a good grinding of pepper. Whisk together the vinegar and orange juice, and drizzle over the salad just before serving.

Broccoli salad

serves 4

ingredients

900g/2lb fresh broccoli
225g/8oz fresh mushrooms,
   sliced
100g/4oz low-fat sour cream
100g/4oz low-fat mayonnaise
1 teaspoon granulated sugar
pinch of freshly ground
   black pepper
1 teaspoon grated onion
1 garlic clove, crushed
225g/8oz canned water
   chestnuts, drained and sliced

- Cut off and discard the tough ends of the broccoli stalks. Break the florets into small clusters, and steam for about 10 minutes until al dente. Refresh in cold water. Drain.
- Mix together the mushrooms, sour cream, mayonnaise, sugar, pepper, onion and garlic in a small bowl.
- In a large salad bowl, combine the broccoli and water chestnuts. Add the creamed mixture, and toss gently. Cover with cling film, and refrigerate for at least 4 hours before serving.

Eggs & Cheese

The beauty of eggs and cheese is that, while they can be eaten on their own or with either bread or toast, it takes little time or effort to whip them up into something worthy of serving to your guests or family at the dinner table. Most of the recipes in this chapter are quick and easy to make: the omelette options can be made in no time at all. And far from being plain or bland, there are unusual and exciting ingredient combinations to be found here, in recipes such as Quail's Eggs and Tomato Salad, Ricotta Cheese and Courgette Rolls, and Feta Cheese and Capers.

Crispy cheese balls

serves 6

ingredients

250ml/8fl oz milk
250g/9oz plain flour
75g/3oz butter
250g/9oz Cheddar cheese,
  grated
1 teaspoon cayenne pepper
3 eggs, beaten
salt
vegetable oil for deep-frying

- Warm the milk in a large heavy saucepan over a medium heat, stirring constantly while gradually adding the flour.
- Add the butter and, once the mixture has thickened, remove from the heat and mix in the cheese.
- Add salt to taste, the cayenne and the beaten eggs.
- Allow the mixture to cool. It should now be thick enough to shape into about 24 balls.
- Heat the oil in a deep heavy saucepan until very hot. Deep-fry the balls in batches of about six until they are golden brown.
- Remove from the pan with a slotted spoon, drain on kitchen paper and serve immediately.

Egg salad

serves 4

ingredients

8 eggs, hard-boiled and
  chopped
50g/2oz butter
4 tablespoons chopped celery
2 tablespoons small capers,
  rinsed and drained
2 teaspoons grain mustard
1 teaspoon chopped fresh
  tarragon
salt and freshly ground
  black pepper

- In a large bowl, mix all the ingredients thoroughly, seasoning to taste with salt and pepper.
- Serve on a bed of crisp lettuce.

Quail's egg & tomato salad
serves 4

ingredients
50g/2oz pine nuts
125ml/4fl oz olive oil
24 cherry tomatoes
24 quail's eggs, hard-boiled and
  chopped
½ teaspoon salt
½ teaspoon granulated sugar
2 tablespoons red wine vinegar

- In a frying pan over a medium heat, fry the pine nuts in a teaspoon of the oil until golden brown, taking care not to scorch.
- Put the tomatoes and quail's eggs in a serving bowl. Sprinkle the pine nuts over the top.
- Blend the remaining olive oil, salt, sugar and red wine vinegar together in a screwtop glass jar until thoroughly mixed.
- Pour the dressing over the eggs. Let stand for 10 minutes to allow the flavours to infuse before serving.

Eggs with spinach
serves 2

ingredients
450g/1lb fresh spinach
25g/1oz butter
1 small onion, finely chopped
pinch of ground nutmeg
4 eggs
salt and freshly ground
  black pepper

- Cook the spinach for 1–2 minutes in boiling water until the leaves have just wilted, then drain and squeeze out the excess water.
- In a heavy frying pan, melt the butter and sweat the onion for 5 minutes until soft.
- Add the spinach and cook for a further 5 minutes, stirring frequently. Season with a pinch of nutmeg and salt and pepper.
- Make four holes in the spinach, and break an egg into each space.
- Cover the pan and cook for 5 minutes until the egg whites are cooked through.
- Serve with bread.

Feta cheese & capers
serves 6

ingredients
½ teaspoon mixed peppercorns
8 coriander seeds
350g/12oz feta cheese, cubed
2 garlic cloves, thinly sliced
1 bay leaf
1 tablespoon capers, rinsed and
  drained
1 sprig of fresh oregano or thyme
olive oil to cover
16 black olives
hot toast

- Using a mortar and pestle, lightly crush the peppercorns and coriander seeds.
- In a screwtop glass jar, layer the feta cheese, garlic, bay leaf, ground peppercorns and coriander seeds, capers and a fresh sprig of thyme or oregano.
- Pour in enough oil to cover the cheese, and marinate for 2 weeks in the refrigerator.
- Serve the feta cheese on hot toast together with the black olives and a drizzling of oil.

Camembert with garlic
serves 4

ingredients
1 whole Camembert housed in a
  wooden box
4 garlic cloves, thickly sliced
4 thick slices brown bread,
  crusts removed
4 teaspoons cranberry sauce
fresh watercress, to garnish

- Preheat the oven to 200°C/ 400°F/Gas mark 6.
- Remove the cheese from its packaging, retaining the wooden box. Quarter the cheese, then put back in the wooden box, excluding any paper.
- Slip the garlic slices in the gaps between the quarters. Bake in the oven for 8–10 minutes until the cheese is very soft and warm.
- Serve on a bed of lightly toasted brown bread accompanied by the cranberry sauce and garnished with watercress.

Fried mozzarella

serves 6

ingredients
4 eggs
15g/½oz plain flour, seasoned
  with salt and freshly ground
  black pepper
15g/½oz dried white
  breadcrumbs
600g/1¼lb mozzarella cheese
sunflower oil for deep-frying

- Beat the eggs in a bowl. Spread some seasoned flour on one plate and some breadcrumbs on another.
- Slice the mozzarella into 5mm/¼in pieces. Dredge the slices with the flour first, then dip into the beaten egg, then into the breadcrumbs. Dip again into the egg and again into the breadcrumbs to coat well.
- Pour the sunflower oil into a deep heavy frying pan so that it is at least 2.5cm/1in in depth. Heat until a piece of bread dropped into the oil sizzles immediately.
- Fry the coated cheese in the oil until golden. Remove with a spatula, drain on kitchen paper and serve hot.

Parmesan balls

serves 6

ingredients
vegetable oil for deep-frying
175g/6oz Parmesan cheese,
  freshly grated
2 egg whites, stiffly beaten
½ teaspoon cayenne pepper

- Heat the oil in a large heavy pan until very hot.
- Mix the Parmesan with the egg whites and cayenne, keeping aside a small quantity of cheese for dusting the balls.
- Using the remaining cheese to dust your hands, form the mixture into 12 small balls.
- Deep-fry the balls in two batches until golden brown. Drain and serve immediately.

Ricotta cheese & courgette rolls

serves 2

ingredients

2 large courgettes, cut
    lengthways into 1cm/½in slices
2 tablespoons vegetable oil
50g/2oz ricotta cheese, softened
2 tablespoons chopped fresh
    flat-leaf parsley
2 tablespoons chopped tomatoes
salt and freshly ground
    black pepper

- Brush the courgette slices with the oil, and grill on each side until lightly browned. Drain on kitchen paper and leave to cool.
- Mix the ricotta with the parsley, and season with salt and pepper. Spread this mixture on each courgette slice.
- Top each slice with some of the tomatoes and roll up, securing with a toothpick. Serve.

Baked Brie with sun-dried tomatoes

serves 6

ingredients

225g/8oz Brie cheese
1 tablespoon chopped fresh
    flat-leaf parsley
1 tablespoon chopped sun-dried
    tomatoes in oil

- Preheat the oven to 230°C/ 450°F/Gas mark 8.
- Trim the rind from the top of the Brie, and place the Brie on a baking tray. In a small bowl, mix together the parsley and tomato.
- Spread the tomato mixture on top of the cheese, and bake in the oven for 10 minutes or until the cheese is heated through. Serve straight away.

Chive omelette stir-fry

serves 6

ingredients

2 eggs
2 tablespoons snipped fresh
    chives
1 tablespoon groundnut oil
1 garlic clove, chopped
1cm/½in piece of fresh root
    ginger, chopped
2 celery sticks, cut into shreds
2 carrots, cut into shreds
2 small courgettes, cut into
    shreds
1 bunch of radishes, sliced
4 spring onions, cut into shreds
100g/4oz beansprouts
¼ head Chinese leaves,
    shredded
1 tablespoon sesame oil
salt and freshly ground
    black pepper

- Whisk together the eggs and chives in a bowl. Season with salt and
  pepper, and whisk again. Heat about 1 teaspoon of the groundnut oil in
  a small frying pan, and pour in just enough of the egg mixture to cover
  the bottom of the pan. Cook for about 1 minute until set, then turn over
  and cook the omelette on the other side for a further minute.
- Tip out the omelette onto a plate, and cook the rest of the egg mixture in
  the same way to make two or three small omelettes, adding extra oil to
  the pan if necessary. Roll up each omelette and slice thinly. Keep the
  omelettes warm until required.
- Heat the remaining groundnut oil in a wok or large frying pan, add the
  garlic and ginger, and stir-fry for a few seconds.
- Add the celery, carrots and courgettes, and stir-fry for about 1 minute.
  Add the radishes, spring onions, beansprouts and Chinese leaves, and
  stir-fry for a further 3 minutes until all the vegetables are tender but still
  with a bite. Sprinkle the sesame oil over the vegetables, and toss gently.
- Serve the vegetables at once, with the omelette scattered over the top.

Egg curry
serves 4

ingredients

2 large onions, finely chopped
100g/4oz desiccated coconut
5 fresh red chillies
4 tablespoons tamarind pulp
2 teaspoons coriander seeds

pinch of asafoetida powder
pinch of cumin seeds
pinch of salt
2 eggs
2 tablespoons olive oil

- To make the spice paste, put one-third of 1 onion in a large frying pan or wok over a medium heat with the coconut, chillies, tamarind, coriander seeds, asafoetida and cumin seeds. Toast for 5 minutes, stirring constantly. Remove from the heat and set aside to cool.
- Transfer the toasted spice mixture to a grinder, and grind for 2–3 minutes. Then, in a large heavy saucepan, combine the ground spices with the remaining two-thirds of 1 onion and 400ml/14fl oz water. Bring the mixture to the boil, reduce the heat and simmer for 5 minutes, stirring occasionally.
- Add the salt, then carefully break the eggs into the saucepan. Cover and cook for 5 minutes.
- In a frying pan, heat the oil, then add the remaining onion and cook over a high heat, stirring, until brown. Remove from the heat and pour the contents of the frying pan over the eggs. Serve hot.

● ●

French omelette
serves 2

ingredients

6 eggs
50g/2oz butter

salt and freshly ground
black pepper

- Place a medium frying pan over a medium heat. Whisk the eggs in a bowl with salt and pepper until frothy. Put half the butter in the pan, tilting the pan to coat, then add half the eggs.
- Using the flat of a fork, stir the centre vigorously for 5 seconds, tilting the pan to move the uncooked egg to the edges. Remove from the pan while the middle is still slightly creamy, as the egg will continue cooking from residual heat. Repeat with the remaining butter and egg, and serve hot.

Pasta frittata
serves 4

ingredients

350g/12oz spaghetti
4 eggs
¼ teaspoon ground black pepper
50g/2oz Parmesan cheese, freshly
   grated
2 tablespoons olive oil

100g/4oz mozzarella cheese,
   diced
2 tomatoes, diced
2 onions, chopped
50g/2oz prosciutto, sliced
2 tablespoons chopped fresh
   flat-leaf parsley

- Add the spaghetti to a large saucepan of salted boiling water. Cook
  until al dente, drain, then cut into 2.5cm/1in lengths. Beat the eggs in a
  large bowl. Mix in the spaghetti, pepper and Parmesan.
- Heat the oil in a non-stick frying pan over a medium heat. Add half of
  the pasta mixture, spreading it out to the edges like a pancake. Spread
  the mozzarella in a single layer on top, then layer on the tomatoes,
  onions and prosciutto. Finish by spreading the remaining pasta on top
  and pouring any egg left in the bowl over it.
- Cook over a low heat for about 5 minutes. When the bottom has set and
  is golden brown, flip the frittata over. Cook, uncovered, for another
  5 minutes or until the bottom is crisp and golden.
- To serve, cut into four wedges and sprinkle with parsley. Serve warm.

Apple & Brie omelette
serves 4

ingredients

2 apples, peeled, cored and thinly
   sliced
25g/1oz butter
8 eggs

50ml/2fl oz single cream
100g/4oz Brie cheese, crumbled
salt and freshly ground
   black pepper

- Sauté the apple in half the butter over a medium heat. Beat together the
  eggs, cream and salt and pepper until blended but not frothy.
- Melt the remaining butter in a frying pan over a high heat until the foam
  begins to recede. Pour in the egg mixture. Cook the omelette, beating to
  lighten but allowing to set on the bottom. Fill with sautéed apples and
  Brie. Fold or roll, and slide out of the pan onto a heated plate. Serve.

Vegetable omelette

serves 6

ingredients

For the filling

25g/1oz butter

100g/4oz mushrooms,
   thinly sliced

1 courgette, cut into julienne

1 tomato, deseeded and coarsely
   chopped

¼ teaspoon salt

⅛ teaspoon ground black pepper

2 tablespoons chopped fresh
   basil leaves

50g/2oz Parmesan cheese, grated

For the omelette

12 eggs

1 tablespoon soda water

50g/2oz butter

salt and freshly ground
   black pepper

- To make the filling, heat the butter in a frying pan over a medium heat until melted. Add the mushrooms and sauté for 2 minutes. Add the courgette, and continue to sauté for 2 minutes.
- Add the tomato and cook over a high heat for 2 minutes to evaporate any excess liquid from the tomato. Add the salt, pepper and basil, and mix well. Taste for seasoning. Cover to keep warm.
- To prepare each omelette, whisk 2 eggs with a pinch of salt, a pinch of pepper and ½ teaspoon club soda until smooth.
- Melt 15g/½oz of the butter in a frying pan over a medium heat until it begins to sizzle.
- Pour in the egg mixture, and stir it in the centre of the pan with the flat side of a fork. Using the prongs of the fork, lift the edges of the omelette so that any uncooked mixture runs to the edge of the pan. Vigorously slide the pan back and forth over the heat until the omelette begins to slip around freely.
- When the omelette is lightly cooked but still creamy in the centre, spoon about 2 tablespoons of the filling over the half of the omelette closer to the pan's handle. Sprinkle 1 tablespoon of the Parmesan over the filling.
- Fold the omelette in half, and slide the folded omelette onto a serving dish. Serve immediately. Repeat with the remaining eggs.

Indian eggs & chillies
serves 4

ingredients

6 large eggs
3 tablespoons vegetable oil
4 green chillies, slit lengthways
2.5cm/1in piece of fresh root
    ginger, peeled and finely
    chopped
20 curry leaves
3 onions, finely sliced
3 tomatoes, sliced
¼ teaspoon ground turmeric
¼ teaspoon chilli powder
pinch of salt

- In a saucepan of water, slowly bring the eggs to the boil and simmer for 10 minutes until hard-boiled. Drain, remove the shells and set aside to cool.
- Heat the oil in a large pan and sauté the chillies, ginger and curry leaves for 2–3 minutes. Add the onions and fry until half-cooked.
- Add the tomatoes, turmeric, chilli powder and salt. Cook for 5 minutes or until thick. Add the whole eggs to the sauce, and mix gently until they are covered with the sauce. Remove from the heat, and serve hot with rice.

Piperade
serves 4

ingredients

1 onion, diced
75ml/3fl oz olive oil
3 red peppers, seeded and
    diced
1½ teaspoons red chilli flakes
4 ripe plum tomatoes, peeled
    and quartered
8 eggs
salt and freshly ground
    black pepper

- In a heavy pan over a low heat, sweat the onion in 3 tablespoons of the olive oil until soft and translucent.
- Add the peppers and chilli flakes. Continue to sweat over a low heat, stirring frequently, for 5–8 minutes.
- Add the tomatoes to the pan, season with salt and pepper, and cook until the mixture is thick and the tomatoes have broken down.
- Scramble the eggs in the remaining oil, seasoning to taste with salt and pepper. Fold the pepper purée into the eggs, and serve hot.

Spanish omelette

serves 4

ingredients
2 large potatoes, quartered
6 eggs
2 tablespoons olive oil
1 Spanish onion, chopped
salt and freshly ground black pepper

- Boil the potatoes in a saucepan of salted water for 15–20 minutes until just tender. Drain and leave until cool enough to handle, then cut the potatoes into slices.
- Beat the eggs in a bowl with salt and pepper to taste.
- Heat the oil in a deep non-stick frying pan over a low heat, add the onion and diced potatoes, and sauté for 10–15 minutes, stirring frequently, until soft and golden. Preheat the grill to hot.
- Add the eggs to the frying pan, and cook undisturbed for 5 minutes or until the eggs are just beginning to set in the centre. Slide the frying pan under the hot grill, and cook for a few minutes until the top is golden brown. Serve the omelette hot or cold, cut into wedges.

Pasta, Grains & Pulses

Grains and pasta are incredibly versatile – they can be used with virtually any other ingredient you can think of – and offer the foundation to a huge range of dishes. Recipes in this chapter invite you to use not just all types of pasta and noodles, but also rice, couscous, chickpeas and other pulses. Here you will find your essential recipes for such classics as spaghetti bolognese and paella, as well as more innovative recipes for dishes such as Hazelnut Pesto Tagliatelle and Rice-stuffed Courgettes.

Pasta with caviar
serves 4

ingredients
225g/8oz fresh vermicelli
75g/3oz unsalted butter
100g/4oz good-quality caviar
8 fresh chives, chopped
8 quail's eggs, soft-boiled and
    peeled
1 lemon, thinly sliced

- Cook the pasta in lightly salted boiling water until al dente, then drain, retaining a very little of the cooking water, and toss in the butter. Arrange in swirls on four small serving plates.
- Put a dollop of caviar in the centre of each mound of pasta, and sprinkle the chives over the top.
- Garnish each serving with two quail's eggs and lemon slices.

Spinach tagliatelle with veal
serves 4

ingredients
450g/1lb thin veal escalopes, cut
    into thin strips
plain flour, seasoned
50g/2oz butter
1 onion, sliced
125ml/4fl oz dry white wine
4 tablespoons chicken stock

175ml/6fl oz double cream
600g/1¼lb fresh spinach
    tagliatelle
3 tablespoons freshly grated
    Parmesan cheese
salt and freshly ground
    black pepper

- Dredge the veal strips with the seasoned flour. Melt the butter in a frying pan. Add the veal strips and sauté until browned. Remove with a slotted spoon, and set aside.
- Add the onion to the pan and sauté until soft and golden. Pour in the wine and cook rapidly to reduce the liquid. Add the stock and cream, and season with salt and pepper. Reduce the sauce again until it is thick and creamy, adding the veal towards the end.
- Meanwhile, cook the tagliatelle in a large pan of lightly salted boiling water until al dente. Drain and transfer to a warm serving dish.
- Stir 1 tablespoon of the Parmesan through the sauce, then pour the sauce over the pasta and toss gently to mix through. Serve immediately, sprinkled with the remaining Parmesan.

Pasta salad
serves 6–8

ingredients

450g/1lb penne
100g/4oz fresh basil leaves
2 garlic cloves, crushed
50g/2oz Parmesan cheese,
  freshly grated
2 tablespoons pine nuts, toasted
75ml/3fl oz olive oil
250g/9oz cherry tomatoes,
  halved
1 small red onion, sliced into
  thin wedges
150g/5oz pitted black olives

- Cook the pasta in lightly salted boiling water until al dente. Drain, retaining a very little of the cooking water to keep moist. Set aside to cool while you make the pesto.
- Blend or process the basil, garlic, Parmesan and pine nuts until roughly chopped. With the motor running, add the oil in a thin stream until well combined.
- Put the pasta in a large bowl, stir in the pesto and mix well. Add the tomatoes, onion and olives. Stir gently. Chill for 1 hour, then serve.

Pesto chicken salad
serves 4

ingredients

450g/1lb dried spiral pasta
  such as fusilli
125ml/4fl oz olive oil
2 tablespoons chopped pine nuts
2 tablespoons chopped fresh
  basil leaves
1 small onion, chopped
1 garlic clove, minced
900g/2lb skinless chicken thigh
  fillet, cubed
125ml/4fl oz red wine
1 tomato, diced
2 small carrots, chopped
salt and freshly ground
  black pepper

- Cook the pasta in lightly salted boiling water until al dente. Drain, retaining a little of the cooking water to keep moist. Cool while you make the rest of the salad.
- To make the dressing, mix the olive oil, pine nuts, basil, onion and garlic in a bowl. Season with salt and pepper. Refrigerate while you cook the chicken.
- Simmer the chicken cubes over a medium-high heat with 1 teaspoon salt and the red wine, stirring constantly, for about 10 minutes. When done, drain off the liquid.
- Toss together the chicken, dressing, tomato, carrots and pasta to serve.

Couscous salad

serves 2

ingredients

175g/6oz couscous
50g/2oz cooked peas
Pinch of curry powder
2 spring onions (sliced)
1 small egg (hard-boiled and
    chopped)
2 tablespoons olive oil
2 teaspoons lemon juice
Salt and pepper

- Cook the couscous according to the packet instructions. Mix the couscous with the peas, curry powder, spring onions and egg.
- Toss with the olive oil and lemon juice, and season well with salt and pepper. Serve.

Rice salad

serves 6–8

ingredients

300g/11oz long-grain rice
75g/3oz frozen peas
3 spring onions, sliced
1 green pepper, finely diced
1 red pepper, finely diced
275g/10oz canned sweetcorn
    kernels, drained
15g/½ oz fresh mint, chopped

For the dressing
125ml/4fl oz extra virgin
    olive oil
2 tablespoons freshly squeezed
    lemon juice
1 garlic clove, crushed
1 teaspoon granulated sugar
salt and freshly ground
    black pepper

- Bring a large heavy pan of water to the boil, and stir in the rice. Return to the boil and cook for 12–15 minutes until tender. Drain and cool.
- Cook the peas in a small pan of boiling water for about 2 minutes. Rinse under cold water. Drain well.
- To make the dressing, whisk together the oil, juice, garlic and sugar in a small jug, then season with salt and pepper.
- Combine the rice, peas, spring onions, peppers, sweetcorn and mint in a large bowl.
- Pour over the dressing and mix well. Cover the salad with cling film, and refrigerate for 1 hour before serving.

Bean croquettes
serves 6

ingredients

600g/1¼lb canned cooked red
kidney beans, drained
4 tablespoons butter
1 teaspoon vinegar
¼ teaspoon dried ground bay leaf

1 egg
12 tablespoons dried breadcrumbs
vegetable oil for deep-frying
salt and freshly ground
 black pepper

- Blend the beans in a food processor until they form a smooth paste. Add the butter, vinegar and bay leaf. Season with salt and pepper. Blend for 2 minutes. Separate the mixture into 12 portions shaped like fingers.
- Beat the egg with some water, and put in a shallow dish. Put the breadcrumbs in another shallow dish.
- Coat the fingers, or croquettes, first with the egg, then with the breadcrumbs. Repeat the egg and breadcrumbs process to ensure that the croquettes are well coated. Chill for 1 hour.
- Heat enough oil for deep-frying in a heavy frying pan over a medium-high heat. When the oil is hot enough, deep-fry the croquettes until golden brown. Remove from the pan using a spatula or slotted spoon, and drain on kitchen paper. Serve hot.

● ●

Spinach & rice salad
serves 6?–8

ingredients

225ml/8fl oz vinaigrette
1 teaspoon granulated sugar
300g/11oz cooked long-grain
 rice
200g/7oz fresh spinach, thinly
 sliced
100g/4oz celery, thinly sliced
150g/5oz spring onion, thinly
 sliced
100g/4oz streaky bacon,
 cooked and crumbled

- Put the vinaigrette, soy sauce and sugar in a large salad bowl, and combine well. Add the rice and mix through well. Cover in cling film, and chill until ready to serve.
- Add the rest of the ingredients just before serving, and mix well.

Mixed bean salad
serves 4–6

ingredients

75g/3oz dried red kidney beans,
    soaked in cold water overnight
75g/3oz dried black-eyed
    beans, soaked in cold water
    overnight
75g/3oz dried borlotti beans,
    soaked in cold water overnight
125ml/4fl oz vinaigrette
1 tablespoon chopped fresh
    coriander leaves
1 onion, sliced into rings
salt and freshly ground
    black pepper

- Drain the kidney, black-eyed and borlotti beans. Put in a saucepan, cover with water and bring to the boil. Boil rapidly for 10 minutes, then simmer gently for 1½ hours until tender. Drain the cooked beans thoroughly, and put them in a large salad bowl.
- Combine the vinaigrette and coriander, and pour over the beans while they are still warm. Toss thoroughly and leave to cool for 30 minutes.
- Mix the onion into the beans, and season well with salt and pepper. Chill for 2–3 hours before serving.

Chickpea salad
serves 6

ingredients

500g/1lb 2oz dried chickpeas,
    soaked in cold water
    overnight
2 large carrots
1 large onion
3 cloves garlic
4 tablespoons extra virgin
    olive oil
1 teaspoon salt
2 tablespoons white wine
    vinegar
freshly ground black pepper

- Drain the beans and put in a saucepan. Cover with water and bring to the boil with the carrots, onion, garlic and 3 tablespoons of the olive oil. Simmer for 2 hours.
- Add the salt and simmer for a further hour until the chickpeas are cooked. Add water if necessary to keep them covered.
- Drain, reserving the liquid, but discarding the carrot, onion and garlic. Serve the chickpeas hot with a little of the liquid, a teaspoon of vinegar, the remaining olive oil and a sprinkling of pepper.

Rice-stuffed courgettes

serves 4

ingredients

4 courgettes, about 175g/6oz each
1 teaspoon sunflower oil
1 garlic clove, crushed
1 teaspoon ground lemon grass
finely grated zest and juice of
   ½ lemon
100g/4oz cooked long-grain rice
175g/6oz cherry tomatoes, halved
2 tablespoons cashew nuts, toasted
salt and freshly ground black pepper

- Preheat the oven to 200°C/400°F/Gas mark 6.
- Halve the courgettes lengthways, and use a teaspoon to scoop out the centres. Blanch the shells in boiling water for 1 minute, then drain well.
- Chop the courgette flesh finely, and put in a saucepan with the oil and garlic. Stir over a medium heat until softened but not browned.
- Stir in the lemon grass, lemon zest and juice, rice, tomatoes and cashew nuts. Season well with salt and pepper.
- Spoon the mixture into the courgette shells. Put the shells in a baking dish or roasting tin, and cover with foil. Bake for 25–30 minutes until the courgettes are tender.

Lentil & rice salad

serves 6

ingredients

175g/6oz green lentils
200g/7oz basmati rice
4 large red onions, thinly sliced
4 garlic cloves, crushed
250ml/9fl oz olive oil
50g/2oz butter
2 teaspoons ground cinnamon
2 teaspoons sweet smoked
    paprika (pimenton dulce)
2 teaspoons ground cumin
2 teaspoons ground coriander
2 spring onions, chopped
salt and freshly ground
    black pepper

- Cook the lentils and rice in separate pans of water until the grains are just tender, then drain.
- In a heavy pan over a low heat, very gently sweat the onions and garlic in the oil and butter for 30 minutes until very soft and caramelized. Stir in the cinnamon, paprika, cumin and coriander, and cook for a further 2 minutes until the spices are aromatic.
- Combine the onion and spice mixture with the drained rice and lentils. Stir in the spring onions, and season with salt and pepper. Serve warm.

Spiced noodle salad

serves 4

ingredients

250g/9oz cooked rice noodles
175g/6oz broccoli, blanched
175g/6oz mangetout, blanched
2 teaspoons sesame oil
2 tablespoons plum sauce
4 tablespoons soy sauce
1 fresh red chilli, seeded and
    finely chopped

- Mix the noodles with the broccoli and mangetout, and toss with the sesame oil, plum and soy sauces.
- Sprinkle with the chilli, and serve.

Stir-fried broccoli pasta
serves 8

ingredients

450g/1lb angel hair pasta
3 tablespoons olive oil
3 garlic cloves, finely chopped
1 head broccoli, broken into florets
2 red peppers, seeded and diced

250ml/9fl oz double cream
175g/6oz Parmesan cheese,
  freshly grated
pinch of freshly grated nutmeg
salt and ground black pepper

- Cook the pasta in lightly salted boiling water for 8–10 minutes until just al dente. Drain, retaining just a little of the cooking water, then toss with 1 tablespoon of the oil. Keep warm.
- Heat the remaining oil in a heavy frying pan over a medium heat. Add the garlic and sauté lightly until soft (but do not brown). Add the broccoli and peppers, and sauté until tender.
- Remove the vegetables from the pan and set aside. Add the cream and bring to the boil. Reduce the heat and simmer for about 5 minutes until it starts to thicken. Add the Parmesan and a pinch of nutmeg, and cook for a further 2 minutes to thicken a bit more.
- Return the vegetables to the pan with the pasta, and toss together well. Season with salt and pepper if needed. Serve immediately.

● ●

Curried rice salad
serves 6–8

ingredients

225ml/8fl oz vinaigrette
1 tablespoon curry powder
½ teaspoon salt
250g/9oz cold cooked
  long-grain rice
6 scallions, chopped
4 celery sticks, finely chopped
2 red peppers, seeded and
  finely chopped

- In a small bowl, whisk together the vinaigrette, curry powder and salt to make the dressing.
- Put the remaining ingredients in a medium bowl. Add the dressing, and toss until combined.
- Cover with cling film, and chill for at least 2 hours before serving.

Mushroom risotto

serves 4

ingredients

1 onion, finely chopped

2 tablespoons olive oil

450g/1lb portobello mushrooms,
    stalks removed if woody, halved
    and thickly sliced

350g/12oz risotto rice such as
    Arborio or Carnaroli

150ml/5fl oz dry white wine

1 litre/1¾pt hot vegetable stock

25g/1oz butter

3 tablespoons freshly grated
    Parmesan cheese

- In a large heavy saucepan over a gentle heat, sweat the onion in the olive oil for about 15 minutes unti soft and caramelized.
- Increase the heat and add the mushrooms, sautéeing for 3–4 minutes until browned. Add the rice and cook, stirring, for a further minute until the grains are coated in oil.
- Pour in the white wine and simmer, stirring constantly, until the liquid has been almost completely absorbed.
- Meanwhile, keep a pan of the vegetable stock simmering on the stove. Add a ladleful of vegetable stock to the rice. Simmer, stirring, until the liquid has been absorbed. Continue adding the stock in this way, stirring continuously, until all the stock has been used and the rice is tender.
- Remove from the heat, stir in the butter and Parmesan, and serve hot.

Fresh herb risotto
serves 4–6

ingredients

1 tablespoon olive oil
1 onion, finely chopped
2 garlic cloves, finely chopped
225g/8oz risotto rice such as
   Arborio or Carnaroli
215ml/4fl oz dry white wine
700ml/1¼pt hot vegetable stock

3 tablespoons chopped fresh
   mixed herbs such as basil,
   parsley, chives and chervil
finely grated zest of 1 lemon
salt and ground black pepper
Parmesan cheese shavings,
   to serve

- Heat the oil in a medium heavy pan over a low heat. Gently sweat the onion and garlic until soft and starting to caramelize.
- Add the rice, and cook, stirring, over a low to medium heat for 1–2 minutes until all the grains are coated in oil.
- Pour in the white wine and simmer, stirring constantly, until the liquid has been almost completely absorbed.
- Meanwhile, keep a pan of the stock simmering on the stove. Add a ladleful of stock to the rice. Simmer, stirring, until the liquid has been absorbed. Continue adding the stock in this way, stirring, until all the stock has been used and the rice is tender.
- Remove from the heat, stir in 2 tablespoons of the herbs and the lemon zest. Season well with salt and pepper. Serve hot, garnished with the remaining herbs and Parmesan shavings.

Spaghetti with garlic & chilli oil
serves 2

ingredients

250g/9oz dried spaghetti
75ml/3fl oz extra virgin olive oil
4 garlic cloves, crushed
1 small fresh red chilli, seeded
   and finely chopped
6 tablespoons chopped fresh
   flat-leaf parsley

- Cook the pasta in a large pan of salted boiling water until al dente.
- Meanwhile, heat the olive oil over a gentle heat, and sauté the garlic and chilli for about 3 minutes until the garlic turns lightly golden.
- Remove from the heat and pour over the drained cooked pasta, and mix in the parsley. Serve hot.

Seafood spaghetti
serves 4

ingredients
350g/12oz dried spaghetti
500g/1lb 2oz mussels
700g/1½lb squid, cleaned
500g/1lb small littleneck clams
300g/11oz shrimps
4 cloves garlic
6 tablespoons extra virgin olive oil
250ml/9fl oz dry white wine
3 tablespoons chopped fresh
   flat-leaf parsley
2 dried red chillies, finely chopped
salt and freshly ground black pepper

- Soak the mussels and clams in water for an hour. Discard any broken mussels or clams, or open ones that don't close when tapped on the work surface. Under cold running water, scrub the mussels and clams thoroughly to remove any grit, pulling out the beards from the mussels.
- In a large deep frying pan over a medium heat, sweat 1 clove of the garlic in 2 tablespoons of the oil. Increase the heat to high, and add the mussels and clams with half of the wine. Cover with a tight-fitting lid, and cook for about 5 minutes until the shells are open (discard any that remain closed). Remove from the heat and discard the garlic.
- Slice the squid into rings and finely chop the remaining garlic. Heat the remaining oil in another pan, and sauté the garlic, parsley and chillies for a few minutes. Add the squid and cook until the edges curl.
- Pour in the remaining wine and cover. Cook for 10 minutes. Add the shrimps (just the tails) and cook for a few more minutes before adding the clams and mussels. Simmer for another few minutes, then remove from the heat.
- Meanwhile, bring a large saucepan of salted water to the boil, add the spaghetti and cook until al dente. Drain and add the seafood mixture to the spaghetti, mixing well.Stir over a low heat for a couple of minutes. Serve piping hot.

Cheese-stuffed rice balls
serves 3

ingredients

200g/7oz long-grain rice,
  cooked and cooled
2 eggs, lightly beaten
100g/4oz mozzarella cheese,
  cubed
100g/4oz coarse dried
  breadcrumbs
vegetable oil for deep-frying

- Mix together the rice and egg until well combined. Take a teaspoon of the rice and put a mozzarella cube in the centre. Top with another teaspoon of rice. Press together to form a ball. Continue until all the rice mixture has been used.
- Coat the rice balls with the breadcrumbs. Place on a baking tray, and refrigerate for at least 30 minutes. Heat enough oil for deep-frying in a heavy pan. Fry the rice balls, in batches, for 5 minutes until golden brown. Serve hot.

Broad bean, pea & goat's cheese salad
serves 4

ingredients

250g/9oz goat's cheese
1 bunch of watercress leaves
1 tablespoon chopped fresh
  tarragon
1 tablespoon chopped fresh
  flat-leaf parsley
2 spring onions, finely sliced
75g/3oz peas
100g/4oz broad beans, skinned
4 tablespoons olive oil
1 tablespoon lemon juice
1 tablespoon freshly grated
  Parmesan cheese
salt and ground black pepper

- Preheat the grill until hot. Cut the goat's into thick slices, and season with salt and pepper. Cook under the grill for 3–4 minutes until the cheese starts to melt.
- Toss the herbs with the spring onions, peas, broad beans, oil, lemon juice and Parmesan. Season with salt and pepper.
- Top the salad with the goat's cheese, and serve straight away.

Chinese lettuce wraps
serves 4

ingredients

450g/1lb minced beef

12–16 iceberg lettuce leaves

225g/8oz canned water
   chestnuts, drained and
   chopped

200g/7oz onion, chopped

2 tablespoons minced garlic

2 tablespoons light soy sauce

50ml/2fl oz hoisin sauce

2 teaspoons minced fresh
   root ginger

1 tablespoon rice wine vinegar

1 tablespoon chilli sauce

1 bunch of spring onions,
   chopped

3 teaspoons dark sesame oil

• Sauté the beef and onion in a large frying pan over a medium heat. Add the garlic, soy sauce, hoisin sauce, ginger, vinegar and chilli sauce. Continue stirring and cooking until browned.

• Add the water chestnuts, spring onions and sesame oil. Stir and cook for a further 1–2 minutes.

• To serve, arrange the lettuce leaves on the outer rim of a large serving plate. Put the meat mixture in the centre of the plate. To eat, spoon the meat mixture on the lettuce and wrap the leaf around the filling.

• •

Marinated tomato & rice salad
serves 4

ingredients

6 ripe tomatoes, diced

2 tablespoons chopped fresh
   basil

125ml/4fl oz cider vinegar

1 tablespoon granulated sugar

300g/11oz brown rice

2 cucumbers, halved lengthways,
   seeded and chopped

50g/2oz fresh flat-leaf parsley,
   chopped

125ml/4fl oz olive oil

9 spring onions, thinly sliced

1 teaspoon salt

½ teaspoon ground black pepper

• Put the tomatoes in a medium bowl. Add the vinegar, basil and sugar, and stir to mix well. Cover with cling film, and marinate in the refrigerator for 1 hour.

• Cook the rice according to the packet instructions. Drain and cool to room temperature.

• Combine the rice, cucumber and parsley in a large bowl, and stir in the olive oil. Add the spring onion, marinated tomatoes, salt and pepper, and stir to mix well. Serve.

Spaghetti bolognese
serves 4

ingredients

1 tablespoon olive oil
1 onion, finely chopped
2 garlic cloves, finely chopped
1 carrot, chopped
1 celery stick, chopped
50g/2oz streaky bacon, diced
350g/12oz minced beef
400g/14oz canned peeled
  plum tomatoes
2 teaspoons dried oregano
125ml/4fl oz red wine
2 tablespoons tomato purée
salt and freshly ground black pepper
700g/1½lb dried spaghetti

- Heat the oil in a large frying pan over a medium heat, then add the onion and sweat for 3 minutes.
- Add the garlic, carrot, celery and bacon, and sauté for 3–4 minutes until just beginning to brown.
- Add the beef and cook over a high heat for another 3 minutes until all of the meat has browned. Stir in the tomatoes (breaking up slightly with a wooden spoon), oregano and wine, and bring to the boil.
- Reduce the heat and leave to simmer gently for at least 45 minutes. Stir in the tomato purée, and season with salt and pepper.
- Cook the spaghetti in a pan of lightly salted boiling water for 8–10 minutes until al dente. Drain thoroughly.
- Transfer the spaghetti to a large serving bowl, and pour the sauce over it. Toss to mix well, and serve hot.

Smoked ham linguine
serves 4

ingredients
450g/1lb dried linguine
450g/1lb broccoli florets
225g/8oz smoked ham, cut into
   thin strips

For the cheese sauce
25g/1oz butter
1 tablespoon plain flour
250ml/9fl oz milk
2 tablespoons single cream
pinch of ground nutmeg
50g/2oz Cheddar cheese, grated
1 tablespoon freshly grated
   Parmesan cheese
salt and freshly ground black pepper

- Bring a large pan of lightly salted water to the boil. Add the linguine and broccoli, and cook for 10 minutes until the pasta is al dente. Drain the linguine and broccoli thoroughly, then set aside and keep warm.
- Meanwhile, make the cheese sauce. Melt the butter in a non-stick saucepan, stir in the flour and cook for 1 minute. Gradually pour in the milk, stirring all the time using a wooden spoon. Stir in the cream and season with the nutmeg, salt and pepper. Simmer the sauce for 5 minutes to reduce, then remove from the heat and stir in the cheeses. Stir until the cheeses have melted and blended into the sauce.
- Toss the linguine, broccoli and ham in the cheese sauce, then gently warm through over a very low heat. Divide the pasta among four serving bowls, and serve immediately.

Clam & Prosecco spaghetti

serves 4

ingredients

3 tablespoons extra virgin
   olive oil
3 garlic cloves, finely chopped
2 dried red chillies, crumbled
3kg/6½lb small clams
250ml/9fl oz Prosecco
350g/12oz spaghetti
salt and freshly ground
   black pepper
2 tablespoons chopped fresh
   flat-leaf parsley, to garnish

- Heat the oil in a heavy pan. Add the garlic, and sauté until just coloured. Add the chillies, clams and Prosecco, cover and cook over a high heat for about 3 minutes until the clams open. (Discard any clams that do not open.) Season with salt and pepper. Keep warm.
- Cook the spaghetti in lightly salted boiling water until al dente, drain and add to the clam sauce. Toss together over a high heat for 2 minutes. Remove any empty shells. Check the seasoning, and serve garnished with the parsley.

Note See instructions on page 144 for preparing clams.

Spaghetti with courgettes

serves 2

ingredients

200g/7oz spaghetti
about 3 tablespoons olive oil
2 courgettes, finely sliced
50g/2oz Parmesan cheese,
   freshly grated
salt and freshly ground
   black pepper

- Bring a large pan of lightly salted water to the boil, and cook the spaghetti until al dente.
- Heat 1 tablespoon of the oil in a large frying pan, and sauté the courgettes in batches until golden, adding more oil when necessary.
- Drain the spaghetti well, add ½ tablespoon of the oil and season generously with salt and pepper.
- Toss the courgettes with the pasta, then divide between two warmed serving bowls. Sprinkle with the Parmesan just before serving.

Tuna & tomato noodles
serves 4

ingredients

3 tablespoons olive oil

2 garlic cloves, finely chopped

2 dried red chillies, seeded and chopped

1 large red onion, finely sliced

175g/6oz canned tuna in oil, drained

100g/4oz pitted black olives

400g/14oz canned peeled plum tomatoes

2 tablespoons chopped fresh flat-leaf parsley

350g/12oz fresh egg noodles such as fettucine

salt and freshly ground black pepper

- Heat the oil in a large frying pan. Add the garlic and dried chillies, sauté for a few seconds, then add the onion. Sauté, stirring, for about 5 minutes until the onion softens.
- Add the tuna and olives to the pan, and stir until well mixed. Stir in the tomatoes and any juices, and bring to the boil. Season with salt and pepper, add the parsley, then reduce the heat and simmer gently for about 5 minutes until the tomatoes have broken down.
- Meanwhile, cook the noodles in lightly salted boiling water for 3–4 minutes until just tender. Drain well, toss the noodles with the sauce and serve immediately.

Hazelnut pesto tagliatelle
serves 4

ingredients

2 garlic cloves, crushed

25g/1oz fresh basil leaves

25g/1oz hazelnuts

200g/7oz soft cheese such as mascarpone

225g/8oz dried tagliatelle

salt and freshly ground black pepper

- Put the garlic, basil leaves, hazelnuts and cheese in a blender or food processor, and purée to a thick paste.
- Cook the tagliatelle in lightly salted boiling water until al dente, then drain well.
- Spoon the sauce onto the hot pasta, tossing until melted through. Season with salt and pepper, and serve immediately.

Peppered chicken pasta
serves 4–6

ingredients

700g/1½lb skinless chicken breast
    fillet, cut into strips
2 teaspoons cracked black
    peppercorns
2 garlic cloves, minced
3 tablespoons olive oil
350g/12oz dried ribbon noodles
    such as fettucine

350ml/12fl oz chicken stock
1 tablespoon freshly squeezed
    lemon juice
75g/3oz Parmesan cheese,
    freshly grated
salt and freshly ground
    black pepper

- Toss the chicken with the peppercorns, garlic and 1 tablespoon of the oil. Cover and marinate in the refrigerator for at least 1 hour.
- Heat the remaining olive oil in a frying pan over a medium-high heat. Add the chicken and lightly brown all over for about 3 minutes. Add the stock and lemon juice, and reduce the heat to a simmer. Simmer the sauce for about 8 minutes. Season with salt and pepper.
- Meanwhile, cook the pasta in lightly salted boiling water until al dente. Drain well and toss with the chicken. Serve immediately, with the Parmesan in a separate bowl for sprinkling over the top.

Fig & chilli tagliatelle
serves 4

ingredients

350g/12oz egg tagliatelle
2 tablespoons extra virgin
    olive oil
8 black figs, each cut into
    8 wedges
2 dried red chillies, crumbled
finely grated zest of 2 lemons
    and juice of 1
125ml/4fl oz double cream
50g/2oz Parmesan cheese,
    freshly grated
salt and ground black pepper

- Bring a large pan of lightly salted water to the boil, and cook the tagliatelle until al dente. Drain.
- Meanwhile, heat a large frying pan, add the oil and, when smoking, carefully put the figs in the pan, turning them immediately to caramelize. Season with salt and pepper, and add the chilli.
- Stir the lemon zest and juice into the cream, and mix into the cooked pasta. Add the figs and serve hot, scattered with the Parmesan.

Roasted vegetable pasta
serves 4

ingredients

50g/2oz butter, melted
2 tablespoons chopped fresh
   flat-leaf parsley
1 tablespoon finely grated
   lemon zest
1 small red pepper, seeded and cut
   into thin strips

1 small green pepper, seeded and
   cut into thin strips
100g/4oz button mushrooms,
   halved
8 cherry tomatoes, halved
350g/12oz dried farfalle
salt and ground black pepper

- Preheat the oven to 200°C/400°F/Gas mark 6. In a small bowl, mix half the butter with the parsley and lemon zest. Set aside.
- Brush the remaining butter over the peppers and arrange, in a single layer, on a baking tray. Cook in the oven for 10 minutes. Add the mushrooms and tomatoes, and cook for a further 5 minutes.
- Meanwhile, cook the pasta in lightly salted boiling water until al dente and drain. Toss the pasta with the roasted vegetables and the herb mixture. Season with salt and pepper, and serve immediately.

Tagliolini with herbs
serves 2–4

ingredients

50g/2oz fresh thyme, chopped
75g/3oz fresh sage, chopped
50g/2oz fresh mint, chopped
50g/2oz fresh marjoram,
   chopped
2 garlic cloves, finely chopped
125ml/4fl oz extra virgin
   olive oil
500g/1lb 2oz tagliolini (also
   known as taglierini)
100g/4oz Parmesan cheese,
   freshly grated
2 tomatoes, cut into wedges
salt

- Put the thyme, sage, mint and marjoram in a bowl with the garlic and the oil. Leave for at least 1 hour, stirring occasionally.
- Bring a pan of lightly salted boiling water to the boil, and cook the pasta until al dente. Drain.
- Toss the pasta with the herb dressing. Serve sprinkled with the Parmesan and a little salt, and topped with the tomatoes.

Special chow mein

serves 4–6

ingredients

50ml/2fl oz vegetable oil
2 garlic cloves, sliced
1 teaspoon chopped fresh root ginger
2 fresh red chillies, seeded and
  chopped
1 skinless chicken breast fillet, thinly
  sliced
16 raw tiger prawns, peeled and
  deveined, with tails left intact
450g/1lb egg noodles
100g/4oz green beans
225g/8oz beansprouts
50g/2oz garlic chives
2 tablespoons light soy sauce
1 tablespoon oyster sauce
1 tablespoon sesame oil
salt and freshly ground black pepper

- Heat 1 tablespoon of the oil in a wok or large frying pan, and stir-fry the garlic, ginger and chillies. Add the chicken, prawns and beans. Stir-fry for 4–5 minutes over a high heat until the chicken and prawns are both cooked. Transfer the mixture to a bowl and set aside.
- Cook the egg noodles in a saucepan of slightly salted boiling water for 2–3 minutes until tender.
- Heat the rest of the oil in the same wok used for the chicken and prawn mixture. Add the beansprouts and garlic chives. Stir-fry for 1–2 minutes. Add the noodles and toss to mix. Next, add the soy sauce and oyster sauce, and season with salt and pepper.
- Return the prawn mixture to the wok. Reheat and mix well with the noodles. Stir in the sesame oil, and serve immediately.

Smoked salmon pasta

serves 4

ingredients

1 tablespoon olive oil
1 garlic clove, crushed
375ml/13fl oz double cream
3 tablespoons chopped fresh
  chives
¼ teaspoon mustard powder
200g/7oz smoked salmon, cut
  into strips
2 teaspoons lemon juice
450g/1lb fettuccine
3 tablespoons chopped sun-dried
  tomatoes
2 tablespoons freshly grated
  Parmesan cheese
salt and freshly ground
  black pepper

- Heat the oil in a pan, and sweat the garlic briefly over a low heat. Add the cream, chives and mustard powder. Season with salt and pepper, and bring to the boil. Reduce the heat and stir until the sauce thickens.
- Add the salmon and lemon juice, and stir until heated through. Keep the sauce warm.
- Meanwhile, cook the fettuccine in a large pan of lightly salted boiling water until al dente. Drain well and return to the same pan.
- Toss the sauce through the pasta, and serve immediately topped with the tomatoes and Parmesan.

Singapore fried noodles

serves 4

ingredients

175g/6oz rice noodles
50ml/2fl oz vegetable oil
½ teaspoon salt
75g/3oz peeled and deveined
  cooked prawns
175g/6oz cooked pork, cut into
  thin strips
1 green pepper, seeded and cut
  into thin strips
½ teaspoon granulated sugar
2 teaspoons curry powder
75g/3oz Thai fish cakes
2 teaspoons light soy sauce

- Soak the noodles in water for about 10 minutes, drain well, then pat dry with kitchen paper.
- Heat the wok, then add half the oil. When the oil is hot, add the noodles and half the salt. Stir-fry for 2 minutes. Transfer to a serving dish and keep warm.
- Heat the remaining oil, and add the prawns, pork, pepper, sugar, curry powder and remaining salt. Stir-fry for 1 minute. Return the noodles to the wok with the fish cakes. Stir-fry for 2 minutes. Stir in the soy sauce. Serve immediately.

Lemon & garlic pasta
serves 4

ingredients
1 teaspoon olive oil
2 garlic cloves, minced
125ml/4fl oz dry white wine
50ml/2fl oz freshly squeezed
  lemon juice
150g/5oz tomatoes, chopped
100g/4oz spinach angel
  hair pasta
100g/4oz semolina angel
  hair pasta
25g/1oz chopped fresh basil
2 tablespoons freshly grated
  Parmesan cheese
salt and freshly ground
  black pepper

- In a frying pan, heat the oil and sauté the garlic over a medium heat until the garlic just begins to colour. Remove the frying pan from the heat, and pour in the wine.
- Return the pan to the heat. Cook for another 2 minutes until the wine has been reduced by half. Stir in the lemon juice and tomatoes, and remove the pan from the heat.
- Meanwhile, put both pastas in a large saucepan of lightly salted boiling water, and cook until al dente. Drain and put the pasta into a warmed serving bowl. Add the basil, Parmesan and tomato mixture. Season with salt and pepper. Toss and serve at once.

Bottarga spaghetti
serves 4

ingredients
200g/7oz bottarga (Italian dried
  salted fish roe), grated
juice of 2 lemons
125ml/4fl oz extra virgin
  olive oil
350g/12oz dried spaghetti
2 dried red chillies, crumbled
salt and freshly ground
  black pepper

- In a bowl, combine three-quarters of the bottarga and the lemon juice to create a cream. Gradually stir in the oil to form a thick sauce.
- Cook the spaghetti in lightly salted boiling water until al dente. Drain; reserve a little of the cooking water.
- Stir the hot cooking water into the bottarga cream to loosen. Add the chilli, and season with salt and pepper. Add the spaghetti to the sauce and toss to coat thoroughly.
- Serve immediately, scattered with the remaining bottarga.

Ginger & coriander noodles
serves 4–6

ingredients

handful of fresh coriander sprigs
225g/8oz dried egg noodles
50ml/2fl oz groundnut oil
5cm/2in piece of fresh root ginger,
  finely shredded

7 spring onions, shredded
2 tablespoons light soy sauce
salt and freshly ground
  black pepper

- Strip the leaves from the coriander sprigs. Pile them on a chopping board and chop roughly using a cleaver or a large sharp knife.
- Cook the noodles according to the packet instructions. Rinse under cold water and drain well. Toss them in 1 tablespoon of the oil.
- Heat a wok until hot, add the remaining oil and swirl it around the wok. Add the ginger and stir-fry for a few seconds, then add the noodles and spring onions. Stir-fry for 3–4 minutes until hot.
- Sprinkle in the soy sauce, and season with salt and pepper. Toss well, then serve immediately.

Red fried rice
serves 2

ingredients

100g/4oz basmati rice
2 tablespoons groundnut oil
1 small red onion, chopped
1 red pepper, chopped

225g/8oz cherry tomatoes, halved
2 eggs, beaten
salt and freshly ground
  black pepper

- Put the rice in a colander, and rinse under cold running water. Drain well. Bring a large saucepan of lightly salted water to the boil, add the rice and cook for 10–12 minutes until tender.
- Meanwhile, heat the oil in a wok until very hot. Add the onion and red pepper, and stir-fry for 2–3 minutes. Add the tomatoes, and stir-fry for a further 2 minutes. Pour in the eggs. Cook for 30 seconds without stirring, then stir to break up the egg as it sets.
- Drain the cooked rice thoroughly, add to the wok and toss it over the heat with the vegetable and egg mixture for 3 minutes. Season with salt and pepper, and serve hot.

Paella

serves 4

ingredients

12 black mussels

125ml/4fl oz white wine

1½ small red onions, chopped

125ml/4fl oz olive oil

1 small skinless chicken breast
fillet, cut into bite-size pieces

12 raw prawns, peeled and
deveined

100g/4oz cleaned squid rings

100g/4oz skinless cod fillet, cut
into bite-size cubes

1 rasher smoked back bacon,
finely chopped

4 garlic cloves, crushed

1 red pepper, seeded and finely
chopped

1 tomato, peeled and chopped

75g/3oz chorizo, thinly sliced

pinch of cayenne pepper

200g/7oz long-grain rice

¼ teaspoon saffron threads

500ml/18fl oz chicken stock

75g/3oz fresh peas

2 tablespoons finely chopped fresh
flat-leaf parsley

salt and ground black pepper

- Scrub the mussels with a stiff brush and pull out the hairy beards.
  Discard any broken mussels or open ones that do not close when tapped
  on the work surface.
- Heat the wine and onion in a large pan. Add the mussels, cover and
  gently shake the pan for 4–5 minutes over a high heat. After 3 minutes,
  begin removing any opened mussels and set aside. At the end of
  5 minutes, discard any unopened mussels. Reserve the cooking liquid.
- Heat half the oil in a large frying pan. Pat the chicken dry with kitchen
  paper, then cook for 5 minutes or until golden brown. Remove from the
  pan and set aside. Add the prawns, squid and cod to the pan, and cook
  for 1 minute. Remove from the pan and set aside.
- Heat the remaining oil in the same pan. Add the bacon, garlic and red
  pepper. Cook for 5 minutes, then add the tomato, chorizo and cayenne.
  Season with salt and pepper. Stir in the reserved cooking liquid, then
  add the rice and mix well.
- In a heavy saucepan, blend the saffron with the stock and mix well.
  Bring slowly to the boil. Reduce the heat to low. Simmer, uncovered, for
  15 minutes, without stirring.
- Put the peas, chicken, prawns, squid and cod on top of the rice. Using a
  wooden spoon, push pieces into the rice, cover and cook over a low
  heat for 10–15 minutes until the rice is tender and seafood cooked. Add
  the mussels for the last 2 minutes to heat. Serve sprinkled with parsley.

Sausage & ricotta penne

serves 4

ingredients

4 pepperoni sausages
1 onion, finely chopped
1 fennel bulb, chopped
1 tablespoon extra virgin olive oil
150ml/5fl oz red wine
100ml/3½fl oz passata or
  tomato sauce
3 tablespoons chopped fresh
  basil leaves
300g/11oz dried penne
100g/4oz ricotta cheese
50g/2oz Parmesan cheese,
  freshly grated
salt and freshly ground
  black pepper

- Put the sausages in a frying pan and cover with water. Bring to the boil, then simmer until the water evaporates. Cool, remove the meat from the casings and crumble.
- Fry the onion and fennel in the oil until soft. Add the sausage, wine and passata or tomato sauce. Cook for 10 minutes. Add the basil and season with salt and pepper.
- Cook the penne in lightly salted boiling water until al dente, then drain. Stir in the sauce.
- Put 1 tablespoon ricotta on each plate. Spoon the pasta over the top, and sprinkle with Parmesan.

Cajun chicken pasta

serves 2

ingredients

100g/4oz linguine
2 skinless chicken breast fillet
  halves, cut into thin strips
2 teaspoons Cajun seasoning
25g/1oz butter
1 green pepper, sliced
1 red pepper, sliced
4 mushrooms, sliced
1 onion, sliced
300ml/10fl oz double cream
¼ teaspoon dried basil
¼ teaspoon lemon pepper
¼ teaspoon salt
⅛ teaspoon garlic powder
⅛ teaspoon ground black pepper

- Cook the pasta in lightly salted boiling water until al dente. Drain.
- Meanwhile, put the chicken and Cajun seasoning in a bowl. Toss to coat. In a large frying pan over a medium heat, sauté the chicken in the butter for 5–7 minutes until almost tender. Add the peppers, mushrooms and onion, then cook, stirring for 2–3 minutes.
- Reduce the heat, and add the cream, basil and seasonings. Tip in the linguine, and toss gently. Heat through and serve immediately.

Pies & Tarts

People often think that working with pastry is difficult, but there is no longer any need to worry – this chapter will show you how to get it right. These recipes are diverse and include not only old favourites such as chicken pie, shepherd's pie and Cornish pasties, but also flans, tarts and quiches. Recipes such as Sorrel Tart, Terrace Crab Pie and Continental Flan are destined to become valued additions to your cooking repertoire.

Crab quiche
serves 4

ingredients

For the pastry
175g/6oz flour, sifted
75g/3oz butter, cubed
pinch of salt

For the filling
225g/8oz cooked crabmeat
2 eggs
300ml/5fl oz double cream
1 tablespoon finely chopped fresh
  flat-leaf parsley
1 tablespoon finely chopped
  fresh fennel
1 spring onion, chopped
salt and freshly ground black pepper

- Preheat the oven to 190°C/375°F/Gas mark 5.
- Put the flour, butter and pinch of salt in a bowl, and work with the tips of
  your fingers until the mixture resembles breadcrumbs. Add 2 tablespoons
  water, and mix to a dough. Knead the pastry on a floured surface until
  smooth. Form into a slightly flattened disk, wrap in cling film and chill for
  30–45 minutes.
- Roll out the pastry and use to line a 20cm/8in pie dish. Break up the
  crabmeat with a fork, and scatter over the bottom of the pastry shell.
- Put the eggs, cream and parsley in a bowl. Season with salt and pepper.
  Beat together until the mixture is smooth, then pour over the crabmeat.
- Bake in the oven for 40 minutes until the filling is set and the top is
  golden. Serve hot or warm, garnished with the spring onion.

Leek pie
serves 6

ingredients

225g/8oz shortcrust pastry
900g/2lb leeks, thinly sliced
450g/1lb button mushrooms
50g/2oz butter

3 egg yolks
300ml/10fl oz crème fraîche
salt and freshly ground
    black pepper

- Preheat the oven to 190°C/375°F/Gas mark 5. Roll out the pastry and line a greased 20cm/8in pie tin.
- In a frying pan, sweat the leeks and mushrooms in the butter until tender. Spoon into the pie tin. In a bowl, beat together the egg yolks and crème fraîche. Season with salt and pepper. Pour the mixture onto the leeks.
- Bake in the oven for 25–30 minutes until the filling is set. Serve warm.

• •

Onion tart
serves 6

ingredients

For the pastry
25g/1oz self-raising flour
50g/2oz butter
pinch of salt

For the filling
6 onions, sliced
150ml/5fl oz boiling water

4 rashers streaky bacon, diced)
50g/2oz butter
1 teaspoon dried mixed herbs
2 egg yolks
50ml/2fl oz double cream
salt and freshly ground
    black pepper

- Preheat the oven to 180°C/350°F/Gas mark 4. Grease a medium-sized baking tin.
- To make the pastry, sift the flour into a bowl and rub in the butter. Add a pinch of salt to 50ml/2fl oz water, then gradually add to the bowl until the mixture forms a ball. Roll out and use to line the bottom of the tin.
- For the filling, sweat the onions in the boiling water for 5 minutes. Drain.
- Fry the bacon in a little of the butter until crisp. Add the remaining butter, onions, mixed herbs, salt and pepper, and cook for 15 minutes.
- Beat the egg yolks and cream together. Add to the onion mixture, and pour into the baking tin. Bake in the oven for 40–45 minutes. Serve hot.

Spinach tart
serves 4

ingredients

900g/2lb spinach leaves
25g/1oz butter
4 eggs
375ml/13fl oz double cream
50g/2oz granulated sugar

1 teaspoon finely grated
  lemon zest
1 teaspoon ground coriander
pinch of ground nutmeg
450g/1lb shortcrust pastry

- Preheat the oven to 180°C/350°F/Gas mark 4.
- Blanch the spinach for 1 minute in boiling water. Put in a colander, and refresh under cold running water. Drain, squeeze out the excess water and chop. In a frying pan, melt the butter and add the chopped spinach. Sauté for 2 minutes.
- Whisk 3 of the eggs, the cream and the sugar together in a bowl. Add the lemon zest, coriander and nutmeg. Add the mixture to the frying pan, and stir through.
- Roll out two-thirds of the dough to line a baking dish, reserving the extra third to form a lattice top. Fill with the spinach mixture and cover with strips of the remaining dough. Beat the yolk of the remaining egg with 1 tablespoon water. Brush the lattice top with the mixture.
- Bake in the oven for 30 minutes or until the pastry is lightly browned.

Cheese pie
serves 6

ingredients

200g/7oz puff pastry
275g/10oz Camembert or Brie

1 egg, beaten
freshly ground black pepper

- Preheat the oven to 230°C/450°F/Gas mark 8.
- Roll out half of the pastry into a 20cm/8in round. Put the cheese in the centre, and sprinkle with black pepper.
- Roll out the remaining dough, cover the cheese and seal the edges to make a parcel. Brush the surface with the egg. Jake a hole for the steam to escape by cutting a short slit in the pastry with a sharp knife.
- Put on a baking tray lined with baking parchment, and bake in the oven for 15–20 minutes until the pastry is puffed and golden. Serve hot.

Anchovy tart

serves 6

ingredients

butter for greasing
350g/12oz shortcrust pastry
300g/11oz onions, chopped
90ml/3½fl oz olive oil

10 anchovy fillets in oil, drained
7 black olives, pitted and halved
1 teaspoon dried fennel
freshly ground black pepper

- Preheat the oven to 200°C/400°F/Gas mark 6. Grease a baking sheet with butter.
- Roll out the dough to a 20cm/8in square, 5mm/1/2in thick. Place on the baking sheet and roll the edges to make a rim. Prick the dough all over.
- Fry the onion in 75ml/3fl oz olive oil until golden and spread over the dough.
- Soak the anchovies in water for a few minutes, then rinse and dry them on kitchen paper.
- Arrange the anchovies over the onion in a diamond shape. Decorate each diamond with the halved olives and sprinkle with freshly ground pepper, the fennel and the remainder of the olive oil.
- Bake in the oven for 30 minutes. Serve immediately with a tomato salad.

Courgette flan

serves 6

ingredients

olive oil for greasing
6 courgettes, sliced
4 eggs, separated
175g/6oz Parmesan cheese, freshly grated
pinch of freshly grated nutmeg
salt

- Preheat the oven to 180°C/350°F/Gas mark 4. Grease a baking dish with oil.
- Blanch the courgettes in boiling water for 2 minutes. Cool slightly.
- Put the egg yolks, Parmesan and nutmeg in a bowl. Add the courgettes, and mix through.
- Beat the egg whites until stiff. Fold into the courgette mixture.
- Fill the baking dish with the mixture and bake for 25 minutes until the flan is golden on top. Remove from the oven, and serve piping hot.

Leek tart

serves 6

ingredients

6 large leeks, white part only
100g/4oz raw ham, diced
200g/7oz veal or lamb, minced
200g/7oz lean pork, minced
200ml/7fl oz olive oil
100ml/3½fl oz dry red wine
pinch of saffron threads, soaked in
2 tablespoons boiling water

pinch of grated nutmeg
300g/11oz olive oil other
shortcrust pastry
25g/1oz Parmesan cheese,
freshly grated
salt and freshly ground
black pepper

- Preheat the oven to 190°C/375°C/Gas mark 5. Grease a 20cm/8in pie dish. Cut the leeks lengthways into 5cm/2in strips, soak in cold water for 5 minutes, then drain.
- Brown the ham and minced meat in a frying pan, using half the olive oil. Add the wine, saffron and its soaking liquid, and the nutmeg. Season with salt and pepper. Cook for a further 2 minutes, stirring, until the wine has evaporated.
- Sweat the leeks for 3 minutes in a saucepan using the remainder of the oil, and season with salt.
- Line the pie dish with three-quarters of the pastry. Pour in the meat mixture and spread evenly over the bottom of the tart shell. Arrange the leeks on top of the meat, and sprinkle with the Parmesan.
- Cut the remaining pastry into strips, and arrange over the top of the pie in a lattice pattern. Bake in the oven for 40 minutes or until the top of the filling is golden brown. Serve hot.

Cheese & courgette quiche

serves 6

ingredients

350g/12oz shortcrust pastry
1 onion, chopped
15g/½oz butter
450g/1lb courgettes, grated

2 eggs
4 tablespoons crème fraîche
25g/1oz Gruyère cheese, grated
salt and ground black pepper

- Preheat the oven to 200°C/400°F/Gas mark 6. Grease a 25cm/10in pie dish.
- Roll out the pastry and use to line the pie dish. Cover with greaseproof paper or baking parchment and line with baking beans. Bake in the oven for 15 minutes then remove the greaseproof paper and beans.
- Reduce the oven temperature to 190°C/375°F/Gas mark 5.
- Sweat the onion in butter until soft, then add the courgettes and sweat for a further minute. Spoon the mixture into the pie dish. Mix together the crème fraîche and cheese. Season with salt and pepper, and pour over the courgettes. Bake in the oven for 30 minutes until set. Serve hot.

Sorrel tart

serves 6

ingredients

225g/8oz shortcrust pastry
225g/8oz sorrel leaves
75g/3oz granulated sugar
½ teaspoon ground cinnamon

25g/1oz unsalted butter
3 egg yolks
3 digestive biscuits, crumbled
1 tablespoon lemon juice

- Preheat the oven to 180°C/350°F/Gas mark 4.
- Roll out the pastry and use to line a greased 20–23cm/8–9in tart tin or pie dish. Bake blind for 15 minutes (see above).
- Using a mortar and pestle, grind the sorrel and pour the resulting juice into a saucepan. If little juice appears, then wrap the sorrel in cheesecloth and squeeze the juice out this way.
- Add the sugar, cinnamon, butter, egg yolks, biscuit crumbs and lemon juice to the pan. Cook over a low heat until the mixture thickens.
- Scoop the mixture into the pastry shell and bake in the oven for 30 minutes or until the filling has turned golden brown. Serve hot.

Cottage cheese flan

serves 6

ingredients
250g/8oz butter, plus extra
  for greasing
175g/6oz plain flour
salt
2 eggs, beaten, plus 4 extra,
  separated
175ml/6fl oz sour cream
900g/2lb cottage cheese
4 eggs, separated
1 tablespoon finely chopped
  fresh dill

- Preheat the oven to 200°C/400°F/Gas Mark 6. Grease a 20cm/8in tart tin with a little butter.
- Put the flour and a pinch of salt on a work surface. Make a well in the centre, and pour in the 2 beaten eggs and 150ml/5fl oz of the sour cream. Add 175g/6oz of the butter, cut into pieces, and work into a smooth dough with your hands. Knead for 10 minutes. Cover the dough with a cloth, and leave in a cool place for 1 hour.
- Mix the cottage cheese with the remaining butter, egg yolks, dill and salt to taste. In a separate bowl, whisk the egg whites until stiff, then fold into the cottage cheese mixture.
- Line the prepared tart tin with the pastry. Trim the edges, and spread the cottage cheese mixture evenly over the bottom of the pastry.
- Brush the top of the mixture with the remaining sour cream, and bake in the oven for 30 minutes or until the filling is set. Serve hot.

Cornish pasties
serves 6

ingredients
175g/6oz rump steak, finely
    chopped
1 potato, finely chopped
1 onion, finely chopped
1 carrot, finely chopped
2 teaspoons Worcestershire sauce
2 tablespoons beef stock
salt and freshly ground black pepper
1 egg, lightly beaten

For the pastry
butter for greasing
275g/10oz plain flour
pinch of salt
100g/4oz butter, cubed
4–5 tablespoons iced water

- Lightly grease a medium baking tray.
- To make the pastry, sift the flour and pinch of salt into a large bowl, and rub in the butter with your fingertips until the mixture resembles fine breadcrumbs. Make a well in the centre and add almost all the water. Mix together with a flat-bladed knife or spatula, using a cutting action, until the mixture comes together in small beads, adding more water if the dough is too dry. Turn out onto a floured work surface, and form into a ball. Cover with cling film and refrigerate for 20 minutes.
- Preheat the oven to 210°C/425°F/Gas mark 7. Mix together the steak, potato, onion, carrot, Worcestershire sauce and stock in a bowl, and season well with salt and pepper.
- Divide the dough into six portions. Roll out each portion to 3mm/⅛in thick. Using a 16cm/6½in plate as a guide, cut out six circles. Divide the filling evenly between the circles. Brush the edges with the egg and bring the pastry together to form a semicircle. Pinch the edges into a frill.
- Put the pasties on the prepared baking tray. Brush with the beaten egg, and bake for 15 minutes. Reduce the oven temperature to 180°C/350°F/Gas mark 4, and cook for a further 25–30 minutes until golden. Serve hot or cold.

Chicken pie
serves 12

ingredients

125ml/4fl oz olive oil
900g/2lb skinless chicken breast
   fillets, halved horizontally
6 garlic cloves, crushed
2 tablespoons chopped
   fresh oregano
2 tablespoons chopped fresh
   flat-leaf parsley
3 large onions, sliced
450g/1lb courgettes, sliced
450g/1lb aubergines, thinly sliced
675g/1½lb puff pastry

3 beefsteak tomatoes, peeled,
   quartered and seeded
1 egg, beaten
salt and freshly ground
   black pepper

For the sauce
50g/2oz butter
2 teaspoons plain flour
450ml/¾pt double cream
125ml/4fl oz horseradish sauce
125ml/4fl oz white wine

- Preheat the oven to 220°C/425°F/Gas mark 7. Grease a large baking tray.
- Heat 4 tablespoons of the oil in a large frying pan, add half the chicken and sprinkle with half the garlic and herbs. Season lightly. Sauté the chicken on both sides to seal and remove with a slotted spoon. Sauté the remaining chicken, garlic and herbs. Remove from the pan. Add the onions to the pan. Sauté gently for 5 minutes. Add the courgettes and aubergines, and sauté for a further 5 minutes, adding more oil if needed. Allow to cool.
- On a floured work surface, roll out a third of the pastry into a 40 x 20cm/16 x 8in rectangle. Place on the baking tray. Lay half the chicken to within 2.5cm/1in of the pastry edges, cover with half the vegetables, then arrange half the tomatoes over the top. Repeat the layering to use all the ingredients. Brush the pastry edges with some of the beaten egg.
- Thinly roll half the remaining pastry to a rectangle. Cut diagonally into strips and lay over the filling, leaving a gap between the strips. Press the ends to seal. Brush with beaten egg. Roll out the remaining pastry, cut strips and lay them over the pie in a lattice pattern. Press the edges of the pastry firmly together to seal; trim off the excess with a knife. Brush with beaten egg.
- Bake for 15 minutes. Reduce the temperature to 180°C/350°F/Gas mark 4 and bake for a further 40 minutes until risen and golden.
- To make the sauce, melt the butter in a small pan and blend in the flour. Cook for 1 minute, stirring. Remove from the heat and stir in the cream and horseradish. Return to the heat and cook, stirring, until thickened, then add the wine. Serve hot with the pie.

Prawn pies

serves 4

ingredients

225g/8oz plain flour, plus extra
 for dusting
100g/4oz butter, cubed, plus extra
 for greasing
1 tablespoon dried vegetable oil
5cm/2in piece of fresh root
 ginger, grated
3 garlic cloves, crushed
900g/2lb raw prawns, peeled and
 deveined
75ml/3fl oz sweet chilli sauce
75ml/3fl oz lime juice
75ml/3fl oz double cream
25g/1oz fresh coriander, chopped
1 egg yolk, lightly beaten

- Sift the flour into a large bowl, add the butter and rub into the flour with your fingertips until the mixture resembles fine breadcrumbs. Make a well, add 3 tablespoons water and mix with a flat-bladed knife, using a cutting action, until the mixture comes together in beads. Gather the dough together and lift out on to a lightly floured surface. Press into a ball and flatten into a disc. Wrap in cling film and chill for 15 minutes.
- Preheat the oven to 200°C/400°F/Gas mark 6. Grease two baking trays with butter.
- Heat the oil in a large frying pan, and sauté the ginger, garlic and prawns for 3 minutes. Remove the prawns and set aside. Add the chilli sauce, lime juice and cream to the pan, and simmer over a medium heat until the sauce has reduced by a third. Return the prawns to the pan and add the coriander. Stir through, then leave to cool.
- Divide the pastry into four, and roll out each portion, between sheets of baking parchment, into a 20cm/8in circle. Divide the filling into four, and place a portion in the centre of each pastry, leaving a wide border. Fold the edges loosely over the filling, and slide the pies onto the prepared baking trays. Brush the pastry with the egg yolk. Bake for 25 minutes or until golden. Serve hot.

Continental flan
serves 4

ingredients

50g/2oz butter, plus extra
   for greasing
4 slices white bread
2 eggs, beaten
100g/4oz Cheddar cheese,
   grated
50ml/2fl oz milk
50g/2oz onion, finely chopped
50g/2oz green pepper, seeded
   and finely chopped
½ teaspoon mustard powder
salt and ground black pepper

- Preheat the oven to 200°C/
  400°F/Gas mark 6. Grease a large
  baking dish with butter.
- Butter the bread, remove the crusts
  and cut into quarters diagonally.
  Line the sides of the baking dish
  with the bread, overlapping slightly.
- In a large bowl, mix together the
  eggs, cheese, milk, onion, pepper
  and mustard. Season with salt and
  pepper, and pour over the bread.
- Cook in the oven for 20–25
  minutes. Serve either hot or cold.

Beef & cabbage pie
serves 6

ingredients

butter for greasing
200g/7oz potatoes, shredded
200g/7oz Cheddar cheese,
   grated
450g/1lb minced beef

1 tablespoon vegetable oil
175g/6oz cabbage, shredded
100g/4oz canned chopped green
   chillies, drained
125ml/4fl oz taco sauce
salt and ground black pepper

- Preheat the oven to 180°C/350°F/Gas mark 4. Lightly grease a
  23cm/9in pie plate with butter.
- Combine the potatoes with half the cheese and season with salt and
  pepper. Press into the bottom and up the sides of the prepared pie plate.
  Bake in the oven for 20 minutes.
- In a large frying pan, brown the beef in the oil and drain. Add the
  cabbage and sauté until crisp. Remove from the heat and add the
  chillies and taco sauce. Season with salt and pepper. Spoon the mixture
  into the crust, and bake for a further 20 minutes.
- Sprinkle with the remaining cheese, and continue baking until the cheese
  melts. Allow to stand for about 10 minutes before serving.

Game pie
serves 6

ingredients

225g/8oz onions, sliced
1 teaspoon butter
2 garlic cloves, finely chopped
675g/1½lb game meat, off the
   bone, diced
plain flour for sprinkling
1½ teaspoons vegetable oil

225g/8oz streaky bacon, diced
1 bay leaf
150ml/5fl oz chicken stock
150ml/5fl oz red wine
225g/8oz button mushrooms
350g/12oz puff pastry
1 egg, beaten

- Preheat the oven to 180°C/350°F/Gas mark 4.
- Sauté the onions lightly in the butter until golden. Add the garlic and sauté for a further 1 minute. Sprinkle the game meat with flour, and brown gently in the oil.
- Stew the meat slowly in a large covered saucepan with the bacon, onions, garlic, bay leaf, stock and wine. Just before the meat is done, add the mushrooms. Continue cooking until tender. Allow to cool.
- Line a small pie dish with the puff pastry, leaving enough to make a lid. Fill with the meat mixture, cover with pastry and seal the edges. Brush with the egg. Bake for 25 minutes or until golden brown. Serve hot.

Terrace crab pie
serves 6

ingredients

25g/1oz butter
100g/4oz onion, sliced
   into rings
100g/4oz celery, chopped
150g/5oz cooked crabmeat
150g/5oz Cheddar cheese,
   grated
23cm/9in unbaked pastry shell
3 eggs
50ml/2fl oz single cream
1 teaspoon salt
½ teaspoon ground black pepper

- Preheat the oven to 200°C/ 400°F/Gas mark 6.
- In a frying pan, melt the butter and sauté the onion and celery until the onion is soft and golden. Spoon alternate layers of the crabmeat, cheese and onion mixture into the pastry shell.
- In a bowl, beat together the eggs, cream, salt and pepper. Pour into the pastry shell over the other ingredients. Bake in the oven for 30–40 minutes until set. Serve hot.

Apple & Cheddar pie

serves 6

ingredients

150g/5oz plain flour, sifted
250g/9oz Cheddar cheese, grated
½ teaspoon salt
150g/5oz vegetable shortening
75ml/3fl oz iced water
350g/12oz cooking apples, cored
  and chopped
100g/4oz granulated sugar
2 teaspoons self-raising flour
½ teaspoon ground cinnamon
2 teaspoons butter
1 egg yolk, beaten
1 tablespoon water

- Preheat the oven to 200°C/400°F/Gas mark 6. Grease a 23cm/9in pie dish with butter.
- Mix together the plain flour, cheese and salt in a bowl. Using a pastry blender or two knives, cut in the shortening until the mixture resembles coarse breadcrumbs. Sprinkle the iced water over, and toss the crumbs until a dough is formed. Press the dough firmly into a ball.
- Divide the pastry almost in half and roll out the larger half, on a lightly floured surface, to a 30cm/12in circle. Use to line the greased pie dish, trimming the edges to 1cm/½in beyond the rim of the pie plate.
- Put the apples, sugar, self-raising flour and cinnamon in a bowl, and mix well. Arrange the apple mixture in the pastry shell. Roll out the remaining pastry to a 30cm/12in circle. Place on top of the filling, trimming the crust to 2.5cm/1in beyond the rim of the pie dish. Flute the edges to form a rim.
- Combine the egg yolk with 1 tablespoon water to make an egg wash, then brush over the top crust and rim.
- Bake the pie in the oven for 45–50 minutes until apples are tender and the crust is a golden brown. Cool on a wire rack before serving.

Seafood pie

serves 4

ingredients

700g/1½lb potatoes, peeled and
  thinly sliced
salt and freshly ground black pepper
450g/1lb cod fillet
450ml/¾pt milk
75g/3oz butter, plus extra for
  greasing
350g/12oz trimmed leeks, sliced
freshly grated nutmeg
25g/1oz plain flour
100g/4oz Stilton cheese
50ml/2fl oz single cream
225g/8oz peeled and deveined
  cooked prawns
salt and freshly ground black pepper

- Preheat the oven to 190°C/375°F/Gas mark 5. Lightly grease a
  1.7-litre/3pt pie dish and place on a baking tray.
- Cook the potatoes in a pan of salted boiling water for 5 minutes or until
  partially softened, then drain thoroughly.
- Put the cod in a shallow pan. Pour over 50ml/2fl oz of the milk and
  season lightly with salt and pepper. Cover and poach for 5 minutes until
  tender. Drain, reserving the liquid. Flake the cod, discarding the skin
  and bones.
- Melt 25g/1oz of the butter in a pan and sauté the leeks for 3 minutes,
  adding nutmeg to taste.
- Melt the remaining butter in another small pan. Add the flour and cook,
  stirring, for 1 minute. Remove from the heat, and gradually blend in the
  remaining milk and the reserved fish liquid, stirring until smooth.
- Return the pan to the heat. Cook, stirring, until the sauce has thickened.
  Crumble in the Stilton and add the cream. Season with salt and pepper.
- Put the cod, leeks and prawns in the prepared pie dish. Spoon over half
  the sauce, add the potatoes and pour over the remaining sauce. Cook
  the pie in the oven for 45 minutes. Serve immediately.

Tuna mornay

serves 4

ingredients

50g/2oz butter
25g/1oz plain flour
500ml/16fl oz milk
½ teaspoon mustard powder
75g/3oz Cheddar cheese, grated
600g/1lb 5oz canned tuna, drained
2 tablespoons chopped fresh
    flat-leaf parsley
2 eggs, hard-boiled and chopped
25g/1oz fresh white breadcrumbs
salt and freshly ground black pepper

- Preheat the oven to 180°C/350°F/Gas mark 4.
- Melt the butter in a small pan. Add the flour and stir over a low heat for
  1 minute or until pale and foaming. Remove the pan from the heat, and
  gradually stir in the milk. Return the pan to the heat and stir constantly
  until the sauce boils and thickens. Reduce the heat and simmer for
  2 minutes. Remove from the heat and whisk in the mustard and 50g/2oz
  of the cheese until melted and smooth.
- Flake the tuna with a fork and mix into the sauce with the parsley and
  egg. Season with salt and pepper. Spoon into 4 x 250ml/9fl oz
  ramekins. Mix the breadcrumbs and remaining cheese, and sprinkle over
  the top of each ramekin. Bake in the oven for 15–20 minutes until the
  topping is golden brown. Serve hot.

Chicken & sausage pie

serves 6–8

ingredients

For the pastry

150g/5oz butter, plus extra
 for greasing
450g/1lb plain flour
1 tablespoon dried mixed herbs
salt and freshly ground
 black pepper
1 egg, beaten

For the filling

450g/1lb spinach
freshly grated nutmeg
450g/1lb skinless chicken breast
 fillet, cubed
225g/8oz sausage meat
1 bunch of spring onions, chopped
25g/1oz chopped fresh
 flat-leaf parsley
4 fresh apricots, stoned and
 chopped
1 teaspoon grated lemon zest
1 egg, beaten

- Preheat the oven to 200°C/400°F/Gas mark 6. Grease a 23cm/9in round loose-bottomed cake tin with butter.
- For the pastry, mix together the flour and herbs, and season with salt and pepper. Melt the butter in a pan with 250ml/9fl oz water, then bring to the boil. Quickly stir in the flour mixture, mixing to form a soft dough. Cool slightly, then turn out and knead briefly on a lightly floured work surface. Wrap in cling film and leave to cool.
- To make the filling, wash the spinach, then place in a large pan with no water and cook, covered, for 5 minutes until the spinach is wilted and tender. Drain well, pressing out any excess liquid. Chop, then season to taste with nutmeg, salt and pepper.
- Put the chicken in a bowl with the sausage meat, spring onions, parsley, apricots, lemon zest and egg. Combine thoroughly with your hands. Add the spinach, season with salt and pepper, and mix well.
- Roll out two-thirds of the pastry and use to line the prepared cake tin. Fill the pastry with the chicken mixture.
- Dampen the pastry edges, then roll out the remaining pastry to cover the pie, pinching the edges together to seal.
- Bake in the oven for 1–1¼ hours until golden. Leave to cool in the tin for 20 minutes, then remove and cool completely before serving.

Mushroom & veal pie

serves 4

ingredients

25g/1oz plain flour
¼ teaspoon salt
½ teaspoon freshly ground
  black pepper
450g/1lb stewing veal, trimmed
  and cut into bite-size pieces
1 tablespoon vegetable oil
1 onion, chopped
1 garlic clove, minced
2 carrots, chopped
200g/7oz mushrooms, sliced
½ teaspoon dried sage
150ml/5fl oz water

500ml/18fl oz beef stock
2 tablespoons dry vermouth
1 tablespoon tomato purée
1 teaspoon Worcestershire sauce
175g/6oz frozen peas

For the topping
200g/7oz plain flour
1 tablespoon chopped fresh
  flat-leaf parsley
2 teaspoons baking powder
25g/1oz butter
175ml/6fl oz Greek-style yogurt
salt and ground black pepper

- In a plastic bag, combine the flour with the salt and half the pepper. Toss the veal in the flour mixture, in batches if necessary.
- In large frying pan, heat half the oil over a medium-high heat, and brown the veal in batches, adding the remaining oil as necessary. Transfer to a plate and set aside.
- Stir the onion, garlic, carrots, mushrooms, sage and 1 tablespoon water into the pan and cook, stirring, for about 7 minutes until golden. Stir in the remaining water, the stock, vermouth, tomato purée, Worcestershire sauce, remaining pepper and veal. Bring to the boil, then reduce the heat and simmer, covered, stirring occasionally, for 1 hour.
- Preheat the oven to 230°C/450°F/Gas mark 8.
- Uncover the pan and cook for about 15 minutes until the veal is tender and the sauce has thickened. Stir in the peas and leave to cool. Pour into a 20cm/8in square baking dish.
- To make the topping, in a large bowl, stir together the flour, parsley, baking powder and seasoning. Cut in the butter until the mixture resembles coarse breadcrumbs.
- On lightly floured surface, gently knead the dough until smooth. Gently pat out the dough into a 20cm/8in square. Cut into 16 equal squares and place over the veal mixture in four rows.
- Bake in the oven for 25–30 minutes until the crust is golden. Serve hot.

Filo mince pie
serves 4

ingredients

1 tablespoon vegetable oil
450g/1lb minced lamb
1 red onion, sliced
2 tablespoons chopped fresh
  coriander leaves
25g/1oz plain flour
50g/2oz canned cooked
  chickpeas, drained

300ml/10fl oz lamb stock
1 teaspoon ground cumin
225g/8oz filo pastry
100g/4oz dried apricots
1 courgette, sliced
25g/1oz butter, melted
salt and freshly ground
  black pepper

- Preheat the oven to 190°C/375°F/Gas mark 5.
- Heat the oil in a large pan. Add the lamb and brown for 5 minutes. Stir in the onion, coriander and flour. Cook for a further 1 minute. Add the chickpeas, stock, cumin, salt and pepper. Cook for 20 minutes.
- Line a deep ovenproof dish with 4 sheets of filo pastry. Spoon in the mince mixture. Top with the apricots and courgettes. Lay 2 sheets of pastry on top of the filling, and brush with the melted butter. Fold the remaining sheets on top. Pour over the rest of the butter, and cook the pie in the oven for 40 minutes. Serve hot.

Tomato & ham pie
serves 6

ingredients

200g/7oz puff pastry
175g/6oz cooked ham, sliced
450g/1lb tomatoes, peeled
  and sliced
2 eggs
150ml/5fl oz double cream
100g/4oz Cheddar cheese, cut
  into slices
salt and freshly ground
  black pepper
chopped fresh flat-leaf parsley,
  to garnish

- Preheat the oven to 220°C/ 425°F/Gas mark 7.
- Roll out the pastry and use to line an 18cm/7in baking dish. Put the ham, then the tomatoes on top.
- Beat together the eggs, cream and Cheddar cheese. Season with salt and pepper, and pour over the tomatoes.
- Bake for 40 minutes. Sprinkle with chopped parsley and serve.

Shepherd's pie

serves 4

ingredients

100g/4oz unsmoked streaky bacon,
  cut into strips
450g/1lb lean beef mince
2 tablespoons olive oil
225g/8oz onion, diced
175g/6oz carrot, diced
2 garlic cloves, chopped
150ml/5fl oz red wine
300ml/10fl oz chicken stock
450g/1lb canned chopped tomatoes
1 bay leaf
2 teaspoons dried oregano
2 tablespoons Worcestershire sauce
3 tablespoons tomato ketchup
900g/2lb mashed potatoes
salt and freshly ground black pepper

- Fry the streaky bacon in a hot frying pan until it is almost crisp, then transfer to a heavy saucepan. Brown the beef in the frying pan, then add to the same saucepan.
- Add the olive oil to the bacon fat, and sweat the onion, carrot and garlic until soft but not brown, adding them to the saucepan when done.
- Preheat the oven to 220°C/425°F/Gas mark 7.
- Deglaze the frying pan with the red wine, and add this to the saucepan, topping up to cover with the stock. Add the tomatoes and their liquid, bay leaf, oregano, Worcestershire sauce and tomato ketchup. Stir, bring to the boil and simmer, uncovered, over a very low heat for 3 hours, seasoning with salt and pepper halfway through.
- Put the contents of the saucepan into a deep rectangular ovenproof dish, cover with the mashed potatoes and brown in the oven for 20 minutes. Serve hot.

Steak & onion pie
serves 4

ingredients

For the pastry
300g/11oz butter
1 egg
2 egg yolks
550g/1lb 4oz plain flour, sifted
½ teaspoon salt
3 tablespoons iced water

For the filling
50g/2oz butter
450g/1lb trimmed leeks, washed and thinly sliced
225g/8oz chestnut mushrooms, sliced
100g/4oz Gruy?re cheese, grated
50g/2oz Parmesan cheese, freshly grated
225g/8oz sliced smoked cooked ham, diced
4 tablespoons wholegrain mustard
200ml/7fl oz fromage frais
1 egg, beaten
salt and freshly ground black pepper

- To make the pastry, put the butter, egg and yolks in a blender or food processor, and process until pale. Add the flour and salt, and pulse until the mixture just comes together. Add the iced water, process for 1 second, then tip the dough out into a bowl and use your hands to bring together. Divide in two, with one piece slightly larger than the other. Wrap in cling film, and chill for 30 minutes.
- Preheat the oven to 200°C/400°F/Gas mark 6.
- Roll out the smaller piece of dough into a large rectangle measuring about 23 x 28cm/9 x 11in. Slide the dough onto a greased baking tray. Prick all over with a fork and bake for 10–15 minutes. Cool.
- To make the filling, melt the butter in a frying pan, add the leeks and mushrooms and cook for about 10 minutes until soft. Stir in the cheeses and season well with salt and pepper. Spread half of this mixture over the pastry base, leaving a border around the edge. Cover with the ham.
- Mix the mustard with the fromage frais, season with salt and pepper, and spread over the ham. Top with the remaining leek and mushroom mixture. Lightly brush the edges with water.
- Roll out the remaining dough on a large piece of baking parchment. Carefully place on top of the pie and remove the parchment. Press the dough down to seal. Brush all over with beaten egg.
- Bake in the oven for 35 minutes until the pastry is golden and crisp. Serve either hot or cold.

Cottage pie
serves 4

ingredients
2 tablespoons vegetable oil
1 onion, finely chopped
1 carrot, finely chopped
100g/4oz mushrooms, chopped
500g/1lb 2oz minced lamb
300ml/10fl oz lamb stock
1 tablespoon plain flour
1 bay leaf
3 teaspoons Worcestershire sauce
1 tablespoon tomato purée
700g/11/2lb potatoes, boiled
25g/1oz butter
3 tablespoons hot milk
salt and freshly ground black pepper

- Heat the oil in a heavy saucepan, add the onion, carrot and mushrooms, and cook, stirring occasionally, until browned. Stir the lamb into the pan and continue to cook, stirring to break up the lumps, until lightly browned. Blend a few spoonfuls of the stock with the flour, then stir this mixture into the pan.
- Pour in the remaining stock and bring to a simmer, stirring constantly. Add the bay leaf, Worcestershire sauce and tomato purée, then cover the pan and cook very gently for 1 hour, stirring occasionally. Remove the lid from the pan towards the end of cooking to allow any excess water to evaporate, if necessary, but do not let it boil dry or stick to the pan.
- Preheat the oven to 190°C/375°F/Gas mark 5.
- Mash the potatoes with the butter and milk, and season with salt and pepper. Season the mince mixture, then spoon into an ovenproof dish. Cover with an even layer of potato, and make a pattern on the top using the prongs of a fork.
- Bake for 25 minutes until golden brown. Serve hot.

Casseroles & Stews

There is nothing more comforting and heart-warming than a hot bowlful of stew or casserole on a winter's evening, and with all the ingredients cooked in one pot this is a great way to offer complete nourishment with a minimum of fuss. There are virtually no limits to the ingredients you can use to make a tasty casserole, and there are recipes here to suit everyone – from meat lovers, to fish lovers, to vegetarians. This chapter is also where you can readily reap the benefits of slow cooking, with its meltingly tender results and its rich, appetizing flavours.

casseroles & stews

Beef & stout casserole
serves 4

ingredients
700g/1½lb beef
175g/6oz lean bacon, cubed
1 tablespoon vegetable oil
15g/½oz butter
2 tablespoons plain flour
1 bottle of stout
450g/1lb shallots
3 garlic cloves, crushed
1 tablespoon sugar
1 tablespoon wine or
   cider vinegar
salt and freshly ground
   black pepper

- Preheat the oven to 150°C/
  300°F/Gas mark 2.
- Sauté the beef and bacon in the
  oil. Drain off the excess liquid.
  Remove the meat and set aside.
- Add the butter to the pan and melt.
  Stir in the flour to make a roux;
  cook, stirring, for a minute or two.
  Gradually stir in the stout.
- Put the meat and the shallots in a
  deep casserole dish, and season
  with salt and pepper. Add the
  garlic. Sprinkle the sugar on top,
  and pour in the sauce. Cover and
  put in the oven. Cook very gently
  for up to 3 hours.
- Remove from the oven and mix
  in the vinegar. Serve hot with
  boiled potatoes.

Beef hotpot
serves 4

ingredients
900g/2lb rump steak, cubed
350g/12oz carrots,
   thickly sliced
2 onions, thickly sliced
700g/1½lb potatoes,
   thickly sliced
500ml/18fl oz beef stock
salt and freshly ground
   black pepper

- Preheat the oven to 170°C/
  325°F/Gas mark 3.
- Arrange a layer of beef in a
  casserole dish. Sprinkle over a little
  salt and pepper, then top with a
  layer of carrots, onions and
  potatoes. Pour in the stock.
- Cover and bake for 2–2½ hours
  until the meat is tender. Increase
  the oven temperature to 200°C/
  400°F/Gas mark 6, and cook for
  another 30 minutes or until
  potatoes are brown. Serve hot.

One-pot beef dinner

serves 6

ingredients

3 tablespoons vegetable oil
1 small onion, chopped
1 large egg, lightly beaten
450g/1lb minced beef
50g/2oz plain breadcrumbs
1½ teaspoons onion powder
1½ teaspoons garlic salt
4 medium potatoes, sliced
450g/1lb frozen carrots

- Heat the oil in a frying pan over a medium-high heat. Reduce the heat to medium once the oil is hot. Add the onion to the pan, and sweat until soft.
- In a large bowl, mix the egg, beef, 50ml/2fl oz water, breadcrumbs, onion powder and garlic salt. Press the meat into the bottom of the bowl to form a rounded loaf. Invert the bowl to remove, and put the loaf on top of the onion. Put the sliced potatoes around the loaf and the carrots on top of the potatoes.
- Sprinkle with additional seasonings if desired. Cover and cook for about 1 hour. After 30 minutes, turn the meatloaf over and stir the vegetables. Serve hot.

Green chilli & meat stew

serves 5

ingredients

2½lb stewing beef, cubed
1.2 litres/2pt water
100g/4oz fresh green chillies, roasted, peeled, seeded and chopped
2 teaspoons garlic powder
1 teaspoon cornflour
salt and freshly ground black pepper

- Cover the meat with water in a large heavy pan, bring to the boil and simmer gently for 4 hours.
- Add the chillies and garlic powder Season with salt and pepper.
- Dissolve the cornflour in 2 teaspoons water to form a paste, and stir in rapidly. When the mixture has thickened, simmer for about 45 minutes. Serve hot.

One-pot spaghetti
serves 2

ingredients
100g/4oz minced beef
1 tablespoon chopped onion
225g/8oz tomato sauce
75g/3oz spaghetti
100g/4oz Parmesan cheese,
 freshly grated

- Crumble the beef into a microwave-proof casserole dish and add the onion.
- Microwave on High for 2½ minutes or until no longer pink, stirring once. Drain and stir to break the meat into smaller pieces. Add the tomato sauce, 400ml/14fl oz water and spaghetti.
- Cover with the casserole lid. Microwave for 10–11 minutes until the spaghetti is al dente, stirring twice. Serve hot with the Parmesan sprinkled over the top.

Mexican nacho casserole
serves 4

ingredients
450g/1lb minced beef
1 tablespoon dried mixed herbs
100g/4oz canned refried beans
50g/2oz onions, chopped
200g/7oz nacho chips
1 green pepper, seeded
 and diced
100g/4oz Cheddar
 cheese, grated

- Preheat the oven to 200°C/ 400°F/Gas mark 6.
- Cook the minced beef and herbs in a frying pan, mixing well and stirring to break up any lumps.
- Spread the refried beans in the bottom of a medium casserole dish, then sprinkle with the onions. Layer the meat over the beans. Bake in the oven for 15 minutes.
- Tuck the nacho chips around the edges of the casserole, then top with the pepper and cheese, and bake for a further 5 minutes. Serve immediately.

Beef paprikash
serves 8

ingredients

1.4kg/3lb stewing beef, cubed
150g/5oz onions, sliced
1 garlic clove, minced
225ml/8fl oz tomato ketchup
3 tablespoons Worcestershire
  sauce
¾ teaspoon mustard powder
1 tablespoon paprika
1½ tablespoons soft brown sugar
2 tablespoons cornflour, mixed
  with 75ml/3fl oz water

- Mix all the ingredients except the cornflour paste in a flameproof casserole dish. Cover and cook over a low heat for 4 hours.
- Increase the heat to high, and stir in the cornflour paste. Cook for 15–20 minutes until thickened.
- Serve hot with potatoes (these can be cooked separately, or added to the casserole 25–30 minutes before the end of the cooking time if you like) or on a bed of noodles.

• •

Lamb hotpot with dumplings
serves 4–6

ingredients

700g/1½lb neck of lamb, chopped
2 teaspoons redcurrant jelly
2 onions, chopped
3 carrots, chopped
1 turnip, chopped
175g/6oz mushrooms, sliced
1 parsnip, chopped and blanched
1 tablespoon tomato purée

600ml/1pt vegetable stock
salt and freshly ground
  black pepper

For the dumplings
100g/4oz self-raising flour, sifted
50g/2oz suet, shredded
1 teaspoon chopped fresh parsley

- Preheat the oven to 190°C/375°F/Gas mark 5.
- Put the pieces of meat in the bottom of a large casserole dish. Spread them with the redcurrant jelly, and put in the oven for 15 minutes. Remove and add the vegetables and a little salt and pepper. Stir the tomato purée into the stock. Pour over the meat and vegetables. Return the casserole to the oven, reduce the temperature to 180°C/350°F/Gas mark 4 and cook for about 1½ hours until the meat is tender.
- To make the dumplings, mix together the flour, suet and seasoning with enough water to form a stiff dough. This makes about 6 small dumplings. Add the dumplings to the hotpot for the last 30 minutes of cooking.

Lamb hotpot
serves 4

ingredients
675g/1½lb lean lamb neck cutlets
2 lamb's kidneys
675g/1½lb potatoes, thinly sliced
1 large onion, thinly sliced
2 tablespoons chopped fresh thyme

150ml/5fl oz lamb stock
25g/1oz butter, melted
salt and freshly ground black
  pepper

- Preheat the oven to 180°C/350°F/Gas mark 4.
- Remove any excess fat from the lamb. Skin and core the kidneys, and cut them into slices.
- Arrange a layer of potatoes in the bottom of a 1.8-litre/3pt ovenproof dish.Arrange the lamb neck cutlets on top of the potatoes, and cover with the kidneys, onion and thyme. Pour the stock over the meat, and season with salt and pepper. Layer the remaining potato slices on top, overlapping to completely cover the meat and onion.
- Brush the potato slices with the butter, cover the dish and cook in the oven for 1½ hours. Remove the lid and cook for a further 30 minutes until golden brown on top. Serve hot.

Lamb & leek stew
serves 4

ingredients
8 small lamb cutlets, trimmed of
  all fat, cut into cubes
450g/1lb leeks, thickly sliced
3 carrots, thickly sliced
2 turnips, cut into chunks
900ml/1½pt lamb stock
450g/1lb potatoes, cut into
  large chunks
2 tablespoons chopped fresh
  flat-leaf parsley
salt and freshly ground
  black pepper

- Put all the ingredients except the potatoes and parsley in a large saucepan. Season with salt and pepper. Bring to the boil and skim the surface. Reduce the heat, part-cover the pan and simmer gently for 1 hour.
- Add the potatoes and a little more seasoning, and simmer for a further 30 minutes or until the potatoes and meat are tender. Serve hot.

Ulster Irish stew

serves 4

ingredients

900g/2lb neck of lamb, cubed
900g/2lb potatoes, sliced
450g/1lb onions, thickly sliced
1 sprig of fresh thyme
salt and freshly ground
   black pepper

- Layer the meat, potatoes and onion in a casserole dish, seasoning each layer well with salt and pepper. Finish with a layer of potatoes. Fill to about two-thirds full with water, add the thyme and cover with a lid.
- Bring to the boil and simmer for 1–2 hours until the lamb is really tender. Serve hot.

Lamb & vegetable stew

serves 4

ingredients

2 tablespoons olive oil
400g/14oz lean lamb
   fillet, cubed
1 red onion, sliced
1 garlic clove, crushed
1 potato, cubed
400g/14oz canned chopped
   plum tomatoes
1 red pepper, seeded
   and chopped
200g/7oz canned chickpeas
1 aubergine, cut into chunks
200ml/7fl oz lamb stock
1 tablespoon red wine vinegar
1 teaspoon chopped fresh thyme
1 teaspoon chopped fresh
   rosemary
1 teaspoon chopped fresh
   oregano
8 pitted black olives, halved
salt and ground black pepper

- Preheat the oven to 170°C/ 325°F/Gas mark 3.
- Heat 1 tablespoon of the oil in a flameproof casserole dish and, over a high heat, brown the lamb. Reduce the heat and add the remaining oil, the onion and the garlic. Cook until soft.
- Add the potato, tomatoes, pepper, drained chickpeas, aubergine, stock, vinegar and herbs to the casserole dish. Season with salt and pepper, stir and bring to the boil. Cover and cook in the oven for 1–1½ hours until tender.
- About 15 minutes before the end of cooking time, add the olives. Serve hot.

Lamb & okra stew
serves 8

ingredients

2 large onions, chopped
2 garlic cloves
50g/2oz butter
900g/2lb lamb, cubed
900g/2lb okra, chopped

225g/8oz tomatoes, sliced
1 tablespoon tomato purée
juice of 1 lemon
salt and freshly ground
   black pepper

- Fry the onions and garlic in the butter until both are golden and the garlic is aromatic. Add the lamb and brown all over. Add the okra and fry gently for about 10 minutes.
- Add the tomatoes, continue to cook for a few more minutes, and cover with water in which you have diluted the tomato purée. Season with salt and pepper, and stir well. Bring to a boil and simmer over a low heat for 1½ hours or more until the meat and vegetables are very tender and the sauce is reduced, adding a little more water if necessary.
- Remove from the heat and add the lemon juice. Serve hot.

Irish lamb stew
serves 6

ingredients

2kg/4½lb lamb shoulder
3 onions, thickly sliced
700g/1½lb carrots, thickly sliced
900g/2lb potatoes, peeled
   and halved
2 teaspoons Worcestershire
   sauce
1 bay leaf
salt and freshly ground
   black pepper

- Trim a fair amount of fat off the meat and reserve. Cut the meat into large cubes. In a heavy pan, render down the fat over a low heat. Brown the meat in the fat, then set aside and brown the onions and carrots. Drain off any excess fat.
- Return the meat to the pan with the potatoes, Worcestershire sauce and bay leaf. Season with salt and pepper. Pour in enough water to cover. Simmer for 2–3 hours until the meat is tender and the potatoes are soft and melting. Skim off the fat from the surface, and serve hot.

Irish hotpot
serves 6

ingredients
6 potatoes, thinly sliced
2 onions, thinly sliced
3 carrots, thinly sliced
75g/3oz cooked long-grain rice
400g/14oz canned peas
600g/1lb 5oz pork and herb
   sausages
425g/15oz canned condensed
   tomato soup, diluted
salt and freshly ground
   black pepper

- Preheat the oven to 190°C/
  375°F/Gas mark 5.
- Layer the potatoes, onions and
  carrots in a large casserole dish,
  seasoning as you go with salt and
  pepper. Sprinkle with the rice and
  peas, and top with the sausages.
  Pour the diluted soup over all.
- Bake in the oven, covered, for
  1 hour. Remove the lid from the
  casserole, turn the sausages and
  bake, uncovered, for a further
  1 hour. Serve hot.

Sausage & sweet pepper casserole
serves 4–6

ingredients
2 tablespoons olive oil
450g/1lb spicy sausages,
   cut into 5cm/2in slices
700g/1½lb green peppers,
   seeded and sliced
225g/8oz tomatoes, skinned
   and quartered
1 teaspoon chopped fresh
   flat-leaf parsley
salt and freshly ground
   black pepper

- Heat the oil in a pan, and gently
  fry the sausages until lightly
  browned. Add the peppers, and
  fry for a further 3 minutes, stirring
  continuously.
- Add the tomatoes and parsley to
  the pan. Season with salt and
  pepper. Cover the pan and cook
  gently for about 10 minutes until
  the sausages are cooked through.
  Serve hot.

One-pot sausage jambalaya

serves 4

ingredients

2 Italian sausages,
  coarsely chopped
500g/1lb 2oz canned chopped
  plum tomatoes
200g/7oz long-grain rice
1 teaspoon dried basil
1 red pepper, seeded
  and chopped

- In large wide non-stick saucepan over a medium-high heat, brown the sausages for 8 minutes, then drain off any fat.
- Add the tomatoes, then stir in 550ml/18fl oz water, the rice and the basil.
- Cover and bring to the boil, then reduce the heat to low and simmer for 20 minutes, stirring once. Stir in the pepper, cover, and simmer for 5 minutes. Serve hot.

One-pot pork chop supper

serves 4

ingredients

1 tablespoon vegetable oil
4 pork chops
400g/14oz canned tomato soup
1 teaspoon Worcestershire sauce
½ teaspoon salt
½ teaspoon caraway seeds
3 potatoes, quartered
4 carrots, cut into
  5cm/2in pieces

- In a large frying pan, brown the chops in the oil. Pour off any fat, then add the soup, 125ml/4fl oz water, Worcestershire sauce, salt, caraway, potatoes and carrots.
- Cover and simmer for 45 minutes or until tender. Serve hot.

Ham & cheese casserole

serves 8

ingredients
100g/4oz plain flour
75g/3oz butter
600ml/1pt milk
300g/11oz ham, chopped
600g/1lb 5oz potatoes,
   thinly sliced
250g/9oz Cheddar cheese,
   grated
1 onion, chopped
1 green pepper, seeded
   and chopped
salt and freshly ground
   black pepper

- Preheat the oven to 180°C/ 350°F/Gas mark 4.
- Season the flour with salt and pepper. Melt the butter in a saucepan, then add the flour mixture. Cook over a medium heat for 1 minute, stirring constantly. Remove from the heat and stir in the milk. Return to the heat and cook until thick.
- In a very large bowl, mix the remaining ingredients with the sauce. Bake in a casserole dish for 1½ hours, keeping the casserole covered for the first 30 minutes of cooking. Allow to cool for 15 minutes before serving.

Pork & apricot casserole

serves 4

ingredients
4 lean pork loin chops
1 onion, finely chopped
2 yellow peppers, seeded
   and sliced
2 teaspoons medium curry
   powder
1 tablespoon plain flour
250ml/9fl oz chicken stock
100g/4oz dried apricots
2 tablespoons wholegrain
   mustard
salt and freshly ground
   black pepper

- Trim the excess fat from the pork and fry without fat in a large heavy pan until lightly browned. Add the onion and peppers, and stir over a medium heat for 5 minutes. Stir in the curry powder and the flour.
- Add the stock, stirring, then add the apricots and mustard. Cover and simmer for 25–30 minutes until tender. Season with salt and pepper, and serve hot.

Baked bean
& bacon casserole
serves 3

ingredients

6 rashers rindless back bacon
450g/1lb canned baked beans
2 tablespoons minced onion
2 tablespoons tomato ketchup
1 teaspoon prepared mustard
2 tablespoons Demerara sugar

- Preheat the oven to 190°C/ 375°F/Gas mark 5.
- Dry-fry the bacon in a frying pan until very crisp.
- In a deep casserole dish, combine the beans, onion, ketchup, mustard and sugar. Mix thoroughly.
- Crumble the bacon, and sprinkle over the baked bean mixture.
- Heat in the oven, uncovered, for 10 minutes or until the sauce is bubbly. Serve hot.

Bacon & lentil stew
serves 4–6

ingredients

450lb/1lb rindless smoked back
   bacon rashers, diced
1 onion, chopped
2 carrots, sliced
2 celery sticks, chopped
1 turnip, chopped
1 large potato, chopped
75g/3oz green lentils such as
   Puy, rinsed and drained
1 bouquet garni
900ml/1½pt chicken stock
salt and freshly ground
   black pepper

- Heat a large flameproof casserole and add the bacon. Cook over a medium heat, stirring, for 5 minutes or until the fat runs. Add the onion, carrots, celery, turnip and potato, and cook, stirring, for 5 minutes
- Add the lentils, bouquet garni and stock. Bring to the boil, reduce the heat andsimmer for 1 hour or until the lentils are tender.
- Remove and discard the bouquet garni, and season with salt and pepper. Serve immediately.

Veal & spinach stew
serves 4

ingredients
900g/2lb loin of veal, chopped
    into 2.5cm/1in cubes
900g/2lb spinach
2 onions, chopped
25g/1oz butter
salt and freshly ground
    black pepper

- Put all the ingredients in a large casserole dish. Pour in 225ml/8fl oz water, cover and cook over a high heat for about 35 minutes.
- Serve hot.

Tuscan veal broth
serves 4

ingredients
50g/2oz dried peas, soaked for
    2 hours and drained
900g/2lb boned neck of
    veal, diced
1.2 litres/2pt beef stock
50g/2oz barley
1 carrot, diced
1 turnip, diced
1 leek, thinly sliced
1 red onion, finely chopped
100g/4oz tomatoes, chopped
1 sprig of fresh basil
100g/4oz dried vermicelli
salt and freshly ground
    black pepper

- Put the peas, veal, stock and 600ml/1pt water in a large pan. Bring to the boil over a low heat. Using a slotted spoon, skim off any scum that rises to the surface.
- When all the scum has been removed, add the barley and a pinch of salt. Simmer gently over a low heat for 25 minutes.
- Add the carrot, turnip, leek, onion, tomatoes and basil to the pan, and season with salt and pepper. Leave to simmer for about 2 hours, skimming the surface from time to time to remove any scum. Remove the pan from the heat and set aside for 2 hours.
- Set the pan over a medium heat and bring to the boil. Add the vermicelli and cook for 12 minutes. Season with salt and pepper, then remove and discard the basil. Serve immediately.

Liver & macaroni casserole

serves 4

ingredients

350g/12oz pigs' livers,
  thinly sliced
25g/1oz butter
2 onions, thinly sliced
3 tablespoons plain flour
150ml/5fl oz chicken stock

400g/14oz canned chopped
  plum tomatoes
2 teaspoons chopped fresh sage
100g/4oz macaroni
salt and freshly ground
  black pepper

- Preheat the oven to 180°C/350°F/Gas mark 4.
- Brown the liver in half the butter in a flameproof casserole dish for
  1 minute on each side. Remove from the pan with a slotted spoon.
- Add the remaining butter, and sauté the onions for 3 minutes until soft
  and lightly golden. Add the flour and cook, stirring, for 1 minute. Blend
  in the stock and tomatoes. Bring to the boil, stirring, for 1 minute.
- Return the liver to the pan and add the sage and a little salt and pepper.
  Cover and cook in the oven for 1 hour.
- Cook the pasta until al dente. Drain. Stir into the casserole. Serve hot.

Liver hotpot

serves 6

ingredients

500g/1lb 2oz lamb's liver
25g/1oz plain flour
2 large onions, thinly sliced
850g/13/4lb potatoes,
  thinly sliced

500ml/18fl oz lamb stock
6 rashers streaky bacon
salt and freshly ground
  black pepper

- Preheat the oven to 180°C/350°F/Gas mark 4. Lightly grease a large
  casserole dish. Remove the skin and tubes from the liver. Season the flour
  with salt and pepper. Dredge each slice of liver in the seasoned flour.
- Arrange layers of liver, onion and potatoes in the casserole dish, ending
  with a neat layer of potatoes. Heat the stock and pour in just enough to
  cover the potatoes. Cover the casserole dish and bake for about 1 hour
  until the liver is tender. Remove the lid and arrange the bacon rashers on
  top. Continue cooking, uncovered, until the bacon is crisp. Serve hot.

Calves' kidney stew

serves 6–8

ingredients

350g/12oz calves' kidney,
   peeled and diced
plain flour, seasoned with salt
   and freshly ground black
   pepper, for coating
50g/2oz butter
100g/4oz onions, chopped
175g/6oz carrots, chopped
1 turnip, finely chopped
3 celery sticks, finely chopped
1.7 litres/3pt beef stock
salt and freshly ground
   black pepper

- Put the kidney in a bowl and cover with cold water and a good pinch of salt. Leave to soak while you prepare the vegetables, then drain and dry with kitchen paper and toss in the seasoned flour.
- Melt the butter in a saucepan, add the kidney and vegetables, and toss for 1–2 minutes in the butter. Season with salt and pepper, and add the stock. Bring to the boil, reduce the heat and simmer for 45–60 minutes until tender.
- Put the stew in a blender or food processor, and blend for 2 minutes, then reheat and serve hot.

● ●

Spicy goatmeat stew

serves 6

ingredients

900g/2lb goatmeat
2 onions, sliced
1 teaspoon fresh thyme
1 teaspoon curry powder
75ml/3fl oz groundnut oil
225g/8oz fresh red chillies
900g/2lb tomatoes
200ml/7fl oz tomato purée
salt and freshly ground
   black pepper

- Season the goatmeat with salt, put in a deep heavy frying pan and add the onions, thyme, curry powder and half of the oil. Cook for 30–40 minutes until tender.
- In another pan, heat the remaining oil, and fry the chillies and tomatoes for 20 minutes until fairly dry. Add the tomato purée and stir thoroughly, then add the fried goatmeat pieces. Simmer gently for another 10 minutes, stirring frequently until well blended. Drain off any excessive oil that rises to the top, and serve hot.

Woodpigeon casserole
serves 4

ingredients
2 pig's trotters
25g/1oz butter
1 tablespoon vegetable oil
4 woodpigeon
12 pickling onions
1 carrot, diced
1 celery stick, diced
100g/4oz streaky back bacon, cut
   into strips
1 cinnamon stick
1 bay leaf
2 sprigs of fresh thyme
1½ tablespoons plain flour
16 prunes, pitted
2 sprigs of fresh flat-leaf parsley
300ml/10fl oz red wine
salt and freshly ground black pepper

- Put the trotters in a pan and cover with water. Bring to the boil, cover
  and simmer for 1 hour, skimming off any scum that rises to the surface.
  Reserve the liquid and trotters.
- Melt the butter and oil in a flameproof casserole dish. Quickly brown the
  pigeons, then remove and reserve. Add the onions, carrot, celery and
  bacon to the pan with the cinnamon, bay leaf and thyme. Stir to coat
  with the fat, then reduce the heat, cover and sweat gently for
  10 minutes. Sprinkle with the flour and stir.
- Return the pigeons to the pan, together with the trotters, prunes, parsley,
  wine and 600ml/1pt of the reserved cooking liquid. Season lightly with
  salt and pepper. Bring to the boil, cover and simmer gently, turning the
  pigeons occasionally, for 45–60 minutes, until tender. Serve hot.

Venison & wild rice casserole

serves 5

ingredients

375ml/13fl oz cream of
  mushroom soup
75g/3oz button mushrooms
250g/9oz wild rice
6 lean venison chops
1 medium onion, thinly sliced
3 rashers lean back bacon
salt and freshly ground
  black pepper

- Preheat the oven to 180°C/
  350°F/Gas mark 4.
- Put 500ml/18fl oz water, the soup
  and the mushrooms in a large
  casserole dish.
- Rinse the rice in cold water a few
  times, drain and add to the
  casserole dish. Spread the venison
  chops out in the sauce. Season
  with salt and pepper, and arrange
  the onions on top, then the bacon.
- Cover and bake in the oven for
  1–1½ hours until the meat and rice
  are soft and cooked. Serve hot.

Grouse stew

serves 4

ingredients

1 grouse, cut into bite-size pieces
plain flour for dredging
25g/1oz butter
1.8 litres/3pt boiling water
1 teaspoon dried thyme
200g/7oz sweetcorn
2 potatoes, cubed
¼ teaspoon cayenne pepper
3 onions, sliced
400g/14oz canned chopped
  plum tomatoes
salt and freshly ground
  black pepper

- Roll the grouse pieces in the flour
  seasoned with salt and pepper.
  Melt the butter in a large heavy
  frying pan, and brown the grouse
  on all sides.
- Put the grouse and all the other
  ingredients except the tomatoes in
  a large casserole dish. Add the
  boiling water, then cover and
  simmer for 1½–2 hours. Add the
  tomatoes and continue to simmer
  for a further 1 hour. Serve hot.

Rabbit casserole
serves 4

ingredients

25g/1oz butter
900g/2lb rabbit pieces
200g/7oz tomatoes
1 tablespoon cornflour
100g/4oz carrot, coarsely grated
1 tablespoon finely grated
  orange zest

1 teaspoon dried oregano
50ml/2fl oz brandy
25ml/1fl oz white wine vinegar
375ml/13fl oz warm water
2 bay leaves

- Preheat the oven to 180°C/350°F/Gas mark 4.
- Melt the butter in a large frying pan and brown the rabbit pieces well, turning frequently, then transfer the pieces to a large casserole dish.
- Put the tomatoes in a bowl of boiling water; leave for 2 minutes. Peel off the skins and chop the flesh into small cubes. Add to the casserole dish.
- Combine the cornflour, carrot, orange zest and oregano in a small bowl. Pour in the brandy, vinegar and warm water, and stir well. Pour over the contents of the casserole dish and add the bay leaves.
- Cover and bake for 1½ hours or until the rabbit is tender. Serve hot.

Pheasant casserole
serves 4

ingredients

2 tablespoons beef dripping
2 pheasants, jointed, breast and
  legs only
1 onion, chopped
1 carrot, chopped
1 celery stick, chopped
350ml/12fl oz red wine
salt and freshly ground
  black pepper

- Preheat the oven to 180°C/350°F/Gas mark 4.
- Heat the dripping in a frying pan and brown the pheasant joints. Remove from the pan, and put in a casserole dish. Put the vegetables in the frying pan, and cook for 2 minutes, then add the red wine and bring to the boil.
- Pour the mixture over the pheasant joints, season with salt and pepper, and cover the casserole dish.
- Cook in the oven for 1–1½ hours until tender. Serve hot.

Pheasant &
wild rice casserole

serves 6

ingredients

400g/14oz pheasant, diced
250g/9oz wild rice
225g/8oz mushrooms, sliced
75g/3oz butter
1 onion, chopped
50g/2oz plain flour
300ml/10fl oz chicken stock
300ml/10fl oz milk
2 tablespoons chopped fresh
   flat-leaf parsley
50g/2oz slivered almonds, toasted
salt and freshly ground black pepper

- Preheat the oven to 180°C/350°F/Gas mark 4.
- Poach the pheasant in simmering water for 1 hour or until tender.
- Prepare the rice according to the packet instructions.
- Sauté the mushrooms in half of the butter, then remove from the pan and reserve. Sauté the onion in the remaining butter until softened. Remove from the heat, and stir in the flour until smooth. Gradually stir the stock into the flour mixture, then add the milk. Return to the heat and cook, stirring constantly, until thick.
- Add the rice, mushrooms, pheasant and parsley, and season with salt and pepper. Transfer the mixture to a large casserole dish, and sprinkle with the almonds. Bake in the oven for 25–30 minutes. Serve hot.

Guinea fowl stew
serves 4

ingredients

50ml/2fl oz groundnut oil

900g/2lb guinea fowl, cut into
   bite-size pieces

1 teaspoon dried thyme

1 teaspoon curry powder

2 large onions, sliced

225g/8oz fresh red chillies,
   seeded and chopped

900g/2lb tomatoes

225g/8oz tomato purée

2 garlic cloves

2 onions, sliced

- In a large frying pan, heat half of the oil and brown the guinea fowl pieces, in batches if necessary, with the thyme and curry powder. Remove to a plate and keep warm.
- Add the remaining oil to the pan and sweat the onions and chillies for a few minutes, then add the tomatoes and cook for about 20 minutes until fairly dry. Add the tomato purée, stir thoroughly and add the guinea fowl pieces.
- Simmer gently for another 10 minutes, stirring frequently. Serve hot.

• •

Quail stew
serves 4

ingredients

8 medium quails

1 tablespoon ground cumin

1 tablespoon vegetable oil

15g/½oz butter

2 large onions, finely chopped

1 tablespoon crushed garlic

1 teaspoon tomato purée

1 teaspoon allspice

4 green cardamom pods

salt and ground black pepper

- Wash the quails thoroughly inside and out, removing all fat from the tops and bottoms of the quails. Cut each quail in two, with bottoms and chests separated. Season with the cumin.
- In a large cooking pan, heat the oil and butter. Add the onions and garlic, and stir until the onions begin to brown. Put the quails in the pan, turning to brown all over. Next, add the tomato purée, cover the pan and reduce the heat. Season with salt and pepper, and add the allspice, cardamom and enough boiling water just to keep a thick sauce. Leave to cook for 30 minutes until well done.
- Remove the cardamom, and serve hot.

Rabbit hotpot

serves 4

ingredients

900g/2lb rabbit, jointed
2 onions, sliced
2 tablespoons wholegrain mustard
12 prunes, pitted
4 bay leaves
450ml/¾pt dry cider
450ml/¾pt chicken stock
4 tablespoons plain flour, seasoned
   with salt and freshly ground
   black pepper
2 tablespoons vegetable oil
15g/½oz butter
450g/1lb parsnips, cut into chunks
400g/14oz canned cooked kidney
   beans, drained

- Put the rabbit joints, onions, mustard, prunes and bay leaves into a bowl, cover with the cider and stock. Mix, cover tightly, and marinate in the refrigerator overnight.
- Preheat the oven to 180°C/350°F/Gas mark 4.
- Remove the rabbit joints and prunes from the marinade; reserve. Pat the rabbit dry with kitchen paper, and dredge in the seasoned flour.
- Heat the oil and butter in a large flameproof casserole dish, add the joints and fry until browned. Sprinkle with any remaining flour. Add the reserved marinade and the parsnips, and bring to the boil.
- Cover and transfer to the oven. Bake for 40 minutes. Add the prunes and kidney beans, and bake for 20–30 minutes until tender. Serve hot.

Spanish partridge & chocolate stew

serves 4

ingredients

2 partridges, halved
2 tablespoons olive oil
1 large onion, chopped
8 garlic cloves
2 cloves
1 bay leaf
300ml/10fl oz dry white wine
1 tablespoon sherry vinegar
25g/1oz plain chocolate, grated
salt and freshly ground
   black pepper

- Brown the partridges in the oil in a frying pan over a high heat, and transfer to a casserole dish. Fry the onion in the same oil, then transfer to the casserole dish.
- Add all the remaining ingredients to the casserole dish except the chocolate, and bring to a gentle simmer, cover tightly and continue simmering for 45–50 minutes until the partridges are tender. Transfer the meat to a serving dish and keep warm.
- Stir the chocolate into the remaining liquid in the pan, and simmer for a further 3 minutes. Stir and adjust the seasoning. Pour the sauce over the partridges, and serve immediately.

Hare stew
serves 6

ingredients

225g/8oz smoked back bacon,
   cut into strips
125ml/4fl oz olive oil
225g/8oz onions, sliced
2 garlic cloves, chopped
plain flour for dredging
1.8kg/4lb hare, cut into 12 pieces
600ml/1pt red wine
600ml/1pt chicken stock
1 bouquet garni
24 pickling onions
25g/1oz butter
225g/8oz button mushrooms
2 tablespoons chopped fresh
   flat-leaf parsley
salt and freshly ground black pepper

- Fry the bacon slowly in 2 tablespoons of the oil until almost crisp, then transfer to a casserole dish with a slotted spoon. Fry the onions in this fat until soft and translucent. Add the garlic and cook for a further 2 minutes, then add the onions and garlic to the casserole dish.
- Season the hare with salt and pepper, and dredge in the flour. Add 2 tablespoons of the oil to the pan, increase the heat to medium and brown the hare pieces on all sides. Transfer to the casserole dish.
- Increase the heat under the frying pan, add the wine and deglaze, scraping up any bits clinging to the pan. Pour the wine mixture over the hare ,and add the stock, bouquet garni and salt and pepper. Bring to the boil, skim off any scum that rises to the surface, then reduce the heat, cover and simmer for about 1 hour.
- About 15 minutes before the end of the cooking time, fry the pickling onions in the butter and remaining oil. Season lightly with salt and pepper, and sauté for 5–10 minutes until golden brown. Transfer to a dish and keep warm while you fry the button mushrooms. Add these to the onions, and stir both into the casserole dish.
- Scatter the parsley over the top, and serve hot.

Pot roast of venison

serves 4

ingredients

1.8kg/4lb boned joint of venison
75ml/3fl oz vegetable oil
4 cloves
8 black peppercorns, lightly crushed
250ml/9fl oz red wine
100g/4oz streaky back bacon,
    chopped
2 onions, finely chopped
2 carrots, chopped
150g/5oz mushrooms, sliced
1 tablespoon plain flour
250ml/9fl oz chicken stock
2 tablespoons redcurrant jelly
salt and freshly ground black pepper

- Put the venison in a bowl, add half of the oil, the spices and wine, cover and leave in a cool place for 24 hours, turning the meat occasionally.
- Preheat the oven to 160°C/325°F/Gas mark 3. Remove the venison from the bowl and pat dry with kitchen paper. Reserve the marinade. Heat the remaining oil in a shallow pan, then brown the venison evenly. Transfer to a plate.
- Stir the bacon, onions, carrot and mushrooms into the pan, and cook for about 5 minutes.
- Stir in the flour and cook for 2 minutes, then remove from the heat and stir in the marinade, stock and redcurrant jelly. Season with salt and pepper. Return to the heat and bring to the boil, stirring, then simmer for 2–3 minutes.
- Transfer the venison and sauce to a casserole dish, cover and cook in the oven, turning the joint occasionally, for about 3 hours until tender. Serve hot.

Spiced chicken casserole

serves 4

ingredients

4 chicken portions, skinned
2 tablespoons plain flour
1 teaspoon paprika
25g/1oz butter
1 teaspoon curry powder
300g/11oz canned condensed
  mushroom soup
2 teaspoons chopped gherkins
salt and freshly ground
  black pepper

- Preheat the oven to 180°C/ 350°F/Gas mark 4.
- Toss the chicken portions in the flour, season with a little salt and pepper and dust with the paprika.
- Melt the butter in a flameproof casserole dish, and brown the chicken on all sides. Remove from the pan and set aside. Drain off any excess fat.
- Sprinkle the curry powder into the casserole dish and add the soup. Bring to the boil, stirring. Add the chicken and gherkins, cover and cook in the oven for 1½–2 hours until the chicken is cooked. Serve hot.

Chicken & leek casserole

serves 6

ingredients

25g/1oz butter
4 skinless chicken breast fillets
2 leeks, chopped
275g/10oz canned condensed
  vegetable soup
225ml/8fl oz white wine
1 tablespoon cornflour

- Preheat the oven to 180°C/ 350°F/Gas mark 4.
- In a frying pan, brown the chicken in the butter over a medium-high heat. Add the leeks and cook until soft. Add the soup and wine, and sprinkle the cornflour over the top.
- Mix together, then simmer for about 20 minutes until the mixture really starts to thicken.
- Pour the mixture into a large casserole dish. Bake in the oven for about 30 minutes. Serve hot.

Chicken & potato bake

serves 4

ingredients

2 tablespoons olive oil
4 chicken breasts
1 bunch of spring onions,
    trimmed and chopped
350g/12oz carrots, sliced
100g/4oz green beans, trimmed
    and sliced
600ml/1pt chicken stock
350g/12oz new potatoes
2 tablespoons cornflour
salt and freshly ground
    black pepper

- Preheat the oven to 190°C/375°F/Gas mark 5.
- Heat the oil in a large flameproof casserole dish, and add the chicken breasts. Gently fry for 5–8 minutes until browned on both sides. Lift from the casserole dish with a slotted spoon and set aside.
- Add the spring onions, carrots and green beans to the dish, and gently fry for 3–4 minutes.
- Return the chicken to the casserole dish, and pour in the stock. Add the potatoes, season with salt and pepper, and bring to the boil. Cover the casserole dish, transfer to the oven and bake for 40–50 minutes until the potatoes are tender.
- Blend the cornflour with 3 tablespoons cold water. Add to the casserole, stirring until blended and thickened. Cover and cook for a further 5 minutes. Serve immediately.

Turkey one-pot
serves 4

ingredients
100g/4oz dried kidney beans,
   soaked overnight and drained
25g/1oz butter
2 herby pork sausages
450g/1lb turkey casserole meat
3 leeks, sliced
2 carrots, finely chopped
400g/14oz canned chopped
   plum tomatoes
3 teaspoons tomato purée
1 bouquet garni
400ml/14fl oz chicken stock
salt and freshly ground black pepper

- Cook the beans in boiling water for 40 minutes, then drain well.
- Meanwhile, heat the butter in a flameproof casserole dish, then cook the sausages until browned and the fat runs. Remove and drain on kitchen paper. Stir the turkey into the casserole dish and cook until lightly browned all over, then transfer to a bowl using a slotted spoon.
- Stir the leeks and carrots into the casserole dish and brown lightly. Add the tomatoes and tomato purée, and simmer gently for about 5 minutes.
- Chop the sausages and return to the casserole dish with the beans, turkey, bouquet garni, stock and seasoning. Cover and cook gently for about 1¼ hours until the beans are tender and there is very little liquid. Serve hot.

Chicken pasanda

serves 4

ingredients

4 green cardamom pods
6 black peppercorns
½ cinnamon stick
½ teaspoon cumin seeds
2 teaspoons garam masala
1 teaspoon chilli powder
1 teaspoon grated fresh root ginger
1 garlic clove, finely chopped
4 tablespoons Greek-style yogurt
pinch of salt
700g/1½lb skinless chicken breast
    fillets, diced
5 tablespoons groundnut oil
2 onions, finely chopped
3 fresh green chillies, seeded
    and chopped
2 tablespoons chopped fresh
    coriander leaves
125ml/4fl oz single cream

- Put the cardamom pods in a dish with the peppercorns, cinnamon, cumin, garam masala, chilli powder, ginger, garlic, yogurt and salt. Add the chicken and stir well to coat. Cover and leave to marinate in the refrigerator for 2 hours.
- Heat the oil in a wok. Add the onions and cook over a low heat, stirring occasionally, for 5 minutes, then add the chicken and marinade, and cook over a medium heat, stirring, for 15 minutes.
- Stir in the chillies and coriander, and pour in the cream. Heat through but do not allow to boil. Serve immediately.

Duck, tomato & pepper stew
serves 4

ingredients

4 duck legs, each cut into
   2 pieces
3 tablespoons olive oil
1 small red onion, chopped
3 garlic cloves, finely chopped
1 red pepper, seeded and cut
   into strips
1 green pepper, seeded and cut
   into strips
700g/1½lb tomatoes, skinned
   and roughly chopped
2 sprigs of fresh thyme
1 sprig of fresh rosemary
15g/½oz plain chocolate,
   finely chopped
salt and freshly ground
   black pepper

- Brown the duck legs briskly in the oil over a high heat in a wide deep frying pan. Set aside.
- Reduce the heat and sweat the onion, garlic and peppers gently in the oil until soft. Add the tomatoes, thyme, rosemary, salt and pepper and 150ml/5fl oz water. Bring to the boil, return the duck to the pan and simmer for 40 minutes.
- Stir in the chocolate and cook for a further 5 minutes. Taste, adjust the seasoning and serve hot.

Chicken macaroni casserole
serves 4

ingredients

225g/8oz macaroni
200g/7oz cooked chicken,
   cubed
275g/10oz canned condensed
   mushroom soup
125ml/4fl oz milk
1 tablespoon chopped fresh
   flat-leaf parsley
175g/6oz Cheddar cheese,
   grated

- Preheat the oven to 200°C/ 400°F/Gas mark 6.
- Cook the macaroni in salted boiling water until al dente, then rinse and drain.
- Combine the macaroni with the remaining ingredients, reserving enough cheese to sprinkle over the top. Put in a casserole dish, cover and bake for about 20 minutes. Serve hot.

Chicken broccoli casserole
serves 4

ingredients

500g/1lb 2oz broccoli florets

500g/1lb 2oz cooked chicken, cubed

275g/10oz canned condensed chicken soup

125ml/4fl oz mayonnaise

100g/4oz Parmesan cheese, freshly grated

½ teaspoon curry powder

100g/4oz fresh bread, cubed

25g/1oz butter, melted

• Preheat the oven to 180°C/ 350°F/Gas mark 4. Lightly grease a large baking dish with a little vegetable oil.

• Cook the broccoli in water in a covered saucepan until al tender but still with a bite, then drain.

• Put the broccoli in the prepared baking dish.

• Combine the chicken, soup, mayonnaise, cheese and curry powder, then spoon over the broccoli. Top with the bread and butter. Bake in the oven, uncovered, for 25–30 minutes until heated through. Serve hot.

Duck casserole
serves 4

ingredients

25g/1oz plain flour

1 duck, jointed and skinned

4 shallots, finely chopped

100g/4oz mushrooms, finely chopped

400ml/14fl oz beef stock

225g/8oz shelled green peas

1 teaspoon chopped fresh mint

salt and freshly ground black pepper

• Preheat the oven to 190°C/ 375°F/Gas mark 5.

• Season the flour with salt and pepper, and use to coat the duck. Put the shallots and mushrooms with the duck in a casserole dish.

• Add enough stock to cover, put on a lid and cook in the oven for 45 minutes. Add the peas and mint and continue cooking for a further 30 minutes until the duck is tender. Serve hot.

Chicken casserole with yogurt

serves 6

ingredients
50g/2oz cornflour
1 teaspoon paprika
1.2kg/3lb chicken fillets, skinned
  and trimmed
1 packet chicken noodle soup
250ml/9fl oz warm water
1 garlic clove, crushed
1 teaspoon Worcestershire sauce
50ml/2fl oz dry sherry
125ml/4fl oz freshly squeezed
  lemon juice
2 tablespoons Greek-style yogurt
1 tablespoon finely chopped
  fresh flat-leaf parsley

- Preheat the oven to 180°C/
  350°F/Gas mark 4.
- Mix together the cornflour and
  paprika, and toss the chicken fillets
  in the mixture. Arrange the fillets in
  the bottom of a large shallow
  casserole dish.
- Combine the remaining ingredients
  and pour over the chicken.
- Cook in the oven, uncovered, for
  about 40 minutes until the chicken
  is tender. Serve hot.

Swiss chicken casserole

serves 4

ingredients
500g/1lb 5oz cooked chicken,
  chopped into bite-size pieces
175g/6oz celery, sliced
200g/7oz herb stuffing,
  broken up
225ml/8fl oz salad dressing
125ml/4fl oz milk
50g/2oz onion, chopped
225g/8oz Emmenthaler
  cheese, grated
50g/2oz toasted slivered
  almonds
salt and freshly ground
  black pepper

- Preheat the oven to 180°C/
  350°F/Gas mark 4.
- Combine the chicken, celery,
  stuffing, salad dressing, milk, onion
  and cheese in a large casserole
  dish. Season with salt and pepper,
  and sprinkle with the almonds.
- Cover the casserole with a lid and
  bake in the oven for 25 minutes.
  Remove the lid and continue
  baking for a further 10 minutes.
  Serve hot.

French-style pot-roast poussin

serves 4

ingredients

1 tablespoon olive oil
1 onion, sliced
1 garlic clove, sliced
50g/2oz smoked back bacon
2 fresh poussins, about
    450g/1lb each
25g/1oz butter, melted
2 baby celery hearts, quartered
8 baby carrots
2 small courgettes, cut into chunks

8 small new potatoes
600ml/1pt chicken stock
150ml/5fl oz dry white wine
1 bay leaf
2 sprigs of fresh thyme
2 sprigs of fresh rosemary
1 tablespoon butter, softened
1 tablespoon plain flour
salt and freshly ground
    black pepper

- Preheat the oven to 190°C/375°F/Gas mark 5.
- Heat the olive oil in a large flameproof casserole dish, and add the onion, garlic and bacon. Sauté for 5–6 minutes until the onions are soft.
- Brush the poussin with a little of the melted butter and season well with salt and pepper. Lay on top of the onion mixture, and arrange the prepared vegetables around them. Pour the stock and wine around the poussin, and add the herbs.
- Cover and bake in the oven for 20 minutes, then remove the lid and brush the pousssins with the remaining melted butter. Cook for a further 25–30 minutes until golden.
- Transfer the poussins to a warmed serving platter, and cut each one in half using poultry shears or scissors. Remove the vegetables with a slotted spoon, and arrange them around the birds. Cover with foil and keep warm.
- Discard the herbs from the pan juices. In a bowl, mix together the softened butter and flour to form a paste. Bring the liquid in the pan to the boil, then whisk in teaspoonfuls of the paste until thickened. Season the sauce with salt and pepper, and serve with the poussin and vegetables.

One-pot chicken couscous
serves 8

ingredients

900g/2lb boneless, skinless
   chicken breasts, cut into
   2.5cm/1in chunks
50ml/2fl oz olive oil
4 large carrots, peeled and sliced
2 onions, diced
3 garlic cloves, crushed
500g/1lb 2oz canned
   chicken soup
250g/9oz couscous
2 teaspoons Tabasco sauce
½ teaspoon salt
200g/7oz raisins
200g/7oz slivered almonds,
   toasted
50g/2oz fresh parsley, chopped

- In a large frying pan over a medium-high heat, cook the chicken in the oil until well browned on all sides. Using a slotted spoon, remove the chicken to a plate.
- Reduce the heat to medium.
- In the remaining drippings, cook the carrots and onion for 5 minutes. Add the garlic and cook for a further 2 minutes, stirring frequently.
- Add the soup, Tabasco sauce, salt and chicken. Bring to the boil, then reduce the heat to low, cover and simmer for 5 minutes. Stir in the raisins, almonds and parsley. Heat through, and serve immediately.

One-pot Cajun chicken gumbo
serves 2

ingredients

1 tablespoon sunflower oil
4 chicken thighs
1 small onion, diced
2 celery sticks, diced
1 green pepper, seeded
   and diced
100g/4oz long-grain rice
300ml/10fl oz chicken stock
1 fresh red chilli, seeded and
   thinly sliced
225g/8oz okra, trimmed
1 tablespoon tomato purée
salt and freshly ground
   black pepper

- Heat the oil in a wide pan. Fry the chicken until golden. Remove the from the pan. Stir in the onion, celery and pepper, and fry for 1 minute. Pour off any excess oil.
- Add the rice and fry, stirring, for a further minute. Add the stock and heat until boiling. Add the chilli, okra and tomato purée. Season with salt and pepper.
- Return the chicken to the pan and stir. Cover tightly and simmer gently for 15 minutes or until the rice is tender and the chicken is cooked. Serve immediately.

Turkey, pea & ham pot pie

serves 6

ingredients

50g/2oz plain flour
500g/1lb 2oz turkey thighs, diced
4 tablespoons vegetable oil
1 onion, chopped
250ml/9fl oz chicken stock
175g/6oz ham, cut into
   bite-size chunks
150g/5oz frozen peas
2 teaspoons chopped fresh tarragon
2 teaspoons chopped fresh chives
2 tablespoons crème fraîche
375g/13oz ready-rolled puff pastry
1 egg, beaten
salt and freshly ground black pepper

- Preheat the oven to 200°C/400°F/Gas mark 6.
- Put the flour in a bowl, season with salt and pepper, and toss the turkey until coated. Heat half of the oil in a large frying pan and brown the turkey on all sides. Remove the turkey from the pan using a slotted spoon. Set aside.
- Heat the remaining oil in the same pan, and sweat the onion for about 10 minutes until soft. Stir in the remaining flour and cook for 1 minute.
- Pour in the stock, bring to the boil and simmer until thickened. Return the turkey to the pan, add the ham, peas and herbs, and simmer for 5 minutes. Stir in the crème fraîche. Transfer the mixture to a medium baking dish and allow to cool.
- Lay out the puff pastry, rolling if necessary, to a size just larger than the top of the baking dish. Brush the edge of the dish with a little egg and lay the pastry on top, pressing gently to seal. Crimp lightly around the edges with your fingers or a fork. Brush the top of the pastry with the beaten egg. Make small slits in the top for steam to escape.
- Bake for 30–35 minutes until the filling is completely heated through and the pastry golden brown. Serve hot.

Turkey casserole

serves 8

ingredients
75g/3oz butter
2 tablespoons plain flour
150ml/5fl oz single cream
225g/8oz cooked turkey, diced
225g/8oz Cheddar cheese,
   grated
450g/1lb potatoes, cooked
   and mashed
225g/8oz dry stuffing mix
salt and freshly ground
   black pepper

- Preheat the oven to 180°C/ 350°F/Gas mark 4.
- Melt half the butter in a saucepan over a low heat, then stir in the flour until thoroughly mixed. Slowly stir in the cream and 225ml/8fl oz cold water. Season with salt and pepper. Stir over a low heat for 5 minutes. Remove from the heat.
- Put the turkey in a lightly greased baking dish. Pour the sauce over the turkey, then sprinkle with the cheese. Spread the mashed potatoes over the cheese.
- Melt the remaining butter and add to the stuffing mix, then sprinkle the stuffing over the potato. Bake in the oven, uncovered, for 45 minutes. Serve hot.

• •

Chicken & crackers casserole

serves 6

ingredients
2 packets Ritz or other butter
   crackers, crushed
100g/4oz butter, melted
6 skinless chicken breast fillets,
   cooked and chopped into
   bite-size pieces
400g/14oz canned cream of
   chicken soup
225g/8oz sour cream
225ml/8fl oz chicken stock

- Preheat the oven to 150°C/ 300°F/Gas mark 2.
- Put half the crackers in the bottom of a large casserole dish. Drizzle half the butter over the crackers.
- Mix the chicken with the soup, sour cream and stock, then pour over the crackers.
- Sprinkle the remaining crackers over the chicken mixture. Drizzle with the remaining butter. Bake in the oven for 30–45 minutes. Serve immediately.

Chicken & sweetcorn stew
serves 4

ingredients

4 skinless chicken breast fillets,
  chopped into chunks
plain flour for dredging
2 tablespoons olive oil
1 onion, sliced
1 garlic clove, crushed
150g/5oz canned sweetcorn
2 chicken stock cubes
1 tablespoon clear honey
125ml/4fl oz tomato sauce
salt and freshly ground
  black pepper

- Season the chicken with salt and pepper, and dredge in the flour. Shake off any excess.
- Sauté the chicken in the oil until golden. Remove from the pan.
- Sweat the onion and garlic in the same pan until soft. Add the chicken, sweetcorn, stock cubes, honey and tomato sauce. Simmer over a medium-high heat for at least 20 minutes, stirring regularly. Serve hot.

Chicken & pasta broth
serves 4

ingredients

2 tablespoons sunflower oil
350g/12oz skinless chicken
  breast fillets, diced
1 onion, diced
250g/9oz carrots, diced
250g/9oz cauliflower florets
900ml/1½pt chicken stock
2 teaspoons dried mixed herbs
100g/4oz pasta shapes
salt and freshly ground
  black pepper

- Heat the oil in a large saucepan and quickly sauté the chicken, onion, carrots and cauliflower until they are lightly coloured. Stir in the chicken stock and herbs, and bring to the boil.
- Add the pasta and return to the boil. Cover the pan and leave the broth to simmer for 10 minutes, stirring occasionally to prevent the pasta shapes sticking together.
- Season the broth with salt and pepper, and serve immediately.

Winter chicken stew

serves 4

ingredients
4 chicken fillet portions,
   skinned and chopped into
   bite-size pieces
25g/1oz butter
1 onion, sliced
4 carrots, sliced
1 swede, sliced
100g/4oz pearl barley
900ml/1½pt chicken stock
3 potatoes, cut into bite-size
   chunks
1 green cabbage, shredded
salt and freshly ground
   black pepper

- Brown the chicken in the butter in a large saucepan. Remove from the pan with a slotted spoon.
- Add the onion, carrots and swede to the same pan, and sauté for 2 minutes, stirring.
- Add the barley and stock, and return the chicken to the pan. Season with salt and pepper.
- Bring to the boil, then simmer for 45 minutes. Add the potatoes and cabbage, cover and continue cooking for 20 minutes or until all ingredients are tender. Serve hot.

Tortilla chicken casserole

serves 6–8

ingredients
6 skinless chicken breast fillet
   halves, cooked and chopped
100g/4oz canned chopped
   green chillies
225g/8oz Cheddar cheese,
   grated
275g/10oz canned condensed
   mushroom soup
225ml/8fl oz milk
12 corn tortillas
175g/6oz plain potato
   crisps, crushed

- Preheat the oven to 180°C/350°F/Gas mark 4. Lightly grease a 23cm/9in square baking dish with vegetable oil.
- Combine the chicken, green chillies, cheese, soup and milk.
- Place 4 tortillas in the bottom of the prepared baking dish, and spread one-third of the chicken mixture over the tortillas. Repeat the layers until all tortillas are used, ending with chicken mixture. Top with the crisps. Bake for 30 minutes until bubbly. Serve immediately.

Duck & pomegranate stew

serves 4

ingredients

2 small pomegranates
2kg/4lb duck, cut into 8 pieces
3 tablespoons sunflower oil
1 onion, chopped
225g/8oz shelled walnuts,
   coarsely ground
450ml/¾pt chicken stock
1 cinnamon stick
2 cloves
juice of ½ lemon
pinch of granulated sugar
salt and freshly ground black pepper

- Squeeze the juice from one of the pomegranates using a lemon squeezer. Extract the seeds of the other pomegranate and reserve.
- Brown the duck pieces briskly in half of the oil, and transfer to a flameproof casserole dish. Fry the onion in the same fat until it is tender, and transfer to the casserole dish. Add the walnuts to the pan, and fry until they begin to change colour, then scrape into the casserole dish.
- Return the frying pan to the heat and pour in the stock. Bring to the boil, stirring up any pan residue. Pour into the casserole dish and add the cinnamon stick, cloves, pomegranate juice, lemon juice and sugar. Season with salt and pepper.
- Cover and simmer for 30 minutes. Remove the lid and continue simmering, uncovered, for 20–30 minutes until the meat is very tender and the sauce is thick. Taste and adjust the seasoning, and serve hot with the pomegranate seeds sprinkled over the top.

Sherry chicken casserole
serves 4

ingredients
4 chicken fillet portions, skinned and chopped
25g/1oz butter
1 large onion, finely chopped
100g/4oz button mushrooms, quartered
400g/14oz canned chopped tomatoes
125ml/4fl oz sherry
2 tablespoons tomato purée
1 bouquet garni
salt and freshly ground black pepper

- Preheat the oven to 180°C/ 350°F/Gas mark 4.
- Brown the chicken in the butter in a flameproof casserole dish. Remove with a slotted spoon, then add the onion and fry for 2 minutes. Add the mushrooms and cook for a further 1 minute. Return the chicken to the pan.
- Add the tomatoes. Blend the sherry with the tomato purée, and stir in. Add the bouquet garni and season with salt and pepper. Bring to the boil, then cover and cook in the oven for 1½ hours or until the chicken is tender. Skim off any fat, and serve the casserole hot.

• •

Duck stew with turnips & onions
serves 4

ingredients
25g/1oz butter
1 duck, cut in pieces
1 tablespoon plain flour
2 onions, quartered
8 turnips, quartered
salt and freshly ground black pepper

- Melt the butter in a heavy frying pan, and sauté the duck quickly until browned.
- Add the flour, stirring all the time.
- Add 1.2 litres/2pt water, bring to the boil and boil for 3 minutes.
- Transfer the contents of the pan to a casserole dish. Add the onions and turnips, and season with salt and pepper. Cover and cook slowly for 45–50 minutes until the duck is tender. Serve hot.

Almond chicken casserole
serves 6

ingredients

700g/1½lb chicken, boned, skinned
   and diced
200ml/7fl oz mayonnaise
200ml/7fl oz Greek-style yogurt
400g/14oz canned mushroom soup
450ml/¾pt chicken stock
2 tablespoons freshly squeezed
   lemon juice
3 tablespoons chopped onion
350g/12oz cooked rice
225g/8oz canned sliced
   water chestnuts
225g/8oz slivered almonds
175g/6oz celery, chopped
100g/4oz butter
150g/5oz cornflakes
salt and freshly ground black pepper

- Preheat the oven to 180°C/350°F/Gas mark 4.
- Mix the chicken, mayonnaise, yogurt, soup, stock, lemon juice, onion, rice, water chestnuts, half of the almonds and the celery together. Season with salt and pepper. Put in a large casserole dish.
- Mix the remaining almonds with the butter and cornflakes, and use this mixture to top the casserole. Bake in the oven for 35–45 minutes. Serve hot.

Chilli chicken casserole
serves 4

ingredients

plain flour for dredging
200g/7oz chicken, chopped
25g/1oz butter
2 tablespoons vegetable oil
2 medium onions, chopped
1½ teaspoons poultry seasoning
4 tablespoons soy sauce
125ml/4fl oz tomato purée
2 tablespoons chilli powder
175ml/6fl oz medium dry sherry
salt and freshly ground
   black pepper

- Preheat the oven to 180°C/ 350°F/Gas mark 4.
- Season the flour with salt and pepper. Dredge the chicken pieces in the seasoned flour, then brown in a casserole dish with the butter and oil over a medium-high heat.
- Add the remaining ingredients to the casserole dish and mix well. Cover and bake in the oven for 1 hour or until the chicken is tender. Serve hot.

Chicken macaroni stew
serves 2

ingredients

225g/8oz canned chopped
   plum tomatoes
200g/7oz frozen mixed
   vegetables
100g/4oz elbow macaroni
50g/2oz onion, chopped
¼ teaspoon chopped fresh oregano

⅛ teaspoon garlic powder
1 bay leaf
225ml/8fl oz chicken stock
200g/7oz cooked chicken, diced
salt and freshly ground
   black pepper

- Put all the ingredients except the chicken in a saucepan and bring to the boil. Reduce the heat and boil gently for about 15 minutes, uncovered, until the macaroni is tender. Stir several times to prevent the macaroni from sticking together.
- Add the chicken and heat to serving temperature. Remove the bay leaf and serve immediately.

Pumpkin turkey stew

serves 6

ingredients

2 tablespoons canola oil
4 onions, finely chopped
2 teaspoons grated fresh root ginger
700g/1½lb skinless turkey thigh fillet,
    cut into 4cm/1½in cubes
400g/14oz canned chopped
    plum tomatoes
200g/7oz pumpkin purée
½ teaspoon salt
¼ teaspoon pepper
2 tablespoons chopped fresh
    coriander leaves

- Heat 1 tablespoon of the oil in a large flameproof casserole dish over a medium heat. Sweat the onions for 3 minutes until softened. Add the ginger and cook for a further 2 minutes. Transfer to a bowl.
- Heat the remaining oil in the casserole dish. Brown the turkey in batches, allowing 3–4 minutes per batch. Return the onions and ginger to the casserole dish. Stir in the tomatoes, pumpkin purée, salt, pepper and 225ml/8fl oz water. Bring to the boil.
- Reduce the heat to low and simmer, part-covered, for 40 minutes, until the turkey is tender. Stir occasionally. Add the coriander and cook for a further 2 minutes, then serve hot.

French-style stewed duck

serves 4

ingredients

1 oven-ready duck, about 1.8kg/4lb
25g/1oz butter
12 pearl onions
600ml/1pt chicken stock
225g/8oz frozen peas
1 tablespoon chopped fresh mint
1 tablespoon chopped fresh
    oregano
1 tablespoon chopped fresh
    flat-leaf parsley
1 teaspoon grated nutmeg
25g/1oz plain flour
salt and freshly ground black pepper

* Preheat the oven to 200°C/400°F/Gas mark 6.
* Remove the giblets and wipe the duck inside and out with kitchen paper. Prick all over with a fork.
* Melt the butter in a flameproof casserole dish, and brown the duck on all sides. Remove the duck and put to one side, and brown the onions. Pour off any fat and return the duck to the dish. Add the stock and a little salt and pepper, and bring to the boil. Cover and cook in the oven for 30 minutes.
* Skim off any fat from the surface, then add all the remaining ingredients except the flour. Reduce the oven temperature to 180°C/350°F/Gas mark 4, and cook for a further 1½ hours. Remove the duck and keep warm. Again, skim off any fat.
* Blend the flour with a little water and stir into the casserole dish. Simmer, stirring, for 3 minutes. Taste and adjust the seasoning if necessary.
* Carve the duck, discarding the skin, and transfer to warmed serving plates. Spoon the sauce over and serve immediately.

Tarragon chicken casserole
serves 10

ingredients

275g/10oz canned condensed chicken soup

275g/10oz canned condensed mushroom soup

175ml/6fl oz single cream

4 teaspoons dried tarragon

½ teaspoon ground black pepper

450g/1lb linguine, cooked and drained

600g/1lb 5oz cooked chicken, cubed

100g/4oz Parmesan cheese, freshly grated

- Preheat the oven to 180°C/350°F/Gas mark 4.
- In a large bowl, combine the soups, cream, tarragon and pepper. Stir in the linguine and chicken, and transfer the contents of the bowl to a large baking dish. Sprinkle with the Parmesan.
- Bake, uncovered, for 30 minutes or until heated through. Serve hot.

Butter bean & chicken casserole
serves 4

ingredients

425g/15oz canned cooked butter beans

50ml/2fl oz tomato ketchup

200g/7oz chicken, cooked and cubed

1 teaspoon minced onion

75g/3oz green pepper, chopped

½ teaspoon Worcestershire sauce

200g/7oz Cheddar cheese, grated

salt and freshly ground black pepper

- Preheat the oven to 170°C/325°F/Gas mark 5.
- Put the beans, ketchup, chicken, onion, pepper and Worcestershire sauce in a large casserole dish. Bake, uncovered, in the oven for 20 minutes. Top with the cheese and return to the oven until the cheese is melted and golden. Serve hot.

Salmon & potato casserole
serves 4–6

ingredients

250g/9oz smoked salmon,
  flaked
900g/2lb white potatoes,
  thinly sliced
1 onion, chopped
25g/1oz butter
2 tablespoons chopped fresh
  flat-leaf parsley
¼ teaspoon freshly ground
  black pepper

- Preheat the oven to 180°C/
  350°F/Gas mark 4. Lightly grease
  a large casserole dish with a little
  vegetable oil.
- Layer half of the salmon, potato,
  onion, butter, parsley and pepper
  in the casserole dish. Repeat
  the layers.
- Gently pour 75ml/3fl oz water
  over the layers in the casserole
  dish, then cover. Bake for about
  1¼ hours until the potatoes are
  tender. Serve hot.

Crab & seafood one-pot
serves 4

ingredients

225g/8oz cooked crabmeat,
  shredded
225g/8oz peeled and deveined
  cooked prawns, chopped
125ml/4fl oz sour cream
150g/5oz green chillies, sliced
1 teaspoon chilli powder
½ teaspoon ground cumin
¼ teaspoon salt
225g/8oz tortilla chips, crushed
225ml/8fl oz ready-made salsa
200g/7oz Cheddar cheese,
  grated
100g/4oz pitted black
  olives, halved
2 spring onions, sliced

- Preheat the oven to 180°C/
  350°F/Gas mark 4.
- In large bowl, mix together the
  crabmeat, prawns, sour cream,
  chillies, chilli powder, cumin
  and salt.
- Line the bottom of a large baking
  dish with tortilla chips. Spoon the
  crab mixture over the chips and
  top with salsa, cheese, olives and
  spring onions. Bake in the oven for
  15 minutes or until heated through
  and the cheese has melted.
  Serve immediately.

Oyster & cauliflower stew
serves 4

ingredients

25g/1oz butter
600ml/1pt canned shucked oysters
  with liquid
100g/4oz cauliflower florets,
  blanched

1 tablespoon cornflour
400ml/14fl oz milk
¼ teaspoon salt
¼ teaspoon cracked black pepper
¼ teaspoon onion powder

- Put the butter in a large microwave-safe baking dish. Cover with kitchen paper. Heat in the microwave on high for 45 seconds or until melted.
- Drain the oysters, reserving the liquid. Add the oysters to the butter, and cook on high for 1 minute. Using a slotted spoon, remove the oysters to a container or pot with the cauliflower.
- Gradually add the cornflour to the oyster liquid, and stir until blended. Add the milk and transfer the liquid to the baking dish. Add the salt, pepper and onion powder. Cook on high for 4–5 minutes until slightly thickened, stirring twice. Add the oysters and cauliflower to the dish, and cook on high for 2 minutes. Serve hot.

Hearty fish stew
serves 4

ingredients

1 large onion, thinly sliced
2 carrots, thinly sliced
1 large potato, diced
1 parsnip, diced
1 turnip, diced
¼ small green cabbage, shredded
25g/1oz butter

400g/14oz canned chopped
  tomatoes
1 fish stock cube
350g/12oz cod fillet, skinned
  and cubed
½ teaspoon dried mixed herbs
salt and ground black pepper

- Put all the vegetables in a large saucepan with the butter. Cook, stirring, for 5 minutes. Add the tomatoes, 300ml/10fl oz water and crumbled stock cube. Bring to the boil, reduce the heat, part-cover and simmer for 15 minutes or until the vegetables are nearly tender.
- Add the fish, a little salt and pepper, and the herbs, and cook for a further 5 minutes. Taste and adjust the seasoning if necessary. Serve hot.

Clam stew
serves 6

ingredients

18 fresh clams
2 tablespoons olive oil
175g/6oz onion, chopped
1 teaspoon chopped garlic
850g/1¾lb canned chopped
   plum tomatoes
175ml/6fl oz tomato purée

50g/2oz fresh basil, chopped
2 teaspoons paprika
¼ teaspoon freshly ground
   black pepper
225ml/8fl oz dry white wine
700g/1½lb swordfish, cut into
   2.5cm/1in pieces

- Wash the clams under cold running water to release any grit. Set aside.
- Heat the oil in a large saucepan over a medium heat. Add the onion and garlic, and cook until tender. Add the tomatoes, tomato purée, basil, paprika and pepper. Cover and bring to a boil, then reduce the heat and simmer for 10 minutes, stirring occasionally.
- Add the wine, clams and fish. Cover and simmer over a medium heat until the clams open. Remove the clam meat from the shells and return to the stew, discarding the shells. Heat through, mix thoroughly and serve.

• •

Halibut stew
serves 3

ingredients

25g/1oz butter
1 large onion, finely chopped
2 garlic cloves, finely minced
1 small green pepper, seeded and
   diced

1 tomato, peeled and chopped
250g/9oz potatoes, diced
1 teaspoon dried marjoram
5 halibut fillets
salt and ground black pepper

- Melt the butter in a microwave-safe baking dish for 1 minute on high, then mix in the onion, garlic and green pepper and mix well. Microwave on high for 2 minutes. Stir well. Mix in the tomato, potatoes, 125ml/4fl oz water and marjoram. Season with salt and pepper. Stir well. Microwave for 5 minutes on a medium-high setting.
- Cut the fish into individual servings. Arrange over the hot vegetable mixture. Lightly season, cover and microwave for 5 minutes on high. Let stand for 3 minutes before serving.

casseroles & stews

Trout stew
serves 4

ingredients
1 teaspoon salt
1 onion, thinly sliced
225ml/8fl oz tomato juice
2 garlic cloves, crushed
4 small potatoes, diced
1 green pepper, seeded
   and chopped
1 medium tomato, peeled
   and chopped
1.2kg/2½lb trout fillets
275g/10oz frozen green beans

- Combine all the ingredients except
  the trout and green beans in a
  large microwave-safe casserole
  dish. Add 50ml/2fl oz water.
  Cover and microwave for
  10 minutes on high or until the
  potatoes are tender.
- Add the fish and green beans to
  the stew, cover, and microwave
  for a further 5 minutes on high.
  Let stand for a minute or two
  before serving.

One-pot tuna pasta
serves 4

ingredients
2 chicken stock cubes
1/8 teaspoon freshly ground
   black pepper
1 teaspoon dried basil
225g/8oz elbow macaroni
100g/4oz red pepper, seeded
   and diced
250g/9oz frozen green beans,
   chopped
225ml/8fl oz milk
100g/4oz Cheddar cheese,
   grated
400g/14oz canned tuna in oil,
   drained
50g/2oz fresh flat-leaf parsley,
   chopped

- Bring 600ml/1pt water, the stock
  cubes, pepper and basil to the boil
  in large casserole dish.
- Gradually add the pasta, keeping
  the water at boiling point. Cover
  and simmer for 7 minutes, stirring
  occasionally.
- Stir the red pepper, green beans
  and milk into the casserole dish.
  Cover and simmer for 6–8 minutes
  until the pasta and beans are
  tender. Stir in the cheese, tuna and
  parsley until the cheese is melted.
  Serve immediately.

Sea bass stew

serves 10

ingredients

450g/1lb back bacon rashers
1.3kg/3lb sea bass fillet, cubed
3 onions, sliced
8 celery sticks, sliced
450g/1lb carrots, sliced
600ml/1pt fish stock
4 bay leaves
850g/1¾lb canned chopped
   plum tomatoes
4 large potatoes, cubed
salt and freshly ground
   black pepper

- Dry-fry the bacon slowly in a large frying pan and reserve the grease.
- Steam the sea bass over 750ml/1¼pt water for 15 minutes.
- In a large casserole dish, sauté the onions in the reserved bacon grease until light golden brown. Add the celery, carrots and fish, and stir lightly to coat.
- Pour in the stock and 750ml/1¼pt water. Add the bay leaves and tomatoes, and season with salt and pepper. Bring to the boil, add the potatoes, reduce the heat and simmer for 40 minutes, stirring occasionally. Serve hot.

Red snapper casserole

serves 6

ingredients

700g/1½lb red snapper fillets
plain flour for dredging
50g/2oz butter
175g/6oz green chilli sauce
350g/12oz Cheddar cheese,
   grated
2 tablespoons chopped fresh
   flat-leaf parsley
salt and freshly ground
   black pepper

- Preheat the oven to 180°C/350°F/Gas mark 4.
- Season a little flour with salt and pepper. Dredge the snapper fillets in the seasoned flour.
- Heat the butter in a frying pan, and lightly sauté the fillets on both sides, in batches if necessary.
- Transfer the fillets to a large casserole dish. Divide the chilli sauce and cheese among them. Bake for about 12 minutes.
- Sprinkle with the parsley, and serve immediately.

Calamari stew
serves 4

ingredients
3 garlic cloves, minced
2 tablespoons white wine vinegar
1 tablespoon light soy sauce
900g/2lb fresh squid, cleaned
    and cut into rings
salt and freshly ground
    black pepper

- Put the garlic, vinegar, soy sauce, 1 tablespoon water and salt and pepper to taste in a frying pan over a medium heat, and bring to the boil.
- Add the squid while the mixture is still boiling, and cook for another 3–4 minutes, stirring occasionally. Serve immediately.

● ●

Cod stew
serves 4–6

ingredients
50g/2oz butter
4 carrots, chopped
2 onions, chopped
900g/2lb potatoes, sliced
4 tomatoes, sliced
1½ tablespoons plain flour
125ml/4fl oz milk
3 cod fillets
salt and freshly ground
    black pepper

- Melt the butter in a heavy saucepan. Add the carrots and onions, and sweat until soft.
- Add the potatoes and tomatoes, and season with salt and pepper.
- Pour in enough water to come to just below the top layer of tomatoes and bring to the boil. Boil slowly for 20 minutes.
- Mix the flour and milk together until smooth, and stir into the stew. Lay the cod on top of the stew, and cook for 10–20 minutes. Serve hot.

Prawn & spinach stew
serves 4

ingredients

175g/6oz mushrooms, sliced
1 onion, chopped
1 garlic clove, minced
25g/1oz butter
25g/1oz plain flour
⅛ teaspoon ground nutmeg
⅛ teaspoon ground black pepper
1 bay leaf
400ml/14fl oz vegetable stock
225ml/8fl oz milk
225g/8oz peeled and deveined
  cooked prawns
200g/7oz fresh spinach, torn
75g/3oz Gruy?re cheese,
  grated

- In a medium saucepan, cook the mushrooms, onion and garlic in the butter until soft. Stir in the flour, nutmeg and pepper, and add the bay leaf.
- Add the stock and milk, and cook, stirring, until the mixture has thickened. Add the prawns and cook for a further 2 minutes. Add the spinach and cheese.
- Cook and stir until the spinach wilts and the cheese melts. Remove and discard the bay lea. Serve hot.

• •

Dover sole stew
serves 4

ingredients

400ml/14fl oz chicken stock
275g/10oz canned condensed
  French onion soup
200g/7oz potatoes, cubed
175g/6oz celery, sliced
450g/1lb Dover sole, cut into
  2.5cm/1in pieces
150g/5oz baby carrots
150g/5oz courgette,
  thinly sliced
400g/14oz canned chopped
  tomatoes
½ teaspoon dried thyme
½ teaspoon dried rosemary

- Put the stock, soup, potatoes and celery in a large casserole dish, and bring to the boil. Reduce the heat to medium, cover and cook for 5 minutes.
- Add the remaining ingredients and cook, covered, for a further 10 minutes or until the fish is cooked and the vegetables are tender. Serve hot.

Thai jasmine rice & prawn casserole

serves 3

ingredients

500g/1lb 2oz cold cooked
   jasmine rice
30 peeled and deveined cooked
   tiger prawns, chopped
400g/14oz canned sweetcorn
   kernels, drained
200g/7oz carrots, thinly sliced
600g/1lb 5oz ready-made mild
   ginger stir-fry sauce

- Put the cooked rice in a large heavy frying pan.
- Add the prawns, sweetcorn and carrots, and cook, stirring, over a high heat for 5 minutes, until the carrots are tender.
- Pour in the sauce, and simmer for a further 5 minutes. Serve hot.

Cheese & crabmeat casserole

serves 4

ingredients

450g/1lb Cheddar cheese,
   cubed
8 slices bread, crusts removed,
   cubed
275g/10oz frozen crabmeat
5 eggs
600ml/1pt milk
75g/3oz butter, melted

- Preheat the oven to 180°C/ 350°F/Gas mark 4.
- Alternate layers of cheese, bread and crabmeat in a casserole dish.
- Whisk together the eggs, milk and melted butter, and pour over the layered mixture.
- Set the casserole dish in a baking tray. Carefully fill the tray with water to come halfway up the sides. Bake the casserole in the oven for 1–1½ hours. Serve hot

Halibut casserole
serves 8

ingredients
450g/1lb halibut
2 bay leaves
½ onion, sliced
25g/1oz butter
4 tablespoons plain flour
400ml/14fl oz milk
225g/8oz Cheddar cheese,
  grated
salt and freshly ground
  black pepper

- Preheat the oven to 180°C/
  350°F/Gas mark 4.
- Steam the halibut, bay leaves and
  onion for 30 minutes.
- Prepare a white sauce by
  combining the butter, flour, milk,
  salt and pepper (see method for
  Béchamel sauce on page 728).
- Break the halibut into bite-size
  pieces, and layer in a large
  casserole dish with the cheese and
  white sauce. Cover and bake in
  the oven for 35 minutes. Serve hot.

• •

Salmon casserole
serves 4

ingredients
425g/15oz canned salmon
250g/9oz elbow macaroni
350g/12oz canned sweetcorn
  kernels, drained
150g/5oz canned chopped
  plum tomatoes
50g/2oz onion, chopped
250g/9oz celery, sliced
275g/10oz canned condensed
  cream of mushroom soup
2 tablespoons freshly squeezed
  lemon juice
salt and freshly ground
  black pepper

- Preheat the oven to 180°C/
  350°F/Gas mark 4.
- Drain the salmon, reserving the
  juices. Cook the macaroni in salted
  boiling water until al dente, drain
  and transfer to a deep casserole
  dish. Mix in the salmon.
- In a bowl, mix together the
  sweetcorn, tomatoes, onion, celery,
  soup and lemon juice. Season with
  salt and pepper, and pour over the
  salmon mixture. Bake in the oven
  for 30 minutes. Serve hot.

Tuna fish casserole
serves 4

ingredients

200g/7oz thin egg noodles,
  boiled and drained
275g/10oz canned tuna in oil,
  drained
275g/10oz canned condensed
  mushroom soup
125ml/4fl oz sour cream
150g/5oz mushrooms, chopped
100g/4oz Cheddar cheese,
  grated

- Preheat the oven to 180°C/
  350°F/Gas mark 4.
- Mix together the noodles, tuna,
  soup, sour cream and mushrooms
  in a large casserole dish. Sprinkle
  all over with the cheese.
- Bake in the oven for about
  20 minutes until cooked through.
  Serve hot.

Scallop casserole
serves 2

ingredients

100g/4oz celery, chopped
100g/4oz onion, chopped
150g/5oz green pepper,
  roughly chopped
200g/7oz broccoli, chopped
350g/12oz scallops, chopped
3 eggs, beaten
200g/7oz Cheddar cheese,
  grated
1 teaspoon salt

- Preheat the oven to 190°C/
  375°F/Gas mark 5.
- In a frying pan, sauté the celery,
  onions and green pepper for
  3–4 minutes. Cool slightly.
- Remove from the heat and drain.
  Cook the broccoli until tender.
- Put the scallops and vegetables in
  a casserole dish. Mix gently to
  distribute evenly.
- Whisk together the eggs, cheese
  and salt. Pour over the top of the
  scallops and vegetables. Bake in
  the oven for 35–40 minutes, and
  serve hot.

Okra stew with prawns

serves 4

ingredients

1 tablespoon lime juice
450g/1lb peeled and deveined
   raw prawns
50g/2oz butter
6 tablespoons chopped
   spring onion
225g/8oz okra, topped, tailed
   and sliced
225g/8oz canned sweetcorn
3 tomatoes, peeled and chopped
2 fresh red chillies, seeded
   and sliced
1 bay leaf
1 tablespoon tomato purée
salt and ground black pepper

- Mix the lime juice with the prawns and set aside.
- Heat the butter in a frying pan and sauté the onions for 3 minutes. Add all the remaining ingredients except the prawns to the pan, and simmer for 10 minutes.
- Add the prawns and bring to the boil, then simmer for 5 minutes. Remove and discard the bay leaf, and serve hot.

Squid casserole

serves 4

ingredients

3 tablespoons olive oil
1 large onion, thinly sliced
2 garlic cloves, crushed
700g/1½lb squid rings
1 red pepper, seeded and sliced
2 sprigs of fresh rosemary
150ml/5fl oz dry white wine
400g/14oz canned chopped
   plum tomatoes
2 tablespoons tomato purée
1 teaspoon paprika
salt and freshly ground
   black pepper

- Heat the oil in a casserole dish and fry the onion and garlic until soft. Add the squid, increase the heat and continue to cook for about 10 minutes until sealed and beginning to colour.
- Add the red pepper, rosemary, wine and 250ml/9fl oz water, and bring to the boil. Cover and simmer gently for 45 minutes.
- Discard the rosemary, and add the tomatoes, tomato purée and paprika. Season with salt and pepper. Continue to simmer gently to 45–60 minutes until tender. Serve hot.

Brown fish stew
serves 4

ingredients
900g/2lb red snapper fillets
juice of 2 limes
2 tablespoons vegetable oil
2 tomatoes, chopped
1 tablespoon pimento berries
1 garlic clove, chopped
½ fresh red chilli, seeded
    and chopped
2 onions, sliced
salt and freshly ground
    black pepper

- Clean the fish, then rub with the lime juice and pat dry with kitchen paper.
- Heat the oil in a frying pan until smoking. Add the fish and fry on both sides until crisp and brown.
- Drain the oil from the pan, leaving enough to coat the bottom. Add the tomatoes, pimento berries, garlic, chilli and onions. Season with salt and pepper. Sauté until the onion is soft.
- Add 350ml/12fl oz water. Bring to the boil and reduce by half, then cover and simmer for 10 minutes. Serve hot.

Hot prawn stew
serves 4

ingredients
2.4 litres/4pt fish stock
4 potatoes, cubed
1 large carrot, cubed
1 large onion, sliced
3 cloves
1 teaspoon ground
    mustard seeds
1 teaspoon granulated sugar
6 fresh red chillies, seeded
    and finely chopped
2 tablespoons Worcestershire
    sauce
450g/1lb large raw prawns,
    peeled and deveined

- In a large flameproof casserole dish, bring the stock to the boil, then add the potatoes, carrot and onion, and simmer for 5 minutes.
- Add the remaining ingredients except the prawns, and simmer for 15 minutes. Add the prawns and simmer for a further 6 minutes. Serve immediately.

Cheese & rice casserole
serves 4

ingredients

200g/7oz brown rice, cooked and cooled

3 onions, chopped

200g/7oz cottage cheese

1 teaspoon dried dill

50g/2oz Parmesan cheese, grated

125ml/4fl oz milk

- Preheat the oven to 180°C/350°F/Gas mark 4. Lightly grease a large casserole dish with a little vegetable oil.
- Combine all the ingredients in a bowl, making sure that they are well mixed, then pour into the prepared casserole dish. Bake in the oven for 15–20 minutes until hot and melting. Serve hot.

Bean & celery stew
serves 4

ingredients

1 onion, thickly sliced

4 celery sticks, chopped

1 tablespoon olive oil

2 garlic cloves, crushed

400g/14oz canned cooked haricot beans, drained

400g/14oz canned chopped plum tomatoes

1 tablespoon tomato purée

1 vegetable stock cube

salt and freshly ground black pepper

- Sweat the onion and the celery in the oil in a large flameproof casserole dish over a medium heat until the onion is soft and starting to caramelize. Add the garlic and fry for a few more minutes.
- Add the beans, tomatoes and the tomato purée, and mix well.
- Season with salt and pepper, then crumble in the stock cube. Simmer for a further 10 minutes, then serve immediately.

Potato & leek casserole
serves 4

ingredients

300g/11oz leeks, cut into
   1cm/½in pieces
150g/5oz carrots, grated
2 tablespoons olive oil
1 teaspoon dried rosemary

900g/2lb potatoes, sliced into
   thin rounds
225ml/8fl oz vegetable stock
50g/2oz fresh parsley, chopped
salt and ground black pepper

- Preheat the oven to 190°C/375°F/Gas mark 5. In a deep frying pan, coat the leeks and carrots with oil. Cover and sweat over a low heat until soft. Add the rosemary, season with salt and pepper, and mix well.
- Layer a casserole dish with one-third of the potatoes, then half of the seasoned vegetables. Repeat the layers and finish with the last third of the potatoes. Pour the stock evenly into the casserole dish. Cover and bake in the oven for 50 minutes.
- Remove the lid and bake, uncovered, for a further 20 minutes. Garnish withthe parsley and serve hot.

● ●

Brown rice stew
serves 8

ingredients

500ml/16fl oz chicken stock
200g/7oz long-grain brown rice
850g/1¾lb canned chopped
   plum tomatoes
3 carrots, sliced
3 onions, chopped
1 large onion, chopped
1 celery stick, sliced
3 garlic cloves, chopped
1 bay leaf
3 knackwurst sausages, sliced
1 teaspoon dried oregano
1 teaspoon dried basil
½ teaspoon dried thyme

- Put the stock, rice, tomatoes, carrots, onions, celery, garlic and bay leaf in a large flameproof casserole dish. Cover and cook over a high heat for 10 minutes or until boiling, then stir.
- Reduce the heat to medium and simmer, covered, for 45–60 minutes until the rice is tender.
- Stir in the sausages, oregano, basil and thyme, and leave to stand, covered, for 15 minutes. Discard the bay leaf, and serve immediately.

One-pot macaroni & cheese

serves 2

ingredients

200g/7oz elbow macaroni
250g/9oz Cheddar cheese,
    grated
25g/1oz butter
2 tablespoons double cream
pinch of paprika
pinch of ground white pepper
pinch of cayenne pepper

- Bring a large saucepan of salted water to a boil. Stir in the pasta and return the water to a rapid boil. Continue boiling for 4 minutes, stirring occasionally.
- Reduce the heat to medium, and continue to boil the pasta, stirring frequently, for a further 7 minutes.
- Drain the pasta in a colander, then return to the pan. Stir in the remaining ingredients, stirring well until the cheese is melted.
- Serve immediately

Armenian stew

serves 4

ingredients

200g/7oz dried apricots,
    soaked in 125ml/4fl oz water
    for 1 hour
100g/4oz dried chickpeas,
    soaked overnight in water
1.2 litres/2pt water
200g/7oz red lentils, picked
    and rinsed
3 onions, sliced
salt and freshly ground
    black pepper

- In a large pan, bring the apricots and their soaking water to the boil. Add the chickpeas and 150ml/5fl oz water, and simmer for 30 minutes. (Do not add salt at this point, as this will toughen the beans' skins.)
- Add the lentils, onions and 1 litre/1¾pt water to the pan, and bring to the boil once again.
- Reduce the heat, cover and cook for about 2 hours until the beans are tender. Season with salt and pepper. Serve hot.

Autumn barley stew
serves 10

ingredients
200g/7oz pearl barley
1.8 litres/3pt vegetable stock
2 onions, chopped
3 potatoes, cut into chunks
1 large sweet potato, cut
    into chunks
450g/1lb Brussels sprouts
2 tablespoons tamari
1 teaspoon chopped fresh
    flat-leaf parsley
2 teaspoons dried oregano
1 teaspoon dried dill
3 tomatoes, chopped

- Put the barley and stock in large flameproof casserole dish, and bring to the boil.
- Add the remaining ingredients, except the tomatoes. Reduce the heat, cover and simmer for about 50 minutes.
- Add the tomatoes, and cook for a further 10 minutes until the tomatoes are soft. Serve hot.

● ●

Aromatic green casserole
serves 4

ingredients
75g/3oz sugarsnap peas,
    cut into bite-size pieces
75g/3oz Brussels sprouts
75g/3oz broccoli, cut into
    bite-size pieces
50g/2oz walnuts, chopped
2 tablespoons vegetable oil
½ teaspoon chopped fresh dill
¼ teaspoon sage
½ teaspoon salt
juice of ½ lemon
pinch of cayenne pepper

- Steam the beans, Brussels sprouts and broccoli for 8 minutes. Reserving the sprouts and broccoli, combine the beans with the remaining ingredients.
- Transfer to a blender or food processor. Add 50ml/2fl oz water, and purée until smooth.
- Pour the sauce over the vegetables. Serve hot or cold.

Japanese tofu hotpot
serves 2

ingredients
50g/2oz dried fish flakes
300g/11oz firm tofu, cubed
2 tablespoons light soy sauce
1 tablespoon granulated sugar
1 tablespoon sake
1 large egg, beaten
7 spring onions, roughly
  chopped

• Spread the fish flakes evenly in the
  bottom of a flameproof casserole
  dish, and arrange the tofu on top.
• Add the soy sauce, sugar, sake
  and 125ml/4fl oz water.
• Cover and bring to the boil over
  a medium heat, then reduce the
  heat and simmer for 5 minutes.
• Pour in the egg evenly over the top
  of the casserole, and sprinkle with
  the spring onions. Simmer for a
  further 30 seconds, covered, then
  serve immediately.

Baked bean
& vegetable casserole
serves 4

ingredients
450g/1lb canned baked beans
100g/4oz celery, finely diced
100g/4oz carrot, finely grated
100g/4oz courgette, finely
  grated
25g/1oz shallots, finely chopped
1 tablespoon chopped fresh
  flat-leaf parsley
50g/2oz fresh red chilli, seeded
  and finely chopped
1 garlic clove, crushed

• Mix all the ingredients together
  in a bowl.
• Put in a heavy saucepan, and
  cook, covered, over a medium-high
  heat for 10 minutes, stirring
  occasionally. Serve hot.

Stewed cabbage hotpot
serves 4

ingredients

300g/11oz Chinese cabbage,
  shredded
200g/7oz tofu, cubed and
  dry-fried
8 dried Chinese mushrooms,
  soaked and chopped
1 carrot, sliced
2 teaspoons salt
1 tablespoon chopped fresh
  flat-leaf parsley

- Put all the ingredients except the parsley in a large flameproof casserole dish, and pour over enough water to cover.
- Bring to the boil, reduce the heat and simmer for about 15 minutes until the vegetables are tender.
- Scatter with the parsley, and serve immediately.

Potato, pancetta & sage one-pot roast
serves 4

ingredients

25g/1oz butter
750g/1lb 11oz potatoes, sliced
100g/4oz pancetta, thinly sliced
12 fresh sage leaves
juice of ½ lemon
300ml/10fl oz hot
  vegetable stock
150g/5oz Gruyère cheese,
  coarsely grated
salt and freshly ground
  black pepper

- Preheat the oven to 190°C/ 375°F/Gas mark 5. Lightly butter an ovenproof dish.
- Scatter the potato slices, pancetta and sage leaves into the dish, seasoning with salt and pepper as you go.
- Stir the lemon juice into the stock, and pour over the potatoes. Dot the butter over the top.
- Roast in the oven for 1 hour until the top is golden and the potatoes are tender. Top with the cheese, and serve immediately.

Barley & pine nut casserole
serves 6–8

ingredients
200g/7oz pearl barley
75g/3oz butter
75g/3oz pine nuts
1 onion, chopped
100g/4oz fresh flat-leaf parsley,
   minced
100g/4oz fresh chives, minced
900ml/1¾pt canned condensed
   beef soup
salt and freshly ground black pepper

- Preheat the oven to 190°C/375°F/Gas mark 4.
- Rinse the barley in cold water and drain well. Set aside.
- Melt 25g/1oz of the butter in a frying pan over a medium heat, then add the pine nuts and cook until lightly toasted, stirring constantly and taking care not to scorch. Remove the pine nuts with a slotted spoon, and set aside.
- Heat the remaining butter in the pan until melted, then add the barley and onion. Cook, stirring constantly, until the barley is lightly toasted and the onion is tender. Remove from the heat and stir in the reserved pine nuts, parsley and chives. Season with salt and pepper.
- Spoon the barley mixture into a casserole dish.
- Bring the beef soup to the boil in a medium saucepan, pour over the barley mixture in the casserole dish and stir well. Cook in the oven, uncovered, for 1 hour 10 minutes or until the barley is tender and the liquid has been absorbed. Serve hot.

Sweet potato casserole

serves 10

ingredients

900g/2lb sweet potatoes, boiled,
 peeled and mashed
2 eggs, beaten
50g/2oz butter, melted
50g/2oz soft brown sugar
225ml/8fl oz buttermilk
¼ teaspoon baking powder
¼ teaspoon freshly grated nutmeg

- Preheat the oven to 180°C/
 350°F/Gas mark 4.
- Combine all the ingredients in a
 large casserole dish, and mix
 together well.
- Bake in the oven, covered, for
 1 hour. Serve hot.

Rice verde one-pot

serves 3

ingredients

50g/2oz butter
1 small onion, finely chopped
200g/7oz cold cooked
 long-grain rice
275g/10oz spinach, chopped
225ml/8fl oz milk
1 egg, lightly beaten
½ teaspoon salt
225g/8oz Cheddar cheese,
 grated

- Preheat the oven to 180°C/
 350°F/Gas mark 4.
- Melt the butter in a large casserole
 dish and sauté the onion until it is
 transparent. Stir in the rice,
 spinach, milk, egg, salt and
 cheese. Mix well with a fork.
- Cover and bake for about
 30 minutes, until the mixture is hot
 and the top is crisp.

Peas pilaf one-pot
serves 8

ingredients

200g/7oz tomatoes, chopped
150g/5oz green peas
50ml/2fl oz Greek-style yogurt
4 teaspoons minced garlic
4 teaspoons minced root ginger
2 teaspoons ground coriander
1 teaspoon ground cumin
1 teaspoon garam masala
¼ teaspoon ground turmeric
2 tablespoons canola oil
200g/7oz onion, finely diced

2 fresh green chillies, seeded
  and chopped
2 cinnamon sticks
16 black peppercorns
2 teaspoons cumin seeds
350g/12oz potatoes, cut into
  bite-sized pieces
200g/7oz basmati rice, rinsed
  and drained
salt and freshly ground
  black pepper

- Put the tomatoes, peas, yogurt, garlic, ginger, coriander, cumin, garam masala and turmeric in a large bowl. Season with salt and pepper, and stir to combine.
- Heat the oil in a large saucepan. Add the onion, chillies, cinnamon, peppercorns and cumin seeds, and sauté until the onion starts to turn golden. Add the tomato mixture and stir through. Cover and cook over a medium heat for 10 minutes, stirring occasionally.
- Add 700ml/1¼pt water, ¾ teaspoon salt and the potatoes, and stir well. Cover and bring to the boil. Add the rice, stir gently and cook, covered for about 10 minutes until almost all the liquid has been absorbed. Reduce the heat to low, and cook for 10–15 minutes until the rice is tender. Serve hot.

Yellow split pea casserole

serves 4

ingredients

2 tablespoons ghee or butter
1 teaspoon black mustard seeds
1 onion, finely chopped
2 garlic cloves, crushed
1 carrot, grated
2.5cm/1in piece of fresh root
   ginger, grated
1 fresh green chilli, seeded and
   finely chopped
1 tablespoon tomato purée
250g/9oz yellow split peas,
   soaked in water for 2 hours,
   rinsed and drained

400g/14oz canned chopped
   plum tomatoes
500ml/16fl oz vegetable stock
225g/8oz pumpkin, cubed
225g/8oz cauliflower, cut
   into florets
2 tablespoons vegetable oil
1 large aubergine, cubed
1 tablespoon chopped fresh
   coriander leaves
1 teaspoon garam masala
salt and freshly ground
   black pepper

- Melt the ghee or butter over a medium heat in a large heavy pan. Add the mustard seeds and, when they start to splutter and pop, add the onion, garlic, carrot and ginger.
- Sweat for about 5 minutes until soft. Add the chilli and stir in the tomato purée, then stir in the drained split peas. Add the tomatoes and stock, and bring to the boil. Season well with salt and pepper. Simmer for 40 minutes, stirring occasionally.
- Add the pumpkin and cauliflower, and simmer for a further 30 minutes, covered, until the split peas are soft.
- Meanwhile, heat the oil in a frying pan over a high heat. Add the aubergine and stir until sealed on all sides, then remove and drain on kitchen paper.
- Stir the aubergine into the split pea mixture with the coriander and garam masala. Serve immediately.

Greek-style chickpea casserole

serves 4

ingredients

450g/1lb spinach
25g/1oz butter
1 garlic clove, crushed
400g/14oz canned cooked
  chickpeas, drained
100g/4oz feta cheese, cubed
pinch of ground cinnamon
4 tomatoes, peeled and chopped
125ml/4fl oz crème fraîche
salt and freshly ground
  black pepper

- Wash the spinach thoroughly under running water, and remove any tough stems. Drain well, then cut into shreds.
- Heat the butter in a heavy saucepan, and sauté the spinach and garlic, stirring, for 4 minutes. Add the chickpeas, cheese and cinnamon, and season with salt and pepper. Toss over a gentle heat for 2 minutes.
- Add the tomatoes and crème fraîche, and heat through, tossing and stirring. Serve hot.

Spinach & artichoke casserole
serves 4

ingredients

275g/10oz frozen spinach, thawed
450g/1lb mushrooms, sliced
1 tablespoon vegetable oil
1 onion, chopped
175g/6oz marinated artichoke hearts, with liquid
5 eggs, beaten
1 garlic clove, crushed
75g/3oz Parmesan cheese, freshly grated
75g/3oz Cheddar cheese, grated

- Preheat the oven to 180°C/ 350°F/Gas mark 4.
- In a heavy frying pan, sauté the mushrooms and onion in the oil until the onion is translucent.
- Combine all the ingredients in a large casserole dish and mix well.
- Cook in the oven, covered, for 30–40 minutes. Serve hot.

Chickpea & artichoke stew
serves 4

ingredients

1.2 litres/2pt vegetable stock
2 onions, chopped
2 garlic cloves, minced
1 tablespoon olive oil
1 teaspoon ground turmeric
1 teaspoon paprika
4 potatoes, cubed
5 fresh sage leaves, crushed
200g/7oz cooked sweet potato, puréed
900g/2lb canned cooked chickpeas, rinsed and drained
400g/14oz canned artichoke hearts, quartered
salt and freshly ground black pepper

- In a large heavy saucepan, bring the stock to a simmer.
- Meanwhile, in a large frying pan, sweat the onions and garlic in the oil for about 8 minutes until soft. Stir in the turmeric and paprika, and sauté for 1 minute.
- Add the potatoes, sage and the simmering stock. Cook for about 12 minutes until the potatoes are tender. Stir in the sweet potato, and add the chickpeas and artichoke hearts. Season with salt and pepper.
- Stir through gently, then return the stew to a simmer. Heat through and serve immediately.

Baked lentil & vegetable stew
serves 4

ingredients

450g/1lb fresh Brussels sprouts
200g/7oz green lentils such as
  Puy, picked and rinsed
200g/7oz onions, chopped
150g/5oz celery, chopped
200g/7oz carrots, sliced
400g/14oz rutabaga, chopped
4 bay leaves
1 tablespoon grated fresh
  root ginger
2 tablespoons tamari

• Preheat the oven to 180°C/
  350°F/Gas mark 4.
• Cut a cross in the bottom of each
  sprout. Combine the sprouts and
  remaining ingredients except the
  tamari in a large baking dish.
  Gently pour in 700ml/1½pt water.
• Cook in the oven for about 1 hour,
  stirring occasionally, until the lentils
  and vegetables are tender. Top up
  with more water while cooking if
  necessary – green lentils require
  more cooking than other varieties.
• Stir in the tamari and serve warm.

Courgette & corn casserole
serves 8

ingredients

50g/2oz potato flour
75g/3oz rice flour
1 teaspoon baking powder
600g/1lb 5oz courgettes,
  grated
425g/15oz canned creamed
  sweetcorn
200g/7oz red pepper,
  finely diced
100g/4oz onion, finely diced
50g/2oz Cheddar cheese,
  finely grated
2 tablespoons olive oil
2 eggs, lightly beaten
salt and freshly ground
  black pepper

• Preheat the oven to 200°C/
  400°F/Gas mark 6. Lightly grease
  a casserole dish with butter.
• Sift the potato flour, rice flour and
  baking powder together.
• Put the courgettes, sweetcorn, red
  pepper, onion and cheese in a
  large bowl. Stir to mix through
  evenly. Add the sifted flours, oil
  and eggs, and mix well using a
  metal spoon until well combined.
  Season with salt and pepper.
• Pour the mixture into the prepared
  casserole dish. Bake for 30 minutes
  or until set in the centre. Serve hot.

Apple cranberry casserole
serves 2

ingredients

250g/9oz cooking apples
  such as Granny Smith
200g/7oz cranberries
175g/6oz granulated sugar
75g/3oz soft brown sugar
100g/4oz oatmeal
100g/4oz pecan nuts, chopped
50g/2oz butter

- Preheat the oven to 170°C/
  325°F/Gas mark 3.
- Peel, core and dice the apples.
  Scatter the apples and cranberries
  in a layer over the bottom of a
  large casserole dish.
- Mix together the granulated and
  brown sugar, oatmeal and nuts,
  and scatter evenly over the fruit.
- Dot the butter over the top, and
  bake in the oven for 1 hour.
  Serve hot.

● ●

Lentil hotpot
serves 4

ingredients

1 tablespoon olive oil
1 onion, chopped
1 garlic clove, crushed
2 potatoes, diced
2 carrots, finely chopped
2 celery sticks, chopped
225g/8oz red lentils, picked
  and rinsed
425g/15oz canned chopped
  plum tomatoes
2 tablespoons tomato purée
1 bay leaf
½ teaspoon dried oregano
1 vegetable stock cube
salt and freshly ground
  black pepper

- Heat the oil in a large heavy pan,
  and sweat the onion and garlic
  until the onion is softened. Add the
  potatoes, carrots, celery and
  lentils, and sweat for a further
  2 minutes.
- Add the tomatoes, tomato purée,
  bay leaf and oregano, and season
  with salt and pepper.
- Crumble in the stock cube, and stir
  in 450ml/¾pt water. Bring to the
  boil, then reduce the heat and
  simmer for 25–30 minutes until the
  lentils and vegetables are tender.
- Ladle the hotpot into warmed
  bowls, and serve immediately.

Chinese vegetable casserole
serves 4

ingredients

4 tablespoons vegetable oil
2 carrots, sliced
1 courgette, sliced
4 baby sweetcorn, halved
   lengthways
100g/4oz cauliflower florets
1 leek, sliced
100g/4oz water chestnuts, halved
225g/8oz firm tofu, diced

300ml/10fl oz vegetable stock
1 teaspoon salt
2 teaspoons soft dark brown sugar
   such as muscovado
2 teaspoons light soy sauce
2 tablespoons dry sherry
1 tablespoon cornflour
1 tablespoon chopped fresh
   coriander leaves, to garnish

- Heat the oil in a preheated wok until it is almost smoking. Reduce the heat slightly, and add the carrots, courgette, sweetcorn, cauliflower and leek. Stir-fry for 2–3 minutes.
- Stir in the water chestnuts, tofu, stock, salt, sugar, soy sauce and sherry, and bring to the boil. Reduce the heat, cover and simmer for 20 minutes.
- Blend the cornflour with 2 tablespoons water to form a smooth paste. Stir the paste into the wok, bring the sauce to the boil and cook, stirring constantly, until it thickens and turns glossy.
- To serve, scatter the coriander over the top, and serve immediately.

Aubergine, mozzarella & Cheddar hotpot
serves 4

ingredients

4 large white potatoes, thinly sliced
2 tablespoons olive oil
1 aubergine, sliced
1 large onion, sliced
275g/10oz canned chopped
  plum tomatoes
425g/15oz canned cooked
  chickpeas, drained
25g/1oz green lentils such as Puy,
  picked and rinsed

2 garlic cloves, crushed
2 tablespoons chopped fresh
  flat-leaf parsley
25g/1oz mozzarella cheese,
  finely grated
25g/1oz Cheddar cheese,
  finely grated
1 tablespoon boiling water
salt and freshly ground
  black pepper

- Put the potatoes in a saucepan of salted cold water. Bring to the boil, and cook until beginning to soften – do not cook completely. Drain and set aside.
- Heat the oil in a frying pan and gently sauté the aubergine until it begins to brown. Turn and repeat on the other side. As each piece is done, remove to kitchen paper.
- When the aubergine is cooked, stir the onion in the frying pan until softened, but not browned. Stir in the tomatoes, chickpeas, lentils, garlic, parsley and seasoning. Cook over a medium heat for 40 to 45 minutes, or until the lentils are tender.
- Preheat the oven to 200°C/400°F/Gas mark 6.
- Mix the cheeses together. Add the boiling water to make a paste.
- When the tomato mixture is ready, spoon the remaining mixture over the bottom of a large casserole dish. Cover with half the aubergine and add another third of the tomato mixture. Layer on the remaining aubergine.
- Spread a third of the cheese mixture on to the aubergine. Add half the potatoes, another third of the cheese and then the remaining potatoes. Finish with the final third of cheese.
- Cover and bake in the middle of oven for 30 minutes. Remove the lid and bake for a further 10 minutes to brown.

Baked squash casserole
serves 10

ingredients
1.8kg/4lb butternut squash, peeled,
    seeded and chopped
1 egg
200g/7oz coorse dried
    breadcrumbs
75g/3oz soft brown sugar
½ tablespoon chopped onion
100g/4oz green pepper, diced
salt and freshly ground black pepper

- Preheat the oven to 180°C/350°F/Gas mark 4.
- Drop the squash into a large saucepan with enough boiling water to cover. Return to the boil, reduce the heat and cook until tender, then drain, reserving the cooking liquid. Mash the squash.
- In a bowl, combine the squash and its cooking liquid, egg, two-thirds of the breadcrumbs, the sugar, onion and green pepper. Season with salt and pepper.
- Turn the mixture into a large casserole dish, and cover with the remaining breadcrumbs. Bake in the oven for about 30 minutes until lightly browned. Serve hot.

Chunky vegetable chilli
serves 8–10

ingredients

150g/5oz quick-cooking barley
1 aubergine, diced
½ large red pepper, seeded
  and chopped
½ large green pepper, seeded
  and chopped
1 onion, chopped
3 garlic cloves, minced

400g/14oz canned chopped
  plum tomatoes
425g/15oz canned cooked
  black beans, drained
½ teaspoon chilli powder
150g/5oz fresh spinach, chopped
salt and freshly ground
  black pepper

- Bring 1.2 litres/2pt water to the boil in a large deep heavy frying pan. Stir in the barley. Cover and reduce the heat. Simmer for about 10 minutes until the barley is tender.
- Add the aubergine, peppers, onion and garlic. Stir thoroughly, cover and cook over a medium heat for about 20 minutes until the aubergine is softened and the other vegetables are tender, removing the lid to stir frequently to prevent the mixture catching on the bottom of the pan.
- Tip in the tomatoes and black beans, add the chilli powder, and season with salt and pepper. Stir to combine, and cook for a further 5 minutes. Add the spinach, stir through and cook for 2–3 minutes until the spinach is wilted. Serve immediately.

Bean stew
with herb dumplings
serves 4

ingredients

425g/15oz canned cooked red kidney beans, drained

425g/15oz canned cooked haricot beans, drained

400g/14oz canned chopped plum tomatoes

1 tablespoon tomato purée

200g/7oz canned sweetcorn kernels, drained

1 garlic clove, crushed

1 bay leaf

300ml/10fl oz vegetable stock

275g/10oz green beans, topped and tailed, cut into lengths

1 tablespoon chopped fresh flat-leaf parsley, to serve

salt and freshly ground black pepper

For the herb dumplings

100g/4oz self-raising flour

25g/1oz butter

1 teaspoon dried mixed herbs

- Put the kidney and haricot beans in a large heavy saucepan or flameproof casserole dish. Add the tomatoes, tomato purée, sweetcorn, garlic and bay leaf, and stir to mix through evenly.

- Pour in the stock, and season lightly with salt and pepper. Bring to the boil, reduce the heat and simmer gently for 5 minutes.

- Meanwhile, sift the flour into a bowl with a little salt and pepper. Rub in the butter with your fingertips until the mixture resembles rough crumbs. Stir in the herbs. Mix with just enough cold water to form a soft but not too sticky dough.

- Add the green beans to the vegetable mixture. Shape the dough into eight round balls, and carefully drop into the top of the stew. Cover and simmer gently for 15–20 mintues until the dumplings are fluffy and risen.

- To serve, discard the bay leaf. Sprinkle the stew with the parsley, and serve hot, allowing two dumpling for each serving.

Baked barley & broad bean casserole
serves 4

ingredients

50g/2oz onion, minced
about 2 tablespoons vegetable oil
150g/5oz skinned cooked
  broad beans
100g/4oz cooked pearl barley
225ml/8fl oz soy milk
75g/3oz raw wheatgerm

25g/1oz plain flour
3 tablespoons prepared mustard
75ml/3fl oz clear honey
75ml/3fl oz tomato ketchup
½ teaspoon garlic powder
½ teaspoon onion powder
½ teaspoon chilli powder

- Sweat the onion in a little oil for a few minutes until soft and translucent. Using a slotted spoon, transfer to a large bowl and cool slightly.
- Once the onion is cool enough, add 1 tablespoon oil to the bowl together with all the other remaining ingredients. Mix together and leave to stand for 30 minutes.
- Preheat the oven to 180°C/350°F/Gas mark 4. Turn the mixture into an oiled casserole dish, and bake for 40 minutes. Serve hot.

Meat
& Game

Now we come to the heart of any meal, a meaty main course. Whether cooking to impress or whipping up something tasty for the family at the weekend, you'll find a recipe here to suit every occasion. And all types of meat are used, from the staples of beef, pork, and lamb, to less frequently used fare such as veal, rabbit, venison and other game. You will find recipes for traditional roasts, as well as recipes for cooking chops and cutlets, stir-fries, meatloaf, and meat in a range of delicious sauces.

Beef goulash
serves 4

ingredients

450g/1lb stewing beef, cubed
1 onion, chopped
2 teaspoons sunflower oil
175ml/6fl oz beer
175ml/6fl oz water
50ml/2fl oz tomato purée
1 tablespoon paprika
¼ teaspoon salt
¼ teaspoon caraway seeds
450g/1lb potatoes
225g/8oz canned sauerkraut
2 tablespoons snipped fresh
    flat-leaf parsley

- In a frying pan, cook the beef and onion in the oil until the beef is brown. Add the beer, water, tomato purée, paprika, salt and caraway seeds. Cover and simmer for 1¼–1½ hours.
- Add the potatoes, undrained sauerkraut and parsley to the pan. Cook, covered, for about 20 minutes until the vegetables are tender. Remove the lid from the pan and cook, uncovered, for a further 10 minutes or until the mixture is thickened and most of the liquid has evaporated.
- Serve hot with rice.

Beef fajitas
serves 4

ingredients

1 tablespoon vegetable oil
1 onion, cut into strips
2 garlic cloves, minced
1 tablespoon Mexican chilli powder
450g/1lb minced beef
75g/3oz ready-prepared salsa
1 red pepper, seeded and chopped
1 green pepper, seeded and
   chopped
1 courgette, thinly sliced
4 x 25cm/10in flour tortillas
salt and freshly ground black pepper

- Preheat the oven to 180°C/350°F/Gas mark 4.
- In a non-stick frying pan, heat the oil over a medium-high heat. Cook the onion, garlic, chilli powder and seasoning, stirring, for 5 minutes or until the onion is softened.
- Add the beef and salsa, and cook, breaking up the beef with the back of a spoon, for about 3 minutes until the beef is no longer pink. Add the peppers and courgette, and cook, stirring, for 3 minutes or until the liquid has evaporated.
- Meanwhile, wrap the tortillas in foil and heat in the oven for 5 minutes or until warmed through.
- Divide the beef mixture among the tortillas, and roll up. Serve the fajitas immediately while still piping hot.

Orange beef
with green peppers
serves 6

ingredients

700g/1½lb flank steak
175ml/6fl oz orange juice
3 tablespoons light soy sauce
2 tablespoons smooth peanut butter
1½ tablespoons orange zest
2 garlic cloves (crushed)
1½ teaspoons curry powder
½ teaspoon red wine vinegar
½ teaspoon red pepper flakes
1 tablespoon vegetable oil
2 green peppers, cut into 1cm/½in
   wide strips

- Diagonally cut the beef, against the grain, into slices 1cm/½in thick.
- In a bowl, combine the orange juice, soy sauce, peanut butter, orange zest, garlic, curry, vinegar and red pepper flakes. Stir to blend. Add the beef and toss to coat evenly. Cover and set aside to marinate for 2 hours at room temperature.
- Heat the oil in a heavy frying pan or wok over a high heat. Add the marinated beef mixture. Stir-fry for 2 minutes. Remove the beef with a slotted spoon and set aside on a plate.
- Add the green peppers to the pan, then stir-fry for about 5 minutes until the peppers are browned around the edges.
- Return the beef to the pan, and stir-fry for a further 1 minute to heat through. Serve hot.

Spiced beef & onions
serves 4

ingredients
50ml/2fl oz olive oil
700g/1½lb baby onions
900g/2lb chuck steak, trimmed and
   cut into bite-size cubes
3 garlic cloves, halved lengthways
125ml/4fl oz red wine
1 cinnamon stick
4 cloves
1 bay leaf
1 tablespoon red wine vinegar
2 tablespoons tomato purée
375ml/13fl oz water
2 tablespoons currants
salt and freshly ground black pepper

- Heat the oil over a medium heat in a large heavy saucepan. Add the
  onions and sauté, stirring, for 5 minutes or until golden. Remove from the
  pan and drain on kitchen paper.
- Add the meat to the pan, and stir over a high heat for 10 minutes or
  until the meat is well browned and almost all the liquid has evaporated.
- Add the garlic, wine, spices, bay leaf, vinegar and tomato purée.
  Season with salt and pepper. Pour 375ml/13fl oz water into the pan,
  and bring to the boil. Reduce the heat, cover and simmer for 1 hour,
  stirring occasionally.
- Return the onions to the saucepan, add the currants and stir gently.
  Simmer, covered, for 15 minutes. Discard the cinnamon before serving.

Thai beef curry
serves 4

ingredients
1 tablespoon tamarind pulp
2 tablespoons vegetable oil
700g/1½lb stewing beef (cubed)
500ml/18fl oz coconut milk
4 cardamom pods, bruised
500ml/18fl oz coconut cream
2 tablespoons curry paste
2 tablespoons Thai fish sauce
8 pickling onions
8 baby potatoes
2 tablespoons granulated sugar
75g/3oz unsalted peanuts, roasted
    and ground

- Put the tamarind pulp and 125ml/4fl oz boiling water in a bowl, and set aside to cool. Mash the pulp with your fingertips to dissolve it, then strain and reserve the liquid, discarding the pulp.
- Heat a non-stick wok over a high heat, add the oil and swirl to coat. Add the beef in batches, and stir-fry over a high heat for 5 minutes for each batch or until browned all over. Reduce the heat, add the coconut milk and cardamom pods, and simmer for 1 hour or until the beef is tender. Remove the beef from the wok, then strain the cooking liquid into a bowl and keep to one side.
- Heat the coconut cream in the wok, and stir in the curry paste. Cook for 10 minutes or until the oil starts to separate from the cream. Add the fish sauce, onions, potatoes, beef mixture, sugar, peanuts, tamarind water and the reserved cooking liquid. Simmer for 25–30 minutes until the meat is tender. Serve hot.

Fillet of beef with porcini & sweet peppers

serves 8

ingredients

1.4kg/3lb trimmed beef fillet
25g/1oz dried porcini mushrooms, soaked and drained
250g/9oz jar sliced red and yellow peppers in oil, drained
375g/13oz pancetta slices
2 tablespoons extra virgin olive oil

2 teaspoons plain flour
150ml/5fl oz Italian red wine
300ml/10fl oz beef stock
2 tablespoons Marsala
2 teaspoons dried mixed herbs
salt and freshly ground black pepper

- Preheat the oven to 190°C/375°F/Gas mark 5.
- Cut a slit along the side of the fillet, keeping both ends attached. Open it out with your fingers a little, to make a pocket.
- Roughly chop the porcini, reserving half for the sauce. Mix the remainder with half of the peppers, and use to fill the pocket in the beef. Grind black pepper over the meat, then wrap the pancetta around the fillet to enclose it completely. Tie with string at regular intervals.
- Heat the oil in a large non-stick frying pan, add the meat and sear on all sides. Lift the fillet out of the oil, draining over the pan. Reserve the juices in the pan for the sauce.
- Transfer the fillet to a roasting tin, and roast in the oven for 45 minutes. Remove from the oven, cover with foil and leave to rest in a warm place for 10–15 minutes.
- Meanwhile, reheat the reserved juices in the frying pan, sprinkle in the flour and cook, stirring, over a medium heat for 2–3 minutes. Gradually stir in the red wine and the stock, then bring to the boil, stirring. Reduce the heat and add the Marsala and mixed herbs. Season with salt and pepper, and simmer until thickened, stirring constantly.
- Add the remaining peppers and porcini, and heat through.
- Remove the string from the beef fillet and carve the meat into neat slices. Using a slotted spoon, remove the peppers and onions from the sauce and use to garnish the meat. Serve immediately, drizzled with the sauce.

Beef Wellington
serves 8

ingredients

1.6kg/3½lb beef fillet, larded and
   tied with string
350g/12oz mushrooms, finely
   chopped
50g/2oz butter
225g/8oz pâté de foie gras
450g/1lb puff pastry
1 egg white, whisked lightly
1 large egg yolk, beaten with
   1 teaspoon water

125ml/4fl oz Madeira
2 teaspoons arrowroot, dissolved in
   1 tablespoon cold water
125ml/4fl oz beef stock
2 tablespoons finely chopped
   black truffles
salt and freshly ground
   black pepper

- Preheat the oven to 200°C/400°F/Gas mark 6. In a roasting tin, roast the beef in the middle of the oven for 25–30 minutes. Turn off the oven and allow the beef to cool completely, then discard the larding fat and strings. Skim the fat from the pan juices; reserve the juices.
- In a heavy frying pan, cook the mushrooms in butter over a medium-low heat, stirring, until all liquid has evaporated and the mixture is dry. Season with salt and pepper and allow to cool completely.
- Spread the beef evenly with the foie gras, covering the top and sides, and spread the mushrooms evenly over the foie gras.
- On a floured work surface, roll the puff pastry into a rectangle of about 50cm/20in x 30.5cm/12in or large enough to enclose the beef completely. Invert the beef in the middle of the pastry, and fold up the long sides to enclose it, brushing the edges of the pastry with some egg white to seal. Fold the ends of the pastry over the beef; seal with the egg white.
- Transfer the beef, seam side down, to a baking tin, and brush the pastry with the egg yolk wash. Chill for at least 1 hour.
- Preheat the oven 200°C/400°F/Gas mark 6. Bake the fillet in the middle of the oven for 30 minutes. Reduce the heat to 180°C/350°F/Gas mark 4, and bake for a further 5–10 minutes until the pastry is cooked through. Leave to stand for 15 minutes.
- In a saucepan, boil the reserved pan juices and the Madeira until the mixture is reduced by a quarter. Add the arrowroot mixture, stock and truffles. Season with salt and pepper. Cook the sauce over a medium heat, stirring, for 5 minutes or until thickened, being careful not to let it boil. Serve the beef cut into thick slices, accompanied by the sauce.

Crispy shredded beef
serves 4

ingredients

2 eggs

¼ teaspoon salt

4 tablespoons plain flour

350g/12oz beef rump steak, cut
  into thin strips

vegetable oil for deep-frying

2 carrots, finely shredded

2 spring onions, thinly shredded

1 garlic clove, finely chopped

3 small fresh red chillies, seeded
  and thinly sliced

4 tablespoons granulated sugar

3 tablespoons rice vinegar

1 tablespoon light soy sauce

2 tablespoons beef stock

1 teaspoon cornflour

- Beat the eggs in a bowl with the salt and flour, adding a little water if necessary to make a batter.
- Add the beef to the batter, and mix well until coated.
- Heat a wok over a high heat, then add the oil and heat until smoking. Add the beef and deep-fry for 5 minutes, stirring to separate the strips. Remove with a slotted spoon, and drain on kitchen paper.
- Add the carrots to the wok, and deep-fry to about 1–1½ minutes, then remove with a slotted spoon and drain on kitchen paper.
- Pour off the excess oil, leaving about 1 tablespoon in the wok. Add the spring onions, garlic, chillies and deep-fried carrots, and stir-fry for 1 minute. Add the sugar, vinegar, soy sauce and stock to the wok, and bring to the boil. Stir in the cornflour, and simmer for a few minutes to thicken the sauce.
- Return the beef to the wok, and stir until well coated with the sauce. Serve immediately.

meat & game

Beef stroganoff
serves 4

ingredients
15g/1/2oz dried porcini mushrooms
2 tablespoons olive oil
100g/4oz shallots, sliced
175g/6oz chestnut mushrooms
350g/12oz beef fillet, cut into
   5mm/¼in slices)
½ teaspoon Dijon mustard
75ml/3fl oz double cream
salt and freshly ground black pepper

- Put the porcini mushrooms in a bowl, cover with hot water and leave to soak for 20 minutes. Drain, reserving the soaking liquid, and chop the porcini. Sieve the soaking liquid through a fine-mesh sieve and reserve.
- Heat half the oil in a large frying pan. Add the shallots, and cook over a low heat, stirring occasionally, for 5 minutes or until softened. Add the porcini, reserved soaking water and chestnut mushrooms. Cook, stirring frequently, for 10 minutes or until almost all of the liquid has evaporated, then transfer the mixture to a plate.
- Heat the remaining oil in the frying pan, add the beef (in batches if necessary to avoid crowding the pan) and cook, stirring frequently, for 4 minutes or until browned. Return the mushroom mixture to the frying pan, and season with salt and pepper.
- Put the mustard and cream in a small bowl and stir to mix, then fold into the mixture. Heat through and serve.

Chilli beef in tortillas
serves 6–8

ingredients

For the tortillas
850g/1¾lb plain flour
4 teaspoons baking powder
1 teaspoon salt
4 tablespoons vegetable oil

For the filling
3 tablespoons vegetable oil
1 large onion, finely chopped
2 teaspoons dried oregano
1 teaspoon ground cumin
1 teaspoon chilli powder
1 teaspoon paprika
850g/1¾lb minced beef
1 green pepper, seeded and finely
    chopped
2 garlic cloves, crushed
50g/2oz tomato purée

- To make the tortillas, mix the flour and baking powder with the salt. Mix in the oil using a fork, then add enough lukewarm water to enable you to gather the dough into a ball with your hands. Knead lightly to smooth, then leave covered in the bowl for at least 20 minutes.
- Divide the dough into 24 balls, and roll out each one on a lightly floured surface into a thin pancake, or tortilla.
- Heat a non-stick frying pan without any oil, and cook each tortilla until the top surface bubbles up. Puncture the blisters and turn to cook the other side. Wrap the tortillas in a clean cloth to keep warm.
- Meanwhile, to make the filling, heat the oil and sweat the onion gently with the oregano, cumin, chilli powder and paprika until the onion is just soft. Add the beef, green pepper and garlic, and stir gently using a wooden spoon until the meat changes colour and breaks into granules.
- Put the tomato purée into a bowl, and mix with its own volume of cold water. Stir into the meat and cook, covered, for about 10 minutes. Serve hot with the warm tortillas.

Beef & pumpkin curry
serves 4–6

ingredients
3 tablespoons sesame oil
2 teaspoons dried chilli flakes
1 teaspoon ground turmeric
600g/1¼lb sirloin steak, cut into
   2.5cm/1in cubes
300ml/10fl oz beef stock
1 teaspoon soft brown sugar
450g/1lb pumpkin, peeled, seeded
   and cut into 2.5cm/1in cubes
½ teaspoon salt

For the spice paste
2 large onions, chopped
4 garlic cloves, chopped
2 stalks lemon grass, tough outer
   layer removed, chopped
2.5cm/1in piece of fresh root ginger,
   chopped

- Put all the ingredients for the spice paste in a blender or food processor, and work into a coarse paste.
- Heat the oil in a large flameproof casserole dish, add the spice paste and fry over a gentle heat, stirring for about 5 minutes until softened and aromatic. Add the chilli flakes and turmeric, and fry for a further 2 minutes.
- Add the steak to the pan, stir well to coat in the spice mixture and fry, stirring frequently, for 5 minutes. Add the stock and sugar to the curry, and bring to the boil. Reduce the heat, cover the pan and cook, stirring occasionally, for 35 minutes or until the steak is tender.
- Add the pumpkin and salt to the pan, and stir gently to mix. Cover and cook for a further 10 minutes or until the pumpkin is tender. Adjust the seasoning to taste. Serve hot.

Asparagus & bean beef
serves 4

ingredients
225g/8oz beef, cut across the grain
   into thin slices
¼ teaspoon baking powder,
   dissolved in 2 teaspoons water
1 tablespoon groundnut oil
½ teaspoon salt
450g/1lb asparagus
1 tablespoon vegetable oil
1 tablespoon Chinese fermented
   black beans, minced with
   4 garlic cloves
1 tablespoon rice wine
2 teaspoons light soy sauce

For the marinade
1 teaspoon cornflour
1 teaspoon light soy sauce
½ teaspoon rice wine
½ teaspoon granulated sugar
½ teaspoon salt

- Put the beef in a bowl or glass dish. Stir the baking powder solution into the beef to help tenderize it. Stir together the marinade ingredients, and marinate the beef for 1 hour in the refrigerator.
- In a heavy pan, heat the groundnut oil over a high heat. Add the salt, asparagus and 50ml/2fl oz water. Cover the pan for 2 minutes and cook. When done, transfer the asparagus to a platter.
- Place the pan over a high heat, and add the vegetable oil. Stir-fry the black bean and garlic mixture for a few seconds.
- Add the beef and stir-fry quickly until barely cooked. Add the rice wine and soy sauce, and heat until sizzling. Stir in the asparagus and toss quickly to heat through. Serve immediately.

Steak, kidney & mushroom pie

serves 4

ingredients

2 tablespoons vegetable oil
100g/4oz bacon, chopped
1 onion, chopped
500g/1lb 2oz chuck steak, diced
2 tablespoons plain flour
100g/4oz lamb's kidneys
1 bouquet garni
400ml/14fl oz beef stock
100g/4oz button mushrooms
225g/8oz ready-made puff pastry
beaten egg, to glaze
salt and freshly ground black pepper

- Preheat the oven to 170°C/325°F/Gas mark 3.
- Heat the oil in a heavy pan, add the bacon and onion, and sauté, stirring, until lightly browned. Toss the steak in the flour, add to the pan in batches and sauté, stirring, until browned.
- Toss the kidneys in the flour, and add to the pan with the bouquet garni. Sauté until browned.
- Transfer the mixture to a casserole dish, then pour in the stock, cover and cook in the oven for 2 hours.
- Remove from the oven, stir in the mushrooms and season with salt and pepper. Leave to cool.
- Preheat the oven to 220°C/425°F/Gas mark 7. Roll out the pastry to 2cm/1in larger than the top of a 1.2 litre/2pt pie dish. Cut off a strip and fit around the dampened rim of the dish to make a collar. Brush the pastry with water.
- Tip the meat mixture into the dish. Lay the pastry round over the dish and press the edges together to seal. Knock up the edges with the back of a knife. Make a small slit in the pastry, brush with the beaten egg and bake in the oven for 20 minutes.
- Reduce the oven temperature to 180°C/350°F/Gas 4, and bake for a further 20 minutes. Serve hot.

Beef daube

serves 6–8

ingredients

25g/1oz butter
1 large onion, cut into wedges
2 celery sticks, chopped
1 green pepper, seeded and
  chopped
450g/1lb sirloin steak, trimmed and
  cut into strips
1kg/2½lb lean braising steak, cubed
50g/2oz plain flour, seasoned with
  salt and black pepper
600ml/1pt beef stock
2 garlic cloves, crushed
150ml/5fl oz red wine
2 tablespoons red wine vinegar
2 tablespoons tomato purée
½ teaspoon Tabasco sauce
1 teaspoon chopped fresh thyme
2 bay leaves
½ teaspoon Cajun spice mix

- Heat the butter in a large heavy casserole dish. Add the onion wedges and sauté until browned on all sides. Remove with a slotted spoon and set aside.
- Add the celery and pepper to the dish, and cook until softened. Remove the vegetables with a slotted spoon and set aside.
- Coat the meat in the seasoned flour, add to the pan and sauté until browned on all sides. Add the stock, garlic, wine, vinegar, tomato purée, Tabasco and thyme, and heat gently.
- Return the onions, celery and pepper to the pan. Tuck in the bay leaves and sprinkle with the Cajun seasoning.
- Bring to the boil, transfer to the oven and cook for 3 hours or until the meat and vegetables are tender. Serve with French bread.

Beef & pork ragù

serves 4

ingredients

15g/½oz dried porcini mushrooms
225g/8oz boneless beef chuck,
    trimmed of all fat
225g/8oz lean boneless pork,
    trimmed of all fat
50g/2oz butter
3 shallots, chopped
1 celery stick, finely chopped
1 carrot, finely chopped
2 tablespoons chopped fresh
    flat-leaf parsley
1 tablespoon flour
175ml/6fl oz beef stock
150ml/5fl oz dry white wine
salt and freshly ground black pepper

- Soak the porcini mushrooms in 250ml/9fl oz warm water for
  30 minutes. Drain the porcini, reserving the liquid and squeezing excess
  water out of the porcini and into the bowl. Chop the porcini. Strain the
  soaking liquid and reserve.
- Cut the beef and pork into 1cm/½in dice.
- Melt the butter in a large pan over a medium-low heat. Add the shallots,
  celery, carrot and porcini mushrooms. Increase the heat to medium and
  sauté for about 5 minutes until lightly coloured. Stir in the parsley.
- Reduce the heat and add the meat. Brown lightly on all sides. Stir in the
  flour, pour in the reserved porcini liquid, beef stock and wine, and
  season with salt and pepper.
- Stir, cover and simmer very gently for 2½–3 hours, stirring occasionally,
  until the meat begins to disintegrate and the sauce thickens. Serve hot
  with freshly cooked pasta.

Roast beef &
Yorkshire pudding
serves 6–8

ingredients

1.8kg/4lb joint of beef
splash of red wine
300ml/10fl oz reduced beef stock
salt and freshly ground
    black pepper

For the Yorkshire pudding
175g/6oz plain flour
1 teaspoon salt
300ml/10fl oz cold milk
3 eggs, beaten
60g/2½oz beef dripping

- To prepare the Yorkshire pudding batter, sift the flour into a mixing bowl with the salt. In another large bowl, mix together the milk and 150ml/10fl oz water, and whisk with the beaten eggs. Add this to the flour in a thin stream, whisking to a smooth batter. Leave to stand for 60 minutes at room temperature.
- Preheat the oven to 240°C/475°F/Gas mark 9.
- Season the joint of beef heavily with salt and pepper, rubbing it in all over. Sit the joint on a rack in a roasting tin, and roast in the oven for 25 minutes, then reduce the temperature to 200°C/400°F/Gas mark 6 and continue roasting for a further 25 minutes. It is important not to open the oven door for more than a few seconds at any time from start to finish.
- Remove the meat from the oven and allow to rest on its rack for about 30 minutes in a warm place, covered with foil. Increase the oven temperature to 230°C/450°F/Gas mark 8.
- While the meat is resting, cook the Yorkshire pudding. Put the beef dripping into a metal pan at least 6.5cm/2½in deep, and put in the oven until smoking hot. Give the prepared batter a final whisk, and pour into the fat. Bake for 25–30 minutes, when the pudding will be well risen with a crisp, golden crust.
- Make a gravy by pouring off the fat from the roasting tin. Place the pan over a high heat, and deglaze it with a splash of red wine. Add the stock and boil fiercely, scraping the stuck-on sediment with a wooden spoon. Taste and adjust the seasoning if necessary.
- Serve the roast beef cut in slices, accompanied by the gravy, Yorkshire pudding and roasted vegetables.

Meatloaf

serves 4

ingredients

25g/1oz butter
450g/1lb minced beef
1 onion, chopped
2 garlic cloves, crushed
50g/2oz bulgur wheat, soaked
25g/1oz Parmesan cheese
1 celery stick trimmed and sliced
2 tablespoons horseradish sauce
2 tablespoons tomato purée

2 tablespoons instant oatmeal
1 tablespoon chopped fresh
   thyme leaves
salt and freshly ground
   black pepper

For the relish
2 tablespoons horseradish sauce
150ml/5fl oz sour cream

- Grease and line the bottom of a 700g/1½lb loaf tin. Preheat the oven to 180°C/350°F/Gas mark 4.
- Melt the butter in a large pan, and add the minced beef, onion and garlic. Sauté, stirring, for 7 minutes until the meat is brown and sealed.
- Transfer the mixture to a bowl, and add the remaining ingredients. Mix well, season and spoon into the prepared tin. Cover with foil.
- Stand the loaf tin in a roasting tin, and add 2.5cm/1in of water. Carefully place in the oven and cook for 1½ hours.
- Mix together the relish ingredients in a bowl. Turn out the meatloaf and garnish with the fresh thyme. Serve with fresh vegetables and the relish as a condiment.

Beef olives in gravy

serves 4

ingredients

8 ready-prepared beef olives
4 tablespoons chopped fresh
    flat-leaf parsley
4 garlic cloves, finely chopped
4 rashers smoked streaky bacon,
    finely chopped
grated zest of ½ small orange
2 tablespoons olive oil
300ml/10fl oz dry red wine
1 bay leaf
1 teaspoon granulated sugar
50g/2oz pitted black olives,
    drained
salt and freshly ground black pepper

- Flatten out the beef olives as thinly as possible, using a meat tenderizer or mallet.
- Mix together the parsley, garlic, bacon and orange zest. Season with salt and pepper. Spread this mixture evenly over each beef olive. Roll up each beef olive tightly, then secure with a cocktail stick or toothpick.
- Heat the oil in a frying pan, and sauté the beef olives on all sides for 10 minutes until browned.
- Drain the beef olives, reserving the pan juices, and keep warm. Pour the wine into the juices, add the bay leaf and sugar. Season with salt and pepper. Bring to the boil, and boil rapidly for 5 minutes to reduce slightly, stirring.
- Return the cooked beef olives to the pan along with the black olives, and heat through for a further 2 minutes. Discard the bay leaf and carefully pull out the cocktail sticks or toothpicks.
- Transfer the beef olives and gravy to a serving dish. Serve immediately.

Beef, tomato & olive kebabs
serves 8

ingredients
450g/1lb rump or sirloin steak
16 cherry tomatoes
16 large green olives, pitted

For the baste
4 tablespoons olive oil
1 tablespoon sherry vinegar
1 garlic clove, crushed
salt and freshly ground black pepper

For the relish
6 plum tomatoes
1 tablespoon olive oil
½ red onion, finely chopped
1 garlic clove, chopped
1 tablespoon chopped fresh
   flat-leaf parsley
1 tablespoon freshly squeezed
   lemon juice

- Soak 8 bamboo skewers in cold water for at least 30 minutes to prevent them burning.
- Using a sharp knife, trim any fat from the steak, and cut the meat into roughly 24 evenly sized pieces.
- Thread the pieces of steak onto the skewers, alternating the beef with the cherry tomatoes and the green olives.
- To make the baste, combine all the baste ingredients in a bowl.
- To make the relish, plunge the tomatoes in a bowl of boiling water, then drain and transfer to a bowl of cold water. Peel off and discard the skin, and chop the flesh.
- Heat the oil in a small pan, and sauté the onion and garlic for 3–4 minutes until softened. Add the tomatoes and cook for a further 2–3 minutes. Stir in the parsley and lemon juice, and season with salt and pepper. Set aside and keep warm.
- Barbecue the kebabs over hot coals for 5–10 minutes, basting and turning frequently. Serve with the relish.

Beef & mushroom burgers
serves 4

ingredients
1 small onion, chopped
150g/5oz small cup mushrooms
450g/1lb lean minced beef
50g/2oz fresh wholemeal
  breadcrumbs
1 teaspoon dried mixed herbs
1 tablespoon tomato purée
flour for shaping
salt and freshly ground black pepper

- Put the onion and mushrooms in a blender or food processor, and whiz until finely chopped. Add the beef, breadcrumbs, herbs and tomato purée, and season with salt and pepper. Blend for a few seconds until the mixture binds together but still has some texture.
- Divide the mixture into 8 to 10 pieces, then press into burger shapes using lightly floured hands.
- Cook the burgers in a non-stick frying pan or under a hot grill for 12–15 minutes, turning once, until evenly cooked. Serve hot.

Veal Marsala
serves 2

ingredients
2 veal escalopes
flour for dredging
½ teaspoon dried oregano, crumbled
8 field mushrooms, stalks removed
   and caps thinly sliced
about 25g/1oz butter
2 tablespoons olive or sunflower oil
150ml/5fl oz Marsala
salt and freshly ground black pepper

- If necessary, put the veal escalopes between two sheets of greaseproof paper or cling film, and gently pound with a meat mallet or wooden rolling pin to flatten. Trim any rough edges if necessary.
- Put enough flour for dredging in a shallow bowl or plate. Season with salt and pepper, and the oregano. Dredge the escalopes in the seasoned flour, gently shaking off any excess. (If you like, you can omit this step, and simply season the veal without dredging in the flour.)
- Put the oil and a knob of butter in a heavy frying pan over a medium heat. When the butter has melted and is starting to foam (do not allow to burn), add the escalopes and fry for 2 minutes on each side. Remove to a plate, cover with foil and keep warm.
- Pour the Marsala into the pan and boil it down, deglazing the pan by scraping up any bits stuck to the pan using a wooden spoon. Add the cooked mushrooms and toss through.
- Put an escalope on each of two serving plates, pour over the mushroom sauce and serve immediately.

Veal chops & mushrooms

serves 4

ingredients

25g/1oz margarine or butter
4 lean loin veal chops
1 onion, chopped
450g/1lb mushroom caps
225g/8oz white onions
1 tablespoon plain flour
1 tablespoon tomato purée
175ml/6fl oz chicken stock
150ml/5fl oz dry white wine
50g/2oz chopped fresh chives
1 teaspoon chopped fresh tarragon
1 teaspoon chopped fresh basil
1 small bay leaf
1 tablespoon chopped fresh
  flat-leaf parsley

- Preheat the oven to 170°C/325°F/Gas mark 3.
- Melt the margarine or butter in a large heavy frying pan. Add the veal chops and brown over a high heat. Transfer to a shallow casserole dish.
- In the same frying pan, sauté the onions. Add the remaining ingredients except the parsley. Cover the pan and cook for 5 minutes.
- Pour the mixture over the chops. Cover the casserole dish and bake in the oven for 1 hour. Sprinkle with the parsley before serving hot.

Pork with port & coffee sauce

serves 6

ingredients

1.8kg/4lb pork loin, boned
225ml/8fl oz strong espresso coffee
125ml/4fl oz single cream
75ml/3fl oz port
2 teaspoons granulated sugar
2 teaspoons cornflour

- Preheat oven to 180°C/350°F/Gas mark 4.
- Remove the rind from the pork and trim the fat to make a 1cm/½in layer. Roll and tie the meat with string. Put the meat in a roasting tin, and roast in the oven for 30 minutes.
- Combine the coffee, half the cream, half the port and the sugar, and pour over the pork. Continue roasting the pork for 1½ hours, basting it every 15 minutes with the coffee mixture.
- Remove the pork from the oven when cooked. Keep covered in a warm place while making the sauce. Skim off the fat from the pan juices, and transfer the juices to a small saucepan. Add 50ml/2fl oz water, the remaining cream and port, and the cornflour. Cook until thickened, then strain. Slice the pork thinly and drizzle with sauce. Serve immediately.

Ginger &
honey-glazed gammon
serves 10

ingredients
4.5–6.8kg/10–15lb unsmoked
   gammon on the bone
2 shallots, peeled and halved
6 cloves
3 bay leaves
2 celery sticks, cut into 5cm/2in
   lengths
2 tablespoons English mustard
5cm/2in piece of fresh root ginger,
   thinly sliced

For the glaze
225g/8oz dark muscovado sugar
2 tablespoons clear honey
125ml/4fl oz brandy

- Put the gammon in a heavy pan with the shallots, cloves, bay leaves, celery and enough cold water to cover. Bring to the boil, cover and simmer gently for about 5 hours. Skim off any scum using a slotted spoon. Lift the ham out of the pan, discard the vegetables and herbs, and allow the gammon cool.
- Preheat the oven to 200°C/400°F/Gas mark 6.
- Using a sharp knife, carefully cut away the gammon's thick skin to leave an even layer of fat. Score a diamond pattern in the fat. Put the gammon in a roasting tin, smother evenly with the mustard and tuck the ginger into the scored fat.
- To make the glaze, put the sugar, honey and brandy in a pan, and heat until the sugar has dissolved. Brush over the gammon.
- Cook the gammon in the oven for 30–40 minutes, basting every 10 minutes. Serve either hot or cold, cut into slices.

Chargrilled pork fillet with apple sauce

serves 4

ingredients
450g/1lb pork fillet, trimmed
150ml/5fl oz cider
1 tablespoon light muscovado sugar
1 teaspoon Dijon mustard
2 garlic cloves, crushed
2 sprigs of fresh rosemary sprigs,
    bruised
2 tablespoons olive oil
finely grated zest and juice of
    2 lemons
2 tablespoons golden sultanas
1 teaspoon chopped fresh
    thyme leaves
2 dessert apples
salt and freshly ground black pepper

- Trim the pork fillets of any fat, and cut into 1cm/½in thick rounds before placing in a bowl. Mix together half of the the cider with the sugar, mustard, garlic, rosemary sprigs, oil, half of the lemon zest and 1 tablespoon of the lemon juice. Pour over the pork, and rub all over the meat. Cover and chill until needed.
- To make the sauce, put the remaining lemon zest in a small mixing bowl with 2 tablespoons lemon juice, the remaining cider, the sultanas and thyme leaves. Peel, core and finely dice the apples, one at a time, mixing them in as you go. Season with salt and pepper, and set aside.
- Preheat the grill until hot. Remove the meat from its marinade, and season with salt and pepper. Cook the meat under the grill for 3 minutes per side, removing as soon as it is just cooked through, so that it retains its tenderness. Serve with the apple sauce.

Pork tenderloin Diane
serves 4

ingredients
450g/1lb pork tenderloin, cut
    crossways into 8 pieces
2 teaspoons lemon pepper
25g/1oz butter
2 tablespoons freshly squeezed
    lemon juice
1 tablespoon Worcestershire sauce
1 teaspoon Dijon mustard
1 tablespoon chopped fresh parsley

- Press each tenderloin piece into a 2.5cm/1in thick medallion, and sprinkle the surfaces with lemon pepper.
- Melt the butter in large heavy- frying pan over a medium heat. Add the medallions and cook for 3–4 minutes on each side. Remove from the pan and place on a serving platter. Cover to keep warm.
- Stir the lemon juice, Worcestershire sauce and mustard into the juices in the pan. Cook, stirring, until heated through. Pour the sauce over the medallions, and sprinkle with parsley. Serve immediately.

Aubergine with pork & prawns

serves 6

ingredients

4 large aubergines
150g/5oz minced pork
200g/7oz prawns, peeled and
   deveined
3 shallots, chopped
1 tablespoon vegetable oil
4 garlic cloves, crushed
1 tablespoon malt vinegar
1 tablespoon Thai fish sauce
2 tablespoons canned cooked soya
   beans, rinsed
1 teaspoon granulated sugar
salt and freshly ground black pepper

- Preheat the oven to 230°C/450°F/Gas mark 8. Cook the aubergines
  whole in the oven or barbecue them directly over a strong heat until the
  skins are burnt. Toss the aubergines into cold water, then peel and cut
  the flesh into large pieces. Put the pieces in a serving dish.
- Mix the pork and prawns together. Season with salt and pepper, and
  set aside.
- Sauté the shallots in the oil until browned. Remove the shallots and drain
  on kitchen papper. Use the oil remaining in the pan to sauté the garlic.
  When the garlic is soft and golden, add the pork and prawn mixture
  and sauté for a few minutes over a medium heat.
- Add the vinegar, fish sauce, soya beans and sugar, and mix in well.
  Cover and cook for a few minutes. Top the aubergine pieces with the
  pork and prawn mixture, and sprinkle with the sugar. Serve hot.

Baked cranberry pork chops
serves 4

ingredients
4 pork chops
1 teaspoon onion powder
300ml/10fl oz cranberry sauce
2 tablespoons soft brown sugar
1 teaspoon ground ginger
pinch of ground nutmeg
250g/9oz carrots, cut into strips
1 teaspoon cornflour
1 tablespoon chopped fresh
   flat-leaf parsley

- Preheat the oven to 190°C/375°F/Gas mark 5.
- Sprinkle the chops with the onion powder on both sides, and set aside.
- In a medium saucepan, heat the cranberry sauce, brown sugar, ginger, nutmeg and 2 tablespoons water for about 2 minutes until the cranberry sauce is melted.
- Put the carrots in a large casserole dish, and arrange the pork chops over the carrots. Spoon the cranberry sauce mixture evenly over the pork chops. Cover and bake the oven for about 45 minutes until the pork is thoroughly cooked.
- Remove the chops to a serving plate and scatter the carrots over them.
- Pour the sauce remaining in the casserole into a medium saucepan.
- Combine the cornflour with 1 tablespoon water to make a paste. Stir into the saucepan and cook for about 2 minutes, stirring, until sauce is clear and thickened.
- Spoon over the pork chops and sprinkle with parsley. Serve immediately.

White pork with pak choi

serves 4

ingredients

100g/4oz boneless pork shoulder
1 tablespoon cornflour
450g/1lb pak choi
3 tablespoons groundnut oil
½ teaspoon minced garlic
½ teaspoon minced fresh root ginger
¼ teaspoon salt
50ml/2fl oz chicken stock
½ teaspoon granulated sugar
1 teaspoon dry sherry

- Slice the pork against the grain into thin strips about 5cm/2in x 1cm/½in. Combine the cornflour with 1½ tablespoons water to make a paste.
- Separate the outer fleshy stalks from the centre stalk of the pak choi and discard the centre stalk. Wash the outer stalks and diagonally slice into 8cm/3in pieces.
- Swirl the oil around in a very hot wok. When the oil begins to smoke, add the pork and stir-fry for about 1 minute until the meat is seared. Add the pak choi, garlic and ginger. Stir-fry until the green leaves are bright and shrivelled, stirring constantly.
- Add the salt, stock, sugar and sherry. When the liquid begins to boil, cover the wok and steam for 30 seconds or less on high heat, until the stalks are tender but still crisp.
- Remove the meat and vegetables using a slotted spoon and set aside. Stir the cornflour paste into the remaining cooking liquid to make a light sauce. Serve immediately.

Pork with Stilton

serves 4

ingredients

350g/12oz boneless pork steaks,
    cut into 1cm/½in cubes
plain flour for coating
25g/1oz butter
1 tablespoon white wine vinegar
75ml/3fl oz red wine
75g/3oz Stilton cheese, crumbled
salt and freshly ground black pepper

- Season the flour with salt and pepper. Dredge the pork thoroughly in the seasoned flour. Heat the butter in a frying pan, and gently fry the pork until lightly browned and cooked through. Remove from the pan using a slotted spoon, and keep warm.
- Drain the fat from the pan and pour in the vinegar and wine. Stir, scraping up all the meat residues, and bring to the boil. Reduce the heat to very low, and stir in the Stilton until it has melted. Taste and season with salt and pepper.
- Spoon the sauce over the pork, then serve immediately.

Pork & brown bean sauce
serves 4–6

ingredients
50ml/2fl oz brown bean sauce
2 tablespoons hoisin sauce
175ml/6fl oz chicken stock
½ teaspoon granulated sugar
2 tablespoons groundnut oil
3 garlic cloves, finely chopped
6 spring onions, sliced, white and
   green parts separated
650g/1lb 6oz minced pork
500g/1lb 2oz fresh noodles

- In a small bowl, combine the bean and hoisin sauces, stock and sugar, and mix until smooth.
- Heat a wok over a high heat, add the oil and swirl. Add the garlic and white part of the spring onions, and stir-fry for 15 seconds. Add the pork and stir-fry over a high heat for 3 minutes or until the meat has browned. Add the bean mixture, reduce the heat and simmer for 7–8 minutes.
- Meanwhile, cook the noodles in a large saucepan of boiling water for 4–5 minutes until tender. Drain and rinse, then serve with the pork.

Roast fillet of pork with peaches
serves 6

ingredients
¼ teaspoon ground coriander
¼ teaspoon ground cinnamon
¼ teaspoon freshly ground
   black pepper
2 pork fillets
2 tablespoons vegetable oil
3 tablespoons clear honey
2 tablespoons water
3 peaches, halved and stoned
salt

- Preheat the oven to 220°C/425°F/Gas mark 7. Grease a medium roasting tin.
- In a small bowl, mix the coriander, cinnamon and pepper. Lay the pork in the roasting tin, and sprinkle the mixed spices over the top. Spoon the oil over. Bake the pork in the oven for 20 minutes.
- Meanwhile, put the honey and water in a small pan, and warm very gently, stirring, until the honey has dissolved.
- After the first 20 minutes' cooking time, put the peach halves, cut side up, around the pork. Pour the honey mixture over the pork and peaches, and season the pork with salt. Cook for a further 20 minutes, basting from time to time.
- Remove from the oven, and leave to rest for 5 minutes before serving the pork accompanied by the peaches and pan juices.

Italian pork escalopes
serves 4

ingredients
2 tablespoons olive oil
4 garlic cloves, finely sliced
small bunch of fresh sage leaves
4 pork escalopes, around
   50g/2oz each
4 slices Parma ham
4 tablespoons grated Gruyère cheese
flour for dredging
150ml/5fl oz crème fraîche
50g/2oz spring onions, chopped
1 tablespoon white wine vinegar
salt and freshly ground black pepper

- Heat 1 tablespoon of the oil in a frying pan. Sauté the garlic and sage leaves until golden brown. Remove and drain on kitchen paper. Cool, reserving some for the garnish.
- Put each escalope between two pieces of cling film, and beat with a rolling pin until very thin.
- Put a slice of ham, 1 tablespoon of the Gruyère and some of the garlic and sage leaves on each escalope. Season with salt and pepper. Fold the pork in half and season again. Flatten the open edges with a knife to seal. Dust lightly with flour.
- Heat the remaining oil in a heavy frying pan over a medium heat. Cook the pork for 3–4 minutes each side.
- Mix the crème fraîche, spring onions and vinegar together.
- Serve the pork, garnished with the reserved garlic and sage, and a grinding of pepper, and accompanied by the crème fraîche mixture.

Sausage & bean casserole

serves 4

ingredients

8 pepperoni sausages
1 tablespoon olive oil
1 large onion, chopped
2 garlic cloves, chopped
1 green pepper, seeded and cut
   into strips
400g/14oz canned chopped plum
   tomatoes
2 tablespoons sun-dried tomato paste
400g/14oz canned cooked
   cannellini beans

- Prick the sausages all over with a fork. Cook under a preheated grill for 10–12 minutes, turning occasionally, until brown all over. Set aside and keep warm.
- Heat the oil in a large frying pan. Add the onion, garlic and green pepper, and sweat for 5 minutes, stirring occasionally, until softened.
- Add the tomatoes to the frying pan and leave the mixture to simmer for about 5 minutes, stirring occasionally, or until slightly thickened.
- Stir the sun-dried tomato paste, cannellini beans and reserved sausages into the mixture in the frying pan. Cook for 4–5 minutes until the mixture is piping hot. Add 4–5 tablespoons water if the mixture becomes too dry during cooking.
- Transfer the casserole to serving plates, and serve hot with mashed potato or rice.

Chinese spare ribs
serves 4

ingredients
150ml/5fl oz light soy sauce
2.5cm/1in piece of fresh root ginger,
  grated
3 teaspoons five-spice powder
¼ teaspoon dried red chilli flakes
4 garlic cloves, crushed
125ml/4fl oz sunflower oil
1kg/2¼lb pork spare ribs, chopped
  into 5cm/2in pieces
3½ tablespoons clear honey

- In a large bowl, mix together the soy sauce, ginger, five-spice powder, chilli flakes, garlic and 3½ tablespoons of the sunflower oil. Add the pork and toss to coat.
- Cover the top with cling film, and marinate in the refrigerator for 24 hours, shaking occasionally.
- Drain the pork through a colander into a saucepan. Put a heavy frying pan with the remaining sunflower oil over a medium heat. When very hot, add the ribs a few at a time and sear, transferring to the saucepan with the marinade when browned. Bring the contents of the saucepan to the boil, reduce the heat and cover with a lid. Simmer gently for 30–45 minutes until the meat is tender.
- Remove the lid and stir in the honey. Increase the heat and reduce the sauce, tossing and stirring until the water content has evaporated and the ribs are covered with a rich glaze. Serve warm.

Pork crumble
serves 4

ingredients

For the filling

1 green dessert apple, plus extra
    apple slices, to garnish
1 tablespoon freshly squeezed
    lemon juice
1 tablespoon vegetable oil
450g/1lb minced pork
1 onion, sliced
25g/1oz plain flour
150ml/5fl oz milk
150ml/5fl oz vegetable stock
50g/2oz broccoli florets
50g/2oz canned sweetcorn
    kernels, drained

For the topping

50g/2oz instant oatmeal
50g/2oz plain flour
15g/1½oz butter
25g/1oz Red Leicester
    cheese, grated

- Preheat the oven to 180°C/350°F/Gas mark 4.
- For the filling, peel, core and dice the apple, and toss in the lemon juice (do not cut the apple slices until ready to garnish).
- Heat the oil in a large pan and fry the pork for 5 minutes. Add the onion and continue to fry for a further 3 minutes. Stir in the flour and cook for 1 minute. Pour in the milk and stock and bring to the boil, stirring all the time. Add the broccoli, sweetcorn and diced apple. Spoon the mixture into four individual ovenproof dishes.
- For the topping, mix together the oatmeal and flour, then rub in the butter using your fingertips until the mixture resembles coarse crumbs.
- Spoon the topping onto the pork mixture, and press down using the back of a spoon. Scatter the cheese over the top, and place in the oven. Cook for 45 minutes. Garnish with slices of apple and serve at once.

Herbed pork cutlets

serves 4

ingredients

1 egg
75g/3oz dried breadcrumbs
50g/2oz fresh basil, chopped
2 tablespoons chopped
   fresh oregano
1 tablespoon freshly grated
   Parmesan cheese
1 teaspoon chopped fresh thyme
450g/1lb pork cutlets
2 tablespoons vegetable oil
salt and freshly ground black pepper

- In a shallow dish, lightly beat the egg. In a separate dish, stir together the breadcrumbs, basil, oregano, Parmesan, thyme, salt and pepper.
- Dip the pork into the egg to coat well, then press into the breadcrumb mixture, turning to coat all over.
- In a large frying pan, heat half the oil over a medium heat. Working in batches, cook the pork for 8–10 minutes until just a hint of pink remains inside, turning once during the cooking time and adding the remaining oil if necessary. Remove from the pan and divide among four serving plates. Serve hot with accompanying salad or vegetables.

Braised pork slices

serves 4

ingredients

700g/1½lb boned pork steaks
3 tablespoons groundnut oil
3 garlic cloves, minced
1 teaspoon white wine vinegar
2 tablespoons medium sherry
175ml/6fl oz chicken stock
1 tablespoon cornflour, mixed
 with 25ml/1fl oz water to form
 a paste
900ml/1½pt vegetable oil for
 deep-frying

2 egg yolks, beaten with
 1 teaspoon water)
150g/5oz fresh breadcrumbs

For the paste
2 tablespoons cooked
 long-grain rice
½ teaspoon granulated sugar
1 teaspoon dried baker's yeast
2 tablespoons light soy sauce
2 tablespoons warm water

- To make the paste, use a mortar and pestle to pulverize the rice. Combine with the sugar, yeast, soy sauce and warm water, and leave to stand in a warm place for 30 minutes to activate the yeast.

- Slice the pork steaks across the grain into strips. Heat the groundnut oil in a wok until it begins to smoke. Add the pork strips and stir-fry until they lose their pinkness, repeating in batches until all the pork is browned. Add the garlic to the wok and stir briefly. Pour in the prepared paste, vinegar, sherry and stock, then bring to the boil and add all the pork slices. Reduce the heat, add the cornflour paste and stir well. Cover and simmer for 30 minutes. Remove the pork to a large platter, reserving the sauce in the wok, and leave the pork to cool.

- Heat the vegetable oil in a clean wok. Dip the pork pieces in the egg mixture, then in the breadcrumbs, to cover thoroughly. When the oil is hot, slip in a slice of pork as a test – it should lightly brown in about 1 minute. Deep-fry the pork in batches for 1½–2 minutes. Reheat the sauce, and pour over the pork. Serve immediately.

Pork with apples

serves 4

ingredients

500g/1lb 2oz lean pork fillet
2 teaspoons sunflower oil
150ml/5fl oz vegetable stock
150ml/5fl oz dry rosé wine
1 tablespoon chopped fresh thyme
1 tablespoon clear honey
2 green dessert apples, cored, sliced
   and tossed in 1 tablespoon freshly
   squeezed lemon juice
175g/6oz fresh blackberries
2 teaspoons cornflour
4 teaspoons lemon juice
salt and freshly ground black pepper

- Trim away any fat and silvery skin from the pork fillet, and cut into
  1cm/½in thick slices.
- Heat the oil in a non-stick frying pan, add the pork slices and sauté for
  4–5 minutes until browned all over. Using a slotted spoon, remove the
  pork and drain on kitchen paper. Reserve the pan juices.
- Pour the stock and wine into the pan with the juices, and add the thyme
  and honey. Mix well, bring to a simmer and add the pork and apples.
  Continue to simmer, uncovered, for 5 minutes.
- Add the blackberries, season with salt and pepper, and simmer for a
  further 5 minutes. Mix the cornflour with the lemon juice and add to the
  pan – stir until the sauce has thickened. Serve hot with boiled potatoes.

Loin of pork in wine sauce
serves 4

ingredients
1 tablespoon vegetable oil
1 garlic clove, crushed
5 black peppercorns, crushed
4 pork chops
50g/2oz plain flour
1 onion, finely chopped
50g/2oz red pepper, seeded and
    chopped
50ml/2fl oz beef stock
50ml/2fl oz dry white wine
1 tablespoon red wine vinegar

- Heat the oil in a frying pan, and add the garlic and peppercorns. Pat the pork dry with kitchen paper, and dredge in the flour. Sauté on both sides until golden brown. Remove from the pan and set aside.
- Add the onion and red pepper to the pan, and sauté until softened. Add the stock, wine and vinegar, and stir well.
- Return the pork to the pan, and simmer slowly, uncovered, for 30 minutes, turning halfway through. Serve hot with boiled rice.

Pork chow mein
serves 4

ingredients
250g/9oz egg noodles
4 tablespoons vegetable oil
2 tablespoons light soy sauce
250g/9oz pork fillet, cooked and
    sliced into thin shreds
100g/4oz French beans, topped
    and tailed
1 teaspoon salt
½ teaspoon sugar
1 tablespoon Chinese rice wine
2 spring onions, finely sliced
½ teaspoon sesame oil

- Cook the noodles in boiling water according to the packet instructions, then drain and rinse under cold water. Drain again, then toss with 1 tablespoon of the vegetable oil.
- Heat 1 tablespoon of the vegetable oil in a wok until hot. Add the noodles, and stir-fry for 2–3 minutes with 1 tablespoon of the soy sauce, then remove to a serving dish and keep warm.
- Heat the remaining oil, and stir-fry the pork and beans for 2 minutes. Add the salt, sugar, rice wine, remaining soy sauce and half the spring onions to the wok.
- Stir the mixture in the wok, adding a little water if necessary, then pour on top of the noodles and sprinkle with the sesame oil and the remaining spring onions. Serve hot.

Chilli-flavoured pork

serves 4

ingredients

2 tablespoons dried wood ear
   mushrooms

250g/9oz pork fillet, thinly sliced

1 teaspoon salt

1 teaspoon cornflour, mixed
   with 1½ teaspoons water to
   form a paste)

3 tablespoons vegetable oil

1 garlic clove, finely chopped

½ teaspoon finely chopped fresh
   root ginger

2 spring onions, finely chopped,
   with the white and green parts
   separated

2 celery sticks, thinly sliced

½ teaspoon granulated sugar

1 tablespoon light soy sauce

1 tablespoon chilli sauce

2 teaspoons rice vinegar

1 teaspoon rice wine

a few drops of sesame oil

- Soak the wood ear mushrooms in warm water for about 20 minutes, then rinse in cold water until the water is clear. Drain well, then cut into thin shreds.
- Mix the pork in a bowl with a pinch of salt and about half the cornflour paste until well coated.
- Heat 1 tablespoon of the vegetable oil in a smoking-hot wok. Add the pork and stir-fry for about 1 minute until the colour changes, then remove with a slotted spoon and set aside until needed.
- Add the remaining oil to the wok and heat. Add the garlic, ginger, the white parts of the spring onions, the wood ears and celery, and stir-fry for 1 minute.
- Return the pork strips to the wok together with the remaining salt, sugar, soy sauce, chilli sauce, vinegar and wine. Blend well and continue stirring for another minute.
- Finally, add the green parts of the spring onions and blend in the remaining cornflour paste and sesame oil. Stir until the sauce has thickened. Transfer the chilli-flavoured pork to a warmed serving dish, and serve immediately.

Tangy pork fillet
serves 4

ingredients
400g/14oz lean pork fillet
3 tablespoons orange marmalade
grated zest and juice of 1 orange
1 tablespoon white wine vinegar
dash of Tabasco sauce
salt and freshly ground black pepper

For the sauce
1 tablespoon olive oil
1 small onion, chopped
1 small green pepper, seeded and
   thinly sliced
1 tablespoon cornflour
150ml/5 fl oz orange juice

- Preheat a charcoal barbecue until hot. Lay a large piece of double-thickness foil in a shallow dish. Put the pork fillet in the centre of the foil, and season with salt and pepper.
- Heat the marmalade, orange zest and juice, vinegar and Tabasco in a small pan, stirring until the marmalade melts and the ingredients combine. Carefully pour the mixture over the pork, and wrap the meat in the foil, making sure that the parcel is well sealed so that the juices cannot run out.
- Place the parcel over the hot barbecue coals, and barbecue for about 25 minutes, turning the parcel occasionally.
- For the sauce, heat the oil and sweat the onion for 2–3 minutes until soft. Add the pepper and sauté for a further 3–4 minutes.
- Remove the pork from the foil and set on the barbecue rack. Pour the juices into the pan with the onion and green pepper.
- Barbecue the pork for a further 10–20 minutes, turning, until cooked through and golden on the outside.
- In a small bowl, mix the cornflour with a little of the orange juice to form a paste. Add to the sauce with the remaining orange juice, and cook, stirring, until the sauce thickens. Slice the pork, spoon the sauce over, and serve with rice and a green salad.

Pork stroganoff
serves 4

ingredients

350g/12oz lean pork fillet
1 tablespoon vegetable oil
1 onion, chopped
2 garlic cloves, crushed
25g/1oz plain flour
2 tablespoons tomato purée
400ml/14fl oz chicken stock
100g/4oz button mushrooms, sliced
1 large green pepper, seeded
   and diced
½ teaspoon ground nutmeg
4 tablespoons low-fat Greek-style
   yogurt
salt and freshly ground black pepper

- Trim away any excess fat and silver skin from the pork, then cut the meat into slices 1cm/½in thick.
- Heat the oil in a large saucepan, and gently sauté the pork, onion and garlic for 4–5 minutes until lightly browned.
- Stir in the flour and tomato purée, pour in the stock and stir to mix thoroughly. Add the mushrooms, green pepper and nutmeg. Season with salt and pepper. Bring to the boil, cover and simmer for 20 minutes until the pork is tender and cooked through.
- Remove the pan from the heat and stir in the yogurt. Serve the pork and sauce immediately, on a bed of boiled rice.

Pork steaks with gremolata

serves 4

ingredients

2 tablespoons olive oil

4 lean pork shoulder steaks, about 175g/6oz each

1 onion, chopped

2 garlic cloves, crushed

2 tablespoons tomato purée

400g/14oz canned chopped plum tomatoes

150ml/5fl oz dry white wine

1 bouquet garni

3 anchovy fillets in oil, drained and chopped

salt and freshly ground black pepper

For the gremolata

3 tablespoons chopped fresh flat-leaf parsley

grated zest of ½ lemon

grated zest of 1 lime

1 garlic clove, chopped

- Heat the oil in a large flameproof casserole dish, add the pork steaks and brown on both sides. Remove the pork from the dish and set aside.
- Add the onion to the dish, and sweat for a few minutes until soft and beginning to colour. Add the garlic and sweat for 1–2 minutes, then stir in the tomato purée, tomatoes and wine. Add the bouquet garni. Bring to the boil, then boil rapidly for a further 3–4 minutes to reduce the sauce and thicken slightly.
- Return the pork to the casserole dish, then cover and cook for about 30 minutes. Stir in the anchovies. Cover the casserole and cook for a further 15 minutes or until the pork is tender.
- To make the gremolata, mix together the parsley, lemon and lime zests and garlic.
- When ready, remove the pork steaks and discard the bouquet garni. Reduce the sauce over a high heat if necessary to thicken. Taste and adjust the seasoning if required.
- Return the pork to the casserole dish, then sprinkle with the gremolata. Cover and cook for a further 5 minutes, then serve hot.

Lamb with cashew nut curry
serves 4

ingredients

½ teaspoon saffron threads
50ml/2fl oz boiling water
75g/3oz ghee or butter
150g/5oz onion, chopped
2 teaspoons salt
125ml/4fl oz Greek-style yogurt
700g/1½lb lamb, cubed
2 tablespoons finely chopped
    fresh coriander
1 tablespoon freshly squeezed
    lemon juice

For the masala
50g/2oz unsalted cashew nuts
3 dried red chillies
2.5cm/1in piece of fresh root
    ginger
5cm/2in cinnamon stick
¼ teaspoon cardamom seeds
3 cloves
2 garlic cloves
2 tablespoons poppy seeds
1 tablespoon coriander seeds
1 teaspoon cumin seeds

- To make the masala, put the cashew nuts, chillies, ginger and 225ml/ 8fl oz cold water in a blender or food processor. Whiz at high speed for 1 minute. Add the cinnamon, cardamom, cloves, garlic, poppy seeds, coriander seeds and cumin. Blend again until the mixture is completely pulverized. Set the masala aside.
- Put the saffron in a small bowl, add the boiling water and leave to soak for at least 10 minutes.
- In a heavy frying pan, heat the ghee or butter over a medium heat. Add the onion and, stirring constantly, sauté for 8 minutes until soft and golden brown.
- Stir in the salt and the masala, then add the yogurt. Cook over a medium heat, stirring occasionally, until the ghee lightly films the surface.
- Add the lamb, turning it about with a spoon to coat the pieces evenly. Stir the saffron and its soaking liquid into the pan. Reduce the heat to low, cover tightly and cook for 20 minutes, turning the lamb from time to time. Scatter half the coriander over the lamb and continue cooking, tightly covered, for a further 10 minutes or until the lamb is tender.
- To serve, transfer the entire contents of the pan to a warmed serving dish, and sprinkle the top with the lemon juice and the remaining coriander. Serve hot with boiled basmati rice.

Lamb with mint sauce
serves 4

ingredients
8 lamb noisettes, 2.5cm/1in thick
2 tablespoons vegetable oil
50ml/2fl oz white wine
salt and freshly ground black pepper

For the mint sauce
2 teaspoons granulated sugar
1 bunch of fresh mint leaves, finely
   chopped
2 tablespoons white wine vinegar

- To make the mint sauce, stir 2 tablespoon boiling water and the sugar together until the sugar has dissolved, then add the mint and vinegar. Season with salt and pepper. Leave to stand for 30 minutes to allow the flavours to mingle.
- Season the lamb with pepper. Heat the oil in a large frying pan, then sauté the lamb, in batches if necessary, for about 3 minutes on each side for pink meat.
- Transfer the lamb to a warmed serving plate, and season with salt, then cover and keep warm. Transfer the mint sauce to a jug or sauceboat.
- Pour the wine into the cooking juices, and stir with a wooden spoon to dislodge the sediment and any other bits from the bottom of the pan. Bring to the boil and let the juices bubble for a couple of minutes, then pour the sauce over the lamb.
- Serve the lamb noisettes and mint sauce at once, accompanied by roasted new potatoes and carrots.

Cajun lamb with rice
serves 2

ingredients
900g/2lb boneless lamb
   sirloin roast
2 tablespoons vegetable oil
1 small onion, chopped
1 red pepper, seeded and diced
1 green pepper, seeded and diced
450g/1lb tomatoes, sliced
350ml/12fl oz chicken stock
½ teaspoon basil
½ teaspoon grated lemon zest
½ teaspoon chilli powder
225g/8oz long-grain rice

For the spice mix
1 teaspoon salt
½ teaspoon cayenne pepper
¼ teaspoon freshly ground
   black pepper
¼ teaspoon paprika
⅛ teaspoon garlic powder

- Preheat the oven to 180°C/350°F/Gas mark 4.
- Trim the lamb of any excess fat. Combine the spice mix ingredients, and rub over the lamb. Leave to stand for 15 minutes.
- Heat the oil in a frying pan, and sear the lamb on all sides until browned. Remove the lamb to a roasting tin, and roast in the oven for 35–40 minutes.
- Add the onion and peppers to the frying pan, and sauté until soft. Add the tomatoes, stock, basil, lemon zest and chilli powder. Bring to a boil and add the rice. Reduce the heat and simmer until the liquid has been absorbed. Serve hot with the lamb.

Indian spicy lamb
serves 4

ingredients
2 teaspoons ground turmeric
500g/1lb 2oz lamb, cut into small
   pieces
100ml/3½fl oz vegetable oil
2 onions, finely sliced
3 garlic cloves, mashed
1 green chilli
½ teaspoon ground coriander
10 curry leaves
2.5cm/1in piece of fresh root ginger,
   finely chopped
½ teaspoon ground black pepper
½ teaspoon garam masala
100g/4oz desiccated coconut
salt

- Put 450ml/1¾pt water in a large heavy saucepan, add ½ teaspoon of the turmeric and 1 teaspoon salt, and bring to the boil. Add the lamb pieces and simmer, uncovered, for 15 minutes until the lamb is well cooked and the water has almost evaporated.
- Remove the pan from the heat and set aside.
- Heat the oil in a large frying pan. Add the onions and sauté until golden and caramelized. Add the garlic, chilli, coriander and remaining turmeric. Mix well, then add the curry leaves and ginger. Cook, stirring, for 2 minutes.
- Drain any excess water from the lamb, and stir the meat into the onion mixture. Add the ground pepper and garam masala, and stir-fry for 5 minutes or until the mixture becomes quite dry.
- Add the coconut and season with salt. Give the dish a final stir, then serve immediately.

Herb-scented lamb
with balsamic dressing
serves 6

ingredients
50g/2oz fresh thyme sprigs, plus
   1 tablespoon extra chopped
   thyme leaves
50g/2oz fresh rosemary sprigs
850g/1¾lb lamb fillets, trimmed
6 garlic cloves
150ml/5fl oz olive oil
150g/5oz spring onions,
   thinly sliced
225g/8oz cherry tomatoes
3 tablespoons balsamic vinegar
300ml/10fl oz lamb stock

- Preheat the oven to 200°C/400°F/Gas mark 6.
- Put 2 or 3 sprigs of the thyme and rosemary on a board, put one lamb fillet over them, season with pepper, then top with a further 2 or 3 herb sprigs. Tie the herbs and lamb into a bundle with string, secured at about 5cm/2in intervals. Repeat the process with the remaining lamb and herbs.
- Put the lamb in a roasting tin with the garlic cloves, and drizzle with 4 tablespoons of the oil. Roast in the oven for 25–30 minutes.
- Remove the lamb from the roasting tin, and put to one side in a warm place, covered with foil. Put the pan juices and garlic cloves into a bowl to one side. Heat the remaining oil in the roasting tin, then add the reserved garlic cloves, the spring onions and the tomatoes. Sauté gently for 5 minutes, lift out and put to one side. Pour the vinegar into the tin, and bubble to reduce by half. Add the stock and reserved pan juices, bring to the boil and bubble for 5–10 minutes. Add the chopped thyme and return the garlic, spring onions and tomatoes to the tin.
- Remove the string from the meat, and cut the lamb into thick slices. Serve with the hot dressing spooned over.

Crown roast of lamb
serves 6

ingredients

½ onion, chopped
1 garlic clove, chopped
25g/1oz butter
finely grated zest of ½ lemon
3 fresh sage leaves, finely chopped
175g/6oz cooked skinned chestnuts,
    crumbled
1 tablespoon freshly squeezed
    lemon juice
50g/2oz fresh white breadcrumbs
1 tablespoon chopped fresh
    flat-leaf parsley
1 egg, lightly beaten
1 prepared crown of lamb
salt and freshly ground black pepper

- Preheat the oven to 180°C/350°F/Gas mark 4.
- To make the stuffing, sweat the onion and garlic gently in the butter until
  tender but without browning. Mix with all the remaining ingredients
  except the lamb, adding just enough of the egg to bind. Fill the centre of
  the crown with the stuffing, then cover the stuffing with a piece of foil.
- Roast the crown for about 1 hour, removing the foil after 40 minutes.
  Baste the joint from time to time as it cooks, then allow to rest for
  10 minutes before serving.

Lamb & mint stir-fry

serves 4

ingredients

2 tablespoons vegetable oil
850g/1¾lb lamb loin fillets, thinly
    sliced across the grain
2 garlic cloves, finely chopped
1 red onion, cut into wedges
1 fresh red chilli, seeded and finely
    chopped
15g/½oz fresh mint, chopped

For the sauce
50ml/2fl oz freshly squeezed
    lime juice
2 tablespoons sweet chilli sauce
2 tablespoons Thai fish sauce

- To make the sauce, combine the lime juice and chilli and fish sauces in a small bowl.
- Heat a wok over a high heat, add 1 tablespoon of the oil and swirl it around to coat the side of the wok. Add the lamb in batches, stir-frying each batch for 2 minutes or until browned. Remove from the wok.
- Heat the remaining oil in the wok, add the garlic and onion, and stir-fry for 1 minute, then add the chilli and cook for 30 seconds. Return the lamb to the wok, pour in the sauce and cook for 2 minutes over a high heat. Stir in the mint, then serve immediately.

Turkish lamb stew
serves 4

ingredients
2 tablespoons olive oil
400g/14oz lamb fillet, cubed
1 red onion, sliced
1 garlic clove, crushed
1 large potato, cubed
400g/14oz canned chopped plum
   tomatoes
1 red pepper, seeded and sliced
200g/7oz canned cooked chickpeas
1 aubergine, cut into chunks
200ml/7fl oz lamb stock
1 tablespoon red wine vinegar
1 teaspoon chopped fresh thyme
1 teaspoon chopped fresh oregano
1 teaspoon chopped fresh rosemary
8 black olives, pitted and halved
salt and freshly ground black pepper

- Preheat the oven to 170°C/325°F/Gas mark 3.
- Heat half of the oil in a flameproof casserole dish, and brown the lamb over a high heat. Reduce the heat and add the remaining oil, the onion and the garlic, then sweat until soft.
- Add the potato, tomatoes, pepper, chickpeas, aubergine, stock, vinegar and chopped herbs to the pan. Season with salt and pepper, stir and bring to the boil.
- Cover, put in the oven and cook for 1–1½ hours until tender.
- About 15 minutes before the end of cooking time, add the olives to the stew. Serve hot.

Roast rack of lamb

serves 2

ingredients

25g/1oz stale fine breadcrumbs
25g/1oz butter, melted
2 tablespoons chopped fresh herbs
   such as parsley, chives and thyme
1 garlic clove, crushed
1 prepared rack of lamb
vegetable oil for greasing
salt and freshly ground black pepper

- Preheat the oven to 230°C/450°F/Gas mark 8.
- In a bowl, mix the breadcrumbs with the butter, herbs and garlic. Season with salt and pepper. Using your hands, keep turning the mixture over until the crumbs have soaked up all the butter evenly.
- Lay the lamb, fat side upward, in a lightly oiled roasting tin. Pat the crumb mixture firmly and thickly on the fat side.
- Roast the rack for 20–30 minutes, depending on how well cooked you like your lamb. Let the meat rest for 5 minutes before serving.

Moussaka

serves 6

ingredients

salt and ground black pepper
3 large aubergines, sliced
   lengthways
olive oil for brushing
50g/2oz Parmesan cheese, grated
½ teaspoon ground cinnamon

450g/1lb tomatoes, chopped
1 teaspoon sugar
1½ teaspoons ground cinnamon
1 tablespoon chopped fresh
   oregano
3 tablespoons chopped fresh
   flat-leaf parsley

For the meat sauce
1 large onion, chopped
2 garlic cloves, chopped
3 tablespoons olive oil
450g/1lb minced lamb
1 glass of dry white wine
2 tablespoons tomato purée

For the white sauce
50g/2oz butter
50g/2oz flour
600ml/1pt milk
50g/2oz Parmesan cheese, grated
1 egg plus 1 egg yolk

- Preheat the oven to 190°C/375°F/Gas mark 5. Sprinkle the slices of aubergine with salt, and leave for at least 30 minutes.

- To make the meat sauce, sweat the onion and garlic gently in the olive oil in a large frying pan until soft but not coloured. Add the lamb and stir until it loses its raw look. Add all the remaining meat sauce ingredients except the parsley, and season with salt and pepper. Simmer for 20–30 minutes until thick. Stir in the parsley.

- To make the white sauce, melt the butter and stir in the flour. Cook, stirring, for about 1 minute. Remove from the heat. Gradually stir in the milk. Return to a gentle heat. Simmer for 10–15 minutes, stirring, until the sauce is fairly thick. Remove from the heat, stir in the Parmesan and season with salt and pepper. Just before using, beat in the egg and yolk.

- Rinse the aubergine slices and pat dry with kitchen paper. Lay them on oiled baking sheets. Brush generously with olive oil, and bake in the oven for about 20 minutes until tender and patched with brown. Reduce the oven temperature to 180°C/350°F/Gas mark 4.

- Lightly brush a rectangular baking dish with oil. Lay half the aubergine slices on the bottom, overlapping if necessary, then spread half the meat sauce on top. Repeat the layers, and spoon the white sauce over the top, covering the meat completely. Sprinkle with the Parmesan and cinnamon. Bake for 50–60 minutes until browned. Rest for 5 minutes before serving.

Basil-stuffed lamb roast

serves 10–12

ingredients

For the roast

2.7kg/6lb leg of lamb, boned and butterflied (you can ask your butcher to do this)

1 teaspoon crushed dried rosemary

For the stuffing

50ml/2fl oz olive oil

175g/6oz onion, chopped

75g/3oz celery, chopped

2 garlic cloves, minced

2 eggs, beaten

50g/2oz fresh flat-leaf parsley, snipped

3 tablespoons snipped fresh basil

¼ teaspoon crushed dried marjoram

¼ teaspoon ground black pepper

1.4kg/3lb plain croûtons

4 tablespoons freshly grated Parmesan cheese

- Preheat the oven to 170°C/325°F/Gas mark 3.
- To make the stuffing, heat the oil in a pan and sweat the onion, celery and garlic until soft but not browned.
- In a medium bowl, stir together the eggs, parsley, basil, marjoram and pepper. Add the onion mixture, and stir in the croûtons and Parmesan. Drizzle with 125ml/4fl oz water to moisten, tossing lightly. Set aside.
- Pound the meat to an even thickness and sprinkle with the rosemary. Spread the stuffing over the lamb, then roll up and tie the meat securely. Put the roast, seam side down, on a rack in a shallow roasting pan.
- Roast for 1½–2 hours. Leave to rest for 15 minutes before carving.

Persian lamb

serves 4–6

ingredients

2 tablespoons chopped fresh mint
225ml/8fl oz Greek-style yogurt
2 garlic cloves, crushed)
¼ teaspoon ground black pepper
6 lean lamb chops
2 tablespoons freshly squeezed
    lemon juice

For the tabbouleh
250g/9oz couscous
500ml/18fl oz boiling water
2 tablespoons olive oil
2 tablespoons freshly squeezed
    lemon juice
½ onion, finely chopped
4 tomatoes, chopped
25g/1oz fresh coriander, chopped
2 tablespoons chopped fresh mint
salt and freshly ground black pepper

- To make the marinade, combine the mint, yogurt, garlic and pepper.
- Put the chops into a non-porous dish, and rub all over with the lemon juice. Pour the marinade over the chops, cover and marinate in the refrigerator for 2–3 hours.
- To make the tabbouleh, put the couscous in a heatproof bowl and pour the boiling water over it. Leave for 5 minutes. Drain and put into a sieve. Steam over a pan of barely simmering water for 8 minutes. Toss in the oil and lemon juice. Add the onion, tomatoes and herbs. Season with salt and pepper, and set aside.
- Cook the lamb over a medium-hot barbecue for 15 minutes, turning once. Serve with the tabbouleh.

Kleftiko

serves 4

ingredients
4 lamb shanks
5 tablespoons olive oil
450g/1lb onions, thinly sliced
4 garlic cloves, crushed and
   chopped
300ml/10fl oz dry white wine
450g/1lb canned chopped
   plum tomatoes
1 bay leaf
1 teaspoon dried oregano
salt and freshly ground black pepper

- Rub the lamb shanks with salt and pepper, then brown them all over in a frying pan in 3 tablespoons of the olive oil. Put into a casserole dish with a tight-fitting lid.
- Add some more of the olive oil to the frying pan and, over a low heat, sweat the onions until soft and translucent. Add the garlic and sauté for 2 minutes. Transfer to the casserole dish, distributing around the shanks.
- Over a high heat, deglaze the pan with the wine, stirring and scraping up any bits using a wooden spoon, then pour the liquid over the lamb. Add the tomatoes with their liquid, the bay leaf and oregano.
- Bring to the boil, put on the lid and reduce the heat to a simmer. After 1½ hours, test to see whether the meat is done. If not, continue cooking until it is tender.
- Remove the shanks and keep warm on serving plates. Discard the bay leaf, and transfer the tomato and onion mixture to a blender or food processor. Whiz briefly and pass through a sieve. Spoon the sauce around the shanks and serve immediately.

Lamb & tomato koftas
serves 4

ingredients

225g/8oz finely minced lean lamb
1½ onions
2 garlic cloves, crushed
1 dried red chilli, finely chopped
2 teaspoons garam masala
2 tablespoons chopped fresh
  mint leaves
2 teaspoons freshly squeezed
  lemon juice

2 tablespoons vegetable oil
4 small tomatoes, quartered
salt

For the dressing
150ml/5fl oz low-fat Greek-style
  yogurt
5cm/2in piece of cucumber, grated
2 tablespoons fresh mint
½ teaspoon cumin seeds, toasted

- If using bamboo or wooden skewers, soak in water for at least 30 minutes to prevent them burning.
- Put the lamb in a bowl. Finely chop 1 onion, and add to the bowl with the garlic and chilli. Stir in the garam masala, mint and lemon juice, and season well with salt. Mix well.
- Divide the mixture in half, then divide each half into 10 equal portions. Form each portion into a small ball – you will have 20 meatballs, or koftas, in all. Roll the koftas in half of the oil to coat. Quarter the remaining onion half, and separate into layers.
- Preheat the grill until hot. Alternately thread 5 of the koftas, 4 tomato quarters and some of the onion layers onto each of four skewers.
- Brush the vegetables with the remaining oil, and cook the koftas under a hot grill for about 10 minutes, turning frequently, until they are browned all over.
- Meanwhile, prepare the dressing. In a small bowl, mix together the yogurt, cucumber, mint and cumin seeds.
- Serve the koftas hot with the yogurt dressing.

French braised lamb
serves 6

ingredients
1/2 small leg of lamb, about
    900g/2lb, trimmed of all fat
1 large onion, cut into thick wedges
2 garlic cloves, crushed
1 teaspoon dried mixed herbs
600ml/1pt lamb stock
4 tablespoons red wine
3 large leeks, cut into chunks
2 turnips, cut into chunks
450g/1lb carrots, cut into chunks
450g/1lb small potatoes
salt and freshly ground black pepper

- Preheat the oven to 180°C/350°F/Gas mark 4.
- Put the lamb in a flameproof casserole dish with the onion, garlic, herbs, stock and wine. Season with salt and pepper. Bring to the boil, cover and transfer to the oven. Cook for 1½ hours.
- Add the remaining vegetables and return to the oven for a further 45 minutes or until the meat is falling off the bone and the vegetables are tender.
- Lift out the lamb. Remove the meat from the bone and cut into neat pieces, discarding the bone and any remaining fat. Skim off any fat from the surface of the casserole. Spoon everything into six warmed serving bowls and serve immediately.

Lamb with mushroom sauce
serves 4

ingredients
2 tablespoons vegetable oil
350g/12oz lean boneless lamb
 fillets, cut into thin strips
3 garlic cloves, crushed
1 leek, sliced
175g/6oz mushrooms, sliced
½ teaspoon sesame oil

For the sauce
1 teaspoon cornflour
4 tablespoon light soy sauce
3 tablespoons Chinese rice wine
½ teaspoon chilli sauce

- To make the sauce, mix together all the sauce ingredients, add 3 tablespoons water and mix again. Set aside.
- Heat a wok or heavy frying pan over a high heat. Add the vegetable oil and, when hot, add the lamb, garlic and leek. Stir-fry for 2–3 minutes.
- Add the mushrooms to the wok or pan, and stir-fry for 1 minute.
- Stir in the sauce, and cook for 2–3 minutes until the lamb is cooked through and tender.
- Sprinkle the sesame oil over the top, and transfer the contents of the work or pan to a warmed serving dish. Serve immediately.

Lamb & anchovies with thyme

serves 4

ingredients

1 teaspoon olive oil
15g/½oz butter
600g/1lb 5oz lamb shoulder or leg,
    cut into 2.5cm/1in chunks
4 garlic cloves, peeled but left whole
3 sprigs of fresh thyme, stalks
    removed
6 anchovy fillets in oil, drained
150ml/5fl oz red wine
150ml/5fl oz vegetable stock
1 teaspoon granulated sugar
50g/2oz black olives, pitted
    and halved
2 tablespoons chopped fresh
    flat-leaf parsley, to garnish

- Heat the oil and butter in a large frying pan. Add the lamb and sauté
  for 4–5 minutes, stirring, until the meat is browned all over.
- Using a mortar and pestle, grind together the garlic, thyme and
  anchovies to make a smooth paste.
- Add the wine and stock to the frying pan. Stir in the anchovy paste and
  the sugar. Bring the mixture to the boil, reduce the heat, cover and leave
  to simmer for 30–40 minutes until the lamb is tender. For the last
  10 minutes of the cooking time, remove the lid in order to allow the
  sauce to reduce slightly.
- Stir the olives into the sauce and mix through. Transfer the lamb and its
  sauce to a serving bowl, garnish with parsley and serve hot.

Stir-fried lamb with orange
serves 4

ingredients
450g/1lb minced lamb
2 garlic cloves, crushed
1 teaspoon cumin seeds
1 teaspoon ground coriander
1 red onion, sliced
finely grated zest and juice of
    1 orange
2 tablespoons light soy sauce
1 orange, peeled and segmented
salt and freshly ground black pepper

- Heat a wok or large heavy frying pan, without adding any oil. Add the lamb to the wok, and dry-fry for 5 minutes until evenly browned. Drain away any excess fat from the wok.
- Add the garlic, cumin, coriander and onion to the wok or pan, and stir-fry for a further 5 minutes.
- Stir in the orange zest and juice and the soy sauce, mixing thoroughly. Cover, reduce the heat and leave to simmer, stirring occasionally, for 15 minutes. Remove the lid, increase the heat and add the orange segments. Stir to mix. Season with salt and pepper, and heat through for a further 2–3 minutes.
- Transfer the stir-fry to warmed serving plates, and serve immediately.

Liver, bacon & onions

serves 4

ingredients
900g/2lb liver, cubed
450ml/¾pt milk
225g/8oz bacon, cubed
2 large onions, chopped
2 tablespoons vegetable oil
200g/7oz plain flour
2 tablespoons cornflour
pinch of dried basil
pinch of dried thyme
salt and freshly ground black pepper

- Soak the liver in the milk and leave in the refrigerator for 24 hours.
- Heat the oil in a heavy frying pan. Fry the bacon and onions, and set aside. Dredge the liver in the flour and season with salt and pepper.
- Add the liver to the frying pan, and fry until slightly pink in the middle. Remove and set aside.
- Mix the cornflour and 3 tablespoons water, and pour into the frying pan while off the heat, adding the basil and thyme. Add the liver, bacon and onions to the gravy, and simmer for 15 minutes. Serve immediately.

Peppered liver
serves 4

ingredients
1 tablespoon plain flour
2 tablespoons crushed black
  peppercorns
225g/8oz lambs' liver, very
  thinly sliced
25g/1oz low-fat spread
1 tablespoon freshly squeezed
  lemon juice
1 small onion, grated
2 tablespoons chopped fresh
  flat-leaf parsley
3 tablespoons Worcestershire sauce

- Mix the flour with the peppercorns, and use to coat the liver.
- Melt the low-fat spread in a large frying pan, and fry the liver on one side until golden underneath. Turn over and cook until the pink juices rise to the surface.
- Remove from the pan, and transfer to warmed serving plates.
- Add the remaining ingredients to the juices in the pan, and cook, stirring, for 1 minute, scraping up any residue in the pan. Spoon over the liver, and serve immediately.

Thai-style rabbit
serves 4

ingredients

300ml/10fl oz dry white wine
350g/12oz onion, diced
4 garlic cloves, chopped
3 tablespoons sesame oil
3 tablespoons Thai fish sauce
2 x 2.5cm/1in pieces of
  galangal, grated
2 fresh red chillies, seeded and
  thinly sliced
1 rabbit, head removed, jointed and
  cut into three
50ml/2fl oz sunflower oil
2 celery sticks, thinly sliced
300ml/10fl oz chicken stock
salt and freshly ground black pepper
1 lemon grass stalk
2 kaffir lime leaves

- In a large bowl, mix the wine, two-thirds of the onion, half of the garlic, the sesame oil, the fish sauce, half of the galangal and the chillies. Put in the rabbit pieces and turn to coat in the marinade. Cover in cling film and marinate in the refrigerator overnight.
- Just before cooking, sear the rabbit pieces in 1 tablespoon of the sunflower oil in a heavy frying pan, and transfer to a plate. They should still be raw in the middle.
- Add the remaining oil to the pan, and fry the remaining onion and garlic and the celery until softened, then add the remaining galangal and stir before returning the rabbit to the pan.
- Add the stock with any remaining marinade, and season with salt and pepper. Add the lemon grass and lime leaves. Cover the pan and simmer for 10–15 minutes.
- Check that the rabbit is done. Discard the lemon grass, and serve the rabbit immediately.

Rabbit with parsley sauce

serves 4

ingredients

100ml/3½fl oz light soy sauce
5 drops of Tabasco sauce
½ teaspoon ground white pepper
1 tablespoon sweet smoked paprika
1 teaspoon dried basil
1.4kg/3lb rabbit, cut into pieces
3 tablespoons olive oil
75g/3oz plain flour
1 large onion, finely sliced
250ml/9fl oz dry white wine
250ml/9fl oz chicken stock
2 garlic cloves, finely chopped
4 tablespoons chopped fresh
  flat-leaf parsley
2 teaspoons salt

- Combine the soy sauce, Tabasco, white pepper, paprika and basil in a medium bowl. Add the rabbit pieces and turn them over in the mixture so that they are coated thoroughly. Leave to marinate in the refrigerator for at least 1 hour.
- Preheat the oven to 180°C/350°F/Gas mark 4.
- Heat the oil in a flameproof casserole dish. Coat the rabbit pieces lightly in the flour, shaking off the excess. Brown the rabbit pieces in the hot oil for 5–6 minutes, turning them frequently. Remove with a slotted spoon and set aside on a plate or dish.
- Add the onion to the casserole dish, and cook over a low heat for 8–10 minutes until softened. Increase the heat, add the wine and stir well to mix in all the cooking juices.
- Return the rabbit and any juices to the casserole dish. Add the stock, garlic, parsley and salt. Mix well and turn the rabbit to coat with the sauce. Cover and transfer to the oven. Cook for about 1 hour until the rabbit is tender, stirring occasionally. Serve hot with mashed potatoes or boiled rice.

Sweet & sour venison

serves 4

ingredients

1 tablespoon vegetable oil

350g/12oz venison steak, cut into
  thin strips

1 garlic clove, crushed

2.5cm/1in piece of fresh root
  ginger, finely chopped

1 bunch of spring onions, trimmed
  and cut into 2.5cm/1in pieces

1 red pepper, halved, seeded and
  cut into 2.5cm/1in pieces

100g/4oz mangetout, topped
  and tailed

100g/4oz baby sweetcorn

3 tablespoons light soy sauce, plus
  extra for serving

1 tablespoon white wine vinegar

2 tablespoons dry sherry

2 teaspoons clear honey

225g/8oz canned pineapple
  pieces in natural juice, drained

25g/1oz beansprouts

- Heat the oil in a large frying pan or wok until hot, and stir-fry the
  venison, garlic and ginger for 5 minutes.
- Add the spring onion, red pepper, mangetout and baby sweetcorn to the
  pan, then add the 3 tablespoons soy sauce and the vinegar, sherry and
  honey. Stir-fry for a further 5 minutes, keeping the heat high.
- Carefully stir in the pineapple and beansprouts, and cook for a further
  1–2 minutes to heat through. Serve hot.

Venison with plums
serves 4

ingredients
2 tablespoons olive oil
500g/1lb 2oz venison fillet, cut into
    1cm/½in strips
4 plums, halved, stoned and sliced
1 teaspoon chopped fresh sage
6 spring onions, cut into 2.5cm/1in
    lengths
1 tablespoon cornflour
2 tablespoons freshly squeezed
    orange juice
150ml/5fl oz chicken stock
4 tablespoons port
1 tablespoon redcurrant jelly
1 tablespoon brandy
salt and freshly ground black pepper

• Heat the oil in a heavy frying pan, and sauté the venison over a high
  heat for about 2 minutes until browned. Remove from the pan with a
  slotted spoon and set on a plate.
• Add the plums, sage and spring onions to the pan, and cook for
  2 minutes, stirring occasionally.
• Mix the cornflour with the orange juice, and add to the pan. Add the
  stock, port and redcurrant jelly, and heat, stirring, until thickened.
• Return the venison to the pan, season with salt and pepper, and pour in
  the brandy. Heat through and serve immediately.

Mixed game pie
serves 4

ingredients

450g/1lb mixed game meat, off
   the bone
1 small onion, halved
2 bay leaves
2 carrots, halved
4 black peppercorns
1 tablespoon vegetable oil
75g/3oz rindless streaky bacon,
   chopped
1 tablespoon plain flour
2 tablespoons sweet sherry
2 teaspoons ground ginger
grated zest and juice of ½ orange
350g/12oz ready-made puff pastry
beaten egg or milk, to glaze
salt and freshly ground black pepper

- Put the game meat in a deep pan with half an onion, the bay leaves, carrots and black peppercorns. Cover with water and bring to the boil. Simmer until the liquid is reduced to about 300ml/10fl oz, then strain the stock and keep to one side.
- Cut the game meat into bite-size pieces. Chop the remaining onion half. Heat the oil in a frying pan, sauté the onion until softened. Add the bacon and game meat, and sauté quickly to seal. Sprinkle on the flour and stir until beginning to brown. Gradually add the reserved stock, stirring as it thickens, then add the sherry, ginger, orange zest and juice. Season with salt and pepper. Simmer for 20 minutes.
- Transfer the contents of the pan to a 900ml/1½pt pie dish, and allow to cool slightly. Put a pie funnel in the centre of the filling to help hold up the pastry.
- Preheat the oven to 220°C/425°F/Gas mark 7. Roll out the pastry until slightly larger than the dish. Place over the top of the dish, and brush with egg or milk. Bake in the oven for 15 minutes.
- Reduce the oven temperature to 190°C/375°F/Gas mark 5, and bake for a further 25–30 minutes. Serve hot.

Madeira roast pheasant

serves 6

ingredients

200g/7oz butter
1 onion, coarsely chopped
3 celery sticks, coarsely chopped
2 carrots, coarsely chopped
2 bay leaves
2 tablespoons dried mixed herbs
3 pheasants
4 chicken wings

2 chicken breasts
50ml/2fl oz Madeira
600ml/1pt chicken stock
1 tablespoon plain flour
sprigs of fresh flat-leaf parsley,
   to garnish
salt and freshly ground
   black pepper

- Preheat the oven to 230°C/450°F/.Gas mark 8.
- Melt 25g/1oz of the butter in a large roasting tin. Stir in the onion, celery, carrots, bay leaves and half of the mixed herbs. Top with the pheasant giblets and necks, and the chicken wings and breasts. Roast in the oven for about 40 minutes until well browned, turning frequently.
- Meanwhile, make the herb butter by mixing half of the remaining butter with the remaining mixed herbs.
- Reduce the oven temperature to 190°C/375°F/Gas mark 5.
- Pat the pheasant dry inside and out. Loosen the breast skin on each by gently sliding your fingers under the neck flap and down between the breast meat and skin, being careful not to tear the skin. Spread the herb butter evenly over the breast. Sprinkle each cavity with salt and pepper. Put 2 tablespoons herb butter into each cavity. Truss the pheasants to hold their shape. Arrange on their sides on top of the vegetable mixture.
- Roast in the oven for 15 minutes, basting frequently with the pan juices. Turn over and roast for a further 15 minutes, basting frequently.
- Turn the pheasants breast side up. Add the Madeira to the tin, and roast for about 15 minutes until the juices run pale pink when the thickest part of the thigh is pierced, basting frequently. Transfer the pheasants to a platter and discard the string. Tent with foil.
- Add the stock to the roasting tin. Boil for about 6 minutes until reduced to 600ml/1pt liquid, scraping up any browned bits. Melt the remaining butter in a small heavy pan over a low heat. Add the flour and stir for 3 minutes. Whisk in the sauce in a thin stream. Simmer for 5 minutes, stirring frequently.
- Garnish the pheasant with parsley, and serve with the sauce.

Fried venison steaks
serves 4

ingredients

1 orange
1 lemon
75g/3oz fresh cranberries
1 teaspoon grated fresh
   root ginger
1 sprig of fresh thyme
1 teaspoon Dijon mustard
4 tablespoons redcurrant jelly

150ml/5fl oz ruby port
2 teaspoons sunflower oil
4 venison steaks, about
   100g/4oz each
2 shallots, finely chopped
salt and freshly ground
   black pepper

- Pare the zest from half the orange and half the lemon using a vegetable peeler, then cut into very fine strips.
- Blanch the strips in a small pan of boiling water for about 5 minutes until tender. Drain the strips and refresh under cold water.
- Squeeze the juice from the orange and lemon, then pour into a small pan. Add the cranberries, ginger, thyme, mustard, redcurrant jelly and port. Cook over a low heat until the jelly melts.
- Bring the sauce to the boil, stirring occasionally, then cover the pan and reduce the heat. Cook gently for about 15 minutes, until the cranberries are just tender. Remove from the heat.
- Heat the oil in a heavy frying pan, add the venison steaks and cook over a high heat for 2–3 minutes.
- Turn the steaks over and add the shallots to the pan. Cook the steaks on the other side for 2–3 minutes, depending on whether you want them rare or medium.
- Just before the end of cooking, pour in the sauce and add the strips of zest. Leave the sauce to bubble for a few seconds to thicken slightly, then remove the thyme sprig and season with salt and pepper. Transfer the steaks to serving plates, and spoon the sauce over the top. Serve immediately with mashed potato and broccoli.

Pheasant breast with cinnamon marmalade

serves 4

ingredients

4 boneless pheasant breasts
25g/1oz butter
25g/1oz plain flour
¼ teaspoon ground cinnamon
125ml/4fl oz freshly squeezed
    orange juice
2 tablespoons orange marmalade
¾ teaspoon instant chicken bouillon
1 tablespoon orange liqueur
100g/4oz green seedless grapes
1 orange, peeled and cut
    into sections
50g/2oz toasted almonds

- Preheat the oven to 170°C/325°F/Gas mark 3.
- Line a 20cm/8in square baking dish with foil, leaving a small foil collar. Wash the pheasant breasts and pat dry. Arrange in the prepared dish.
- Melt the butter in a saucepan over a medium heat. Stir in the flour and cinnamon. Cook until smooth. Stir in the orange juice, marmalade and bouillon.
- Cook until thickened, stirring constantly. Stir in the liqueur. Spoon over the pheasant and seal the foil tightly.
- Bake in the oven for about 30 minutes until the pheasant is tender. Spoon the grapes and orange sections over the pheasant, and bake, uncovered, for a further 5 minutes. Sprinkle with the almonds and serve hot with rice.

Chicken & Other Poultry

Chicken has long been a favourite all around the world, but this chapter also introduces you to cooking with other poultry such as turkey, duck, goose, quail and guinea fowl. Familiar dishes such as coq au vin and traditional fried chicken sit alongside recipes for Bacon-wrapped Turkey Burgers, Duck with Cumberland Sauce and Guinea Fowl with Fennel, showing you the limitless possibilities of cooking with chicken and other poultry.

Parsley, walnut & orange chicken
serves 6

ingredients
125ml/4fl oz extra virgin olive oil
100g/4oz onion, finely chopped
75g/3oz walnuts, finely chopped
grated zest and juice of 1 large
   orange
6 tablespoons chopped fresh
   flat-leaf parsley
1 tablespoon cranberry sauce
1 large egg, beaten
6 chicken breasts
1 tablespoon Dijon mustard
salt and freshly ground black pepper

- Heat 3 tablespoons of the oil in a small heavy pan and add the onion. Cover and sweat for 10 minutes or until soft and starting to caramelize, then cool. In a bowl, combine the walnuts, orange zest, parsley, cranberry sauce and egg, and season well with salt and pepper. Stir in the cooled onion mixture, and put to one side.
- Preheat the oven to 200°C/400°F/Gas mark 6. Gently ease up the chicken skin and push in the stuffing. Reshape the chicken and put in a large roasting tin.
- Spread with the mustard and season with salt and pepper. Drizzle over 2 tablespoons of the oil and roast for 25–30 minutes, basting occasionally. Leave to cool, reserving the roasting juices.
- When the chicken is cold, slice thickly and arrange in a serving dish. Whisk together 2 tablespoons orange juice with the remaining oil and some salt and pepper. Add the strained chicken juices (skim off any fat from the surface first), pour the sauce over the chicken and serve.

Pepper chicken with ginger & garlic

serves 4

ingredients

3 garlic cloves, roughly chopped
2.5cm/1in piece of fresh root
   ginger, sliced
4 tablespoons vegetable oil
2 onions, finely sliced
10 curry leaves
1 fresh green chilli, slit lengthways
1 teaspoon ground coriander
½ teaspoon ground turmeric
pinch of salt
500g/1lb 2oz skinless chicken
   breast fillets, cubed
1 teaspoon garam masala
½ teaspoon ground black pepper

- Using a mortar and pestle, pound the garlic and ginger to a fine paste. Set aside.
- Heat the oil in a large frying pan. Add the onions, curry leaves and green chilli and cook over a medium heat until the onions are brown.
- Add the garlic-ginger paste and cook for 5 minutes, stirring occasionally. Add the coriander, turmeric and salt. Mix well and cook for a further 5 minutes.
- Add the chicken to the frying pan, stir through, then add 225ml/8fl oz water and the garam masala. Mix well, cover and cook over a low heat for 5 minutes or until the chicken is cooked through.
- Stir the ground pepper into the mixture, then remove the pan from the heat and serve.

Vietnamese chicken & sweet potato curry

serves 4–6

ingredients

450g/1lb sweet potato, peeled and
   cut into 2.5cm/1in chunks
4 tablespoons groundnut oil
1 tablespoon hot curry powder
1 teaspoon ground turmeric
1 teaspoon dried red chilli flakes
450g/1lb skinless chicken breast
   fillets, cut into bite-size pieces
300ml/10fl oz chicken stock
150ml/5fl oz coconut milk
salt and freshly ground black pepper

For the paste
1 large onion, roughly chopped
3 garlic cloves, chopped
1 lemon grass stalk, tough outer
   layer removed, finely chopped

- Put all the ingredients for the paste in a blender or food processor, and purée to produce a thick paste. Set aside.
- Cook the potato in a pan of boiling salted water for 8–10 minutes until tender. Drain and set aside.
- Heat the oil in a wok. Add the paste and fry over a gentle heat, stirring, for about 5 minutes until softened but not coloured. Stir in the curry powder, turmeric and chilli flakes, and fry for 30 seconds until aromatic.
- Add the chicken to the wok, stir to coat it evenly in the spice mixture and fry, stirring, for 2 minutes. Add the stock, bring to the boil, then reduce the heat and simmer gently for 10 minutes or until most of the stock has evaporated. Stir in the coconut milk, then season with salt and pepper. Cook the curry gently, stirring occasionally, for a further 10 minutes.
- Stir in the cooked sweet potato, and heat through for 3–4 minutes. Taste and adjust the seasoning if necessary. Serve hot with rice.

Khara masala balti chicken

serves 4

ingredients

3 curry leaves
¼ teaspoon mustard seeds
¼ teaspoon fennel seeds
¼ teaspoon onion seeds
½ teaspoon crushed dried red chillies
½ teaspoon cumin seeds
½ teaspoon fenugreek seeds
½ teaspoon crushed pomegranate seeds
1 teaspoon salt

1 teaspoon shredded fresh root ginger
3 garlic cloves, sliced
50ml/2fl oz corn oil
4 fresh green chillies, slit lengthways
1 large onion, sliced
1 tomato, sliced
700g/1½lb skinless chicken breast fillets, cubed

- In a large bowl, mix together the curry leaves, mustard seeds, fennel seeds, onion seeds, crushed red chillies, cumin seeds, fenugreek seeds and crushed pomegranate seeds. Add the salt, ginger and garlic.
- Heat a wok until very hot. Add the oil and, when the oil is hot, add the spice mixture, then the green chillies. Stir-fry for a minute or so. Add the onion to the wok and stir-fry over a medium heat for 5–7 minutes.
- Add the tomato and chicken pieces to the wok and cook over a medium heat for 7 minutes or until the chicken is cooked through and the sauce has reduced slightly.
- Stir the mixture over the heat for a further 3–5 minutes, then serve hot.

Chicken with ciabatta & Parma ham

serves 6

ingredients

2 tablespoons olive oil

800g/1lb 12oz leeks, trimmed and cut into 1cm/½in slices

150ml/5fl oz dry sherry

200ml/7fl oz chicken stock

400ml/14fl oz crème fraîche

2 tablespoons wholegrain mustard

3 tablespoons chopped fresh sage

1 tablespoon chopped fresh flat-leaf parsley

700g/1½lb skinless chicken breast fillets, cut into 1cm/½in strips

100g/4oz Gruyère cheese, finely grated

salt and freshly ground black pepper

For the topping

200g/7oz ciabatta breadcrumbs

3 tablespoons olive oil

75g/3oz Parma ham, roughly torn

2 tablespoons chopped fresh flat-leaf parsley

- Heat the oil in a large non-stick frying pan, add the leeks and cook over a gentle heat for 15–20 minutes until softened. Remove with a slotted spoon and put to one side. Add the sherry and stock, bring to the boil and bubble until reduced by about a quarter. Allow to cool.
- Preheat the oven to 190°C/375°F/Gas mark 5.
- In a bowl, mix the crème fraîche, flour, mustard, sage and parsley together with some salt and pepper,. Mix in the reduced stock and leeks.
- Put the chicken into a 2.3 litre/4pt ovenproof dish, and pour the sauce mixture over. Sprinkle the cheese on top.
- To make the topping, put the breadcrumbs in a bowl with the oil, ham and parsley. Toss together and sprinkle over the chicken.
- Cook the chicken in the oven for 50–60 minutes or until bubbling at the sides. Serve hot

Medium balti chicken
serves 6

ingredients

2 tablespoons vegetable oil
900g/2lb skinless chicken breast
  fillets, cubed
1 onion, sliced
225g/8oz green beans, cut into
  5cm/2in lengths
350g/12oz tomatoes, chopped
15g/½oz fresh basil, roughly torn
salt and freshly ground
  black pepper

For the sauce
4 tablespoons vegetable oil
2 large onions, chopped
3 garlic cloves, chopped
2 tablespoons finely chopped fresh
  root ginger

4 fresh green chillies, chopped
15 cloves
seeds from 10 green
  cardamom pods
1 teaspoons ground coriander
1 teaspoon paprika
1 teaspoon ground cinnamon
1 teaspoon ground turmeric
2 teaspoons ground cumin
1 teaspoon ground fenugreek
1 teaspoon mustard powder
400g/14oz tinned chopped
  plum tomatoes
600ml/1pt vegetable stock
2 tablespoons freshly squeezed
  lemon juice
pared zest of 1 lemon

- To make the sauce, heat the oil in a heavy pan, and fry the onions,
  garlic and ginger for 2 minutes. Add the chillies and cook for a further
  2 minutes. Add the spices and stir-fry for 30 seconds until aromatic. Add
  the tomatoes, stock, lemon juice and lemon zest. Bring to the boil and
  simmer, uncovered, for 30 minutes. Discard the lemon zest.
- Heat the oil in a large balti pan or wok, and stir-fry the chicken for
  5 minutes until golden. Add the onion and green beans, and continue to
  stir-fry for 1 minute.
- Pour in the sauce and simmer gently for 8 minutes, stirring occasionally.
  Stir in the tomatoes and basil, and cook for a further 2 minutes or until
  the chicken is tender. Season with salt and pepper. Serve hot.

Garlic & nut butter chicken

serves 12

ingredients

225g/8oz roasted salted mixed nuts,
  roughly chopped
5 garlic cloves, roughly chopped
450g/1lb butter, softened
4 tablespoons chopped fresh
  flat-leaf parsley
2 lemons
225g/8oz puff pastry
1 large egg, beaten
1 tablespoon poppy seeds
1 tablespoon caraway seeds
12 small skinless chicken breast fillets
900ml/1½pt hot chicken stock
freshly ground black pepper

- Combine the nuts and garlic with the butter, parsley and 2 tablespoons of lemon juice, and season well with pepper. Cover and chill.
- Roll out the puff pastry thinly. Prick well and leave to rest for 30 minutes.
- Preheat the oven to 200°C/400°F/Gas mark 6. Brush the pastry with beaten egg and, using a small cutter, stamp out shapes. Sprinkle with the poppy and caraway seeds, and bake in the oven for 10 minutes.
- Arrange the chicken breasts in a roasting tin, and half-cover with the hot stock. Cover with foil and cook for 30 minutes or until cooked through.
- To serve, melt the nut butter mixture. Drain the cooked chicken breasts from the stock, and put on a heated serving dish. Spoon the melted butter over, and garnish with the pastry shapes.

Indonesian-style satay chicken

serves 4

ingredients

50g/2oz raw peanuts
3 tablespoons vegetable oil
1 small onion, finely chopped
2.5cm/1in piece of fresh root
    ginger, finely chopped
1 garlic clove, crushed
700g/11/2lb skinless chicken thigh
    fillets, cubed
100g/4oz creamed coconut,
    roughly chopped
1 tablespoon chilli sauce
2 tablespoons crunchy peanut butter
1 teaspoon soft dark brown sugar
150ml/5fl oz milk
¼ teaspoon salt

- Shell the peanuts and remove the skins by rubbing them between the palms of your hands. Put them in a small bowl, add just enough water to cover and soak for 1 minute. Drain the nuts and cut into slivers.

- Heat the wok and add 1 teaspoon of the oil. When the oil is hot, stir-fry the peanuts for 1 minute until crisp and golden. Remove with a slotted spoon and drain on kitchen paper.

- Add the remaining oil to the hot wok. When the oil is hot, add the onion, ginger and garlic, and stir-fry for 2–3 minutes until softened but not browned. Remove with a slotted spoon and drain on kitchen paper.

- Add the chicken pieces to the wok and stir-fry for 3–4 minutes until crisp and golden on all sides. Thread onto bamboo skewers and keep warm.

- Add the creamed coconut to the hot wok in small pieces, and stir-fry until melted. Add the chilli sauce, peanut butter and ginger mixture, and simmer for 2 minutes. Stir in the sugar, milk and salt, and simmer for a further 3 minutes.

- Serve the skewered chicken hot with a dish of the hot sauce sprinkled with the roasted peanuts and vegetables.

Chicken green masala
serves 4

ingredients

2 tablespoons vegetable oil
2 onions, finely chopped
1 medium chicken, cleaned and cut
    into small pieces
4 tomatoes, finely chopped
salt

For the spice paste
1 large bunch of fresh coriander
    leaves, roughly chopped
1 large onion, roughly chopped
10 fresh green chillies

5 garlic cloves
5cm/2in piece of fresh root ginger,
    chopped
2 cinnamon sticks, about
    5cm/2in each
2 teaspoons coriander seeds
1 teaspoon cumin seeds
1 teaspoon peppercorns
1 teaspoon poppy seeds
¼ teaspoon ground turmeric
2 cardamom pods
2 cloves

- Put all the ingredients for the spice paste in a blender or food processor, and work to a very fine paste. Set aside.
- In a large saucepan, heat the oil over a medium heat. Add the onions and sauté for 5 minutes or until the onions are golden brown. Stir in the spice paste, reduce the heat and cook for a further 5 minutes.
- Add the chicken, tomatoes and a little salt, and mix well. Cover and cook gently for 15 minutes, stirring occasionally.
- Remove the lid from the pan and continue cooking, uncovered, for a further 5–10 minutes until the chicken is done. Serve hot.

Chicken & chickpea stew

serves 4

ingredients

4 skinless chicken breast fillets
2 tablespoons extra virgin olive oil
1 onion, halved and sliced
2 garlic cloves, minced
1 carrot, sliced
1 bay leaf
1 cinnamon stick
1 teaspoon ground cumin
1 teaspoon ground coriander
1 teaspoon ground ginger
½ teaspoon dried red chilli flakes
2 pinches of saffron powder
1 red pepper, seeded and cut into
  2.5cm/1in squares
1 yellow pepper, seeded and cut
  into 2.5cm/1in squares

100g/4oz fennel bulb,
  thinly sliced
50ml/2fl oz dry white wine
400g/14oz canned chopped plum
  tomatoes, drained
225ml/8fl oz vegetable stock
550g/1lb 4oz canned cooked
  chickpeas, rinsed and drained
10 large green olives, pitted and
  cut into slivers
2 tablespoons freshly squeezed
  lemon juice
1 tablespoon grated lemon zest
2 tablespoons chopped fresh
  flat-leaf parsley
salt and ground black pepper

- Cut the chicken breasts on the diagonal into 5cm/2in strips and season with salt and pepper. Heat 1 tablespoon of the oil in a large non-stick frying pan over a medium-high heat, and sauté the chicken in batches for 1–2 minutes until it is no longer pink on the outside. Remove the chicken from the pan and set aside.

- Heat the remaining oil over a medium heat, and sauté the onion, garlic, carrot, bay leaf and all the spices for 10 minutes or until the vegetables begin to soften. Add the red and yellow peppers, fennel and wine, and cook for about 5 minutes until the pan is nearly dry.

- Stir in the tomatoes and stock, and bring to the boil. Reduce the heat and simmer the mixture, covered, for 10 minutes. Add the reserved chicken and chickpeas to the pan, and continue to simmer, covered, for another 15–20 minutes until the stew has thickened.

- Just before serving, stir in the olives, lemon juice, lemon zest and parsley. Serve hot on a bed of rice or couscous.

Chicken with lime stuffing

serves 4

ingredients
1 chicken, about 2.3kg/5lb
vegetable oil for brushing
225g/8oz courgette, cut into strips
25g/1oz butter
juice of 1 lime

For the stuffing
100g/4oz courgettes, trimmed and
   coarsely grated
100g/4oz soft cheese
finely grated zest of 1 lime
2 tablespoons fresh breadcrumbs
salt and freshly ground black pepper

- Preheat the oven to 190°C/375°F/Gas mark 5.
- To make the stuffing, mix the courgette with the cheese, lime zest, breadcrumbs and seasoning.
- Carefully ease the skin away from the breast of the chicken with your fingertips, taking care not to split the skin. Push the stuffing under the skin, to cover the breast evenly.
- Put the chicken in a roasting tin, brush with the oil and roast in the oven for 20 minutes per 500g/1lb 2oz plus 20 minutes, or until the juices run clear when the thickest part of the thigh is pierced with a skewer. Remove from the oven, cover with foil and rest for 5 minutes.
- Sauté the courgettes in the butter and lime juice until just tender, then serve hot with the chicken.

Apple-stuffed chicken

serves 2

ingredients

900g/2lb chicken, halved
   lengthways
75g/3oz butter, melted
175g/6oz dessert apples
½ onion, chopped
50g/2oz celery sticks, chopped
200g/7oz croûtons
75ml/3fl oz water
salt and freshly ground black pepper

- Preheat the grill. Break the wing, hip and drumstick joints of the chicken so that it will remain flat during cooking. Place the chicken skin side up in a baking tray, brush with 15g/1/2oz of the butter and season with salt and pepper.
- Grill for about 20 minutes until lightly browned. Turn and brush the cavity side with 15g/1/2oz butter and season. Grill for a further 15–20 minutes until tender.
- Peel, core and chop the apples. In a small heavy saucepan, cook the apples, onion and celery in the remaining butter until tender. Add the croûtons and 75ml/3fl oz water, and season with salt and pepper.
- Put the apple mixture into the chicken cavity, and grill the chicken for a further 5 minutes. Serve hot.

Soy-braised chicken
serves 6–8

ingredients
1 chicken, about 1.4kg/3lb
1 tablespoon ground black
  peppercorns
2 tablespoons minced fresh
  root ginger
75ml/3fl oz light soy sauce
3 tablespoons Chinese rice wine
1 tablespoon light brown sugar
vegetable oil for deep-frying
600ml/1pt chicken stock
2 teaspoons salt
25g/1oz crystallized sugar

- Rub the chicken both inside and out with the peppercorns and ginger.
  Marinate the chicken with the soy sauce, rice wine and brown sugar for
  at least 3 hours in the refrigerator, turning it several times.
- Heat a wok until very hot. Add the oil and, when the oil is hot enough,
  remove the chicken from the marinade (reserving the marinade), and
  deep-fry for 6 minutes or until brown all over. Remove and drain on
  kitchen paper.
- Pour off any excess oil, add the marinade with the stock, salt and
  crystallized sugar, and bring to the boil. Return the chicken to the pan,
  cover and braise the chicken in the sauce for 35–40 minutes, turning
  once or twice.
- Remove the chicken from the wok and allow it cool a little before
  chopping it into bite-size pieces. Pour the sauce over the chicken and
  serve immediately.

Chicken & ricotta in wine

serves 4

ingredients
100g/4oz frozen spinach, thawed
100g/4oz ricotta cheese
pinch of grated nutmeg
4 skinless chicken breast fillets,
    about 175g/6oz each
4 Parma ham slices
25g/1oz butter
1 tablespoon olive oil
12 small shallots
100g/4oz button mushrooms, sliced
1 tablespoon plain flour
150ml/5fl oz dry white wine
300ml/10fl oz chicken stock
salt and freshly ground black pepper

- Preheat the oven to 200°C/400°F/Gas mark 6.
- Put the spinach in a sieve, and press out the water with a spoon. Mix with the ricotta and nutmeg, and season with salt and pepper.
- Using a sharp knife, slit each chicken breast through the side and enlarge each cut to form a pocket. Fill with the spinach mixture, then reshape the chicken breasts. Wrap each breast tightly in a slice of ham, and secure with cocktail sticks. Cover and chill in the refrigerator.
- Heat the butter and oil in a frying pan, and brown the chicken breasts for 2 minutes on each side. Transfer the chicken to a large shallow ovenproof dish, and keep warm until required.
- Sauté the shallots and mushrooms for 2–3 minutes until lightly browned. Stir in the flour, then gradually add the wine and stock. Bring to the boil, stirring constantly. Season with salt and pepper, and spoon the mixture around the chicken.
- Cook the chicken in the oven for 20 minutes. Turn the chicken over and cook for a further 10 minutes. Remove the cocktail sticks, and serve the chicken with the sauce.

Chicken in peanut sauce

serves 4

ingredients

100g/4oz shelled unsalted
   raw peanuts
1.4kg/3lb chicken, jointed
2 tablespoons sunflower oil
1 onion, finely chopped
100g/4oz tomatoes, peeled and
   roughly chopped
1 tablespoon tomato purée
1 teaspoon cayenne pepper
1 tablespoon paprika
½ teaspoon ground ginger
½ teaspoon ground cinnamon
½ teaspoon ground coriander
pinch of salt
450ml/3/4pt chicken stock

- Preheat the oven to 200°C/400°F/Gas mark 6.
- Spread the peanuts on a baking tray, and toast in the oven for to
  6–8 minutes until lightly browned, shaking and checking frequently.
  Cool, then grind to a powdery paste.
- Heat the oil in a frying pan and brown the chicken. Transfer to a
  flameproof casserole dish. Sweat the onion gently in the same oil until
  golden. Add the tomatoes, tomato purée, spices and salt. Stir for about
  3 minutes, then pour in the stock. Bring to the boil, stirring, then pour
  over the chicken. Cover, reduce the heat and simmer for 30 minutes.
- Stir in the peanuts. Continue to simmer, covered, for a further
  10–15 minutes, until the chicken is tender and the sauce has thickened.
  Skim off any fat from the surface, then check the seasoning and adjust if
  necessary. Serve hot.

Thai chicken green curry

serves 6

ingredients

100g/4oz fresh coriander
3 fresh red chillies, halved
  lengthways and seeded
3 spring onions, chopped
3 garlic cloves, chopped
1 tablespoon olive oil
1½ teaspoons grated lime zest
2 tablespoons freshly squeezed
  lime juice
2 teaspoons light soy sauce
1 teaspoon anchovy paste
1 teaspoon ground ginger

1 teaspoon ground cumin
1 teaspoon ground coriander
½ teaspoon salt
3 large carrots, thinly sliced
450g/1lb small red potatoes, cut
  into chunks
900g/2lb skinless chicken thigh
  fillets, cut into chunks
400ml/14fl oz milk
¾ teaspoon coconut essence
225g/8oz frozen peas

- Put the fresh coriander, chillies, spring onions, garlic, oil, lime zest, lime juice, soy sauce, anchovy paste, ginger, cumin, ground coriander and salt in a blender or food processor. Purée to a paste.
- In a large frying pan over a low heat, cook the paste for 5 minutes. Add the carrots, potatoes and 175ml/6fl oz water, and bring to the boil. Reduce the heat and simmer for 5 minutes.
- Add the chicken and cook for 5 minutes. Stir in the milk and coconut essence, and simmer for 10 minutes or until the chicken is cooked through. Stir in the peas, and cook for 3 minutes or until heated through. Serve hot.

Traditional fried chicken

serves 8

ingredients

2 small chickens, each cut into
    8 pieces
250g/9oz plain flour
1 teaspoon salt
½ teaspoon mustard powder
½ teaspoon ground black pepper
400g/14oz lard

For the gravy
25g/1oz butter melted
1 tablespoon plain flour
175ml/6fl oz chicken stock
50ml/2fl oz single cream
salt and freshly ground black pepper

- Wash each piece of chicken under cold running water. Pat dry with kitchen paper.
- Put the flour, salt, mustard and pepper in a large bag. Shake to blend the ingredients. Drop the chicken pieces into the bag a few at a time, and shake the bag vigorously until each piece is thoroughly coated. Remove the chicken pieces from the bag, and shake off the excess flour.
- Heat the lard in a heavy frying pan over a medium heat. The fat should fill the pan to a depth of about 5cm/2in. Add more lard if necessary.
- When the fat is hot but not smoking, begin frying the chicken. Put in the thigh and legs first, and cover the pan. Lift the cover occasionally to check that the chicken is not burning. When it turns a dark brown, flip each piece over, cover, and again cook until dark brown. Cook the other chicken pieces in the same way.
- To make the gravy, pour out the frying fat from the pan and replace it with the butter, then stir in the flour. When bubbly, stir in the stock and cream, and cook until the sauce thickens. Season with salt and pepper. Serve the sauce separately.

Coronation chicken

serves 8

ingredients

½ lemon
2.3kg/5lb chicken
1 onion, quartered
1 carrot, quartered
8 black peppercorns, crushed
1 teaspoon salt

For the sauce
1 small onion, chopped
15g/½oz butter
1 tablespoon curry paste

1 tablespoon tomato purée
125ml/4fl oz red wine
1 bay leaf
juice of ½ lemon
2–3 teaspoons apricot jam
300ml/10fl oz mayonnaise
125ml/4fl oz double or whipping
cream, whipped
salt and freshly ground
black pepper
watercress, to garnish

- Put the lemon in the cavity of the chicken, then put the chicken in a saucepan that it just fits. Add the onion, carrot, peppercorns and salt to the pan.
- Add sufficient water to come two-thirds of the way up the chicken, bring to the boil, then cover and cook gently for about 1½ hours until the chicken juices run clear.
- Transfer the chicken to a large bowl, pour the cooking liquid over it and leave to cool. When cold, strip the meat from the chicken, discarding the skin and bones, then chop or tear the meat into bite-size pieces.
- To make the sauce, take a frying pan and sweat the onion in the butter until soft. Add the curry paste, tomato purée, wine, bay leaf and lemon juice, then cook for 10 minutes. Add the jam, then push the mixture through a sieve and leave to cool.
- Beat the mixture into the mayonnaise. Fold in the cream, then season with salt and pepper. Stir in the chicken pieces until evenly coated. Chill until ready to serve, garnished with a little watercress.

Chicken & beef satay

serves 4

ingredients

2cm/¾in piece of tamarind pulp
100ml/3½fl oz hot water
2 skinless chicken breast fillets
350g/12oz flash-fry steak
1 teaspoon coriander seeds
1 teaspoon cumin seeds
1 onion, chopped
1 tablespoon light soy sauce
2 garlic cloves, crushed
2 tablespoons vegetable oil
1 teaspoon ground turmeric
1 teaspoon five-spice powder
pinch of salt

For the peanut sauce
100g/4oz smooth peanut butter
100g/4oz creamed coconut,
   crumbled
4 teaspoons freshly squeezed
   lemon juice
1 tablespoon light soy sauce
1 tablespoon soft brown sugar
1 teaspoon chilli powder

- Soak the tamarind pulp in the hot water for a few minutes, then hold the pulp over the bowl and squeeze to extract as much liquid as possible. Discard the pulp and set the tamarind liquid aside.
- Prepare the satay by using a sharp knife to cut the chicken and the steak into small chunks. Put in a deep baking tray and set aside.
- Heat a small frying pan, add the coriander and cumin seeds, and dry-roast for 1–2 minutes until aromatic, stirring constantly. Remove from the heat and pound to a fine powder using a mortar and pestle.
- Put the pounded spices in a blender or food processor with the onion, tamarind liquid, soy sauce, garlic, vegetable oil, turmeric, five-spice powder and a pinch of salt. Whiz for a few seconds, then pour over the meat. Cover and leave to marinate in the refrigerator for 4 hours, turning the meat occasionally.
- Thread the meat onto soaked bamboo skewers. Put under a hot grill or on a barbecue, and grill for 10–15 minutes, turning frequently and basting with any extra marinade.
- To make the peanut sauce, put the peanut butter, coconut, lemon juice, soy sauce, sugar and chilli powder in a clean pan. Add 300ml/10fl oz water, and bring slowly to the boil. Reduce the heat and simmer gently for 5 minutes until the coconut has dissolved and the sauce thickens. Adjust the seasoning to taste.
- Serve the satay sticks hot on a platter with a small bowl of peanut sauce.

Chicken with sage & lemon
serves 4

ingredients
4 skinless, boneless chicken breasts
2 tablespoons finely shredded
   fresh sage leaves
grated zest and juice of 2 lemons
salt and freshly ground black pepper

- Preheat the oven to 200°C/400°F/Gas mark 6. Cut four pieces of foil
  large enough to wrap each chicken breast.
- Put a chicken breast in the centre of each piece of foil, and season
  generously with salt and pepper. Sprinkle with a quarter of the sage and
  lemon zest, then drizzle some lemon juice over the top (reserving a little
  of the juice for serving). Wrap the foil around the chicken to make a
  parcel and fold over the edges to seal. Repeat the process with the
  remaining chicken.
- Put the chicken parcels on a baking sheet, and bake in the oven for
  15 minutes until the chicken has cooked through and the juices run clear.
- To serve, unwrap the chicken and divide among four warmed plates.
  Drizzle with the remaining lemon juice. Serve immediately with rice.

Coq au vin

serves 4

ingredients

4 tablespoons plain flour
1.4kg/3lb chicken cut into 8 pieces
1 tablespoon olive oil
4 tablespoons butter
20 button onions
75g/3oz rindless bacon, diced
20 button mushrooms, wiped with
   damp kitchen paper
2 tablespoons brandy
1 bottle red Burgundy
1 bouquet garni
1 teaspoon soft brown sugar
15g/½oz butter, softened
salt and freshly ground black pepper

- Put 3 tablespoons of the flour in a large plastic bag, and dredge each chicken piece in it until lightly coated. Shake off any excess.
- Heat the oil and butter in a large flameproof casserole dish. Add the onions, bacon and mushrooms, and sauté for 3–4 minutes. Remove with a slotted spoon and set aside. Add the chicken pieces to the hot oil and cook for 5–6 minutes until browned on all sides.
- Pour in the brandy and, standing well back from the pan, very carefully light it with a match, then shake the pan gently until the flames subside. Pour in the wine, then add the bouquet garni and sugar. Season with salt and pepper.
- Bring to the boil, cover and simmer for 1 hour, stirring occasionally.
- Return the reserved onions, bacon and mushrooms to the casserole dish, cover, and cook for 30 minutes. Transfer the chicken, vegetables and bacon to a warmed dish. Remove the bouquet garni, and boil rapidly for 2 minutes to reduce the liquid slightly.
- Cream together the butter and remaining flour. Whisk this into the liquid in the casserole dish, a teaspoon at a time, until the liquid has thickened slightly. Pour over the chicken. Serve hot.

Chicken chow mein

serves 4

ingredients
350g/12oz noodles
225g/8oz skinless chicken
 breast fillets
3 tablespoons light soy sauce
1 tablespoon rice wine
1 tablespoon dark sesame oil
4 tablespoons vegetable oil
2 garlic cloves, finely chopped
50g/2oz mangetout, topped
 and tailed
100g/4oz beansprouts
50g/2oz ham, finely shredded
4 spring onions, finely chopped
salt and freshly ground black pepper

- Cook the noodles in a saucepan of boiling water until tender. Drain, rinse under cold water and drain well.
- Slice the chicken into fine shreds, about 5cm/2in in length. Put the chicken in a bowl, and add 2 tablespoons of the soy sauce, the rice wine and the sesame oil.
- Heat half of the vegetable oil in a wok or frying pan over a high heat. When it starts smoking, add the chicken mixture. Stir-fry for 2 minutes, then transfer the chicken to a plate and keep warm.
- Wipe the wok clean and heat the remaining oil. Stir in the garlic, mangetout, beansprouts and ham. Stir-fry for a further 1 minute, then add the cooked noodles.
- Continue to stir-fry until the noodles are heated through. Add the remaining soy sauce to taste, and season with salt and pepper. Return the chicken and any juices to the noodle mixture, add the chopped spring onions and stir through. Serve immediately.

Kung po chicken

serves 4

ingredients

250g/9oz skinless chicken
   breast fillets
¼ teaspoon salt
½ egg white
1 teaspoon cornflour
1 green pepper, seeded
4 tablespoons vegetable oil
1 spring onion, cut into short sections
a few small slices of fresh root ginger
5 dried red chillies, soaked, seeded
   and shredded
2 tablespoons yellow bean sauce
1 teaspoon rice wine
100g/4oz roasted cashew nuts
a few drops of sesame oil

- Cut the chicken into small cubes about the size of sugar lumps. Put the chicken in a small bowl, and mix with the salt and egg white. Mix a few drops of water with the cornflour to form a paste, and add to the bowl.
- Cut the green pepper into cubes, about the same size as the chicken pieces.
- Heat the oil in a wok, add the chicken, spring onion and ginger, and stir-fry for 1 minute, then add the chillies with the yellow bean sauce and wine. Blend well and stir-fry for another minute. Finally, stir in the roasted cashew nuts and sesame oil.
- Serve hot with boiled rice.

Chicken chop suey

serves 4

ingredients

4 tablespoons light soy sauce
2 teaspoons soft brown sugar
500g/1lb 2oz skinless chicken
  breast fillets
3 tablespoons vegetable oil
2 onions, quartered
2 garlic cloves, crushed
350g/12oz beansprouts
3 teaspoons sesame oil
1 tablespoon cornflour
450ml/¾pt chicken stock

- Mix the soy sauce and sugar together in a small bowl, stirring until the sugar has dissolved.
- Trim any fat away from the chicken, and cut into thin strips. Put the meat in a shallow dish, and spoon the soy mixture over it, turning to coat. Marinate in the refrigerator for 20 minutes.
- Heat the oil in a wok, and stir-fry the chicken for 2–3 minutes until golden brown. Add the onions and garlic, and stir-fry for a further 2 minutes. Add the beansprouts, stir-fry for 4–5 minutes, then add the sesame oil.
- Mix together the cornflour and 3 tablespoons water to form a smooth paste. Pour the stock into the wok, add the cornflour paste and bring to the boil, stirring until the sauce is thickened and clear. Serve hot.

Chicken korma with green beans

serves 4

ingredients

2 tablespoons vegetable oil
350g/12oz skinless chicken breast
    fillets, cut into bite-size pieces
1 onion, sliced
2½ teaspoons korma curry powder
150ml/5fl oz chicken stock
1 teaspoon tomato purée
2 teaspoons caster sugar
75g/3oz tomatoes, roughly chopped
150ml/5fl oz single cream
a little salt
100g/4oz green beans, topped and
    tailed, cut into 2.5cm/1in lengths
25g/1oz ground almonds

- Heat the oil in a saucepan, add the chicken and onion, and sauté over a gentle heat, stirring occasionally, for 6 minutes or until the onion is soft and the chicken is lightly coloured. Stir in the curry powder and cook for a further 2 minutes.
- Add the stock, tomato purée, sugar, tomatoes, cream and a little salt. Stir to combine the ingredients, bring to the boil, then reduce the heat, cover the pan and simmer gently for 10 minutes, stirring occasionally.
- Stir the beans into the curry and cook, covered, for a further 15–20 minutes, stirring occasionally, until the chicken is cooked and the beans are tender. Stir the ground almonds into the curry, and simmer for 1 minute to thicken the sauce. Taste and adjust the seasoning if necessary. Serve with rice.

Warm chicken & feta salad

serves 4

ingredients
4 skinless chicken breast fillets
4 garlic cloves, peeled
2 tablespoons olive oil
3 tablespoons freshly squeezed
   lemon juice
1 onion, cut into wedges
175g/6oz French beans
assorted salad leaves
200g/7oz feta cheese, cubed
175g/6oz cherry tomatoes, halved
50g/2oz black olives
1 red pepper, seeded and sliced

- Put the chicken breasts in a shallow dish. Crush 1 of the garlic cloves and blend with 1 tablespoon of the olive oil and all of the lemon juice. Pour over the chicken, cover and marinate in the refrigerator for at least 30 minutes, turning at least once.
- Heat a frying pan until smoking hot. Drain the chicken and cook for 6–8 minutes on each side. Remove from the heat and allow to stand for 5 minutes.
- Heat the remaining oil in a heavy frying pan. Sauté the remaining garlic with the onion wedges. Cook, stirring occasionally, for 8–10 minutes.
- Cook the French beans in a pan of lightly salted water for 5 minutes. Drain and reserve.
- Arrange the salad leaves in a serving bowl with the feta cheese, cherry tomatoes, beans, black olives and red pepper. Put the onion mixture on top of the salad leaves, then add the chicken and serve drizzled with a little olive oil.

Chinese-style chicken

serves 4

ingredients

½ cucumber, peeled, seeded and
cut into matchsticks
1 teaspoon salt
4 boneless chicken breasts
4 tablespoons soy sauce
pinch of five-spice powder
1 tablespoon freshly squeezed
lemon juice
3 tablespoons sunflower oil
2 tablespoons sesame oil
1 tablespoon sesame seeds
2 tablespoons dry sherry

2 carrots, cut into matchsticks
8 spring onions, shredded
75g/3oz beansprouts

For the sauce
4 tablespoons crunchy
peanut butter
2 teaspoons freshly squeezed
lemon juice
2 teaspoons sesame oil
¼ teaspoon hot chilli powder
1 spring onion, finely chopped

- Put the cucumber matchsticks in a colander, sprinkle with the salt and cover with a plate with a weight on top. Set the colander in a bowl or on a deep plate to catch the drips, and leave to drain for 30 minutes.
- Put the chicken portions in a large pan and just cover with water. Add 1 tablespoon of the soy sauce, the five-spice powder and the lemon juice, cover and bring to the boil. Reduce the heat and simmer for about 20 minutes.
- Lift out the poached chicken with a slotted spoon, and leave until cool enough to handle. Remove and discard the skin. Bash the chicken lightly with a rolling pin to loosen the fibres. Slice into thin strips. Reserve.
- Heat the oils in a large frying pan or wok. Add the sesame seeds, fry for 30 seconds, then stir in the remaining 3 tablespoons of soy sauce and the sherry. Add the carrots, and stir-fry for 2–3 minutes until just tender. Remove from the heat and reserve.
- Rinse the cucumber well, pat dry with kitchen paper and put in a bowl. Add the spring onions, beansprouts, cooked carrots, pan juices and shredded chicken, and mix together. Transfer to a shallow dish. Cover and chill for about 1 hour, turning the mixture once or twice.
- To make the sauce, cream the peanut butter with the lemon juice, sesame oil and chilli powder, adding a little hot water to form a paste, then stir in the spring onion.
- Arrange the chicken mixture on a serving dish, and serve with the peanut sauce.

Cajun chicken jambalaya

serves 4

ingredients

1.4kg/2½lb fresh chicken
1½ onions
1 bay leaf
4 black peppercorns
1 sprig of fresh flat-leaf parsley,
   plus extra, chopped, to garnish
2 tablespoons vegetable oil
2 garlic cloves, chopped
1 green pepper, seeded and
   chopped
1 celery stick, chopped
225g/8oz long-grain rice
100g/4oz chorizo sausage,
   chopped

100g/4oz cooked ham, chopped
400g/14oz canned chopped
   plum tomatoes
½ teaspoon hot chilli powder
½ teaspoon cumin seeds
½ teaspoon ground cumin
1 teaspoon dried thyme
100g/4oz peeled and deveined
   cooked prawns
dash of Tabasco sauce
salt and freshly ground
   black pepper

- Put the chicken in a large flameproof casserole dish, and pour over 600ml/1pt water. Add the onion half, bay leaf, peppercorns and parsley sprig, and bring to the boil. Reduce the heat, cover and simmer gently for about 1½ hours.
- When the chicken is cooked, lift it out of the stock, remove the skin and carcass, and chop the meat. Strain the stock, leave to cool and reserve.
- Chop the remaining onion and heat the oil in a large frying pan. Add the onion, garlic, green pepper and celery. Fry for about 5 minutes, then stir in the rice, coating the grains with the oil. Add the sausage, ham and chopped chicken. Fry for a further 2–3 minutes, stirring frequently.
- Pour in the tomatoes and 300ml/10fl oz of the reserved stock, and add the chilli, cumin and thyme. Bring to the boil, then reduce the heat, cover and simmer gently for 20 minutes or until the rice is tender and the liquid has been absorbed.
- Stir in the prawns and Tabasco. Cook for a further 5 minutes, then season well with salt and pepper, and serve hot, garnished with the extra chopped parsley.

Tuscan chicken

serves 4

ingredients

8 chicken thighs, skinned
1 teaspoon olive oil
1 onion, thinly sliced
2 red peppers, seeded and sliced
1 garlic clove, crushed
300ml/10fl oz puréed tomatoes
150ml/5fl oz dry white wine
1 teaspoon dried oregano
400g/14oz canned cooked
　cannellini beans, drained
3 tablespoons fresh breadcrumbs
salt and freshly ground black pepper

- Heat the oil in a heavy pan, and sauté the chicken until golden brown. Remove and keep warm. Add the onion and red peppers to the pan, and gently sauté until softened but not coloured. Stir in the garlic and sauté for a minute or so.
- Add the chicken, tomatoes, wine and oregano. Season well with salt and pepper, bring to a boil, then cover the pan tightly.
- Reduce the heat and simmer gently, stirring occasionally, for 30–35 minutes until the chicken is tender and the juices run clear.
- Preheat the grill until hot.
- Stir the cannellini beans into the chicken mixture, and simmer for a further 5 minutes until heated through. Sprinkle with the breadcrumbs, and cook under the grill until golden brown.

Pan-fried chicken with red wine sauce

serves 6

ingredients
25g/1oz butter
1 tablespoon oil
6 chicken breasts, about
    150g/5oz each
175g/6oz rindless streaky bacon,
    chopped
225g/8oz button mushrooms, wiped
    with damp kitchen paper
225g/8oz button onions
100ml/31/2fl oz brandy
350ml/12fl oz red wine
700ml/1¼pt chicken stock
4 tablespoons redcurrant jelly
salt and freshly ground black pepper

- Preheat the oven to 150°C/300°F/Gas mark 2.
- Melt the butter and oil in a pan. Add the chicken breasts and cook in batches over a high heat for 3 minutes on each side or until golden. Remove from the pan, and put in a baking dish in the oven to finish cooking while you make the sauce.
- Add the bacon, mushrooms and onions to the frying pan. Cook for 4–5 minutes until golden. Remove from the pan and set aside. Add the brandy, wine, stock and redcurrant jelly. Bring to the boil, and bubble furiously for 15–20 minutes until the sauce is syrupy.
- Return the chicken, bacon, mushrooms and onions to the pan. Bring to the boil, season with salt and pepper, and serve hot.

Sautéed chicken with herbs
serves 4

ingredients
2–3 tablespoons olive oil
1 chicken, cut into 8 pieces
3 garlic cloves, sliced
2 shallots, finely chopped
3 tablespoons dried mixed herbs
juice of ½ lemon
salt and freshly ground black pepper

- Heat the oil in a heavy frying pan over a high heat. Brown the chicken pieces in the oil in two batches.
- When browned, reduce the heat to medium-high and return all the chicken to the pan. Cover the pan and leave to cook for about 10 minutes.
- Turn the chicken pieces, spooning their juices over them, then sprinkle the garlic, shallots, half of the herbs over them. Season with salt and pepper. Cover again and cook for a further 8 minutes.
- When cooked, lift the chicken pieces out with the cooked shallots, garlic and pan juices. Squeeze the lemon juice over the chicken, sprinkle with the remaining herbs and serve hot.

Mustard chicken

serves 4

ingredients

50g/2oz butter
1 onion, finely chopped
450g/1lb skinless chicken breast
    fillets, thinly sliced
1 tablespoon cornflour
1 garlic clove, crushed
150ml/5fl oz chicken stock
1 teaspoon chilli paste
2 teaspoons ground coriander
1 tablespoon wholegrain mustard
1 tablespoon sesame seeds
salt and freshly ground black pepper

- Heat the butter in a saucepan, add the onion and sweat for about 5 minutes until soft but not coloured.
- Mix together the chicken pieces and cornflour, and add to the pan with the garlic. Cook quickly, stirring occasionally, until golden brown.
- Stir in the stock, chilli paste, coriander and mustard. Season with salt and pepper. Bring just to the boil, stirring, and simmer gently for about 10 minutes.
- Just before serving, stir in the sesame seeds, and serve hot with pasta or potatoes.

Fragrant saffron chicken
serves 10

ingredients

2 chickens, about 1.6kg/3½lb each
1 carrot, sliced
2 celery sticks, sliced
6 black peppercorns
2 bay leaves
50g/2oz butter
225g/8oz onion, finely chopped
1 teaspoon saffron threads
4 dried apricots
grated zest of 1 lemon
300ml/10fl oz dry white wine
3 tablespoons clear honey
1 teaspoon mild curry paste
300ml/10fl oz mayonnaise
300ml/10fl oz double cream
salt and freshly ground black pepper

- Put the chickens in two separate large saucepans. Cover with cold water and add the carrot, celery, peppercorns and ½ bay leaf to each. Bring slowly to the boil, cover and simmer very gently for about 1 hour. Pierce the thigh joints with a skewer to test if cooked – the juices should run clear. Leave the chickens to cool in their poaching liquid.
- Drain the chickens. Remove and discard the skin, strip off the meat and discard the bones. Cut the meat into bite-size pieces. Set aside.
- Melt the butter in a medium saucepan, and sauté the onion until soft. Grind the saffron strands to a powder using a mortar and pestle. Stir into the onions with the apricots, lemon zest, white wine, honey, curry paste and 1 bay leaf. Bring to the boil. Simmer, uncovered, for about 10 minutes until well reduced and the consistency of chutney.
- Cool and purée in a blender or food processor, then sieve.
- Fold the cold saffron mixture into the mayonnaise. Whip the cream until it just holds its shape. Fold into the mayonnaise mixture, and season with salt and pepper.
- Mix together the chicken pieces and the mayonnaise mixture, and serve on a bed of rice.

Chinese chicken with cashew nuts

serves 4

ingredients

4 skinless chicken breast fillets,
  sliced into strips
3 garlic cloves, crushed
4 tablespoons soy sauce
2 tablespoons cornflour
225g/8oz dried egg noodles
3 tablespoons sunflower oil
1 tablespoon sesame oil
100g/4oz roasted cashew nuts
6 spring onions, cut into
  5cm/2in pieces

- Put the chicken in a bowl with the garlic, soy sauce and cornflour, and mix until the chicken is well coated. Cover with cling film, and chill for about 30 minutes.
- Meanwhile, bring a pan of water to the boil and add the egg noodles. Turn off the heat and leave to stand for 5 minutes. Drain well. Reserve.
- Heat the oils in a large frying pan or wok over a high heat, and add the chilled chicken and marinade juices. Stir-fry for 3–4 minutes until golden brown. Add the cashew nuts and spring onions to the pan or wok, and stir-fry for 2–3 minutes.
- Add the drained noodles, and stir-fry for a further 2 minutes. Toss the noodles well and serve immediately.

Garlic & herb chicken
serves 4

ingredients
4 skinless chicken breast fillets
100g/4oz full-fat soft cheese
  flavoured with herbs and garlic
8 slices Parma ham
150ml/5fl oz red wine
150ml/5fl oz chicken stock
25g/1oz Demerara sugar

- Using a sharp knife, make a horizontal slit along the length of each chicken breast to form a pocket.
- Beat the cheese with a wooden spoon to soften it. Spoon the cheese into the pocket of the chicken breasts.
- Wrap 2 slices of Parma ham around each chicken breast, and secure firmly in place with string.
- Pour the wine and stock into a large frying pan and bring to the boil. When just starting to boil, add the sugar and stir well to dissolve.
- Add the chicken breasts to the mixture in the frying pan. Leave to simmer for 12–15 minutes until the chicken is tender and the juices run clear.
- Remove the chicken from the pan, set aside and keep warm. Reheat the sauce and boil until reduced and thickened. Remove the string from the chicken, and cut into slices. Pour the sauce over the chicken, and serve hot with a green salad.

Chicken in spicy yogurt
serves 6

ingredients

3 dried red chillies
2 tablespoons coriander seeds
2 teaspoons ground turmeric
2 teaspoons garam masala
4 garlic cloves, crushed
½ large onion, chopped
2.5cm/1in piece of fresh root
    ginger, grated
2 tablespoons freshly squeezed
    lime juice
1 teaspoon salt
125ml/4fl oz low-fat Greek-style
    yogurt
1 tablespoon olive oil
6 chicken pieces, about 2kg/4½lb
    in total

- Grind together the chillies, coriander seeds, turmeric, garam masala, garlic, onion, ginger, lime juice and salt using a mortar and pestle.
- Gently heat a frying pan and add the spice mixture. Stir for 2 minutes, then turn into a shallow dish. Add the yogurt and oil to the spice paste, and mix well to combine.
- Remove the skin from the chicken pieces, and make three slashes in the flesh of each piece. Add the chicken to the dish containing the yogurt and spice mixture, and coat the pieces completely in the marinade. Cover with cling film and chill for at least 4 hours. Remove the dish from the refrigerator, take off the cling film and leave, covered, at room temperature for 30 minutes before cooking.
- Heat a barbecue or grill until very hot. Wrap the chicken pieces in foil, sealing well so that the juices cannot escape. Cook the chicken pieces over the barbecue or under the grill for about 15 minutes, turning once.
- Remove the foil and brown the chicken for 5 minutes. Serve hot.

Grilled chicken with hot salsa

serves 4

ingredients

4 skinless chicken breast fillets,
  about 175g/6oz each
pinch of celery salt
pinch of cayenne pepper
2 tablespoons vegetable oil

For the salsa
275g/10oz watermelon
175g/6oz cantaloupe melon
1 small red onion, finely chopped
2 fresh green chillies, seeded
  and chopped
2 tablespoons freshly squeezed
  lime juice
4 tablespoons chopped fresh
  coriander leaves
pinch of salt

- Preheat a grill to medium. Slash the chicken breasts deeply to speed up the cooking time.
- Season the chicken with the celery salt and cayenne pepper, brush with the oil and grill for about 15 minutes.
- To make the salsa, remove the rind and seeds from the melons. Finely dice the flesh and put into a bowl. Mix in the onion and chillies.
- Add the lime juice and chopped coriander, and season with a pinch of salt. Turn the salsa out into a small serving bowl.
- Arrange the grilled chicken on a plate, and serve hot with the salsa.

Chicken & vegetable terrine
serves 6

ingredients
1 small green pepper, seeded
  and diced
1 small red pepper, seeded
  and diced
2 small carrots, diced
1 courgette, diced
1 butternut squash, diced
750g/11/2lb skinless chicken
  breast fillets, diced
1 garlic clove, crushed
½ teaspoon ground nutmeg
2 tablespoons freshly squeezed
  lemon juice
3 eggs
350ml/12fl oz evaporated
  skimmed milk
75g/3oz mixed fresh herbs such as
  basil, tarragon, dill and parsley

- Blanch the peppers, carrots, courgette and squash lightly in boiling water. Refresh in cold water, drain and reserve.
- In a blender or food processor, purée the chicken. Add the garlic, nutmeg and lemon juice, and whiz briefly. With the motor running, add the eggs one at a time. Process again and add the evaporated milk and chopped herbs. Mix well.
- Pour the chicken mixture into a bowl, and chill for 1 hour.
- Preheat the oven to 180°C/350°F/Gas mark 4.
- Fold the reserved vegetables into the chicken mixture, then spoon the mixture into a 9 x 20cm/3½ x 8in loaf tin.
- Bake in the oven for 1–1½ hours. Leave to cool, then chill overnight in the refrigerator. To serve, cut into slices.

Roast baby chickens
serves 4

ingredients

4 small poussins, weighing about
350–500g/12oz–1lb 2oz each
175g/6oz wild rice, cooked

For the marinade
4 garlic cloves, peeled
2 fresh coriander roots
1 tablespoon light soy sauce
salt and freshly ground
black pepper

For the stuffing
4 lemon grass stalks, tough outer
layer removed
4 kaffir lime leaves
4 slices of fresh root ginger
75ml/3fl oz coconut milk,
for brushing

- Preheat the oven to 180°C/355°F/Gas mark 4. Wash the poussins and pat dry with kitchen paper.
- To make the marinade, put the garlic, coriander and soy sauce in a blender or food processor, and purée until smooth. Season to taste with salt and pepper.
- Rub the marinade mixture evenly into the skin of the poussins.
- Place a stalk of lemon grass, a lime leaf and a piece of ginger in the cavity of each poussin. Put the poussins in a roasting tin, and brush lightly with the coconut milk. Roast for about 30 minutes in the oven.
- Remove from the oven, brush again with coconut milk, return to the oven and cook for a further 15–25 minutes until golden and cooked through, depending on the size of the poussins. The juices should run clear when the thickest part of the thigh is pierced with a skewer.
- Serve the poussins on a bed of wild rice with the pan juices poured over.

Indian charred chicken
serves 4

ingredients
4 skinless chicken breast fillets
2 tablespoons curry paste
1 tablespoon sunflower oil
1 tablespoon light muscovado sugar
1 teaspoon ground ginger
½ teaspoon ground cumin

For the cucumber raita
¼ cucumber
150ml/5fl oz low-fat
　Greek-style yogurt
¼ teaspoon chilli powder
salt

- Put the chicken breasts between two sheets of baking parchment or cling film. Pound with the flat side of a meat mallet or a rolling pin to flatten.
- Mix together the curry paste, oil, sugar, ginger and cumin in a small bowl. Spread the mixture over both sides of the chicken. Leave to marinate in the refrigerator for at least 2 hours.
- To make the raita, cut the cucumber in half lengthways, peel and scoop out the seeds with a spoon.
- Grate the flesh into a colander, sprinkle with salt and leave to stand for 10 minutes. Rinse off the salt, and squeeze out any moisture by pressing the cucumber with the back of a spoon.
- Mix the cucumber with the yogurt, and stir in the chilli powder. Refrigerate until required.
- Heat a charcoal barbecue until hot. Transfer the chicken to an oiled rack, and barbecue over the hot coals for 10 minutes, turning once. Serve with the raita.

Jerk chicken
serves 4

ingredients
4 lean chicken portions
1 bunch of spring onions, trimmed
1 Scotch Bonnet chilli, deseeded
1 garlic clove
5cm/2in piece of fresh root ginger,
    roughly chopped
½ teaspoon dried thyme
½ teaspoon paprika
¼ teaspoon ground allspice
pinch of ground cinnamon
pinch of ground cloves
4 tablespoons white wine vinegar
3 tablespoons light soy sauce
¼ teaspoon freshly ground
    black pepper

- Rinse the chicken portions, and pat dry with kitchen paper. Put in a shallow dish.
- Put all the remaining ingredients in a blender or food processor, and purée until smooth. Pour the mixture over the chicken, turning the chicken portions so that they are well coated in the marinade. Cover and marinate in the refrigerator for 24 hours.
- Heat a charcoal barbecue or grill to medium. Remove the chicken from the marinade, and barbecue over the coals or under the grill for about 30 minutes, turning the chicken and basting occasionally with any remaining marinade, until the meat is browned and cooked through.
- Transfer the chicken to individual serving plates, and serve immediately.

Chicken breasts & balsamic vinegar

serves 4

ingredients

4 skinless chicken breast fillets
2 tablespoons plain flour
¼ teaspoon freshly ground
  black pepper
3 tablespoons olive oil
6 garlic cloves, peeled but left whole
350g/12oz small mushrooms
4 tablespoons balsamic vinegar
175ml/6fl oz chicken stock

- Split each chicken breast in half lengthways.
- Season the flour with pepper, and dredge the chicken in the mixture. Shake off any excess flour.
- Heat the oil in a heavy frying pan over a medium-high heat, and cook the chicken breasts for 4 minutes or until nicely browned on one side. Add the garlic, turn the chicken pieces and continue to cook for a minute of so.
- HAdd the mushrooms and cook for about 7 minutes, then add the vinegar and stock. Cover tightly, reduce the heat to medium-low and cook for 10 minutes, turning the chicken occasionally.
- Transfer the chicken to a warmed serving plate and set aside in a warm place. Let the sauce with the mushrooms cook, uncovered, over a medium-high heat for about 6 minutes.
- Remove the pan from the heat, pour the sauce over the chicken and serve immediately.

Chicken peperonata

serves 4

ingredients

8 skinless chicken thighs
2 tablespoons wholemeal flour
2 tablespoons olive oil
1 small onion, thinly sliced
1 garlic clove, crushed
1 large red pepper, seeded and
   thinly sliced
1 large green pepper, seeded and
   thinly sliced
1 large yellow pepper, seeded and
   thinly sliced
400g/14oz canned chopped
   tomatoes
1 tablespoon chopped fresh
   oregano, plus extra to garnish
salt and freshly ground black pepper

- Toss the chicken in the flour, then shake off any excess.
- Heat the oil in a wide frying pan, and sauté the chicken quickly until sealed and lightly browned, then remove from the pan.
- Add the onion to the pan and gently sauté until soft. Add the garlic, peppers, tomatoes and the 1 tablespoon chopped oregano, then bring to the boil, stirring.
- Arrange the chicken over the vegetables, season well with salt and pepper, then cover the pan tightly and simmer for 20–25 minutes until the chicken is tender and the juices run clear. Check the seasoning, adjusting if necessary.
- Garnish the chicken with the extra oregano, and serve hot.

Chicken with beansprouts

serves 4

ingredients

100g/4oz chicken breast fillet.
   skinned and cut into thin strips
1 teaspoon salt
¼ egg white, lightly beaten
1 teaspoon cornflour mixed
   with 1½ teaspoons water to form
   a paste
300ml/10fl oz vegetable oil
1 small onion, thinly shredded
1 small green pepper, seeded and
   thinly shredded
1 small carrot, thinly shredded
100g/4oz fresh beansprouts
½ teaspoon granulated sugar
1 tablespoon light soy sauce
1 teaspoon rice wine
¼ teaspoon sesame oil

- Put the chicken in a bowl. Add a pinch of the salt, the egg white and the cornflour paste, and mix well.
- Heat a work or large frying pan over a high heat. Add the vegetable oil and, when the oil is hot enough, add the chicken and stir-fry for about 1 minute, separating the chicken strips. Remove with a slotted spoon and drain on kitchen paper.
- Pour off the oil, leaving about 2 tablespoons in the wok. Add the onion, green pepper and carrot, and stir-fry for about 2 minutes. Add the beansprouts and stir-fry for a few seconds.
- Return the chicken to the wok or pan with the remaining salt and the sugar, soy sauce and rice wine. Blend well and add 3 tablespoons water. Sprinkle with the sesame oil, and serve immediately.

Yellow bean chicken

serves 4

ingredients

1 egg white, beaten
1 tablespoon cornflour
450g/1lb skinless chicken breast
    fillets, cut into 2.5cm/1in cubes
1 tablespoon rice wine vinegar
1 tablespoon light soy sauce
1 teaspoon caster sugar
3 tablespoons vegetable oil
1 garlic clove, crushed
1cm/½in piece of fresh root
    ginger, grated
1 green pepper, seeded and diced
2 large mushrooms, sliced
3 tablespoons yellow bean sauce

- Mix the egg white and cornflour in a bowl. Add the chicken and turn in the mixture to coat. Set aside for 20 minutes.
- Mix the rice wine vinegar, soy sauce and sugar in a bowl. Remove the chicken from the egg white mixture.
- Heat a wok over a high heat. Add the oil and, when hot enough, add the chicken and stir-fry for 3–4 minutes until golden brown. Remove the chicken from the wok with a slotted spoon, set aside and keep warm.
- Add the garlic, ginger, pepper and mushrooms to the wok, and stir-fry for 1–2 minutes. Add the yellow bean sauce and cook for 1 minute.
- Stir in the vinegar mixture, and return the chicken to the wok. Cook for 1–2 minutes, and serve hot.

Spicy masala chicken
serves 6

ingredients
12 skinless chicken thighs
75ml/3fl oz freshly squeezed
  lemon juice
1 teaspoon grated fresh root ginger
1 garlic clove, crushed
1 teaspoon crushed dried red chillies
1 teaspoon salt
1 teaspoon Demerara sugar
2 tablespoons clear honey
2 tablespoons chopped fresh
  coriander leaves
1 fresh green chilli, finely chopped
2 tablespoons sunflower oil

- Prick the chicken with a fork, rinse and pat dry with kitchen paper.
- In a large mixing bowl, mix together the lemon juice, ginger, garlic, red chillies, salt, sugar and honey. Transfer the chicken to the spice mixture and coat well. Set aside to marinate for about 45 minutes.
- Preheat the grill to medium. Add the coriander and green chilli to the chicken thighs, and put them in a shallow flameproof dish.
- Pour any remaining marinade over the chicken and, using a pastry brush, baste with the oil.
- Grill the chicken thighs under the grill for 15–20 minutes, turning and basting occasionally, until cooked through and browned. Transfer to a serving dish, and serve immediately.

Chicken & vegetables
serves 4

ingredients
25g/1oz cornflour
300ml/10fl oz skimmed milk
1 teaspoon low-fat spread
1 teaspoon English mustard
75g/3oz low-fat Cheddar
   cheese, grated
350g/12oz cooked mixed chopped
   vegetables
175g/6oz cooked chicken,
   skin removed
¼ teaspoon freshly grated nutmeg
salt and freshly ground black pepper

- Preheat the grill to medium.
- Blend the cornflour in a saucepan with the milk. Add the low-fat spread. Bring to the boil and cook for 1 minute, stirring all the time.
- Stir in a little salt and pepper, the mustard and two-thirds of the cheese. Fold in the vegetables and the chicken, and season with the nutmeg and a little more salt and pepper if required. Heat through.
- Turn into a flameproof serving dish, top with the remaining cheese and put under the grill until golden and bubbling. Serve immediately.

Sage chicken & rice

serves 4

ingredients

1 large onion, chopped
1 garlic clove, crushed
2 celery sticks, sliced
2 carrots, diced
2 sprigs of fresh sage
300ml/10fl oz chicken stock
350g/12oz skinless chicken breast
    fillets, cut into 2.5cm/1in cubes
225g/8oz wild rice
400g/14oz canned chopped
    plum tomatoes
dash of Tabasco sauce
2 courgettes, thinly sliced
100g/4oz lean ham, diced
salt and freshly ground black pepper

- Put the onion, garlic, celery, carrots and sage in a large saucepan, and pour in the stock. Bring to the boil, cover the pan and simmer for 5 minutes.
- Stir the chicken into the pan with the vegetables. Cover the pan and continue to cook for a further 5 minutes. Stir in the rice and tomatoes.
- Add the Tabasco sauce and season well with salt and pepper. Bring to the boil, cover and simmer for 25 minutes.
- Stir in the courgettes and ham, and continue to cook, uncovered, for a further 10 minutes, stirring occasionally, until the rice is just tender. Remove and discard the sage, and serve hot.

Garlic & lime chicken
serves 4

ingredients
4 large skinless chicken breast fillets
50g/2oz garlic butter, softened
3 tablespoons chopped fresh
   coriander leaves
1 tablespoon sunflower oil
finely grated zest and juice of
   2 limes
25g/1oz Demerara sugar

- Put each chicken breast between two sheets of cling film, and pound with a rolling pin until flattened to about 1cm/½in thick.
- Mix together the garlic butter and coriander, and spread over each chicken breast. Roll the chicken up like a Swiss roll and secure with a cocktail stick.
- Heat a wok or heavy frying pan until hot. Add the oil, and when it is hot enough, add the chicken and cook, turning, for 15–20 minutes until cooked through.
- Remove the chicken from the wok or pan, and transfer to a chopping board. Loosely cover with foil to rest for a few minutes, then cut each chicken roll into slices.
- Add the lime zest, juice and sugar to the wok and heat gently, stirring, until the sugar has dissolved. Increase the heat and allow to bubble for 2 minutes.
- Arrange the chicken slices on warmed individual serving plates, and spoon the pan juices over to serve. Serve warm with boiled rice.

Chicken jalfrezi

serves 4

ingredients

1 teaspoon mustard oil
3 tablespoons vegetable oil
1 large onion, finely chopped
3 garlic cloves, crushed
1 tablespoon tomato purée
2 tomatoes, peeled and chopped
1 teaspoon ground turmeric
½ teaspoon ground cumin
½ teaspoon ground coriander

½ teaspoon chilli powder
½ teaspoon garam masala
1 teaspoon red wine vinegar
1 small red pepper, seeded
   and chopped
100g/4oz frozen broad beans
500g/1lb 2oz cooked chicken,
   cut into bite-size pieces
salt

- Heat the mustard oil in a large frying pan set over a high heat for about 1 minute until it begins to smoke. Add the vegetable oil, reduce the heat and add the onion and garlic. Fry until they are golden.
- Add the tomato purée, chopped tomatoes, turmeric, cumin, coriander, chilli powder, garam masala and vinegar to the frying pan. Stir the mixture until fragrant.
- Add the red pepper and beans, and stir for 2 minutes until the pepper is softened. Stir in the chicken and season with salt.
- Simmer gently for 6–8 minutes until the chicken is heated through and the beans are tender. Serve hot.

Turkey gumbo
serves 4

ingredients

25g/1oz margarine

225g/8oz fresh okra, chopped into
   2.5cm/1in pieces

150g/5oz celery, chopped

1 onion, chopped

1 small green pepper, seeded
   and chopped

2 garlic cloves, minced

225g/8oz tomato purée

400g/14oz canned chopped
   plum tomatoes

200g/7oz cooked turkey, chopped

- Melt the margarine in a large frying pan. Add the okra and sauté for about 5 minutes until the okra loses its shiny appearance. Remove the okra pieces to a bowl.
- Add the celery, onion, green pepper and garlic to the pan. Sweat over a medium heat until the onion is soft and transparent. Add the tomato purée, tomatoes, 450ml/¾pt water, okra mixture and turkey.
- Reduce the heat to low, and cook for 10 minutes or until the turkey is heated through. Serve hot with rice.

Turkey & tomato hotpot
serves 4

ingredients

25g/1oz white bread, crusts
  removed
2 tablespoons milk
1 garlic clove, crushed
½ teaspoon caraway seeds
225g/8oz minced turkey
1 egg white
350ml/12fl oz chicken stock
400g/14oz canned chopped
  plum tomatoes
1 tablespoon tomato purée
100g/4oz easy-cook rice
salt and freshly ground black pepper

- Cut the bread into small cubes and put into a mixing bowl. Sprinkle the milk over them, and leave to soak for 5 minutes.
- Add the garlic, caraway seeds and turkey. Season with salt and pepper, and mix well.
- Whisk the egg white until stiff, then fold, half at a time, into the turkey mixture. Refrigerate for 10 minutes.
- While the turkey mixture is chilling, put the stock, tomatoes and tomato purée into a large saucepan and bring to the boil. Add the rice, stir and cook for 5 minutes. Reduce the heat to a gentle simmer.
- Meanwhile, shape the turkey mixture into 16 small balls. Carefully drop them into the stock, and simmer for a further 8–10 minutes until both the turkey balls and rice are cooked. Serve immediately.

Turkey meatloaf
serves 4

ingredients
1 tablespoon olive oil
1 onion, chopped
1 green pepper, seeded and finely
  chopped
1 garlic clove, chopped
450g/1lb minced turkey
50g/2oz fresh white breadcrumbs
1 egg, beaten
50g/2oz pine nuts
12 sun-dried tomatoes in oil, drained
  and chopped
75ml/3fl oz milk
2 teaspoons chopped fresh rosemary
1 teaspoon fennel seeds
½ teaspoon dried oregano
salt and freshly ground black pepper

- Preheat the oven to 190°C/375°F/Gas mark 5.
- Heat the oil in a frying pan. Add the onion, green pepper and garlic, and sweat over a low heat for 8–10 minutes, stirring frequently, until the vegetables are just softened. Remove from the heat and leave to cool.
- Put the minced turkey in a large bowl. Add the onion mixture and all the remaining ingredients, and mix thoroughly.
- Transfer to a 21 x 11cm/8 x 4in loaf tin, packing down firmly. Bake in the oven for 1 hour until golden brown. Serve hot.

Bacon-wrapped turkey burgers

serves 3

ingredients

12 rashers back bacon
450g/1lb minced turkey
200g/7oz dried breadcrumbs
1 teaspoon Worcestershire sauce
½ teaspoon garlic salt
salt and freshly ground black pepper

- Preheat the grill until hot.
- In a frying pan, dry-fry the bacon until beginning to crisp. Remove and set to one side.
- Mix together the turkey, breadcrumbs, Worcestershire sauce and garlic salt. Season with salt and pepper. Shape the mixture into 6 patties.
- Crisscross 2 rashers of bacon on each patty, tucking the ends under and securing with cocktail sticks. Cook under the hot grill for about 4 minutes on each side until the turkey springs back when touched and is no longer pink. Serve hot.

Chillies stuffed with turkey

serves 6

ingredients

vegetable oil for greasing
4 large fresh green chillies
100g/4oz low-fat Cheddar
  cheese, grated
350g/12oz cooked turkey breast,
  cut into 1cm/½in strips
100g/4oz plain flour
½ teaspoon baking powder
¼ teaspoon salt
125ml/4fl oz skimmed milk
3 eggs
150g/5oz mature Cheddar
  cheese, grated

- Preheat the oven to 230°C/450°F/Gas mark 8. Lightly brush a large baking dish with vegetable oil.
- Slit the chillies on one side, remove the seeds and open out flat.
- Fill each chilli with a mixture of the low-fat Cheddar cheese and turkey. Fold over the edges of the chillies, and put seam side down in the prepared baking dish.
- In a medium bowl, combine the flour, baking powder and salt.
- In a small bowl, whisk the milk and eggs together, then slowly add to the flour mixture, beating until smooth. Pour over the chillies. Bake in the oven for 15 minutes.
- Remove from the oven, and sprinkle with the mature Cheddar cheese. Serve hot.

Turkey & macaroni cheese
serves 4

ingredients

1 onion, chopped
150ml/5fl oz vegetable stock
25g/1oz low-fat spread
25g/1oz plain flour
300ml/10fl oz skimmed milk
50g/2oz low-fat Cheddar
  cheese, grated
1 teaspoon mustard powder
225g/8oz macaroni
4 rashers smoked turkey, halved
3 tomatoes, sliced
3 fresh basil leaves
1 tablespoon freshly grated
  Parmesan cheese
salt and freshly ground black pepper

- Put the onion and stock in a non-stick frying pan. Bring to the boil, stirring occasionally, and cook for 5–6 minutes until the stock has reduced entirely and the onion is transparent.
- Put the low-fat spread, flour and milk in a saucepan, and season with salt and pepper. Whisk together over a medium heat until thickened and smooth. Draw aside and add the Cheddar, mustard and onion.
- Preheat the grill until medium-hot. Cook the macaroni in a large pan of lightly salted boiling water until al dente. Drain the macaroni thoroughly, and stir into the sauce. Transfer to a shallow ovenproof dish.
- Arrange the turkey rashers and tomatoes overlapping on top of the macaroni cheese. Tuck in the basil leaves, then sprinkle with the Parmesan and set under the grill to lightly brown the top. Serve hot.

Turkey spinach lasagne

serves 8

ingredients
100g/4oz frozen chopped spinach
vegetable oil for greasing
50g/2oz low-fat ricotta cheese
475g/1lb 1oz chopped
  cooked turkey
500ml/18fl oz ready-prepared
  spaghetti sauce
225g/8oz low-fat mozzarella
  cheese, sliced
50g/2oz Parmesan cheese,
  freshly grated

- Preheat the oven to 180°C/350°F/Gas mark 4.
- Thaw the spinach and squeeze out any liquid. Put about one-third of the spinach in the bottom of a lightly oiled casserole dish.
- Spread half of the ricotta over the spinach. Sprinkle on half of the turkey, and spoon over half of the spaghetti sauce. Top with half of the mozzarella. Repeat the layering process, finishing with the final third of spinach. Sprinkle the Parmesan cheese over the top.
- Bake in the oven for 45–50 minutes. Serve hot.

Duck with tomatoes
serves 4

ingredients
1 duck
350g/12oz cherry tomatoes
100g/4oz pitted black olives
300ml/10fl oz red wine
salt and freshly ground black pepper

- Preheat the oven to 220°C/425°F/Gas mark 7.
- Wipe the duck dry, pull out excess fat and prick the thick fatty bits of the skin using a skewer, particularly the area between legs and breast. Rub the skin with salt and pepper, and season the inside.
- Put the duck on a rack in a roasting tin, breast side up, and roast on the lowest shelf of the oven for 20 minutes. Turn the duck over and roast for a further 30 minutes.
- Reduce the oven temperature to 200°C/400°F/Gas mark 6, pour out the fat and roast for a further 15 minutes, breast-side up. Pour out any remaining fat, add the tomatoes, olives and wine, and roast for a further 15 minutes.
- Remove from the oven and allow the duck to rest for about 10 minutes before carving. Spoon the tomatoes and olives over each serving.

Mushroom & ginger duck

serves 4

ingredients

2.5kg/5½lb duck
1 teaspoon granulated sugar
50ml/2fl oz soy sauce
2 garlic cloves, crushed
8 dried Chinese mushrooms, soaked
    in 350ml/12fl oz warm water for
    15 minutes
1 onion, sliced
5cm/2in piece of fresh root ginger,
    cut into matchsticks
200g/7oz baby sweetcorn
½ bunch of spring onions,
    white bulbs left whole and green
    tops sliced
2 tablespoons cornflour mixed
    with 4 tablespoons water to form
    a paste
salt and freshly ground black pepper

- Cut the duck along the breast, open it up and cut along each side of the backbone. (Any trimmings of fat can be rendered in a frying pan, to use later in the recipe.) Cut each leg and each breast in half. Put in a bowl, rub with the sugar, then pour over the soy sauce and garlic.
- Drain the mushrooms, reserving the soaking liquid. Trim and discard the stalks.
- Fry the onion and ginger in the duck fat, in a heavy frying pan, until they give off a good aroma. Push to one side. Lift the duck slices out of the soy sauce, and fry them until browned. Add the mushrooms and the reserved soaking liquid.
- Add 600ml/1pt water to the pan. Season with salt and pepper, cover and cook over a gentle heat for about 1 hour until the duck is tender.
- Add the sweetcorn and the white part of the spring onions. Cook for a further 10 minutes. Remove from the heat and add the cornflour paste. Return to the heat and bring to the boil, stirring. Cook for 1 minute until glossy. Garnish with the green spring onion tops.
- Serve hot with plain boiled rice.

Mahogany duck

serves 4

ingredients

2 ducks
2 slices white bread
2 spring onions
750ml/1¼pt beer

1 teaspoon crushed black
    peppercorns
175ml/6fl oz light soy sauce
2 tablespoons clear honey
2 tablespoons dark brown sugar

For the marinade
50ml/2fl oz Scotch whisky
3 tablespoons grated fresh
    root ginger
1½ teaspoons chopped garlic
2 tablespoons grated orange zest
1 teaspoon crushed
    coriander seeds

For the sauce
375ml/13fl oz beef stock
2 teaspoons arrowroot dissolved in
    3 tablespoons cold water

- Rinse the ducks, then pat dry with kitchen paper and remove any excess fat from the body cavities. Truss the ducks and arrange them, breast side up, several inches apart on a rack set over a large roasting tin.
- Combine all the marinade ingredients in a bowl. Leave to stand, covered and chilled, for 3 hours. Stir the marinade, and press through a fine sieve into a small bowl. Brush the ducks with some of the marinade, every 30 minutes, for 2½ hours, while keeping them refrigerated.
- Preheat the oven to 180°C/350°F/Gas mark 4.
- Stuff each duck with 1 bread slice and 1 spring onion. Spoon any remaining marinade into the cavities. Prick the ducks, except for the breast area, with a fork.
- Pour the beer into the roasting tin. Roast the ducks on the rack in the lower third of the oven for 30 minutes, then tent them with foil and roast for a further 30 minutes. Discard the foil and roast for another 30 minutes.
- Remove the stuffing ingredients with a spoon, and discard them and the pan juices. Pour the juices from the cavities through a fine sieve into a small bowl. Skim off the fat and reserve 50ml/2fl oz of the juices. Arrange the ducks on a platter and keep warm.
- In a saucepan, bring the stock to the boil, simmer for 15 minutes and stir in the reserved juices. Bring the mixture to a simmer. Stir the arrowroot mixture and add to the pan. Cook the mixture over medium-low heat, being careful not to boil, until thickened. Serve the duck with the sauce.

Duck with Cumberland sauce

serves 4

ingredients

4 duck portions
grated zest and juice of
  1 lemon
grated zest and juice of
  1 large orange
4 tablespoons redcurrant jelly
4 tablespoons port
pinch of ground ginger
1 tablespoon brandy
salt and freshly ground black pepper

- Preheat the oven to 190°C/375°F/Gas mark 5.
- Place a wire rack in a roasting tin. Prick the duck portions all over with a fork, and sprinkle with salt and pepper. Put on the rack and cook in the oven for 45–50 minutes until the juices run clear.
- Simmer the lemon and orange juices and zests together in a saucepan for 5 minutes. Stir in the redcurrant jelly until melted, then stir in the port. Bring to the boil, add the ginger and season with salt and pepper.
- Transfer the duck to a large serving plate, ensuring it is kept warm. Pour away the fat from the roasting tin, leaving the cooking juices. With the roasting tin over a low heat, stir in the brandy and bring to the boil. Stir in the port sauce, and serve with the duck.

Duck vindaloo

serves 4

ingredients

700g/1½lb boneless duck breasts
6 dried red chillies, seeded and
   chopped
150ml/5fl oz distilled malt vinegar
6 garlic cloves, chopped
2cm/1in piece of fresh root
   ginger, grated
1 teaspoon crushed mustard seeds
1 tablespoon ground coriander
1 tablespoon ground cumin
1 teaspoon ground turmeric
1 tablespoon vegetable oil
1 teaspoon salt
1 tablespoon soft brown sugar

- Slice the duck breasts diagonally into 2cm/1in thick slices, and put them in a shallow non-reactive dish.
- Put the chillies, vinegar, garlic, ginger and mustard seeds in a blender or food processor, and purée to a smooth paste. Stir the ground coriander, cumin and turmeric into the paste.
- Pour this spice mixture over the duck slices, and mix until they are evenly coated. Cover and leave to marinate for 3 hours at room temperature or overnight in the refrigerator.
- Heat the oil in a heavy saucepan. Remove the duck from the marinade, reserving the marinade, and add the duck to the pan with the salt. Cook over a gentle heat for 5 minutes, then pour away any excess fat from the pan. Add the reserved marinade and 150ml/5fl oz water, and stir well. Cover and simmer, stirring, for 30 minutes or until the duck is tender.
- Stir in the sugar, increase the heat and cook the vindaloo over a medium-high heat for 6–8 minutes, stirring frequently to prevent it sticking. The sauce should be of a thick coating consistency. Serve hot with basmati rice.

Duck breasts with orange

serves 4

ingredients
4 duck breasts
1 tablespoon sunflower oil
2 oranges
150ml/5fl oz freshly squeezed
    orange juice
1 tablespoon port
2 tablespoons orange marmalade
15g/½oz butter
1 teaspoon cornflour
salt and freshly ground black pepper

- Season the duck breast skin with salt and pepper. Heat the oil in a frying pan over a medium heat, and add the duck breasts, skin side down. Cover and cook for 3–4 minutes until lightly browned. Turn the breasts over, reduce the heat slightly and cook, uncovered, for 5–6 minutes.
- Peel the skin and pith from the oranges. Working over a bowl to catch any juice, slice either side of the membranes to release the orange segments, then set aside with the juice.
- Remove the duck breasts from the pan with a slotted spoon, drain on kitchen paper and keep warm in the oven while making the sauce.
- Drain off the fat from the pan. Add the segmented oranges, all but 2 tablespoons of the orange juice, the port and the orange marmalade to the pan. Bring to the boil, then reduce the heat slightly.
- Blend the cornflour with the reserved orange juice, pour into the pan and stir until slightly thickened. Add the duck breasts, and cook gently for about 3 minutes. Serve hot with the sauce.

Duck with pineapple
serves 4

ingredients

3 tablespoons vegetable oil
1 small onion, thinly shredded
3 slices of fresh root ginger,
   thinly shredded
1 spring onion, thinly shredded
1 small carrot, thinly shredded
175g/6oz cooked duck meat, cut
   into thin strips
100g/4oz canned pineapple cut
   into small slices, drained, with
   2 tablespoons syrup reserved
½ teaspoon salt
1 tablespoon red rice vinegar
1 teaspoon cornflour mixed to a
   paste with 1½ teaspoons water

- Heat the oil in a wok or large heavy frying pan. Add the onion and
  stir-fry until opaque. Add the ginger, spring onion and carrot, and stir-fry
  for 1 minute.
- Add the duck meat and pineapple to the wok together with the salt,
  vinegar and reserved pineapple syrup. Stir until the mixture is well
  blended. Add the cornflour paste, and stir for 1–2 minutes until the
  sauce has thickened. Serve hot.

Duck with leek & cabbage

serves 4

ingredients

4 duck breasts
350g/12oz green cabbage,
  thinly shredded
225g/8oz leeks, sliced
finely grated zest of 1 orange
125ml/4fl oz oyster sauce
1 teaspoon sesame seeds, toasted

- Heat a large wok, and dry-fry the duck breasts with the skin on for about 5 minutes on each side. Remove from the wok, transfer to a clean board and slice thinly with a sharp knife.
- Remove all but 1 tablespoon of the duck fat from the wok and discard.
- Add the cabbage, leeks and orange zest to the wok, and stir-fry for about 5 minutes until the vegetables have softened.
- Return the duck to the wok, and heat through for 2–3 minutes. Drizzle the oyster sauce over the mixture in the wok, toss well until all the ingredients are combined, and heat through.
- Scatter the stir-fry with the sesame seeds, transfer to a warm serving dish and serve hot.

Sweet & spicy duck

serves 4

ingredients

125ml/4fl oz dry sherry
125ml/4fl oz strong black tea
125ml/4fl oz light soy sauce
1 garlic clove, crushed
2 tablespoons clear honey
1 teaspoon ground cloves
salt and freshly ground black pepper
4 small duck breasts, skinned
15g/½oz low-fat spread

- Mix together the sherry, tea, soy sauce, garlic, honey, cloves and a little salt and pepper in a shallow dish. Add the duck and leave to marinate for 1 hour.
- Remove the duck from the marinade, and place on a grill rack. Preheat the grill to medium-high.
- Pour the marinade into a pan, and heat until reduced by half. Stir in the low-fat spread. Brush over the duck, and grill for 10–12 minutes on each side under the grill until golden and cooked through, brushing regularly with the marinade. Serve hot.

Quails with bacon & juniper

serves 4

ingredients

4 quails
3 tablespoons juniper berries
1 teaspoon black peppercorns
1 tablespoon chopped fresh sage
50g/2oz unsalted butter, slightly
   softened
8 rashers smoked streaky bacon

For the rösti
450g/1lb potatoes, peeled
1 bunch spring onions,
   finely chopped
1 red pepper, seeded and
   finely diced
3 tablespoons vegetable oil

- Preheat the oven to 200°C/400°F/Gas mark 6.
- Rinse the quails and pat dry with kitchen paper. Put in a roasting tin.
- Crush the juniper berries and black peppercorns together in a bowl, then mix with the sage leaves and butter to form a paste. Spread evenly over the quails, then place 2 rashers of bacon over each quail. Roast in the oven for 25–30 minutes until cooked through.
- To make the rösti, cook the potatoes in salted boiling water for 15 minutes, drain and allow to cool.
- Coarsely grate the potatoes into a large bowl, add the spring onions and red pepper, and mix well. Divide the mixture into eight, and shape into rounds.
- Heat the oil in a frying pan, and cook the rösti for 2–4 minutes on each side until golden brown and crisp. Keep warm.
- To serve, arrange each quail on 2 rösti rounds, and spoon any juices over. Serve immediately.

Guinea fowl with fennel

serves 4–6

ingredients

4 garlic cloves, chopped
2 tablespoons chopped rosemary
    leaves
2 guinea fowl, each cut into
    8 pieces
olive oil for drizzling
1 red onion, cut into 8 wedges
3 fennel bulbs, cut into 8 pieces
10 slices pancetta, cut into
    1cm/½in pieces
250ml/9fl oz white wine
salt and freshly ground black pepper

- Preheat the oven to 200°C/400°F/Gas mark 6.
- Mix the garlic and rosemary with a pinch of salt and pepper in a small bowl.
- Put the guinea fowl in a separate bowl, drizzle with olive oil and add the garlic mixture. Make sure that each piece is thoroughly coated.
- Transfer the guinea fowl to a roasting tin, and add the red onion, fennel and pancetta. Drizzle with olive oil, and roast for 30 minutes.
- Add the wine and roast for a further 20 minutes. Increase the heat for the last few minutes to brown, and serve hot.

Poached guinea fowl

serves 4

ingredients
1.4kg/3lb guinea fowl
1 teaspoon salt
4 carrots, quartered
2 celery sticks, halved
1 bunch of spring onions, halved
2cm/1in piece of fresh root
   ginger, sliced
2 bay leaves
10 black peppercorns

- Put the guinea fowl in a large pan with the salt. Cover with water and bring to the boil, skimming off the scum from the surface now and then. Add the carrots, celery, spring onions, ginger, bay leaves and peppercorns, and leave to simmer for 45 minutes or until the juices run clear when the thigh is pierced with a skewer.
- Lift the guinea fowl onto a plate, and leave to cool slightly. Strain the remaining stock into a large shallow pan, bring back to the boil and boil rapidly for about 10 minutes until reduced and well flavoured.
- Remove the skin from the guinea fowl, then cut into joints. To do this, first cut off the legs and cut them in half at the joint. Carefully cut the breast meat away from the bones in two large pieces, then cut each one across into two smaller pieces.
- Serve hot with potatoes.

Poussins in vermouth

serves 4

ingredients

4 oven-ready poussins, about
   450g/1lb each
50g/2oz butter, softened
2 shallots, chopped
4 tablespoons chopped fresh
   flat-leaf parsley
225g/8oz white grapes, halved
   and seeded
150ml/5fl oz dry white vermouth
1 teaspoon cornflour
60ml/2½fl oz double cream
salt and freshly ground black pepper

- Preheat the oven to 200°C/400°F/Gas mark 6.
- Rinse the poussins and pat dry with kitchen paper. Spread the butter all over the birds, and put a hazelnut-sized piece in the cavity of each bird.
- Mix together the shallots and parsley. Put a quarter of the shallot mixture inside each bird.
- Put the birds in a roasting tin, and roast in the oven for 40–50 minutes until the juices run clear when the thigh is pierced with a skewer. Transfer to a serving platter and keep warm.
- Skim off most of the fat from the tin, then add the grapes and vermouth. Put the tin over a low heat for a few minutes to warm the grapes. Lift the grapes out of the tin with a slotted spoon, and scatter them around the birds. Keep covered.
- Stir the cornflour into the cream, then add to the pan juices. Cook gently for a few minutes, stirring, until the sauce has thickened. Taste and adjust the seasoning. Pour the sauce around the poussins, and serve hot.

Baked Cornish game hens

serves 6

ingredients

150g/5oz butter, melted
1 onion, chopped
1 celery stick, chopped
½ green pepper, seeded
  and chopped
225g/8oz mushrooms, chopped
1 garlic clove, minced
2 tablespoons chopped fresh
  basil leaves
1 teaspoon dried oregano
2 tablespoon chopped fresh
  flat-leaf parsley
6 Cornish game hens
salt and freshly ground black pepper

- Preheat the oven to 170°C/325°F/Gas mark 3.
- Put 100g/4oz of the butter in a large saucepan. Add the onion, celery, green pepper, mushrooms, garlic, basil and parsley. Gently sweat until the vegetables are tender but not browned.
- Rinse the hens well and pat dry with kitchen paper. Season inside and out with salt and pepper. Stuff each of them with equal amounts of the vegetable mixture, and put them in a baking dish, breast side up.
- Drizzle with the remaining butter, cover and roast in the oven for 1½ hours. Remove from the oven and rest, covered with foil, for a few minutes, then serve hot.

Autumn fruit game hens

serves 8

ingredients

8 Cornish game hens
12 garlic cloves, crushed
4 tablespoons chopped
  fresh oregano
200ml/7fl oz red wine vinegar
150ml/1/4pt olive oil
200g/7oz prunes, pitted
175g/6oz dried apricots
150g/5oz pitted green olives
50g/2oz capers, rinsed
  and drained
8 bay leaves
175g/6oz soft brown sugar
225ml/8fl oz dry white wine
4 tablespoons chopped fresh parsley
salt and freshly ground black pepper

- Clean the hens well under running cold water. Pat dry with kitchen paper. In a large bowl, combine the hens, garlic, oregano, vinegar, oil, prunes, apricots, olives, capers and bay leaves. Season with salt and pepper. Cover and marinate in the refrigerator overnight.
- Preheat the oven to 180°C/350°F/Gas mark 4. Arrange the game hens in shallow roasting tins. Spoon the marinade over the top. Sprinkle evenly with the brown sugar, and pour the wine around them. Roast for 1–1¼ hours, basting frequently, until golden.
- Transfer the hens, fruit, olives and capers to a serving platter. Moisten with the pan juices and sprinkle with the parsley. Serve hot, passing around the remaining pan juices in a sauceboat.

Honey-glazed goose

serves 6

ingredients
5.4kg/12lb goose

For the marinade
3 tablespoons clear honey
1 teaspoon chopped fresh thyme
1 teaspoon chopped fresh coriander
4 tablespoons light soy sauce
3 garlic cloves, crushed
1 teaspoon grated fresh root ginger
1 teaspoon five-spice powder
1 teaspoon ground coriander
pinch of ground cinnamon

- Rinse the goose inside and out, and pat dry with kitchen paper. Remove the wing tips, neck and gizzard. Truss the goose, and place in a non-metallic dish.
- Mix together all the marinade ingredients in a large jug, and pour over the goose. Cover and leave to marinate in the refrigerator overnight, turning and basting occasionally.
- Preheat the oven to 220°C/425°F/Gas mark 7.
- Remove the goose from the marinade, and pat dry with kitchen paper. Weigh the bird, transfer to a rack in a roasting tin and cover with foil. Roast for 20 minutes, then reduce the temperature to 200°C/400°F/Gas mark 6, and roast for 15 minutes per 450g/1lb.
- Serve with roast potatoes and vegetables.

Fish & Seafood

Whether you prefer a spicy meal or a more subtle taste sensation, this chapter offers you a fantastic range of ways to cook all types of fish and seafood, ranging from Salmon Burgers and Prawn Kebabs, to more formal recipes including Sole Véronique, Stuffed Crabs, and Squid with Wine and Rosemary. And cooking with fish and seafood employs a wide range of cooking techniques, from frying and grilling to poaching and baking, so this chapter will also help you to hone your cooking skills.

Grilled stuffed sole

serves 4

ingredients

1 tablespoon olive oil
25g/1oz butter
1 small onion, finely chopped
1 garlic clove, chopped
3 sun-dried tomatoes, chopped
2 tablespoons fresh lemon
    thyme leaves
50g/2oz fresh breadcrumbs
1 tablespoon freshly squeezed
    lemon juice
4 small whole sole, gutted and
    cleaned
lemon wedges, to garnish
salt and freshly ground black pepper

- Preheat the grill. Heat the oil and butter in a frying pan until it just begins to foam. Add the onion and garlic to the frying pan, and cook, stirring, for 5 minutes, or until just softened.
- To make the stuffing, mix together the tomatoes, thyme, breadcrumbs and lemon juice in a bowl, then season with salt and pepper.
- Add the stuffing mixture to the pan, and stir to mix.
- Using a sharp knife, pare the skin from the bone inside the gut hole of the fish to make a pocket. Spoon the stuffing into the pocket.
- Cook the fish, under the grill, for 6 minutes on either side, or until golden brown. Transfer to serving plates, garnish with lemon wedges and serve immediately.

Spicy coconut prawns
serves 3–4

ingredients

3 fresh red chillies, seeded
  and chopped
2 shallots, chopped
1 lemon grass stalk, chopped
3 garlic cloves, chopped
1 teaspoon ground turmeric
1 teaspoon ground coriander
1 tablespoon groundnut oil
2 kaffir lime leaves
1 teaspoon soft brown sugar
2 tomatoes, peeled and chopped
250ml/9fl oz coconut milk
700g/1½lb large raw prawns,
  peeled and deveined
squeeze of lemon juice
salt

- Using a mortar and pestle, pound together the chillies, shallots, lemon grass, garlic, turmeric and coriander until the mixture forms a paste.
- Heat a wok until hot, add the oil and swirl it around. Add the spice paste and stir-fry for 2 minutes. Pour in 250ml/9fl oz water and add the lime leaves, sugar and tomatoes. Simmer for 8–10 minutes until most of the liquid has evaporated.
- Add the coconut milk and prawns, and cook gently, stirring, for 4 minutes until the prawns are pink. Season with lemon juice and salt to taste. Serve immediately.

Seafood lasagne
serves 4

ingredients

50g/2oz butter
50g/2oz plain flour
1 teaspoon mustard powder
600ml/1pt milk
2 tablespoons olive oil, plus extra
  for oiling
1 onion, chopped
2 garlic cloves, finely chopped
1 tablespoon fresh thyme leaves
450g/1lb mixed mushrooms, sliced
150ml/5fl oz white wine

400g/14oz canned chopped
  plum tomatoes
450g/1lb mixed skinless white fish
  fillets, cubed
225g/8oz scallops, trimmed
4–6 sheets fresh lasagne
225g/8oz mozzarella cheese,
  chopped
salt and freshly ground
  black pepper

- Preheat the oven to 200°C/400°F/Gas mark 6.
- Melt the butter in a saucepan over a low heat. Add the flour and mustard powder, and stir until smooth. Cook gently for 2 minutes without colouring.
- Gradually add the milk, whisking until smooth. Bring to the boil and simmer for 2 minutes. Remove from the heat and reserve. Cover the surface of the sauce with cling film to prevent a skin forming.
- Heat the oil in a large frying pan over a low heat. Add the onion, garlic and thyme, and sweat for 5 minutes until softened. Add the mushrooms and cook for a further 5 minutes until softened. Stir in the wine, and boil rapidly until nearly evaporated. Stir in the tomatoes. Bring to the boil, reduce the heat slightly and simmer, covered, for 15 minutes. Season with salt and pepper.
- Lightly oil a lasagne dish. Spoon half of the tomato sauce over the bottom of the dish, and top with half of the fish and scallops. Layer half of the lasagne over this, and cover with half of the white sauce. Dot with half of the mozzarella. Repeat the layers, finishing with the mozzarella.
- Bake in the oven for 30–40 minutes until bubbling, golden and cooked through. Remove from the oven and leave to stand for 10 minutes before serving hot.

Basque tuna stew
serves 4

ingredients
2 tablespoons olive oil
1 onion, chopped
2 garlic cloves, chopped
200g/7oz canned chopped
    plum tomatoes
700g/11/2lb potatoes, cut into
    5cm/2in chunks
3 green peppers, seeded and
    roughly chopped
900g/2lb fresh tuna, cut into chunks
salt and freshly ground black pepper

- Heat the olive oil in a saucepan over a low heat. Add the onion and cook for 8–10 minutes until soft and golden. Add the garlic and cook for a further 1 minute. Add the tomatoes, cover and simmer for about 30 minutes until thickened.
- Meanwhile, mix together the potatoes and peppers in a large clean saucepan. Add 300ml/10fl oz water, which should just cover the vegetables. Bring to the boil over a medium heat, and simmer for 15 minutes until the vegetables are almost tender.
- Add the tuna chunks and the tomato mixture to the potatoes and peppers, and season with salt and pepper. Cover and simmer for 6–8 minutes until the tuna is tender. Transfer to four warmed large individual bowls, and serve immediately.

Californian prawn
& scallop stir-fry
serves 6

ingredients
3 tablespoons vegetable oil
4 tablespoons pine nuts
450g/1lb raw prawns
450g/1lb scallops, quartered
   if large
2 teaspoon grated fresh root ginger
1 fresh green chilli, deseeded and
   finely chopped
2 garlic cloves, finely chopped
1 red pepper, seeded and chopped
225g/8oz spinach, stalks removed
4 onions, sliced
4 tablespoons fish stock
4 tablespoons light soy sauce
4 tablespoons rice wine
1 tablespoon cornflour

- Heat the oil in a wok and add the pine nuts. Cook over a low heat, stirring continuously, until lightly browned. Remove with a slotted spoon and drain on kitchen paper. Set aside.
- Add the prawns and scallops to the oil remaining in the wok and stir over a moderate heat until the scallops are beginning to look opaque and firm, and the prawns are pink.
- Add the ginger, chilli, garlic and pepper, and cook for a few minutes over a medium-high heat. Add the spinach and onion, and stir-fry briefly. Mix the remaining ingredients together in a bowl, and pour over the ingredients in the wok.
- Increase the heat to bring the liquid quickly to a boil, stirring the ingredients continuously. Once the liquid thickens, stir in the reserved pine nuts, and serve immediately.

Mild prawn curry
serves 4

ingredients

75g/3oz desiccated coconut
300ml/10fl oz boiling milk
1 onion, finely chopped
3 tablespoons sunflower oil
2.5cm/1in piece of of fresh root
    ginger, chopped
2 tablespoons Thai fish sauce
350g/12oz basmati rice
1kg/21/4lb raw tiger prawns,
    peeled and deveined

For the masala
½ tablespoon cumin seeds
½ tablespoon coriander seeds
seeds from 6 green
    cardamom pods
½ teaspoon black peppercorns
1 teaspoon dried red chilli flakes
½ teaspoon ground turmeric

- Make the masala by toasting the cumin, coriander and cardamom seeds, peppercorns, chilli flakes and turmeric in a dry frying pan over a low heat for 2–3 minutes until aromatic. Grind to a powder using a mortar and pestle.
- Put the coconut in a bowl, and pour the milk over it. Leave to steep for 20 minutes.
- Sweat the onion in the oil until translucent. Add the masala, stir through and fry gently for 2–3 minutes. Add the ginger, and strain the coconut milk into the mixture through a sieve. Simmer for 10–15 minutes, then add the fish sauce.
- Cook the rice in rapidly boiling water for 8–10 minutes, but do not overcook. Drain.
- Add the prawns to the sauce, and cook for 5–6 minutes until the prawns turn pink. Serve hot with the basmati rice.

Squid sambal
serves 4

ingredients
3 tablespoons groundnut oil
1 tablespoon tamarind pulp, soaked
   in 150ml/5fl oz water for
   10 minutes
1½ teaspoons paprika
1 teaspoon granulated sugar
½ teaspoon salt
450g/1lb small squid with tentacles,
   cleaned

For the spice paste
2 large onions, chopped
2 garlic cloves, chopped
1 teaspoon dried shrimp paste
1½ tablespoons sambal oelek
1 tablespoon chopped fresh
   lemon grass

- Put the ingredients for the spice paste in a blender or food processor, and blend to produce a thick paste.
- Heat the oil in a large saucepan, add the paste and fry over a medium heat for 8 minutes, stirring constantly, until the paste is cooked and lightly golden.
- Strain the tamarind pulp through a sieve, discard the pulp and add the strained tamarind liquid to the pan with the paprika, sugar and salt. Cook the sambal sauce over a very heat, stirring occasionally, for about 10 minutes.
- Cut the squid tubes into 2.5cm/1in thick rings, and add them and the tentacles to the pan.
- Increase the heat and cook the squid sambal, stirring constantly, for 5–6 minutes or until the squid is cooked and the sauce is thick. Serve hot.

Fish fillets in wine sauce
serves 3–4

ingredients
vegetable oil for deep-frying
900g/2lb sole fillets, cut into
    5 x 2.5cm/2 x 1cm pieces
2 egg whites, lightly beaten
3 tablespoons cornflour

For the sauce
3 tablespoons vegetable oil
2 teaspoons caster sugar
125ml/4fl oz dry white wine
50ml/2fl oz rice wine
1 teaspoon salt
2 tablespoons cornflour
175ml/6fl oz fish stock

- In a small deep heavy skillet or frying pan, heat the oil for deep-frying over a medium heat. When the oil is hot, dip each piece of fish in the egg whites, then dredge through the cornflour to coat thoroughly.
- Deep-fry each piece of sole quickly to crisp the outside, about 1 minute each. Remove from the oil with a slotted spoon and drain on kitchen paper. Continue until all the sole is fried.
- For the sauce, heat the oil in a wok over a medium heat. Add the sugar, white wine, rice wine and salt, stirring all the time.
- Blend the cornflour and stock together, add to the wok and stir until the sauce thickens. Carefully put the sole pieces in the wok, and turn them a few times to coat. Serve hot.

Fish loaf
serves 4

ingredients

50g/2oz butter, melted, plus extra
    for greasing
900g/2lb cod fillets, minced
1 small onion, chopped
2 tablespoons fresh white
    breadcrumbs
1 teaspoon salt
2 eggs
2 tablespoons sour cream

For the sauce
1 small onion, finely chopped
25g/1oz butter
1 tablespoon flour
300ml/10fl oz milk
1 teaspoon lemon juice
225g/8oz mushrooms, thinly sliced
1 tablespoon sour cream
salt and freshly ground
    black pepper

- Preheat the oven to 180°C/350°F/Gas mark 4. Grease a 1.2 litre/2pt loaf tin with butter.
- Mix the cod, onion, breadcrumbs, salt, eggs, sour cream and melted butter together in a large bowl. Scrape into the prepared loaf tin, and press down firmly. Bake in the oven for 45 minutes.
- To make the sauce, sweat the onion in the butter until transparent. Add the flour and cook for 1 minute. Add the milk, lemon juice and mushrooms. Season with salt and pepper. Cook until the sauce thickens.
- Add the sour cream to the sauce just before serving. Serve the fish loaf hot with the accompanying sauce.

Pan-seared halibut
serves 4

ingredients
1 teaspoon olive oil
4 skinless halibut steaks, about
    175g/6oz each
½ teaspoon cornflour, mixed
    with 2 teaspoons cold water to
    form a paste
salt and freshly ground black pepper

For the relish
2 red onions, grated
6 shallots, grated
1 tablespoon freshly squeezed
    lemon juice
2 teaspoons olive oil
2 tablespoons red wine vinegar
2 teaspoons caster sugar
150ml/5fl oz fish stock

- To make the relish, put the onions and shallots in a small bowl, and toss in the lemon juice.
- Heat the oil for the relish in a frying pan over a medium heat. Tip in the onions and shallots, and sauté for 3–4 minutes until just softened. Add the vinegar and sugar, and continue to cook for a further 2 minutes over a high heat. Pour in the stock, and season well with salt and pepper. Bring to the boil and simmer gently for 10 minutes until the sauce has thickened and slightly reduced.
- Brush a frying pan with the oil, and heat over a medium-high heat until hot. Press the fish into the pan to seal, reduce the heat and cook for 4 minutes. Turn the fish over and cook for 5 minutes until cooked through. Drain on kitchen paper and keep warm.
- Stir the cornflour paste into the relish and heat through, stirring, until it has thickened. Check and adjust the seasoning if necessary. Pile the relish onto serving plates and top with the halibut.

fish & seafood

Salmon with lemon mash

serves 4

ingredients
4 salmon steaks, about
150g/5oz each
225g/8oz spinach leaves

For the lemon mash
450g/1lb potatoes, cubed
25g/1oz butter
2 tablespoons milk
finely grated zest of ½ lemon

For the sauce
25g/1oz butter
25g/1oz plain flour
200ml/7fl oz skimmed milk
finely grated zest of ½ lemon
4 tablespoons chopped fresh herbs
1 red pepper, finely chopped
1 egg, lightly beaten
salt and freshly ground black pepper

- Cook the potatoes in boiling water for 15–20 minutes until tender.
- Meanwhile, make the sauce. Melt the butter in a saucepan, add the flour and cook, stirring, for 1 minute. Remove from the heat and gradually stir in the milk.
- Return to the heat and bring to the boil, stirring, until thickened and smooth. Add the lemon zest, herbs, red pepper and egg. Season with salt and pepper. Stir well.
- Heat a non-stick frying pan, and cook the salmon for 3–5 minutes on each side until golden brown. Transfer to a flameproof dish.
- Spoon the sauce over the fish, and put under a hot grill until the sauce is set and the salmon is just cooked through.
- Meanwhile, lightly steam the spinach for 8 minutes in a steamer set over a pan of boiling water.
- Drain and mash the potatoes, then stir in the butter, milk and lemon zest. Serve with the fish and spinach.

Seafood balti

serves 4

ingredients

For the seafood

225g/8oz cod fillet, skinned
   and cubed
225g/8oz peeled and deveined
   cooked prawns
6 crab sticks, halved lengthways
1 tablespoon freshly squeezed
   lemon juice
1 teaspoon ground coriander
1 teaspoon chilli powder
1 teaspoon salt
1 teaspoon ground cumin
40g/1½oz cornflour

For the vegetables

300ml/10fl oz corn oil
2 onions, chopped
½ cauliflower, cut into florets
100g/4oz French beans, cut into
   2.5cm/1in lengths
175g/6oz sweetcorn
1 teaspoon shredded fresh
   root ginger
1 teaspoon chilli powder
1 teaspoon salt
4 fresh green chillies, sliced
2 tablespoons chopped fresh
   coriander leaves

- Put the cod, prawns and crab sticks in a mixing bowl.
- In a separate bowl, mix together the lemon juice, ground coriander, chilli powder, salt and cumin. Pour this over the seafood, and mix together thoroughly using your hands.
- Sprinkle on the cornflour, and mix again until the seafood is well coated. Set aside in the refrigerator for about 1 hour to allow the flavours to develop.
- To make the vegetable mixture, heat half of the oil in a preheated wok. Add the onions and stir-fry until lightly browned.
- Add the cauliflower, beans, sweetcorn, ginger, chilli powder, salt and chillies. Stir-fry for 7–10 minutes over a medium heat.
- Spoon the fried vegetables around the edge of a shallow dish, leaving a space in the middle for the seafood.
- Wash the pan, then heat the remaining oil to fry the seafood pieces. Fry in two or three batches until the pieces are golden brown. Remove with a slotted spoon and drain on kitchen paper.
- Arrange the seafood in the middle of the dish of vegetables, and serve immediately.

Seafood kebabs

serves 6

ingredients

700g/1½lb salmon fillet, skinned
  and cut into 2.5cm/1in chunks
12 queen scallops, halved if they
  are large
12 raw king prawns, peeled and
  deveined, but tail left intact
4 tablespoons freshly squeezed
  lime juice
2 tablespoons olive oil
4 fresh basil leaves, shredded
12 fresh bay leaves
salt and freshly ground black pepper

For the sauce
1 teaspoon grated fresh root ginger
1 tablespoon freshly squeezed
  lime juice
12 fresh basil leaves, chopped
100g/4oz butter, softened
75ml/3fl oz dry white wine

- Soak 12 bamboo skewers in water for at least 30 minutes to prevent them burning.
- Put all the seafood in a bowl, and mix with the lime juice, oil and basil. Season with salt and pepper.
- Thread the salmon, prawns and scallops alternately onto the skewers, adding a bay leaf to each skewer.
- To make the sauce, beat together the ginger, lime juice, basil and butter with a little seasoning until well combined.
- Cook the kebabs under a medium grill or on a barbecue for 8–10 minutes, turning occasionally, until evenly cooked and lightly browned on all sides.
- Meanwhile, boil the wine until it is reduced to 2 tablespoons. Remove from the heat, and gradually whisk into the sauce. Serve the hot kebabs with the sauce.

Mediterranean plaice rolls

serves 4

ingredients

75g/3oz butter, plus extra
   for greasing
4 plaice fillets, about 225g/8oz
   each, skinned
1 small onion, chopped
1 celery stick, finely chopped
100g/4oz fresh white breadcrumbs
3 tablespoons chopped fresh
   flat-leaf parsley
2 tablespoons pine nuts, toasted
4 pieces sun-dried tomatoes in oil,
   drained and chopped
50g/2oz canned anchovy fillets,
   drained and chopped
freshly ground black pepper

- Preheat the oven to 180°C/350°F/Gas mark 4. Grease an ovenproof
  dish with a little butter.
- Cut the plaice fillets in half lengthways to make 8 smaller fillets. Melt the
  butter in a pan, and add the onion and celery. Cover and sweat for
  15 minutes, until soft. Do not allow to brown.
- Combine the breadcrumbs, parsley, pine nuts, sun-dried tomatoes and
  anchovies. Stir in the softened vegetables with the buttery juices and
  season with pepper.
- Divide the stuffing into eight portions. Taking one portion at a time, form
  the stuffing into balls, then roll up each one inside a plaice fillet. Secure
  each roll with a cocktail stick.
- Put the rolled-up fillets in the ovenproof dish. Bake for about 20 minutes
  until the fish flakes easily when tested with a fork. Remove the cocktail
  sticks, then serve the hot plaice rolls with a little of the cooking juices
  drizzled over.

Poached red emperor
serves 4

ingredients
900ml/1½pt coconut milk
2 teaspoons grated fresh root ginger
3 fresh red chillies, finely chopped
1 tablespoon chopped coriander
6 shallots, finely chopped
6 kaffir lime leaves
2 lemon grass stalks, white part
  only and tough outer layer
  removed, sliced
2 teaspoons grated lime zest
500ml/18fl oz fish stock
75ml/3fl oz Thai fish sauce
75ml/3fl oz freshly squeezed lime
  juice, strained
4 red emperor fillets, about
  250g/9oz each

- Bring the coconut milk to the boil in a saucepan, and boil for 3 minutes. Add the ginger, chillies, coriander, shallots, lime leaves, lemon grass and lime zest, and bring back to the boil. Add the stock and fish sauce, and simmer for 15 minutes.
- Pass through a sieve, and add the lime juice.
- Heat the sauce in a wide frying pan and, when it comes to the boil, add the fish, then reduce the heat and simmer gently for 10–15 minutes until just cooked through.
- Transfer the fish to a serving platter and drizzle the sauce over the top. Serve immediately.

Smoked haddock quiche
serves 4

ingredients

225g/8oz ready-made shortcrust
    pastry
25g/1oz butter
1 onion, sliced
15g/½oz plain flour
125ml/4fl oz milk
3 eggs, beaten
75g/3oz Cheddar cheese, grated
225g/8oz cooked smoked
    haddock, flaked
3 tomatoes, chopped
salt and freshly ground black pepper

- Preheat the oven to 180°C/350°F/Gas mark 4. Roll out the pastry and use to line a 23cm/9in flan dish.
- Melt the butter in a saucepan, and sweat the onion until soft. Stir in the flour, then the milk, and bring to the boil, stirring continuously.
- Remove the sauce from the heat and add the eggs and half of the cheese. Season with salt and pepper.
- Arrange the flaked fish and tomatoes on the pastry, and pour the sauce over the top. Sprinkle with the remaining cheese.
- Bake in the oven for 30–40 minutes until set and golden brown.

Fish Wellington
serves 6

ingredients
50g/2oz butter
3 onions, thinly sliced
2 skinless monkfish fillets, about
    300g/11oz each
½ teaspoon sweet smoked paprika
2 red peppers
1 large aubergine, cut into
    1cm/½in slices
vegetable oil for brushing
375g/13oz block frozen puff pastry,
    thawed
25g/1oz dried breadcrumbs
1 egg, lightly beaten
salt and freshly ground black pepper

- Melt the butter in a saucepan, add the onion and stir to coat. Cover and sweat gently over a low heat, stirring occasionally, for 15 minutes. Uncover and cook, stirring, for another 15 minutes. Cool, then season with salt and pepper.
- Preheat the oven to 220°C/ 425°F/Gas mark 7.
- Rub one side of each monkfish fillet with the paprika, and put one fillet on top of the other.
- Cut the peppers into quarters, remove the seeds and cook, skin side up, under a hot grill until the skin blackens. Let them cool, then peel off and discard the skin and dice the flesh.
- Put the aubergine on a baking tray. Brush with oil and sprinkle with salt and pepper. Grill until golden, then turn and brown the other side.
- Roll out the pastry on a floured work surface until large enough to enclose the fish. Sprinkle the breadcrumbs lengthways along the centre of the pastry, and put the fish on top of the breadcrumbs. Top with the onion, then the red pepper, then the aubergine.
- Brush the pastry edges with the egg. Fold the pastry over, pressing firmly together to seal. Brush with egg, then bake in the oven for 30 minutes. Slice and serve hot.

Mixed seafood chowder
serves 6–8

ingredients

1 onion, finely chopped
1 green pepper, seeded and
  finely chopped
2 celery sticks, finely sliced
1 carrot, finely chopped
3 garlic cloves, finely minced
3 tablespoons olive oil
450g/1lb canned chopped
  plum tomatoes
250ml/9fl oz tomato purée
1 tablespoon chopped fresh basil
  leaves

1 bay leaf
1 teaspoon salt
½ teaspoon freshly ground
  black pepper
450g/1lb halibut steak
12 fresh mussels
375ml/13fl oz dry white wine
250g/9oz raw prawns, peeled
  and deveined
250g/9oz scallops

- Put the onion, green pepper, celery, carrot, garlic and olive oil in a
  heavy saucepan or casserole dish, and sauté the vegetables on a
  medium heat for 15–20 minutes. Stir in the tomatoes, tomato purée,
  basil, bay leaf, salt and pepper.

- Increase the heat and bring to a rolling boil for 1–2 minutes, then reduce
  the heat to low and simmer for 2 minutes.

- Meanwhile, skin and wash the halibut and cut into bite-size pieces.
  Scrub the mussels thoroughly, removing the beards. Discard any that are
  damaged or do not close when tapped on the work surface.

- Stir the white wine into the sauce, and remove and discard the bay leaf.
  Add the halibut, prawns and scallops, and simmer for 10 minutes.
  Arrange the mussels in a layer on top of the fish in the saucepan. Cover
  tightly and steam for about 10 minutes or until the shells are fully opened
  and the halibut flakes easily. Discard any mussels that do not open in
  the cooking.

- Ladle into individual serving bowls and serve immediately.

Prawn & paneer kebabs

serves 4

ingredients

3 tablespoons Greek-style yogurt

450g/1lb large prawns, peeled and deveined but tails left intact

½ red pepper, seeded and cut into chunks

½ yellow pepper, seeded and cut into chunks

½ red onion, cut into small chunks

100g/4oz paneer cheese, cubed

75ml/3fl oz vegetable oil

1 teaspoon mustard seeds

3 curry leaves

25g/1oz grated coconut

For the spice paste

5 fresh green chillies

3 fresh red chillies

2 garlic cloves

2.5cm/1in piece of fresh root ginger, chopped

2 tablespoons freshly squeezed lemon juice

2 tablespoons vinegar

1 tablespoon cumin seeds

1 tablespoon garam masala

pinch of ground turmeric

- To make the spice paste, put all the ingredients in a blender or food processor and add 75ml/3fl oz water. Purée to a fine paste.
- Transfer the paste to a large bowl, add the yogurt and mix well. Stir in the prawns, peppers and onion, and marinate in the refrigerator for 1 hour.
- Spear the prawns, vegetables and paneer alternately onto bamboo or metal skewers.
- Heat 4 tablespoons of the oil in a large frying pan over a medium heat. Put the kebabs in the pan and cook for 10 minutes, turning regularly to brown evenly.
- In a separate frying pan, heat the remaining oil, then add the mustard seeds and curry leaves. As the mustard seeds begin to pop, pour the contents of the pan over the cooked kebabs.
- Transfer the kebabs to serving plates, garnish with the coconut and serve immediately.

Note You can substitute feta or similar white cheese for the paneer if you cannot find it, but it will be much saltier.

Pan-fried crusted fish curry

serves 4

ingredients

4 dried red chillies

100g/4oz shallots

3 garlic cloves, chopped

2 lemon grass stalks, white part only
   and tough outer layer removed,
   finely sliced

4 fresh coriander roots

2 teaspoons grated lime zest

½ teaspoon green peppercorns,
   roughly chopped

125ml/4fl oz vegetable oil

4 skinless snapper fillets, about
   200g/7oz each

125ml/4fl oz coconut milk

1 tablespoon Thai fish sauce

4 kaffir lime leaves, finely shredded

2 tablespoons freshly squeezed
   lime juice

- Soak the chillies in a bowl of boiling water for 15 minutes. Drain and chop roughly.
- Put the chillies, shallots, garlic, lemon grass, coriander, lime zest, peppercorns and 1 tablespoon of the oil in a blender or food processor, and purée until a smooth paste forms. Spread the paste over one side of each snapper fillet.
- Heat the remaining oil in a large heavy pan. Cook the snapper fillets for 3 minutes on each side until just cooked.
- Stir together the coconut milk, fish sauce, lime leaves and lime juice in a bowl or jug. Pour over the snapper fillets, and simmer for 3 minutes. Serve hot.

Salmon in aspic
serves 10

ingredients
1.8kg/4lb whole fresh salmon
1 teaspoon aspic jelly crystals
2 tablespoons redcurrant jelly

For the sauce
150ml/5fl oz red wine vinegar
1 onion, sliced
3 bay leaves
12 black peppercorns
450ml/¾pt water

- Put the sauce ingredients in a large pan, and simmer for 20 minutes. Cool and drain through a sieve.
- Put the salmon in a large heavy roasting tin, and pour the sauce over it. Cover the tin and poach very gently for 20–30 minutes. Leave to cool.
- When completely cold, gently lift the fish out of the roasting tin. Carefully peel off the skin and scrape off any dark brown flesh.
- Strain the cooking liquid through muslin, pour into a large pan and boil over a high heat until the liquid has reduced to 300ml/10fl oz. Add the aspic and redcurrant jelly, and stir to dissolve. Leave to cool and chill until nearly set.
- Arrange the salmon on a plate, and brush with the liquid aspic. Chill before serving.

Tuna with pak choi
serves 4

ingredients
4 tuna fillets, about 175g/6oz each
3 fresh red chillies, thinly sliced
2 garlic cloves, thinly sliced
225ml/8fl oz red wine
1 tablespoon olive oil
200g/7oz pak choi, coarsely
  chopped
100g/4oz button mushrooms,
  halved lengthways
salt and freshly ground black pepper

- Put the pieces of tuna in a single layer in a glass or ceramic dish.
  Sprinkle the chillies and garlic over the tuna, and pour the wine over the
  top. Cover and marinate in the refrigerator for 1 hour.
- Lift the tuna out of the marinade, drain on kitchen paper and season with
  a little salt.
- Pour the marinade into a small pan, season with salt and pepper, then
  simmer for a few minutes until reduced by about half. Remove from the
  heat, cover and keep warm.
- Heat a ridged cast-iron grill pan until very hot. Dip a wad of kitchen
  paper in oil, and wipe it over the hot pan. Put the tuna in the pan, and
  chargrill for 3–4 minutes.
- Heat the remaining oil in a wok or large deep frying pan until very hot.
  Add the pak choi and mushrooms, and stir-fry over a high heat for about
  3 minutes. Season with salt and pepper.
- To serve, cut the tuna fillets in half, mound the vegetables on warmed
  plates and top with the tuna and marinade. Serve hot.

Creamy fish gratin
serves 8

ingredients

100g/4oz butter
175g/6oz leeks, roughly chopped
450ml/¾pt fish stock
300ml/10fl oz vermouth
4 tablespoons Pernod
350g/12oz monkfish fillet, cut into
   large pieces
350g/12oz salmon fillet, cut into
   large pieces
225g/8oz raw prawns, peeled
   and deveined

225g/8oz raw scallops, halved
175g/6oz onions, chopped
100g/4oz plain flour
150ml/5fl oz double cream
450ml/¾pt milk
75g/3oz Parmesan cheese, grated
75g/3oz Gruyère cheese, grated
1 tablespoon Dijon mustard
4 eggs, separated
15g/½oz coarse breadcrumbs
salt and ground black pepper

- Preheat the oven to 190°C/375°F/Gas mark 5.
- Melt 25g/1oz of the butter in a pan. Add the leeks and cook, stirring, for 4–5 minutes until golden. Pour in the stock, vermouth and Pernod, and bring to the boil. Add the monkfish and salmon, and simmer for 2–3 minutes, then add the prawns and scallops, and simmer for another 3 minutes. Remove the fish, reserve the liquor and wipe out the pan.
- Add 50g/2oz of the butter and the onions to the pan, and cook for 10 minutes or until soft and golden. Stir in 50g/2oz of the flour, and cook for a further minute, stirring. Pour in the reserved poaching liquor and the cream, whisking to prevent lumps forming. Bring to the boil and bubble hard for 10 minutes. Season with salt and pepper. Put the fish and leeks in a 2.4-litre/4pt ovenproof dish, then pour the hot sauce over the top.
- Melt the remaining butter in a large pan, add the remaining flour and cook, stirring, for 1 minute. Pour in the milk and, whisking continuously, bring the mixture to the boil. Stir in 100g/4oz of the cheeses and the mustard. Cool slightly, then stir in the egg yolks. Season well.
- Whisk the egg whites in a bowl until they form soft peaks, then fold them into the sauce. Spoon the topping over the fish, and sprinkle with the remaining cheeses and the breadcrumbs. Cook for 1 hour and serve hot.

Fried squid curry
serves 4–6

ingredients

3 tablespoons vegetable oil
900g/2lb small squid, cleaned
    and cut into 2.5cm/1in rings
1 teaspoon soft brown sugar

For the curry sauce
2 small onions, finely chopped
3 garlic cloves, crushed
8 curry leaves
7cm/3in piece of cinnamon stick,
    broken in half

1 lemon grass stalk, tough outer
    layer removed, bruised
½ teaspoon ground ginger
1 teaspoon ground turmeric
1 teaspoon chilli powder
1 tablespoon Sri Lankan curry
    powder
3 tablespoons freshly squeezed
    lime juice
600ml/1pt coconut milk
salt

- Put all the ingredients for the curry sauce into a heavy saucepan and bring to the boil. Reduce the heat and simmer the sauce for about 45 minutes until it is very thick.
- Heat half of the the oil in a large frying pan, and add half of the squid. Cook over a fairly high heat, stirring constantly, for 1–2 minutes until the squid has turned white and is just cooked. Using a slotted spoon, transfer the squid to the curry sauce, and repeat the process with the remaining oil and squid.
- Stir the sugar into the squid curry, and simmer the curry gently for 5 minutes to heat through. Taste and adjust the seasoning if necessary. Serve at once.

Prawn burgers

serves 4

ingredients

12 large raw prawns, peeled and
  deveined
2 tablespoons freshly squeezed
  lemon juice
1 tablespoon sesame seeds
100g/4oz fresh white breadcrumbs
2 tablespoons chopped fresh
  coriander leaves
1 egg, lightly beaten
2 teaspoons chilli sauce
plain flour for dusting
olive oil for frying
75g/3oz mayonnaise
1 spring onion, finely chopped
1 tablespoon tomato ketchup
1 teaspoon Worcestershire sauce
4 hamburger buns, halved

- Flatten the prawns slightly to open out, and mix with the lemon juice.
- Combine the sesame seeds, breadcrumbs and coriander on a sheet of
  baking parchment. Combine the egg and chilli sauce in a bowl. Dredge
  the prawns in the flour and shake off the excess. Dip in the egg and
  press firmly in the breadcrumbs. Put on a tray covered in baking
  parchment, cover and chill for 10 minutes.
- Heat a little oil in a frying pan. Cook the prawns in batches over a
  medium heat for 2–3 minutes on each side. Remove and drain on
  kitchen paper.
- Combine the mayonnaise, spring onion, tomato and Worcestershire
  sauces in a bowl.
- Put the prawns in the burger buns, and serve with the sauce.

Salt & pepper squid
serves 6

ingredients

900g/2lb squid hoods, halved
    lengthways
250ml/9fl oz freshly squeezed
    lemon juice
250g/9oz cornflour
1½ tablespoons salt
1 tablespoon ground white pepper
2 teaspoons caster sugar
4 egg whites, lightly beaten
vegetable oil for deep-frying
lemon wedges, to serve

- Open out the squid hoods, wash and pat dry with kitchen paper. Lay
  on a chopping board with the insides facing upwards. Score a fine
  diamond pattern in the squid, being careful not to cut all the way
  through. Cut into pieces about 5 x 3cm/2 x 1¼in. Put in a flat glass or
  ceramic dish, and pour the lemon juice over. Cover and refrigerate for
  15 minutes. Drain and pat dry with kitchen paper.
- Combine the cornflour, salt, white pepper and sugar in a bowl. Dip
  the squid in the egg white, and dredge in the flour mixture, shaking off
  any excess.
- Fill a deep heavy pan one-third full with oil, and heat until a cube of
  bread browns in 15 seconds. Deep-fry the squid, in batches, for
  1–2 minutes until the squid turns white and curls. Drain on kitchen paper.
  Serve immediately with lemon wedges.

Seafood fajitas
serves 4

ingredients
250g/9oz scallops
300g/11oz raw prawns
250g/9oz skinless hake fillets
3 tomatoes, finely chopped
1 red chilli, finely chopped
2 spring onions, finely sliced
Salt and pepper
75ml/3fl oz lime juice
1 garlic clove, crushed
1 avocado
2 tablespoons freshly squeezed
  lemon juice
4 flour tortillas
1 onion, thinly sliced
1 green pepper, seeded and sliced

- Slice or pull off any vein, membrane or white muscle from the scallops, leaving any roe attached. Peel and devein the prawns. Cut the hake into bite-size pieces.
- Preheat the oven to 160°C/325°F/Gas mark 3. Combine the tomato, chilli and spring onion in a bowl, and season with salt and pepper.
- Combine the scallops, prawns, hake, lime juice and garlic in another bowl, cover and refrigerate while preparing the other ingredients.
- Slice the avocado and brush with the lemon juice to prevent browning.
- Wrap the tortillas in foil and heat in the oven for 10 minutes.
- Heat a lightly oiled cast-iron grill pan until very hot, add the onion and pepper and cook, turning occasionally, until lightly brown. Push them all to one side of the pan. Drain the seafood thoroughly, and cook briefly until it is seared all over and cooked through.
- To serve, wrap the seafood, onion, green pepper, avocado and tomato mixture in the tortillas. Serve immediately.

Kettle-cooked sea bass

serves 8

ingredients

1.8kg/4lb sea bass, gutted, with
    head and tail left on
1 large bunch of spring onions,
    shredded
2 celery sticks, cut into matchsticks
5cm/2in piece of fresh root ginger,
    cut into matchsticks
vegetable oil for brushing
50ml/2fl oz light soy sauce
50ml/2fl oz dry sherry
salt and freshly ground black pepper

- Wash the fish inside and out, then pat dry thoroughly. Using a sharp knife, make several deep diagonal slashes on both sides of the fish.
- Pour water under the rack of a fish kettle, and put half of the spring onion, celery and ginger on the rack. Brush the outside of the fish lightly with oil, then place over the flavourings on the rack. Sprinkle the remaining spring onion, celery and ginger over the fish, then the soy sauce and sherry. Season with salt and pepper.
- Cover the kettle with its lid, bring the water slowly to the boil, then simmer for 20 minutes. Serve immediately.

Alaskan salmon chowder
serves 6

ingredients
200g/7oz canned Alaskan
  pink salmon
100g/4oz onions, chopped
100g/4oz celery, chopped
1 garlic clove, minced
25g/1oz margarine
225g/8oz potatoes, diced
175g/6oz carrots, diced
450ml/¾pt fish stock
½ teaspoon dried thyme
¼ teaspoon black pepper
100g/4oz broccoli, chopped
375ml/13fl oz evaporated milk
275g/10oz frozen sweetcorn
  kernels, thawed

- Drain and flake the salmon, reserving the liquid.
- Sauté the onions, celery and garlic in margarine in a large frying pan until soft. Add the potatoes, carrots, reserved salmon liquid, fish stock, thyme and pepper. Simmer, covered, for 20 minutes or until the vegetables are nearly tender.
- Add the broccoli and cook for 5 minutes. Add the flaked salmon, evaporated milk and sweetcorn, and heat thoroughly. Serve immediately.

Dover sole with capers

serves 4

ingredients
olive oil for drizzling
4 Dover sole, skinned
2 tablespoons capers, rinsed
  and drained
2 tablespoons finely chopped
  fresh marjoram
salt and freshly ground black pepper
2 lemons, cut into wedges, to serve

- Preheat the oven to 220°C/425°F/Gas mark 7.
- Heat two flat baking trays, scatter them with salt and pepper, and drizzle with olive oil.
- Lay the Dover sole on the trays. Scatter over the capers and marjoram, season with salt and pepper, and drizzle with olive oil.
- Put the trays in the oven, and roast the fish for 10–15 minutes until the flesh comes away easily from the bone when tested with a knife. Serve hot with the lemon wedges for squeezing over.

Sole Véronique
serves 4

ingredients

12 sole fillets
250ml/9fl oz fish stock, made from
   stock cubes
50ml/2fl oz white wine
1 shallot, finely sliced
1 bay leaf
6 black peppercorns
15g/½oz butter
3 teaspoons flour
125ml/4fl oz milk
50ml/2fl oz single cream
125g/4½oz seedless white
   grapes, peeled

- Preheat the oven to 180°C/350°F/Gas mark 4.
- Roll the fillets into coils with the skin on the inside. Secure with toothpicksm and put in a well-greased ovenproof dish.
- Combine the stock, wine, shallot, bay leaf and peppercorns in a jug, and pour over the fish. Cover with greased foil and bake for 15 minutes or until the fish flakes when tested with a fork. Carefully lift the fish out of the liquid with a slotted spoon, put in another dish, cover and keep warm.
- Pour the cooking liquid into a saucepan, and boil for about 2 minutes until reduced by half, then strain.
- In a clean pan, melt the butter, add the flour and stir for 1 minute, or until pale and foaming. Remove from the heat and gradually stir in the milk, cream and strained cooking liquid. Return to the heat, and stir until the mixture boils and thickens.
- Add the grapes, then stir until heated through. Serve immediately, with the sauce poured over the fish.

Seafood medley

serves 4

ingredients
2 tablespoons white wine
1 egg white, lightly beaten
½ teaspoon five-spice powder
1 teaspoon cornflour
300g/11oz raw peeled prawns,
   deveined
100g/4oz prepared squid, cut
   into rings
100g/4oz cod fillets, cut into strips
vegetable oil for deep-frying
1 green pepper, seeded and cut
   into strips
1 carrot, cut into thin strips
4 baby corn cobs, halved
   lengthways

- Mix the wine, egg white, five-spice powder and cornflour in a large bowl. Add the prawns, squid and cod, and stir to coat evenly. Remove with a slotted spoon, reserving any leftover cornflour mixture.
- Heat the oil in a wok, and deep-fry the prawns, squid and cod for 2–3 minutes. Remove from the wok with a slotted spoon and set aside.
- Pour off all but 1 tablespoon of oil from the wok and return to the heat. Add the pepper, carrot and corn cobs, and stir-fry for 4–5 minutes.
- Return the prawns, squid and cod to the wok with any remaining cornflour mixture. Heat through, stirring, and serve hot with rice.

Ceviche

serves 4

ingredients
450g/1lb haddock fillets
1 teaspoon coriander seeds
1 teaspoon black peppercorns
juice of 6 limes
1 teaspoon salt
2 tablespoons olive oil
1 bunch of spring onions,
   finely chopped
4 tomatoes, chopped
Tabasco sauce, to taste
2 tablespoons chopped fresh
   coriander leaves
1 avocado

- To skin the haddock fillets, put them skin side down on a board, dip your fingers in salt, then grip the tail end of the skin. Using a sharp knife, flake off the flesh of the fish by working away from you with a sawing action.
- Wash the fillets, then pat them dry with kitchen paper. Cut diagonally into thin even strips, and put in a bowl.
- Crush the coriander seeds and peppercorns to a fine powder using a mortar and pestle. Mix with the lime juice and salt, then pour over the fish. Cover and chill in the refrigerator for 24 hours, turning the fish occasionally.
- The next day, heat the oil in a pan, add the spring onions and fry gently for 5 minutes. Add the tomatoes and Tabasco sauce to taste, and toss together briskly over the heat for 1–2 minutes. Remove from the heat and leave to cool for 20–30 minutes.
- To serve, drain the fish from the marinade, discarding the marinade. Combine the fish with the spring onion and tomato mixture and the chopped coriander. Halve the avocado, peel and remove the stone. Slice the flesh widthways. Arrange the slices around the edge of a serving bowl, and pile the ceviche in the centre. Serve chilled.

Fresh baked sardines

serves 4

ingredients

2 tablespoons olive oil
2 large onions, sliced into rings
3 garlic cloves, chopped
2 large courgettes, cut into sticks
3 tablespoons fresh thyme leaves
8 sardine fillets
75g/3oz Parmesan cheese,
   freshly grated
4 eggs, beaten
150ml/5fl oz milk
salt and freshly ground black pepper

- Preheat the oven to 180°C/350°F/Gas mark 4.
- Heat 1 tablespoon of the oil in a frying pan. Add the onions and garlic, and sauté for 2–3 minutes. Add the courgettes and cook for about 5 minutes until golden. Stir 2 tablespoons of the thyme into the mixture.
- Put half of the onions and half of the courgettes in the bottom of a large ovenproof dish. Top with the sardine fillets and half of the Parmesan. Put the remaining onions and courgettes on top, and sprinkle with the remaining thyme.
- Mix the eggs and milk together in a bowl, and season with salt and pepper. Pour the mixture over the vegetables and sardines in the dish. Sprinkle the remaining Parmesan over the top.
- Bake in the oven for 20–25 minutes until golden and set. Serve immediately.

Ocean pie

serves 4

ingredients
500g/1lb 2oz cod fillet, skinned
225g/8oz salmon steak
450ml/¾pt skimmed milk
1 bay leaf
900g/2lb potatoes, coarsely
   chopped
50g/2oz peeled and deveined
   prawns
50g/2oz margarine
25g/1oz plain flour
3 tablespoons white wine
1 teaspoon chopped fresh dill
2 tablespoons rinsed and
   drained capers
salt and freshly ground black pepper

- Preheat the oven to 200°C/400°F/Gas mark 6.
- Put the cod and salmon into a saucepan with 300ml/10fl oz of the milk and the bay leaf. Season with salt and pepper. Bring to the boil, cover and simmer gently for 10–15 minutes until tender.
- Cook the potatoes in salted boiling water for about 15 minutes until tender.
- Drain the fish, reserving the cooking liquid. Flake the fish, discarding any bones, and put in a shallow ovenproof dish. Add the prawns.
- Melt half of the margarine in a saucepan, add the flour and cook, stirring, for 1 minute. Gradually stir in the reserved cooking liquid and the wine, and bring to the boil. Add the dill, capers and salt and pepper to taste, and simmer until thickened. Pour over the fish and mix well.
- Drain the potatoes and mash them, adding the remaining margarine and the remaining milk. Season with salt and pepper.
- Spread the mashed potatoes over the fish, and cook in the oven for about 25 minutes or until piping hot and browned. Serve immediately.

Skate with black butter

serves 4

ingredients

175g/6oz butter, chopped, plus a
  little extra
900g/2lb small skate wings
600ml/1pt fish stock
75ml/3fl oz malt vinegar

- To clarify the butter, melt in a pan over a low heat without stirring.
  Remove from the heat and cool slightly. Skim off the foamy mixture from
  the surface. Pour off the clear yellow liquid and reserve. Discard the
  milky sediment left in the pan.
- Pat the skate dry with kitchen paper. Cut fillets from either side of the
  cartilage using a sharp knife, cutting close to the cartilage. Place skin
  side down on a chopping board and, using a sawing motion, cut along
  the length of the wing. Cut into similar-sized pieces.
- Put the stock and vinegar in a large heavy pan, and bring to the boil.
  Add the skate and poach for 8 minutes. Drain well and pat dry with
  kitchen paper.
- Melt a little butter in a frying pan, and cook the skate for 1–2 minutes on
  each side until tender. Put on a serving dish and keep warm.
- Heat the clarified butter in a pan until brown and foaming. Pour over the
  skate, and serve immediately.

Smoked fish with white sauce

serves 6–8

ingredients

900g/2lb haddock fillets, cut into
   serving-sized pieces
225ml/8fl oz milk
225ml/8fl oz water

For the white sauce
600ml/1pt milk
1 onion, halved
1 bay leaf
pinch of ground white pepper
50g/2oz butter
40g/1½oz plain flour
1–2 tablespoons chopped fresh
   flat-leaf parsley
salt and freshly ground black pepper

- For the white sauce, combine the milk in a small pan with the onion, bay leaf and white pepper. Heat slowly to a simmer, then remove from the heat and allow to stand for 3 minutes before straining into a jug. Melt the butter in a pan over a low heat, stir in the flour and cook for 1 minute or until pale and foaming.
- Remove from the heat and gradually stir in the milk.
- Return to the heat and stir constantly until the sauce boils and thickens. Reduce the heat and simmer for 2 minutes. Remove from the heat and season with salt and pepper. Stir in the parsley. Keep warm.
- Put the haddock pieces in a large frying pan. Combine the milk with 225ml/8fl oz water. Pour into the pan to cover the haddock. Bring to the boil, reduce the heat to low and gently cook the fish until it flakes easily at the thickest part when tested with a fork.
- Lift the haddock out of the pan using a slotted spoon. Drain on kitchen paper, and place on serving plates. Top with the white sauce, and serve immediately.

Stuffed crabs

serves 6

ingredients

6 cooked medium blue
   swimmer crabs
50g/2oz butter
2 garlic cloves, finely chopped
½ red pepper, seeded and
   finely chopped
½ green pepper, seeded and
   finely chopped
1 small onion, finely chopped
1 celery stick, finely chopped
½ fresh red chilli, finely chopped
¼ teaspoon celery salt
¼ teaspoon dried thyme
175ml/6fl oz canned condensed
   seafood bisque
75g/3oz fresh breadcrumbs
salt and freshly ground black pepper

* Preheat the oven to 200°C/400°F/Gas mark 6.
* Pull away the crab legs and claws, crack open and extract the meat
  from the legs.
* Reserve 2 front claws on each crab. Lift the flap on the underside of the
  crab and prise off the top shell. Remove the soft organs and pull off the
  gills. Scrub the crab back shells and set aside. Shred the crab meat,
  picking out the shell fragments.
* Melt the butter in a pan, and add the chopped garlic, peppers, onion,
  celery and chilli. Cook, stirring, over a medium heat, for about 5
  minutes. Add the celery salt, thyme and bisque, and cook for 3 minutes.
  Add the crab meat with half the breadcrumbs. Stir until combined and
  season with salt and pepper.
* Spoon the mixture into the crab shells, smooth the tops and press the
  remaining crumbs over the surface. Put the crabs on a baking tray, and
  bake in the oven for about 15 minutes until heated through and golden,
  adding the extra claws close to the end of cooking to warm through.
  Serve hot.

Prawn & spinach lasagne

serves 6

ingredients

225g/8oz fresh egg lasagne,
  unrolled
1½ teaspoons salt

For the filling
900g/2lb fresh spinach, stems
  removed
50g/2oz butter

1 large onion, finely chopped
450g/1lb raw prawns, peeled
  and deveined
½ teaspoon salt
125ml/4fl oz plain tomato sauce
600ml/1pt béchamel sauce (see
  page 728)
50g/2oz Parmesan cheese, grated

- Roll the lasagne as thinly as possible. With a knife, cut into sheets of
  8 x 11cm/3½ x 4½in and let them rest on dry tea towels for at least
  15 minutes.
- Bring a large saucepan of water to the boil. Add the salt, and slip in the
  pasta, two or three pieces at a time, leaving to cook for 1 minute.
  Remove with a slotted spoon, and immerse immediately in cold water.
  Lay the pasta on damp tea towels.
- To make the filling, put the spinach in a large deep pan with no water.
  Cook, tossing occasionally, for 5–10 minutes. Remove from the heat,
  chop finely and set aside.
- Warm the butter in a frying pan and add the onion. Sauté over a
  medium heat for 4 minutes. Add the prawns and sauté quickly, stirring to
  cook evenly. Remove the pan from the heat and stir in the chopped
  spinach and salt.
- Preheat the oven to 200°C/400°F/Gas mark 6.
- Combine the tomato and béchamel sauces. Select a 25 x 35cm/
  10 x 14in baking dish. Smear a very thin layer of sauce on the bottom
  of the baking dish. Carefully place a layer of the pasta over the sauce,
  to cover the entire area. Smear a thin layer of sauce over the pasta.
  Spoon some of the spinach and prawn mixture over it, and sprinkle with
  some Parmesan. Repeat the process of layering, ending with a layer of
  pasta, topped with sauce and cheese.
- Bake for about 20 minutes or until the sauce forms a light golden crust.
  Remove the dish from the oven and leave to stand for 10 minutes before
  serving, cut into slices.

Baked stuffed lobster

serves 4

ingredients

50ml/2fl oz vegetable oil
1 large onion, finely chopped
4 garlic cloves, finely chopped
250ml/9oz tomato purée
150ml/5fl oz red wine
225g/8oz cooked canned clams,
    with their juice
450g/1lb dried white breadcrumbs
1½ teaspoons dried oregano
1 teaspoon garlic salt
1 tablespoon freshly grated
    Parmesan cheese
1 tablespoon chopped fresh
    flat-leaf parsley
3 or 4 medium or large lobsters,
    halved, intestines removed

- Preheat the oven to 200°C/400°F/Gas mark 6.
- Heat the oil and sauté the onion and garlic in a frying pan over a medium heat for about 5 minutes until they are translucent. Add the tomato purée and cook for 3 minutes, then add the wine and the clams and their juice. Cook for 5 minutes.
- In a large mixing bowl, mix together the breadcrumbs, oregano, garlic salt, Parmesan and parsley. Make a well in the middle, and pour in the sauce. Stir and mix into a very soft dough. Cover and set aside.
- Put each lobster on a chopping board, and stuff carefully with the prepared mixture, making sure that the holes are well filled. Push the halves together to encase the stuffing. Repeat the exercise with the remaining lobsters and stuffing.
- Lightly grease a baking tray, and place the lobsters on it. Bake in the oven for 45–60 minutes, checking halfway through. Serve hot with a crisp green salad.

Prawn gumbo
serves 4

ingredients
50ml/2fl oz vegetable oil, plus
   2 tablespoons extra
6 rashers bacon, finely chopped
2½ tablespoons plain flour
2 onions, finely chopped
½ teaspoon cayenne pepper
1 red pepper, seeded and chopped
1 green pepper, seeded
   and chopped
16 okra, trimmed, halved lengthways
1 bay leaf
850g/1¾lb canned tomatoes
900g/2lb raw prawns, peeled and
   deveined, but with tails left intact
1 teaspoon Tabasco sauce
salt and freshly ground black pepper

- Heat the 50ml/2fl oz oil in a large saucepan, add the bacon and cook over a medium heat for 5 minutes. Stir in the flour and cook, stirring, until the flour turns nutty brown. Remove from the pan. This mixture, known as a roux, will be used to thicken and flavour the gumbo.
- Heat the extra 2 tablespoons oil in the saucepan, add the onion, cayenne and peppers, and cook, stirring, over a medium heat for 5 minutes or until the onion is golden brown.
- Add the okra, bay leaf and tomatoes to the saucepan, and bring to the boil. Reduce the heat and simmer for 30 minutes. You may need to add water if the mixture is too thick.
- Stir the prawns and the roux into the mixture, add the Tabasco and season with salt and pepper. Cook for 5 minutes or until the prawns are cooked. Serve hot.

Salmon & asparagus linguine
serves 4

ingredients

150g/5oz asparagus, cut into
   5cm/2in lengths
2 eggs
juice of ½ lemon
2 tablespoons chopped fresh dill
275g/10oz fresh linguine
175g/6oz smoked salmon
   trimmings, cut into strips
salt and freshly ground black pepper

- Cook the asparagus in salted boiling water for 2–5 minutes until just
  tender. Remove with a slotted spoon and drain on kitchen paper,
  keeping the water hot in the pan.
- Break the eggs into a round-bottomed bowl, and add the lemon juice.
  Set the bowl over a separate pan of hot water, making sure that the
  bottom of the bowl does not touch the water. Whisk the eggs until
  warmed, pale and very frothy. Season with salt and pepper, and stir in
  half of the dill, then remove the bowl from the pan and set aside in a
  warm place.
- Top up the asparagus water with boiling water, and bring back to the
  boil. Add the linguine, and boil for 7–8 minutes.
- Drain the linguine, reserving the water, then return the linguine to the
  pan. Add the asparagus and salmon with 1 ladleful of the cooking water
  and the lemon sauce. Toss and add more water if necessary.
- Season with the rest of the dill, and serve immediately.

Moules marinière

serves 4

ingredients

1.1kg/2½lb mussels
1 onion, finely chopped
1 tablespoon olive oil
1 garlic clove, crushed
200ml/7fl oz dry white wine
1 bay leaf
1 tablespoon fresh thyme leaves
2 tablespoons chopped fresh parsley
salt and freshly ground black pepper

- Rinse the mussels well in cold water, and scrape off any barnacles with a small, sharp knife. Remove the beards. Discard any mussels that are damaged or do not close when tapped sharply against the work surface.
- In a deep lidded saucepan, sweat the onion in the oil until softened. Add the garlic and stir for 1 minute, then add the wine, bay leaf, thyme and drained mussels. Stir well, cover tightly and cook rapidly for 5–10 minutes until the mussels have opened. Discard any mussels that remain closed.
- Remove from the heat, and add the parsley. Season with salt and pepper, and serve immediately.

Prawn jambalaya

serves 6

ingredients

900g/2lb large raw prawns, peeled
    and deveined (reserve the heads,
    shells and tails)
2 onions, chopped
2 celery sticks, chopped
225ml/8fl oz dry white wine
50ml/2fl oz vegetable oil
200g/7oz spicy sausage, chopped
1 red pepper, seeded and chopped
400g/14oz canned chopped
    plum tomatoes
½ teaspoon cayenne pepper
½ teaspoon cracked black pepper
½ teaspoon dried thyme
½ teaspoon dried oregano
400g/14oz long-grain rice

- Put the reserved prawn heads, shells and tails in a pan with half of the onion, half of the celery, the wine and 1.2 litres/2pt water. Bring to the boil, then reduce the heat and simmer for 20 minutes. Strain.
- Heat the oil in a large heavy pan. Cook the sausage for 5 minutes or until browned. Remove from the pan with a slotted spoon, and set aside.
- Add the rest of the onion, celery and the red pepper to the pan and cook, stirring occasionally, for 5 minutes. Add the tomato, cayenne, black pepper and dried herbs, and bring to the boil. Reduce the heat and simmer, covered, for 10 minutes.
- Return the sausage to the pan, and add the rice and prawn stock. Bring back to the boil, reduce the heat and simmer, covered, for 25 minutes until almost all the liquid has been absorbed and the rice is tender.
- Add the prawn meat to the pan, and stir through gently. Cover and cook for another 5 minutes. Serve immediately.

Taglierini & seafood sauce

serves 4–6

ingredients

225g/8oz raw prawns, peeled
  and deveined
1 tablespoon olive oil
50g/2oz butter
2 garlic cloves, finely chopped
450g/1lb canned plum tomatoes,
  drained and chopped
125ml/4fl oz dry white wine
450g/1lb whole sea bass, gutted
  and washed
225g/8oz cod fillets
⅛ teaspoon saffron threads, crushed
450g/1lb fresh egg pasta, cut into
  taglierini (fine noodles)
salt and freshly ground black pepper

- Rinse the prawns, dry well with a tea towel, then dice and set aside.
- Warm the oil and 40g/1½oz of the butter in a wide deep frying pan. Add the garlic and sauté for 3–4 minutes until softened. Add the tomatoes and simmer for 5 minutes over a medium heat.
- Stir in the wine, and allow it to evaporate for 2 minutes. Put the sea bass and cod in the pan. Cook for 10 minutes over a medium heat, turning once. Remove the pan from the heat.
- Lift the whole sea bass out of the pan, and remove its bones and skin. Flake the meat finely, and return to the pan.
- Warm the remaining butter in a small frying pan and add the prawns. Sauté for about 3 minutes. Add the prawns, saffron and salt to the sauce, and heat through. Season with pepper and remove the heat.
- Meanwhile, bring a large saucepan of water to the boil. Add the pasta and 1½ tablespoons salt. Let the water return to the boil, then cook for 15 seconds.
- Drain the pasta and toss with the seafood sauce in the frying pan, then serve immediately.

Piri piri prawns

serves 4

ingredients

100ml/3½fl oz tablespoons oil
2 teaspoons dried red chilli flakes
4 garlic cloves, crushed
1 teaspoon salt
900g/2lb medium raw prawns,
    peeled and deveined
75g/3oz butter
50ml/2fl oz freshly squeezed
    lemon juice

- Put the oil, chilli flakes, garlic and salt in a large glass bowl and mix well. Stir the prawns into the oil and chilli mixture, cover and refrigerate for 3 hours, stirring and turning occasionally.
- Preheat the grill to very hot. Put the prawns in a single layer on a baking tray, and brush with any of the remaining oil and chilli mixture. Grill for about 5 minutes until tender.
- Melt the butter with the lemon juice in a small pan, and pour into a serving jug.
- Serve the prawns hot, drizzled with the lemon butter, with boiled rice.

Seafood chimichangas

serves 4–6

ingredients

15g/½oz butter
1.4kg/3lb large raw prawns,
  peeled and deveined
100g/4oz spring onion tops, finely
  chopped
225g/8oz mushrooms
3 garlic cloves, finely chopped
350g/12oz fresh spinach,
  thinly sliced
½ teaspoon salt

3 teaspoons freshly squeezed
  lemon juice
6 thin tortillas
vegetable oil for deep-frying

To serve
Cheddar cheese, grated
guacamole
sour cream
diced tomatoes

- Melt the butter in a heavy saucepan, and sauté the prawns, spring onion tops, mushrooms, garlic, spinach, salt and lemon juice for 7–10 minutes until the vegetables go limp.
- Spread out the tortillas, and divide the seafood mixture equally between them, spooning it over the middle of each one. Roll up each tortilla, and tuck in the ends to form solid packages. Secure with toothpicks.
- Heat the oil in a deep heavy saucepan. Fry each chimichanga for about 3 minutes until golden, turning it over as it cooks to brown on all sides.
- Remove from the oil and drain on paper towels. Serve hot with cheese, guacamole, sour cream and diced tomatoes.

Soused herrings

serves 6

ingredients
6 herrings, filleted
1 carrot, thinly sliced
1 onion, sliced into thin rings

For the marinade
300ml/10fl oz white wine vinegar
225g/8oz onion, sliced into
    thin rings
1 carrot, sliced
8 sprigs of fresh flat-leaf parsley
3 bay leaves
sprig of fresh tarragon
½ tablespoon salt
12 black peppercorns

- To make the marinade, put all the marinade ingredients in a pan and bring to the boil. Reduce the heat and simmer gently for 20–30 minutes. Remove from the heat and allow to cool completely.
- Arrange the herring fillets skin side down in a flameproof roasting pan, pour the marinade over them and slowly bring to the boil on the top of the stove. Immediately remove from the heat and allow to cool.
- To finish the dish, blanch the carrot in salted boiling water for 2–3 minutes, then refresh in cold water and drain.
- Arrange the cooled herring fillets on a serving plate, and spoon some of the marinade over them. Scatter the carrot slices over the fish, and arrange rings of onion on top. Serve.

Spaghetti marinara with seafood

serves 6

ingredients

20 black mussels
200g/7oz medium raw prawns,
  peeled and deveined
50ml/2fl oz white wine
50ml/2fl oz fish stock
1 garlic clove, crushed
350g/12oz spaghetti
25g/1oz butter
100g/4oz calamari rings
100g/4oz skinless cod fillets,
  cubed
200g/7oz canned clams, drained

For the marinara sauce
2 tablespoons olive oil
1 onion, finely chopped
1 carrot, sliced
2 garlic cloves, crushed
400g/14oz canned peeled
  plum tomatoes, crushed
125ml/4fl oz white wine
1 teaspoon sugar

- To make the marinara sauce, heat the olive oil in a pan, add the onion and carrot, and stir over a medium heat for 10 minutes or until the vegetables are lightly browned.
- Add the garlic, tomatoes, white wine and sugar. Bring to the boil, reduce the heat and gently simmer for 30 minutes, stirring occasionally.
- Scrub the mussels with a stiff brush and pull out all the hairy beards. Discard any damaged mussels or open ones that do not close when tapped on the work surface. Rinse well.
- Heat the wine together with the stock and garlic in a large pan. Add the mussels. Cover the pan and shake it over a high heat for 4–5 minutes. After 3 minutes, start removing any opened mussels and set them aside. After 5 minutes, discard any unopened mussels and reserve the liquid.
- Cook the spaghetti in a large pan of salted boiling water until al dente. Drain and keep warm.
- Melt the butter in a frying pan, add the calamari rings, fish and prawns in batches, and stir-fry for 2 minutes or until just cooked through. Remove from the heat, and add the reserved cooking liquid, mussels, calamari, fish, prawns and clams to the marinara sauce. Stir gently until heated through. Gently combine the sauce with the pasta, and serve at once.

Seafood pilaki

serves 4

ingredients

2 tablespoons olive oil
2 garlic cloves, crushed
1 large onion, chopped
2 celery sticks, chopped
3 large carrots, sliced
finely grated zest and juice of
   1 lemon
400g/14oz canned chopped
   plum tomatoes

900g/2lb mussels
700g/1½lb monkfish fillet, trimmed
   and cut into chunks
450g/1lb cleaned squid, cut
   into rings
½ tablespoon chopped fresh
   flat-leaf parsley
salt and freshly ground
   black pepper

- Heat the oil in a large heavy pan. Add the garlic, onion, celery, carrots and lemon zest, and cook for about 5 minutes, stirring all the time.
- Add the lemon juice and the tomatoes with their juice, cover and cook over a low heat for about 25 minutes until the vegetables are very tender, stirring occasionally.
- Meanwhile, scrub the mussels with a stiff brush and pull out all the hairy beards. Discard any damaged mussels or open ones that do not close when tapped on the work surface. Rinse well.
- Add the fish and squid and a little water to the pan with the vegetables. Cover and cook for 3–5 minutes until the fish is just tender. Arrange the mussels on the top, cover the pan tightly and cook for about 5 minutes, stirring occasionally. The mussels should have opened; discard any that remain shut. Stir in the parsley and season with salt and pepper. Serve hot or cold.

Pan-fried scallops

serves 2

ingredients
6 large scallops
2 tablespoons olive oil
12.5g/½ oz butter

For the salsa
2 large ripe plum tomatoes
1 small ripe mango, peeled, stoned
  and diced
1 large shallot, finely chopped
juice of 1 lime
¼ teaspoon Tabasco sauce
salt and freshly ground black pepper

- First, make the salsa. Put the tomatoes in a bowl of just-boiled water, then peel off skin and dice the flesh. Put the tomatoes, mango and shallot in a bowl, and add the lime juice and Tabasco. Season with salt and pepper. Stir well to mix, then cover and chill in the refrigerator until ready to serve.
- Pat the scallops dry with kitchen paper. Heat the oil in a non-stick frying pan, add the butter and stir until foaming. Add the scallops to the pan, and cook for 3–4 minutes, turning them once, until lightly golden on both sides and tender to the touch.
- To serve, spoon the salsa on to two plates. Sit the scallops on top, and serve immediately.

Layered fish & potato pie
serves 4

ingredients
900g/2lb potatoes, sliced
75g/3oz butter
1 red onion, halved and sliced
50g/2oz plain flour
150ml/5fl oz milk
150ml/5fl oz double cream
225g/8oz smoked haddock
   fillet, cubed
225g/8oz cod fillet, cubed
1 red pepper, seeded and diced
100g/4oz broccoli florets
50g/2oz Parmesan cheese,
   freshly grated
salt and freshly ground black pepper

- Bring a large saucepan of lightly salted water to the boil over a medium heat. Add the potatoes and cook for 10 minutes. Drain and reserve.
- Meanwhile, melt the butter in a saucepan over a low heat. Add the onion, and sweat gently for 3–4 minutes.
- Add the flour and cook, stirring, for 1 minute. Blend in the milk and cream, and bring to the boil, stirring, until the sauce has thickened.
- Arrange half of the potato slices in the bottom of a shallow ovenproof dish. Preheat the oven to 180°C/350°F/Gas mark 4.
- Add the fish, red pepper and broccoli to the sauce, and cook over a low heat for about 10 minutes. Season with salt and pepper, then spoon the mixture over the potatoes in the dish.
- Arrange the remaining potato slices in a layer over the fish mixture, then sprinkle the Parmesan over the top. Cook in the oven for 30 minutes or until the potatoes are cooked and the topping is golden. Serve hot.

Barbecued monkfish

serves 4

ingredients

4 tablespoons olive oil
grated zest of 1 lime
2 teaspoons Thai fish sauce
2 garlic cloves, crushed
1 teaspoon grated fresh root ginger
2 tablespoons chopped fresh basil
700g/1½lb monkfish fillet, cut
   into chunks
2 limes, each cut into 6 wedges
salt and freshly ground black pepper
noodles or rice, to serve

- Soak bamboo skewers in water for 30 minutes to prevent burning.
- Mix the olive oil, lime zest, fish sauce, garlic, ginger and basil together. Season with salt and pepper.
- Wash the monkfish under cold running water, and pat dry with kitchen paper. Add to the marinade and mix well. Cover and leave to marinate in the refrigerator for 2 hours, stirring occasionally.
- Preheat a charcoal barbecue or grill until hot. Lift the monkfish pieces from the marinade, and thread them onto the skewers, alternating with the lime wedges.
- Cook the skewers for 5–6 minutes on the hot barbecue or under the grill, turning regularly, until the fish is tender.
- Serve with noodles or rice.

Squid with wine & rosemary

serves 4

ingredients

8 squid, cleaned and gutted
6 canned anchovies, drained
  and chopped
2 garlic cloves, chopped
2 tablespoons fresh rosemary,
  chopped
2 sun-dried tomatoes, chopped
150g/5oz breadcrumbs
1 tablespoon olive oil
1 onion, finely chopped
200ml/7fl oz white wine
200ml/7fl oz fish stock

- Remove the tentacles from the squid bodies, and chop them finely.
- Grind the anchovies, garlic, rosemary and tomatoes to a paste using a
  mortar and pestle. Add the breadcrumbs and the squid tentacles, and
  mix to form a paste, adding water if necessary.
- Spoon the paste into the body sacs of the squid, then tie around the end
  of each sac with cotton to fasten.
- Heat the oil in a frying pan. Add the onion and cook, stirring, for
  3–4 minutes until golden. Add the stuffed squid to the pan, and cook for
  a further 3–4 minutes until they are brown all over.
- Add the wine and stock, and bring to the boil. Reduce the heat, cover
  and leave to simmer for 15 minutes.
- Remove the lid and cook for a further 5 minutes or until the squid is
  tender and the juices reduced. Serve hot with boiled rice or noodles.

Prawn omelette

serves 4

ingredients

3 tablespoons sunflower oil
2 leeks, sliced
4 tablespoons cornflour
1 teaspoon salt
350g/12oz raw tiger prawns,
    peeled and deveined
175g/6oz mushrooms, sliced
175g/6oz beansprouts
6 eggs

- Heat a wok or large frying pan over a medium heat. Add the oil and, when the oil is hot enough, add the leeks and stir-fry for 3 minutes.
- Mix the cornflour and salt together in a large bowl. Add the prawns to the cornflour and salt mixture, and toss to coat all over.
- Add the prawns to the wok, and stir-fry for 2 minutes or until the prawns have changed colour and are almost cooked through.
- Now add the mushrooms and beansprouts to the wok, and stir-fry for a further 2 minutes.
- Beat the eggs with 3 tablespoons water in a small bowl. Pour the egg mixture into the wok and cook, stirring, until the egg sets, carefully turning the omelette over once.
- Turn the omelette out onto a clean board, divide into four and serve hot.

Monkfish & mussel skewers
serves 4

ingredients
1 teaspoon olive oil
2 tablespoon freshly squeezed
  lemon juice
1 teaspoon paprika
1 garlic clove, crushed
450g/1lb monkfish, skinned, boned
  and cut into 2.5cm/1in chunks
4 rashers turkey bacon
8 cooked mussels
8 raw tiger prawns, peeled and
  deveined, but with tails left intact
1 tablespoon chopped fresh dill
salt and freshly ground black pepper

• If using bamboo or wooden skewers, soak in water for 30 minutes to prevent them burning.
• Mix together the oil, lemon juice, paprika and garlic, and season with salt and pepper.
• Put the monkfish in a shallow glass dish. Pour the marinade over the fish and toss to coat evenly. Cover and leave in a cool place for 30 minutes.
• Preheat the grill to high. Cut the turkey rashers in half, and wrap each strip around a mussel. Thread onto 4 skewers, alternating with the fish cubes and prawns. Grill the kebabs for 7–8 minutes, turning once and basting with the marinade.
• Sprinkle with the chopped dill and salt. Serve hot with salad and rice.

Sea bream in a salt crust

serves 4

ingredients
1kg/2¼lb whole sea bream
1 shallot, sliced thinly
1 sprig of fresh flat-leaf parsley
1 sprig of fresh tarragon
2 garlic cloves, roughly chopped
2.5kg/5½lb coarse sea salt
lemon wedges, to garnish

For the sauce
2 shallots, very finely chopped
4 tablespoons freshly squeezed
    lemon juice
300g/11oz butter, diced
salt and freshly ground black pepper

- Preheat the oven to 220°C/425°F/Gas mark 7.
- Wash the sea bream under cold running water, and pat dry with kitchen paper.
- Stuff the body cavity with the shallot, parsley, tarragon and garlic.
- Sprinkle a thick layer of the salt into the bottom of a roasting tin large enough to hold the fish with lots of space around it. Top with the fish, then pour the remaining salt over the fish to completely cover it. Sprinkle water lightly over the salt. Bake in the oven for about 25 minutes.
- To make the sauce, put the shallots and lemon juice in a saucepan, and simmer gently over a low heat for 5 minutes. Increase the heat until the lemon juice is reduced by half. Reduce the heat and add the butter, piece by piece, whisking constantly, until all the butter is incorporated and the sauce is thick. Season with salt and pepper, and keep warm.
- Remove the fish from the oven and leave to stand for 5 minutes before cracking open the salt. Remove the fish, garnish with lemon wedges and serve hot with the sauce.

Baked cod with tomatoes
serves 4

ingredients
vegetable oil for greasing
2 teaspoons olive oil
1 onion, chopped
2 garlic cloves, finely chopped
450g/1lb canned chopped plum
    tomatoes, drained
1 teaspoon tomato purée
4 tablespoons dry white wine
4 tablespoons chopped fresh
    flat-leaf parsley
4 cod cutlets
2 tablespoons dried breadcrumbs
salt and freshly ground black pepper

- Preheat the oven to 190°C/375°F/Gas mark 5. Lightly grease a large baking dish.
- Heat the oil in a frying pan, and sauté the onion for about 5 minutes. Add the garlic, tomatoes, tomato purée and wine. Season with salt and pepper.
- Bring the sauce just to the boil, then reduce the heat slightly and cook, uncovered, for 15–20 minutes until thick. Stir in the parsley.
- Put the cod cutlets in the prepared baking dish, and spoon an equal quantity of the tomato mixture onto each. Sprinkle the breadcrumbs over the top. Bake in the oven for 20–30 minutes, basting the fish occasionally with the sauce, until the fish is tender and cooked through, and the breadcrumbs are golden and crisp.
- Serve hot with new potatoes and a green salad.

Crunchy-topped cod
serves 4

ingredients

4 pieces skinned cod fillet, about
    100g/4oz each
2 tomatoes, sliced
50g/2oz fresh wholemeal
    breadcrumbs
2 tablespoons chopped fresh
    flat-leaf parsley
finely grated zest and juice of
    ½ lemon
1 teaspoon sunflower oil
salt and freshly ground black pepper

- Preheat the oven to 200°C/400°F/Gas mark 6. Put the cod fillets in a wide ovenproof dish. Arrange the tomato slices on top.
- In a bowl, mix together the breadcrumbs, parsley, lemon zest and juice, and oil. Season with salt and pepper.
- Spoon the crumb mixture evenly over the fish, then bake in the oven for 15–20 minutes. Serve hot.

Red mullet & coconut loaf

serves 6

ingredients
225g/8oz red mullet fillets, skinned
  and finely chopped
2 small tomatoes, finely chopped
2 green peppers, seeded and
  finely chopped
1 onion, finely chopped
1 fresh red chilli, finely chopped
150g/5oz fresh breadcrumbs
600ml/1pt coconut milk
salt and freshly ground black pepper

For the sauce
125ml/4fl oz tomato ketchup
1 teaspoon hot pepper sauce
¼ teaspoon hot mustard

- Preheat the oven to 200°C/400°F/Gas mark 6.
- Mix the red mullet with the tomatoes, peppers, onion and chilli. Stir in
  the breadcrumbs and coconut milk. Season with salt and pepper.
- Grease and line a 500g/1lb 2oz loaf tin, and add the mullet mixture.
  Bake for 1–1½ hours until set.
- To make the sauce, mix together all the sauce ingredients until smooth
  and creamy.
- To serve, cut the loaf into slices and serve hot or cold, drizzled with
  the sauce.

Red prawn curry

serves 4

ingredients

2 tablespoons vegetable oil
1 garlic clove, finely chopped
1 tablespoon red curry paste
200ml/7fl oz coconut milk
2 tablespoon Thai fish sauce
1 teaspoon granulated sugar
12 large raw prawns, peeled
  and deveined
2 kaffir lime leaves, finely shredded
1 fresh red chilli, deseeded and
  finely sliced
10 leaves fresh Thai basil, plus
  extra to garnish

For the curry paste
3 dried long red chillies
½ teaspoon ground coriander
¼ teaspoon ground cumin
½ teaspoon freshly ground
  black pepper
2 garlic cloves, chopped
2 lemon grass stalks, chopped
1 kaffir lime leaf, finely chopped
1 teaspoon grated fresh root ginger
½ teaspoon salt

- To make the curry paste, put all the ingredients into a blender or food processor, and purée to a smooth paste, adding a little water if necessary. Transfer to a bowl and reserve.
- Heat a wok or frying pan over a medium heat. Add the oil and heat until almost smoking. Add the garlic and fry until golden. Add the curry paste and cook for a further minute. Add half of the coconut milk, the fish sauce and the sugar. Stir well. The mixture should thicken slightly.
- Add the prawns and simmer for 3–4 minutes until they turn pink. Add the remaining coconut milk, the lime leaves and the chilli. Cook for a further 2–3 minutes until the prawns are just tender.
- Add the basil leaves, stir until wilted and transfer the contents of the wok or pan to a large serving dish. Garnish with the extra basil, and serve immediately.

Fish pasties

serves 4

ingredients

450g/1lb self-raising flour, plus
  extra for dusting
pinch of salt
225g/8oz butter, plus extra
  for greasing
3 tablespoons cold water
1 egg, lightly beaten

For the filling
50g/2oz butter
75g/3oz leek, diced

75g/3oz onion, finely chopped
75g/3oz carrot, diced
225g/8oz potato, peeled
  and diced
350g/12oz cod fillets, cut into
  2.5cm/1in pieces
4 teaspoons white wine vinegar
25g/1oz Cheddar cheese, grated
1 teaspoon chopped fresh tarragon
salt and freshly ground
  black pepper

- Preheat the oven to 200°C/400°F/Gas mark 6.
- To make the pastry, sift the flour and salt together into a large bowl. Add the butter, and rub it in with your fingertips until the mixture resembles coarse breadcrumbs. Add just enough of the cold water to form a dough. Knead briefly until smooth. Wrap in cling film and leave to chill in the refrigerator for 30 minutes.
- To make the filling, melt half the butter in a large frying pan over a low heat. Add the leek, onion and carrot, and cook gently for 7–8 minutes until the vegetables are softened. Remove from the heat and leave to cool slightly.
- Put the vegetable mixture into a bowl, and add the potato, cod, vinegar, remaining butter, cheese and tarragon. Season with salt and pepper.
- Remove the pastry from the refrigerator, and roll out thinly. Using a pastry cutter, press out four 19cm/7½in discs. Divide the filling between the discs.
- Moisten the edges of the pastry, and fold over to form a half-moon. Pinch and crimp the edges to seal. Put the pasties on a lightly greased baking tray. Brush generously with the beaten egg.
- Bake in the oven for 15 minutes. Remove from the oven, and brush again with the egg glaze. Return to the oven for a further 20 minutes until the pastry is golden. Serve warm.

Smoked snapper
serves 4–6

ingredients

450ml/¾pt malt vinegar
3 onions, sliced
1½ teaspoons pimento berries
1.4kg/3lb red snapper
juice of 2 limes
4 teaspoons freshly ground
   black pepper
4 teaspoons salt
140ml/5fl oz vegetable oil

- In a large stainless-steel or other non-reactive saucepan, combine the vinegar, onions and pimento berries. Simmer until the onions are tender, then remove from the heat and allow to cool.
- Sprinkle the snapper with the lime juice, and season with the salt and pepper.
- Heat the oil to smoking point in a heavy frying pan, and fry the fish on both sides until crisp. Put the fish in a deep dish, and pour over the onion and vinegar mixture.
- Chill overnight in the refrigerator before serving.

Sardinian red mullet

serves 4

ingredients
50g/2oz sultanas
150ml/5fl oz red wine
2 tablespoons olive oil
2 medum onions, sliced
1 courgette, cut in half lengthways
   and into 5cm/2in sticks
2 oranges
4 red mullet, boned and filleted
50g/2oz canned anchovy
   fillets, drained
2 tablespoons chopped
   fresh oregano

- Put the sultanas in a bowl. Pour the red wine over them, and leave to soak for 10 minutes.
- Heat the oil in a large frying pan. Add the onions and sauté for 2 minutes. Add the courgette to the pan, and sauté for a further 3 minutes or until they are tender.
- Using a zester, pare long, thin strips from one of the oranges. Using a sharp knife, remove all the peel and pith from both oranges, then segment them by slicing between the membrane.
- Add the orange zest to the frying pan. Add the wine-soaked sultanas and any liquid, the mullet and the anchovies to the pan. Leave to simmer for 10–15 minutes until the fish is cooked through. Stir in the oregano and orange segments, set aside and leave to cool.
- Put the mixture in a large bowl and leave to chill, covered, in the refrigerator for at least 2 hours. Transfer to serving plates, and serve.

French mussels
serves 4

ingredients
900g/2lb fresh mussels
3 tablespoons olive oil
1 onion, chopped
3 garlic cloves, finely chopped
2 teaspoons fresh thyme leaves
150ml/5fl oz red wine
850g/1¾lb canned chopped
    plum tomatoes
2 tablespoons chopped fresh parsley
salt and freshly ground black pepper

- Clean the mussels by scrubbing or scraping the shells and pulling out any beards that are attached to them. Discard any mussels with broken shells or any that do not close when tapped on a work surface.
- Put the mussels into a large saucepan with just the water that clings to their shells. Cook the mussels, tightly covered, over a high heat for 3–4 minutes until the mussels have opened. Discard any mussels that remain closed. Strain, reserving the cooking liquid.
- Heat the oil in a large saucepan over a low heat. Add the onion and sweat gently for 8–10 minutes until softened but not coloured. Add the garlic and thyme, and cook for a further 1 minute. Add the wine and simmer rapidly until reduced and syrupy. Add the tomatoes and reserved mussel cooking liquid, and bring to the boil. Cover and simmer for 30 minutes. Uncover and cook for a further 15 minutes.
- Add the mussels and cook for a further 5 minutes until heated through. Stir in the parsley, season with salt and pepper and serve immediately.

Salmon burgers
serves 4

ingredients
350g/12oz canned boneless,
    skinless pink salmon
1 egg white, beaten
100g/4oz seasoned
    fresh breadcrumbs
100g/4oz onions, chopped
½ teaspoon dried thyme
½ teaspoon cracked black pepper
1 teaspoon salt
1 tablespoon corn oil
4 iceberg lettuce leaves
1 tomato, sliced
2 small pitta breads, halved
    crossways

- Drain the canned salmon, reserving 2 tablespoons of the liquid.
- In a mixing bowl, combine the reserved liquid, egg white, breadcrumbs, onion, thyme, pepper and salt. Add the drained salmon and mix well. Shape the mixture into 4 patties about 1cm/½in thick.
- In a frying pan, cook the patties in the oil over a medium heat for 2–3 minutes until brown on the underside. Turn and cook for a further 2 minutes.
- Serve each patty warm, with lettuce and tomato, in half a pitta bread.

Trout with almonds
serves 4

ingredients

4 small rainbow trout, cleaned
50g/2oz low-fat spread
25g/1oz flaked almonds
2 tablespoons chopped fresh
   flat-leaf parsley
1 tablespoon freshly squeezed
   lemon juice
salt and freshly ground black pepper
450g/1lb potatoes, boiled, to serve

- Rinse the trout and pat dry with kitchen paper. Remove the heads
  if preferred.
- Melt 25g/1oz of the low-fat spread in a large frying pan, and fry the
  fish for 5 minutes on each side until golden brown and cooked through.
  Transfer to serving plates and keep warm.
- Melt the remaining low-fat spread in the juices in the pan. Add the
  almonds and fry until golden brown. Throw in the parsley, a little salt
  and pepper and the lemon juice. Spoon the sauce over the trout, and
  serve immediately with the potatoes.

Thai fish green curry
serves 4

ingredients

2 tablespoons vegetable oil
1 garlic clove, chopped
1 small aubergine, diced
125ml/4fl oz coconut cream
2 tablespoons Thai fish sauce
1 teaspoon granulated sugar
225g/8oz cod fillet, cut
  into pieces
125ml/4fl oz fish stock
2 kaffir lime leaves,
  finely shredded
15 fresh Thai basil leaves

For the curry paste
5 fresh green chillies, seeded
  and chopped
2 teaspoons chopped lemon grass
1 large shallot, chopped
2 garlic cloves, chopped
1 teaspoon grated fresh
  root ginger
2 fresh coriander roots, chopped
½ teaspoon ground coriander
¼ teaspoon ground cumin
1 kaffir lime leaf, finely chopped
½ teaspoon salt

- To make the curry paste, put all the ingredients in a blender or food processor, and purée to a smooth paste, adding a little water if needed.
- Heat the vegetable oil in a large frying pan or preheated wok over a medium heat until almost smoking. Add the garlic and fry until golden. Add the curry paste and stir-fry for a few seconds before adding the aubergine. Stir-fry for 4–5 minutes until softened.
- Add the coconut cream, bring to the boil and stir until the cream thickens and curdles slightly. Add the fish sauce and sugar to the frying pan, and stir well.
- Add the cod and stock. Simmer for 3–4 minutes, stirring occasionally, until the fish is just tender. Add the lime leaves and basil, then cook for a further minute.
- Transfer to a warmed large serving dish, and serve immediately.

Fish with coconut & basil

serves 4

ingredients

2 tablespoons vegetable oil
450g/1lb skinless cod fillet
25g/1oz plain flour, seasoned
   with salt and freshly ground
   black pepper
1 garlic clove, crushed
2 tablespoons red curry paste
1 tablespoon fish sauce
300ml/10fl oz coconut milk
175g/6oz cherry tomatoes, halved
20 fresh basil leaves

- Heat the oil in a large preheated wok. Using a sharp knife, cut the fish into large cubes, removing any bones.
- Put the flour in a bowl, add the fish and mix until well coated. Add to the wok, and stir-fry over a high heat for 3–4 minutes until the fish begins to brown.
- Mix together the garlic, curry paste, fish sauce and coconut milk. Pour the mixture over the fish, and bring to the boil.
- Add the tomatoes to the mixture in the wok, and leave to simmer for 5 minutes.
- Roughly chop or tear the basil leaves. Add the basil to the wok and stir.
- Transfer to serving plates, and serve hot with fragrant rice.

Tuna almondine
serves 11

ingredients
vegetable oil for greasing
1½ teaspoons powdered gelatine
225ml/8fl oz boiling water
450g/1lb low-fat cottage cheese,
   whipped
2 tablespoons freshly squeezed
   lemon juice
½ teaspoon garlic powder
¼ teaspoon salt
75g/3oz onions, finely chopped
2 tablespoons chopped red pepper
400g/14oz canned tuna, drained
   and flaked
225g/8oz almonds, sliced and
   lightly toasted

- Grease a 1.2-litre/2pt fish mould and set aside.
- In a large bowl, sprinkle the gelatine over 125ml/4fl oz cold water and leave to stand for 1 minute. Add the boiling water and stir until the gelatine has dissolved completely.
- Using a hand-held mixer, blend in the cottage cheese until smooth.
- Stir in the lemon juice, garlic powder and salt. Fold in the onions, red pepper, tuna and half of the almonds.
- Pour the mixture into the prepared mould, and chill until firm. Before serving, unmould onto a platter and garnish with the remaining almonds.

Curried prawns in coconut milk
serves 4

ingredients

600ml/1pt coconut milk
2 tablespoons Thai curry paste
1 tablespoon Thai fish sauce
½ teaspoon salt
1 teaspoon granulated sugar
450g/1lb king prawns, peeled and
    deveined, but with tails left intact
225g/8oz cherry tomatoes
1 fresh red chilli, seeded
    and chopped
juice of ½ lime

- Pour half of the coconut milk into a pan or wok, and bring to the boil.
  Add the curry paste, stir until it disperses, then simmer for about
  10 minutes.
- Add the fish sauce, salt, sugar and remaining coconut milk. Simmer for
  another 5 minutes.
- Add the prawns, cherry tomatoes and chilli. Simmer gently for about
  5 minutes until the prawns are pink and tender. Serve immediately,
  sprinkled with the lime juice.

Salt cod fritters

serves 6

ingredients

100g/4oz self-raising flour
1 egg, beaten
150ml/5fl oz milk
250g/9oz salt cod, soaked in cold
    water overnight
1 small red onion, finely chopped
1 small fennel bulb, finely chopped
1 fresh red chilli, finely chopped
2 tablespoons vegetable oil

- Sift the flour into a large bowl. Make a well in the centre of the flour, and add the egg. Using a wooden spoon, gradually draw in the flour while slowly adding the milk, and mix to form a smooth batter. Leave to stand for 10 minutes.
- Drain the salt cod and rinse under cold running water. Drain again thoroughly. Remove and discard the skin and any bones, then mash the flesh with a fork.
- Put the fish in a large bowl, and combine with the onion, fennel and chilli. Add the mixture to the batter, and blend together.
- Heat the oil in a large frying pan and, taking about 1 tablespoon of the mixture at a time, spoon carefully into the hot oil. Cook the fritters, in batches, for 3–4 minutes on each side until golden and slightly puffed. Keep warm while cooking the remaining mixture. Serve with vegetables and rice.

Noodles with cod & mango
serves 4

ingredients
250g/9oz dried egg noodles
450g/1lb skinless cod fillet, cut into
   thin strips
1 tablespoon paprika
2 tablespoons sunflower oil
1 red onion, diced
1 yellow pepper, seeded and sliced
1 red pepper, seeded and sliced
1 green pepper, seeded and sliced
100g/4oz baby corn cobs, halved
1 mango, peeled, stoned and sliced
100g/4oz beansprouts
2 tablespoons tomato ketchup
2 tablespoons light soy sauce
2 tablespoons medium sherry
1 teaspoon cornflour

- Put the noodles in a large bowl, and pour over enough boiling water to cover. Leave to stand for about 10 minutes.
- Meanwhile, put the cod in a large bowl, add the paprika and toss well to coat the fish evenly.
- Heat the oil in a preheated wok or large heavy frying pan over a medium heat. Add the onion, peppers and baby corn cobs, and stir-fry for about 5 minutes.
- Add the cod to the wok or pan together with the sliced mango. Stir-fry for a further 2–3 minutes until the fish is tender. Add the beansprouts to the wok and toss well to combine.
- Mix the tomato ketchup, soy sauce, sherry and cornflour together. Add the mixture to the wok and cook, stirring occasionally, until the juices thicken.
- To serve, drain the noodles well, and divide among four warmed serving bowls. Divide the cod and mango stir-fry among the bowls, and serve immediately.

Vegetables & Vegetarian

This chapter includes a variety of vegetable and vegetarian main courses. If you are cooking for guests, some of whom are vegetarian, you can either go all-out vegetarian or, with some of these recipes, offer both a meat and vegetarian option. But the recipes in this chapter are so hearty and delicious that most meat eaters would never think to miss it. Again, as with other parts of the book, the recipes in this chapter are diverse, and include bakes, soufflés, gratins, roasts, curries and stir-fries.

Vegetarian spaghetti sauce

serves 8

ingredients

4 carrots, finely chopped
1 onion, finely chopped
1 tablespoon olive oil
2 garlic cloves, finely minced
400g/14oz canned cooked kidney
  beans, drained
400g/14oz canned cooked
  cannellini beans, drained
1 tablespoon chopped fresh basil
1 tablespoon chopped fresh oregano
2 x 400g/14oz cans chopped
  plum tomatoes
50ml/2fl oz tomato purée
100g/4oz mushrooms, sliced
275g/10oz broccoli
¼ teaspoon freshly ground
  black pepper

- Sweat the carrots and onion in the oil in a large non-stick saucepan for 5 minutes until softened. Add the garlic and sweat for a further 30 seconds.
- Add the kidney and cannellini beans, basil, oregano, tomatoes, tomato purée and mushrooms. Simmer, covered, for 25 minutes. Add the broccoli and pepper, and cook for about 5 minutes until the broccoli is tender but still with a bite.
- Serve hot over freshly cooked spaghetti.

Asparagus cashew stir-fry
serves 4

ingredients
225g/8oz raw cashew nuts
2 tablespoons sunflower oil
450g/1lb fresh asparagus
4 spring onions, chopped
1 red pepper, seeded and chopped
1 garlic clove, minced
900g/2lb freshly cooked brown
   rice, to serve

For the sauce
3 tablespoons light soy sauce
2 tablespoons cornflour
350ml/12fl oz water
1 tablespoon minced fresh
   root ginger
1 teaspoon sesame oil
1/4 teaspoon crushed red
   pepper flakes

- Spread the cashew nuts over a baking sheet. Toast under a hot grill until
  golden, turning them frequently. Set aside.
- To make the sauce, combine the soy sauce and cornflour in a small
  bowl, stirring until smooth. Stir in the remaining sauce ingredients, and
  set aside.
- Heat the oil in a wok over a medium-high heat. Stir-fry the asparagus,
  spring onions, pepper and garlic until the vegetables are tender. Stir the
  sauce mixture, pour it over the vegetables and stir-fry until the sauce is
  thickened and glossy. Reduce the heat and fold in the cashew nuts.
- Cover and cook for 1 minute until the cashews are heated through.
  Serve immediately with the hot brown rice.

Batter-dipped tofu

serves 4–6

ingredients

225g/8oz firm tofu
125g/4½oz plain flour
2 tablespoons toasted wheatgerm
½ teaspoon dried thyme
¼ teaspoon dried dill
¼ teaspoon garlic powder
¼ teaspoon paprika
¼ teaspoon freshly ground
  black pepper
1 egg
1 tablespoon milk
1 teaspoon hot pepper sauce
2 tablespoons sunflower oil

For the ginger dipping sauce
100ml/3½fl oz rice vinegar
50g/2oz granulated sugar
2 tablespoons light soy sauce
1 teaspoon cornflour
1 tablespoon finely minced fresh
  root ginger

- To make the ginger dipping sauce, put the vinegar, sugar, soy sauce and 175ml/6fl oz water in a small saucepan. Bring to the boil, reduce the heat and simmer, stirring occasionally, for 5 minutes.
- Meanwhile, in a small bowl, combine the cornflour and 1 teaspoon water, and stir into the sauce. Keep stirring until the sauce is clear and thickened. Remove the pan from the heat, and stir in the ginger. Keep warm until needed.
- Cut the tofu into 2.5cm/1in squares about 8mm/¼in thick. Set aside.
- Combine the flour, wheatgerm, thyme, dill, garlic powder, paprika and pepper in a medium bowl.
- In a separate bowl, lightly whisk the egg using a fork. Add the milk and hot pepper sauce, and whisk again to combine.
- Heat the oil in a large wok over a medium-high heat. Piece by piece, dip the tofu in the flour, then in the egg mixture, and again in the flour. Fry the pieces of tofu for about 3 minutes on each side until golden brown (if necessary, cook in batches so that the temperature of the oil does not drop). Drain on kitchen paper.
- Serve immediately with a bowl of the ginger sauce for dipping.

Brinjal curry

serves 4

ingredients

300g/11oz aubergine, cut into
   2.5cm/1in cubes
75ml/3fl oz vegetable oil
a little salt
1 teaspoon mustard seeds
20 curry leaves
1 teaspoon skinned and split
   urad dal
150g/5oz onions, finely sliced
200g/7oz tomatoes
1 tablespoon tomato purée
½ teaspoon chilli powder
½ teaspoon ground coriander
½ teaspoon ground turmeric

- Soak the aubergine in cold water for 10 minutes. Drain and pat dry with kitchen paper.
- In a large frying pan, heat 4 tablespoons of the oil over a medium heat. Add the aubergine and a little salt, and cook for 10 minutes or until the aubergine is brown and soft. Drain the aubergine on kitchen paper, and set aside in a warm place.
- Heat the remaining oil in the same pan. Add the mustard seeds and, as they begin to pop, add the curry leaves and urad dal. Cook, stirring, for a few minutes or until the dal is golden, then add the onions and a little salt and cook until the onions are starting to colour, stirring occasionally.
- Add the tomatoes, tomato purée, chilli powder, coriander and turmeric, and mix well. Add the aubergine and cook for a further 5 minutes, stirring occasionally, until the tomatoes break down. Transfer the mixture to a serving dish, and serve immediately.

Potato & onion pizza
serves 4

ingredients

For the dough
1 teaspoon dried yeast
½ teaspoon granulated sugar
pinch of salt
250ml/9fl oz warm water
175g/6oz white bread flour
150g/5oz wholemeal plain flour

For the topping
1 red pepper
1 potato, very thinly sliced
1 large onion, sliced
100g/4oz soft goat's cheese,
    crumbled into small pieces
3 tablespoons capers, rinsed
    and drained
1 tablespoon dried oregano
1–2 tablespoons olive oil

- To make the dough, mix the yeast, sugar, salt and water in a bowl. Leave in a warm place for 10 minutes or until foamy. Sift both flours into a bowl. Make a well, add the yeast mixture and mix to a firm dough. Knead on a lightly floured surface for 5 minutes or until smooth. Put in a lightly oiled bowl, cover with cling film and leave in a warm place for 1–1½ hours until doubled in size.

- Preheat the oven to 200°C/400°F/Gas mark 6. Brush a 30cm/12in pizza tray with oil. Punch down the dough and knead for 2 minutes. Roll out to a 35cm/14in round. Put the dough on the tray and fold the edge over to form a rim.

- To make the topping, cut the pepper into large flat pieces and remove the seeds. Put the pepper, skin side up, under a hot grill until blackened. Cool, then peel away and discard the skin, and slice the flesh.

- Arrange the potato over the base with the pepper, onion and half of the cheese. Sprinkle with the capers and oregano, and drizzle with a little oil. Brush the crust edge with a little more oil, and bake the pizza in the oven for 15–20 minutes. Add the remaining cheese and bake until the crust is golden and crisp. Serve hot.

Spinach & mushroom bhaji

serves 8

ingredients

1 tablespoon mustard seeds
2 teaspoons coriander seeds
1 teaspoon cumin seeds
2 garlic cloves, roughly chopped
2.5cm/1in piece of fresh root
  ginger, roughly chopped
50ml/2fl oz vegetable oil
2 large onions, thinly sliced
2 teaspoons ground turmeric
1½ teaspoons chilli powder

450g/1lb button mushrooms,
  thickly sliced
400g/14oz canned chopped
  plum tomatoes
900g/2lb fresh spinach,
  roughly shredded
4 tablespoons desiccated or
  shredded coconut, to garnish
salt and freshly ground
  black pepper

- Put the mustard, coriander and cumin seeds in a large heavy flameproof casserole dish, and dry-roast over a medium heat for 2–3 minutes until aromatic, stirring all the time. Remove from the dish and, using a mortar and pestle, crush into a paste with the garlic and ginger.

- Heat the oil in the casserole dish, add the onions and sauté gently, stirring frequently, for about 10 minutes until soft and golden. Add the spice paste, turmeric and chilli powder, and sauté gently, stirring all the time, for 5 minutes.

- Add the mushrooms and stir to coat well with the spiced mixture, then add the tomatoes and bring to the boil, stirring all the time. Simmer for 10 minutes, stirring occasionally.

- Add the spinach and stir well, then season with salt and pepper. Reduce the heat, cover and simmer for 15 minutes, stirring frequently to blend in the spinach.

- Check the seasoning and adjust if necessary, then turn the mixture into a warmed serving dish. Sprinkle with the coconut, and serve immediately.

Tofu & broccoli stir-fry

serves 4

ingredients

2 tablespoons dry sherry
2 tablespoons light soy sauce
4 teaspoons cornflour
1 teaspoon ground ginger
1 tablespoon vegetable oil
2 garlic cloves, minced
350g/12oz broccoli, cut into
    bite-size pieces
100g/4oz onion, cut into wedges
200g/7oz beansprouts
450g/1lb firm tofu, cut into
    1cm/½in pieces
250g/9oz freshly cooked brown
    rice, to serve

- Put the sherry, soy sauce, cornflour and ginger in a bowl. Add 150ml/5fl oz water, and stir together.
- Heat the oil in a wok or large frying pan over a medium heat. Add the garlic and stir-fry for 15 seconds. Add the broccoli and onion, and stir-fry for 5 minutes, then add the beansprouts and stir-fry for a further 1 minute.
- Tip the sauce mixture to the wok and stir until the sauce is thickened and glossy. Stir in the tofu and heat through. Serve with the hot brown rice.

Braised Chinese vegetables
serves 4

ingredients

15g/½oz dried Chinese mushrooms
225g/8oz firm tofu, cubed
50ml/2fl oz vegetable oil
75g/3oz straw mushrooms
75g/3oz sliced bamboo shoots,
  drained
50g/2oz mangetout, topped
  and tailed
175g/6oz Chinese leaves such as
  pak choi, shredded
1 teaspoon salt
½ teaspoon soft brown sugar
1 tablespoon light soy sauce

- Soak the Chinese mushrooms in cold water for 20–25 minutes, then drain, discarding any hard stalks.
- Harden the tofu pieces by putting them in a wok of boiling water for about 2 minutes. Remove and drain.
- Tip the water out of the wok, and wipe dry. Heat the oil in the wok, and lightly brown the tofu pieces on both sides. Remove with a slotted spoon and drain on kitchen paper.
- Stir-fry the vegetables in the wok for 1½ minutes, then add the tofu, salt, sugar and soy sauce. Continue stirring for 1 minute, then cover and braise for 2–3 minutes. Serve immediately.

Broccoli & asparagus fusilli
serves 4

ingredients
225g/8oz dried fusilli
1 tablespoon olive oil
1 head broccoli, cut into florets
2 courgettes, sliced
225g/8oz fresh asparagus spears
100g/4oz mangetout
100g/4oz frozen green peas
25g/1oz butter
2 tablespoons vegetable stock
4 tablespoons double cream
2 tablespoons chopped fresh
  flat-leaf parsley
2 tablespoons freshly grated
  Parmesan cheese
salt and freshly ground black pepper

- Bring a large saucepan of lightly salted water to the boil. Add the fusilli and oil and cook until al dente. Drain, return to the pan with a very little of the cooking liquid, cover and keep warm.
- Meanwhile, steam the broccoli, courgettes, asparagus and mangetout over a pan of salted boiling water until they are just beginning to soften. Remove from the heat and refresh in cold water. Drain and set aside.
- Bring a small saucepan of lightly salted water to the boil. Add the peas and cook for 3 minutes, then drain.
- Put the butter and stock in a saucepan over a medium heat. When the butter has melted, add the vegetables, and toss until heated through. Stir in the cream, and heat through gently without boiling. Season with salt and pepper.
- Transfer the pasta to a warmed serving dish, and stir in the parsley. Spoon the sauce over the pasta, then sprinkle the Parmesan over the top. Serve immediately.

Cabbage & tofu
serves 4

ingredients
3 tablespoons vegetable oil
2½ tablespoons tamari
1 tablespoon Worcestershire sauce
½ teaspoon ground allspice
550g/1lb 4oz firm tofu, cubed
1 onion, chopped
500g/1lb 2oz cabbage, shredded

For the sauce
2 tablespoons tomato purée
1 tablespoon vinegar
1 teaspoon dried dill
1 teaspoon salt
½ teaspoon paprika

- Preheat the oven to 190°C/375°F/Gas mark 5.
- In a baking dish, combine 1 tablespoon of the vegetable oil with the tamari, Worcestershire sauce and allspice to make a marinade. Add the tofu and cook in the oven for about 35 minutes, turning the cubes two or three times during the cooking.
- Sweat the onion in the remaining oil until translucent. Add the cabbage and cook, stirring occasionally, for 5 minutes. Toss the cabbage mixture in the baked tofu.
- Combine the sauce ingredients in a bowl. Add 50ml/2fl oz water, and pour the sauce over the cabbage, onion and tofu. Stir to coat the ingredients evenly. Remove from the heat.
- Cover and return the dish to the oven for 30 minutes. Serve hot over rice or mashed potatoes.

Chickpea chole
serves 4–6

ingredients

3 tablespoons vegetable oil
1 onion, chopped
2 garlic cloves, crushed
2.5cm/1in piece of fresh root
   ginger, grated
4 teaspoons ground cumin
1 tablespoon ground coriander
2 teaspoons chilli powder
1 teaspoon ground turmeric
2 x 425g/14oz cans cooked
   chickpeas, drained and rinsed

400g/14oz canned chopped
   plum tomatoes
1½ teaspoons Demerara sugar
2 tablespoons freshly squeezed
   lime juice
4 tablespoons torn fresh
   coriander leaves
salt

- Heat the oil in a heavy saucepan. Add the onion, garlic and ginger, and sweat over a gentle heat, stirring frequently, for about 5 minutes until softened.
- Stir in the ground cumin, coriander, chilli powder and turmeric, and fry for 2 minutes until aromatic. Add the chickpeas, tomatoes and sugar. Season with salt, and stir to combine the ingredients. Cover the pan and simmer the curry gently, stirring occasionally, for 10 minutes.
- Stir in 1 tablespoon of the lime juice and the torn coriander leaves, and heat through for a further 2 minutes. Taste the curry and add the remaining lime juice and more salt if necessary. Serve hot.

Baked peanut tofu
serves 3–4

ingredients

4 tablespoons smooth peanut butter
2 tablespoons tamari
1 garlic clove, crushed
450g/1lb firm tofu, cubed
1½ tablespoons arrowroot

- In a small bowl, mix together the peanut butter, tamari and garlic. Slowly stir in 225ml/8fl oz water. Mix well until the water in incorporated. Put the tofu in a shallow dish and pour the liquid over it.
- Leave the tofu to marinate for at least 30 minutes.
- Preheat the oven to 190°C/375°F/Gas mark 5.
- Remove the tofu cubes from the marinade, and put them on a well-greased baking tray. Reserve the marinade to make the sauce.
- Bake the tofu cubes in the oven for 30–45 minutes until the desired crispness is reached.
- Mix the arrowroot with the remaining marinade. Put the mixture in a heavy saucepan, and cook over a high heat, stirring constantly, until the sauce thickens. Put the baked tofu on a bed of rice or pasta. Cover with the sauce, and serve immediately.

Spicy okra
serves 4

ingredients

3 tablespoons ghee or butter
1 large onion, sliced
2 garlic cloves, sliced
1 tablespoon ground coriander
1 teaspoon freshly ground
  black pepper
1 teaspoon ground turmeric
½ teaspoon salt
450g/1lb okra, topped, tailed and
  cut into 1cm/½in pieces
½ teaspoon garam masala

- Melt the ghee or butter in a large frying pan over a low heat. Add the onions and garlic, and sweat until soft but not caramelized.
- Add the ground coriander, pepper, turmeric and salt, and sweat for a further 4 minutes, stirring constantly.
- Add the okra. Coat with the mixture, then stir in 600ml/1pt water. Cover and simmer for 5–10 minutes until the okra is tender. Stir in the garam masala, and serve immediately.

Okra with mango & lentils
serves 4

ingredients

100g/4oz green lentils such as Puy,
  picked and rinsed
50ml/2fl oz corn oil
½ teaspoon onion seeds
2 onions, sliced
1 teaspoon fresh root ginger pulp
1 teaspoon garlic pulp
1½ teaspoons chilli powder
¼ teaspoon ground turmeric
1 teaspoon ground coriander
1 green or unripe mango, peeled
  and stoned
450g/1lb okra, chopped
2 fresh red chillies, seeded
  and sliced
1 tomato, sliced

- Put the lentils a saucepan with just enough water to cover. Bring to the boil, and boil for a couple of minutes, then reduce the heat. Simmer for about 20 minutes until soft, topping up with water if necessary. Drain.
- Heat the oil in a wok or large heavy frying pan. Add the onion seeds and fry until they begin to pop. Add the onions and sauté until they are golden. Reduce the heat and add the ginger, garlic, chilli powder, turmeric and coriander. Stir for a minute or so.
- Slice the mango, then add with the okra. Stir well, then add the chillies. Stir-fry for about 3 minutes until the okra is well cooked. Stir in the cooked lentils and tomato, then cook for a further 3 minutes. Serve immediately.

Chestnut & sprout sauté

serves 8

ingredients

900g/2lb fresh chestnuts
600ml/1pt vegetable stock
900g/2lb fresh Brussels sprouts
100g/4oz butter
450g/1lb onions, quartered, with
    layers separated
225g/8oz celery, trimmed and cut
    into 2.5cm/1in pieces
freshly grated zest of 1 lemon
salt and freshly ground black pepper

- Snip the brown outer skins of the chestnuts, and put the chestnuts in boiling water for 3–5 minutes. Lift out a few at a time, then peel off both the brown and inner skins.
- Put the chestnuts in a saucepan, cover with the stock and simmer for 40–45 minutes until tender. Drain well.
- Meanwhile, trim the sprouts and, with a sharp knife, make a cross in the stalk end of each one.
- Cook the sprouts in boiling salted water for 3–4 minutes only; drain well.
- Melt the butter in a large heavy frying pan. Add the onions, celery and lemon zest, and sauté for 2–3 minutes until softened. Add the cooked chestnuts and sprouts, and season with salt and pepper. Sauté for a further 1–2 minutes, and serve immediately.

Vegetable raisin curry
serves 4

ingredients

1 tablespoon vegetable oil
1 large onion, coarsely chopped
1 teaspoon freshly minced garlic
1 tablespoon plain flour
2 teaspoons curry powder
¼ teaspoon cayenne pepper
450g/1lb frozen mixed vegetables
100g/4oz raisins
½ teaspoon salt
500ml/18fl oz vegetable stock
225g/8oz quick-cooking couscous
50g/2oz sliced almonds, toasted

- In a frying pan, heat the oil and sauté the onion and garlic for a few minutes until soft. Stir in the flour, curry powder and cayenne, and cook for 1 minute, stirring constantly. Stir in the vegetables, raisins, salt and half of the stock. Cover and bring to a boil over a high heat.
- Reduce the heat to low and continue cooking, covered, for 10 minutes, stirring occasionally.
- Bring the remaining stock to the boil in a small saucepan. Stir in the couscous and remove from the heat. Cover and leave to stand for 5 minutes or until the liquid is absorbed. Fluff the grains with a fork.
- To serve, put the curry on a bed of couscous, sprinkle with the almonds and serve immediately.

Tofu with mushrooms

serves 4

ingredients

3 tablespoons light soy sauce
2 tablespoons Chinese rice wine
2 teaspoons brown sugar
1 garlic clove, crushed
1 tablespoon grated fresh root ginger
½ teaspoon five-spice powder
225g/8oz firm tofu, cut into
   2.5cm/1in cubes
6 dried Chinese mushrooms
1 teaspoon cornflour
2 tablespoons groundnut oil
6 spring onions, sliced into
   2.5cm/1in lengths, white and
   green parts separated

- In a small bowl, mix together the soy sauce, rice wine, sugar, garlic, ginger and five-spice powder.
- Put the tofu in a shallow dish. Pour the marinade over, toss well and leave to marinate for about 30 minutes. Drain, reserving the marinade.
- Meanwhile, soak the dried Chinese mushrooms in warm water for 20–30 minutes until soft. Drain, reserving 75ml/3fl oz of the soaking liquid. Squeeze out any excess liquid from the mushrooms, remove the stalks and slice the caps. In a bowl, blend the cornflour with the reserved marinade and mushroom soaking liquid.
- Heat the oil in a wok or large heavy frying pan until hot. Add the tofu and stir-fry for 3 minutes or until evenly golden. Remove from the wok using a slotted spoon, and set aside.
- Add the mushrooms and white parts of the spring onions to the wok, and stir-fry for 2 minutes. Pour in the marinade mixture and stir for 1 minute until thickened.
- Return the tofu to the wok with the green parts of the spring onions. Simmer gently for 1–2 minutes. Serve immediately with rice noodles.

Pineapple & coconut curry

serves 6

ingredients

2 tablespoons groundnut oil
1 red onion, sliced
2 garlic cloves, crushed
2 whole cloves, bruised
5cm/2in cinnamon stick
¼ teaspoon ground cardamom
½ teaspoon ground turmeric
2 teaspoons ground cumin
1 tablespoon ground coriander
1 large fresh red chilli, deseeded
   and sliced
½ teaspoon salt
1 ripe pineapple, peeled, cored and
   cut into 2.5cm/1in chunks
75g/3oz creamed coconut,
   dissolved in 250ml/9fl oz
   boiling water

- Heat the oil in a flameproof casserole dish, add the onion, garlic, cloves and cinnamon stick, and sauté over a gentle heat, stirring frequently, for about 5 minutes until softened.
- Add the ground cardamom, turmeric, cumin, coriander, chilli and salt to the pan, and sauté for a further 2 minutes. Add the pineapple chunks and stir well to coat them evenly in the spice mixture.
- Stir in the coconut milk, stir to mix and bring to the boil. Reduce the heat and cook the curry very gently, stirring frequently, for 2–3 minutes until the pineapple is tender but not mushy and the sauce is very thick. Taste and adjust the seasoning if necessary, and serve immediately.

Quinoa & butter beans

serves 4

ingredients

25g/1oz butter
175g/6oz onion, finely chopped
1 tablespoon minced fresh ginger
175ml/6fl oz freshly squeezed
   orange juice
2 tablespoons clear honey
½ teaspoon salt
¼ teaspoon ground coriander
¼ teaspoon ground cardamom
⅛ teaspoon ground nutmeg
225g/8oz sweet potato, cut into
   2cm/½in pieces
225g/8oz butternut squash, cut into
   2cm/½in pieces
225g/8oz canned cooked butter
   beans, drained and rinsed
225g/8oz quinoa
50g/2oz cranberries, chopped

- Melt the butter in a large saucepan over a medium-high heat. Add the onion and ginger, and sauté, stirring, until the onion is softened. Stir in the orange juice, 150ml/5fl oz water, honey, salt, coriander, cardamom and nutmeg, and bring to the boil.
- Stir in the sweet potato and squash, and bring back to the boil. Reduce the heat to a simmer and cook, uncovered, for 7 minutes. Stir in the butter beans and quinoa, and return to the boil. Reduce the heat and simmer, covered, for 15 minutes.
- Stir in the cranberries and simmer, covered, for a further 5 minutes. Serve hot.

Pepper & onion pizza
serves 4

ingredients

2 large red peppers
4 tablespoons olive oil, plus extra
    for drizzling
2 large onions, sliced
450g/1lb white bread and pizza mix
200g/7oz mozzarella cheese, sliced
400g/14oz canned chopped plum
    tomatoes, drained
3 garlic cloves, thinly sliced
salt and freshly ground black pepper

- Preheat the oven to 200°C/400°F/Gas mark 6. Halve the peppers and roast in the oven until blackened all over. Leave until cold enough to handle, then carefully peel off the skins. Cut the flesh into thick strips, discarding the seeds. Leave the oven on.
- Heat 2 tablespoons olive oil in a frying pan, and sweat the onions gently for 5 minutes until softened but not coloured. Set aside.
- Make up the pizza dough following the packet instructions, substituting 2 tablespoons oil for a similar amount of the liquid measurement. Roll out into a 30cm/12in round on a floured work surface, then slide onto a baking tray.
- Cover the pizza base with the mozzarella. Scatter over the tomatoes, onions and peppers, then the garlic. Season with salt and pepper, drizzle with olive oil and leave in a warm place for 20–30 minutes until the dough has doubled in thickness.
- Bake in the oven for 15–20 minutes until golden and bubbling. Serve hot.

Potato curry
serves 4

ingredients
2 tablespoons vegetable oil
1 teaspoon mustard seeds
2 dried red chillies
3 curry leaves
2 onions, chopped
½ teaspoon ground coriander
½ teaspoon garam masala
½ teaspoon ground turmeric
¼ teaspoon chilli powder
2 tomatoes, quartered
400g/14oz potatoes, cut into chunks
125ml/4fl oz coconut milk

- Heat the oil in a large saucepan over a medium heat. Add the mustard seeds, chillies and curry leaves. As the mustard seeds begin to pop, add the onions and sauté, stirring, until lightly browned.
- Stir in the coriander, garam masala, turmeric and chilli powder. Sauté for a minute or so. Add the tomatoes and cook for 5 minutes.
- Add the potatoes and cook over a gentle heat for 5 minutes, stirring constantly. Pour in the coconut milk and 125ml/4fl oz water. Cook for 15–20 minutes until the potatoes are tender. Serve hot.

Casseroled beans & penne

serves 4

ingredients

225g/8oz dried haricot
  beans, soaked overnight,
  rinsed and drained
900ml/1½pt vegetable stock
100ml/3½fl oz olive oil
2 large onions, sliced
2 garlic cloves, chopped
2 bay leaves
1 teaspoon dried oregano
75ml/3fl oz red wine

2 tablespoons tomato purée
225g/8oz dried penne
2 celery sticks, sliced
100g/4oz mushrooms, sliced
225g/8oz tomatoes, sliced
1 teaspoon muscovado sugar
4 tablespoons dried white
  breadcrumbs
salt and freshly ground
  black pepper

- Preheat the oven to 180°C/350°F/Gas mark 4.
- Put the haricot beans in a large heavy saucepan, and add enough cold water to cover. Bring to the boil and continue to boil vigorously for 20 minutes. Drain.
- Put the beans in a large flameproof casserole dish. Add the vegetable stock, and stir in all but 1 tablespoon of the oil, the onions, garlic, bay leaves, oregano, wine and tomato purée. Bring to the boil, then cover and cook in the oven for 2 hours.
- Bring a large saucepan of lightly salted water to the boil. Add the penne and the remaining oil, and cook for about 3 minutes. Drain.
- Add the penne, celery, mushrooms and tomatoes to the casserole dish, and season with salt and pepper. Stir in the muscovado sugar, and sprinkle the breadcrumbs over the top. Cover the dish and cook in the oven for a further 1 hour. Serve hot.

Tabbouleh & tofu

serves 8

ingredients

225g/8oz bulgur wheat
600ml/1pt lukewarm water
75ml/3fl oz olive oil
75ml/3fl oz freshly squeezed
   lemon juice
4 garlic cloves, finely chopped
25g/1oz chopped fresh
   flat-leaf parsley
25g/1oz chopped fresh mint
4 tomatoes, peeled and chopped
1 bunch of spring onions, trimmed
   and finely chopped
200g/7oz marinated tofu
salt and freshly ground black pepper

- Soak the bulgur wheat in the water for 30 minutes, then drain in a sieve, squeezing it with your hands to extract the water. Tip out onto a clean tea towel, gather the corners together and wring out the water so that the bulgur is as dry as possible.
- Whisk the oil and lemon juice together in a bowl with the garlic, parsley and mint. Season with salt and pepper. Add the bulgur and toss to coat in the dressing.
- Add the tomatoes, spring onions and tofu. Fork through until evenly distributed. Taste and adjust the seasoning, and serve the tabbouleh at room temperature.

Stuffed peppers

serves 4

ingredients

3 green peppers
3 red peppers
2 yellow peppers
5 tablespoons olive oil
2 onions, chopped
4 garlic cloves, crushed
350g/12oz tomatoes, seeded
  and chopped
1 tablespoon tomato purée

1 teaspoon sugar
3 tablespoons chopped fresh
  coriander leaves
225g/8oz risotto rice such as
  Arborio or Carnaroli
½ teaspoon ground cinnamon
salt and freshly ground
  black pepper

- Cut a slice off the top of each pepper and reserve. Remove the cores, seeds and membranes, and discard. Wash the peppers and pat dry with kitchen paper.
- Heat 4 tablespoons of the oil in a large frying pan, add the peppers and sauté gently for 10 minutes, turning them frequently so that they soften and colour on all sides. Remove from the pan with a slotted spoon, and drain on kitchen paper.
- To make the stuffing, drain off all but 2 tablespoons of oil from the pan, then add the onion and garlic, and seat very gently for about 15 minutes. Add the tomatoes and sweat gently to soften, stirring constantly. Increase the heat and cook rapidly to drive off the liquid – the mixture should be thick and pulpy.
- Reduce the heat, and add the tomato purée, sugar. Season with salt and pepper, and simmer gently for 5 minutes. Remove the pan from the heat and stir in the chopped fresh coriander and the risotto rice. Spoon the stuffing into the peppers, dividing it equally between them.
- Stand the peppers close together in a flameproof casserole dish. Sprinkle with the cinnamon, then the remaining 1 tablespoon oil. Put the reserved 'lids' on top.
- Carefully pour 150ml/5fl oz water into the bottom of the pan, then bring to the boil. Reduce the heat, cover with a plate or saucer that just fits inside the rim of the dish, then place weights on top.
- Simmer gently for 1 hour, then remove from the heat and leave to cool. Chill in the refrigerator overnight, with the weights still on top. Serve the stuffed peppers chilled, with garlic bread and a salad.

Courgette quiche

serves 4

ingredients

For the pastry
175g/6oz plain flour
pinch of salt
100g/4oz butter, cut into pieces
100g/4oz Cheddar cheese, grated
1 egg yolk, beaten
a little egg white, to seal

For the filling
350g/12oz courgettes, cut into
    2.5cm/1in chunks
3 eggs
150ml/5fl oz double cream
2 teaspoons chopped fresh basil
finely grated zest of 1 lime
a little egg white
salt and freshly ground
    black pepper

- Make the pastry by sifting the flour into a bowl with a pinch of salt. Add the butter in pieces and rub in thoroughly with fingertips until the mixture resembles fine breadcrumbs.
- Stir in the cheese, then the egg yolk. Gather the mixture together with your fingers to make a smooth ball of dough. Wrap the dough in cling film and chill in the refrigerator for about 30 minutes.
- Preheat the oven to 200°C/400°F/Gas mark 6.
- To make the filling, plunge the courgette pieces into salted boiling water, bring back to the boil, then simmer for 3 minutes. Drain and set aside.
- Put the eggs in a jug, and beat lightly together with the cream. Stir in the basil and lime zest, and sprinkle with salt and pepper. Set aside.
- Roll out the chilled dough on a floured work surface, and use to line a loose-bottomed 23cm/9in flan tin. Refrigerate for 15 minutes.
- Prick the base of the dough with a fork, then line with foil. Stand the tin on a preheated baking sheet, and bake in the oven for 10 minutes.
- Remove the foil and brush the inside of the pastry case with the egg white to seal. Return to the oven for 5 minutes.
- Stand the courgette chunks upright in the pastry case, then slowly pour in the egg and cream mixture. Return to the oven for 20 minutes until set and golden. Serve hot or cold.

Spicy Japanese noodles

serves 4

ingredients

500g/1lb 2oz fresh Japanese
  noodles such as soba
1 tablespoon sesame oil
1 tablespoon sesame seeds
1 tablespoon sunflower oil
1 red onion, sliced
100g/4oz mangetout
175g/6oz carrots, thinly sliced
350g/12oz white cabbage,
  shredded
3 tablespoons sweet chilli sauce
2 spring onions, sliced

- Bring a large saucepan of water to the boil. Add the noodles to the pan, and cook for 2–3 minutes. Drain the noodles thoroughly. Toss the noodles with the sesame oil and sesame seeds, and set aside.
- Heat the sunflower oil in a large preheated wok. Add the onion slices, mangetout, carrot slices and shredded cabbage, and stir-fry for about 5 minutes.
- Add the sweet chilli sauce to the wok and cook, stirring occasionally, for a further 2 minutes. Add the sesame noodles to the wok, toss thoroughly to combine and heat for a further 2–3 minutes.
- Transfer the Japanese noodles and spicy vegetables to warm individual serving bowls, scatter over the spring onions and serve immediately.

Vegetarian pizza
serves 4

ingredients

1 large ready-prepared pizza base
 (or see dough on page 517)
200ml/7fl oz tomato purée
4 spinach leaves, stalks removed
1 tomato, sliced
1 celery stick, thinly sliced
½ green pepper, thinly sliced
1 baby courgette, sliced
25g/1oz fresh asparagus tips
25g/1oz sweetcorn kernels
25g/1oz fresh or frozen peas

4 spring onions, trimmed and
 chopped
1 tablespoon mixed dried herbs
50g/2oz mozzarella
 cheese, grated
2 tablespoons freshly grated
 Parmesan cheese
1 marinated artichoke heart
olive oil for drizzling
sea salt and freshly ground
 black pepper

- Preheat the oven to 200°C/400°F/Gas mark 6.
- Put the pizza base on a large greased baking tray. Spread the tomato purée over the base, almost to the edge.
- Arrange the spinach leaves on the sauce, followed by the tomato slices. Top with the remaining vegetables and the herbs.
- Mix together the cheeses, and sprinkle over the top. Put the artichoke heart in the centre. Drizzle the pizza with a little oil and season with salt and pepper.
- Bake in the oven for 18–20 minutes until the edges are crisp and golden. Serve immediately.

Nut roast
serves 6

ingredients

2 tablespoons olive oil
1 large onion, diced
2 garlic cloves, crushed
275g/10oz mushroom caps, wiped
    with damp kitchen paper and
    finely chopped
200g/7oz raw cashew nuts
200g/7oz Brazil nuts
100g/4oz Cheddar cheese, grated
25g/1oz Parmesan cheese,
    freshly grated
1 egg, lightly beaten
2 tablespoons chopped fresh chives
75g/3oz fresh wholemeal
    breadcrumbs
salt and freshly ground black pepper

- Grease a 14 x 21cm/5 1/2 x 8 1/2 in loaf tin, and line the bottom with baking parchment.
- Heat the oil in a frying pan over a medium heat, and add the onion, garlic and mushrooms. Sweat until soft, then cool.
- Process the nuts in a blender or food processor until finely chopped.
- Preheat the oven to 180°C/350°F/Gas mark 4.
- Combine the cooled mushrooms, chopped nuts, Cheddar, Parmesan, egg, chives and breadcrumbs in a bowl. Mix well and season with salt and pepper.
- Press the mixture into the loaf tin, and bake for 45 minutes or until firm. Remove from the oven and leave in the tin for 5 minutes, then turn out and cut into slices. Serve hot with potatoes.

Mushroom vol-au-vent

serves 4

ingredients
500g/1lb 2oz ready-prepared
    puff pastry
1 egg, beaten, for glazing

For the filling
30g/1oz butter
700g/1½lb mixed mushrooms
100ml/3½fl oz white wine
4 tablespoons double cream
2 tablespoons chopped fresh chervil
salt and freshly ground black pepper

- Preheat the oven to 220°C/425°F/Gas mark 7.
- Roll out the pastry to a 20cm/8in square on a lightly floured work
  surface. Using a sharp knife, mark a square 2cm/1in from the pastry
  edge, cutting halfway through the pastry. Score the top in a diagonal
  pattern. Knock up the edges with a kitchen knife and put on a baking
  tray. Brush the top with beaten egg.
- Bake in the oven for 35 minutes or until puffed and golden.
- Cut out the central square. Discard the soft pastry inside the case,
  leaving the base intact. Return to the oven, with the central square, for
  10 minutes.
- Make the filling by melting the butter in a frying pan and sautéeing the
  mushrooms, stirring, over a high heat for 3 minutes. Add the wine and
  cook, stirring occasionally, for 10 minutes, until the mushrooms have
  softened. Stir in the cream and chervil, and season with salt and pepper.
- Pile the filling into the pastry case. Top with the pastry square, and
  serve immediately.

Chargrilled peppers & sweet potatoes

serves 4–6

ingredients
2 red peppers
2 yellow peppers
2 green peppers
1 sweet potato
about 2 tablespoons olive oil

For the dressing
1 teaspoon cumin seeds
2 teaspoons clear honey
2 tablespoons balsamic vinegar
1 tablespoon walnut oil
1 tablespoon olive oil
salt and freshly ground black pepper

- Halve the peppers lengthways and discard the stalks, cores and seeds. Cut each half lengthways into four pieces. Peel the sweet potato and slice into rings about 8mm/¼in thick.
- To make the dressing, in a small frying pan, dry-roast the cumin seeds over a low heat for a few minutes until aromatic, taking care not to burn them. Put them in a bowl with the honey, vinegar and oils, and whisk together. Season with salt and pepper.
- Heat a ridged cast-iron grill pan until very hot. Put the sweet potato slices on the pan, and lightly brush each piece with a little of the oil. Cook for about 10 minutes, turning the pieces over once, then remove from the pan and keep warm.
- Add half the pepper pieces, brush with a little oil and cook for about 8 minutes, turning them over several times. Remove and add to the sweet potatoes, then repeat with the remaining peppers.
- To serve, put the vegetables on a large shallow dish, and drizzle the dressing over them. Serve warm with rice.

Tomatoes au gratin

serves 6

ingredients

900g/2lb tomatoes
50g/2oz butter, softened
3 garlic cloves, chopped
1 teaspoon sugar
4 teaspoons chopped fresh basil
300ml/10fl oz double cream
50g/2oz dried breadcrumbs
25g/1oz Parmesan cheese,
    freshly grated
salt and freshly ground black pepper

- Preheat the oven to 180°C/350°F/Gas mark 4.
- Put the tomatoes in a bowl of just-boiled water, and leave for 30 seconds. Peel off the skin and thinly slice the flesh.
- Brush the inside of an ovenproof dish liberally with some of the butter.
- Arrange a layer of tomato slices in the bottom of the dish, then sprinkle with a little of the garlic, sugar and basil. Season with salt and pepper. Pour over a thin layer of cream. Repeat these layers until all the ingredients have been used.
- Mix the breadcrumbs and Parmesan together, then sprinkle over the top of the tomatoes and cream. Dot with the remaining butter.
- Bake in the oven for 20–30 minutes until the topping is golden brown. Serve hot.

Couscous vegetable loaf

serves 6–8

ingredients

1.2 litres/2pt vegetable stock
450g/1lb quick-cooking couscous
25g/1oz butter
3 tablespoons olive oil
2 garlic cloves, crushed
1 onion, finely chopped
1 tablespoon ground coriander
1 teaspoon ground cinnamon
1 teaspoon garam marsala
225g/8oz cherry tomatoes,
   quartered
1 courgette, finely chopped
150g/5oz canned sweetcorn
   kernels, drained

8 large fresh basil leaves, plus
   50g/2oz fresh basil, chopped
150g/5oz sun-dried peppers in oil

For the dressing
75ml/3fl oz freshly squezed
   orange juice
1 tablespoon freshly squeezed
   lemon juice
3 tablespoons chopped fresh
   flat-leaf parsley
1 teaspoon honey
1 teaspoon ground cumin

- Bring the stock to the boil in a saucepan. Put the couscous and butter in a large bowl, cover with the hot stock and set aside for 10 minutes.
- Heat 1 tablespoon of the oil in a large frying pan, and sweat the garlic and onion over a low heat for 5 minutes or until the onion is soft. Add the spices and cook for 1 minute until fragrant. Remove from the pan.
- Add the remaining oil to the pan and sauté the tomatoes, courgette and corn over a high heat in batches until soft.
- Line a 3 litre/5pt loaf tin with cling film, allowing it to overhang the sides. Arrange the basil leaves along the bottom of the tin. Drain the peppers, reserving 2 tablespoons oil, then roughly chop. Add the garlic and onion mixture, sautéed vegetables, pepper and chopped basil to the couscous and mix together. Press the mixture into the tin, and fold the cling film over to cover. Weigh down and refrigerate overnight.
- To make the dressing, put all the ingredients in a screwtop glass jar, and shake well to combine.
- Turn out the loaf and serve with the dressing and potatoes.

Pasticcio

serves 4–6

ingredients

1 red pepper, seeded
  and chopped
1 yellow pepper, seeded
  and chopped
1 aubergine, chopped
1 large courgette, chopped
2 garlic cloves, crushed
1 teaspoon dried mixed herbs
2 tablespoons olive oil
225g/8oz short pasta such elbow
  macaroni
200ml/7fl oz vegetable stock
300g/11oz mozzarella
  cheese, diced
salt and freshly ground
  black pepper

For the tomato sauce
30g/1oz sun-dried tomatoes,
  chopped
400g/14oz canned chopped
  tomatoes
½ teaspoon sugar
500g/1lb 2oz ripe plum tomatoes,
  seeded and chopped
2 teaspoons balsamic vinegar

- Preheat the oven to 200°C/400°F/Gas mark 6.
- For the tomato sauce, put the sun-dried tomatoes in a saucepan with the canned tomatoes and sugar. Bring to a simmer, and continue to simmer for 5 minutes. Add the diced plum tomatoes and cook gently for 10 minutes, stirring occasionally. Remove the pan from the heat, and stir in the balsamic vinegar. Set aside.
- Put the peppers, aubergine and courgette chunks in a large non-stick roasting tin, and mix in the garlic, dried herbs and oil. Season with salt and pepper. Roast in the oven for 30–40 minutes, stirring occasionally.
- Cook the pasta in salted boiling water until al dente. Drain well. In a separate pan, heat the tomato sauce with the stock.
- Put the vegetables and pasta in a large baking dish, and mix well. Pour the tomato sauce over them and mix through, then put the mozzarella cubes on top. Bake in the oven for 15–20 minutes until melted and golden. Leave to stand for 5–10 minutes before serving.

Gado gado

serves 4

ingredients

100g/4oz white cabbage, shredded

100g/4oz French beans, each cut into three

100g/4oz carrots, cut into matchsticks

100g/4oz cauliflower florets

100g/4oz beansprouts

For the dressing

100ml/4fl oz vegetable oil

100g/4oz unsalted peanuts

2 garlic cloves, crushed

1 small onion, finely chopped

½ teaspoon chilli powder

½ teaspoon soft brown sugar

salt

juice of ½ lemon

- Cook the vegetables separately in a saucepan of salted boiling water for 4–5 minutes. Drain well and chill.
- To make the dressing, heat the oil in a frying pan and fry the peanuts, tossing frequently, for 3–4 minutes. Remove from the pan with a slotted spoon, and drain on kitchen paper. Chop the peanuts in a blender or food processor, or crush with a rolling pin, until fine but not ground to a powder – leave a little texture.
- Pour all but 1 tablespoon of the oil from the pan, and fry the garlic and onion for 1 minute. Add the chilli powder, sugar, a pinch of salt and 450ml/¾pt water, and bring to the boil.Stir in the peanuts, reduce the heat and simmer for 4–5 minutes until the sauce thickens. Add the lemon juice and set aside to cool.
- Arrange the cold vegetables in a serving dish, and put the peanut dressing in a small bowl in the centre. Serve.

Spinach & ricotta pie

serves 4

ingredients

225g/8oz spinach
25g/1oz pine nuts
100g/4oz ricotta cheese
2 large eggs, beaten
50g/2oz ground almonds
40g/1½oz Parmesan cheese,
    freshly grated
250g/9oz ready-prepared
    puff pastry
1 small egg, beaten, to glaze

- Preheat the oven to 220°C/425°F/Gas mark 7.
- Rinse the spinach, put in a large pan and cook with just the water
  clinging to the leaves for 4–5 minutes until wilted. Transfer to a colander
  and drain thoroughly. When the spinach is cool enough to handle,
  gently squeeze out the excess liquid.
- Put the pine nuts on a baking tray, and lightly toast under a medium grill
  for 2–3 minutes until golden brown – be careful not to scorch them.
- Put the ricotta, spinach and eggs in a bowl, and mix together. Add the
  pine nuts, beat well, then stir in the ground almonds and Parmesan.
- Roll out the puff pastry into two squares, each about 20cm/8in wide.
  Trim the edges, reserving the pastry trimmings.
- Put one of the pastry squares on a baking tray. Spoon over the spinach
  mixture to within 1cm/½in of the edge of the pastry. Brush the edges
  with beaten egg, and put the second square over the top.
- Using a round-bladed knife, press the pastry edges together by tapping
  along the sealed edge. Use the pastry trimmings to decorate the pie.
- Bake in the oven for 10 minutes. Reduce the oven temperature to
  190°C/375°F/Gas mark 5, and bake for a further 25–30 minutes.
  Serve hot.

Sweet & sour tofu

serves 4

ingredients
2 tablespoons vegetable oil
2 garlic cloves, crushed
2 celery sticks, sliced
1 carrot, cut into matchsticks
1 green pepper, seeded and diced
75g/3oz mangetout, halved
8 baby corn cobs
150g/5oz beansprouts
450g/1lb firm tofu, cubed

For the sauce
2 tablespoons soft brown sugar
2 tablespoons wine vinegar
225ml/8fl oz vegetable stock
1 teaspoon tomato purée
1 tablespoon cornflour

- Heat the vegetable oil in a preheated wok until it is almost smoking. Reduce the heat slightly, then add the garlic, celery, carrot, pepper, mangetout and baby corn. Stir-fry for 3–4 minutes.
- Add the beansprouts and tofu to the wok, and stir-fry for 2 minutes.
- To make the sauce, combine the sugar, wine vinegar, stock, tomato purée and cornflour, stirring well to mix. Stir into the wok, bring to the boil and cook, stirring, until the sauce thickens and turns glossy. Continue for cook for 1 minute.
- Serve immediately with rice or noodles.

Satay noodles

serves 4

ingredients

275g/10oz wide rice noodles
3 tablespoons groundnut oil
2 garlic cloves, crushed
2 shallots, sliced
225g/8oz green beans, sliced
100g/4oz cherry tomatoes, halved
1 teaspoon red chilli flakes
4 tablespoons crunchy peanut butter
150ml/5fl oz coconut milk
1 tablespoon tomato purée

- Put the noodles in a large bowl and pour over enough boiling water to cover. Leave to stand for 10 minutes or according to instructions on the packet.
- Heat the groundnut oil in a large preheated wok or heavy frying pan. Add crushed garlic and sliced shallots to the wok or frying pan, and stir-fry for 1 minute.
- Drain the noodles thoroughly. Add the green beans and drained noodles to the wok, and stir-fry for about 5 minutes. Add the cherry tomatoes and mix through well.
- Mix together the chilli flakes, peanut butter, coconut milk and tomato purée. Pour the chilli mixture over the noodles, toss well until all the ingredients are thoroughly combined and heat through.
- Transfer the satay noodles to warmed serving dishes or bowls, and serve immediately.

Mushroom pizza
serves 4

ingredients

For the dough
15g/½oz active dry yeast
1 teaspoon sugar
250ml/9fl oz hot water
350g/12oz plain flour
1 teaspoon salt
1 tablespoon olive oil

For the topping
400g/14oz canned chopped
  plum tomatoes
2 garlic cloves, crushed
1 teaspoon dried basil
1 tablespoon olive oil
2 tablespoons tomato purée
200g/7oz mushrooms, chopped
175g/6oz mozzarella
  cheese, grated
salt and freshly ground
  black pepper

- Put the yeast and sugar in a measuring jug and mix with 4 tablespoons of the hot water. Leave in a warm place for 15 minutes or until frothy.
- Mix the flour with the salt in a large bowl, and make a well in the centre. Add the oil, the yeast mixture and the remaining water. Using a wooden spoon, mix to form a dough. Turn the dough out onto a floured work surface, and knead for 4–5 minutes until smooth. Return the dough to the bowl, cover with an oiled sheet of cling film and leave to rise in a warm place for 30 minutes or until doubled in size.
- Preheat the oven to 200°C/400°F/Gas mark 6.
- Remove the dough from the bowl and knead for 2 minutes. Using a rolling pin, roll out the dough to form an oval or circle shape, and put on an oiled baking tray, pushing out the edges until even. The dough should be no more than 8mm/¼in thick, as it will rise during cooking.
- To make the topping, put the tomatoes, garlic, dried basil and olive oil in a large heavy pan. Season with salt and pepper, and simmer for 20 minutes or until the sauce has thickened. Stir in the tomato purée and leave to cool slightly.
- Spread the sauce over the pizza base, leaving a border around the edge. Top with the mushrooms, and scatter the mozzarella evenly over the top. Bake in the oven for 25 minutes, and serve hot.

Beetroot fettuccine

serves 4

ingredients

50g/2oz butter
400g/14oz courgettes, shredded
1 small onion, grated
225ml/8fl oz double cream
3 tablespoons freshly grated
　Parmesan cheese
pinch of grated nutmeg
450g/1lb fresh beetroot fettucine
salt and freshly ground black pepper

- Melt the butter in a large deep frying pan. Add the courgettes and onion. Stir and sauté for about 4 minutes until the onion is starting to soften. Cover the pan, and sauté for a further 3 minutes until soft and translucent. Stir in the cream, and allow it to come to a gentle simmer.
- Remove the pan from the heat, and stir in the Parmesan and nutmeg. Season with salt and pepper. Keep warm.
- Bring a large saucepan of lightly salted water to the boil, and add the fresh fettuccine. Return to the boil, then cook for 15 seconds. Drain and add to the frying pan with the sauce. Toss everything together, and serve immediately.

Fusilli with tomato & mozzarella

serves 4

ingredients

1kg/2½lb vine-ripened
  tomatoes, chopped
100g/4oz mozzarella
  cheese, diced
125ml/4fl oz extra virgin olive oil
2 garlic cloves, chopped
20 large fresh basil leaves, torn
  into pieces
5 anchovy fillets in oil, drained and
  cut into small pieces
¼ teaspoon chopped fresh oregano
½ teaspoon salt
450g/1lb dried fusilli
freshly ground black pepper

- Put the tomatoes in a serving bowl. Add mozzarella, oil, garlic, basil, anchovies, oregano and salt. Season with pepper, and mix well. Leave to marinate for 1–3 hours at room temperature to enable the flavours to mingle and develop.
- Bring a large saucepan of salted water to the boil. Cook the fusilli until al dente, stirring frequently to prevent sticking. Drain and add to the bowl with the sauce, tossing everything together. Serve immediately.

Vegetable jalousie

serves 4

ingredients

500g/1lb 2oz ready-prepared
  puff pastry
1 egg, beaten, to glaze

For the filling
25g/1oz butter
1 leek, finely chopped
2 garlic cloves, crushed
1 red pepper, seeded and sliced
1 yellow pepper, seeded
  and sliced

50g/2oz mushrooms, wiped with
  damp kitchen paper and sliced
75g/3oz small fresh asparagus
  spears, ends trimmed
2 tablespoons plain flour
100ml/3½fl oz vegetable stock
100ml/3½fl oz milk
4 tablespoons dry white wine
1 tablespoon chopped fresh
  oregano
salt and ground black pepper

- Preheat the oven to 200°C/400°F/Gas mark 6.
- Melt the butter in a frying pan, and sauté the leek and garlic, stirring frequently, for 2 minutes. Add the peppers, mushrooms and asparagus, and cook for 3–4 minutes.
- Add the flour and fry for 1 minute. Remove the pan from the heat, and stir in the vegetable stock, milk and white wine. Return the pan to the heat and bring to the boil, stirring, until thickened. Stir in the oregano, and season with salt and pepper.
- Roll out half of the pastry on a lightly floured surface to form a rectangle measuring 38 x 15cm/15 x 6in. Roll out the other half of the pastry to the same shape, but a little larger all round. Put the smaller rectangle on a baking tray lined with dampened baking parchment.
- Spoon the filling evenly on top of the smaller rectangle, leaving a 1cm/½in margin around the edges.
- Using a sharp knife, cut parallel diagonal slits across the larger rectangle to within 2cm/1in on each of the long edges.
- Brush the edges of the smaller rectangle with beaten egg, and place the larger rectangle on top, pressing the edges to seal.
- Brush the whole jalousie with egg to glaze, and bake in the oven for 30–35 minutes until risen and golden. Serve immediately.

Spiced fruity couscous

serves 4–6

ingredients

2 teaspoons cumin seeds
500ml/18fl oz vegetable stock
200g/7oz quick-cooking couscous
75g/3oz ready-to-eat prunes
75g/3oz ready-to-eat dried apricots
2 tablespoons extra virgin olive oil
2 tablespoons chopped fresh
    coriander leaves
salt and freshly ground black pepper

- Dry-roast the cumin seeds over a low heat in a non-stick frying pan for a few minutes, stirring constantly. Crush the seeds finely using a mortar and pestle, and set aside.
- Bring the stock to the boil in a large saucepan, add the couscous and stir well. Turn off the heat, cover the pan and leave to stand for 10 minutes. Use a fork to fluff the couscous.
- Using scissors, snip the dried fruit into the couscous, then add the cumin seeds, oil and half of the coriander. Season with salt and pepper. Fork through until evenly mixed.
- Turn into a serving bowl and sprinkle with the remaining coriander. Serve hot or at room temperature.

Spinach & ricotta ravioli

serves 4

ingredients

450g/1lb fresh egg pasta
1 egg white
salt

For the filling
700g/1½lb fresh spinach
700g/1½lb ricotta cheese, drained
2 egg yolks
¼ teaspoon freshly grated nutmeg
½ teaspoon salt
¼ teaspoon freshly ground
   black pepper
50g/2oz Parmesan cheese, grated
1 tablespoon chopped fresh
   flat-leaf parsley

- To make the filling, put the spinach in a deep saucepan with no water except the drops still clinging to the leaves after washing. Cover with a lid, and steam the spinach for 5–10 minutes until tender, tossing occasionally. Drain the spinach thoroughly in a colander, and squeeze out as much water as you can. Chop the spinach and set aside.
- Combine all the ingredients for the filling in a bowl, blending well with a wooden spoon. Cover and refrigerate.
- Divide the pasta dough into six portions. Working with one portion at a time, roll the dough as thinly as possible into 10cm/4in wide strips. Work with two strips at a time, keeping the others covered with a damp cloth, and work quickly to prevent the dough drying out.
- Put a teaspoon of filling at 5cm/2in intervals in rows along one of the pasta strips. Dip a pastry brush in the egg white, and paint around each spoonful of filling. Put the second rolled-out sheet of pasta over the filled sheet. Press down firmly around each mound of filling to seal it, forcing out any trapped air. Use a knife to cut the ravioli into squares. Put the squares on a tray, and leave to dry for 2 hours.
- Bring a pan of salted water to the boil, and cook the ravioli in batches for 3–5 minutes, lifting out with a slotted spoon. Transfer to a serving dish. Serve immediately, either buttered or with tomato sauce.

Falafels
serves 4–6

ingredients

800g/1lb 14oz canned cooked
    chickpeas, drained and rinsed
¼ onion
2 garlic cloves
15g/¼oz flat-leaf parsley leaves
15g/¼oz fresh coriander leaves
1 teaspoon ground cumin
1 tablespoon freshly squeezed
    lemon juice
¼ beaten egg
about 2 tablespoons olive oil

For the dressing
1 small handful of fresh mint
1 garlic clove
200g/7oz Greek-style yogurt
salt and freshly ground black pepper

- To make the falafels, purée the chickpeas, onion, garlic, parsley, coriander, cumin and lemon juice in a blender or food processor. Turn the mixture into a bowl, and beat in the egg, then cover and chill in the refrigerator for 30–60 minutes, or longer if more convenient.
- Preheat the oven to 180°C/350°F/Gas mark 4.
- With wet hands, shape the mixture into 20 equal-size balls. Put the falafels on an oiled baking sheet, and flatten them slightly, then brush with a little oil. Bake in the oven for 20 minutes, turning the falafels over halfway through the cooking time.
- To make the dressing, blend or process the mint, garlic and yogurt until smooth, turn into a bowl and season with salt and pepper.
- To serve, put the falafels on a serving platter, and spoon the dressing over the top. Serve hot.

Kidney bean Kiev

serves 4

ingredients

For the garlic butter
100g/4oz butter
3 garlic cloves, crushed
1 tablespoon chopped fresh
flat-leaf parsley

For the bean patties
700g/1½lb canned cooked red
kidney beans, drained
150g/5oz fresh white
breadcrumbs

25g/1oz butter
1 leek, chopped
1 celery stick, chopped
1 tablespoon chopped fresh
flat-leaf parsley
1 egg, beaten
vegetable oil for shallow-frying
salt and freshly ground
black pepper

- To make the garlic butter, put the butter, garlic and parsley in a bowl and blend together using a wooden spoon. Put the garlic butter on a sheet of baking parchment, roll into a cigar shape and wrap in the baking parchment. Chill in the refrigerator until required.
- Using a potato masher, mash the red kidney beans in a mixing bowl and stir in half of the breadcrumbs until thoroughly blended.
- Melt the butter in a heavy frying pan. Add the leek and celery, and sweat over a low heat, stirring constantly, for 3–4 minutes.
- Add the bean mixture to the pan, together with the parsley and a pinch of salt. Mix thoroughly. Remove the pan from the heat, and set aside to cool slightly.
- Divide the kidney bean mixture into four equal portions, and shape them into ovals.
- Slice the garlic butter into four pieces, and place a slice in the centre of each bean patty. With your hands, mould the bean mixture around the garlic butter to encase it completely. Dip each bean patty into the beaten egg to coat, then roll in the remaining breadcrumbs.
- Heat a little oil in a frying pan over a medium heat, and fry the patties, turning once, for 7–10 minutes until golden brown. Serve immediately.

Spinach & ricotta conchiglioni

serves 4

ingredients

20 dried conchiglioni (jumbo
   pasta shells)
1 tablespoon extra virgin olive oil
1 onion, finely chopped
450g/1lb fresh spinach, chopped
700g/1½lb ricotta cheese
25g/1oz Parmesan cheese,
   freshly grated
225g/8oz tomato pasta sauce

- Cook the pasta in a pan of salted boiling water for 8–10 minutes until al dente, then drain thoroughly.
- Heat the oil in a pan, add the onion and sauté, stirring, over a medium heat for 3 minutes or until lightly golden. Add the spinach and stir over a low heat until wilted. Stir in the ricotta cheese until combined.
- Spoon the mixture into the pasta shells, and sprinkle with Parmesan. Put the shells on a cold lightly oiled grill tray. Cook under a medium-high heat for 3 minutes, or until lightly browned and heated through.
- Meanwhile, put the tomato pasta sauce in a small pan and stir over a high heat for 1 minute, or until heated through. Spoon the sauce onto a serving platter and top with the shells.

Tunisian vegetables
serves 4–6

ingredients
1 large aubergine, finely diced
4 tablespoons olive oil
1 large onion, finely chopped
2 garlic cloves, crushed
1 red pepper, seeded and diced
4 medium courgettes, diced
450g/1lb ripe tomatoes, chopped
2 tablespoons tomato purée
2 teaspoons chilli powder
pinch of sugar
salt and freshly ground black pepper

- Put the aubergine in a colander, sprinkle liberally with salt and cover with a plate or saucer. Put a heavy weight on top, then leave for 30 minutes.
- Rinse the aubergine under cold running water, then drain thoroughly. Heat the oil in a large flameproof casserole dish, add the aubergine and onion, and cook gently, stirring frequently, until softened.
- Add the garlic, pepper, courgettes and tomatoes. Stir well to mix, then pour in 300ml/10fl oz water and bring to the boil, stirring. Reduce the heat, then add the tomato purée, chilli powder and sugar. Season with salt and pepper.
- Cover and simmer gently for 30 minutes, stirring occasionally and adding more water if the mixture becomes dry. Taste and adjust the seasoning, before serving hot.

Macaroni cheese

serves 4–6

ingredients
225g/8oz macaroni
100g/4oz butter
2 spring onions, finely sliced
2 tablespoons plain flour
225ml/8fl oz evaporated milk
225g/8fl oz single cream
2 tablespoons mayonnaise
275g/10oz Cheddar
  cheese, grated
2 eggs, lightly beaten
100g/4oz Parmesan cheese,
  freshly grated

- Bring a large saucepan of lightly salted water to the boil. Carefully pour the macaroni into the boiling water, and cook for about 10 minutes until al dente. Do not overcook. Remove from the heat, drain and set aside.
- Preheat the oven to 180°C/350°F/Gas mark 4. Grease a large casserole dish.
- In a heavy frying pan, melt the butter and sauté the spring onions over a medium heat until soft. Add the flour and stir to mix well. Continue to sauté for about 3 minutes, then blend in first the evaporated milk, then the cream, then the mayonnaise. Finally, add the Cheddar cheese.
- Stir the beaten eggs through the macaroni until evenly combined.
- Mix the macaroni with the cheese sauce, and pour into the casserole dish. Sprinkle the top with the Parmesan, and bake in the oven for 20–30 minutes until the top has browned and the macaroni is piping hot. Turn off the heat and allow the macaroni cheese to cool a little. Serve warm.

Veggie burgers

serves 2

ingredients

100g/4oz fresh green beans
100g/4oz bulgur wheatt
225ml/8fl oz boiling water
1 small courgette
1 small carrot
½ Granny Smith apple
100g/4oz canned cooked
    chickpeas, rinsed and drained
1 tablespoon minced onion
1 tablespoon peanut butter
1 ½ tablespoons vegetable oil
½ teaspoon curry powder
½ teaspoon chilli powder
100g/4oz fresh breadcrumbs
salt and freshly ground black pepper

- Cook the green beans in boiling water until tender but still with a bite. Refresh in cold water, drain and chop finely.
- Cook the bulgur in boiling water for 1 minute. Remove from the heat, cover and leave to stand.
- Grate the courgette and carrot, then peel, core and grate the apple. Wrap in a clean tea towel and squeeze out excess moisture. Combine with the green beans in a mixing bowl.
- In a blender or food processor, purée the chickpeas, onion, peanut butter, oil, curry powder and chilli powder until smooth. Season with salt and pepper. Add to the grated vegetables.
- Drain the bulgur through a strainer, pressing with the back of a spoon to extract excess liquid. Add to the bowl. Add the breadcrumbs and refrigerate for 1 hour.
- With wet hands, shape the mixture into four burgers. Cook under a medium grill for 3 minutes on each side. Serve hot.

Ratatouille

serves 4

ingredients

2 large aubergines,
   coarsely chopped
4 courgettes, coarsely chopped
150ml/5fl oz olive oil
2 onions, sliced
2 garlic cloves, chopped
1 large red pepper, seeded and
   coarsely chopped
2 large yellow peppers, seeded and
   coarsely chopped
sprig of fresh rosemary
sprig of fresh thyme
1 teaspoon coriander seeds, crushed
3 plum tomatoes, chopped
8 fresh basil leaves, torn
salt and freshly ground black pepper

- Sprinkle the aubergines and courgettes with salt, then place them in a colander with a plate and a weight on top to extract the bitter juices and excess water. Leave to stand for about 30 minutes.
- Heat the oil in a large heavy pan. Add the onions, sweat gently for 6–7 minutes until just softened, then add the garlic and sweat for another 2 minutes.
- Rinse the aubergines and courgettes, and pat dry with kitchen paper. Add to the pan with the peppers, increase the heat and sauté until the peppers are just turning brown. Add the herbs and coriander seeds, then cover the pan and cook gently for about 40 minutes.
- Add the tomatoes and season well with salt and pepper. Cook gently for 10 minutes until the vegetables are soft but not too mushy.
- Remove the herb sprigs. Stir in the basil leaves, and check the seasoning. Serve hot.

Vegetable biryani

serves 4

ingredients

4 tablespoons vegetable oil
2 onions, sliced
2 garlic cloves, crushed
2cm/1in piece of fresh root
   ginger, sliced
1 teaspoon ground turmeric
½ teaspoon chilli powder
1 teaspoon ground coriander
2 teaspoons ground cumin
100g/4oz red lentils, picked
   and rinsed

3 tomatoes, chopped
1 aubergine, cut into cubes
1.8 litres/3pt vegetable stock
1 red pepper, seeded and diced
350ml/12oz basmati rice
100g/4oz French beans, halved
225g/8oz cauliflower florets
225g/8oz mushrooms, quartered
50g/2oz unsalted cashew nuts

- Heat the oil in a saucepan, add the onions and fry gently for 2 minutes. Stir in the garlic, ginger and spices, and fry gently, stirring frequently, for 1 minute.
- Add the lentils, tomatoes, aubergine and 600ml/1pt of the stock. Stir well, then cover and simmer gently for 20 minutes.
- Add the pepper and cook for a further 10 minutes or until the lentils are tender and all the liquid has been absorbed.
- Meanwhile, rinse the rice under cold running water. Drain and place in another pan with the remaining stock. Bring to the boil, add the French beans, cauliflower and mushrooms, then cover and cook gently for 15 minutes or until the rice and vegetables are tender. Remove from the heat and set aside, covered, for 10 minutes.
- Add the lentil mixture and the cashews to the cooked rice, and mix lightly together. Serve hot.

Vegetable paella

serves 4

ingredients

2 small fennel bulbs, halved
   lengthways
225g/8oz cherry tomatoes, halved
3 tablespoons olive oil
2 teaspoons coriander seeds,
   crushed
900ml/1½pt vegetable stock
100g/4oz wild rice
200g/7oz long-grain white rice
2 tablespoons chopped fresh
   coriander leaves
juice of ½ lemon
salt and freshly ground black pepper

- Preheat the oven to 200°C/400°F/Gas mark 6.
- Put the fennel and tomatoes in a roasting tin, drizzle with the oil and
  sprinkle with the coriander seeds. Season with salt and pepper. Roast the
  vegetables, turning them once or twice, for 40 minutes or until tender.
- Meanwhile, bring the stock to the boil in a large heavy saucepan. Add
  the wild rice and simmer for 30 minutes. Add the long-grain rice and
  continue to cook for 15–20 minutes or until both types of rice are tender.
  Drain through a sieve.
- Turn the rice and roasted vegetables into a large bowl, and toss to mix.
  Sprinkle over the chopped coriander and lemon juice. Serve hot.

Spring vegetable stir-fry
serves 4

ingredients

1 tablespoon groundnut oil
1 garlic clove, sliced
2.5cm/1in piece of fresh root
    ginger, finely chopped
100g/4oz baby carrots
100g/4oz patty-pan squash,
    roughly chopped
100g/4oz baby corn
100g/4oz green beans, topped
    and tailed
100g/4oz sugarsnap peas, topped
    and tailed

100g/4oz young fresh asparagus,
    cut into 7.5cm/3in pieces
8 spring onions, trimmed and cut
    into 5cm/2in pieces
100g/4oz cherry tomatoes

For the dressing
juice of 2 limes
1 tablespoon clear honey
1 tablespoon soy sauce
1 teaspoon sesame oil

- Heat the groundnut oil in a wok or large heavy frying pan. Add the garlic and ginger, and stir-fry for about 1 minute.
- Add the carrots, patty-pan squash, baby corn and beans, and stir-fry for a further 3–4 minutes.
- Next, add the peas, asparagus, spring onions and cherry tomatoes, and stir-fry for a further 1–2 minutes.
- To make the dressing, mix all the ingredients together. Add to the wok or pan, stir well, then cover the wok or pan. Cook for 2–3 minutes more until the vegetables are tender but still crisp. Serve immediately.

Pasta with Sicilian sauce

serves 4

ingredients

50g/2oz sultanas
450g/1lb tomatoes, halved
25g/1oz pine nuts
50g/2oz canned anchovies,
    drained and halved lengthways
2 tablespoons tomato purée
675g/1lb 8oz dried penne

- Soak the sultanas in a bowl of warm water for about 20 minutes. Drain thoroughly and set aside.
- Cook the tomatoes under a preheated grill for about 10 minutes. Leave to cool slightly, then peel off the skin and dice the flesh.
- Put the pine nits on a baking tray, and lightly toast under the grill for 2–3 minutes until golden brown. Be careful not to scorch them.
- Put the tomatoes, pine nuts and sultanas in a small saucepan and gently heat through. Add the anchovies and tomato purée, heating the sauce for a further 2–3 minutes until hot. Keep warm.
- Meanwhile, cook the pasta in a saucepan of salted boiling water for 8–10 minutes until al dente. Drain thoroughly.
- Transfer the pasta to a serving dish. Pour the hot sauce over the top and toss through gently. Serve immediately.

Blue cheese hotpot

serves 4

ingredients

2 carrots, sliced
1 turnip, diced
2 celery sticks, sliced
8 small leeks, quartered
25g/1oz low-fat spread
25g/1oz plain flour
450ml/¾pt vegetable stock
1 teaspoon yeast extract
425g/15oz canned cooked haricot
    beans, drained
3 tablespoons chopped fresh
    flat-leaf parsley
450g/1lb potatoes, thinly sliced
50g/2oz blue cheese, crumbled
salt and freshly ground black pepper

- Preheat the oven to 180°C/350°F/Gas mark 4.
- Sauté the carrots, turnip, celery and leeks in the low-fat spread in a flameproof casserole dish for 3 minutes, stirring. Stir in the flour.
- Remove from the heat and gradually blend in the stock and yeast extract. Return to the heat, bring to the boil and cook for 2 minutes, stirring. Stir in the beans and parsley, and season with salt and pepper. Arrange the potatoes in a layer over the top, overlapping them slightly.
- Cover with a lid and bake in the oven for 1 hour. Remove the lid, sprinkle with the cheese and continue cooking, uncovered, for a further 30 minutes. Serve straight from the pot.

Courgette & asparagus parcels
serves 4

ingredients

2 medium courgettes
1 medium leek
225g/8oz young fresh asparagus,
    trimmed
4 sprigs of fresh tarragon
4 whole garlic cloves, unpeeled
1 egg, beaten, to glaze
salt and freshly ground black pepper

- Preheat the oven to 200°C/400°F/Gas mark 6.
- Using a potato peeler, carefully slice the courgettes lengthways into thin strips. Cut the leek into very fine julienne, and cut the asparagus evenly into 5cm/2in lengths.
- Cut out four sheets of baking parchment measuring 30 x 38cm/12 x 15in and fold in half. Draw a large curve to make a heart shape when unfolded. Cut along the line, and open out.
- Divide the courgettes, asparagus and leek evenly between each paper heart, positioning the filling on one side of the fold line and topping each with a tarragon sprig and a garlic clove. Season with salt and pepper. Brush the edges lightly with the egg and fold over. Twist the edges together so that each parcel is completely sealed.
- Lay the parcels on a baking tray, and cook in the oven for 10 minutes. Serve immediately, laying the parcels on the serving plates to be opened at the table.

Baked potatoes with salsa

serves 4

ingredients

4 baking potatoes, about
225g/8oz each
1 large avocado
1 teaspoon freshly squeezed
lemon juice
175g/6oz smoked tofu, diced
2 garlic cloves, crushed
1 onion, finely chopped
1 tomato, finely chopped
100g/4oz mixed salad leaves

For the salsa
2 tomatoes, diced
1 tablespoon chopped fresh
coriander leaves
1 shallot, finely diced
1 fresh green chilli, seeded
and diced
1 tablespoon freshly squeezed
lemon juice
salt and freshly ground
black pepper

- Preheat the oven to 190°C/375°F/Gas mark 5.
- Scrub the potatoes and prick the skins with a fork. Rub a little salt into the skins, and put the potatoes on a baking tray. Bake in the oven for 1 hour or until cooked through and the skins are crisp.
- Meanwhile, make the salsa just before the end of the potatoes' cooking time. Put all the ingredients in a bowl, mix through and season with salt and pepper. Set aside.
- Cut the potatoes in half lengthways, and scoop the flesh into a bowl, leaving a thin layer of potato inside the shells.
- Halve and stone the avocado. Using a spoon, scoop out the avocado flesh and add to the bowl containing the potato. Stir in the lemon juice and mash the mixture together with a fork. Mix in the tofu, garlic, onion and tomato. Spoon the mixture into one half of the potato shells.
- Arrange the mixed salad leaves on top of the guacamole mixture, and place the other half of the potato shell on top. Serve immediately with the salsa as an accompaniment.

Roasted Mediterranean vegetables
serves 6

ingredients

1 red pepper, seeded and cut
into chunks
1 yellow pepper, seeded and cut
into chunks
2 Spanish onions, cut into wedges
2 large courgettes, cut into chunks
1 large aubergine, cut into chunks
1 fennel bulb, thickly sliced
2 beef tomatoes
8 garlic cloves
2 tablespoons olive oil
a few sprigs of fresh rosemary
freshly ground black pepper

- Preheat the oven to 220°C/425°F/Gas mark 7.
- Spread the peppers, onions, courgettes, aubergine and fennel in a
  lightly oiled shallow ovenproof dish or roasting tin.
- Cut each tomato in half and place, cut side up, with the vegetables. Tuck
  the garlic cloves in among the vegetables, then brush them with the olive
  oil. Add some sprigs of rosemary, and grind over some black pepper.
- Roast in the oven for 20–25 minutes, turning the vegetables halfway
  through the cooking time. Serve hot.

Leek & herb soufflé

serves 4

ingredients

1 tablespoon olive oil
350g/12oz baby leeks,
  finely chopped
125ml/4fl oz vegetable stock
50g/2oz walnuts
2 eggs, separated
2 tablespoons chopped fresh
  mixed herbs
2 tablespoons Greek-style yogurt
salt and freshly ground black pepper

- Preheat the oven to 180°C/350°F/Gas mark 4. Lightly grease a
  900ml/1½pt soufflé dish with vegetable oil.
- Heat the olive oil in a frying pan. Add the leeks and sauté over a
  medium heat, stirring occasionally, for 2–3 minutes.
- Add the stock to the pan, reduce the heat and simmer gently for a further
  5 minutes.
- Put the walnuts in a blender or food processor, and chop finely. Add the
  leek mixture to the nuts, and process briefly to form a purée. Transfer to
  a bowl.
- Mix together the egg yolks, herbs and yogurt until thoroughly combined.
  Pour the egg mixture into the leek purée. Season with salt and pepper,
  and mix well.
- Put a baking tray into the oven to warm. In a separate bowl, whisk the
  egg whites until firm peaks form. Gently fold the egg whites into the leek
  mixture. Spoon the mixture into the prepared dish, and place on the
  warmed baking tray. Bake in the oven for 35–40 minutes until risen and
  set. Serve immediately.

Tomato rice
serves 4

ingredients

2 tablespoons corn oil
½ teaspoon onion seeds
1 onion, sliced
2 tomatoes, sliced
1 yellow pepper, seeded
   and chopped
1 teaspoon grated fresh root ginger
1 garlic clove, crushed
1 teaspoon chilli powder
2 tablespoons chopped fresh
   coriander leaves
1 potato, diced
1½ teaspoons salt
50g/2oz frozen peas
400g/14oz basmati rice

- Heat the oil and fry the onion seeds for about 30 seconds. Add the onion and fry for about 5 minutes.
- Add the tomatoes, pepper, ginger, garlic, chilli powder, coriander, potato, salt and peas, and stir-fry over a medium heat for a further 5 minutes. Add the rice and stir-fry for about 1 minute.
- Pour in 750ml/1¼pt water and bring to the boil, then reduce the heat to medium. Cover and cook for a further 12–15 minutes. Leave the rice to stand for 5 minutes, and serve hot.

Macaroni & four cheeses
serves 6

ingredients
225g/8oz dried macaroni
25g/1oz margarine
100g/4oz Parmesan cheese,
    freshly grated
100g/4oz Romano cheese, grated
350ml/12fl oz skimmed milk
100g/4oz low-fat cottage cheese
25g/1oz plain flour
¼ onion, sliced
½ teaspoon mustard powder
100g/4oz low-fat mozzarella
    cheese, grated
75g/3oz fresh breadcrumbs

- Preheat the oven to 180°C/350°F/Gas mark 4.
- Cook the macaroni in lightly salted boiling water until al dente. Drain. Toss with half of the margarine.
- In a 1.2 litre/2pt baking dish, layer half of the macaroni and the Parmesan and Romano cheeses. Repeat with the remaining macaroni and cheese.
- In a blender or food processor, purée the milk, cottage cheese, flour, onion and mustard until smooth. Pour the mixture over the macaroni. Sprinkle mozzarella over the top.
- Combine the breadcrumbs and remaining margarine, and sprinkle over the top. Bake for 40 minutes. Serve hot.

Tofu with mushrooms & peas
serves 4

ingredients
25g/1oz dried Chinese mushrooms
450g/1lb firm tofu
25g/1oz cornflour
vegetable oil for deep-frying
2 garlic cloves, finely chopped
2.5cm/1in piece of fresh root
    ginger, grated
100g/4oz fresh peas

- Put the Chinese mushrooms in a large bowl. Pour in enough boiling water to cover, and leave to stand for about 10 minutes.
- Meanwhile, cut the tofu into bite-size cubes using a sharp knife. Put the cornflour in a large bowl. Add the tofu and toss in the cornflour until evenly coated.
- Heat enough oil for deep-frying in a large preheated wok. Add the cubes of tofu. Cooking in batches, deep-fry for 2–3 minutes until golden and crispy. Remove the tofu with a slotted spoon. Drain on kitchen paper.
- Drain off all but 2 tablespoons of oil from the wok. Add the garlic, ginger and Chinese mushrooms, and stir-fry for 2–3 minutes.
- Return the cooked tofu to the wok, and add the peas. Heat through for 1 minute and serve hot.

Bean & tofu enchiladas
serves 10

ingredients

2 tablespoons olive oil
50g/2oz green pepper, seeded
  and chopped
50g/2oz onion, chopped
200g/7oz canned cooked red
  kidney beans, drained
100g/4oz cold cooked
  long-grain rice
100g/4oz firm tofu, cubed
300ml/10fl oz enchilada sauce
10 corn tortillas
200g/7oz Cheddar cheese, grated

- Preheat the oven to150°C/300°F/Gas mark 2. Lightly grease a large baking tin with vegetable oil.
- Heat the oil in a heavy frying pan. Add the green pepper and onion, sauté for a few minutes until soft. Transfer to a large bowl using a slotted spoon. Add the beans, rice and tofu, and mix through. Stir in 2 tablespoons of the enchilada sauce.
- Heat the remaining sauce through, and moisten the tortillas in the warmed sauce. Put a line of the bean mixture down the centre of each tortilla, and roll up.
- Put the enchiladas in the prepared tin, seam side down. Pour any remaining sauce on top of the enchiladas once the pan is filled. Scatter the cheese on top, and bake in the oven for 35–40 minutes. Serve hot.

Broccoli with feta
& tomato sauce
serves 4

ingredients
450g/1lb broccoli, cut into florets
25g/1oz low-fat spread
1 large onion, finely chopped
3 garlic cloves, crushed
850g/1¾lb canned chopped
    plum tomatoes
1 teaspoon dried oregano
2.5cm/1in piece of cinnamon stick
1 tablespoon freshly squeezed
    lemon juice
100g/4oz feta cheese, crumbled
100g/4oz Emmenthaler
    cheese, grated
salt and freshly ground black pepper

- Preheat the oven to 190°C/375°F/Gas mark 5.
- Cook the broccoli in lightly salted boiling water for 5 minutes until just tender. Drain and place in an ovenproof serving dish.
- Melt the low-fat spread in the saucepan. Sauté the onion and garlic for 3 minutes, stirring. Add the tomatoes, oregano and cinnamon. Season with a little salt and pepper. Bring to the boil and simmer for 5 minutes. Discard the cinnamon stick.
- Pour the sauce over the broccoli, and sprinkle with the lemon juice. Sprinkle the two cheeses over the top. Bake in the oven for 25 minutes, and serve immediately.

Mixed mushroom ragout

serves 4

ingredients

1 small onion, finely chopped
1 garlic clove, crushed
1 teaspoon coriander seeds, crushed
1 tablespoon red wine vinegar
1 tablespoon light soy sauce
1 tablespoon dry sherry
2 teaspoons tomato purée
2 teaspoons soft brown sugar
150ml/5fl oz vegetable stock
100g/4oz baby button mushrooms
100g/4oz chestnut mushrooms,
    quartered
100g/4oz oyster mushrooms, sliced
salt and freshly ground black pepper

- Put the onion, garlic, coriander seeds, vinegar, soy sauce, sherry, tomato purée, sugar and stock in a large saucepan. Bring to the boil, reduce the heat and simmer, covered, for 5 minutes
- Remove the lid from the pan, and simmer for 5 more minutes or until the liquid has reduced by half.
- Add the button and chestnut mushrooms, and simmer for 3 minutes. Stir in the oyster mushrooms, and cook for a further 2 minutes. Remove the mushrooms from the pan with a slotted spoon, transfer to a serving dish and keep warm.
- Boil the juices in the pan for about 5 minutes until reduced to about 75ml/3fl oz. Season with salt and pepper.
- Allow to cool for 2–3 minutes, then pour over the mushrooms. Serve hot or well chilled.

Chargrilled kebabs
serves 4

ingredients

2 tablespoons freshly squeezed
   lemon juice
1 tablespoon olive oil
1 garlic clove, crushed
1 tablespoon chopped fresh
   rosemary leaves
1 red pepper, seeded and sliced
   into 2.5cm/1in pieces
1 green pepper, seeded and sliced
   into 2.5cm/1in pieces

1 yellow pepper, seeded andsliced
   into 2.5cm/1in pieces
1 courgette, sliced into
   2.5cm/1in pieces
4 baby aubergines, quartered
   lengthways
2 red onions, each cut into 8
   wedges
salt and freshly ground
   black pepper

- If using bamboo skewers, soak in cold water for at least 30 minutes before using, to prevent them burning.
- Put the peppers, courgette, aubergines and onions in a large bowl.
- In another small bowl, whisk together the lemon juice, olive oil, garlic and rosemary. Season with salt and pepper, and whisk again. Pour the mixture over the vegetables, and stir to coat evenly.
- Preheat the grill to medium. Thread the peppers, courgette, aubergines and onion alternately onto 8 skewers. Arrange the kebabs on the grill rack, and cook for 10–12 minutes, turning frequently until the vegetables are lightly charred. Serve hot.

Vegetable-stuffed conchiglioni

serves 8

ingredients

24 dried conchiglioni (jumbo pasta shells)

275g/10oz chopped fresh spinach

1 egg white

350g/12oz low-fat cottage cheese

350g/12oz mozzarella cheese, grated

100g/4oz onion, finely chopped

2 garlic cloves, minced

50g/2oz fresh flat-leaf parsley, chopped

275g/10oz broccoli, chopped

For the sauce

1 tablespoon olive oil

3 garlic cloves, peeled but left whole

½ medium onion, chopped

400g/14oz canned chopped tomatoes

75g/3oz mushrooms, sliced

½ tablespoon shredded fresh basil leaves

½ tablespoon chopped fresh oregano

1 tablespoon chopped fresh flat-leaf parsley

50g/2oz Parmesan cheese, freshly grated

- Preheat the oven to 180°C/350°F/Gas mark 4. Grease a 33 x 23cm/13 x 9in tin with a little vegetable oil.
- To make the sauce, heat the olive oil in a large heavy saucepan. Add the garlic and sauté until the garlic begins to brown. Remove the garlic from the oil with a slotted spoon; discard. Add the onion to the garlic-infused oil and sauté lightly.
- Add the tomatoes and mushrooms, and cook over a medium heat for about 30 minutes. Add the basil, oregano and parsley, and bring to a boil. Remove from the heat and stir in the Parmesan. Put aside.
- Cook the pasta in a pan of salted boiling water for 8–10 minutes until al dente, then drain thoroughly.
- Combine the spinach, egg white, cottage cheese, mozzarella, onion, garlic, parsley and broccoli in a bowl. Blend well.
- Stuff the shells with the cheese mixture, using about 2 tablespoons for each shell. Arrange in the prepared tin. Pour the sauce over the shells,. bake in the oven for 30–40 minutes. Serve hot.

Chilled noodles & peppers
serves 6

ingredients
250g/9oz ribbon noodles
1 tablespoon sesame oil
1 red pepper
1 yellow pepper
1 green pepper
6 spring onions, cut into
    matchstick strips

For the dressing
5 tablespoons sesame oil
2 tablespoons soy sauce
1 tablespoon tahini
4 drops of hot pepper sauce
salt

- Preheat the grill to medium. Cook the noodles in a large pan of salted boiling water until they are almost tender. Drain in a colander, run cold water through them and drain again thoroughly. Tip the noodles into a bowl, stir in the sesame oil, cover and chill.
- Cook the peppers under the grill, turning them frequently, until they are blackened on all sides. Plunge into cold water, then peel off the skin. Cut in half, remove the core and seeds, and cut the flesh into thick strips. Set aside in a covered container.
- To make the dressing, mix together the sesame oil, soy sauce, tahini and pepper sauce until well combined.
- Pour the dressing on the noodles, reserving 1 tablespoon, and toss well. Add the reserved peppers, gently toss through the noodles and spoon on the reserved dressing. Scatter the spring onion over the top, and serve.

Ratatouille penne bake
serves 6

ingredients

1 small aubergine
2 courgettes, thickly sliced
200g/7oz firm tofu, cubed
3 garlic cloves, crushed
2 teaspoons sesame seeds
1 small red pepper, seeded
  and sliced
1 onion, finely chopped
150ml/5fl oz vegetable stock
3 tomatoes, peeled, seeded and
  quartered
1 tablespoon chopped fresh
  mixed herbs
225g/8oz dried penne
salt and freshly ground black pepper

- Cut the aubergine into 2.5cm/1in cubes. Put into a colander with the courgettes, sprinkle with salt and leave to drain for 30 minutes.
- Mix the tofu with the soy sauce, 1 garlic clove and the sesame seeds. Cover and marinate for 30 minutes.
- Put the pepper, onion and remaining garlic into a saucepan with the stock. Bring to the boil, cover and cook for 5 minutes until tender. Remove the lid, and boil until all the stock has evaporated. Add the tomatoes and herbs to the pan, and cook for a further 3 minutes
- Thoroughly rinse the aubergine and courgettes. Drain, shaking the colander gently to get rid of excess water. Add to the pepper and tomato mixture, and cook until tender. Season with salt and pepper.
- Meanwhile, cook the pasta in a large pan of salted boiling water until al dente, then drain thoroughly. Preheat the grill.
- Toss the pasta with the vegetables and marinated tofu. Transfer to a shallow ovenproof dish, and grill until lightly toasted. Serve hot.

Quorn-stuffed marrow
serves 6

ingredients
1 small marrow
salt and freshly ground black pepper

For the filling
25g/1oz low-fat spread
1 onion, finely chopped
1 carrot, finely chopped
1 celery stick, finely chopped
225g/8oz mushrooms,
    roughly chopped
200g/7oz minced quorn
2 tablespoons tomato purée
150ml/5fl oz vegetable stock
½ teaspoon dried mixed herbs
50g/2oz low-fat Cheddar
    cheese, grated

- Preheat the oven to 180°C/350°F/Gas mark 4.
- Peel the marrow and cut into 8 slices. Discard the pith and seeds. Put in a single layer in a baking tin, and sprinkle with salt and pepper. Add 2 tablespoons water.
- Cover with foil and bake in the oven for 30 minutes.
- To make the filling, melt the low-fat spread in a saucepan. Add the onion, carrot and celery, and sauté, stirring, for 2 minutes. Add the mushrooms, quorn, tomato purée, stock, herbs and a little salt and pepper, and stir well. Bring to the boil, reduce the heat and simmer gently for 20 minutes until the mixture is tender and the liquid is well reduced, stirring occasionally.
- Spoon the mixture into the marrow rings, top each with a little cheese and bake uncovered in the oven for a further 25 minutes or until tender and golden. Serve hot.

Red curry with cashews

serves 4

ingredients

1 tablespoon vegetable oil
250ml/9fl oz coconut milk
1 kaffir lime leaf
¼ teaspoon light soy sauce
50g/2oz baby corn cobs,
  halved lengthways
100g/4oz broccoli florets
100g/4oz French beans, cut into
  5cm/2in pieces
25g/1oz raw cashew nuts
15 fresh Thai basil leaves
1 tablespoon chopped fresh
  coriander leaves
1 tablespoon chopped roasted
  peanuts, to garnish

For the red curry paste
7 fresh red chillies, halved, seeded
  and blanched
2 teaspoons cumin seeds
2 teaspoons coriander seeds
2.5cm/1in piece of galangal,
  chopped
½ lemon grass stalk, tough outer
  layer removed, chopped
1 teaspoon salt
grated zest of 1 lime
4 garlic cloves, chopped
3 shallots, chopped
2 kaffir lime leaves, shredded

- To make the curry paste, grind all the ingredients together using a large mortar and pestle, or a grinder. Alternatively, purée briefly in a blender or food processor until a paste forms.
- Put the oil a wok or large heavy frying pan over a high heat. Add 3 tablespoons of the red curry paste, and stir until aromatic. (Store any leftover paste in a screwtop glass jar in the refrigerator, and use within a few days.)
- Reduce the heat to medium. Add the coconut milk, kaffir lime leaf, soy sauce, baby corn cobs, broccoli florets, French beans and cashew nuts. Bring to the boil and simmer for about 10 minutes, until the vegetables are cooked, but still firm and crunchy.
- Remove and discard the lime leaf, and stir in the basil leaves and coriander. Transfer to a warmed serving dish, garnish with the peanuts and serve immediately.

Leek & carrot gratin
serves 6

ingredients

700g/1½lb leeks, cut into
   5cm/2in pieces
150ml/5fl oz vegetable stock
3 tablespoons white wine
1 teaspoon caraway seeds
pinch of salt
300ml/10fl oz skimmed milk
25g/1oz margarine
25g/1oz plain flour

For the topping
100g/4oz fresh wholemeal
   breadcrumbs
100g/4oz carrot, grated
2 tablespoons chopped fresh
   flat-leaf parsley
75g/3oz Edam cheese,
   coarsely grated
2 tablespoons flaked almonds

- Put the leeks in a large heavy saucepan, and add the stock, wine, caraway seeds and a pinch of salt. Bring to a simmer, cover and cook for 5–7 minutes until the leeks are just tender.
- With a slotted spoon, transfer the leeks to an ovenproof dish. Boil the remaining liquid to half the original volume, then make up to 350ml/12fl oz with the skimmed milk.
- Preheat the oven to 180°C/350°F/Gas mark 4.
- Melt the margarine in a flameproof casserole dish, stir in the flour and cook without allowing it to colour for 1–2 minutes. Gradually add the stock and milk, stirring well after each addition, until smooth. Simmer for 5–6 minutes, stirring constantly, until thickened and smooth, then pour the sauce over the leeks in the dish.
- To make the topping, mix all the ingredients together in a bowl, and sprinkle over the leeks. Bake for 20–25 minutes until golden. Serve hot.

Aubergine cake
serves 4

ingredients
1 large aubergine
300g/11oz tricolour pasta shapes
100g/4oz low-fat soft cheese with
    garlic and herbs
350ml/12fl oz passata
4 tablespoons freshly grated
    Parmesan cheese
1 ½ teaspoons dried oregano
2 tablespoons dried white
    breadcrumbs
salt and freshly ground black pepper

- Preheat the oven to 190°C/375°F/Gas mark 5. Grease and line
  a 20cm/8in round springform cake tin.
- Trim the aubergine and slice lengthways into slices about 5mm/¼in
  thick. Put in a bowl, sprinkle liberally with salt, and set aside for
  30 minutes to remove any bitter juices. Rinse well under cold running
  water, and drain.
- Bring a saucepan of water to the boil, and blanch the aubergine for
  1 minute. Drain and pat dry with kitchen paper.
- Cook the pasta shapes in lightly salted boiling water until al dente. Drain
  well, and return to the saucepan. Add the soft cheese and allow it to
  melt over the pasta. Stir in the passata, Parmesan and oregano, and
  season with salt and pepper.
- Arrange the aubergine over the bottom and sides of the cake tin,
  overlapping the slices and making sure that there are no gaps.
- Pile the pasta mixture into the tin, packing down well, and sprinkle with
  the breadcrumbs. Bake in the oven for 20 minutes, then remove the tin
  from the oven and leave to stand for 15 minutes.
- Loosen the cake around the edge with a palette knife or spatula, and
  release from the tin. Turn out the pasta cake, aubergine side uppermost,
  and serve hot.

Hot Desserts & Puddings

Dessert is many people's favourite part of a meal and, whether treating the family or rounding off a dinner party, or fulfilling a need for comfort food, a hot dessert can be a satisfying indulgence. Relive old memories with traditional favourites such as sticky toffee pudding and apple pie, and master classics such as Christmas pudding, baked Alaska and zabaglione. The mouthwatering recipes in this chapter ensure that you'll find something to tantalize the taste buds every time.

Plum filo pockets
serves 4

ingredients
100g/4oz skimmed milk
  soft cheese
1 tablespoon muscovado sugar
½ teaspoon ground cloves
8 large plums, halved and stoned
8 sheets filo pastry
sunflower oil for brushing
icing sugar, to dust

- Preheat the oven to 220°C/ 425°F/Gas mark 7.
- In a small bowl, mix together the cheese, sugar and cloves.
- Sandwich the plum halves back together using a spoonful of the cheese mixture.
- Spread out the pastry, and cut into 16 pieces, each about 23cm/9in square. Brush one lightly with oil, and place a second diagonally on top. Repeat the process with the remaining squares.
- Put a plum on each pastry square, and pinch the corners together. Place on a baking tray. Bake for 15–18 minutes until golden, then dust with icing sugar. Serve hot.

Fromage frais with hot plum sauce
serves 4

ingredients
450g/1lb plums, halved
  and stoned
1 teaspoon granulated sugar
225g/8oz low-fat fromage frais

- Put the plums in a pan with 2 tablespoons water, and cook very gently until the juice runs.
- Cover and stew over a gentle heat until tender and pulpy. Purée in a blender or food processor, and return to the pan. Add the sugar and reheat.
- Spoon the fromage frais into four individual dishes. Spoon the hot sauce over, and serve immediately.

Bananas with hot lemon sauce

serves 4

ingredients

15g/½oz low-fat spread
2 teaspoons granulated sugar
15g/½oz cornflour
grated zest and juice of ½ lemon
300ml/10fl oz low-fat
 Greek-style yogurt
4 small bananas, sliced

- Put the low-fat spread, sugar and cornflour in a saucepan. Make the lemon juice up to 150ml/5fl oz with water, and stir into the pan. Bring to the boil and cook, stirring, for 2 minutes.
- Divide the yogurt between four serving dishes, and add the banana. Spoon the hot sauce over, and serve immediately.

● ●

Apple brown betty

serves 4–6

ingredients

5 cooking apples, peeled, cored
 and chopped
100g/4oz butter
90g/3½oz Demerara or soft
 brown sugar

finely grated zest of 1 lemon
½ teaspoon ground cinnamon
pinch of ground nutmeg
225g/8oz fresh breadcrumbs

- Preheat the oven to 180°C/350°F/Gas mark 4. Lightly grease a 1.2-litre/2pt ovenproof dish.
- Cook the apples with 15g/½oz of the butter, 15g/½oz of the sugar, the lemon zest, cinnamon and nutmeg for 10–15 minutes until the apples are soft enough to beat to a purée.
- Melt the remaining butter in a frying pan over a low heat, and add the breadcrumbs and remaining sugar. Toss until the crumbs are coated, and continue tossing while you fry the crumbs until they are golden brown.
- Spread one-third of the crumbs in the greased ovenproof dish, and add half of the apple purée in an even layer. Add another third of the crumbs and the remaining apple, then finish with a layer of crumbs. Bake in the oven for 20 minutes or until crisp and golden on top. Serve hot, either plain or with cream or ice cream.

Poppy seed custard with red fruit

serves 6

ingredients

600ml/1pt skimmed milk
2 eggs
1 tablespoon caster sugar
1 tablespoon poppy seeds
100g/4oz strawberries
100g/4oz raspberries
100g/4oz blackberries
1 tablespoon Demerara sugar
60ml/21/2fl oz red grape juice

- Preheat the oven to 150°C/300°F/Gas mark 2. Grease a soufflé dish very lightly with low-fat spread.
- Heat the milk until just below boiling point, but do not boil.
- Beat the eggs in a bowl with the caster sugar and poppy seeds until creamy. Whisk the milk into the egg mixture until very well mixed.
- Stand the prepared soufflé dish in a shallow roasting tin. Pour in enough hot water from the kettle to come halfway up the sides of the dish.
- Pour the custard into the soufflé dish, and bake in the oven for 50–60 minutes until the custard is just set and golden on top.
- While the custard is baking, mix the fruit with the sugar and fruit juice. Chill until ready to serve with the warm baked custard.

Apple & blackcurrant pancakes
serves 10

ingredients
100g/4oz plain wholemeal flour
300ml/10fl oz skimmed milk
1 egg, beaten
1 tablespoon sunflower oil

For the filling
450g/1lb cooking apples
225g/8oz blackcurrants
2 tablespoons water
25g/1oz Demerara sugar

- To make the pancake batter, put the flour in a mixing bowl and make a well in the centre.
- Add a little of the milk with the egg and the oil. Beat the flour into the liquid, then gradually beat in the rest of the milk, keeping the batter smooth and free from lumps. Cover the batter and chill while you prepare the filling.
- Quarter, peel and core the apples. Slice them into a pan and add the blackcurrants and 2 tablespoons water. Cook over a gentle heat for 10–15 minutes until the fruit is soft. Stir in the sugar.
- Lightly grease a pan with a little sunflower oil. Heat and pour in about 2 tablespoons of the batter, swirl it around and cook for about 1 minute. Flip the pancake over with a spatula or palette knife, and cook the other side. Put on a sheet of kitchen paper, and keep hot while cooking the remaining pancakes.
- To serve, fill the pancakes with the apple and blackcurrant mixture, and roll them up. Serve hot.

Lemon syrup pears with pancakes

ingredients

serves 6

For the batter
100g/4oz plain flour
75g/3oz self-raising flour
25g/1oz caster sugar
3 eggs, lightly beaten
350ml/12fl oz milk
50g/2oz butter, melted

For the lemon syrup pears
175g/6oz caster sugar
2 tablespoons honey
125ml/4fl oz freshly squeezed
  lemon juice
5 firm dessert pears
zest of 1 lemon, cut into thin strips
225g/8oz sour cream

- Sift the flours into a large bowl, add the sugar and make a well in the centre. Whisk in the combined eggs, milk and butter. Beat untl smooth, then set aside for 30 minutes.
- To make the lemon syrup pears, combine the sugar, honey, and 350ml/12fl oz water in a saucepan, stirring over a low heat until the sugar has dissolved. Add the lemon juice, bring to the boil, reduce the heat and simmer for 8 minutes.
- Meanwhile, peel and core the pears, and cut into wedges. Skim off any froth from the surface of the syrup mixture, and add the pears. Simmer for a further 5 minutes. Remove from the heat, stir in the lemon zest and leave to cool slightly.
- Heat a lightly greased 20cm/8in frying pan over a medium heat, then pour 50ml/2fl oz of the pancake batter into it. Cook for 2 minutes on each side, tur the pancake with a spatula or palette knife. Continue with the rest of the batter, greasing the pan when necessary. Stack the pancakes between greaseproof paper to prevent them sticking together, and keep warm.
- Strain 125ml/4fl oz of the lemon syrup, and mix with the sour cream to make a sauce for the pancakes. Strain the pairs to serve.
- Serve the pancakes warm, with some of the pears and a little of the sauce drizzled over the top. Decorate with strips of lemon zest.

Exotic fruit pancakes
serves 4

ingredients

For the batter
100g/4oz plain flour
pinch of salt
1 egg plus 1 egg yolk
300ml/10fl oz coconut milk
4 teaspoons sunflower oil, plus
  extra for frying

For the filling
1 banana
1 papaya
juice of 1 lime
2 passion fruit
1 mango
4 lychees
2 tablespoons honey

- To make the batter, sift the flour and salt into a bowl. Make a well in the centre, and add the egg, egg yolk and a little of the coconut milk. Gradually draw the flour into the egg mixture, beating well and slowly adding the remaining coconut milk to make a smooth batter. Stir in the 4 teaspoons sunflower oil. Cover and chill for 30 minutes

- To make the fruit filling, peel and slice the banana, and peel and slice the papaya, discarding the seeds. Put the banana and papaya in a bowl, add the lime juice and mix well.

- Cut the passion fruit in half, and scoop out the pulp and seeds into the fruit bowl. Peel, stone and dice the mango, and add to the other fruit. Peel, stone and halve the lychees, and also add to the fruit. Toss through gently, then stir in the honey.

- Heat a little oil in a 15cm/6in frying pan. Pour in just enough of the pancake batter to cover the bottom of the pan, and tilt the pan so that the batter spreads thinly and evenly.

- Cook until the pancake is just set and the underside is lightly browned, then turn and cook on the other side. Remove from the pan and keep warm. Repeat with the remaining batter to make a total of 8 pancakes.

- Put a little fruit filling in the centre of each pancake, then roll into a cone. Serve immediately.

Fried bananas
serves 4

ingredients

100g/4oz plain flour
½ teaspoon bicarbonate of soda
pinch of salt
2 tablespoons sugar
1 egg
2 tablespoons desiccated or
    shredded coconut
4 firm bananas
vegetable oil for deep-frying
2 tablespoons clear honey
vanilla ice cream, to serve (optional)

- Sift the flour, bicarbonate of soda and a pinch of salt into a bowl. Stir in the sugar. Whisk in the egg and just enough water (you will need about 6 tablespoons, added a tablespoon at a time) to make a thin batter. Whisk in the coconut.
- Heat enough oil for deep-frying in a preheated wok.
- Peel the bananas. Carefully cut each one in half lengthways, then cut in half widthways. Dip in the batter, then gently drop a few pieces at a time into the hot oil. Fry until golden brown.
- Remove the bananas from the oil using a slotted spoon, and drain on kitchen paper. Serve immediately with honey drizzled over and some vanilla ice cream, if you like.

Pears with strawberry sauce
serves 4

ingredients

4 dessert pears

1 tablespoon freshly squeezed
orange juice

2 teaspoons low-fat spread or
butter, melted

5cm/2in cinnamon stick, broken
in half

225g/8oz strawberries

1 teaspoon granulated sugar

1 teaspoon cornflour

1 teaspoon freshly squeezed
lemon juice

- Preheat the oven to 180°C/350°F/Gas mark 4.
- Pare the skin off the pears, but leave whole with the stems attached. Arrange on their sides in a shallow 1.2-litre/2pt casserole dish.
- In a bowl, whisk together 50ml/2fl oz water, the orange juice and the low-fat spread or butter, and pour over the pears. Add the cinnamon stick, and bake in the oven for 20–30 minutes until tender, basting from time to time. Using a slotted spoon, transfer each pear to a dessert dish, reserving the pan juices.
- In a small saucepan, combine the pan juices with the strawberries and bring to the boil.
- In a small bowl, combine 1 tablespoon water, the sugar, cornflour and lemon juice, stirring to dissolve. Add to the saucepan, stirring constantly, and bring to the boil. Reduce the heat and cook, stirring constantly, until thickened. Remove from the heat, and pour over the pears. Serve immediately either plain or with double cream.

Griddle cakes
serves 4–8

ingredients
125g/4oz plain flour
2 teaspoons baking powder
2 tablespoons caster sugar
2 eggs, separated
1 tablespoon melted butter
125ml/4fl oz milk
50g/2oz pitted fresh cherries,
   chopped
50g/2oz ready-to-eat dried
   apricots, chopped
clear honey or golden syrup, gently
   warmed, to serve

- Sift the flour, baking powder and sugar together. Make a well in the centre. Whisk the egg yolks, melted butter and milk together, then stir into the dry ingredients to form a smooth batter.
- Fold the cherries and apricots into the batter.
- Whisk the egg whites until stiff and dry, then fold carefully into the batter.
- Heat a griddle or flat cast-iron grill pan until medium-hot. Brush with a little melted butter. Put spoonfuls of the batter on the griddle, and cook until the top is set and bubbles appear, and the underside is golden. Turn and cook on the other side.
- Serve hot with warmed honey or golden syrup.

Spotted dick
serves 4

ingredients
175g/6oz plain flour
1 teaspoons baking powder
100g/4oz sugar
1½ teaspoons ground ginger
150g/5oz fresh breadcrumbs
50g/2oz sultanas
100g/4oz currants
100g/4oz suet, grated
2 teaspoons finely grated lemon zest
2 eggs, lightly beaten
175ml/6fl oz milk

- Sift the flour, baking powder, sugar and ginger into a large bowl. Add the breadcrumbs, sultanas, currants, suet and lemon zest. Mix with a wooden spoon.
- Combine the egg and milk, add to the dry ingredients and mix well. Add a little more milk if necessary, then set aside for 5 minutes.
- Lay a sheet of baking paper on a work surface, and form the mixture into a roll shape about 20cm/8in long. Roll up the pudding in the paper and fold up the ends – but do not wrap too tightly. Wrap in a tea towel, put it in the top of a steamer, cover and steam for 1½ hours. Do not let the pudding boil dry – replenish with boiling water if necessary as the pudding cooks.
- Serve with hot custard or fresh cream.

Floating islands
in hot plum sauce
serves 4

ingredients
450g/1lb red plums
300ml/10fl oz apple juice
2 egg whites
2 tablespoons concentrated
  apple juice
freshly grated nutmeg

- Halve the plums and remove the stones. Put them in a wide saucepan with the apple juice. Bring to the boil, then cover and simmer gently until the plums have become tender.
- Put the egg whites in a bowl and whisk them until they hold soft peaks.
- Gradually whisk in the concentrated apple juice, whisking until the meringue holds fairly firm peaks.
- Using a tablespoon, scoop the meringue mixture into the gently simmering plum sauce. Cover and simmer gently for 2–3 minutes, until the meringues are set.
- Serve immediately, sprinkled with a little freshly grated nutmeg.

Boozy banana soufflé
serves 6

ingredients

50g/2oz low-fat spread
1 teaspoon artificial
   sweetener granules
2 eggs, separated
150ml/5fl oz white rum
4 bananas
4 tablespoons reduced-fat
   crème fraîche, to serve

- Preheat the oven to 190°C/375°F/Gas mark 5. Lightly grease a
  20cm/8in soufflé dish with low-fat spread.
- Purée the low-fat spread, sweetener, egg yolks, rum and bananas in a
  blender or food processor. Whisk the egg whites until stiff, and fold into
  the mixture with a metal spoon.
- Turn into the prepared dish, and bake in the oven for about 35 minutes
  until risen, golden and just set. Serve hot with the crème fraîche.

Baked apples in honey & lemon
serves 4

ingredients

4 cooking apples

1 tablespoon clear honey

grated zest and juice of 1 lemon

25g/1oz low-fat spread

- Preheat the oven to 180°C/350°F/Gas mark 4.
- Remove the cores from the apples, leaving them whole. With a sharp knife, cut lines through the skin of the apples at intervals, and put them in an ovenproof dish.
- Mix together the honey, lemon zest and juice, and low-fat spread.
- Spoon the mixture into the apples, and cover the dish with foil or a lid. Bake for 40–45 minutes until the apples are tender. Serve hot.

Custard tart
serves 4

ingredients

100g/4oz plain flour

pinch of salt

50g/2oz low-fat spread

2 eggs

½ teaspoon granulated sugar

300ml/10fl oz skimmed milk, warmed

freshly grated nutmeg

- Preheat the oven to 200°C/400°F/Gas mark 6. Lightly grease an 18cm/7in flan tin with low-fat spread.
- Put the flour and salt in a bowl. Add the low-fat spread, and rub in with your fingertips until the mixture resembles crumbs. Adding a tablespoon of water at a time, mix with just enough cold water to form a firm dough. Knead gently on a lightly floured work surface. Roll out and use to line the flan tin. Prick the base with a fork. Fill with crumpled foil, and place on a baking tray.
- Bake in the oven for 15 minutes, removing the foil after 10 minutes to allow the pastry to dry out. Remove the pastry shell from the oven, and reduce the oven temperature to 190°C/375°F/Gas mark 5.
- Whisk together the eggs and sugar, then whisk into the milk. Strain into the pastry shell, and sprinkle with a little grated nutmeg. Bake for about 35 minutes until the custard is set. Serve warm.

Strawberry baked apples
serves 4

ingredients

4 cooking apples
50ml/2fl oz reduced-sugar
  strawberry jam

1 teaspoon sugar
reduced-fat crème fraîche, to serve
  (optional)

- Preheat the oven to 180°C/350°F/Gas mark 4.
- Remove the cores from the apples, and cut a line around the centre of the fruit to prevent the skin bursting. Put in an ovenproof dish.
- Fill the centres of the apples with jam, and sprinkle with the sugar. Add about 2.5cm/1in of water to the dish.
- Bake in the oven for 1 hour until the apples are tender but still holding their shape. Serve hot with the crème fraîche, if you like.

• •

Spiced pear & blueberry parcels
serves 4

ingredients

4 dessert pears
2 tablespoons freshly squeezed
  lemon juice
15g/½oz low-fat spread, melted

150g/5oz blueberries
50g/2oz muscovado sugar
freshly ground black pepper

- Preheat the oven to 200°C/400°F/Gas mark 6.
- Peel the pears, cut in half lengthways and scoop out the core. Brush with lemon juice to prevent browning.
- Cut four squares of double-thickness foil, each large enough to wrap a pear, and brush with melted spread. Place 2 pear halves on each, cut side facing upwards. Gather the foil around them to hold them level.
- Mix the blueberries and sugar together, and spoon them on top of the pears. Sprinkle with black pepper. Wrap the foil over, and cook for 20–25 minutes in the oven. Serve hot.

Hot chocolate custard

serves 4

ingredients
25g/1oz cornflour
25g/1oz cocoa powder
600ml/1pt skimmed milk
artificial sweetener granules or
   a little sugar

- Blend the cornflour and cocoa with a little of the milk in a saucepan. Stir in the remaining milk. Bring to the boil and cook for 3 minutes, stirring until smooth and thick.
- Sweeten with artificial sweetener or sugar to taste. Serve immediately.

• •

Souffléed rice pudding

serves 4

ingredients
50g/2oz short-grain rice
3 tablespoons clear honey
750ml/1¼pt skimmed milk
½ teaspoon vanilla essence
2 egg whites
1 teaspoon freshly
   grated nutmeg

- Put the rice, honey and milk in a heavy or non-stick saucepan, and bring to the boil.
- Reduce the heat, and put the lid on the pan. Leave to simmer gently for 1–1¼ hours, stirring occasionally to prevent sticking, until most of the liquid has been absorbed. Add the vanilla essence.
- Preheat the oven to 220°C/ 425°F/Gas mark 7.
- Put the egg whites in a bowl, and whisk until they hold soft peaks. Using a large metal spoon, carefully fold the egg whites evenly into the rice mixture, and tip into a 1-litre/1¾pt ovenproof dish.
- Sprinkle with grated nutmeg and bake for 15–20 minutes until the pudding is well risen and golden brown. Serve hot.

Nectarines with spiced ricotta
serves 4

ingredients

4 ripe nectarines, halved
  and stoned
100g/4oz ricotta cheese
1 tablespoon Demerara sugar
½ teaspoon ground star anise,
  to decorate

- Arrange the nectarine halves, with the cut side facing upwards, in a shallow flameproof dish.
- Put the ricotta in a small mixing bowl. Stir in the sugar.
- Using a teaspoon, spoon equal amounts of the mixture into the hollow of each nectarine half. Sprinkle with the star anise.
- Cook under a medium-hot grill for 6–8 minutes until the nectarines are hot. Serve warm.

Apple couscous pudding
serves 4

ingredients

600ml/1pt unsweetened
  apple juice
100g/4oz quick-cooking
  couscous
50g/2oz sultanas
½ teaspoon mixed spice
2 cooking apples
2 tablespoons Demerara sugar

- Preheat the oven to 200°C/ 400°F/Gas mark 6.
- Put the apple juice, couscous, sultanas and spice in a pan, and bring to the boil, stirring. Reduce the heat, cover and simmer for 5 minutes.
- Peel, core and slice the apples. Spoon half of the couscous mixture into a 1.2-litre/2pt ovenproof dish. Arrange half of the apple slices over the couscous, and top with the remaining couscous.
- Arrange the remaining apple slices over the top, and sprinkle with the sugar.
- Bake for 25–30 minutes until golden brown. Serve hot.

569

Rhubarb crumble
serves 4–6

ingredients

900g/2lb rhubarb
150g/5oz sugar
100g/4oz butter

75g/3oz plain flour
75g/3oz Demerara sugar
10 amaretti biscuits, crushed

- Preheat the oven to 200°C/400°F/Gas mark 6.
- Trim the rhubarb, cut into short lengths and put in a pan with the sugar. Stir over a low heat until the sugar has dissolved, then cover and simmer for 8–10 minutes until the rhubarb is soft. Spoon into a deep 1.5-litre/ 2½pt ovenproof dish.
- Rub the butter into the flour until the mixture resembles fine breadcrumbs, then stir in the sugar and biscuits.
- Sprinkle the crumble over the stewed rhubarb, and bake for 15 minutes or until the topping is golden brown. Serve with cream or ice cream.

• •

Banana dosa
serves 4

ingredients

4 ripe bananas, peeled
  and mashed
200g/7oz rice flour
100g/4oz plain flour
2 tablespoons white sugar

2 tablespoons vegetable oil
½ teaspoon crushed cardamom
  seeds
pinch of salt

- Put the bananas, rice flour, plain flour, sugar, oil, cardamom and pinch of salt in a large bowl. Make a well in the centre and pour in 100ml/3½floz water. Blend with a wooden spoon to form a thick batter, adding a little more water or flour if required.
- Heat a frying pan over a medium heat. Rub the surface with some oil using a brush or kitchen paper.
- Pour a large spoonful of the batter into the pan, and spread it out lightly. Cook for 5 minutes or until golden brown underneath, then turn over and cook for a further 3 minutes. Continue until all the batter has been used.
- Serve hot with ice cream.

Plum Charlotte
serves 4

ingredients

450g/1lb plums
1 tablespoon caster sugar, plus
  extra for sprinkling

4 slices white bread
25g/1oz butter

- Preheat the oven to 190°C/375°F/Gas mark 5.
- Halve and stone the plums, and put the plum halves in a saucepan with 1 tablespoon water. Poach until tender. Add the 1 tablespoon sugar.
- Spread the bread with the butter, and use two of the slices to line a 20cm/8in ovenproof serving dish. Top with the plums.
- Cut the remaining bread into thin strips, and arrange in a lattice on top of the plums. Sprinkle with extra caster sugar, and bake in the oven for 30–40 minutes until golden brown.

• •

Apple Charlotte
serves 4–6

ingredients

900g/2lb cooking apples
100g/4oz caster sugar
150g/5oz butter

juice of 1 lemon
3 tablespoons sieved apricot jam
8 slices white bread

- Preheat the oven to 180°C/350°F/Gas mark 4.
- Peel, core and slice the apples, and put them in a pan with the caster sugar and 25g/1oz of the butter. Add 3 tablespoons water, cover the pan and poach gently over a low heat for 10 minutes. Remove the lid, stir and turn up the heat, continuing to cook until you have a thick purée. Stir in the lemon juice and apricot jam, and reserve.
- Melt the remaining butter and cut the crusts off the slices of white bread. Cut the bread into fingers, brush with the butter and use them to line a 20cm/8in mould or soufflé dish. Pour in the apple purée, and cover the top with more butter-soaked bread.
- Place the dish on a baking sheet, and bake in the oven for 35 minutes until the top is crisp and golden brown. Allow to cool for 10 minutes before sliding a palette knife round the edge and turning out onto a serving dish. Cut into wedges and serve with cream or ice cream.

Yogurt flapjacks
serves 4

ingredients

700g/1½lb vanilla yogurt
50g/2oz maple syrup
1 egg
350g/12oz pancake mix

450g/1lb chopped fresh fruit such
   as strawberries, grapes,
   blueberries, peaches, etc

- Combine 350g/12oz yogurt with the maple syrup and set aside.
- Combine the remaining yogurt with the egg, and beat well. Add the pancake mix and blend to combine.
- Heat a greased 20cm/8in frying pan over a medium heat. Spoon 50ml/2floz of the batter into the hot pan, and gently spread out. Cook until the edges are firm and the underside is golden. Flip over using a spatula or palette knife, and cook on the other side. Repeat with the remaining batter.
- Serve warm with the chopped fruit and maple yogurt sauce.

● ●

Pear & blackberry crumble
serves 6

ingredients

450g/1lb pears, peeled, cored
   and cut into chunks
juice of 1 lemon
225g/8oz caster sugar
1 teaspoon mixed spice

450g/1lb blackberries
100g/4oz butter, chopped
225g/8oz plain flour
75g/3oz ground almonds

- Preheat the oven to 200°C/400°F/Gas mark 6. Grease a 1.8-litre/3¼pt shallow ovenproof dish.
- Put the pear pieces in a bowl, add the lemon juice and toss well.
- Add 100g/4oz of the sugar and the mixed spice to the pears, then add the blackberries and toss thoroughly to coat with sugar and spice. Tip the mixture into the greased ovenproof dish.
- Put the butter, flour, almonds and remaining sugar into a blender or food processor, and pulse until the mixture begins to look like breadcrumbs. Scatter the topping evenly over the fruit. Bake for 35–45 minutes until the crumble is golden. Serve hot with cream or custard.

Pear & ginger crumble
serves 4

ingredients
4 dessert pears
25ml/1fl oz apple juice
100g/4oz plain flour
1 teaspoon ground ginger

50g/2oz butter
1 teaspoon granulated sugar, plus
  extra for sprinkling

- Preheat the oven to 190°C/375°F/Gas mark 5.
- Peel, core and slice the pears. Put in a 1.2-litre/2pt ovenproof serving dish with the apple juice.
- Sift the flour and ginger into a bowl, then rub in the butter with your fingertips and stir in the sugar. Spoon the mixture over the pears, and press down lightly. Sprinkle with a little extra sugar.
- Bake for 45 minutes until golden. Serve hot with cream or custard.

Queen of puddings
serves 4

ingredients
50g/2oz dark chocolate (at least
  70% cocoa solids), broken into
  small pieces
500ml/18fl oz chocolate-
  flavoured milk

100g/4oz fresh white
  breadcrumbs
100g/4oz caster sugar
2 eggs, separated
4 tablespoons black cherry jam

- Preheat the oven to 180°C/350°F/Gas mark 4.
- Put the chocolate and milk in a saucepan. Heat gently, stirring until the chocolate melts. Bring almost to the boil. Remove the pan from the heat.
- Put the breadcrumbs in a large bowl with 25g/1oz of the sugar. Pour in the chocolate mixture and mix well. Beat in the egg yolks. Spoon the mixture into a 1.2-litre/2pt pie dish. Bake in the oven for 25–30 minutes until set and firm.
- Whisk the egg whites in a large bowl until standing in soft peaks. Gradually whisk in the remaining sugar, and whisk until you have a thick meringue. Spread the jam over the baked chocolate base and pile the meringue on top.
- Return the pudding to the oven for about 15 minutes. Serve immediately.

Glazed berry pudding
serves 8

ingredients

4 eggs, separated
50g/2oz caster sugar
25g/1oz plain flour
150ml/5fl oz double cream
150ml/5fl oz milk
1 teaspoon vanilla essence
225g/8oz icing sugar, plus extra
    for dusting
450g/1lb mixed red berries

- Lightly grease eight 150ml/5fl oz ramekins with butter.
- Combine the egg yolks and caster sugar in a bowl, and beat until pale, then stir in the flour.
- Bring the cream and milk to the boil in a small saucepan, then pour into the yolk mixture, stirring. Return the mixture to the pan, and cook over a gentle heat for 2 minutes, stirring all the time, or until thick and smooth. Turn into a clean bowl, add the vanilla essence, cover and leave to cool.
- Put the egg whites and icing sugar in a large heatproof bowl over a pan of simmering water, whisk for 10 minutes until thick, then remove from the heat and whisk until cool.
- Put 2 tablespoonfuls of the berries in the bottom of each ramekin. Fold the meringue into the custard, and pile the mixture on top of the berries. Chill the filled ramekins in the freezer for at least 7 hours.
- Preheat the oven to 220°C/425°F/Gas mark 7.
- Remove the ramekins from the freezer, put on a baking tray and dust thickly with icing sugar. Bake for 20 minutes, and serve immediately.

Gentlemen's pudding

serves 6

ingredients

150g/5oz butter
75g/3oz caster sugar
150g/5oz self-raising flour
3 large eggs, whisked
4 tablespoons sieved
    raspberry jam

For the sauce
2 egg yolks
1 tablespoon caster sugar
175ml/6fl oz dry sherry
2 tablespoons sieved
    raspberry jam

- Beat the butter with the sugar to a pale cream. Sift in half of the flour, then add one of the eggs, and incorporate. Sift in the remaining flour and beat in, followed by the remaining eggs, to achieve a smooth batter. Add the jam and stir.
- Pour into a buttered 1-litre/1½pt pudding basin. Cover with a cloth and steam for 1½ hours.
- To make the sauce, whisk the egg yolks with the sugar in a heatproof bowl set over a pan of simmering water. As they thicken, add the sherry and sieved jam, and cook for a few minutes, stirring constantly.
- Serve the sauce hot with the pudding.

●●●●●●●●●●●●●●●●●●●●●●●●●●●●●●●●●

Strawberry & apple crumble

serves 4

ingredients

450g/1lb cooking apples,
    peeled, cored and sliced
150g/5oz strawberries, halved
25g/1oz granulated sugar
1/2 teaspoon ground cinnamon
25ml/1fl oz orange juice
hot vanilla custard, to serve

For the crumble
50g/2oz wholemeal flour
50g/2oz porridge or rolled oats
25g/1oz butter, softened

- Preheat the oven to 180°C/ 350°F/Gas mark 4.
- Toss together with the strawberries, sugar, cinnamon and orange juice. Tip the mixture into a 1.2-litre/2pt ovenproof dish.
- To make the crumble, combine the flour and oats in a bowl, and mix in the butter with a fork.
- Sprinkle the crumble mixture evenly over the fruit, and bake in the oven for 40–45 minutes until golden brown. Serve warm with custard.

Sticky toffee pudding
serves 4

ingredients
100g/4oz butter
50g/2oz caster sugar
150ml/5fl oz double cream
100g/4oz muscovado sugar
4 eggs, separated
150g/5oz plain flour
1½ teaspoons baking powder

- Preheat the oven to 180°C/350°F/Gas mark 4. Grease four moulds measuring 300ml/10fl oz.
- In a saucepan, dissolve the caster sugar in 2 tablespoons water over a low heat. Warm the double cream in another pan. When the sugar has dissolved, increase the heat under that pan, and boil until golden brown. Remove from the heat and add the hot cream, stirring. Pour equally between the moulds.
- Using an electric whisk, cream the butter and muscovado sugar until off-white, then whisk in the egg yolks, one at a time.
- In a glass bowl, whisk the egg whites to soft peaks and reserve.
- Sift the flour and baking powder into a bowl, then whisk into the butter cream. Fold the whisked egg whites into the mixture.
- Spoon into the moulds, and cover the tops with buttered rounds of baking parchment. Put into a roasting tin, and pour in enough hot water from the kettle to come halfway up the moulds. Bake in the oven for 40–50 minutes. Serve hot on their own, or with cream or ice cream.

Ginger upside-down pudding

serves 4–6

ingredients

1 tablespoon brown sugar
4 peaches, halved and stoned
8 walnut halves
150g/5oz wholemeal flour
½ teaspoon bicarbonate of soda
1½ teaspoons ground ginger
1 teaspoon ground cinnamon
100g/4oz molasses sugar
1 egg
125ml/4fl oz milk
50ml/2fl oz sunflower oil

- Preheat the oven to 180°/350°F/Gas mark 4. Brush the bottom and side of a 23cm/9in round springform cake tin with a little sunflower oil. Sprinkle the brown sugar over the bottom of the tin.
- Arrange the peaches cut side down in the tin, with the walnut halves in place of the stones.
- For the base, sift together the flour, bicarbonate of soda, ginger and cinnamon, then stir in the sugar. Whisk together the egg, milk and oil, then mix into the dry ingredients until smooth.
- Pour the mixture evenly over the peaches, and bake for 35–40 minutes until firm to the touch. Turn out onto a serving plate. Serve hot with custard, cream or ice cream.

Sticky marmalade pudding
serves 8

ingredients
175g/6oz butter
175g/6oz muscovado sugar
300g/11oz marmalade
2 seedless oranges, peeled,
    all pith removed and sliced
    thinly into rounds
2 large eggs, beaten
175g/6oz self-raising flour
1½ teaspoons ground ginger
50g/2oz fresh root ginger,
    finely chopped

• Preheat the oven to 180°C/375°F/Gas mark 4. Line the bottom of
  a 23cm/9in round cake tin, at least 5cm/2in deep, with non-stick
  baking parchment.
• Warm together 50g/2oz each of the butter and sugar, and half of the
  marmalade. Spoon into the tin, then arrange the orange slices over the
  top of the marmalade mixture.
• Beat together the remaining butter and sugar. Gradually beat in the
  eggs. Sift the flour and ground ginger together, and fold into the mixture
  with the remaining marmalade and the fresh ginger. Carefully pour over
  the oranges, and spread to fill the tin.
• Stand the tin on a baking tray, and bake for 1 hour 10 minutes or until
  just firm to the touch.
• Invert the pudding onto a serving plate, and serve warm with custard.

Caramelized apple tarts
serves 6

ingredients

1 pastry sheet from a 375g/13oz
   pack puff pastry
100g/4oz white marzipan, chilled
   and coarsely grated
4 Braeburn apples, quartered, cored
   and sliced
50g/2oz butter
juice of 1 large lemon
25g/1oz Demerara sugar
½ teaspoon mixed spice

- Preheat the oven to 200°C/400°F/Gas mark 6. Grease the bottoms of six 7.5cm/3in individual tartlet tins.
- Roll out the pastry sheet more thinly. Stamp out six 12.5cm/5in rounds of pastry using a pastry cutter. Use to line the tins, and prick the bases twice with a fork. Chill for 10 minutes.
- Line the pastry with foil and baking beans. Bake blind for 10 minutes. Remove the foil and beans, sprinkle in the marzipan and cook for a further 5 minutes.
- Quarter, core and slice the apples. Heat the butter in a large non-stick frying pan. Add the apples, lemon juice, sugar and mixed spice, and cook over a high heat for 5 minutes, turning as needed, until most of the lemon juice has evaporated and the apples are just tender.
- Pile the apple mixture into the warm pastry cases, then put back in the oven for 2–3 minutes. Serve the tartlets warm with crème fraîche.

Blackberry batter pudding

serves 8

ingredients
350g/12oz blackberries
250g/9oz granulated sugar
3 tablespoons plain flour
grated zest of 1 lemon
¼ teaspoon ground nutmeg

For the topping
225g/8oz plain flour
225g/8oz granulated sugar
1 tablespoon baking powder
pinch of salt
250ml/9fl oz milk
75g/3oz butter, melted

- Preheat the oven to 180°C/350°F/Gas mark 4.
- In a large mixing bowl, combine the blackberries with 225g/8oz sugar.
- Add the flour and lemon zest. Using a large spoon, stir gently to blend. Transfer to a 2-litre/3½pt baking dish.
- To make the topping, sift the flour, sugar, baking powder and salt into a large bowl. Set aside. In a jug, combine the milk and butter. Gradually stir the milk mixture into the dry ingredients, and keep stirring until the batter is just smooth. Spoon the batter over the berries.
- Mix the remaining sugar with the nutmeg, then sprinkle the mixture over the pudding. Bake in the oven for about 50 minutes until the topping is set. Serve hot.

Indian bread pudding
serves 6

ingredients

6 medium slices white bread
75g/3oz ghee or butter
150g/5oz granulated sugar
3 green cardamom pods, husks
  removed

600ml/1pt milk
175ml/6fl oz evaporated milk
½ teaspoon saffron threads

- Cut the bread slices into quarters. Heat the ghee or butter in a large heavy frying pan. Add the bread slices and fry, turning once, until golden brown.
- Put the fried bread in the bottom of a heatproof dish and set aside.
- To make a syrup, put the sugar, 300ml/10fl oz water and cardamom seeds in a saucepan. Bring to the boil over a medium heat, stirring constantly, until the sugar has dissolved. Boil until the syrup thickens. Pour the syrup over the fried bread.
- Put the milk, evaporated milk and saffron in a separate saucepan, and bring to the boil over a low heat. Simmer until it has halved in volume. Pour the mixture over the syrup-coated bread. Serve warm.

• •

Chocolate & pear crumble
serves 4

ingredients

4 pears, cored and sliced
25ml/1fl oz apple juice
100g/4oz plain flour
15g/½oz cocoa powder
50g/2oz butter
2 teaspoons granulated sugar

- Preheat the oven to 190°C/ 375°F/Gas mark 5.
- Peel, core and slice the pears, and put in an ovenproof dish with the apple juice.
- Sift the flour and cocoa into a bowl. Rub the butter into the mixture with your fingertips. Stir in the sugar. Sprinkle over the pears, and press down lightly.
- Bake for about 40 minutes until cooked through. Serve hot.

Oat & fruit puddings
serves 4

ingredients
100g/4oz rolled oats
50g/2oz butter, melted
2 tablespoons chopped almonds
1 tablespoon clear honey

pinch of ground cinnamon
2 dessert pears
1 tablespoon marmalade
custard or yogurt, to serve

- Preheat the oven to 200°C/400°F/Gas mark 6. Lightly oil the bottoms of four individual pudding bowls, and line each one with a small circle of baking parchment.
- Mix together the oats, butter, almonds, honey and cinnamon in a small bowl. Using a spoon, spread two-thirds of the oat mixture over the base and around the sides of the pudding bowls.
- Peel, core and finely chop the pears. Toss together with the marmalade, and spoon into the oat cases. Scatter the remaining oat mixture over to cover the pears and marmalade.
- Bake for 15–20 minutes until golden and crisp. Leave for 5 minutes before removing the pudding bowls. Serve hot with custard or yogurt.

Fruity bread pudding
serves 4

ingredients
75g/3oz mixed dried fruit
150ml/5fl oz unsweetened
  apple juice
3–4 slices day-old white bread,
  cubed

1 teaspoon mixed spice
1 large banana, sliced
150ml/5fl oz milk
1 tablespoon Demerara sugar

- Preheat the oven to 200°C/400°F/Gas mark 6. Put the dried fruit in a small pan with the apple juice, and bring to the boil.
- Remove the pan from the heat and stir in the bread cubes, mixed spice and banana. Spoon the mixture into a shallow 1.2-litre/2pt ovenproof dish and pour the milk over.
- Sprinkle with the sugar, and bake for 25–30 minutes until firm and golden brown. Serve hot or cold.

Treacle pudding
serves 6

ingredients

50g/2oz butter
100g/4oz caster sugar
2 eggs
175g/6oz plain flour

2 teaspoons baking powder
pinch of salt
2 tablespoons milk
4 tablespoons golden syrup

- Cream the butter and sugar in a bowl. Beat in the eggs, one at a time.
- Sift the flour, baking powder and salt together, and fold into the mixture, adding just enough milk to give a dropping consistency.
- Butter a 1.2-litre/2pt pudding basin, then pour the syrup into the bottom. Spoon in the batter to fill the basin. Cover the top with a round of buttered baking parchment, and secure pleated foil over that with string.
- Stand in a pan of simmering water with a lid on, and steam for 1½ hours, topping up with boiling water when necessary. Invert the pudding onto a serving plate. Serve hot.

● ●

Banana chocolate chip soufflés
serves 6

ingredients

3 egg whites
75g/3oz granulated sugar
2 bananas

2½ tablespoons mini chocolate chips

- Preheat the oven to 230°C/450°F/Gas mark 8. Lightly grease six 175ml/6fl oz ramekins.
- In a bowl, beat the egg whites with an electric mixer until soft peaks form, then gradually beat in the sugar until the mixture holds stiff peaks.
- Thinly slice the bananas onto the mixture, and gently fold in the chocolate chips.
- Arrange the ramekins on a baking tray, and divide the mixture evenly among them. Run a knife around the sides of the ramekins, and bake the soufflés in the middle of the oven for 15 minutes or until golden brown. Serve immediately.

Baked coconut rice pudding
serves 4–6

ingredients

100g/4oz short-grain rice
600ml/1 pint coconut milk
300ml/10fl oz milk
50g/2oz caster sugar
1–2 teaspoons butter

- Lightly grease a 1.2-litre/2pt shallow ovenproof dish.
- Mix the rice with the coconut milk, milk and sugar until all the ingredients are well blended.
- Pour the rice mixture into the prepared dish, and dot the surface with the butter. Bake in the oven for about 30 minutes. Serve hot.

• •

Creamy puddings
serves 6

ingredients

300ml/10fl oz double cream
250g/9oz ricotta cheese
50g/2oz caster sugar
100g/4oz white chocolate, broken into pieces

350g/12oz mixed summer fruits, such as strawberries, blueberries and raspberries
2 tablespoons Cointreau

- Whip the cream until soft peaks form. Fold in the ricotta cheese and half the of sugar.
- Put the chocolate in a heatproof bowl set over a saucepan of simmering water. Stir until melted. Remove from the heat and leave to cool, stirring occasionally. Stir into the cheese mixture until well blended.
- Spoon the mixture into six individual pudding moulds, and level the surface of each pudding with the back of a spoon. Put in the freezer and freeze for 8 hours or overnight.
- Put the fruits and the remaining sugar in a pan, and heat gently, stirring occasionally, until the sugar has dissolved. Stir in the Cointreau.
- Dip the pudding moulds in hot water for 30 seconds, and invert onto serving plates. Spoon the hot fruit compote over the puddings, and serve immediately.

Chocolate crêpes
serves 6

ingredients
75g/3oz plain flour
1 tablespoon cocoa powder
1 teaspoon caster sugar
2 eggs, lightly beaten
175ml/6fl oz milk
2 teaspoons dark rum
25g/1oz butter, melted, plus extra
   for brushing

For the filling
5 tablespoons double cream
225g/8oz dark chocolate (at least
   70% cocoa solids)
3 eggs, separated
25g/1oz caster sugar

- Preheat the oven to 200°C/400°F/Gas mark 6.
- Sift the flour, cocoa and sugar into a bowl. Make a well in the centre, add the eggs and beat them in a little at a time, drawing in the flour mixture from the edge of the bowl. Add the milk, rum and butter, and beat until smooth. Cover and set aside for 30 minutes.
- Brush an 18cm/7in crêpe pan with melted butter, and set over a medium heat. Pour 3 tablespoons of the batter into the pan, swirling it to cover the bottom. Cook for 3 minutes, turning once, then slide onto a plate. Cook another 11 crêpes in the same way. Stack, interleaved with baking parchment, and keep warm.
- For the filling, put the cream and chocolate in a pan and melt gently, stirring. In a bowl, beat the egg yolks with half of the sugar until creamy, beat in the chocolate cream and leave to cool. In a separate bowl, whisk the egg whites into soft peaks, add the rest of the sugar and beat until stiff. Stir a spoonful of the whites into the chocolate mixture, then fold in the remainder.
- Spread each crêpe with 1 tablespoon of the filling, then fold into quarters. Brush with melted butter, place on a buttered baking tray and bake in the oven for 20 minutes. Serve hot.

Black cherry crêpes

serves 4

ingredients

For the crêpe batter

100g/4oz plain flour
1 egg
300ml/10fl oz milk

For the filling

375g/13oz fresh black cherries
25g/1oz icing sugar
150g/5oz Greek-style yogurt
2 tablespoons vegetable oil

- To make the crêpe batter, whisk together the flour, egg and milk until smooth. Cover and set aside for 30 minutes.
- For the filling, pit the cherries and halve or quarter them if they are large. Stir the icing sugar into the yogurt.
- Brush a 15cm/6in non-stick crêpe pan very lightly with oil, and heat until hot.
- Whisk the batter well, and thin it with a little extra milk if it is too thick. Pour one-eighth of the batter into the hot pan, and swirl it around to cover the bottom. Cook for 1–2 minutes until golden underneath, then turn over and cook the other side.
- Turn the crêpe out of the pan. Repeat with the remaining mixture until you have 8 crêpes, adding more oil as necessary. Stack them between sheets of greaseproof paper on a plate as you cook them. Rest the plate over a saucepan of simmering water to keep warm.
- To serve, put a spoonful of sweetened yogurt in the centre of each crêpe, and top with a spoonful of cherries. Fold the crêpe into quarters, and serve warm.

Crêpes Suzettes
serves 4

ingredients

For the crêpe batter
100g/4oz plain flour
Pinch of salt
2 eggs
300ml/10fl oz milk
25g/1oz butter, melted
2 teaspoons vegetable oil

For the sauce
50g/2oz butter
25g/1oz caster sugar, sifted
finely grated zest and juice of
   1 large orange
finely grated zest of 1 large lemon
3 tablespoons Cointreau
2 tablespoons brandy

- To make the crêpe batter, put all the ingredients except the oil in a blender or food processor. Add 150ml/5fl oz cold water, and blend to a smooth batter. Alternatively, sift the flour and salt into a bowl, add the eggs and about half of the milk. Whisk to a thick paste. Whisk in the remaining milk and 150ml/5fl oz water for a smooth pouring batter, then add the melted butter. Cover and set aside for 30 minutes.
- Heat ½ teaspoon of the oil in a non-stick 18 cm/7in frying pan. Pour in 4 tablespoons batter and swirl around. Cook for 15 seconds until the edges brown. Turn the pancake over and cook until lightly browned.
- Repeat with the rest of the batter to make about 14 pancakes, adding more oil as necessary. Stack them between sheets of greaseproof paper on a plate as you cook them. Rest the plate over a saucepan of simmering water to keep warm.
- To make the sauce, put the butter, sugar, zests and juice in a frying pan, and warm gently until the butter has melted. Add the pancakes and warm through gently, turning once.
- Pour in the Cointreau and brandy, and swirl carefully over the heat to warm through gently. Once the alcohol is warm, flame the pancakes with a lighted match. Serve immediately.

Apricot soufflé
serves 2

ingredients

8 large fresh apricots, stoned
175ml/6fl oz double cream
2¼ teaspoons plain flour
50g/2oz caster sugar, plus extra
   for dusting

1 teaspoon Kirsch
3 eggs, separated
1 pinch cream of tartar
1 teaspoon butter
Icing sugar for dusting

- Preheat the oven to 230°C/450°F/Gas mark 8. Slice half of the apricots and set aside. Dice the remaining apricots.
- Combine the cream, flour, caster sugar and diced apricots in a large saucepan. Bring to a simmer over a medium heat and cook, whisking until thick, for 3 minutes. Remove from the heat, add the Kirsch, then whisk in the egg yolks one at a time.
- Beat the egg whites in a mixing bowl until stiff.
- Butter a small soufflé dish and dust with caster sugar. Spread 50g/2oz of the apricot mixture on the bottom. Add about a third of the egg whites to the remaining apricot mixture. Gently fold together. Carefully fold in the remaining egg whites in two batches. Spoon over the apricot mixture in the soufflé dish. Bake for 12–15 minutes until lightly browned on top. Dust generously with icing sugar, and arrange sliced apricots on top. Serve immediately.

● ●

Zabaglione
serves 4

ingredients

5 egg yolks
100g/4oz caster sugar

150ml/5fl oz Marsala or sweet
sherry

- Put the egg yolks in a large mixing bowl. Add the caster sugar, and whisk until the mixture is thick, very pale and doubled in volume.
- Set the bowl containing the egg yolk and sugar mixture over a saucepan of gently simmering water. Add the Marsala and continue whisking until the mixture becomes warm. This may take up to 10 minutes.
- Pour the mixture, which should be frothy and light, into four wine glasses. Serve warm.

Apple pie
serves 6

ingredients

6 large cooking apples such as
  Granny Smith
2 tablespoons caster sugar
1 teaspoon finely grated
  lemon zest
pinch of ground cloves
2 tablespoons marmalade
1 egg, lightly beaten
1 tablespoon granulated sugar

For the pastry
225g/8oz plain flour
25g/1oz self-raising flour
150g/5oz butter, chilled and
  cubed
2 tablespoons caster sugar
4–5 tablespoons iced water

- Lightly grease a 23cm/9in pie plate.
- Peel, core and cut the apples into wedges. Put in a saucepan with the sugar, lemon zest, cloves and 2 tablespoons water. Cover and cook over a low heat for 8 minutes or until the apples are just tender, shaking the pan occasionally. Drain and cool completely.
- To make the pastry, sift the flours into a bowl, and rub in the butter using your fingertips, until the mixture resembles fine breadcrumbs. Stir in the sugar, then make a well in the centre. Add almost all the iced water, and mix with a pastry scraper or flat-bladed knife, using a cutting action, until the mixture comes together. Gather together and lift out onto a lightly floured work surface. Press into a ball and divide into two, making one half a little bigger. Cover with cling film and refrigerate for 20 minutes.
- Preheat the oven to 200°C/400°F/Gas mark 6.
- Roll out the larger piece of pastry between two sheets of baking parchment, and line the bottom and side of the pie plate. Using a small sharp knife, trim away any excess pastry. Brush the marmalade over the bottom of the pastry shell, and spoon in the apple mixture.
- Roll out the other pastry ball between the baking parchment until large enough to cover the pie. Brush water around the rim of the pastry shell, and put the pastry on the top. Pinch the edges to seal, and cut a couple of short slits in the top to allow steam to escape.
- Brush the top of the pie with beaten egg, and sprinkle with the sugar, Bake in the oven for 20 minutes, then reduce the oven temperature to 180°C/350°F/Gas mark 4 and bake for another 15–20 minutes until golden. Serve hot with cream or vanilla ice cream.

Bread & butter pudding
serves 6

ingredients

50g/2oz butter, softened
6 slices white bread
25g/1oz currants
25g/1oz sultanas
3 eggs

550ml/18fl oz milk
50g/2oz light muscovado sugar
pinch of mixed spice
single cream for drizzling

- Lightly grease a 1.2-litre/2pt ovenproof dish with a little of the butter. Use the rest to spread evenly over the bread, then cut each slice in half diagonally.
- Arrange the slices in the dish, each one slightly overlapping the last, and sprinkle the currants and sultanas over the top.
- Beat together the eggs, milk, sugar and mixed spice in a bowl, and pour over the bread. Leave to soak for 30 minutes. Preheat the oven to 180°C/350°F/Gas mark 4.
- Bake the pudding for 45–55 minutes until golden brown but still slightly moist in the centre. Serve with a drizzle of single cream.

•••••••••••••••••••••••••••••••••

Hot plum batter
serves 4

ingredients

450g/1lb red plums, quartered
and stoned
200ml/7fl oz skimmed milk
4 tablespoons skimmed
milk powder
1 tablespoon muscovado sugar
1 teaspoon vanilla essence
75g/3oz self-raising flour
2 egg whites
icing sugar for dusting

- Preheat the oven to 220°C/ 425°F/Gas mark 7. Lightly oil a wide shallow ovenproof dish with vegetable oil, and add the plums.
- Put the milk, milk powder, sugar, vanilla essence, flour and egg whites in a food processor. Whiz until smooth.
- Pour the batter over the plums. Bake for 25–30 minutes until well risen and golden. Lightly dust with icing sugar, and serve immediately.

Apple strudel
serves 6–8

ingredients

100g/4oz dried breadcrumbs
900g/2lb cooking apples
juice of 3 lemons
225g/8oz cranberries
225g/8oz seedless raisins
2 teaspoons ground cinnamon

½ teaspoon freshly grated nutmeg
225g/8oz chopped walnuts
175g/6oz soft brown sugar
450g/1lb filo pastry sheets
175g/6oz butter

- Heat a dry frying pan over a medium heat. Pour in the breadcrumbs. Stirring all the time, lightly toast the crumbs for 1–2 minutes. Remove from the heat and set aside to cool.
- Peel, core and dice the apples, put them in a large bowl and toss in the lemon juice to prevent browning. Add the cranberries, raisins, cinnamon, nutmeg, walnuts and sugar. Mix well together.
- Preheat the oven to 180°C/350°F/Gas mark 4.
- Spread a moist tea towel on a clean work surface, and put the sheets of pastry on it. Remove a single sheet of pastry, and place on a second moist tea towel. Quickly cover the remaining pastry with a third moist tea towel.
- Melt some of the butter in a pan, and brush over the single pastry sheet. Sprinkle with some of the breadcrumbs. Uncover the pastry sheets, lift off a second sheet of pastry and place this on top of the first. Cover the remaining sheets as before.
- Brush the second sheet of pastry with melted butter and sprinkle with breadcrumbs. Repeat this procedure with another 2 pastry sheets. Spread half of the apple and walnut filling on the fourth sheet, leaving a border around the edge. Using the tea towel underneath, slowly and carefully roll the sheets of pastry away from you to form a log, tucking the edges of the pastry inwards as you go.
- Repeat the entire procedure until you have 2 pastry logs, keeping the first one moist under a tea towel while making the second.
- Lightly grease a baking tray, and carefully slide the strudel logs onto it. Brush the tops of both logs with the remaining butter, and bake in the oven for 30–40 minutes until brown and crisp. Remove from the oven and allow to cool slightly before serving.

Classic custard
serves 4

ingredients
3 eggs
350ml/12fl oz milk
50g/2oz caster sugar
1 teaspoon vanilla essence

• Whisk the eggs and milk in a heatproof bowl. Add the sugar gradually, whisking to dissolve. Stir in the vanilla essence.
• Put the bowl over a pan of simmering water, making sure that the bottom does not touch the water. Heat gently, stirring, until it thickens and coats the back of a wooden spoon. Serve hot.

Cherry pie
serves 6–8

ingredients
150g/5oz plain flour
25g/1oz icing sugar
100g/4oz butter, cubed
50g/2oz ground almonds

3 tablespoons chilled water
700g/1½lb pitted Morello cherries
1 egg, lightly beaten
caster sugar for sprinkling

• Sift the flour and icing sugar into a bowl. Add the butter and rub in with just your fingertips until the mixture is fine and crumbly. Stir in the ground almonds, then add almost all the water and stir into the flour mixture with a flat-bladed knife until the mixture forms a dough, adding the remaining water if necessary.
• Turn the dough onto a lightly floured work surface and gather together into a ball. Roll out on a sheet of baking parchment into a circle about 26cm/10½in in diameter. Flatten slightly, cover with cling film and refrigerate for 20 minutes.
• Preheat the oven to 200°C/400°F/Gas mark 6.
• Spread the cherries in the bottom of a greased 23cm/9in pie dish.
• Cover the pie dish with the pastry, and trim the overhanging edge. Brush the pastry top all over with beaten egg, and sprinkle lightly with caster sugar. Put the pie dish on a baking tray, and cook for 35–40 minutes until golden brown.
• Serve warm with cream or ice cream.

Mince pies

serves 4–6

ingredients

150g/5oz butter, cut into pieces
225g/8oz plain flour
50g/2oz ground almonds
25g/1oz caster sugar
a few drops of almond essence
grated zest of 1 orange
1 egg yolk
225g/8oz mincemeat
1 egg white, lightly beaten

- Preheat the oven to 200°C/400°F/Gas mark 6. Lightly grease a 12-hole bun tin or muffin pan.
- Rub the butter into the flour using your fingertips until the mixture resembles coarse breadcrumbs. Add the almonds, sugar, almond essence, orange zest, egg yolk and 1 tablespoon water. Mix to form a firm dough. Knead briefly on a floured work surface, then wrap and chill for 30 minutes.
- Roll out thinly, and stamp out 12 rounds, about 7.5cm/3in, using a pastry cutter. Use the pastry to line the holes in the bun tin. Spoon in the mincemeat to come two-thirds of the way up each hole. Use the remaining pastry to cut into seasonal shapes – such as holly leaves or Christmas trees – and place on top of the mincemeat.
- Bake for 20 minutes until crisp and golden brown. Serve warm with cream or brandy butter.

Christmas pudding
serves 8–10

ingredients

250g/9oz sultanas
150g/5oz currants
250g/9oz raisins
300g/11oz mixed dried fruit, chopped
50g/2oz mixed peel
120ml/4fl oz brown ale
2 tablespoons brandy
75ml/3fl oz freshly squeezed orange juice
75ml/3fl oz freshly squeezed lemon juice

1 teaspoon grated orange zest
1 teaspoon grated lemon zest
225g/8oz suet, grated
225g/8oz soft brown sugar
3 eggs, lightly beaten
200g/7oz white breadcrumbs
75g/3oz self-raising flour
pinch of salt
1 teaspoon mixed spice
¼ teaspoon freshly grated nutmeg
100g/4oz blanched almonds, roughly chopped

- Put the sultanas, currants and raisins, mixed dried fruit, mixed peel, brown ale, rum, orange and lemon juices and zests into a large bowl, and stir together. Cover and leave to steep overnight.
- The next day, add the remaining ingredients to the bowl, and mix well.
- Put a 2-litre/3½pt pudding basin on a trivet in a large saucepan with a lid, and pour in enough water to come halfway up the side of the basin. Remove the basin and put the water on to boil.
- Brush the basin with melted butter, and line the bottom with baking parchment. Fill with the pudding mixture, then cover with a round of buttered baking parchment. Top with pleated foil, and secure with string around the rim of the basin.
- Steam the pudding for 8 hours in the saucepan with the lid on, topping up with boiling water when necessary. Invert the pudding onto a serving plate. Serve hot with brandy sauce, cream or ice cream.

Baked Alaska

serves 6

ingredients

1.2 litres/2pt round tub of good-
  quality vanilla ice cream
1 Victoria sponge or other plain
  butter sponge cake
4 egg whites
75g/3oz caster sugar
1 tablespoon raspberry jam

- Freeze the ice cream in the coldest section of the freezer. Cut the sponge to match the top of the ice-cream tub, then freeze the sponge on a baking sheet overnight.
- Preheat the oven to 230°C/450°F/Gas mark 8.
- To make the meringue, whisk the eggs whites with an electric mixer to soft peaks, then increase the mixer speed and gradually add the sugar until the peaks are firm. Take care not to exceed this point or the meringue will separate.
- Spread the sponge with the jam. Turn out the ice cream to sit on top of the jam. Smooth the meringue all over the ice cream with a palette knife, taking it right down to the bottom edge of the cake to seal in the ice cream entirely, making sure to leave no gaps.
- Bake in the oven for 4–5 minutes until the meringue is just beginning to colour. Remove from the oven and serve immediately.

Banana custard

serves 4

ingredients

1 egg, lightly beaten
2 tablespoons custard powder
2 tablespoons sugar
225ml/8fl oz milk
125ml/4fl oz double cream
2 bananas, sliced into discs

- In a heatproof bowl, whisk the egg, custard powder, sugar, milk and cream until smooth.
- Put the bowl over a pan of simmering water. Stir constantly over a low heat for 5 minutes or until the custard thickens slightly and coats the back of a wooden spoon. Remove the bowl from the heat and gently stir in the banana.
- Serve hot.

Rice pudding

serves 4

ingredients

50g/2oz pudding rice
50g/2oz granulated sugar
400g/14oz evaporated milk
300ml/10fl oz fresh milk

pinch of freshly grated nutmeg
25g/1oz butter
strawberry jam, to serve

- Preheat the oven to 150°C/300°F/Gas mark 2. Lightly oil a large ovenproof dish.
- Sprinkle the rice and the sugar into the dish, and mix together.
- Bring the evaporated milk to the boil in a small pan, stirring occasionally. Stir the evaporated and fresh milk into the rice, and mix well until the rice is coated thoroughly.
- Sprinkle over the nutmeg, cover with foil and bake in the oven for 30 minutes.
- Remove the pudding from the oven and stir well, breaking up any lumps. Cover with the same foil. Bake in the oven for a further 30 minutes.
- Remove from the oven and stir well again. Dot the pudding with butter and bake for a further 45–60 minutes until the rice is tender and a brown skin has formed on top.
- Divide the pudding into four individual serving bowls. Top each one with a large spoonful of jam, and serve immediately.

Peach cobbler
serves 4–6

ingredients

4 large peaches, peeled and thickly
   sliced, with stones removed
175ml/6fl oz maple syrup
1 teaspoon ground nutmeg
1 teaspoon ground cinnamon
½ teaspoon ground cloves
½ teaspoon ground ginger
225g/8oz plain flour, sifted
225ml/8fl oz milk
2 egg whites

- Preheat the oven to 190°C/375°F/Gas mark 5.
- Arrange the peaches in a glass dish measuring about 20cm/8in in diameter. Mix together the maple syrup with half of each of the ground nutmeg, cinnamon, cloves and ginger. Drizzle the mixture over the peaches, making sure that each piece of fruit is well coated. Allow to stand for 10–15 minutes.
- In a mixing bowl, combine the flour, milk and egg whites and blend to mix. Pour carefully over the top of the fruit, then sprinkle with the other half of the spices.
- Bake, uncovered, in the oven for 45–50 minutes until the topping is cooked and golden. Serve hot with cream or ice cream.

Semolina
serves 4

ingredients

6 tablespoons pure ghee
3 whole cloves
3 whole cardamom pods
8 tablespoons coarse semolina
½ teaspoon saffron threads
50g/2oz sultanas
150g/5oz caster sugar
300ml/10fl oz water
300ml/10fl oz milk

- Put the ghee in a saucepan, and melt over a medium heat. Add the cloves and the whole cardamoms, and reduce the heat, stirring to mix.
- Add the semolina to the mixture in the pan, and stir-fry until it turns a slightly darker colour. Add the saffron, sultanas and sugar to the semolina mixture, stirring to mix well.
- Pour in the water and milk, and cook the mixture, stirring constantly, until the semolina has softened. Add a little more water if required.
- Remove the pan from the heat, and transfer the semolina to a warmed serving dish. Serve immediately with cream, chopped nuts and shredded coconut, if you like.

Rhubarb & apple cobbler

serves 6

ingredients

900g/2lb rhubarb
450g/1lb cooking apples
6 tablespoons caster sugar
4 tablespoons plain flour
1 tablespoon cornflour
½ teaspoon ground ginger
1 tablespoon butter
grated zest of 1 orange

For the dough
150g/5oz plain flour
2 teaspoons baking powder
pinch of salt
50g/2oz butter, softened
3 tablespoons caster sugar
125ml/4fl oz buttermilk
2 tablespoons double cream
1 teaspoon Demerara sugar

- Preheat the oven to 220°C/425°F/Gas mark 7.
- Cut the rhubarb into 2cm/1in lengths. Peel, core, quarter and slice the apple. Mix together the rhubarb, apples, sugar, flour, cornflour, ginger, butter and orange zest. Put the mixture in a 25cm/10in shallow ovenproof dish, and set aside.
- To make the dough, sift the flour, baking powder and salt into a bowl. Rub in the softened butter using your fingertips until the mixture resembles fine breadcrumbs. Stir in the caster sugar and buttermilk. Spoon the dough onto the rhubarb and apple mixture in small mounds, making sure that it does not completely cover the fruit. Mix the cream with the Demerara sugar, and drizzle on the top.
- Put the dish on a baking tray, and bake for 10 minutes. Reduce the heat to 190°C/375°F/Gas mark 5 and bake for a further 20–30 minutes until puffed and brown, and the fruit is just soft. Remove from the oven and leave to stand for 10 minutes, then serve warm with cream.

Treacle tart
serves 6

ingredients

1 x 23cm/9in shortcrust pastry
  shell, baked
400g/14oz golden syrup
2 tablespoons treacle
150g/5oz slivered almonds
125g/4½oz fresh white
  breadcrumbs
2 eggs
grated zest of ½ lemon

- Preheat the oven to 130°C/
  250°F/Gas mark 1/2. Put the
  pastry shell on a baking sheet.
- In a bowl, mix together the golden
  syrup, treacle, slivered almonds,
  breadcrumbs, eggs and lemon
  zest. Spoon the mixture into the
  pastry case, and bake for about
  1 hour.
- Serve warm with clotted cream or
  double cream.

Chocolate fudge pudding
serves 4

ingredients

50g/2oz butter
75g/3oz soft brown sugar
2 eggs, beaten
350ml/12fl oz milk
50g/2oz chopped walnuts
50g/2oz plain flour
2 tablespoons cocoa powder,
  plus extra for dusting
icing sugar for dusting

- Preheat the oven to 180°C/
  350°F/Gas mark 4. Lightly grease
  a 1.2-litre/2pt ovenproof dish.
- Cream together the butter and
  sugar in a large mixing bowl until
  fluffy. Beat in the eggs.
- Gradually stir in the milk, and add
  the walnuts, stirring to mix.
- Sift the flour and cocoa powder
  into the mixture. Fold in gently with
  a metal spoon until well mixed.
- Spoon the mixture into the
  ovenproof dish, and cook in the
  oven for 35–40 minutes.
- To serve, dust with icing sugar and
  cocoa powder, and serve hot.

Cold Desserts

A cold dessert is a refreshing conclusion to any summer
menu and can provide the perfect counterpoint to a meal,
whether it is hot or cold outside. You are bound to find
something to appeal in the delicious range of ice creams,
sorbets and mousses included in this chapter. Add to these
recipes for trifles, jellies, syllabubs and fools, and you'll have
a treat to cool you down or refresh your palate
on any day of the year.

Apricot fool

serves 4

ingredients

2 tablespoons cornflour
300ml/10fl oz skimmed milk
15g/½oz low-fat spread
¼ teaspoon vanilla essence
½ teaspoon granulated sugar
400g/14oz canned apricots
   in juice

- To make the sauce, blend the cornflour with 2 tablespoons of the milk in a saucepan with a wooden spoon. Add the remaining milk, bring to the boil and cook for 2 minutes until thickened.
- Stir in the low-fat spread, vanilla essence and sugar. Leave to cool.
- Keeping half an apricot aside for decoration, purée the rest with the juice in a blender or food processor. Fold into the sauce.
- Spoon into individual glasses, and chill for 1 hour before serving.

● ●

Strawberry rose-petal pashka

serves 4

ingredients

350g/12oz cottage cheese
175g/6oz low-fat Greek-style
   yogurt
2 tablespoons clear honey

½ teaspoon rose water
275g/10oz strawberries
handful of unsprayed scented pink
   rose petals, to decorate

- Drain any free liquid from the cottage cheese, and tip the cheese into a sieve. Use a wooden spoon to rub through the sieve into a bowl.
- Stir the yogurt, honey and rose water into the cheese. Roughly chop about half the strawberries, and stir them into the cheese mixture.
- Line a new clean flowerpot or a sieve with muslin, and tip the cheese mixture in. Leave to drain over a bowl for several hours or overnight.
- Invert the flowerpot or sieve onto a serving plate, turn out the pashka and remove the muslin. Decorate with rose petals and serve chilled.

Perfumed pineapple salad
serves 4

ingredients
1 small pineapple
1 tablespoon icing sugar
1 tablespoon orange-flower
  water
100g/4oz fresh dates, stoned
  and quartered
225g/8oz strawberries, sliced
fresh mint sprigs, to decorate

- Cut the skin from the pineapple and, using the tip of a vegetable peeler, remove as many brown 'eyes' as possible. Quarter the pineapple lengthways, remove the core from each wedge, then slice.
- Lay the pineapple slices in a shallow serving bowl. Sprinkle with icing sugar, and drizzle the orange-flower water over.
- Add the dates and strawberries to the pineapple, cover and chill for at least 2 hours, stirring once or twice. Serve chilled, decorated with a few mint sprigs.

Pineapple wedges with lime
serves 4

ingredients
1 pineapple, about 800g/1¾lb
1 lime
1 tablespoon muscovado sugar
1 teaspoon ground allspice

- Cut the pineapple lengthways into quarters. Remove the hard core.
- Loosen the flesh on each wedge by sliding a knife between the flesh and the skin. Cut the flesh into slices, leaving it on the skin.
- Using a sharp-pointed knife, remove a few shreds of zest from the lime. Squeeze out the juice.
- Sprinkle the pineapple with the lime juice and zest, sugar and allspice. Chill for 1 hour and serve.

Passion fruit & apple foam

serves 4

ingredients

450g/1lb cooking apples
100ml/3½fl oz unsweetened
  apple juice

3 passion fruit
3 egg whites

- Peel, core and roughly chop the apples. Put them in a pan with the apple juice. Bring the liquid to the boil, then reduce the heat and cover the pan. Cook gently, stirring occasionally, until the apple is very tender.
- Remove from the heat, and beat the apple mixture with a wooden spoon until it forms a fairly smooth purée.
- Cut the passion fruit in half, and scoop out the seeds and pulp into the apple purée. Stir to mix thoroughly.
- Put the egg whites in a bowl, and whisk until soft peaks form. Fold the egg whites into the apple mixture. Spoon the apple foam into four serving dishes. Leave to cool and serve cold.

● ●

Dried fruit fool

serves 4

ingredients

300g/11oz ready-to-eat dried
  fruit, such as apricots,
  peaches or apples
300ml/10fl oz freshly squeezed
  orange juice
250ml/9fl oz low-fat
  fromage frais
2 egg whites

- Put the dried fruit in a saucepan, add the orange juice and heat gently until boiling. Reduce the heat, cover and simmer gently for 3 minutes.
- Cool slightly. Tip into a blender or food processor, and purée until smooth. Stir in the fromage frais.
- Whisk the egg whites in a bowl until stiff enough to hold soft peaks, then slowly fold into the fruit mixture until combined.
- Spoon into four stemmed glasses, then chill the fools for at least 1 hour before serving.

Green fruit salad
serves 6

ingredients

3 galia melons
100g/4oz green seedless grapes
2 kiwi fruit
1 star fruit

1 green dessert apple
1 lime
175ml/6fl oz sparkling grape juice

- Cut the melons in half and scoop out the seeds. Keeping the shells intact, scoop out the fruit with a melon baller. Set aside the melon shells.
- Remove any stems from the grapes, and peel and chop the kiwi fruit. Thinly slice the star fruit. Core and thinly slice the apple, and put the slices in a bowl with the melon, grapes, kiwi fruit and star fruit.
- Thinly pare the zest from the lime, and cut into fine strips. Blanch the strips in boiling water for 10 seconds, then drain and rinse in cold water. Squeeze the juice from the lime, and sprinkle it into the fruit. Toss through gently.
- Spoon the prepared fruit into the melon shells, and chill in the refrigerator until required. Just before serving, spoon the sparkling grape juice over the fruit, and scatter it with the lime zest.

● ●

Cherry mousse
serves 8

ingredients

1 egg
2 tablespoons powdered
   gelatine
1 tablespoon cornflour
150ml/5fl oz cranberry juice
225ml/8fl oz boiling water
450g/1lb fresh cherries, pitted
225ml/8fl oz low-fat
   Greek-style yogurt
150g/5oz granulated sugar

- Combine the egg, gelatine, cornflour, cranberry juice and 1 tablespoon cold water. Stir well to blend. Add the boiling water, and mix together thoroughly.
- Purée the cherries in a blender or food processor, add the gelatine mixture, yogurt and sugar, and blend until smooth.
- Chill for 4–6 hours to set. Blend again just before serving.

Cappuccino creams
serves 8

ingredients

550g/1¼lb fromage frais
2 tablespoons finely ground
   espresso coffee

1 tablespoon icing sugar
17g/6oz dark chocolate, at least
   70% cocoa solids), grated

- Mix the fromage frais with the coffee and icing sugar. Spoon half of the mixture into eight individual ramekins or glass dishes.
- Sprinkle over most of the grated chocolate, and top with the remaining fromage frais mixture, sprinkling the last of the grated chocolate over the top. Chill until ready to serve.

• •

Frozen citrus soufflé
serves 4

ingredients

1 tablespoon powdered gelatine
100ml/3½fl oz very hot water
   (not boiling)
3 eggs, separated
100g/4oz caster sugar
grated zest and juice of 1 lemon

grated zest and juice of ½ lime
grated zest and juice of ½ orange
150ml/5fl oz double or whipping
   cream
100g/4oz fromage frais

- Tie a greaseproof paper callar around a 15cm/6in soufflé dish.
- Sprinkle the gelatine into the hot water, stirring well to dissolve. Leave to stand for 2–3 minutes, stirring occasionally, to give a completely clear liquid. Leave to cool for 10–15 minutes.
- Meanwhile, whisk the egg yolks and sugar together until very pale and light in texture. Add the zest and juice from the fruits, mixing well. Stir in the cooled gelatine liquid, making sure that it is thoroughly mixed in.
- Put the cream in a large chilled bowl, and whip until it holds its shape. Stir the fromage frais into the cream, mixing it in gently. Fold the cream mixture into the citrus mixture using a large metal spoon.
- Using a clean whisk, beat the egg whites in a clean bowl until stiff, then gently fold into the citrus mixture using a metal spoon. Pour the mixture into the prepared dish. Transfer to the freezer, and freeze for at least 2 hours until firm. Remove from the freezer 10 minutes before serving.

Strawberries in raspberry & passion fruit sauce

serves 4

ingredients

350g/12oz fresh raspberries
3 tablespoons caster sugar

1 passion fruit
700g/1½lb small strawberries

- Put the raspberries and sugar in a saucepan, carefully mix through and heat gently until the raspberries release their juices. Allow to simmer for 5 minutes, then leave to cool.
- Cut the passion fruit in half, and scoop out the pulp and any juices into a bowl.
- Tip the raspberry mixture into a blender or food processor, add the passion fruit and purée until smooth. Press the purée through a fine nylon sieve placed over a bowl to remove the seeds.
- Fold the strawberries into the sauce, then spoon into four stemmed glasses. Serve straight away, or chill until needed.

• •

Creamy fruit baskets

serves 6

ingredients

3 oranges
500g/18oz mascarpone cheese
5 tablespoons crème fraîche
2 tablespoons clear honey, warmed

6 half-coated chocolate waffle or brandy snap baskets
100g/4oz strawberries, hulled and sliced

- Finely grate and reserve 1 tablespoon orange zest. Pare off a little extra orange zest, and cut into very thin strips; reserve. Peel all the oranges, removing as much of the white pith as possible. Divide into segments.
- Put the mascarpone cheese in a bowl with the orange zest, and beat until smooth. Add half of the crème fraîche with the honey to taste. Stir through, then add enough of the remaining crème fraîche to give a fairly stiff dropping consistency. Cover and chill for at least 30 minutes.
- To serve, fill the baskets with the crème fraîche mixture, and top with the orange segments and sliced strawberries. Decorate with orange strips.

Hazelnut pavlova
serves 6

ingredients

4 egg whites
225g/8oz caster sugar
1 teaspoon distilled malt vinegar

300ml/10fl oz double cream
50g/2oz toasted hazelnuts,
chopped

- Preheat the oven to 130°C/250°F/Gas mark ½.
- Mix together the egg whites, sugar and vinegar in a clean grease-free heatproof bowl, and put over a pan of gently simmering water. Beat with an electric whisk for 10 minutes or until very stiff and shiny.
- Line a baking sheet with non-stick baking parchment, and spread the meringue mixture into a rectangle using a metal spatula or palette knife. Bake for 40 minutes, turn off the oven and leave the meringue inside to cool completely.
- Whip the cream until it just holds its shape, and spread over the cold pavlova. Sprinkle with the nuts, and chill for 2–3 hours or overnight. Cut into thick slices to serve.

● ●

Orange ice cream
serves 4

ingredients

8 oranges
1 lemon
200g/7oz caster sugar

500ml/18fl oz double cream
4 tablespoons Grand Marnier

- Finely grate the zest of the oranges and the lemon, and put in a bowl. Add the juice of 2 oranges, and leave to steep while preparing the other ingredients.
- Squeeze the juice of the remaining oranges, combine with the sugar and cook to reduce to a thick syrup.
- Whip the cream to soft peaks. Stir the steeped juice and zest into the syrup. Add the juice of the lemon, then stir the syrup into the cream, which will immediately thicken. Add the Grand Marnier.
- Freeze in a shallow container, stirring every 30 minutes for 4 hours, then leave overnight to freeze before serving.

Apricot delice
serves 8

ingredients

850g/13/4lb canned apricots in
   natural juice
50g/2oz granulated sugar
25ml/1fl oz freshly squeezed
   lemon juice

5 teaspoons powdered gelatine
425g/15oz low-fat
   ready-to-serve custard
150ml/5fl oz Greek-style yogurt
1 ripe apricot, sliced, to decorate

- Line the bottom of a 1.2-litre/2pt cake tin with baking parchment.
- Drain the apricots, reserving the juice. Put the apricots in a blender or food processor together with the sugar and 4 tablespoons of the apricot juice. Purée until smooth.
- Measure 2 tablespoons of the apricot juice into a small bowl. Add the lemon juice, then sprinkle over 2 teaspoons of the gelatine. Leave for about 5 minutes until spongy.
- Stir the gelatine into half of the purée, and pour into the prepared tin. Chill in the refrigerator for 1½ hours or until firm.
- Sprinkle the remaining gelatine over 4 tablespoons of the reserved apricot juice. Leave for about 5 minutes until spongy. Mix the remaining apricot purée with the custard, yogurt and gelatine. Pour on to the layer of set fruit purée, and chill for 3 hours.
- To serve, dip the cake tin into hot water for a few seconds, and unmould the delice onto a serving plate. Peel off the lining paper. Decorate the top with the sliced apricot.

Banana lassi
serves 4

ingredients

250g/9oz Greek-style yogurt
200g/7oz banana, peeled and
   cut into chunks
125ml/4fl oz milk
4 teaspoons granulated sugar

- Put all the ingredients in a blender or food processor, and whiz for 2 minutes.
- Pour the lassi into individual glasses and serve straight away, or cover and store in the refrigerator for up to 24 hours.

Port & orange jellies
serves 8

ingredients

450ml/¾pt ruby port
6 tablespoons powdered gelatine

125g/4½oz granulated sugar
8 oranges, segmented

- Splash cold water into eight 150ml/5fl oz fluted moulds and chill.
- Pour the port into a bowl, and sprinkle the gelatine into it. Set aside.
- Put the sugar in a large pan with 600ml/1pt cold water. Heat gently to dissolve, then bring to the boil and simmer until the liquid has reduced by half. Stir in the soaked gelatine until completely dissolved.
- Put the orange segments in the flutes of the mould so that they stand up, pressed against the sides of the mould. Pour in enough of the port and orange liquid to come halfway up the sides. Chill to set, then pour in the rest of the liquid and chill again before serving.

● ●

Amaretti
serves 4–6

ingredients

300g/11oz blanched almonds
300g/11oz caster sugar
5 egg whites

- Preheat the oven to 180°C/ 350°F/Gas mark 4.
- Put the almonds in a mortar, and add 100g/4oz of the sugar little by little, pounding constantly with the pestle.
- Beat the egg whites until stiff. Fold in the remaining sugar, and add the almonds.
- Cut ribbons of greaseproof paper 5cm/2in wide, and put on a baking tray. Spoon teaspoonfuls of the mixture on, about 2cm/¾in apart. Sprinkle with sugar and bake for 20 minutes.
- Allow to cool slightly, then lift off the greaseproof paper and cool on a wire rack. Serve with espresso coffee at the end of a meal.

Coeurs à la crème
serves 4–6

ingredients

225g/8oz cottage cheese
25g/1oz caster sugar
300ml/10fl oz double cream

1 teaspoon lemon juice
2 egg whites, stiffly whisked
150ml/5fl oz single cream

- Press the cottage cheese through a nylon sieve into a bowl. Add sugar and mix well.
- Whip the cream until stiff, then add the lemon juice. Mix into the cheese and sugar mixture. Fold in the stiffly whisked egg whites.
- Spoon the mixture into four or six individual moulds. Refrigerate overnight. Serve with the single cream and/or fresh fruit.

Yogurt ring with tropical fruit
serves 6

ingredients

175ml/6fl oz tropical fruit juice
1 tablespoon powdered gelatine
3 egg whites
150g/5oz low-fat Greek-style yogurt
jinely grated zest of 1 lime

For the filling
1 mango
2 kiwi fruit
12 cape gooseberries
juice of 1 lime

- Put the fruit juice in a saucepan and sprinkle the gelatine over. Heat gently until the gelatine has dissolved.
- Whisk the egg whites in a bowl until they hold stiff peaks. Continue whisking hard, while gradually adding the yogurt and lime zest. Continue whisking hard, and pour in the hot gelatine mixture. Mix in well, and quickly pour the mixture into a 1.5-litre/2½pt ring mould. Chill the mould iuntil set. The mixture will separate into two layers.
- For the filling, halve, stone, peel and dice the mango. Peel and slice the kiwi fruit. Remove the outer leaves from the gooseberries and cut in half. Toss all the fruits together, and stir in the lime juice.
- To serve, run a knife around the edge of the ring to loosen the mixture. Dip the mould quickly into cold water, then invert onto a serving plate. Spoon all the fruit into the centre of the ring, and serve immediately.

Fruited rice ring
serves 4

ingredients
75g/3oz short-grain rice
900ml/1½pt milk
1 cinnamon stick
175g/6oz mixed dried fruit
175ml/6fl oz orange juice
50g/2oz caster sugar
finely grated zest of
   1 small orange

- Put the rice, milk and cinnamon stick in a large pan, and bring to the boil.
- Cover and simmer, stirring occasionally, for about 1½ hours until no free liquid remains.
- Meanwhile, put the dried fruit and orange juice in a pan, and bring to the boil. Cover and simmer very gently for about 1 hour until tender.
- Remove the cinnamon stick from the rice, and stir in the sugar and orange zest.
- Tip the fruit into the bottom of a lightly oiled 1.5-litre/2½pt ring mould. Spoon the rice over, smoothing down firmly. Chill for 1 hour before serving.

Tapioca pudding
serves 6

ingredients
50g/2oz tapioca
125ml/4fl oz cold milk
600ml/1pt hot milk
2 eggs, separated
75g/3oz granulated sugar
pinch of salt
1 teaspoon vanilla essence

- Soak the tapioca in the cold milk for 10 minutes. Transfer to a saucepan, add the hot milk and cook until transparent.
- Beat the egg yolks, sugar and salt together. Add the hot milk mixture gradually, stirring constantly. Cook until it begins to thicken.
- Beat the egg whites until stiff, flavour with the vanilla essence, and fold into the hot mixture. Chill and serve.

Sherry trifle
serves 8

ingredients
1 Victoria or other butter
sponge, halved
3 tablespoons raspberry jam
3 tablespoons apricot jam
150ml/5fl oz brandy
150ml/5fl oz sweet sherry
600ml/1pt double or
whipping cream

For the custard
5 egg yolks
75g/3oz caster sugar
600ml/1pt milk
3 drops of vanilla essence

- Spread one half of the sponge with raspberry jam and the other with apricot jam. Cut each half into four, and put in a dish in which they will just fit, alternating raspberry with apricot. Pour over the brandy and sweet sherry, and leave to macerate for 2 hours.
- To make the custard, whisk the egg yolks with the caster sugar until creamy. Bring the milk to the boil. Pour it over the egg yolks, whisking constantly, then put the bowl over a pan of simmering water and whisk until thick. Stir in the vanilla essence. Pour over the sponge and refrigerate overnight.
- To serve, whip the cream until stiff, and spoon over the top.

Blueberry trifle
serves 6

ingredients
350g/12oz Madeira cake, cut
into cubes
175ml/6fl oz white wine
125ml/4fl oz elderflower cordial
3 tablespoons blueberry
conserve
500g/1lb 2oz custard
250ml/9fl oz double cream
100g/4oz blueberries
1 tablespoon pistachio nuts,
finely chopped

- Put the cake into a 2.4-litre/4pt glass serving bowl. Mix the wine with 2 tablespoons of the cordial, and pour over the cake.
- Dot the blueberry conserve over the cake, then pour the custard on top. Whip the cream into soft peaks, then fold in the remaining cordial and half of the blueberries. Add to the trifle.
- Cover and chill overnight. Scatter with the nuts and remaining blueberries before serving.

Chocolate charlotte
serves 8

ingredients

22 boudoir biscuits

4 tablespoons orange-flavoured
    liqueur such as Cointreau

250g/9oz dark chocolate (at least
    70% cocoa solids), melted

150ml/5fl oz double cream

4 eggs, separated

150g/5oz caster sugar

- Line the bottom of a charlotte mould or a deep 18cm/7in round cake tin with a piece of baking parchment.
- Put the boudoir biscuits on a non-reactive tray, and sprinkle with half of the orange-flavoured liqueur. Use to line the sides of the mould or tin, trimming if necessary to make a tight fit.
- Mix the chocolate with the double cream in a bowl, and beat in the egg yolks. Whisk the egg whites in a large bowl until standing in stiff peaks, then gradually add the caster sugar, whisking until stiff and glossy.
- Carefully fold the egg whites into the chocolate mixture in two batches, taking care not to knock out the air. Pour into the centre of the mould, and trim the biscuits so they are level with the chocolate mixture. Chill for at least 5 hours before serving.

Orange syllabub trifle
serves 3–4

ingredients

For the orange syllabub

finely grated zest and juice of
    1 orange

50g/2oz caster sugar

175g/6oz crème fraîche

225g/8oz thick Greek-style
    yogurt

For the trifle

4 trifle sponges

150ml/5fl oz freshly squeezed
    orange juice

- Put the orange zest and juice in a bowl with the sugar, and leave to marinate for 1 hour. Strain the liquid into a clean bowl, and add gradually the crème fraîche , beating until thick. Fold in the yogurt. Chill overnight.
- Cut the trifle sponges in half lengthways. Lay them in the bottom of a small serving dish, moisten with the orange juice, and finish with a layer of the syllabub. Chill for 2–3 hours before serving.

Raspberry mousse

serves 4

ingredients

3 teaspoons powdered gelatine
225g/8oz vanilla yogurt
400g/14oz fromage frais
4 egg whites
300g/11oz fresh raspberries,
  mashed

- Put 1 tablespoon hot water in a small heatproof bowl, sprinkle the gelatine over the top and leave until spongy. Bring a small pan of water to the boil, remove from the heat and put the bowl into the pan. The water should come halfway up the side of the bowl. Stir the gelatine until dissolved.
- In a large bowl, stir the vanilla yogurt and fromage frais together to combine, then add the cooled gelatine and mix well.
- Using an electric beater, beat the egg whites until stiff peaks form, then fold through the yogurt mixture until just combined.
- Gently fold the raspberries through the mixture. Chill for several hours before serving.

Tofu berry brûlée

serves 4

ingredients

300g/11oz silken tofu
25g/1oz icing sugar
225g/8oz red berries, such as
  strawberries, raspberries and
  redcurrants
75g/3oz Demerara sugar

- Mix the tofu and icing sugar in a blender, and purée until smooth.
- Stir in the fruits, then spoon into a 900ml/1½pt ovenproof dish. Flatten the top.
- Sprinkle the top with enough demerara sugar to cover evenly. Place under a very hot grill until the sugar melts and caramelizes. Chill before serving.

Crème caramel
serves 8

ingredients

175g/6oz granulated sugar
750ml/1¼pt milk
75g/3oz caster sugar

4 eggs
1 teaspoon vanilla essence

- Preheat the oven to 160°C/325°F/Gas mark 3. Brush eight 125ml/4fl oz ramekins or moulds with melted butter.
- Put the granulated sugar and 50ml/2fl oz water in a pan. Stir over a low heat until the sugar has dissolved. Bring to the boil, reduce the heat and simmer until the mixture turns golden and starts to caramelize. Remove from the heat immediately, and pour enough hot caramel into each ramekin to cover the bottom.
- To make the custard, heat the milk in a pan over a low heat until almost boiling. Remove from the heat. Whisk together the caster sugar, eggs and vanilla essence for 2 minutes, then stir in the warm milk. Strain the mixture into a jug, and carefully pour into the ramekins.
- Put the ramekins in a baking dish, and pour in enough boiling water to come halfway up the sides of the ramekins. Bake for 30 minutes or until the custard is set. Allow to cool, and refrigerate for at least 2 hours before serving.

Strawberry mousse
serves 2

ingredients

200ml/7fl oz double cream
4 digestive biscuits
55g/2oz strawberries, sliced
30g/1oz dark chocolate (at least 70% cocoa solids), grated

- Oil the inside of two moulds, and line the insides with cling film.
- Whisk up the cream so that it is thick, and crumble in the digestives. Stir through the strawberries and chocolate.
- Fill the moulds with the mousse, and chill for 10 minutes.
- Turn out onto a plate to serve.

Panna cotta
serves 6

ingredients
750ml/1¼pt double cream
3 teaspoons powdered gelatine

1 vanilla pod, split lengthways
75g/3oz caster sugar

- Lightly grease the insides of six 150ml/5fl oz ramekins with butter.
- Put 3 tablespoons of the double cream in a small bowl, sprinkle the gelatine in an even layer over the surface and leave until spongy.
- Put the remaining cream in a pan with the vanilla pod and sugar. Heat gently, stirring until almost boiling. Remove from the heat and discard the vanilla pod.
- Whisk the gelatine into the cream mixture until dissolved. Pour into the ramekins, and chill for 2 hours.

• •

Iced honey & lemon mousse
serves 4

ingredients
4½ large lemons
1 egg white
6 tablespoons clear honey

- Trim the stalk end from 4 of the lemons so that they stand up. Cut off the tops and seat side. Using a knife and a teaspoon, score around the insides of the lemons and scrape out the flesh. Purée the flesh in a blender or food processor until smooth, then strain into a jug. Put the hollowed lemon skins and tops on a small tray, and freeze.
- Finely grate the zest of the ½ lemon and set aside. In a bowl, whisk the egg white until stiff peaks form. Gradually whisk in the honey until the mixture is thick and shiny. Slowly whisk in 75ml/3fl oz of the lemon juice, and fold in the zest.
- Transfer to a freezer container, and freeze for 2 hours until frozen 2.5cm/1in from the sides of the container. Scrape into a bowl and beat until smooth. Cover with cling film and freeze until set.
- Spoon into a piping bag, and pipe into the frozen lemon skins. Add the tops and freeze until ready to serve.

Mango sorbet
serves 8

ingredients

175g/6oz granulated sugar
3 green cardamom pods, split

2 ripe mangoes
3 egg whites

- Put the sugar and cardamom pods in a heavy saucepan, pour in 600ml/1pt cold water and heat gently, stirring occasionally, until the sugar has dissolved. Increase the heat and bring to the boil, then boil for 7 minutes without stirring. Remove from the heat and leave to cool.
- Meanwhile, peel the mangoes and remove as much flesh as possible from the stones. Purée the flesh in a blender or food processor, then pour into a shallow container.
- Strain the cooled syrup into the mango purée, and stir well to mix. Freeze, uncovered, for 3 hours. Turn the mango mixture into a bowl, and break up the crystals with a fork.
- Whisk the egg whites until stiff. Fold the egg whites into the mango mixture until evenly mixed, then return the mixture to the container. Cover and freeze overnight. Transfer to the refrigerator for 20 minutes to soften slightly before serving.

Orange freeze
serves 4

ingredients

4 large oranges
300g/11oz vanilla ice cream

- Using a sharp knife, carefully cut a lid off each orange. Scoop out the flesh, discarding any pips and thick pith. Put the shells and lids in the freezer, and chop the orange flesh, reserving the juice.
- Whisk together the orange juice, flesh and vanilla ice cream until well blended. Pour into a freezer container, Cover and freeze for 24 hours, stirring occasionally.
- Put 2 large scoops of the ice-cream mixture into each of the frozen orange shells, so that it is overflowing at the top. Put the lids on top, and return to the freezer for 3 hours before serving.

Marshmallow ice cream
serves 4

ingredients

75g/3oz dark chocolate, broken
  into pieces

175g/6oz white marshmallows
150ml/5fl oz milk
300ml/10fl oz double cream

- Put the chocolate and marshmallows into a pan and pour in the milk. Warm over a very low heat until the chocolate and marshmallows have melted. Remove from the heat and leave the mixture to cool completely.
- Whisk the cream until thick, then fold it into the cold chocolate mixture with a metal spoon. Pour into a 450g/1lb loaf tin and freeze for at least 2 hours.

Blackcurrant jelly with coulis
serves 8

ingredients

6 sheets of leaf gelatine
450g/1lb blackcurrants
225g/8oz caster sugar

150ml/5fl oz ruby port
2 tablespoons crème de cassis

- In a small bowl, soak the gelatine in 75ml/3fl oz water until soft. Put the blackcurrants, sugar and 300ml/10fl oz water in a large saucepan. Bring to the boil, reduce the heat and simmer for 20 minutes.
- Strain, reserving the cooking liquid in a large jug. Put half of the blackcurrants in a bowl, and pour 4 tablespoons of the reserved cooking liquid over them. Set the bowl and jug aside.
- Squeeze the water out of the gelatine, and put in a small saucepan with the port, crème de cassis and 75ml/3fl oz water. Heat gently to dissolve the gelatine, but do not allow the mixture to boil. Stir the gelatine mixture into the jug of blackcurrant liquid until well mixed.
- Put eight individual jelly moulds in a roasting tin. Fill with the port mixture. Chill for at least 6 hours until set.
- Tip the bowl of blackcurrants into a blender or food processor, and purée until smooth.
- To serve, turn each jelly out onto a serving plate, and spoon the coulis around each jelly. Decorate with the remaining blackcurrants.

Peach & ginger pashka

serves 4

ingredients

350g/12oz cottage cheese
2 ripe peaches, stoned and
   roughly chopped
100g/4oz Greek-style yogurt
2 pieces of preserved stem
   ginger in syrup, drained
   and chopped (reserve
   2 tablespoons syrup)
½ teaspoon vanilla essence

- Drain the cottage cheese and rub through a sieve into a large bowl.
- Add the peaches, yogurt, stem ginger and reserved syrup, and vanilla essence.
- Line a new, clean flower pot with a piece of cheesecloth. Tip in the cheese mixture, wrap the cloth over the top and weigh down. Leave over a bowl in a cool place to drain overnight.
- The next day, unwrap, invert onto a plate and serve.

Cinnamon & nutmeg ice cream

serves 8

ingredients

½ teaspoon ground cinnamon
½ teaspoon ground nutmeg
50g/2oz caster sugar
150ml/5fl oz double cream
250g/9oz mascarpone cheese
400ml/14fl oz fresh custard

- Put the cinnamon, nutmeg, sugar and cream in a small heavy pan. Bring slowly to the boil, then put to one side to cool.
- Put the mascarpone in a large bowl and beat until smooth. Stir in the custard and the cooled spiced cream. Pour the mixture into a shallow freezer container, and freeze for 2½ hours.
- Beat to break up the ice crystals, and freeze for a further 2½ hours before serving.

Turkish delight ice cream
serves 12

ingredients

350g/12oz pink Turkish delight,
   cut into small pieces
5 tablespoons water
700ml/1pt 4fl oz fresh custard
300ml/10fl oz double cream
3 tablespoons rose water

- Put the Turkish delight in a pan with 5 tablespoons water, and cook over a low heat, stirring, until the mixture has almost melted. Stir into the custard.
- Lightly whip the cream until it forms soft peaks, then fold gently into the custard. Stir in the rose water.
- Pour the mixture into a 1.2-litre/2pt loaf tin lined with cling film, and freeze for at least 4 hours.

Orange granita
serves 6

ingredients

4 large oranges
1 large lemon
150g/5oz granulated sugar

- Thinly pare the orange and lemon zest, and set aside for decoration. Cut the fruits in half, and squeeze the juices into a jug. Set aside.
- Heat the sugar and 500ml/16fl oz water in a heavy saucepan, stirring until the sugar has dissolved. Bring to the boil, then boil without stirring until a syrup forms.
- Remove the syrup from the heat, add some of the orange and lemon zest, and shake the pan. Cover and leave to cool.
- Strain the sugar syrup into a shallow freezer container, and add the fruit juice. Stir well to mix, then freeze, uncovered, for about 4 hours until slushy. Remove the half-frozen mixture from the freezer and mix with a fork, then return to the freezer and freeze again for at least 4 hours.
- To serve, turn into a bowl and leave to soften for about 10 minutes, then break up again and pile into long-stemmed glasses. Decorate with strips of orange and lemon zest.

Vanilla ice cream
serves 6

ingredients

600ml/1pt double cream
1 vanilla pod, split lengthways
pared zest of 1 lemon

4 eggs, beaten, plus 2 egg yolks
175g/6oz caster sugar

- Put the cream in a heavy saucepan and heat gently, whisking.
- Add the vanilla pod, lemon zest, eggs and yolks to the pan, and heat until the mixture nearly reaches boiling point. Reduce the heat and cook for 8–10 minutes, whisking continuously, until thickened.
- Stir the sugar into the cream mixture, set aside and leave to cool. Once cool, strain the mixture through a sieve.
- Slit open the vanilla pod, scrape out the tiny black seeds and stir into the cream. Pour the mixture into a shallow freezing container with a lid, and freeze overnight until set.

Citrus jelly
serves 4

ingredients

3 oranges
1 lemon
1 lime

75g/3oz caster sugar
1 tablespoon powdered gelatine

- With a sharp knife, cut all the peel and white pith from 1 orange and carefully remove the segments. Arrange the segments in the bottom of a 1.2-litre/2pt mould.
- Grate the zest from the lemon, lime and 1 orange. Put all the grated zest in a saucepan with 300ml/10fl oz water and the sugar. Heat gently until the sugar has dissolved. Remove from the heat.
- Squeeze the juice from the lemon, lime and 2 oranges, and stir into the pan. Strain the liquid into a measuring jug to remove the zest. You should have about 600ml/1pt; if necessary, make up the amount with water. Sprinkle the gelatine over the mixture, and stir until dissolved.
- Pour the jelly liquid over the orange segments in the bowl. Refrigerate until set before serving.

Key lime sorbet

serves 4

ingredients

275g/10oz granulated sugar
grated zest of 1 lime
175ml/6fl oz freshly squeezed
    lime juice
25g/1oz icing sugar

- In a small heavy saucepan, dissolve the granulated sugar in 600ml/1pt water, without stirring, over a medium heat. When the sugar has dissolved, boil the syrup for 5–6 minutes. Remove from the heat and leave to cool.
- Mix the cooled sugar syrup and lime zest in a bowl. Stir well. Add the lime juice, and stir in the icing sugar. Freeze the mixture overnight in a shallow freezer container, occasionally breaking up any large crystals with a fork if necessary.

Chocolate rum pots

serves 6

ingredients

225g/8oz dark chocolate (at
    least 70% cocoa solids)
4 eggs, separated
75g/3oz caster sugar
50ml/2fl oz dark rum
75ml/3fl oz double cream

- Melt the chocolate in a heatproof bowl set over a pan of simmering water, and leave to cool slightly.
- Using an electric whisk or balloon whisk, whisk the egg yolks with the caster sugar in a bowl until pale and fluffy.
- Drizzle the chocolate into the mixture and fold through together with the rum and double cream.
- Whisk the egg whites in a separate bowl until standing in soft peaks. Gently fold the egg whites into the chocolate mixture in two batches. Divide the mixture between six ramekins, and chill for at least 2 hours before serving.

Chocolate ice-cream sandwiches
serves 6

ingredients
6 amaretti biscuits
12 dark chocolate digestive biscuits
500ml/16fl oz vanilla ice cream

- Put the amaretti biscuits in a blender or food processor, and whiz until they form coarse crumbs.
- Take one of the digestive biscuits and spread a 2.5cm/1in layer of ice cream on its non-chocolate side. Sandwich another biscuit on top, chocolate side uppermost. Squeeze the biscuits gently together and smooth the ice cream around the edges. Repeat with the remaining biscuits and ice cream.
- Roll the edges of the biscuit sandwiches in the crushed amaretti biscuits to coat them, then place on a tray in the freezer. Freeze for at least 2 hours before serving.

● ●

Mixed berry sorbet
serves 6

ingredients
225g/8oz strawberries
225g/8oz redcurrants
100g/4oz caster sugar

150ml/5fl oz sparkling white wine
2 egg whites

- Hull the strawberries and remove the stalks from the redcurrants, then put all the berries in a saucepan with 2 tablespoons water. Cook for about 10 minutes until soft. Press the berries through a sieve to form a purée.
- Dissolve the sugar in 150ml/5fl oz water over a low heat, and boil gently for 10 minutes. Leave to cool for 1 hour.
- Stir the wine and fruit purée into the cooled syrup. Pour into a shallow freezer container, and freeze for 3 hours.
- Transfer the frozen mixture to a chilled basin, and break up with a fork. Whisk the egg whites until stiff and fold into the mixture. Return to the freezer for 3 hours. Transfer to the refrigerator 30 minutes before serving to soften slightly.

Strawberry frozen yogurt
serves 4

ingredients
400g/14oz canned strawberries
and syrup
500ml/16fl oz Greek-style
yogurt
125ml/4fl oz single cream

- Put the strawberries and syrup in a blender or food processor, and purée until smooth. Add the yogurt and cream, and continue to purée until a uniform colour is achieved.
- Pour into a shallow freezer container, cover with cling film and freeze until set.
- After 30 minutes, remove from the freezer and stir with a fork before returning. Repeat 1 hour later, then leave until set before serving.

Vanilla & caramel parfait
serves 4

ingredients
100g/4oz butter
150g/5oz Demerara sugar
175ml/6fl oz single cream
450ml/¾pt vanilla ice cream

- Heat the butter in a heavy pan. Add the sugar and stir over a low heat, without boiling, until the sugar has dissolved.
- Increase the heat and simmer without boiling for 3 minutes or until golden. Remove from the heat and allow to cool slightly.
- Layer the caramel sauce with the vanilla ice cream into four tall parfait glasses. Serve immediately.

Strawberry & raspberry parfait

serves 6

ingredients

75g/3oz strawberry-flavoured
  jelly crystals
450ml/¾pt boiling water
250g/9oz strawberries, hulled
  and chopped
500g/1lb 2oz vanilla ice cream
100g/4oz raspberries

- Stir the strawberry crystals in the boiling water until the crystals have dissolved, then refrigerate until set.
- Purée 100g/4oz of the strawberries in a blender or food processor for 30 seconds.
- Layer the jelly, ice cream, remaining strawberries, raspberries and purée in six parfait glasses. Serve immediately.

Ginger parfait

serves 10

ingredients

150g/5oz gingernut biscuits
15g/½oz butter, melted
2 eggs

175g/6oz icing sugar
1 tablespoon ground ginger
500ml/18fl oz double cream

- Put the biscuits in a blender or food processor, and whiz briefly to make crumbs.
- Use some of the melted butter to grease a 900g/2lb loaf tin. Line the tin with cling film, then brush the cling film with the rest of the butter. Spoon about 3 tablespoons of the biscuit crumbs into the loaf tin, and put in the freezer for at least an hour.
- Put the eggs, icing sugar and ginger in a bowl, and whisk together for 5–10 minutes until the mixture is thick and mousse-like.
- Whisk the cream until soft peaks form, then fold into the egg mixture. Put 3 tablespoons of the biscuit crumbs to one side, then fold in the remainder. Pour the mixture into the prepared loaf tin, and sprinkle with the reserved biscuit crumbs.
- Cover with cling film and freeze for at least 3 hours. Serve cut into 1cm/½in slices.

Cinnamon ice cream
serves 6

ingredients

3 egg yolks

100g/4oz light muscovado sugar

2 cinnamon sticks, broken in half

300ml/10fl oz milk

300ml/10fl oz double cream

- Whisk together the egg yolks and sugar until thick and pale. Slowly heat the cinnamon sticks in the milk until just boiling. Remove from the heat.
- Discard the cinnamon, and stir the milk into the egg yolk mixture. Return the mixture to the pan and cook, stirring, over a low heat for about 15 minutes until thickened.
- Remove from the heat, strain into a clean freezerproof bowl and leave until cold. Stir occasionally to prevent a skin forming.
- Stir the cream into the custard. Put the bowl in the freezer and leave for 2–3 hours until the mixture is set 2.5cm/1in from the edges. Whisk the mixture to break down the large ice crystals, return to the freezer for a further 1 hour, then whisk again. Transfer to a freezer container and freeze until firm.
- Transfer to the refrigerator to soften slightly 30 minutes before serving.

Mango fool
serves 6

ingredients

3 large mangoes

250ml/9fl oz custard

400ml/14fl oz double cream

- Peel and stone the mangoes, and purée the flesh in a blender or food processor.
- Add the custard and blend to combine.
- Whip the cream until soft peaks form, then gently fold into the mango mixture until just combined.
- Pour the mixture into a serving dish or individual glasses. Refrigerate for at least 1 hour before serving.

Blueberry sundae
serves 4

ingredients

800g/1¾lb fresh blueberries
2 tablespoons lemon juice
1 teaspoon vanilla essence

2 teaspoons cornflour
350g/12oz granulated sugar
600ml/1pt vanilla yogurt

- Reserving a few blueberries for decoration, purée the blueberries in a blender or food processor. In a large saucepan, combine the blueberry purée with the lemon juice and vanilla essence. Cook over a medium heat for 5 minutes.
- Combine the cornflour and 2 tablespoons water, and add to the fruit mixture, stirring constantly for about 3 minutes until thickened. Remove from the heat, and stir in the sugar.
- Using the back of a spoon, press the mixture through a sieve to remove the blueberry skins. Layer in tall glasses, alternating with the vanilla yogurt. Decorate with reserved blueberries. Serve immediately or chill until needed.

Orange-blossom jelly
serves 4

ingredients

75g/3oz caster sugar
25g/1oz powdered gelatine

600ml/1pt fresh orange juice
2 tablespoons orange-flower water

- Put the sugar and 150ml/5fl oz water in a small saucepan, Heat gently to dissolve the sugar. Pour into a heatproof bowl and leave to cool.
- Sprinkle the gelatine over the surface of the syrup. Leave to stand until the gelatine has absorbed all the liquid.
- Gently melt the gelatine over a saucepan of simmering water until it becomes clear. Leave to cool.
- When the gelatine is cold, mix with the orange juice and orange-flower water. Pour into a jelly mould, and chill in the refrigerator for at least 2 hours before serving.

Tuscan pudding
serves 4

ingredients

15g/½oz butter
75g/3oz mixed dried fruit
250g/9oz ricotta cheese
3 egg yolks
50g/2oz caster sugar
1 teaspoon ground cinnamon
grated zest of 1 orange

- Preheat the oven to 180°C/ 350°F/Gas mark 4. Lightly grease four mini pudding basins or ramekins with the butter.
- Put the dried fruit in a bowl and cover with warm water. Leave to soak for 10 minutes.
- Beat the ricotta cheese with the egg yolks in a bowl. Stir in the caster sugar, cinnamon and orange zest, and mix to combine.
- Drain the dried fruit in a sieve set over a bowl. Mix the drained fruit with the ricotta cheese mixture. Spoon the mixture into the basins or ramekins.
- Bake in the oven for 15 minutes. Leave to cool, then refrigerate overnight before serving.

Lemon curd ice cream
serves 6

ingredients

6 eggs
100g/4oz butter
100g/4oz caster sugar
grated zest and juice of
   4 lemons
700ml/1¼pt thick Greek-style
   yogurt

- Put the eggs, butter, sugar and lemon juice and zest in a heavy pan, and cook gently over a low heat, stirring, until the mixture coats the back of a spoon.
- Leave to cool slightly, then whisk in the yogurt. Put in a shallow freezer container and freeze until set, stirring occasionally to break up the ice crystals.
- Transfer to the refrigerator 20 minutes before serving.

Plum & cardamom fool
serves 4

ingredients
1kg/2¼lb dessert plums, stoned
  and sliced
100g/4oz caster sugar
4 greed cardamom pods, split and
  seeds removed and crushed

2 tablespoons fresh lemon juice
150ml/5fl oz fresh custard
200ml/7fl oz Greek-style yogurt

- Set aside 8 slices of plum for decoration. Put the remaining plums, sugar, cardamom seeds and lemon juice in a pan. Cover and bring to the boil, then simmer for 20–25 minutes until the plums are soft. Pour into a cold bowl, and leave for 30 minutes.
- Lift the plums out of the bowl with a slotted spoon, reserving the juices. Purée in a blender or food processor, and pour into a bowl.
- Boil the reserved juices for 3–4 minutes until reduced to 3 tablespoons, then stir into the plum purée with the custard and yogurt until smooth. Spoon into four tumblers and chill for 2 hours.
- Decorate with the reserved plum slices and serve.

Coffee granita
serves 4

ingredients
100g/4oz granulated sugar
250ml/9fl oz very strong
espresso coffee, cooled

- Gently heat the sugar and 500ml/18fl oz water until the sugar has dissolved. Bring to the boil, stirring occasionally. Remove from the heat and allow to cool.
- Stir the coffee and sugar syrup together, put in a freezer container and freeze until solid.
- Just before serving, turn the granita out of the freezer container and chop into chunks. Put in a blender or food processor, and briefly whiz until it forms small crystals.
- Spoon the granita into tall glasses, and serve immediately.

Champagne granita
serves 4

ingredients
100g/4oz granulated sugar
400ml/14fl oz pink Champagne

- Put the sugar and 200ml/7fl oz water in a heavy saucepan. Heat gently, stirring occasionally, until the sugar has dissolved, then boil without stirring until a light sugar syrup is formed. Remove from the heat and allow to cool.
- Mix the Champagne and sugar syrup together, pour into a freezer container and freeze overnight.
- Flake into tall glasses to serve.

● ●

Pineapple sorbet
serves 4

ingredients
850ml/1pt 8fl oz unsweetened
    pineapple juice
375g/13oz granulated sugar
3 tablespoons freshly squeezed
    lemon juice
1 egg white, lightly beaten

- Stir the pineapple juice and sugar in a large pan over a low heat until the sugar has dissolved. Bring to the boil, reduce the heat and simmer for 5 minutes. Skim off any scum that rises to the surface.
- Stir in the lemon juice and pour into a metal tray. Cover with a sheet of greaseproof paper and freeze for 2 hours.
- Transfer the mixture to a blender or food processor, and purée to a slush, then return to the tray and put the tray back in the freezer.
- Repeat the beating and freezing twice more, then beat for a final time, adding the egg white. Process until smooth. Return to the tray, cover with greaseproof paper and freeze until firm.

Brazilian coffee bananas
serves 4

ingredients

4 bananas
1 tablespoon instant coffee
  granules
1 tablespoon hot water
25g/1oz dark muscovado sugar
250ml/9fl oz Greek-style yogurt
2 teaspoons flaked almonds,
  toasted

- Peel and mash 3 of the bananas with a fork in a large mixing bowl. Reserve the remaining banana for decoration. Dissolve the coffee in the hot water and stir into the mashed bananas.
- Spoon a little of the mashed banana mixture into four serving dishes, and sprinkle each one with sugar. Top with a spoonful of yogurt, then repeat the layers until the ingredients have all been used. Refrigerate for 30 minutes.
- To finish, quickly peel the reserved banana and cut into slices. Use to top each dish, and sprinkle with the almonds. Serve immediately.

Raspberry fool
serves 4

ingredients

300g/11oz fresh raspberries
50g/2oz icing sugar
300ml/10fl oz cr?me fra?che

½ teaspoon vanilla essence
2 egg whites

- Put the raspberries and sugar in a blender or food processor, and purée until smooth.
- Reserve 1 tablespoon of the crème fraîche for decorating, and the remaining crème fraîche and the vanilla essence in a bowl. Stir in the raspberry purée.
- Whisk the egg whites in a separate bowl until stiff peaks form. Using a metal spoon, gently fold the egg whites into the raspberry mixture until fully combined.
- Spoon the raspberry fool into individual serving dishes, and chill for at least 1 hour. Decorate with the reserved crème fraîche.

Chocolate banana sundae
serves 4

ingredients
50g/2oz dark chocolate (at least 70% cocoa solids), broken into small pieces
100g/4oz golden syrup
15g/½oz butter
1 tablespoon rum
150ml/5fl oz double cream
12 scoops vanilla ice cream
4 bananas, sliced, tossed in a little lemon juice
75g/3oz flaked almonds, toasted

- Put the chocolate in a heatproof bowl with the syrup and butter. Heat over a pan of simmering water until melted, stirring until well combined. Remove the bowl from the heat, and stir in the rum.
- Whip the cream until just holding its shape. Put a scoop of vanilla ice cream in the bottom of each of four tall sundae glasses. Top with the sliced banana, some chocolate sauce and a sprinkling of nuts.
- Repeat the layers, finishing with a generous dollop of cream.

Apricot and orange jellies
serves 4

ingredients
225g/8oz ready-to-eat dried apricots
300ml/10fl oz unsweetened orange juice
2 tablespoons freshly squeezed lemon juice
3 teaspoon clear honey
1 tablespoon powdered gelatine
4 tablespoons boiling water

- Put the apricots in a saucepan and pour in the orange juice. Bring to the boil, cover and simmer for 15 to 20 minutes until the apricots are plump and soft. Leave to cool for 10 minutes.
- Transfer the mixture to a blender or food processor, and purée until smooth. Stir in the lemon juice and add the honey. Pour the mixture into a measuring jug, and make up to 600ml/1pt with cold water.
- Dissolve the gelatine in the boiling water, and pour into the apricot mixture. Stir to mix completely.
- Pour the mixture into four individual 150ml/5fl oz moulds. Leave to chill until set before serving.

Chocolate brandy cream

serves 4

ingredients

175g/6oz dark chocolate (at
   least 70% cocoa solids),
   broken into pieces
300ml/10fl oz whipping cream
2 tablespoons brandy
1 teaspoon coffee essence
1 egg white

- Put the chocolate in a heatproof bowl placed over a saucepan of simmering water, and leave to melt slowly, stirring occasionally. Allow to cool slightly.
- Pour the cream into a small bowl and whip until soft peaks form.
- Gently stir the brandy and coffee essence into the chocolate. Mix together gently until blended, then fold in the whipped cream using a metal spoon.
- Briskly whisk the egg white in a small bowl until stiff, then gently fold into the chocolate mixture using a metal spoon.
- Spoon the mixture into four tall glasses, and chill for at least 2 hours before serving.

Quick apricot whip

serves 4

ingredients

400g/14oz canned apricot
   halves in juice
1 tablespoon Grand Marnier
175ml/6fl oz Greek-style yogurt
1 tablespoon flaked almonds,
   toasted

- Drain the juice from the apricots, and put the fruit and Grand Marnier in a blender or food processor. Purée until smooth.
- Spoon alternate layers of fruit purée and yogurt into four tall glasses. Top with almonds and chill until ready to serve.

Raspberry sorbet
serves 6–8

ingredients

450g/1lb raspberries
175g/6oz sugar

50ml/2fl oz freshly squeezed
lemon juice

- Purée the raspberries in a blender or food processor, and strain through a sieve.
- Put the sugar and 300ml/10fl oz water in a heavy saucepan, and boil for 5 minutes. Remove from the heat and allow to cool. Add the lemon juice and 100ml/3½fl oz water and the raspberries.
- Freeze the mixture overnight in a shallow freezer container, occasionally breaking up any large crystals with a fork if necessary.

Strawberry shortcake
serves 4

ingredients

450g/1lb strawberries, sliced
¼ teaspoon honey
2 teaspoons freshly squeezed
    orange juice
50g/2oz caster sugar
450g/1lb plain flour
4 tablespoons baking powder

½ teaspoon salt
grated zest of 1 orange
50g/2oz butter
50g/2oz solid shortening
100g/4oz sour cream
600ml/1pt whipping cream

- Preheat the oven to 200°C/400°F/Gas mark 6.
- Combine the strawberries, honey and orange juice in a bowl, and leave to stand at room temperature for 1 hour.
- Sift all the dry ingredients together into a bowl. Add the orange zest, butter and shortening, and work into the flour mixture thoroughly.
- Using a fork, lightly mix in the sour cream to form a soft dough. Roll the dough out onto a lightly floured work surface until 2.5cm/1in thick, and cut into four circles. Put on ungreased baking parchment on a baking tray, and bake in the oven for about 20 minutes until cgolden.
- To serve, whip the cream into soft peaks. Top each shortcake with the berry mixture, and serve with a dollop of whipped cream.

Lemon syllabub
serves 6

ingredients
100g/4oz caster sugar
zest and juice of 2 lemons
3 tablespoons brandy
600ml/1pt double cream

- Whisk together the caster sugar, lemon juice and zest, and brandy.
- In another bowl, whisk the double cream until thick, then slowly whisk in the lemon mixture. Pour into wine glasses, and refrigerate overnight before serving.

● ●

Tiramisù
serves 6

ingredients
500ml/18fl oz strong espresso coffee, cooled
50ml/2fl oz Marsala wine
2 eggs, separated
50g/2oz caster sugar

225g/oz mascarpone cheese
225ml/8fl oz double cream
16 large savoiardi (sponge finger biscuits)
2 tablespoons dark cocoa powder

- Combine the coffee and Marsala in a bowl, and set aside. Beat the egg yolks and sugar in a bowl with an electric mixer for 3 minutes or until thick and pale. Add the mascarpone and mix. Transfer to a large bowl. Whisk the cream in a separate bowl until soft peaks form, then fold into the mascarpone mixture.
- Whisk the egg whites in a small clean dry bowl until soft peaks form. Fold quickly and lightly into the cream mixture.
- Dip half of the biscuits into the coffee mixture, drain off any excess and arrange in a large glass serving dish. Spread half of the mascarpone cream mixture over the biscuits.
- Dip the remaining biscuits into the remaining coffee mixture, and repeat layering. Smooth the surface, and dust liberally with the cocoa powder. Chill in the refrigerator overnight before serving.

Rum & raisin ice cream
serves 8

ingredients

250g/9oz raisins
100ml/3½fl oz dark rum
4 large egg yolks
3 tablespoons golden syrup

1 tablespoon treacle
600ml/1pt double cream,
 whipped

- Put the raisins in a pan, add the rum and bring to the boil. Remove from the heat and leave the mixture to steep.
- Put the egg yolks, syrup and treacle in a small bowl. Whisk with an electric mixer for 2–3 minutes until it has a mousse-like consistency. Pour into the cream, and whisk for 3–4 minutes until thick.
- Pour the mixture into a large roasting tin, and freeze for 1 hour or until it begins to harden around the edges.
- Add the soaked fruit and any remaining liquid to the ice cream, and mix well. Put back in the freezer for 45 minutes, then spoon into a sealable container and freeze for at least 2½ hours.

Brandy trifle
serves 6

ingredients

20cm/8in sponge cake, cut into
 small cubes
150g/5oz apricot jam
125ml/4fl oz brandy
75g/3oz apricot jelly crystals
600ml/1pt boiling water
2 bananas
450ml/¾pt prepared custard
225ml/8fl oz double cream,
 whipped
50g/2oz toasted almonds,
 chopped
pulp of 2 passion fruit

- Put the sponge cubes in a large serving bowl. Combine the jam, brandy and 50ml/2fl oz water, and sprinkle over the sponge.
- Add the jelly crystals to the boiling water, and stir until dissolved. Pour into a rectangular dish and refrigerate until set.
- Cut the jelly into cubes. Scatter over the sponge. Peel and slice the bananas. Top the jelly with the sliced bananas and the custard.
- Decorate the trifle with the whipped cream, almonds and passion fruit. Chill until needed.

Chocolate fluff
serves 2

ingredients
3 egg whites
3 tablespoons caster sugar
½ teaspoon vanilla essence
150ml/5fl oz cream
2 tablespoons melted dark
    chocolate (at least 70%
    cocoa solids)
chopped nuts, to serve

- Beat the egg whites until stiff, then gradually stir in the sugar and vanilla essence.
- Whip the cream until firm. Fold into the egg whites. Gradually fold in the chocolate.
- Put into individual glasses, chill until needed and serve sprinkled with chopped nuts.

Redcurrant filo baskets
serves 6

ingredients
3 sheets filo pastry
1 tablespoon sunflower oil
175g/6oz redcurrants

250ml/9fl oz Greek-style yogurt
1 teaspoon icing sugar

- Preheat the oven to 200°C/400°F/Gas mark 6. Cut the sheets of filo pastry into 18 squares measuring 10cm/4in.
- Brush each filo square very thinly with the oil, then arrange 3 squares in each hole of a six-hole muffin tin, placing each one at a different angle so that they form star-shaped baskets. Bake for 6–8 minutes until crisp and golden. Lift the baskets out carefully. Leave to cool on a wire rack.
- Set aside a few redcurrants for decoration, and stir the rest into the Greek yogurt. Spoon the mixture into the filo baskets. Decorate with the reserved redcurrants, and sprinkle with the icing sugar to serve.

Frozen egg nog

serves 4

ingredients
2 egg yolks
3 tablespoons caster sugar
2 tablespoons dark rum
1 tablespoon brandy
300ml/10fl oz double cream

- Put the egg yolks, rum and brandy in a pan over simmering water and whisk until the mixture is thick and creamy. Remove from the heat and continue whisking until the mixture has cooled slightly. Transfer to a freezerproof container.
- Whip the cream until it stands in soft peaks, then fold carefully into the egg mixture.
- Freeze for a minimum of 4 hours before serving.

Glazed nectarine tart

serves 6

ingredients
175g/6oz ready-to-roll
   puff pastry
25g/1oz butter, melted
600g/1¼lb nectarines,
   quartered, stoned and sliced
2 tablespoons apricot jam

- Preheat the oven to 230°C/ 450°F/Gas mark 8.
- Roll out the pastry thinly to a 28cm/11in round. Put on a non-stick baking sheet ,and prick well all over with a fork. Bake for 8–10 minutes until well browned and cooked through.
- Brush some of the melted butter over the pastry, and arrange the fruit slices on top, right to the edges of the pastry. Drizzle with the remaining butter and grill for 5 minutes or until the fruit is just tinged with colour. Cool slightly.
- Warm the apricot jam with a little water, and brush over the fruit to glaze. Serve warm or cold.

Chocolate cream pudding
serves 6

ingredients
25g/1oz cornflour
75g/3oz unsweetened cocoa
125g/4½oz Demerera sugar
750ml/1¼pt milk
2 teaspoons vanilla essence

• Sift the cornflour with the cocoa and sugar, and put in a saucepan.
• Gradually stir in the milk over a low heat until the mixture is free of lumps. Add the vanilla when slightly cooled, then pour the pudding mixture into a serving dish and refrigerate until needed.

Mango & lime mousse
serves 6

ingredients
grated zest and juice of 2 limes
8g/⅓oz powdered gelatine
3 eggs plus 2 egg yolks
50g/2oz caster sugar
300ml/10fl oz mango purée
100ml/4fl oz double cream, lightly whipped

• Put the lime juice in a small heatproof bowl, sprinkle in the gelatine and leave to soak for 10 minutes.
• In a large bowl, whisk together the whole eggs, egg yolks and sugar for 4–5 minutes until thick and mousse-like. Gently fold the mango purée, whipped cream and the lime zest into the mousse mixture.
• Put the heatproof bowl over a pan of simmering water to dissolve the gelatine and lime juice mixture. Lightly fold into the mango mixture, making sure that everything is evenly combined.
• Pour the mousse into glasses, put in the freezer for 20 minutes, then transfer to the refrigerator for at least 1 hour before serving chilled.

Fruit Desserts

We should all eat more fruit, and here is a chapter of delicious recipes to appeal to all tastes. This chapter offers a range of tempting recipes from simple, fresh fruit salads, to richer and more substantial desserts, such as Eton Mess, Peach Melba, and Californian Baked Pears. And many of these recipes can be adapted to use different fruit or combinations of fruit, so you have plenty of scope to experiment.

Grilled pink grapefruit

serves 4

ingredients
2 pink grapefruit
1 teaspoon granulated sugar
4 scoops vanilla ice cream

- Halve the grapefruit and cut round the edge of each, between the pith and the flesh. Separate the segments. Sprinkle each grapefruit with sugar.
- Put in ramekins to keep them flesh side up, and put on a grill pan. Grill for 2–3 minutes until starting to lightly brown. Put a scoop of vanilla ice cream on top of each, and serve immediately.

Lime sherbet

serves 6

ingredients
8 limes
75g/3oz caster sugar
pinch of salt
crushed ice, to serve

- Squeeze the limes and pour the juice into a large jug. Add the sugar and salt. Stir until dissolved
- Pour in 1.5 litres/2½pt water, and top up with plenty of ice to serve.

Fruit fondue

serves 2

ingredients
50g/2oz soft cheese
150ml/5fl oz hazelnut yogurt
1 teaspoon vanilla essence
1 teaspoon caster sugar
selection of fresh fruits for
   dipping, such as strawberries,
   satsumas, kiwi fruit, grapes,
   all cut into bite-size pieces

- Beat the soft cheese with the yogurt, vanilla essence and sugar in a bowl.
- Spoon the mixture into a glass serving dish set on a platter. Arrange the prepared fruits around the dip, and serve immediately.

Poached peaches with ginger
serves 4

ingredients
4 peaches, halved and stoned
125ml/4fl oz water
2 tablespoons lemon juice
1cm/1/2 in root ginger,
   peeled and grated
1 cinnamon stick
225g/8oz seedless white
   grapes, halved

- Preheat the oven to 180°C/
  350°F/Gas mark 4.
- Put the peach halves skin side up in
  a baking dish. Combine 125ml/
  4fl oz water, the lemon juice,
  ginger and cinnamon stick, and
  pour over the peaches. Poach in
  the oven for 30 minutes.
- Remove from the oven and arrange
  the peaches on four dessert plates.
  Top with the cooking juices, add
  the grapes and serve immediately.

Gooseberry cheese cooler
serves 4

ingredients
500g/1lb 2oz fresh
   gooseberries
finely grated zest and juice of
   1 small orange
1 tablespoon clear honey
250g/9oz cottage cheese

- Top and tail the gooseberries, and
  put them in a pan. Add the orange
  zest and juice, and cook gently,
  stirring occasionally, until the fruit
  is tender. Remove from the heat
  and stir in the honey.
- Purée the gooseberries and their
  juice in a blender or food
  processor until almost smooth.
  Allow to cool.
- Press the cottage cheese through
  a sieve until smooth. Stir half of the
  cooled gooseberry purée into the
  cottage cheese.
- To serve, spoon the cheese mixture
  into four serving glasses. Top each
  one with gooseberry purée, and
  serve chilled.

Nectarines with marzipan & yogurt

serves 4

ingredients
4 nectarines
75g/3oz marzipan
75ml/3fl oz Greek-style yogurt
3 amaretti biscuits, crushed

- Cut the nectarines in half, removing the stones. Cut the marzipan into 8 pieces, and press one piece into the stone cavity of each nectarine half. Preheat the grill.
- Spoon the Greek yogurt on top of the nectarines. Sprinkle the crushed amaretti biscuits over the yogurt. Put the fruits under the grill for 3–5 minutes until the yogurt starts to melt. Serve immediately.

Persian melon cups

serves 4

ingredients
2 small cantaloupe melons
225g/8oz strawberries, hulled and sliced
3 peaches, peeled and cubed
225g/8oz seedless white grapes
25g/1oz caster sugar
1 tablespoon rose water
1 tablespoon freshly squeezed lemon juice
crushed ice, to serve

- Carefully cut the melons in half and remove the seeds. Scoop out the flesh with a melon baller, taking care not to damage the skin. Reserve the melon shells.
- Put the strawberries in a large mixing bowl with the melon balls, peaches, grapes, sugar, rose water and lemon juice.
- Pile the fruit into the melon shells, and chill in the refrigerator for 2 hours.
- To serve, sprinkle with the crushed ice, and serve immediately.

Strawberries in grape jelly
serves 4

ingredients

500ml/18fl oz red grape juice
1 cinnamon stick
pared zest and juice of 1 small
 orange

1 tablespoon powdered gelatine
225g/8oz strawberries, hulled
 and chopped

- Pour the grape juice into a pan, and add the cinnamon stick and orange zest. Cook over a very low heat for 10 minutes, then strain the juice and discard the flavourings.
- Sprinkle the powdered gelatine over the orange juice in a small bowl. When the mixture is spongy, stir into the grape juice until it has completely dissolved.
- Allow the jelly to cool in the bowl until just beginning to set. Stir in the strawberries, and pour into a 900ml/1½pt mould. Chill until set.

● ●

Peach Melba
serves 4

ingredients

300g/11oz fresh raspberries
25g/1oz icing sugar
375g/13oz granulated sugar
1 vanilla pod, split lengthways
4 peaches
4 scoops vanilla ice cream

- Purée the raspberries and icing sugar together in a blender or food processor. Pass through a sieve and discard the seeds.
- Stir the sugar, vanilla pod and 600ml/1pt water in a pan over a low heat until the sugar has completely dissolved.
- Bring the sugar syrup to the boil, and add the peaches, ensuring that they are covered with the syrup. Simmer for 5 minutes or until tender, then remove the peaches with a slotted spoon and carefully remove the skin.
- To serve, put a scoop of ice cream on each plate, add a peach and spoon raspberry purée on top.

Blushing pears
serves 6

ingredients

6 dessert pears
300ml/10fl oz rosé wine
150ml/5fl oz cranberry juice
strip of thinly pared orange zest

1 cinnamon stick
4 whole cloves
1 bay leaf
75g/3oz caster sugar

- Thinly peel the pears with a sharp knife or vegetable peeler, leaving the stalks intact.
- Pour the wine and cranberry juice into a large heavy pan. Add the orange zest, cinnamon stick, cloves, bay leaf and sugar. Heat gently, stirring all the time, until the sugar has dissolved. Add the pears, standing them upright in the pan. Pour in enough cold water to barely cover them.
- Cover and cook gently for 20–30 minutes until just tender, turning and basting with the syrup occasionally. Using a slotted spoon, gently lift the pears out of the syrup and transfer to a serving dish.
- Bring the syrup to the boil, and boil rapidly for 10–15 minutes until it has reduced by half. Strain the syrup and pour over the pears. Serve.

• •

Sweet-stewed dried fruit
serves 4

ingredients

500g/1lb 2oz mixed dried
    fruit salad
450ml/¾pt apple juice
2 tablespoons clear honey
2 tablespoons brandy
grated zest and juice of
    1 lemon
grated zest and juice of
    1 orange

- Put the fruit salad, apple juice, honey, brandy, lemon and orange zests and juices in a small saucepan. Bring to the boil, and simmer for about 1 minute.
- Remove the pan from the heat, and allow the mixture to cool completely. Transfer to a large bowl, cover with cling film and chill in the refrigerator overnight.
- To serve, spoon the stewed fruit into four shallow dishes.

Grapefruit in apricot brandy

serves 4

ingredients

3 grapefruit
125ml/4fl oz apple juice
1½ teaspoons granulated sugar
2.5cm/1in piece of
   cinnamon stick
3 tablespoons apricot brandy
3 ready-to-eat dried apricots,
   chopped

- Cut off all the zest and pith from the grapefruit, working over a shallow pan to catch any juice. Push out the white core using the handle of a teaspoon, then thickly slice the grapefruit.
- Put the apple juice and sugar in the pan with the cinnamon stick. Bring to the boil, and simmer for 3 minutes. Add the fruit and simmer for 6–8 minutes.
- Remove the fruit from the pan and transfer to four warmed serving plates. Add the apricot brandy to the juice. Bring back to the boil, then spoon over the fruit and sprinkle with the chopped apricots. Serve immediately.

Grilled apple stack

serves 4

ingredients

4 large dessert apples, cored
   and peeled
25g/1oz butter
1 x 400g/14oz jar lime
   marmalade
4 scoops vanilla ice cream

- Cut the apples into thin slices across the core, and put on a lightly greased grill tray. Top each slice with a small piece of butter and ½ teaspoon lime marmalade.
- Cook under a hot grill until the butter has melted and the apple is golden brown.
- Serve 4 or 5 slices stacked on top of each other, with a scoop of vanilla ice cream alongside.

Red fruit salad
serves 4

ingredients
250g/9oz strawberries, hulled
and halved
100g/4oz raspberries
250g/9oz cherries, pitted
1 tablespoon Cointreau
1 tablespoon soft brown sugar

- Put the strawberries, raspberries and cherries in a bowl, drizzle with Cointreau, cover and set aside for 20 minutes.
- Put the sugar and 2 tablespoons water in a small pan. Stir over a gentle heat for 3 minutes or until the sugar has dissolved. Cool, pour over the fruit, and serve.

Snow-capped apples
serves 4

ingredients
4 small cooking apples
75ml/3fl oz orange marmalade
2 egg whites
50g/2oz caster sugar

- Preheat the oven to 180°C/350°F/Gas mark 4.
- Core the apples and score through the skins around the middle with a sharp knife.
- Put the apples in a wide ovenproof dish, and spoon 1 tablespoon marmalade into the centre of each. Cover and bake in the oven for 35–40 minutes until tender.
- Whisk the egg whites in a large bowl until stiff enough to hold soft peaks. Whisk in the sugar, then fold in the remaining marmalade.
- Spoon the meringue over the apples, then return to the oven for 10–15 minutes. Serve immediately.

Pineapple & passion fruit salsa
serves 6

ingredients

1 small pineapple
2 passion fruit
150ml/5fl oz Greek-style yogurt
2 tablespoons light
   muscovado sugar

- Cut the top and bottom of the pineapple. Using a large sharp knife, slice off the peel and remove any remaining 'eyes'. Slice the pineapple, and use a small pastry cutter or an apple corer to remove the tough core from each slice.
- Cut the passion fruit in half, and scoop the seeds and pulp into a bowl. Stir in the pineapple slices and yogurt. Cover and chill.
- Stir in the sugar just before serving.

Melon medley
serves 4

ingredients

½ cantaloupe melon
½ honeydew melon
½ watermelon
pulp from 2 passion fruit

- Cut the melons into bite-size pieces, or use a melon baller to slice into balls. Chill, covered, for 30 minutes.
- Drizzle with the passion fruit pulp before serving.

Melon & orange cups

serves 4

ingredients
2 small honeydew melons
1 grapefruit, peeled and
segmented
2 oranges, peeled and
segmented
50g/2oz roasted, unsalted
peanuts
25g/1oz light muscovado sugar
1/4 teaspoon ground cinnamon

- Halve the melons, scoop out the seeds and discard, then remove and chop the flesh. Reserve the melon shells.
- In a bowl, mix together the melon and citrus fruits. Pile the fruits back into the melon shells.
- Chop the peanuts and mix with the sugar and cinnamon. Sprinkle over the fruit and serve.

Grilled fresh figs
with crème fraîche

serves 4

ingredients
8 ripe fresh figs
225g/8oz crème fraîche
50g/2oz light muscovado sugar

- Preheat the grill to high. Lightly butter a shallow flameproof dish, large enough to accommodate the figs in a single layer.
- Cut the figs into quarters without cutting through the base, and gently open each one out a little. Spoon a dollop of crème fraîche into the centre of each fig.
- Sprinkle the sugar evenly between the figs. Put the figs in the prepared dish, and put the hot grill for 2 minutes or until the sugar has melted and the crème fraîche starts to run. Serve immediately.

Poached allspice pears

serves 4

ingredients

4 large dessert pears, peeled,
  cored and halved
300ml/10fl oz orange juice

2 teaspoons ground allspice
50g/2oz raisins
25g/1oz Demerara sugar

- Put the pears in a large saucepan. Add the orange juice, ground allspice, raisins and sugar, and heat gently, stirring, until the sugar has dissolved. Bring the mixture to the boil and continue to boil for 1 minute.
- Reduce the heat to low, and leave to simmer for about 10 minutes. Test to see if the pears are soft and cooked by inserting the tip of a sharp knife. When they are ready, remove the pears from the pan with a slotted spoon and transfer to serving plates.
- Serve hot with the syrup.

● ●

Spiced fruit platter

serves 6

ingredients

1 pineapple
2 papayas
1 small cantaloupe melon

juice of 2 limes
2 pomegranates
chat masala, to taste

- Cut away the top and base of the pineapple, then cut down the sides, removing all the dark 'eyes'. Cut the pineapple into thin slices. Using an apple corer, remove the hard, central core from each slice.
- Peel the papayas. Cut them in half, then into thin wedges. Halve the melon and remove the seeds from the middle. Cut into thin wedges and remove the skin.
- Arrange the fruit on six individual plates, and sprinkle with the lime juice. Cut the pomegranates in half, and scoop out the seeds, discarding any bitter pith. Scatter the seeds over the fruit.
- Serve, sprinkled with a little chat masala to taste.

Pineapple flambé

serves 4

ingredients
1 large ripe pineapple, about
    600g/1¼lb
25g/1oz butter
50g/2oz soft brown sugar
50ml/2fl oz freshly squeezed
    orange juice
25ml/1fl oz vodka
1 tablespoon slivered almonds,
    toasted

- Cut away the top and base of the pineapple, then cut down the sides, removing all the dark 'eyes'. Cut the pineapple into thin slices. Using an apple corer, remove the hard, central core from each slice.
- Melt the butter in a frying pan with the sugar. Add the orange juice and stir until hot. Add as many pineapple slices as the pan will hold, and cook for 1–2 minutes, turning once. As each pineapple slice browns, remove to a plate.
- Return all the pineapple slices to the pan, heat briefly, then pour over the vodka and carefully light with a long match. Let the flames die down, then sprinkle with the almonds and serve at once.

Bananas with chocolate marshmallow sauce

serves 4

ingredients
4 slightly unripe bananas
50g/2oz chocolate chips
24 mini marshmallows

- Preheat the oven to 160°C/325°F/Gas mark 3.
- Trim the ends of the bananas, leaving on the skins. Using a sharp knife, make a lengthways slit in each one.
- Gently prise open each banana, and fill with chocolate chips and marshmallows, then wrap each banana in foil. Bake in the oven for 15–20 minutes, and serve hot.

Strawberries Romanoff
serves 4

ingredients
750g/1lb 11oz strawberries,
  quartered
2 tablespoons Cointreau
½ teaspoon finely grated
orange zest
15g/½oz caster sugar
125ml/4fl oz double cream
20g/¾oz icing sugar

- Combine the strawberries, Cointreau, orange zest and caster sugar in a large bowl, cover and refrigerate for 1 hour. Drain the strawberries, reserving any juices.
- Purée about a quarter of the strawberries with the reserved juices in a blender or food processor. Divide the remaining strawberries among four glasses.
- Beat the cream and icing sugar until soft peaks form, then fold the strawberry purée through the whipped cream. Spoon the mixture over the top of the strawberries, cover and refrigerate until needed.

Summer fruits with ricotta & vanilla dip
serves 6

ingredients
250g/9oz ricotta cheese
250g/9oz mascarpone cheese
150ml/5fl oz crème fraîche
a few drops of vanilla essence
grated zest of 1 lemon
50g/2oz caster sugar
900g/2lb mixed fresh
  summer berries

- Beat the cheeses together with the crème fraîche, vanilla essence, lemon zest and sugar. Spoon into a serving dish, cover and chill for at least 30 minutes.
- To serve, pile the berries onto a serving plate, and spoon the ricotta and vanilla dip on top.

Eton mess

serves 6

ingredients

150ml/5fl oz double cream,
    lightly whipped
200ml/7fl oz Greek-style yogurt
500g/1lb 2oz strawberries,
    hulled
2 tablespoons crème de cassis
5 meringue nests

- Fold the cream into the yogurt and chill for 30 minutes.
- Put 250g/9oz strawberries in a blender or food processor, blend to a purée, then stir in the crème de cassis. Measure out 75ml/3fl oz of the purée and reserve.
- Slice the remaining strawberries into a bowl, reserving 6 for decoration, then pour the purée over and chill in the bowl for 20 minutes.
- Break up the meringue nests, and carefully fold into the cream mixture along with the strawberry mixture. Divide between six serving glasses, then drizzle over the reserved purée.
- Decorate with the reserved strawberries, and serve.

Mulled Florida cocktail

serves 4

ingredients

2 grapefruit
2 oranges
150ml/5fl oz apple juice
1 tablespoon brandy
2 fresh cherries, pitted
    and halved

- Over a saucepan to catch the juice, remove all zest and pith from the grapefruit and oranges, and separate each into segments.
- Put the segments in the saucepan. Add the apple juice and brandy. Heat through until almost boiling.
- Spoon into four glass dishes and top each with half a cherry. Serve warm.

Banana split
serves 4

ingredients
200g/7oz dark chocolate (at
   least 70% cocoa solids)
175ml/6fl oz double cream
25g/1oz butter
4 bananas
12 scoops vanilla ice cream
mixed chopped nuts, to serve

- Put the chocolate, cream and butter in a pan, and stir over a low heat until smooth. Cool slightly.
- Split the bananas in half lengthways, and arrange in four glass dishes. Put 3 scoops of ice cream in each dish, and pour the chocolate sauce over the top.
- Sprinkle with the chopped nuts, and serve immediately.

•••••••••••••••••••••••••••••••

Muscat grape frappé
serves 4

ingredients
½ bottle Muscat wine
450g/1lb Muscat grapes

- Pour the wine into a stainless-steel baking tray, add 150ml/5fl oz water and freeze for 3 hours or until completely solid.
- Scrape the frozen wine with a tablespoon to make a fine ice. Combine the grapes with the ice, and spoon into four shallow glasses. Serve immediately.

Mango & melon ginger salad

serves 4

ingredients

2 avocados, peeled, stoned and flesh cut into slices

1 mango, peeled and cut into slices

1 cantaloupe melon, peeled and cut into slices

Grated zest and juice of 2 limes

100g/4oz Stilton cheese, crumbled

2 tablespoons finely chopped stem ginger

2 passion fruit, halved

- Arrange the slices of avocado, mango and melon decoratively on a serving plate.
- Sprinkle the fruit with the lime zest and juice, Stilton and ginger. Spoon the passion fruit over the salad and serve.

Summer berries in Champagne jelly

serves 8

ingredients

900ml/1½pt Champagne

1½ teaspoons powdered gelatine

250g/9oz granulated sugar

250g/9oz strawberries, hulled and chopped

250g/9oz blueberries

- Pour half of the champagne into a large bowl, and let the bubbles subside. Sprinkle the gelatine over the top in an even layer. Do not stir. Leave until the gelatine is spongy.
- Pour the remaining Champagne into a large saucepan, add the sugar and heat gently, stirring constantly, until all the sugar has dissolved. Remove the pan from the heat, add the gelatine mixture and stir until thoroughly dissolved. Cool completely.
- Divide the berries among eight 125ml/4fl oz stemmed wine glasses, and gently pour the jelly over them. Chill in the refrigerator until set. Remove from the refrigerator 15 minutes before serving.

Californian baked pears

serves 4

ingredients

25g/1oz butter
1 teaspoon granulated sugar
grated zest of ½ lemon
4 dessert pears
300g/11oz canned fruit cocktail
   in syrup
½ teaspoon mixed spice

- Preheat the oven to 190°C/ 375°F/Gas mark 5.
- Melt the butter in a flameproof casserole dish. Add the sugar and lemon zest. Peel the pears, and turn in this mixture. Cover and bake for 30 minutes.
- Add the fruit cocktail and its syrup, and sprinkle with the mixed spice. Return to the oven for 10 minutes.
- Lift the pears out onto warmed plates. Stir the fruit cocktail well into the pan juices. Spoon around the pears, and serve immediately.

Fresh figs in wine

serves 6

ingredients

450ml/¾pt dry white wine
75g/3oz clear honey
50g/2oz caster sugar
1 small orange
8 whole cloves
450g/1lb fresh figs
1 cinnamon stick

- Put the wine, honey and sugar in a heavy saucepan, and heat gently until the sugar dissolves.
- Stud the orange with the cloves, and add to the syrup with the figs and cinnamon. Cover and simmer until the figs are soft.
- Transfer to a serving dish, and leave to cool before serving.

fruit desserts

Mandarins in syrup
serves 4

ingredients

10 mandarin oranges
15g/½oz icing sugar

2 teaspoons orange-flower water
15g/½oz chopped pistachio nuts

- Thinly pare a little of the zest from 1 mandarin, and cut into fine shreds for decoration. Squeeze the juice from 2 mandarins and set aside.
- Peel the remaining mandarins, removing as much of the white pith as possible. Arrange the peeled fruit whole in a large glass dish.
- Mix the reserved mandarin juice, sugar and orange-flower water, and pour it over the fruit. Cover the dish and chill for at least an hour.
- Blanch the shreds of mandarin zest in boiling water for 30 seconds. Drain and leave to cool.
- To serve, sprinkle the shreds of zest and pistachio nuts over the mandarins, and serve immediately.

Orange & date salad
serves 6

ingredients

6 oranges
2 tablespoons orange-flower water
100g/4oz stoned dates, chopped
50g/2oz pistachio nuts, chopped
15g/½oz icing sugar
1 teaspoon toasted almonds

- Peel the oranges with a sharp knife, removing all the pith. Cut into segments, catching all the juice in a bowl. Put the segments in a serving dish.
- Stir in the juice from the bowl and the orange-flower water.
- Sprinkle the dates and nuts over the salad, along with the icing sugar. Chill for 1 hour.
- Just before serving, sprinkle with the toasted almonds.

Cakes & Pastries

Whether you are looking for a tasty tea-time treat or that perfect cake for a special birthday or occasion, this chapter is sure to provide you with plenty of inspiration. Learn to bake single large cakes such as Dundee Cake and Chocolate Cake, or lots of individual cakes in recipes for Madeleines and Butterfly Cakes. Making heavenly classics such as Chocolate Eclairs, Baklava and Mississippi Mud Pie should be a delight with these easy-to-follow recipes.

Sly cakes
serves 8

ingredients

450g/1lb ready-to-roll puff pastry
2 cooking apples
50g/2oz butter
50g/2oz muscovado sugar
225g/8oz sultanas

50g/2oz mixed peel
2 teaspoons ground allspice
1 egg yolk, beaten
icing sugar, to dust

- Preheat the oven to 200°C/400°F/Gas mark 6. Lightly grease a non-stick baking tray.
- Roll out the puff pastry to a thickness of 1cm/½in, then trim and cut into 2 equal rectangles. Put one on the baking tray.
- Peel, core and dice the apple. Fry in the butter. When golden and starting to soften, add the muscovado sugar and toss to coat. Remove from the heat and stir in the sultanas, mixed peel and allspice.
- Spread the mixture onto the pastry rectangle on the baking tray. Put the other rectangle on top, and press down lightly. Divide into 16 squares with a sharp knife, pressing nearly all the way through, and brush the tops with egg yolk.
- Bake in the oven for 15–20 minutes. Transfer to a wire rack to cool. Dust with icing sugar.

Cherry turnover
serves 8

ingredients
450g/1lb shortcrust pastry
450g/1lb pitted sour cherries

double cream, to serve

- Preheat the oven to 180°C/350°F/Gas mark 4.
- Roll out the pastry, and use to line a greased 20cm/8in pie dish, allowing the sides of the pastry to hang over the edge. Fill the lined dish with the cherries. Fold the edges of the dough over the filling, sealing them where they meet in the centre. Prick the pastry top with a fork.
- Bake in the oven for 30 minutes or until the pastry is lightly browned. Serve with cream.

Coconut cake
serves 6–8

ingredients
2 x packets 450g/1lb chocolate
  cake mix
225g/8oz desiccated coconut
2 eggs
125ml/4fl oz sour cream
125ml/4fl oz milk

- Preheat the oven to 180°C/
  350°F/Gas mark 4. Lightly grease
  a loaf tin.
- Beat together the cake mix,
  coconut, eggs, sour cream and
  milk for 3–4 minutes or until
  smooth. Pour the mixture into the
  loaf tin.
- Bake for 45–50 minutes until the
  top is springy to the touch and a
  skewer inserted in the centre comes
  out clean. Turn onto a wire rack to
  cool, and serve cut in slices.

●●●●●●●●●●●●●●●●●●●●●●●●●●●●●●●●●●●

Apple turnovers
serves 6

ingredients
500g/1lb 2oz puff pastry
1 egg white, lightly beaten
caster sugar, to dust

For the filling
200g/7oz stewed apple
25g/1oz caster sugar
50g/2oz raisins, chopped
25g/1oz walnuts, chopped

- Preheat the oven to 210°C/425°F/Gas mark 7. Lightly grease a
  baking tray.
- Roll the pastry on a lightly floured work surface to a rectangle about
  45 x 35cm/18 x 14in. Cut out 12 rounds measuring 10cm/4in.
- To make the apple filling, mix together the ingredients in a mixing bowl.
- Divide the filling among the pastry rounds, then brush the edges with
  water. Fold the pastry in half to make a half-moon, and pinch the edges
  firmly together to seal. Brush the tops with egg white, and dust with
  caster sugar. Make 2 small slits in the top of each turnover. Bake for
  15 minutes, then reduce the temperature to 190°C/375°F/Gas mark 5
  and bake for a further 10 minutes. Serve warm.

Chocolate éclairs
serves 9

ingredients
100g/4oz butter
100g/4oz plain flour, sifted
4 eggs, lightly beaten
300ml/10fl oz double cream,
   whipped
150g/5oz dark chocolate
   (at least 70% cocoa solids),
   broken into pieces

- Preheat the oven to 210°C/425°F/Gas mark 7, and grease two baking trays.
- Combine the butter and 225ml/8fl oz water in a large heavy saucepan. Stir over a medium heat until the butter melts. Increase the heat, bring to the boil, then remove the pan from the heat.
- Add the flour to the saucepan all at once, and quickly beat into the buttery water using a wooden spoon. Return to the heat and continue beating until the mixture leaves the sides of the pan and forms a ball. Transfer to a large bowl and cool slightly.
- Beat the mixture to release any remaining heat. Gradually add the egg, about 3 teaspoonfuls at a time. Beat well after each addition until all the egg has been added and the mixture is glossy. Spoon the mixture into a piping bag fitted with a 1.5cm/⅝in plain nozzle.
- Sprinkle the baking trays lightly with water. Pipe 15cm/6in lengths onto the trays, leaving room for them to expand. Bake for 10–15 minutes. Reduce the oven temperature to 180°C/350°F/Gas mark 4, and bake for a further 15 minutes. Cool on a wire rack.
- Split each cooled éclair and remove any uncooked dough. Fill the centre with cream.
- Melt the chocolate in a bowl set over a saucepan of simmering water. Spread the melted chocolate over to the top of each éclair, in a line along the top. Allow to set, then serve.

Pain au chocolat

serves 6

ingredients

450g/1lb strong plain flour
½ teaspoon salt
½ teaspoon dried yeast
25g/1oz lard
1 egg, beaten lightly
225ml/8fl oz hand-hot water
175g/6oz butter, softened
beaten egg, to seal and glaze
100g/4oz dark chocolate (at least
    70% cocoa solids), broken into
    12 squares

- Lightly grease a baking tray.
- Sift the flour and salt into a mixing bowl, and stir in the yeast. Rub in the fat lard using your fingertips. Add the egg and enough of the water to form a soft dough. Knead the dough for about 10 minutes until elastic.
- Roll the dough out to form a rectangle measuring 38 x 20cm/15 x 8in. Divide the butter into three portions, and dot one portion over two-thirds of the rectangle, leaving a small border around the edge.
- Fold the rectangle into three by first folding the plain third of the dough over, then the other third. Seal the edges of the dough by pressing with a rolling pin. Give the dough a quarter turn. Re-roll and fold again, without butter, then wrap the dough and chill for 30 minutes.
- Repeat the buttering and folding outlined above twice more, chilling the dough each time. Re-roll and fold twice more without butter. Chill for a final 30 minutes.
- Roll the dough to a rectangle measuring 45 x 30cm/18 x 12in, trim and halve lengthways. Cut each half into 6 rectangles, and brush with beaten egg. Put a chocolate square at the end of each rectangle, and roll up to form a sausage.
- Press the ends together and place, seam side up, on the baking tray. Cover and leave to rise for 40 minutes in a warm place.
- Preheat the oven to 220°C/425°F/Gas mark 7.
- Brush the pastries with egg, and bake for 20–25 minutes until golden. Cool on a wire rack. Serve warm or cold.

Sticky plum tart
serves 6

ingredients

100g/4oz plain flour
1 teaspoon ground cinnamon
pinch of salt
75g/3oz butter
1 egg yolk

1 tablespoon chilled water
450g/1lb plums, halved, stoned
   and diced
25g/1oz caster sugar
3 tablespoons apricot jam

- Sift the flour into a blender or food processor, add the ground cinnamon, salt, butter and egg yolk. Process for 30 seconds or until evenly combined. Add the chilled water and process for a further 30 seconds. Knead together lightly, and roll out to a circle about 25.5cm/10in in diameter. Put on a baking tray and chill for 10–15 minutes.
- Preheat the oven to 200°C/400°F/Gas mark 6.
- Prick the pastry all over with a fork. Bake for 20–25 minutes or until golden brown.
- Arrange the plums over the cooked pastry, and sprinkle with the sugar. Put back in the oven for 40–45 minutes until the plums are tender.
- To finish, melt the jam in a small saucepan with 2 tablespoons water, bring to the boil and bubble for 1 minute. Brush or spoon over the warm tart to glaze.

Bakewell tart
serves 6

ingredients

225g/8oz ready-to-roll
   puff pastry
100g/4oz ground almonds
100g/4oz caster sugar
50g/2oz butter
3 eggs
¼ teaspoon almond essence
4 tablespoons strawberry jam

- Preheat the oven to 200°C/ 400°F/Gas mark 6.
- Roll out the pastry on a floured work surface, and use to line a 900ml/1½pt shallow dish.
- Beat the almonds with the sugar, butter, eggs and almond essence.
- Spread the pastry with an even layer of jam. Pour in the filling.
- Bake for 30 minutes or until set. Serve warm with cream.

Chocolate meringue pie

serves 6

ingredients

225g/8oz dark chocolate
  digestive biscuits
25g/1oz butter, melted

For the filling
3 egg yolks
50g/2oz caster sugar
50g/2oz cornflour
600ml/1pt milk
100g/4oz dark chocolate (at least
  70% cocoa solids)

For the meringue
2 egg whites
100g/4oz caster sugar
½ teaspoon vanilla essence

- Preheat the oven to 160°C/325°F/Gas mark 3.
- Put the digestive biscuits in a plastic bag, and crush with a rolling pin. Pour into a mixing bowl. Stir the butter into the biscuit crumbs until well mixed. Press the biscuit mixture firmly into the bottom and up the sides of a 23cm/9in flan tin or dish.
- To make the filling, beat the egg yolks, sugar and cornflour in a large bowl until they form a smooth paste, adding a little of the milk if necessary. Heat the milk until almost boiling, then slowly pour into the egg mixture, whisking well.
- Return the mixture to the saucepan and cook gently, whisking constantly, until it thickens. Remove from the heat. Melt the chocolate in a heatproof bowl set over a pan of simmering water. Whisk the melted chocolate into the mixture in the saucepan. Pour the mixture into the digestive biscuit base.
- To make the meringue, whisk the egg whites in a large mixing bowl until standing in soft peaks. Gradually whisk in about two-thirds of the sugar until the mixture is thick and glossy. Fold in the remaining sugar and the vanilla essence. Spread the meringue over the filling.
- Bake the pie in the centre of the oven for 30 minutes. Serve warm.

Citrus tart
serves 12

ingredients

For the pastry
175g/6oz plain flour
75g/3oz butter
3 tablespoons caster sugar
3 egg yolks

For the filling
finely grated zest of 1 lemon
juice of 3 lemons
juice of 1 orange
2 eggs plus 1 egg yolk
350ml/12fl oz double cream
175g/6oz caster sugar

- To make the pastry, sift the flour into a mixing bowl, make a well in the centre and put the butter, sugar and egg yolks in it. Work with the fingertips of one hand until these are blended, then gradually work in the flour. Continue mixing until the pastry forms a smooth ball. Wrap in cling film and chill for 30 minutes.
- Preheat the oven to 190°C/375°F/Gas mark 5. Grease a 28cm/11in flan dish.
- Roll out the pastry and use to line the tin. Prick the base of the pastry with a fork, and line with foil. Fill with baking beans and bake blind for 15–20 minutes until just brown. Remove from the oven to cool, and reduce the oven temperature to 160°C/325°F/Gas mark 3.
- To make the filling, put the lemon zest in a large bowl with the lemon and orange juice. Add the eggs and yolk, cream and sugar. Whisk the mixture together until the sugar has dissolved and the top is fluffy. Pour the filling into the pastry case and bake in the centre of the oven for 30–35 minutes until the filling is set. Serve warm or cold.

Raspberry buns
serves 4–6

ingredients

175g/6oz plain white flour
pinch of salt
50g/2oz butter
50g/2oz caster sugar, plus extra,
   to dust

1 teaspoon baking powder
1 egg
2 teaspoons milk
1 tablespoon raspberry jam
melted butter for brushing

- Preheat the oven to 200°C/400°F/Gas mark 6. Grease a baking tray.
- Sift the flour and salt into a bowl. Rub the butter into the flour, then add the sugar and baking powder. Whisk the egg and add the milk. Mix with the dry ingredients to form a stiffish dough. Divide the dough into 10 equal portions, and roll into balls.
- Lay the balls of dough on the greased baking tray, and make a hole in the top of each using your thumb. Fill with a small quantity of raspberry jam, and pinch the dough together again. Flatten the buns slightly, brush with melted butter and dust with sugar. Bake for about 15 minutes until the tops of the buns crack open slightly to reveal the jam.

● ●

Cherry clafoutis

serves 6–8

ingredients

25g/1oz butter, melted
400g/1lb fresh cherries, pitted
50g/2oz plain flour
75g/3oz caster sugar

4 eggs, lightly beaten
250ml/9fl oz milk
icing sugar, to dust

- Preheat the oven to 180°C/350°F/Gas mark 4. Brush a 23cm/9in glass or ceramic pie plate with melted butter.
- Spread the cherries on the bottom of the pie plate in a single layer.
- Sift the flour into a bowl, add the sugar and make a well in the centre. Gradually add the combined eggs, milk and butter, whisking until smooth and free of lumps.
- Pour the batter over the cherries, and bake for 30–35 minutes. Remove from the oven and dust generously with icing sugar. Serve immediately.

cakes & pastries

Pear cream pie
serves 8

ingredients

For the shortcrust pastry
300g/11oz plain flour
pinch of salt
175g/6oz butter, cubed
50ml/2fl oz iced water

For the filling
700g1½lb pears
100g/4oz sugar
500ml/18fl oz double cream
¼ teaspoon freshly ground pepper
1 egg yolk, lightly beaten

- To make the shortcrust pastry, sift the flour and the salt together into a large mixing bowl. Add the cubes of butter. Rub the butter and flour together with your fingertips until the mixture has a coarse texture.
- Stirring lightly with a knife, sprinkle water over the dough until it just begins to cohere. Gather the dough together into a ball, pressing it together with your hands. Wrap in cling film and chill for 30 minutes.
- Preheat the oven to 180°C/350°F/Gas mark 4.
- Roll out the dough to a thickness of 3mm/⅛in and use two-thirds of it to line a 23cm/9in pie dish.
- To make the filling, peel, core and slice the pears. Mix the pear slices with the sugar and cream, and add the pepper. Fill the pie with this mixture, and cover with the remaining dough. Glaze with the egg yolk, and cut a small slit in the top so the steam can escape during cooking.
- Bake in the oven for about 50 minutes or until the top is browned. Serve warm or cold.

Almond friands

serves 5

ingredients
150g/5oz butter
75g/3oz flaked almonds
50g/2oz plain flour
175g/6oz icing sugar, plus extra,
    to dust
5 egg whites

- Preheat the oven to 210°C/425°F/Gas mark 7. Lightly grease ten 125ml/4fl oz friand tins.
- Melt the butter in a small saucepan over a medium heat, then cook for 3–4 minutes until the butter turns a deep golden colour. Strain to remove any residue. Remove from the heat and set aside to cool until just lukewarm.
- Put the flaked almonds in a blender or food processor, and chop until finely ground. Transfer to a b owl, and sift in the flour and icing sugar.
- Put the egg whites in a separate bowl, and lightly whisk with a fork until just combined. Add the lukewarm butter to the flour mixture along with the egg whites. Mix gently with a metal spoon until all the ingredients are well combined.
- Spoon some mixture into each friand tin to fill to three-quarters of the way up the side. Put the tins on a baking tray, and bake in the centre of the oven for 10 minutes. Reduce the oven temperature to 180°C/350°F/ Gas mark 4, and bake for another 5 minutes. Remove and leave in the tins for 5 minutes before turning out onto a wire rack to cool completely. Dust with icing sugar before serving.

Fruit salad cake
serves 6–8

ingredients

175g/6oz dried fruit salad,
   roughly chopped
250ml/9fl oz hot tea
225g/8oz wholemeal
   self-raising flour

1 teaspoon grated nutmeg
50g/2oz muscovado sugar
3 tablespoons sunflower oil
75ml/3fl oz skimmed milk
Demerara sugar, to sprinkle

- Soak the dried fruits in the tea for several hours or overnight. Drain and reserve the liquid.
- Preheat the oven to 180°C/350°F/Gas mark 4. Grease an 18cm/7in round cake tin and line the bottom with non-stick greaseproof paper.
- Sift the flour into a bowl with the nutmeg. Stir in the muscovado sugar, fruit salad mixture and tea. Add the oil and milk and mix well.
- Spoon the mixture into the prepared tin. Sprinkle with Demerara sugar. Bake for 50–55 minutes until firm. Turn out and cool on a wire rack.

Alaskan blueberry coffee cake
serves 8

ingredients

350g/12oz plain flour
175g/6oz caster sugar
2½ teaspoons baking powder
1 teaspoon salt
50ml/2fl oz vegetable oil
175ml/6fl oz milk

1 egg
250g/9oz blueberries
100g/4oz Demerara sugar
½ teaspoon ground cinnamon
50g/2oz butter

- Preheat the oven to 190°C/375°F/Gas mark 5. Grease a greased deep 20cm/8in round springform cake tin.
- In a medium bowl, blend together 250g/9oz of the flour with the sugar, baking powder, salt, oil, milk, egg and 225g/8oz of the blueberries. Using a wooden spoon, beat thoroughly for 30 seconds and spread the mixture in the prepared cake tin.
- Combine the remaining flour, Demerara sugar, cinnamon and butter. Sprinkle over the mixture, and top with the remaining berries.
- Bake in the oven for 30–40 minutes. Cool in the tin on a wire rack.

Dundee cake
serves 10

ingredients

175g/6oz butter
175g/6oz caster sugar
4 eggs
50g/2oz ground almonds
300g/11oz self-raising flour
½ teaspoon salt
1 teaspoon baking powder

100g/4oz currants
100g/4oz sultanas
100g/4oz raisins
50g/2oz mixed peel, chopped
25g/1oz whole almonds,
    blanched and split

- Preheat the oven to 240°C/475°F/Gas mark 9. Line a 20cm/8in cake tin with greaseproof paper.
- Cream the butter and sugar until light and fluffy, then beat in the eggs, one at a time, along with the ground almonds.
- Sift the flour with the salt and baking powder, and gradually add to the creamed mixture along with the fruit and peel. Put the mixture in the prepared cake tin, smooth over and lightly arrange the almonds on top.
- Put the cake in the centre of the oven. Immediately reduce the temperature to 170°C/325°F/Gas mark 3, and bake for 1½ hours until the cake is firm and springs back at the touch. Allow to cool in the tin.

Child's birthday cake
serves 10–12

ingredients

275g/10oz butter
275g/10oz caster sugar
5 eggs

350g/12oz self-raising flour
grated zest of 2 oranges

- Preheat the oven to 160°C/325°F/Gas mark 3. Grease a 3.6-litre/6pt ovenproof glass mixing bowl. Line the bottom with greaseproof paper.
- Beat together the butter, sugar, eggs, flour and orange zest. Turn into the bowl and level the surface. Bake for 1 hour 10 minutes until just firm.
- Loosen from the bowl by running around the edge with a knife, then turn out and leave to cool on a wire rack. This is the perfect base cake for brightly coloured icing for a child's birthday.

Banana cake
serves 12

ingredients
475g/1lb 1oz plain flour
1 tablespoon baking powder
½ teaspoon salt
50ml/2fl oz vegetable oil
2 eggs

125ml/4fl oz milk
1 teaspoon vanilla essence
225g/8oz bananas, mashed
2 tablespoons caster sugar
225g/8oz vanilla yogurt

- Preheat the oven to 180°C/350°F/Gas mark 4. Grease 2 x 20cm/8in round cake tins.
- Sift together the dry ingredients into a large mixing bowl.
- Blend the oil, eggs, milk and vanilla essence until smooth in a separate bowl, then stir in the bananas. Add to the dry ingredients and stir well.
- Pour equal amounts into the prepared tins. Bake for 20 minutes, then cool completely on a wire rack. Sprinkle with the caster sugar. Turn one of the cooled cakes upside down, and spread the yogurt on its bottom side. Put the other cake on top, right side up, to make a sandwich.

Molasses cake
serves 8–10

ingredients
1.1kg/2½lb plain flour
250g/9oz butter
250g/9oz sugar
2 teaspoons ground ginger

1 tablespoon bicarbonate of soda
3 tablespoons warm water
225ml/8fl oz sour milk
450g/1lb molasses

- Preheat the oven to 190°C/375°F/Gas mark 5. Grease a 23cm/9in round cake tin.
- Sift the flour in a large bowl, and rub in the butter until the mixture resembles fine breadcrumbs, then mix in the sugar and the ginger.
- Dissolve the bicarbonate of soda in the warm water. Stir in the sour milk and molasses. Add to the flour mixture to make a fairly sticky dough.
- Work the dough thoroughly, and put in the prepared cake tin. Bake in the oven for 50 minutes. Leave to cool in the tin for 30 minutes before turning out to cool completely.

Pineapple upside-down cake

serves 6

ingredients

425g/15oz canned unsweetened
   pineapple pieces, drained with
   juice reserved
4 teaspoons cornflour
50g/2oz soft brown sugar
50g/2oz margarine or butter
grated zest of 1 lemon

For the sponge
50ml/2fl oz sunflower oil
75g/3oz soft brown sugar
150g/5oz plain flour
2 teaspoons baking powder
1 teaspoon ground cinnamon

- Preheat the oven to 180°C/350°F/Gas mark 4. Grease a deep
  18cm/7in cake tin.
- Mix the reserved juice from the pineapple with the cornflour until it forms
  a smooth paste. Put the paste in a saucepan with the sugar, butter or
  margarine, and 125ml/4fl oz water. Stir over a low heat until the sugar
  has dissolved. Bring to the boil and simmer for 2–3 minutes until
  thickened. Set aside to cool slightly.
- To make the sponge, put the oil, sugar and 150ml/5fl oz water in a
  saucepan. Heat gently until the sugar has dissolved – do not allow to
  boil. Remove from the heat and leave to cool. .
- Sift the flour, baking powder and cinnamon into a bowl. Pour over the
  cooled sugar syrup, and beat well to form a batter.
- Put the pineapple pieces and lemon zest on the bottom of the prepared
  tin, and pour over 4 tablespoons pineapple syrup. Spoon the sponge
  batter on top.
- Bake in the oven for 35–40 minutes until set. Invert onto a plate, leave to
  stand for 5 minutes, then remove the tin. Serve with or without the
  remaining syrup.

Coffee & walnut cake
serves 8

ingredients

100g/4oz butter, softened
300g/11oz caster sugar
2 eggs, lightly beaten
200g/7oz flour, sifted with
   1 tablespoon baking powder

150ml/5fl oz strong
   espresso coffee
200g/7oz shelled walnuts,
   finely chopped

- Preheat the oven to 180°C/350°F/Gas mark 4. Grease a 20cm/8in square cake tin.
- Cream the butter and sugar together in a large mixing bowl until light and fluffy, then beat in the eggs. Add the flour alternately with the coffee until the mixture is soft and smooth. Add the nuts and mix well.
- Pour the mixture into the prepared cake tin, and bake in the oven for 1 hour. Leave to cool in the tin for 10 minutes, then turn out onto a wire rack to cool completely. Serve with after-dinner coffee.

Brandied chocolate cake
serves 8–10

ingredients

100g/4oz dark chocolate (at least
   70% cocoa solids, broken into
   small pieces
2 tablespoons strong black coffee
4 eggs

100g/4oz caster sugar
100g/4oz plain flour, sifted
4 tablespoons brandy
whipped cream or ice cream,
   to serve

- Preheat the oven to 180°C/350°F/Gas mark 4. Grease a 20cm/8in round springform cake tin.
- Melt the chocolate in a heatproof bowl set over a pan of simmering water. Stir in the coffee and put aside until cooled.
- Beat the eggs, gradually beat in the sugar and continue beating until soft and creamy. Fold in the flour alternately with the cooled chocolate mixture.
- Pour the mixture into the prepared tin, and bake in the oven for 30–35 minutes. Leave in the tin to cool for 10 minutes before turning out onto a wire rack. While the cake is still warm, sprinkle the brandy over, then chill overnight. Serve with whipped cream or ice cream.

Butterfly cakes
serves 4–6

ingredients
100g/4oz butter, softened
150g/5oz caster sugar
175g/6oz self-raising flour, sifted
125ml/4fl oz milk
2 teaspoons vanilla essence
2 eggs
125ml/4fl oz double cream,
    whipped to soft peaks
100g/4oz strawberry jam
icing sugar, to dust

- Preheat the oven to 180°C/350°F/Gas mark 4. Line a 12-hole shallow muffin tin with paper cases.
- Put the butter, sugar, flour, milk, vanilla essence and eggs in a bowl, and beat with an electric mixer on a low speed for 2 minutes or until well mixed. Increase the speed and beat for another 2 minutes or until smooth and pale.
- Divide the mixture evenly among the cases, and bake for 20 minutes or until cooked and golden. Transfer to a wire rack to cool completely.
- Using a small sharp knife, cut shallow round 'lids' from the top of each cake. Cut these in half, keeping in pairs. Spoon about ½ tablespoon cream into the hole in the top of each cake, then top with a teaspoon of jam. Position two halves of the cake tops in the jam to resemble butterfly wings. Dust the cakes with icing sugar before serving.

Bermuda cheesecake

serves 6–8

ingredients

75g/3oz butter
400g/14oz caster sugar
250g/9oz digestive biscuit crumbs
500g/1lb 2oz cream cheese

75g/3oz cocoa powder
1½ teaspoons vanilla essence
2 eggs
250g/9oz sour cream

- Preheat the oven to 180°C/350°F/Gas mark 4.
- Melt the butter in a pan, and stir in 25g/1oz of the caster sugar and the biscuit crumbs, mixing thoroughly. Press the mixture over the bottom of a 20cm/8in round springform cake tin and chill while preparing the filling.
- Beat the cream cheese until smooth. Beat in 350g/12oz of the sugar, then gradually add the cocoa powder, 1 teaspoon of the vanilla essence and the eggs. When smooth, pour into the crumb crust, and bake for 35 minutes.
- Combine the sour cream with the remaining sugar and vanilla essence. Spread the mixture over the top of the cheesecake, and bake for another 10 minutes. Remove from the oven, cool and chill overnight.

Seed cake

serves 6–8

ingredients

100g/4oz butter
150g/5oz caster sugar
2 eggs
150g/5oz flour, sifted
25g/1oz cornflour
2 teaspoons caraway seeds
½ teaspoon baking powder
50g/2oz glacé cherries, finely chopped
½ teaspoon vanilla essence

- Preheat the oven to 170°C/325°F/Gas mark 3. Grease a 20cm/8in round cake tin, and line with greaseproof paper.
- Cream the butter and sugar together until white and fluffy, then add each egg separately.
- Gradually stir in the flour, cornflour, caraway seeds, baking powder, cherries and vanilla essence, mixing until smooth.
- Pour the mixture into the prepared cake tin, and bake in the oven for 1¼ hours. Turn the cake out onto a wire rack to cool.

Rich fruit cake

serves 8–10

ingredients

450g/1lb sultanas

375g/13oz raisins, chopped

225g/8oz currants

225g/8oz glacé cherries,
quartered

250ml/9fl oz brandy, plus extra
1 tablespoon, to glaze

225g/8oz butter

200g/7oz Demerara sugar

2 tablespoons apricot jam

2 tablespoons treacle

1 tablespoon grated lemon zest

4 eggs

300g/11oz plain flour, sifted

1 teaspoon ground ginger

1 teaspoon mixed spice

1 teaspoon ground cinnamon

- Put the sultanas, raisins, currants and cherries in a bowl with the 250ml/9fl oz brandy, and soak overnight.
- Preheat the oven to 150°C/300°F/Gas mark 2. Lightly grease and line a deep 23cm/9in round cake tin.
- Using an electric mixer, beat the butter and sugar in a large bowl until just combined. Beat in the jam, treacle and lemon zest. Add the eggs, one at a time, beating after each addition.
- Stir the fruit, flour and spices alternately into the mixture, mixing until the ingredients are combined.
- Spoon the mixture into the tin, and smooth the surface. Tap the tin on the bench to remove any air bubbles. and level the surface with wet hands.
- Bake for 3–3¼ hours. Brush the surface with the extra tablespoon of brandy. Cover the top of the cake with baking parchment, and wrap in a tea towel. Allow to cool completely before turning out of the tin.
- To store, wrap the cake in a double thickness of greaseproof paper, and keep in an airtight tin. Leave to 'mature' for a few days before eating.

Date & apple muffins
serves 6–12

ingredients

150g/5oz self-raising
   wholemeal flour
150g/5oz self-raising white flour
1 teaspoon ground cinnamon
1 teaspoon baking powder
25g/1oz margarine, softened
75g/3oz muscovado sugar
250ml/9fl oz apple juice

2 tablespoons pear and
   apple spread
1 egg, lightly beaten
1 dessert apple, peeled, cored
   and diced
75g/3oz chopped dates
1 tablespoon chopped pecan nuts

- Preheat the oven to 200°C/400°F/Gas mark 6. Arrange 12 paper cake cases in a 12-hole muffin tin.
- Put the wholemeal flour in a bowl. Sift in the white flour, cinnamon and baking powder. Rub in the margarine until the mixture resembles breadcrumbs, then stir in the muscovado sugar.
- Stir a little of the apple juice into the pear and apple spread until smooth. Mix in the remaining juice, then add to the flour mixture with the egg. Add the chopped apple and dates. Mix quickly until just combined.
- Divide the mixture among the muffin cases. Sprinkle with the nuts and bake for 20–25 minutes until golden brown and firm in the middle.
- Transfer to a wire rack, and serve while still warm.

Almond cake
serves 8

ingredients

175g/6oz almonds, blanched
grated zest of 1 lemon
3 eggs, lightly beaten

175g/6oz plain flour, sifted
175g/6oz butter
175g/6oz granulated sugar

- Preheat the oven to 170°C/325°F/Gas mark 3. Grease a 23cm/9in tart tin.
- Using a large mortar and pestle, pound the almonds with the lemon zest. Add the remaining ingredients gradually, pounding together to form a thick paste. Spread the paste evenly into the tart tin, and bake in the oven for 1 hour or until the cake is golden on top. Cool on a wire rack.

Chocolate cake

serves 10

ingredients

100g/4oz butter, softened
100g/4oz caster sugar
50g/2oz icing sugar
2 eggs, lightly beaten
1 teaspoon vanilla essence
75g/3oz blackberry jam
150g/5oz self-raising flour, sifted
50g/2oz cocoa powder
1 teaspoon bicarbonate of soda
225ml/8fl oz milk

For the chocolate butter cream
50g/2oz dark chocolate (at least
   70% cocoa solids), broken into
   small pieces
25g/1oz butter
3 teaspoons double cream
3 teaspoons icing sugar, sifted

- Preheat the oven to 180°C/350°F/Gas mark 4. Lightly grease a 20cm/8in square cake tin, and line with greaseproof paper.
- Cream the butter and sugars in a small bowl with an electric beater until light and fluffy. Add the eggs gradually, beating thoroughly after each addition. Beat in the vanilla and jam. Transfer to a large bowl.
- Sift together the flour, cocoa and bicarbonate of soda. Using a wooden spoon, fold the flour mixture into the butter alternately with the milk. Stir until the mixture is just combined and almost smooth.
- Pour into the prepared tin, and smooth the surface. Bake for 45 minutes until a skewer inserted into the centre of the cake comes out clean. Remove from the oven and leave in the tin for 15 minutes before turning onto a wire rack to cool completely.
- To make the butter cream, stir the ingredients in a small pan over a low heat until smooth and glossy. Spread over the top of the cooled cake using a flat-bladed knife. Allow to set.

Chocolate chip muffins
serves 4–6

ingredients

100g/4oz soft margarine
225g/8oz caster sugar
2 large eggs
150ml/5fl oz full-fat Greek-style
  yogurt

5 tablespoons milk
275g/10oz plain flour
1 teaspoon bicarbonate of soda
175g/6oz dark chocolate chips

- Preheat the oven to 190°C/375°F/Gas mark 5. Line a 12-hole muffin tin with paper cases.
- Using a wooden spoon, cream the margarine and sugar in a mixing bowl until light and fluffy. Beat in the eggs, yogurt and milk until combined. Sift together the flour and bicarbonate of soda, and add to the mixture with the chocolate chips. Stir until just blended.
- Spoon the mixture into the paper cases, and bake in the oven for 25 minutes. Leave to cool in the tin for 5 minutes, then transfer the muffins to a wire rack to cool.

Bramble scones
serves 8

ingredients

450g/1lb self-raising flour
1/2 teaspoon salt
2 teaspoons baking powder
75g/3oz butter, cubed

75g/3oz caster sugar
225g/8oz frozen blackberries
200ml/7fl oz buttermilk
1 egg, beaten

- Preheat the oven to 220°C/425°F/Gas mark 7.
- Sift the flour, salt and baking powder together in a large bowl. Rub in the butter until the mixture resembles breadcrumbs. Stir in the sugar and frozen blackberries. Stir in the buttermilk to form a firm dough.
- Knead the dough very lightly. Roll out on a floured surface to 2.5cm/1in thick. Using a 6.5cm/2½in cutter, stamp into rounds, being careful not to cut through the blackberries. Knead and re-roll as necessary.
- Put the scones on a greased baking tray, and brush the tops with beaten egg. Bake in the oven for about 10 minutes until well risen and golden brown. Serve while still hot.

Chocolate roulade

serves 6

ingredients

150g/5oz dark chocolate (at least
   70% cocoa solids)
6 eggs
175g/6oz caster sugar
25g/1oz plain flour
1 tablespoon cocoa powder
icing sugar, to dust

For the filling
300ml/10fl oz double cream,
   whisked
75g/3oz strawberries, sliced

- Preheat the oven to 200°C/400°F/Gas mark 6. Line a 38 x 25cm/
  15 x 10in Swiss roll tin with greaseproof paper.
- In a small saucepan over a medium heat, melt the chocolate in
  2 tablespoons water, stirring constantly. Leave to cool slightly.
- Put the eggs and sugar in a bowl, and whisk for 10 minutes or until the
  mixture is pale and foamy. Whisk in the chocolate in a thin stream. Sift
  the flour and cocoa together, and fold into the mixture. Pour into the tin
  and level the top.
- Bake in the oven for 12 minutes. Dust a sheet of greaseproof paper with
  a little icing sugar, turn the roulade onto it and peel off the lining
  parchment. Roll up the roulade with the fresh paper inside. Put on a wire
  rack, cover with a damp tea towel and leave to cool.
- To finish, unroll the roulade and spread with the cream. Scatter with the
  strawberries and re-roll. Put on a plate and dust with icing sugar. Serve
  cut into slices.

Potato apple cake
serves 2

ingredients

450g/1lb cooked potatoes, mashed
100g/4oz plain flour, sifted
½ teaspoon salt
1–2 Bramley cooking apples, peeled, cored and sliced

25g/1oz butter, plus extra for basting
sprinkling of caster sugar

- Mix together the potatoes, flour and salt. Roll the potato mixture into a round about 2cm/1in thick. Divide into four, and put a couple of layers of apple on top of two of the sections, then sandwich the other two sections on top. Pinch around the edges to seal.
- Melt the 25g/1oz butter in a non-stick frying pan over a medium heat. Cook the cake on both sides for about 20 minutes until browned. Remove the top sections and dot the apple with butter. Sprinkle with sugar. Replace the tops and return to the pan until the butter has melted. Remove carefully to warmed plates, and serve immediately.

• •

Lemon chocolate cake
serves 8

ingredients

100g/4oz butter
225g/8oz soft brown sugar
grated zest of 1 lemon
2 eggs
75g/3oz plain chocolate, grated
300g/11oz self-raising flour, sifted

pinch of salt
100g/4oz sour cream

For the topping
2 tablespoons icing sugar
1 tablespoon grated lemon zest

- Preheat the oven to 180°C/350°F/Gas mark 5. Grease a 23 x 13cm/ 9 x 5in loaf tin.
- Cream the butter, sugar and lemon zest together. Add the eggs and beat well. Mix in the chocolate. Sift the flour and salt together, and add to the mixture alternately with the sour cream. Beat well.
- Pour the mixture into the loaf tin, and sprinkle with the icing sugar and lemon zest. Bake for 50–60 minutes until cooked. Cool on a wire rack.

Pecan & raisin muffins
serves 6

ingredients

350g/12oz plain flour
1 tablespoon baking powder
pinch of salt
100g/4oz caster sugar
2 eggs
150ml/5fl oz milk

50ml/2fl oz corn oil
¼ teaspoon vanilla essence
75g/3oz pecan nuts,
  roughly chopped
75g/3oz raisins

- Preheat the oven to 190°C/375°F/Gas mark 5. Grease a 12-hole muffin tin.
- Sift the flour, baking powder and salt into a bowl. Mix in the sugar and make a well in the centre. Lightly beat the eggs with the milk, oil and vanilla essence, and pour into the centre of the dry ingredients. Mix quickly to blend the flour with the liquid. Do not overmix – the mixture should look slightly lumpy. Lightly stir in the nuts and raisins.
- Divide the mixture equally in the muffin tin and bake for 25 minutes or until well risen, golden brown and cooked through. Leave in the tin to cool for a few minutes. Serve warm or cold.

Spiced date & walnut cake
serves 8

ingredients

300g/11oz wholemeal
  self-raising flour
2 teaspoons mixed spice
150g/5oz dates, chopped

50g/2oz walnuts, chopped
4 tablespoons sunflower oil
100g/4oz dark muscovado sugar
300ml/10fl oz skimmed milk

- Preheat the oven to 180°C/350°F/Gas mark 4. Grease a 900g/2lb loaf tin, and line with greaseproof paper.
- Sift together the flour and spice, tipping any bran in the sieve into the bowl. Stir in the dates and walnuts.
- Mix the oil, sugar and milk together. Stir evenly into the dry ingredients. Spoon the mixture into the prepared tin.
- Bake in the oven for 40–45 minutes until firm and golden brown. Turn out the cake, remove the lining paper and leave to cool on a wire rack.

Rock cakes

serves 10

ingredients

75g/3oz butter, cubed
225g/8oz self-raising flour
100g/4oz caster sugar
75g/3oz mixed dried fruit

½ teaspoon ground ginger
1 egg
50ml/2fl oz milk

- Preheat the oven to 200°C/400°F/Gas mark 6. Grease two baking trays.
- Sift the flour into a large bowl, and rub in the butter with your fingertips until the mixture resembles fine breadcrumbs. Stir in the sugar, dried fruit and ginger.
- In a bowl, whisk together the egg and milk. Add the dry ingredients and mix to a stiff dough. Drop rough heaps of mixture, about 3 tablespoons at a time, onto the baking trays. Bake for 10–15 minutes until golden. Cool on a wire rack.

● ●

Madeira cake

serves 8

ingredients

175g/6oz butter, softened
175g/6oz caster sugar
3 eggs, lightly beaten
2 teaspoons finely grated
   orange zest

150g/5oz self-raising flour, sifted
100g/4oz plain flour
2 tablespoons milk

- Preheat the oven to 160°C/325°F/Gas mark 3. Lightly grease a 20 x 10 x 7cm/8 x 4x 2½in loaf tin, and line the bottom and sides with greaseproof paper.
- Using an electric mixer, cream the butter and sugar in a small bowl until light and fluffy. Add the eggs gradually, beating thoroughly after each addition. Add the zest and mix through. Transfer to a large bowl. Fold in both flours and the milk with a metal spoon. Stir until smooth.
- Spoon into the loaf tin and smooth the surface. Bake for 50 minutes or until a skewer inserted into the centre comes out clean. Cool the cake in the tin for 10 minutes, then turn out onto a wire rack to cool completely.

Plum cake
serves 10–12

ingredients

450g/1lb butter
450g/1lb soft brown sugar
12 eggs
450g/1lb plain white flour
225g/8oz ground almonds
450g/1lb sultanas

450g/1lb raisins
450g/1lb currants
225g/8oz mixed peel
grated zest and juice of 1 lemon
175ml/6fl oz whisky

- Preheat the oven to 180°C/350°F/Gas mark 4. Carefully line a 30cm/12in round cake tin with greaseproof paper.
- Cream the butter and sugar until light and fluffy. Add the eggs one at a time, beating well between each addition. Mix half of the flour and the almonds with the fruit and peel. Stir the other half of the flour into the cake mixture. Stir in the fruit with the lemon juice and zest, and mix well.
- Pour into the tin, smooth the top and bake for 2 hours. Allow to cool in the tin. Poke holes in the cake with a skewer, and pour the whisky over.

● ●

Raisin gingerbread
serves 8

ingredients

150g/5oz granulated sugar
150ml/10fl oz molasses
150ml/10fl oz boiling water
25g/1oz butter
1 teaspoon bicarbonate of soda
75g/3oz raisins

50g/2oz pecan nuts, chopped
1 egg, well beaten
175g/6oz plain flour, sifted
1 teaspoon ground cinnamon
1 teaspoon ground ginger
¼ teaspoon ground cloves

- Preheat the oven to 180°C/350°F/Gas mark 4. Grease a 23cm/9in round cake tin.
- Mix together the sugar, molasses and boiling water. While the mixture is still hot, stir in the butter and the bicarbonate of soda. Leave to cool. Add the raisins, nuts and egg.
- Sift together the flour and spices, and stir into the molasses mixture. Pour the mixture into the cake tin and bake for 35–40 minutes until an inserted skewer comes out clean. Turn out onto a wire rack to cool.

Madeleines

serves 6

ingredients
175g/6oz butter, melted and cooled
100g/4oz plain flour
2 eggs
175g/6oz caster sugar
1 teaspoon finely grated orange zest
2 tablespoons icing sugar, to dust

- Preheat the oven to 180°C/350°F/Gas mark 4. Lightly grease 12 holes in a madeleine tin. Dust the tin with flour, and shake off any excess.
- Combine the eggs and sugar in a heatproof bowl. Put the bowl over a pan of simmering water, and beat the mixture with a whisk or an electric beater until thick and pale yellow. Remove the bowl from the heat, and continue to beat the mixture until it has cooled slightly and increased in volume.
- Sift the flour three times onto baking parchment. Add the flour, butter and orange zest to the egg mixture, and fold in quickly and lightly with a metal spoon until just combined. Spoon the mixture carefully into the madeleine holes.
- Bake for 10–12 minutes until lightly golden. Carefully remove from the tin and place on a wire rack until cold. Dust with icing sugar before serving. Madeleines are best eaten on the day of baking.

Apple galettes
serves 8

ingredients
225g/8oz plain flour
350g/12oz butter, chopped,
125ml/4fl oz chilled water
8 cooking apples
175g/6oz caster sugar

- Put the flour and 225g/8oz of the butter in a bowl. Cut the butter into the flour using two knives until it resembles large crumbs. Gradually add the chilled water, stirring with a knife and pressing together until a rough dough forms.
- Turn onto a lightly floured work surface and roll into a rectangle. The dough is crumbly and hard to manage at this point. Fold the dough and re-roll several times. Wrap the pastry in cling film and refrigerate for 30 minutes, then fold and re-roll a few more times. Wrap again in cling film and refrigerate for another 30 minutes.
- Preheat the oven to 190°C/375°F/Gas mark 5. Roll the pastry until 3mm/½in thick. Cut into 8 x 10cm/4in rounds.
- Peel, core and slice the apples. Arrange in a spiral on the pastry. Sprinkle well with the caster sugar, and dot with the remaining butter. Bake on greased baking trays for 20–30 minutes until the pastry is crisp and golden. Serve warm with cream or ice cream.

Baklava
serves 8–10

ingredients
100g/4oz butter, melted
450g/1lb walnuts, finely chopped
50g/2oz caster sugar
pinch of ground cinnamon
275g/10oz filo pastry

For the syrup
juice of 1 lemon
150g/5oz sugar
½ teaspoon ground cinnamon

- Preheat the oven to 180°C/350°F/Gas mark 4. Lightly grease a 25cm/10in loose-bottomed cake tin.
- Mix together the walnuts, sugar and cinnamon in a bowl.
- Unfold the filo pastry, and cover with a damp tea towel to prevent it drying out. Brush a piece of the filo with melted butter, and fit it into the bottom of the tin with the buttered side down. Let the edges spill over and brush with butter. Repeat with three more buttered filo sheets, making sure that the whole tin is lined.
- Sprinkle with half of the nut mixture. Repeat with four more layers of buttered filo, then scatter the remaining nut mixture over them. Put two more layers of buttered filo on top, then fold the edges in and under.
- Cut the last two pieces of filo so they that fit the tin, place on top and brush generously with butter. Bake for 40 minutes, then increase the temperature to 200°C/400°F/Gas mark 6. Bake for a further 20 minutes or until golden brown.
- To make the syrup, gently heat the lemon juice, sugar and cinnamon until the sugar has dissolved and the syrup has reduced slightly. Pour over the cooked baklava, and leave to cool in the tin for 1–2 hours. Cut into wedges and serve.

Filo rhubarb pie
serves 4

ingredients

500g/1lb 2oz pink rhubarb
1 teaspoon mixed spice
grated zest and juice of 1 orange

1 tablespoon granulated sugar
1 tablespoon low-fat spread
3 sheets filo pastry

- Preheat the oven to 200°C/400°F/Gas mark 6.
- Trim the leaves and ends from the rhubarb stems, and chop into 2.5cm/1in pieces. Put in a medium bowl. Add the mixed spice, orange zest and juice, and sugar, and toss well to coat evenly. Tip the rhubarb into a 1.2 litre/2pt pie dish.
- Melt the spread and brush over the filo sheets. Crumple the filo loosely, and place the pieces on top of the filling to cover.
- Put the dish on a baking tray, and bake the pie for 20 minutes until golden brown. Reduce the temperature to 180°C/350°F/Gas mark 4. Bake for 10–15 minutes more until the rhubarb is tender. Serve warm.

Coffee almond ice-cream cake
serves 8

ingredients

350g/12oz chocolate wafer
  crumbs
50g/2oz butter, melted
350g/12oz coffee ice cream
350g/12oz double cream

1 teaspoon vanilla essence
350g/12oz amaretti biscuits,
  crushed
100g/4oz slivered almonds,
  toasted

- Lightly oil a 20cm/8in round springform cake tin.
- In a bowl, stir together the crumbs and butter with a fork until the mixture is well combined. Press the mixture onto the bottom of the prepared tin and 2.5cm/1in up its sides. Freeze for 30 minutes until firm.
- Spread the ice cream evenly on the crust, and return to the freezer for 30 minutes until the ice cream is firm.
- In a bowl, beat the cream with the vanilla essence using an electric mixer until it holds stiff peaks. Fold in the amaretti biscuits, and spread over the ice cream. Smooth the top of the cake, sprinkle with almonds and freeze for 30–45 minutes or until the top is firm.

Mississippi mud pie
serves 8

ingredients

225g/8oz plain flour
2 tablespoons cocoa powder
150g/5oz butter
25g/1oz caster sugar
450ml/¾pt double cream, whipped

For the filling
175g/6oz butter
350g/12oz muscovado sugar
4 eggs, lightly beaten
4 tablespoons cocoa powder, sifted
150g/5oz dark chocolate
300ml/10fl oz single cream
1 teaspoon chocolate essence

- To make the pastry, sift the flour and cocoa powder into a mixing bowl. Rub in the butter until the mixture resembles fine breadcrumbs. Stir in the sugar and enough cold water (about 2 tablespoons) to mix to a soft dough. Chill for 15 minutes.
- Preheat the oven to 190°C/375°F/Gas mark 5.
- Roll out the pastry dough on a lightly floured work surface, and use to line a greased 23cm/9in loose-bottomed flan tin. Line with foil and baking beans.
- Bake blind in the oven for 15 minutes. Remove the beans and foil, and cook for a further 10 minutes until crisp. Reduce the oven temperature to 170°C/325°F/Gas mark 3.
- To make the filling, beat the butter and sugar in a bowl, and gradually beat in the eggs with the cocoa powder. Melt the dark chocolate in a heatproof bowl set over a pan of simmering water, then beat the melted chocolate, single cream and chocolate essesnce into the egg mixture.
- Pour the mixture into the cooked pastry shell, and bake in the oven for 45 minutes or until the filling is set. Leave in the tin to cool completely, then transfer to a serving plate. Cover with the whipped cream, and chill before serving.

Frangipane tart
serves 10

ingredients

For the pastry
100g/4oz caster sugar
50g/2oz ground almonds
100g/4oz plain flour
75g/3oz butter, cut into small dice
1 large egg
1 egg yolk
grated zest of 1 small lemon
2 teaspoons water
pinch of salt

For the filling
50g/2oz butter
50g/2oz caster sugar
50g/2oz ground almonds
50g/2oz white breadcrumbs
1 large egg
3 drops of almond essence
4 tablespoons raspberry jam

- To make the pastry, put the sugar, almonds and flour into a blender or food processor, and whiz at full speed for a few seconds. Add the butter and work again until just blended. The mixture should resemble fine breadcrumbs.
- Add the egg and egg yolk, the lemon zest, 2 teaspoons water and a pinch of salt. Work again until the pastry balls. Wrap in cling film and refrigerate for 2 hours.
- Preheat the oven to 190°C/375°F/Gas mark 5.
- Roll out the chilled pastry, and use to line a greased 20cm/8in loose-bottomed tart tin. If it breaks it can be repaired by pressing with your fingers. Make the shell as even as possible, with a double thickness round the edges, and pushed right up to the top as it will shrink as it bakes. Be careful to press into the bottom edges to eliminate air between the tin and the pastry.
- To make the filling, put the butter, sugar, almonds and breadcrumbs into the blender and work briefly to mix. With the machine running on full speed, add the egg and almond essence until a smooth paste forms.
- Put the shell on a baking tray, prick the bottom with a fork and line with foil. Fill with baking beans and bake blind for 10 minutes.
- Remove the foil and beans, and leave to cool slightly, then fill the base with a layer of raspberry jam. Cover this with the almond paste. Scrape the surface smooth and level.
- Return to the oven and bake for 25–30 minutes until risen and lightly browned. Serve warm or at room temperature.

Rhubarb cake
serves 8–10

ingredients
10g/5oz butter
350g/12oz caster sugar
200g/7oz flour
2 teaspoons baking powder
pinch of salt
3 eggs, lightly beaten
grated zest and juice of 1 lemon
4 tablespoons milk
600g/1¼lb rhubarb, cut into
    2.5cm/1in lengths
1 teaspoon ground cinnamon

- Preheat the oven to 190°C/375°F/Gas mark 5. Grease a 20cm/8in springform cake tin.
- Cream the butter with 150g/5oz of the sugar until light and fluffy. Sift together the flour, baking powder and salt. Add to the flour mixture alternately with the eggs. Beat in the lemon zest and juice, then the milk. Put the mixture into the prepared cake tin, and level the top.
- Mix the rhubarb with the cinnamon and remaining sugar, and spread on top of the cake mixture. Bake in the oven for 40–45 minutes until the rhubarb is soft and the cake has shrunk slightly from the side of the tin. Leave to cool completely in the tin.

Lime meringue tarts
serves 6

ingredients

For the pastry
50g/2oz pistachio nuts
100g/4oz plain flour, sifted
pinch of salt
75g/3oz butter, diced
50g/2oz icing sugar
2 medium eggs

For the pastry
1 egg plus 3 egg yolks
grated zest and juice of 5 limes
200g/7oz caster sugar
150ml/5fl oz double cream

- Preheat the oven to 190°C/375°F/Gas mark 5. Grease and flour six tartlet tins measuring 8 x 2.5cm/3¼ x 1in.
- To make the pastry, chop the pistachios in a blender or food processor for 30 seconds. Add the flour, salt and butter, and pulse until the mixture resembles crumbs. Add the icing sugar and pulse to mix. Separate the eggs, put 1 egg white to one side for the meringue and discard the other. Add the yolks to the mixture, and pulse until it just holds together.
- Turn the dough on to a lightly floured work surface, and knead gently to bring the mixture together. Roll out the pastry and use to line the tins, pressing well into the edges and trimming off any excess pastry. Cover with cling film and chill for 30 minutes.
- Put the tins on a baking sheet, line with foil and fill with baking beans. Bake for 10 minutes. Remove the foil and beans, and bake for a further 10–12 minutes until just cooked. Remove from the oven, and reduce the temperature to 180°C/350°F/Gas mark 4.
- Meanwhile, to make the filling, put the egg and egg yolks into a small pan, add the lime zest and juice, 150g/5oz of the caster sugar and the cream. Cook over a medium heat for 5 minutes, stirring regularly, until the custard has thickened and is smooth. Pour into a large bowl and allow to cool. Spoon the lime filling into the pastry cases.
- Put the reserved egg white into a bowl and whisk until it stands in stiff peaks. Add the remaining sugar a little at a time, and continue to beat until the mixture is stiff and shiny. Put in a piping bag fitted with a round 1cm/½in nozzle, and pipe around the edge of the tarts.
- Bake the tarts for 10 minutes or until the meringue is hard to the touch. Serve hot or cold.

Chocolate pecan pie

serves 6

ingredients

For the pastry
275g/10oz plain flour
50g/2oz cocoa powder
100g/4oz icing sugar
pinch of salt
200g/7oz butter, diced
1 egg yolk

For the filling
350g/12oz shelled pecan nuts
75g/3oz butter
175g/6oz Demerara sugar
3 eggs
2 tablespoons double cream
2 tablespoons plain flour
75g/3oz dark chocolate (at least
      70% cocoa solids)
1 tablespoon icing sugar, to dust

- Preheat the oven to 180°C/350°F/Gas mark 4.
- To make the pastry, sift the flour, cocoa, sugar and salt into a bowl and make a well in the centre. Put the butter and egg yolk in the well, and mix together, then gradually mix in the dry ingredients. Knead lightly into a ball. Cover with cling film and chill in the refrigerator for 1 hour.
- Unwrap the pastry and roll out on a lightly floured work surface. Use to line a 25cm/10in non-stick springform pie tin, and prick the base with a fork. Line the pastry shell with foil and fill with baking beans. Bake in the oven for 15 minutes. Remove from the oven, discard the beans and foil, and allow to cool. Leave the oven on.
- To make the filling, roughly chop 225g/8oz of the pecan nuts. Mix the butter with 50g/2oz of the Demerara sugar. Beat in the eggs one at a time, then add the remaining Demerara sugar and mix.
- Stir in the double cream, flour and chopped pecan nuts. Melt the chocolate in a heatproof bowl set over a pan of simmering water, then add to the mixture.
- Spoon the filling into the pastry shell, and smooth the surface. Cut the remaining pecan nuts in half, and arrange over the pie.
- Bake in the oven for 30 minutes, then cover the top of the pie with foil to prevent it burning and bake for a further 25 minutes. Remove the pie from the oven and let it cool slightly before removing from the tin and transferring to a wire rack to cool completely. Dust with the icing sugar.

Pumpkin pie
serves 8

ingredients

450g/1lb pumpkin
2 eggs, lightly beaten
150g/5oz Demerara sugar
75ml/3fl oz cream
1 tablespoon sweet sherry
1 teaspoon ground cinnamon
½ teaspoon ground nutmeg
½ teaspoon ground ginger

For the pastry
150g/5oz plain flour
100g/4oz butter, cubed
1 teaspoons caster sugar
75ml/3fl oz iced water
1 egg yolk, lightly beaten, to glaze
1 tablespoon milk, to glaze

- Lightly grease a 23cm/9in round pie dish.
- Peel the pumpkin and discard the seeds. Chop the flesh into small chunks, and steam or boil for 10 minutes or until the pumpkin is just tender. Drain thoroughly, mash and set aside to cool.
- To make the pastry, sift the flour into a large bowl, and rub in the butter using your fingertips until the mixture resembles fine breadcrumbs. Stir in the caster sugar.
- Make a well in the centre, add almost all of the iced water and mix with a flat-bladed knife. Add the remaining water, a little at a time, if necessary to bring the dough together. Gather the dough into a ball, and roll out between two sheets of baking parchment until large enough to cover the base and side of the pie dish. Line the dish with the pastry, trim away any excess and crimp the edges. Chill the pastry-lined dish for about 20 minutes.
- Preheat the oven to 180°C/350°F/Gas mark 4.
- Cut a piece of baking parchment large enough to cover the pie dish. Use to line the pastry shell, then spread baking beans over the paper. Bake blind for 10 minutes, then remove the paper and beans. Return the pie shell to the oven for a further 10 minutes or until lightly golden. Do not turn the oven off.
- To make the filling, whisk the eggs and Demerara sugar in a large bowl. Add the cooled mashed pumpkin, cream, sherry, cinnamon, nutmeg and ginger, and stir thoroughly until combined. Pour the filling into the pastry shell, smooth the surface with the back of a spoon, then bake for 40 minutes or until set.
- Serve the pie warm with ice cream or whipped cream.

Fruit & nut torte

serves 8

ingredients

75g/3oz caster sugar
450g/1lb lemon sponge
500g/1lb 2oz ricotta cheese
100g/4oz plain chocolate-coated
   almonds, finely chopped
75g/3oz soft nougat, finely chopped
50g/2oz mixed peel, finely chopped
finely grated zest of 1 orange
finely grated zest of 1 lemon
75g/3oz sultanas
2 tablespoons Amaretto or
   orange liqueur
175g/6oz flaked almonds, toasted
icing sugar, to dust

- Put the caster sugar in a large pan with 150ml/5fl oz water. Heat gently, stirring occasionally, until the sugar has dissolved. Bring to the boil and boil rapidly without stirring for 10 minutes until syrupy. Leave to cool.
- Line a 23cm/9in round springform cake tin with foil. Cut the lemon sponge into very thin slices. Use to line the bottom and sides of the tin.
- Beat the cheese in a bowl, then gradually add 150ml/5fl oz of the sugar syrup, stirring constantly.
- Stir in the almonds, nougat, mixed peel, orange and lemon zests, sultanas and liqueur. Beat thoroughly, then spoon into the sponge-lined tin. Sprinkle with the toasted almonds. Cover with cling film and chill overnight before serving.

Biscuits & Sweet Treats

This chapter includes those bite-size treats that all the family loves, and are perfect for tea-time, picnics, children's lunchboxes or snacks at any time of day. Whether you are looking to satisfy your sweet craving with a crunchy cookie or wish to succumb to the indulgent pleasure of home-made Turkish delight, you will be sure to find it within this chapter.

Viennese chocolate fingers

serves 8

ingredients

100g/4oz butter
75g/3oz icing sugar
175g/6oz self-raising flour, sifted
25g/1oz cornflour
200g/7oz dark chocolate (at least
   70% cocoa solids)

- Preheat the oven to 190°C/375°F/Gas mark 5. Lightly grease two baking trays.
- Cream the butter and sugar in a mixing bowl until light and fluffy. Gradually beat in the flour and cornflour.
- Melt 75g/3oz dark chocolate in a heatproof bowl set over a pan of simmering water. Beat the chocolate into the biscuit dough.
- Put the mixture in a piping bag fitted with a large star nozzle, and pipe fingers about 5cm/2in long on the baking trays, leaving room for spreading. Bake in the oven for 12–15 minutes.
- Remove from the oven, and leave to cool slightly on the baking trays, then transfer to a wire rack and allow to cool completely.
- Melt the remaining chocolate in a heatproof bowl set over a pan of simmering water, and dip one end of each biscuit in the chocolate, allowing the excess to drip back into the bowl.
- Put the biscuits on a sheet of baking parchment, and leave to set before serving.

Coconut sweet
serves 6

ingredients
75g/3oz butter
200g/7oz desiccated coconut
175ml/6fl oz condensed milk

- Put the butter in a heavy saucepan and melt over a low heat, stirring constantly. Add the desiccated coconut, stirring to mix. Stir in the condensed milk, and keep stirring continuously for 7–10 minutes.
- Remove the sepan from the heat, set aside and leave the coconut mixture to cool slightly.
- Once cool enough to handle, shape the mixture into long blocks and cut into equal-size rectangles. Leave to set for 1 hour.

● ●

Swiss biscuits
serves 6

ingredients
100g/4oz butter
50g/2oz granulated sugar
1 egg
1½ tablespoons freshly squeezed
    orange juice
1 tablespoon grated orange zest

300g/11oz plain flour
⅛ teaspoon bicarbonate of soda
75g/3oz chopped walnuts
100g/4oz dark chocolate (at
    least 70% cocoa solids),
    coarsely grated

- Grease a medium baking tray.
- Cream the butter and sugar until light and fluffy. Add the egg and beat well. Beat in the orange juice and grated zest. In a separate bowl, sift together the flour and bicarbonate of soda, then beat into the creamed mixture. Stir in the walnuts and chocolate. Wrap the mixture in cling film. Chill until firm enough to handle. Shape into a roll about 2.5cm/1in in diameter, wrap and chill again until very firm.
- Preheat the oven to 180°C/350°F/Gas mark 4.
- Cut the roll into slices about 1cm/½in thick, place on the baking tray and bake in the oven for 10–12 minutes. Remove from the oven, slide off the tray using a spatula and cool on a wire rack.

Spicy fruit biscuits
serves 10–12

ingredients
175g/6oz butter, softened
175g/6oz brown sugar
1 teaspoon vanilla essence
1 egg
250g/9oz plain flour, sifted
1 teaspoon mixed spice
½ teaspoon ground ginger
1 teaspoon baking powder
100g/4oz mincemeat

- Preheat the oven to 180°C/350°F/Gas mark 4. Line two baking trays with baking parchment.
- Using a hand-held mixer, cream the butter and sugar together in a small bowl until light and fluffy. Add the vanilla essence and egg, and beat until well combined. Transfer to a large bowl and add the sifted flour, mixed spice, ginger and baking powder.
- Using a knife, mix to a soft dough. Gather together, then divide the mixture into two portions.
- Roll one portion out into a rectangle about 3mm/⅛in thick, and trim the edges. Repeat with the other dough portion. Chill both until just firm.
- Spread each dough rectangle with mincemeat, then roll up like a Swiss roll. Cut the rolls into slices about 1cm/½in thick. Put on the prepared trays, leaving space between each slice.
- Bake in the oven for 10–15 minutes until golden. Cool on the trays for 3 minutes before transferring to a wire rack to cool completely.

Almond shortbread

serves 8

ingredients

150g/5oz plain flour
75g/3oz ground almonds
175g/6oz butter
100g/4oz caster sugar, plus extra
   for dusting
a few drops of almond essence
1 egg white, lightly beaten
50g/2oz flaked almonds

- Preheat the oven to 160°C/325°F/Gas mark 3. Lightly grease an 18 x 28cm/7 x 11in shallow baking tin.
- Combine the flour and ground almonds in a bowl. Cut the butter into small pieces, and rub into the flour and almonds with your fingertips until the mixture resembles breadcrumbs.
- Stir in the sugar and almond essence, then squeeze the mixture together to form a dough. Put the dough in the prepared baking tin. Spread to the edges by pressing it down with a metal spoon.
- Lightly brush the top of the dough with egg white, and sprinkle the flaked almonds over. Bake for 30–35 minutes until lightly browned. Leave to cool in the tin, then cut into individual biscuits. Dust with a little extra sugar just before serving.

Peanut butter slices
serves 8

ingredients

100g/4oz crunchy peanut butter
200g/7oz butter, softened
1 teaspoon vanilla essence
475g/1lb 1oz Demerara sugar

3 eggs
225g/8oz plain flour
½ teaspoon salt
175g/6oz icing sugar, sifted

- Preheat the oven to 180°C/350°F/Gas mark 4. Grease a 23cm/9in square cake tin.
- Beat together the peanut butter, butter and vanilla essence. When well blended, add the sugar and beat until light and fluffy. Beat in the eggs, one at a time, then stir in the flour and salt, sifted together, until blended.
- Spread into the cake tin, and bake for about 35 minutes. Remove from the oven and leave to cool slightly in the tin.
- To make the icing, mix together the icing sugar and 2 teaspoons water. Drizzle over the mixture in the tin.
- When cold, cut into slices.

Orange & ginger cream cheese fudge
serves 6

ingredients

350g/12oz dark chocolate (at least 70% cocoa solids), broken into pieces
75g/3oz cream cheese

275g/10oz icing sugar, sifted
1 satsuma, peeled and chopped
50g/2oz crystallized (candied) ginger, chopped

- Line a 10 x 8cm/4 x 3¾in baking tin with waxed paper.
- Put the chocolate in a small heatproof bowl over a pan of simmering water, and stir occasionally until melted.
- Gradually beat the melted chocolate into the cream cheese, and add the icing sugar a little at a time. Stir in the satsuma and ginger, and spoon the fudge into the baking tin. Refrigerate until firm.
- Cut out shapes or squares. Keep refrigerated, and eat within 7 days.

Easter nests

serves 4

ingredients

1 egg white

75g/3oz caster sugar

25g/1oz cornflour, sifted

50g/2oz dark chocolate (at least 70% cocoa solids), grated

16 mini chocolate eggs

- Preheat the oven to 140°C/275°C/Gas mark 1. Line a baking tray with greaseproof paper.
- Whisk the egg white until stiff. Gradually whisk in half of the sugar, then fold in the remainder with the cornflour and chocolate.
- Transfer the mixture to a piping bag with a large star nozzle, and pipe 6.5cm/2½in nests onto the baking tray.
- Bake in the oven for 45 minutes. Leave to cool, then fill with mini chocolate eggs.

● ●

Chocolate & apricot squares

serves 6

ingredients

100g/4oz butter

175g/6oz white chocolate, broken into small pieces

4 eggs

100g/4oz caster sugar

200g/7oz plain flour, sifted

1 teaspoon baking powder

pinch of salt

100g/4oz ready-to-eat dried apricots, chopped

- Preheat the oven to 180°C/350°F/Gas mark 4. Lightly grease a 23cm/9in square cake tin and line the bottom with baking parchment.
- Melt the butter and chocolate in a heatproof bowl set over a saucepan of simmering water. Stir frequently with a wooden spoon until the mixture is smooth and glossy. Leave the mixture to cool slightly.
- Beat the eggs and caster sugar into the butter and chocolate mixture until well combined.
- Fold in the flour, baking powder, salt and apricots, and incorporate well.
- Pour the mixture into the tin, and bake in the oven for 25–30 minutes. The centre of the cake may not be completely firm, but it will set as it cools. Leave in the tin to cool.
- When completely cold, turn out and slice into squares or bars.

Traditional oat flapjacks

serves 12

ingredients

25g/1oz golden syrup
50g/2oz caster sugar
75g/3oz butter
175g/6oz rolled oats

- Preheat the oven to 170°C/ 325°F/Gas mark 3. Lightly grease a shallow baking tin.
- Melt the syrup, sugar and butter together in a heavy pan. Remove from the heat. Stir in the oats and mix well.
- Press the mixture firmly into the tin, and bake in the oven for about 35 minutes. Leave to cool in the tin slightly, then cut into generous portions while still warm.

Almond slices

serves 8

ingredients

3 eggs
75g/3oz ground almonds
200g/7oz milk powder
200g/7oz granulated sugar
½ teaspoon saffron threads, crumbled
100g/4oz butter
1 tablespoon flaked almonds

- Preheat the oven to 160°C/ 325°F/Gas mark 3. Grease a shallow 15cm/6in ovenproof dish.
- Beat the eggs together in a bowl and set aside.
- Put the ground almonds, milk powder, sugar and saffron in a large mixing bowl, and stir well.
- Melt the butter in a small saucepan. Pour the melted butter over the dry ingredients, and mix well until thoroughly combined.
- Add the beaten eggs to the mixture, and mix well.
- Spread the mixture in the ovenproof dish, and bake for 45 minutes. Cut into slices, and decorate with the flaked almonds. Serve hot or cold.

Turkish delight
serves 6–8

ingredients
450g/1lb granulated sugar
¼ teaspoon tartaric acid
200g/7oz icing sugar, sifted
75g/3oz cornflour
50g/2oz clear honey
a few drops of rose water
red food colouring

To coat
175g/6oz icing sugar
1½ teaspoons bicarbonate of soda
¾ teaspoon citric acid

- Put the granulated sugar in a saucepan with 300ml/10 fl oz water. Heat gently, stirring continuously, until the sugar has dissolved.
- Bring to the boil, add the tartaric acid and remove from the heat.
- Put the icing sugar and cornflour in a saucepan, and gradually blend in 600ml/1pt water. Bring to the boil, stirring well until thick and syrupy.
- Reduce the heat and gradually beat in the sugar syrup. Bring to the boil, and boil steadily for 30 minutes until very pale golden and transparent.
- Beat in the honey and rose water, add a little colouring (add only a drop of two at a time, so that the Turkish delight is a delicate rose colour) and pour into an oiled 18cm/7in square tin. Leave to set.
- Sift together the coating ingredients, cut the Turkish delight into squares and toss in the coating.

Macadamia blondies

serves 12

ingredients

100g/4oz butter, cubed
100g/4oz white chocolate, broken
  into pieces
100g/4oz caster sugar
2 eggs, lightly beaten

1 teaspoon vanilla essence
100g/4oz self-raising flour, sifted
75g/3oz macadamia nuts, roughly
  chopped

- Preheat the oven to 180°C/350°F/Gas mark 4. Lightly grease a
  20cm/8in square tin and line with baking parchment, leaving the paper
  hanging over on two opposite sides.
- Put the butter and white chocolate in a heatproof bowl. Half-fill a
  saucepan with water, and bring to the boil. Remove from the heat. Place
  the bowl over the saucepan, making sure that the bottom of the bowl
  does not sit in the water. Stir occasionally until the butter and chocolate
  have melted and are smooth.
- Add the caster sugar to the bowl, and gradually stir in the eggs. Add the
  vanilla essence, fold in the flour and macadamia nuts, then pour into the
  prepared tin. Bake for 35–40 minutes. Leave to cool in the tin before
  lifting out and cutting into squares.

• •

Truffles

makes 24

ingredients

175g/6oz dark chocolate (at least
  70% cocoa solids)
2 tablespoons Amaretto
25g/1oz butter

50g/2oz icing sugar
50g/2oz ground almonds
50g/2oz milk chocolate, grated

- Melt the dark chocolate with the Amaretto in a heatproof bowl set over a
  saucepan of simmering water, stirring until well combined. Add the
  butter, and stir until it has melted.
- Stir in the icing sugar and ground almonds.
- Leave the mixture in a cool place until firm enough to roll into 24 balls.
- Put the grated chocolate on a plate and roll the truffles in the chocolate
  to coat them. Put the truffles in paper cases, and chill.

Apple brownies

serves 12

ingredients

225g/8oz butter, softened
400g/14oz granulated sugar
2 eggs, well beaten
1 teaspoon vanilla essence
475g/1lb 1oz plain flour
1 teaspoon baking powder
1 teaspoon ground cinnamon
¾ teaspoon salt
500g/1lb 2oz baking apples, peeled, cored and chopped
100g/4oz pecan nuts
icing sugar, to dust

- Preheat the oven to 180°C/ 350°F/Gas mark 4. Grease a 23cm/9in square baking tin.
- In a large mixing bowl, cream the butter, sugar, eggs and vanilla essence using an electric mixer.
- Combine the flour, baking powder, cinnamon and salt, then add to the butter mixture. Mix until the flour is moistened. Fold in the apples and pecan nuts.
- Spread the mixture in the baking tin, and bake in the oven for 45 minutes. Allow to cool in the tin on a wire rack, then cut into squares and dust with icing sugar.

Date flapjacks

serves 12

ingredients

100g/4oz butter
4 tablespoons clear honey
175g/6oz rolled oats
1 tablespoon sesame seeds
100g/4oz chopped dates
1 teaspoon ground cinnamon

- Preheat the oven to 180°C/ 350°F/Gas mark 4. Lightly grease a 20cm/8in square shallow baking tin.
- Melt the butter with the honey in a saucepan. Add the remaining ingredients, and mix thoroughly.
- Press the oat mixture into the baking tin, and bake for about 25 minutes until golden. Allow to cool on a wire rack, and cut into squares while still slightly warm.

Oatmeal cookies

serves 8

ingredients

225g/8oz raisins
475g/1lb 1oz plain flour
1 teaspoon baking powder
1 teaspoon ground cinnamon
½ teaspoon salt
175g/6oz butter
225g/8oz granulated sugar
2 eggs
475g/1lb 1oz oatmeal

- Preheat the oven to 190°C/ 375°F/Gas mark 5. Lightly grease a baking tray.
- Put the raisins in a saucepan, cover with water and cook until tender. Cool in their liquid.
- Sift the flour and add the baking powder, cinnamon and salt.
- Cream the butter and sugar until light and fluffy. Add the eggs, one at a time, beating well between each addition. Blend in the flour mixture. Add the oatmeal and fold in the raisins.
- Drop a teaspoonful of mixture at a time onto the baking tray. Bake for 10 minutes or until barely brown. Cool and store in layers, with waxed paper in between.

Chocolate crunch biscuits

serves 6

ingredients

100g/4oz milk chocolate, broken into pieces
15g/½oz butter
50g/2oz praline, finely crushed

- Grease a 15cm/6in shallow, square baking tin, and line with waxed paper.
- Put the chocolate and butter in a small heatproof bowl over a pan of simmering water, and stir gently until melted.
- Remove the bowl from the heat, and stir in the praline.
- Pour the mixture into the baking tin, and leave to set.
- When set, cut into biscuit-size pieces, ready to serve.

Dutch macaroons
serves 10

ingredients
2 egg whites
225g/8oz caster sugar
175g/6oz ground almonds
225g/8oz dark chocolate (at least
  70% cocoa solids)

- Preheat the oven to 180°C/350°F/Gas mark 4. Cover two baking trays
  with rice paper.
- Whisk the egg whites in a large mixing bowl until stiff, then fold in the
  sugar and almonds.
- Put the mixture in a large piping bag fitted with a 1cm/½in plain nozzle,
  and pipe fingers about 7.5cm/3in long, allowing space for the mixture
  to spread during cooking.
- Bake in the oven for 15–20 minutes until golden. Transfer to a wire rack
  and leave to cool. Remove the excess rice paper from around the edges.
- Melt the chocolate in a heatproof bowl set over a pan of simmering
  water. Dip the base of each biscuit into the chocolate. Put the macaroons
  on a sheet of baking parchment, and allow to set.
- Pipe any remaining chocolate over the biscuits in a drizzle pattern of
  stripes, and leave to set before serving.

Cranberry biscotti
serves 10

ingredients

500g/1lb 2oz plain flour
225g/8oz granulated sugar
½ teaspoon baking powder
½ teaspoon salt
75g/3oz butter, cubed
2 eggs
1 teaspoon vanilla essence
225g/8oz shelled pistachio nuts,
   coarsely chopped
2 tablespoons dried cranberries

- Lightly grease a baking tray. In a large bowl, combine the flour, sugar, baking powder and salt. Using a pastry blender or two knives, cut the butter into the flour mixture until the mixture resembles coarse crumbs.
- Mix in the eggs, one at a time, until a stiff dough forms. Add the vanilla essence, and stir in the pistachios and cranberries.
- Divide the dough in half, and shape each half into a 30 x 5cm/ 12 x 2in log on the baking tray. Cover with cling film, and refrigerate the logs for at least 30 minutes.
- Preheat the oven to 190°C/375°F/Gas mark 5. Remove the cling film from the logs, and bake for 20–25 minutes until the edges start to brown. Cool the logs on the baking tray for 10 minutes.
- Reduce the oven temperature to 170°C/325°F/Gas mark 3. Transfer the logs to a cutting board, and cut crosswise diagonally into 1cm/½in thick slices. Using the same baking tray, arrange the slices so that they lie flat (cut side down) in a single layer.
- Bake the slices for 20–25 minutes, turning once, until they are light golden brown on both sides. Cool completely on a wire rack. Store in an airtight container.

Rosemary biscuits

serves 4–6

ingredients

50g/2oz butter, softened
50g/2oz caster sugar
grated zest of 1 lemon
4 tablespoons freshly squeezed
   lemon juice
1 egg, separated
2 teaspoons finely chopped fresh
   rosemary leaves
200g/7oz plain flour, sieved

- Lightly grease two baking trays.
- In a large mixing bowl, cream together the butter and sugar until pale and fluffy.
- Add the lemon zest and juice, then the egg yolk, and beat until they are thoroughly combined. Stir in the rosemary.
- Add the flour, mixing well until a soft dough is formed. Wrap and leave to chill for 30 minutes.
- Preheat the oven to 180°C/350°F/Gas mark 4.
- On a lightly floured work surface, roll out the dough thinly, then stamp out 25 circles with a 6cm/2½in biscuit cutter. Arrange the dough circles on the prepared baking trays.
- In a bowl, lightly whisk the egg white. Gently brush the egg white over the surface of each biscuit.
- Bake in the oven for about 15 minutes. Transfer the biscuits to a wire rack and leave to cool before serving.

Peanut-frosted brownies
serves 8

ingredients
225g/8oz plain flour
100g/4oz cocoa powder
½ teaspoon baking powder
pinch of salt
100g/4oz butter, softened
350g/12oz soft brown sugar
3 eggs
1 teaspoon vanilla essence
225g/8oz unsalted peanuts

For the peanut frosting
50g/2oz butter
225g/8oz icing sugar, sifted
2 tablespoons smooth peanut butter
1 tablespoon boiling water

- Preheat the oven to 180°C/350°F/Gas mark 4. Grease a 30 x 23cm/ 12 x 9in baking tin.
- Sift the flour, cocoa, baking powder and salt into a bowl. Cream the butter and sugar, then beat in the eggs and the vanilla essence. Stir in the dry ingredients, and beat until smooth. Fold in half of the nuts.
- Spoon the mixture into the greased tin, and bake for 30 minutes.
- To make the peanut frosting, cream the butter and gradually mix in the icing sugar until light and fluffy. Combine the peanut butter with the boiling water and stir into the mixture.
- When the brownies are cooked, spread with the frosting and decorate with the remaining nuts.

Peanut butter cornets
makes 8

ingredients
8 sugar ice-cream cones
100g/4oz milk chocolate, broken into small pieces
4 tablespoons crunchy peanut butter
15g/½oz unsalted peanuts, finely chopped and toasted

- Slice about 2.5cm/1in off the top of each cone, and crush well. Reserve the cones.
- Put the chocolate and the peanut butter in a small saucepan, and heat very gently until melted. Stir in the crushed cone tops.
- Pour or spoon the mixture into the reserved cones, sprinkle with the peanuts and leave to set.

Marzipan cherries
makes 12

ingredients

12 glacé cherries
2 tablespoons brandy
250g/9oz marzipan

100g/4oz dark chocolate (at least
    70% cocoa solids)

- Line a baking tray with baking parchment.
- Cut the cherries in half, and put in a small bowl. Add the brandy and stir well to coat. Leave for at least 1 hour, stirring occasionally.
- Divide the marzipan into 24 pieces, and roll each piece into a ball. Press half a cherry into the top of each marzipan ball.
- Break the chocolate into pieces, place in a heatproof bowl and set over a pan of simmering water. Stir until all the chocolate has melted.
- Dip each sweet into the melted chocolate using a cocktail stick, allowing the excess to drip back into the bowl. Put the chocolate-coated marzipan cherries on the baking tray, and chill in the refrigerator until set.

● ●

Brandy snaps
serves 6

ingredients

75g/3oz caster sugar
25g/1oz butter
1 tablespoon golden syrup
25g/1oz plain flour

2 teaspoons ground ginger
freshly whipped cream, sweetened
    with a little icing sugar, to serve

- Preheat the oven to 150°C/300°F/Gas mark 2. Lightly grease a baking tray.
- Beat the sugar with the butter and golden syrup until light and thick. Sift in the flour and ginger, and stir together. Divide into 12 equal parts, then roll each one into a small ball and put on the baking tray. Bake for 10–15 minutes until they have spread into lacy golden brown biscuits.
- Allow to cool briefly, then lift them off, one at a time. At this point they will be pliable. Wrap them, one at a time, around the handle of a wooden spoon to bend in half. They should set hard very quickly.
- When ready to serve, pipe whipped cream into each brandy snap.

Coconut ice
serves 4–6

ingredients

450g/1lb granulated sugar
150ml/5fl oz milk

150g/5oz desiccated coconut
a few drops of red food colouring

- Grease a 20 x 15cm/8 x 6in shallow tin.
- Put the sugar and milk in a large saucepan and heat gently, stirring, until the sugar has dissolved. Bring to the boil, and boil steadily to 116°C/240°F, the soft-ball stage.
- Remove immediately from the heat, and stir in the coconut. Quickly pour half of the mixture into the greased tin. Add a few drops of red food colouring to the remaining mixture, stir through and quickly but carefully pour over the first layer. Leave to cool, and mark into squares while still slightly warm. Leave to set completely, and cut into bite-size pieces.

Easter biscuits
serves 4–8

ingredients

125g/4oz butter
75g/3oz caster sugar
1 egg, separated
200g/7oz plain flour
pinch of salt
½ teaspoon mixed spice

½ teaspoon ground cinnamon
50g/2oz currants
25g/1oz chopped mixed peel
2 tablespoons milk
caster sugar for sprinkling

- Preheat the oven to 200°C/400°F/Gas mark 6. Lightly grease two baking trays.
- Cream together the butter and sugar, and beat in the egg yolk.
- Sift together the flour, salt and spices. Fold into the creamed mixture with the currants and peel. Add the milk to form a soft dough.
- Knead lightly on a floured work surface, and roll out to 8mm/¼in thick. Cut out using a 6cm/2½in fluted cutter, and put on the baking trays.
- Bake in the oven for 10 minutes, then brush with egg white and sprinkle with caster sugar. Return to the oven for a further 10–15 minutes.
- Remove from the oven, and carefully slide onto a wire rack to cool.

Tollhouse cookies
makes about 20

ingredients
175g/6oz butter, softened
100g/4oz Demerara sugar
100g/4oz granulated sugar
2 eggs, lightly beaten
1 teaspoon vanilla essence
275g/10oz plain flour
1 teaspoon bicarbonate of soda
300g/11oz dark chocolate chips
100g/4oz pecan nuts,
   roughly chopped

- Preheat the oven to 190°C/375°F/Gas mark 5. Line two baking trays with baking parchment.
- Cream the butter and sugars in a bowl with an electric beater until light and fluffy.
- Gradually add the eggs, beating well after each addition. Stir in the vanilla, then the sifted flour and bicarbonate of soda until just combined. Mix in the chocolate chips and pecan nuts.
- Drop tablespoonfuls of the mixture onto the trays, leaving room for spreading. Bake the cookies for 8–10 minutes until lightly golden. Cool slightly on the trays before transferring to a wire rack to cool completely.

Highball cups
makes 10

ingredients

100g/4oz dark chocolate (at least 70% cocoa solids), broken into pieces
100g/4oz fudge

2 teaspoons whisky
2 teaspoons chopped preserved stem ginger

- Melt the chocolate in a heatproof bowl set over a pan of simmering water, then pour evenly between 10 small foil sweet cases or bonbon cups. Tilt the cases to coat the entire inside. When set, remove the cases.
- Put the fudge in a small heatproof bowl over a pan of simmering water, and stir until melted.
- Remove the bowl from the pan, and stir in the whisky. Cool slightly.
- Divide the ginger between the chocolate cups, and spoon some fudge into each one. Leave to set.

● ●

Nougat
serves 4–6

ingredients

75g/3oz clear honey
50g/2oz granulated sugar
50g/2oz liquid glucose

3 egg whites
225g/8oz mixed chopped glacé cherries, angelica and almonds

- Line an 18cm/7in square tin with rice paper.
- Leave the honey to melt in a small bowl over a pan of simmering water.
- Gently heat the sugar and 150ml/5fl oz water in a saucepan, stirring continuously, until the sugar has dissolved. Add the glucose, bring to the boil, and boil steadily.
- Pour the honey into the sugar syrup, and continue boiling.
- Whisk the egg whites in a large bowl until very stiff, and gradually whisk in the hot syrup. Put the bowl over a pan of simmering water, and keep whisking until the mixture is very thick and firm.
- Remove the bowl from the heat, stir in the fruit and nuts, and turn the mixture into the tin. Cover the nougat with more rice paper, place a thick piece of card over the top, and weigh down overnight.
- Turn out and cut into bite-size squares.

Dips, Dressings, Sauces and Stocks

While you can buy most dips, sauces and dressings ready-made, it is disarmingly simple to make your own using quality fresh ingredients – and the results are delicious. Salad dressings, in particular, are very quick and easy to make. Classic dips are ideal for offering before a barbecue or at a party, or even just for a snack. Rich home-made stocks, although requiring more effort, undoubtedly have the edge over any shop-bought stock cubes, and are incredibly useful as the base for numerous soups, sauces and casseroles.

Spicy avocado dip
serves 6–10

ingredients

2 medium-ripe avocados
450ml/³4pt sour cream
1 bunch of spring onions,
   chopped
½ teaspoon cayenne pepper
1½ tablespoons freshly squeezed
   lemon juice
salt and freshly ground
   black pepper

- Halve the avocados and remove the stones. Peel and discard the skin; roughly chop the flesh.
- Put the avocado, sour cream, onions, cayenne and 1 tablespoon of the lemon juice in a blender or food processor. Purée until smooth.
- Spoon into a serving bowl and season with salt and pepper. Add more lemon juice to taste. Cover with a layer of cling film pressed lightly on the surface of the dip, and chill until ready to serve.

Aubergine caviar
serves 8

ingredients

900g/2lb small aubergines
4 tablespoons olive oil
2 garlic cloves
1 teaspoon smoked paprika
3 large pitta breads
1 egg white
2 tablespoons cumin seeds
freshly ground black pepper

- Preheat the oven to 180°C/ 350°F/Gas mark 4.
- Dice the aubergine, and steam in a colander or a bamboo steamer over a pan of boiling water for 30 minutes.
- Heat the oil in a large heavy saucepan over a medium-high heat. Add the steamed aubergine, garlic and paprika. Season with pepper. Simmer for 10 minutes, stirring constantly, until the aubergine is soft.
- To prepare the pitta bread, split each into 2 rounds. Brush with the white of the egg and sprinkle with cumin seeds. Bake in the oven for 15 minutes until crisp. Serve with the aubergine caviar for dipping.

Guacamole
serves 8

ingredients

2 ripe avocados
juice of 1 lemon
2 tablespoons olive oil
1 small onion, finely chopped
1 garlic clove, crushed
225g/8oz tomatoes, peeled,
    seeded and finely chopped

1 small fresh green chilli, seeded
    and finely chopped
chopped fresh coriander leaves,
    to garnish

- Halve the avocados and remove the stones. Peel and discard the skin. Roughly chop the flesh. Transfer to a bowl and, using a fork, mash with the lemon juice.
- Add the remaining ingredients, except for the coriander, and blend the mixture until smooth. Cover with a layer of cling film pressed lightly on the surface of the dip. Chill until needed.
- Garnish with the chopped coriander just before serving.

Taramasalata
serves 4

ingredients

225g/8oz smoked cod's roe
1 onion, finely grated
200ml/7fl oz olive oil

5 slices white bread, crusts
    removed
juice of 3 lemons

- If the roe is fairly salty, soak the cod's roe in water for 2 hours, then drain thoroughly and peel off the skin. If the roe is not too salty and the skins are soft enough, however, simply peel off without soaking first.
- Using a fork, mash the cod's roe in a bowl, and add the onion. Add a little of the olive oil, then transfer to a blender or food processor. Purée into a smooth paste.
- Moisten the bread and gently squeeze out any excess water. Continue blending the cod's roe mixture, alternately adding small bits of moistened bread, the remaining olive oil and the lemon juice. Blend until the taramasalata is smooth and cream in colour. Serve with pitta bread.

Two-cheese dip

serves 8

ingredients

1 red pepper, halved and seeded
1 yellow pepper, halved and
    seeded
110g/4oz dolcelatte cheese
225g/8oz mascarpone cheese
1 tablespoon freshly squeezed
    lemon juice
4 small gherkins
salt and freshly ground
    black pepper

- Grill the peppers for about 5 minutes or until their skins are charred. When cool enough to handle, peel off and discard the skin, and chop the flesh finely.
- Using a fork, mash the dolcelatte in a bowl. Stir in the mascarpone and lemon juice, then add the peppers and gherkins. Season with salt and pepper, and serve with crudités or toasted flatbread such as pitta.

Salmon dip

serves 4

ingredients

3 tablespoons cream cheese
1 tablespoon horseradish sauce
125g/4½oz smoked salmon
squeeze of lemon juice
salt and freshly ground
    black pepper

- Mix the cream cheese with the horseradish. In a blender or food processor, purée the salmon and lemon juice, and add to the cream cheese mixture.
- Season with salt and pepper, and chill before serving.

Gorgonzola dip

serves 12

ingredients

225g/8oz Gorgonzola cheese
300ml/10fl oz whipping cream
1 tablespoon Worcestershire
    sauce
salt and freshly ground
    black pepper

- Mix the cheese and cream together using a wooden spoon, then beat well until thick and creamy.
- Stir in the Worcestershire sauce, and season with salt and pepper. Chill before serving with crudités or toasted flatbread such as pitta.

Anchovy dip

serves 6

ingredients

100g/4oz canned anchovy
  fillets, drained
2 garlic cloves, finely chopped
1 tablespoon mayonnaise
1 tablespoon olive oil
2–3 tablespoons freshly
  squeezed lemon juice
freshly ground black pepper
1 tablespoon chopped fresh
  parsley, to garnish

- Soak the anchovies in cold water for 10 minutes, then drain and pat dry with kitchen paper.
- In a blender or food processor, combine the anchovies, garlic and mayonnaise. Season with pepper. Gradually dribble the oil in a few drops at a time, stirring constantly until thick and smooth.
- Spoon into a serving dish, and stir in lemon juice to taste.
- Garnish with the parsley, and serve with crudités or toasted flatbread such as pitta.

Anchovy & garlic dip

serves 8

ingredients

225g/8oz cream cheese,
  softened
150ml/10fl oz single cream
50g/2oz canned anchovy fillets
  in olive oil, drained
freshly ground black pepper

- Using a wooden spoon, beat the cheese and cream together until light and airy.
- Pat the anchovies dry on kitchen paper, and chop finely.
- Add the anchovies to the cream cheese mixture, and season with black pepper.
- Chill before serving with a selection of crudités or toasted flatbread such as pitta.

Cucumber yogurt dip
serves 12

ingredients
500ml/18fl oz Greek-style yogurt
1 tablespoon olive oil
¾ tablespoon freshly squeezed
  lemon juice
½ teaspoon finely chopped
  fresh mint
1 small garlic clove, crushed
1 large cucumber, peeled,
  seeded and grated
salt
chopped fresh flat-leaf parsley,
  to garnish

- Mix together the yogurt, oil, lemon juice, mint, garlic and salt to taste.
- Stir in the cucumber, and chill for at least 1 hour.
- Sprinkle the parsley on top before serving with crudités or toasted flatbread such as pitta.

Cucumber & herb dip
serves 6–8

ingredients
225g/8oz cream cheese,
  softened
½ cucumber, finely shredded
25g/1oz Emmenthal cheese,
  grated
½ teaspoon chopped fresh dill
½ teaspoon lemon juice
¼ teaspoon freshly minced garlic
salt and freshly ground
  black pepper

- Mix all the ingredients in a blender or food processor until smooth, seasoning to taste.
- Transfer to a serving dish and chill for 2 hours or until ready to serve.
- Serve with crudités or toasted flatbread such as pitta.

Curry & mayonnaise dip
serves 6

ingredients
150g/5oz mayonnaise
2 teaspoons curry powder
1 tablespoon grated onion
½ teaspoon dry mustard powder
1 teaspoon Tabasco sauce
salt and ground black pepper

- Mix all the ingredients together well, seasoning to taste. Chill for at least 2 hours.
- Serve with crudités or toasted flatbread such as pitta.

Blue cheese & avocado dip
serves 6

ingredients
125g/4½oz blue cheese
125g/4½oz chopped avocado
1 tablespoon chopped fresh
   flat-leaf parsley
1 tablespoon chopped
   fresh chives
1 teaspoon chopped fresh chilli
2 tablespoons mayonnaise
salt and ground black pepper

- Blend or process all the ingredients together until smooth, seasoning to taste. Chill for at least 2 hours.
- Serve with crudités or toasted flatbread such as pitta.

Garlic dip
serves 12

ingredients
6 garlic cloves
350g/12oz cold mashed potato
2 tablespoons freshly squeezed
   lemon juice
5 tablespoons olive oil
salt and freshly ground
   black pepper

- Using a mortar and pestle, mash the garlic with a generous pinch of salt until it is a smooth paste.
- Mix into the mashed potato, and blend until well combined.
- Stir in the lemon juice and olive oil. When smooth, season with salt and pepper. Cover and chill.
- Serve with crudités or toasted flatbread such as pitta.

Chilli tomato dip
serves 12

ingredients

1 large onion, finely chopped

400g/14oz canned chopped tomatoes, drained

2 fresh green chillies, seeded and finely chopped

1 fresh red red chilli, seeded and finely chopped

2 teaspoons granulated sugar

1 garlic clove, crushed

¼ teaspoon ground turmeric

1 teaspoon curry powder

125ml/4fl oz sunflower oil

½ teaspoon chilli powder

• Heat the oil in a pan over a low heat, add the onions and sweat gently. Add the tomatoes, and keep stirring until the tomatoes are broken up. Add the remaining ingredients, and stir well.

• Simmer for 20 minutes, stirring regularly to avoid the mixture catching on the bottom of the pan. Continue cooking until the liquid is nearly gone. Remove from the heat and allow to cool.

• Serve at room temperature with toasted flatbread such as pitta.

Tapenade
serves 12

ingredients

50g/2oz canned anchovies in olive oil

250g/9oz pitted black olives

2 tablespoons capers, rinsed and drained

4 tablespoons extra virgin olive oil

squeeze of lemon juice

1 baguette, sliced and toasted

• Put the anchovies, capers and olives into a blender, and chop for a minute or so.

• With the motor running, gradually add the olive oil in a thin constant stream, then add the lemon juice.

• Transfer to a bowl and chill until needed. Serve on freshly toasted slices of baguette.

Note?Tapenade makes a good spread with other ingredients on sandwiches such as muffuletta, panini or focaccia; it can also be used as a condiment. It will keep for up to 2 weeks stored in a glass screwtop jar in the refrigerator.

Hummus
serves 8

ingredients
450g/1lb chickpeas
½ teaspoon baking powder
425g/15oz tahini
1 tablespoon freshly squeezed
   lemon juice salt

- Soak the chickpeas in cold water overnight. Drain, put in a heavy saucepan and cover with water. Add the baking powder, bring to the boil and cook for 10 minutes. Reduce to a simmer, and cook for 1½–2 hours until the chickpeas are soft and mashable.
- Drain the chickpeas, put in a bowl and mash with a fork. Add the remaining ingredients and 200ml/7fl oz water. Mix well and chill for at least 3 hours before serving.

Mayonnaise
makes 300ml/10fl oz

ingredients
2 large egg yolks
1 teaspoon dry English mustard
   powder
pinch of salt
300ml/10fl oz groundnut oil or
   extra virgin olive oil
1 teaspoon white wine vinegar
freshly ground black pepper

- Put the egg yolks into a 900ml/1½pt basin with a narrow base. Add the mustard powder. Season with the pinch of salt and pepper, and mix well using a metal spoon.
- Using an electric whisk, gradually add the oil one drop at a time, whisking thoroughly between each addition. When the mixture begins to thicken, you can begin to add slightly more oil at a time.
- When about half the oil has been incorporated, add the vinegar. Pour in the remaining oil in a steady trickle, whisking all the time.
- Use straight away, or store in a screwtop jar in the refrigerator for no more than a week.

Garlic mayonnaise
makes 300ml/10fl oz

ingredients
4 garlic cloves, minced
2 large egg yolks
pinch of salt
250ml/9fl oz olive oil
juice of 1 small lemon
½ tablespoon boiling water

- Put the garlic, egg yolks and pinch of salt into a 900ml/1½pt basin with a narrow base. Mix well using a metal spoon.
- Using an electric whisk, gradually add the oil one drop at a time, whisking thoroughly between each addition. Once about half the oil is incorporated, start to add in drops of the lemon juice.
- When the mixture begins to thicken, you can begin to add slightly more oil at a time. The mixture should become thick and well combined.
- Stir in the boiling water to prevent the mayonnaise from separating. Use straight away, or store in a screwtop jar in the refrigerator for no more than a week.

• •

Garlic & herb mayonnaise
serves 12

ingredients
1 garlic clove, crushed with salt
250g/9oz mayonnaise
1 tablespoon chopped
fresh chives
1 tablespoon chopped fresh
flat-leaf parsley
1 tablespoon freshly squeezed
lemon juice

- Combine the crushed garlic with the mayonnaise and the remaining ingredients.
- Mix well and chill before serving. This mayonnaise is best used quickly because of the fresh herbs.

French vinaigrette
makes 150ml/5fl oz

ingredients

2 tablespoons red or white
   wine vinegar
125ml/4fl oz light olive oil
1 teaspoon Dijon mustard
1 garlic clove
pinch of sugar
salt and freshly ground
   black pepper

- Combine all the ingredients in a screw-top glass jar. Secure the lid firmly, and shake vigorously. Leave to infuse for 2 hours.
- Remove the garlic clove, then leave the vinaigrette overnight before using. It will keep for up to a week if stored in the refrigerator.

Lemon mustard vinaigrette
makes 150ml/5fl oz

ingredients

1 teaspoon Dijon mustard
3 tablespoons fresh lemon juice
125ml/4fl oz extra virgin
   olive oil
salt and freshly ground
   black pepper

- In a small bowl, whisk the mustard and lemon juice together.
- Whisking constantly, slowly drizzle in the olive oil until everything is combined and an emulsion forms. Season with salt and pepper, and let stand for 30 minutes.
- Use straight away, or store in a glass jar with a tight-fitting lid in the refrigerator for up to a week. Shake well before use.

Variations
- Add finely chopped fresh herbs such as parsley, basil, marjoram and mint.
- Sprinkle in some rinsed and drained capers, or some finely sliced gherkins or diced shallots.
- Add 1½ tablespoons roasting juices, with the oil drained, if using the dressing for a meat salad. Use straight away.

Béchamel sauce
makes 450ml/¾pt

ingredients
450ml/¾pt milk
1 bay leaf
10 whole black peppercorns
1 slice onion, about 1cm/½in thick

50g/2oz butter
25g/1oz plain flour
salt and freshly ground
   black pepper

- Put the milk in a heavy saucepan over a low heat, and add the bay leaf, peppercorns and onion. Cook for about 5 minutes, letting it come slowly to simmering point. Remove the pan from the heat, and strain the milk into a jug, discarding the flavourings.
- Melt the butter gently in a separate pan. As soon as the butter melts, add the flour and, over a medium heat, stir quite vigorously using a wooden spoon to make a smooth paste, or roux.
- Add the milk a little at a time, stirring vigorously between each addition. When about half the milk is in, switch to a whisk and start adding more milk at a time, whisking briskly, until all the milk has been added.
- Reduce the heat to low, and let the sauce simmer gently for 5 minutes, whisking occasionally. Season with salt and pepper.

• •

Barbecue sauce
makes 600ml/1pt

ingredients
2 tablespoons vegetable oil
1 onion, finely chopped
3 garlic cloves, minced
225ml/8fl oz tomato ketchup or
   tomato sauce

350ml/12fl oz cider vinegar
50ml/2fl oz Worcestershire sauce
75g/3oz golden granulated sugar
1 teaspoon chilli powder
½ teaspoon cayenne pepper

- Heat the oil in a saucepan over a medium heat. Add the onion and garlic, and sweat gently, stirring, for about 5 minutes.
- Add the ketchup or tomato sauce, vinegar, Worcestershire sauce, sugar, chilli powder and cayenne.
- Reduce the heat and simmer, partially covered, for about 20 minutes until the sauce has thickened slightly.

Tomato sauce

makes 600ml/1pt

ingredients

300ml/10fl oz white vinegar
1 teaspoon mixed spice
1.4kg/3lb ripe tomatoes, sliced
25g/1oz salt
100g/4oz golden granulated
    sugar such as Demerara

- Put the vinegar and mixed spice in a stainless-steel or enamelled saucepan. Bring to the boil and remove from the heat. Cover and leave to infuse for 3–4 hours.
- Put the tomatoes in a separate heavy saucepan over a medium heat, and simmer gently until pulpy.
- Rub the tomato pulp through a sieve into a bowl. Return the strained pulp to the cleaned pan. Add the salt and simmer gently until the mixture thickens. Add the sugar and infused vinegar, stirring until completely dissolved.
- Continue simmering, stirring occasionally, until the mixture is the consistency of whipped cream. Pot into hot sterilized glass jars, and seal tightly (make sure the lids are vinegar-proof). The tomato sauce will keep for up to 6 months.

Creamed tomato sauce

makes 300ml/10fl oz

ingredients

6 ripe tomatoes
125ml/4fl oz double cream
50ml/2fl oz plain yogurt
salt and freshly ground
    black pepper

- Scald the tomatoes in a bowl of just-boiled water for 30 seconds. Peel, then finely chop the flesh.
- Put the tomatoes in a heavy saucepan, and add 175ml/6fl oz water. Cover the pan, and simmer until the sauce is thick and creamy.
- Stir in the cream and yogurt. Season with salt and pepper, and serve hot or warm.

Chicken stock
makes 1.8 litres/3pt

ingredients

1 x 1kg/2¼lb raw chicken
carcass

100g/4oz carrot, coarsely
chopped

100g/4oz celery, coarsely
chopped

200g/7oz onion, coarsely
chopped

3 garlic cloves

1 teaspoon salt

1 bouquet garni

- Put the chicken carcass in a large stockpot and cover with 3 litres/ 5pt water. Add the remaining ingredients, and bring to the boil over a high heat.
- Skim off any cloudy scum that rises to the surface and, once the scum stops forming, reduce the heat to medium and simmer, uncovered, for 2 hours. If you wish to reduce the stock, stir over a high heat until reduced to the required amount.
- Carefully strain through a fine-mesh sieve and leave to cool. Refrigerate for 8 hours or overnight, then skim off any fat from the surface.
- Store in the refrigerator and use within 3 days, or divide into portions and freeze until needed.

Vegetable stock
makes 500ml/18fl oz

ingredients

1 tablespoon olive oil

2 leeks, roughly chopped

2 carrots, chopped

1 celery stick, chopped

1 small russet potato, chopped

2 garlic cloves, halved

50g/2oz dried red lentils

1 bay leaf

½ teaspoon peppercorns

½ tablespoon light soy sauce

pinch of dried thyme

6 sprigs of fresh flat-leaf parsley

- Put the oil in a large casserole dish over a medium heat. Sauté the leeks, carrots, celery, potato and garlic until slightly browned. Add 1.2 litres/2pt water and the remaining ingredients.
- Bring to the boil, then reduce the heat and simmer, uncovered, for 1 hour. Strain the stock through a fine-mesh sieve and leave to cool.
- Store in the refrigerator and use within 3 or 4 days, or divide into portions and freeze until needed.

Beef stock
makes 1.8 litres/3pt

ingredients

2.7kg/6lb beef bones
1 large onion, sliced
3 large carrots, chopped
2 celery sticks, chopped
1 large tomato
100g/4oz parsnip, chopped
100g/4oz potatoes, cubed

8 whole black peppercorns
4 sprigs of fresh flat-leaf parsley
1 bay leaf
1 tablespoon salt
2 teaspoons dried thyme
2 garlic cloves

- Preheat the oven to 230°C/450°F/Gas mark 8.
- Put the beef bones, onion and carrots in a large shallow roasting pan. Roast in the oven, uncovered, for 30 minutes or until the bones are browned, turning occasionally.
- Drain off any fat. Put the browned bones, onion and carrots in a large stockpot or heavy saucepan. Pour 150ml/5fl oz water into the roasting pan and swirl around the pan. Pour this liquid into the soup pot. Add the celery, tomato, parsnip, potatoes, peppercorns, parsley, bay leaf, salt, thyme and garlic. Pour in 2.8 litres/4¾pt water.
- Bring the mixture to the boil, then skim off any cloudy scum from the surface. Reduce the heat, cover the pan and simmer gently for 5 hours, skimming off scum from time to time as necessary.
- Carefully strain the stock through a fine-mesh sieve. Discard the meat, vegetables and seasonings. Leave the stock to cool completely, then skim off any fat from the surface and discard.
- Store the stock in the refrigerator and use within 3 days, or divide into portions and freeze until needed.

Fish stock

makes 1.8 litres/3pt

ingredients

2.3kg/5lb fish trimmings
5 onions, quartered
5 celery sticks, including leaves,
   chopped
5 sprigs of fresh flat-leaf parsley
5 bay leaves
1 teaspoon dried thyme
750ml/11/4pt dry white wine
salt and freshly ground black pepper

- Put all the ingredients in a large stockpot or heavy saucepan, and add 3 litres/5pt water. Set over a high heat, bring to the boil, then skim off any scum from the surface.
- Reduce the heat and simmer, uncovered, for about 40 minutes, continuing to skim off scum from the surface as it rises. Carefully strain the liquor through a fine-mesh sieve, and discard the seasonings.
- Allow to cool, then refrigerate until needed. Use on the same day the stock is made, or divide into portions and freeze until needed.

Conversion
tables

Weights

Imperial	Approx. metric equivalent	Imperial	Approx. metric equivalent
1/2oz	15g	1 1/4lb	600g
1oz	25g	1 1/2lb	700g
1 1/2oz	40g	1 3/4lb	850g
2oz	50g	2lb	900g
2 1/2oz	60g	2 1/2lb	1.1kg
3oz	75g	3lb	1.4kg
4oz	100g	3 1/2lb	1.6kg
5oz	150g	4lb	1.8kg
6oz	175g	4 1/2lb	2kg
7oz	200g	5lb	2.3kg
8oz	225g	5 1/2lb	2.5kg
9oz	250g	6lb	2.7kg
10oz	275g	6 1/2lb	3kg
11oz	300g	7lb	3.2kg
12oz	350g	7 1/2lb	3.4kg
13oz	375g	8lb	3.6kg
14oz	400g	8 1/2lb	3.9kg
15oz	425g	9lb	4.1kg
16oz (1lb)	450g	9 1/2lb	4.3kg
1lb 2oz	500g	10lb	4.5kg

The Imperial pound (lb), which is 16 ounces (oz), equals approximately 450 grams (g).

Oven temperatures

°C	°F	Gas mark	Temperature
130	250	1/2	Very cool
140	275	1	Very cool
150	300	2	Cool
160–170	325	3	Warm
180	350	4	Moderate
190	375	5	Fairly hot
200	400	6	Fairly hot
210–220	425	7	Hot
230	450	8	Very hot
240	475	9	Very hot

Oven temperatures

Imperial	Approx. metric equivalent	Imperial	Approx. metric equivalent
1fl oz	25ml	9fl oz	250ml
2fl oz	50ml	10fl oz (1/2pt)	300ml
3fl oz	75ml	12fl oz	350ml
3 1/2 fl oz	100ml	15fl oz (3/4pt)	450ml
4fl oz	125ml	18 fl oz	500ml
5fl oz (1/4pt)	150ml	20fl oz (1pt)	600ml
6fl oz	175ml	30fl oz (1 1/2pt)	900ml
7fl oz	200ml	35 fl oz (2pt)	1.2 litres
8fl oz	225ml	40 fl oz (2 1/2pt)	1.5 litres

Spoon measures

All the measurements given in the recipes are for level spoonfuls (British Imperial Standard)
1 teaspoon = 5ml
1 tablespoon = 15ml

The tablespoon measurements below are equivalent to approximately 1oz (25g) of the following ingredients:

Breadcrumbs (dried)	3	Flour, unsifted	3
Breadcrumbs (fresh)	7	Rice (uncooked)	2
Butter/margarine/lard	2	Sugar (granulated, caster)	2
Cheese, grated (Cheddar)	3	Sugar (icing)	3
Cheese, grated (Parmesan)	4	Honey/syrup	1
Cocoa powder	4	Yeast (dried)	2
Cornflour/custard powder	2 1/2		

index

A

Alaskan pink salmon
Alaskan salmon chowder 434
Alaskan salmon chowder 434
Alaskan blueberry coffee cake 670
Almond cake 678
Almond chicken casserole 220
Almond friands 669
Almond shortbread 701
Almond slices 704
Almond soup 10
almonds
    Almond cake 678
    Almond chicken casserole 220
    Almond friands 669
    Almond shortbread 701
    Almond slices 704
    Almond soup 10
    Amaretti 610
    Bakewell tart 664
    Coffee almond ice-cream cake 689
    Dutch macaroons 709
    Frangipane tart 691
    Marzipan 638
    Nutty rice salad 111
    Trout with almonds 472
    Tuna almondine 475
Amaretti 610
anchovies
    Anchovy & garlic dip 721
    Anchovy dip 721
    Anchovy tart 163
    Classic Caesar salad 96
    Lamb & anchovies with thyme 319
    Squid with wine & rosemary 459
    Tapenade 724
Anchovy & garlic dip 721
Anchovy dip 721
Anchovy tart 163
Apple & blackcurrant pancakes 557
Apple & Brie omelette 129
Apple & cheddar pie 172
Apple brown betty 692
Apple brownies 707
Apple Charlotte 571
Apple couscous pudding 569
Apple cranberry casserole 250

Apple galettes 687
Apple pie 589
Apple strudel 591
Apple turnovers 661
apples
    Apple & blackcurrant pancakes 557
    Apple & Brie omelette 129
    Apple & cheddar pie 172
    Apple brown betty 692
    Apple brownies 707
    Apple Charlotte 571
    Apple couscous pudding 569
    Apple cranberry casserole 250
    Apple galettes 687
    Apple pie 589
    Apple strudel 591
    Apple turnovers 661
    Apple-stuffed chicken 343
    Baked apples in honey & lemon 566
    Caramelized apple tarts 669
    Curried carrot & apple soup 38
    Date & apple muffins 678
    Grilled apple stack 647
    Lemon chocolate cake 682
    Passion fruit & apple foam 604
    Pork with apples 296
    Potato apple cake 682
    Rhubarb & apple cobbler 599
    Sly cakes 660
    Snow-capped apples 648
    Strawberry & apple crumble 575
    Strawberry baked apples 567
    Waldorf chicken salad 98
Apple-stuffed chicken 343
Apricot & orange jellies 633
Apricot delice 609
Apricot fool 602
Apricot soufflé 588
apricots
    Apricot delice 609
    Apricot fool 602
    Apricot & orange jellies 633
    Apricot soufflé 588
    Armenian stew 239
    Chocolate & apricot squares 703
    Pork & apricot casserole 191
    Quick apricot whip 634

Spiced fruity couscous 521
Armenian stew 239
Aromatic green casserole 240
Artichoke & prawn cocktail 86
artichokes
 Artichoke & prawn cocktail 86
 Chickpea & artichoke stew 248
 Cream of artichoke soup 42
 Fresh salad with raspberry
  vinaigrette 113
 Grilled artichoke salad 94
 Jerusalem artichoke soup 10
 Spinach & artichoke casserole 248
asparagus
 Asparagus & bean beef 269
 Asparagus & chorizo salad 72
 Asparagus & potato salad 98
 Asparagus cashew stir-fry 481
 Broccoli & asparagus fusilli 488
 Courgette & asparagus parcels 535
 Grilled asparagus & leeks 48
 Salmon & asparagus linguine 447
Asparagus & bean beef 269
Asparagus & chorizo salad 72
Asparagus & potato salad 98
Asparagus cashew stir-fry 481
Aubergine cake 552
Aubergine caviar 718
Aubergine, mozzarella & Cheddar
 hotpot 252
Aubergine with pork & prawns 284
aubergines
 Aubergine cake 552
 Aubergine caviar 718
 Aubergine, mozzarella & Cheddar
  hotpot 252
 Aubergine with pork & prawns 284
 Brinjal curry 483
 Chargrilled kebabs 545
 Chunky vegetable chilli 254
 Moussaka 312
 Pasticcio 512
 Ratatouille 529
 Ratatouille penne bake 548
 Roasted Mediterranean
  vegetables 537
 Tunisian vegetables 526

Turkish lamb stew 310
Autumn barley stew 240
Autumn fruit game hens 403
Avocado cream 87
avocados
 Avocado cream 87
 Blue cheese & avocado dip 723
 Chilled avocado soup 11
 Guacamole 719
 Mango & melon ginger salad 656
 Spicy avocado dip 718

B

bacon see also smoked back bacon
 Bacon & split pea soup 11
 Bacon-wrapped prawns 71
 Bacon-wrapped turkey burgers 385
 Baked bean & bacon casserole 192
 Banana & pecan salad 114
 Beef & stout casserole 182
 Cheesy potato skins 80
 Chicken & bacon kebabs 61
 Classic Caesar salad 96
 Devils on horseback 74
 Game pie 171
 Liver, bacon & onions 321
 Onion tart 161
 Pâté en croûte 78
 Pork & liver pâté 77
 Potato soup 27
 Quails with bacon & juniper 398
 Sea bass stew 229
 Shepherd's pie 178
 Spinach & bacon salad 116
 Steak, kidney & mushroom pie 270
 Succotash 91
 Tomato soup 29
Bacon & lentil stew 192
Bacon & split pea soup 11
Bacon-wrapped prawns 71
Bacon-wrapped turkey burgers 385
Baked Alaska 595
Baked apples in honey & lemon 566
Baked barley & broad bean
 casserole 256
Baked bean & bacon casserole 192
Baked bean & vegetable casserole 241

index

baked beans
Baked bean & bacon casserole 192
Baked bean & vegetable
casserole 241
Baked Brie with sun-dried tomatoes 126
Baked coconut rice pudding 584
Baked cod with tomatoes 463
Baked Cornish game hens 402
Baked cranberry pork chops 285
Baked fennel 84
Baked lentil & vegetable stew 249
Baked mozzarella & tomatoes 83
Baked mushrooms 48
Baked peanut tofu 491
Baked potatoes with salsa 536
Baked seafood salad 110
Baked squash casserole 253
Baked stuffed lobster 445
Bakewell tart 664
baking potatoes
Baked potatoes with salsa 536
Cheesy potato skins 80
Baklava 688
Bamboo shoot salad 117
bamboo shoots
Bamboo shoot salad 117
Hot & sour soup 17
Banana cake 672
Banana & chicory salad 119
Banana & pecan salad 114
Banana chocolate chip soufflés 583
Banana custard 596
Banana dosa 570
Banana lassi 609
Banana split 655
bananas
Banana cake 672
Banana & chicory salad 119
Banana & pecan salad 114
Banana chocolate chip soufflés 583
Banana custard 596
Banana dosa 570
Banana lassi 609
Banana split 655
Bananas with chocolate marshmallow
sauce 652
Bananas with hot lemon sauce 555

Boozy banana soufflé 565
Brazilian coffee bananas 632
Chocolate banana sundae 633
Exotic fruit pancakes 559
Fried bananas 560
Fruity bread pudding 582
Bananas with chocolate marshmallow
sauce 652
Bananas with hot lemon sauce 555
Barbecue sauce 728
Barbecued monkfish 458
barley
Autumn barley stew 240
Baked barley & broad bean
casserole 256
Barley & pine nut casserole 243
Chunky vegetable chilli 254
Scotch broth 29
Barley & pine nut casserole 243
Basil-stuffed lamb roast 313
basmati rice
Lentil & rice salad 140
Red fried rice 156
Saffron rice salad 102
Tomato rice 539
Basque tomatoes 116
Basque tuna stew 409
Batter-dipped tofu 482
Bean & celery stew 237
Bean croquettes 137
Beansprout & pepper salad 117
beansprouts
Beansprout & pepper salad 117
Chicken chop suey 355
Chicken with beansprouts 375
Chinese prawn salad 108
Gado gado 513
Special chow mein 153
Tofu & broccoli stir-fry 486
Béchamel sauce 728
beef see also beef olives and minced beef
and stewing beef
Asparagus & bean beef 269
Beef & pork ragù 272
Beef & stout casserole 182
Beef carpaccio 60
Beef stroganoff 266

Beef Wellington 264
Consommé 32
Fillet of beef with porcini & sweet
  peppers 263
Roast beef & Yorkshire pudding 273
Beef & cabbage pie 170
Beef & lentil soup 21
Beef & pork ragù 272
Beef & pumpkin curry 268
Beef & mushroom burgers 277
Beef & stout casserole 182
beef bones
  Beef stock 731
Beef carpaccio 60
Beef daube 271
Beef fajitas 259
Beef goulash 258
Beef hotpot 182
beef olives
  Beef olives in gravy 275
Beef olives in gravy 275
Beef paprikash 185
Beef satay 72
Beef stock 731
Beef stroganoff 266
Beef, tomato & olive kebabs 276
Beef Wellington 264
beetroot
  Beetroot & chive salad 113
  Beetroot & orange salad 112
  Beetroot & yogurt salad 49
  Borscht 12
  Red onion & beetroot soup 36
Beetroot & chive salad 113
Beetroot & orange salad 112
Beetroot & yogurt salad 49
Beetroot fettuccine 518
beetroot pasta
  Beetroot fettuccine 518
Bermuda cheesecake 676
Black bean & salsa salad 101
black beans
  Black bean & salsa salad 101
  Chunky vegetable chilli 254
black cherries
  Black cherry crêpes 586
Black cherry crêpes 586

black-eyed beans
  Mixed bean salad 138
blackberries
  Blackberry batter pudding 580
  Bramble scones 680
  Pear & blackberry crumble 572
  Poppy seed custard with red fruit 556
Blackberry batter pudding 580
Blackcurrant jelly with coulis 619
blackcurrants
  Apple & blackcurrant pancakes 557
  Blackcurrant jelly with coulis 619
blue cheese
  Blue cheese & avocado dip 723
  Blue cheese hotpot 534
Blue cheese & avocado dip 723
lue cheese hotpot 534
blueberries
  Alaskan blueberry coffee cake 670
  Blueberry sundae 555
  Blueberry trifle 613
  Creamy puddings 584
  Spiced pear & blueberry
    parcels 567
  Summer berries in Champagne
    jelly 656
Blueberry sundae 555
Blueberry trifle 613
Blushing pears 646
Boozy banana soufflé 565
Borlotti bean salad 102
borlotti beans
  Borlotti bean salad 102
  Mixed bean salad 138
Borscht 12
Boston bean soup 12
Bottarga
  Bottarga spaghetti 155
Bottarga spaghetti 155
Braised Chinese vegetables 487
Braised pork slices 295
braising steak
  Beef daube 271
Bramble scones 680
Brandied chocolate cake 674
Brandy snaps 713
Brandy trifle 637

index

Brazil nuts
  Nut roast 507
Brazilian coffee bananas 632
Bread & butter pudding 590
Breaded mushrooms 58
Brie
  Apple & Brie omelette 129
  Baked Brie with sun-dried
    tomatoes 126
  Cheese pie 162
Brinjal curry 483
Broad bean, pea & goat's cheese
  salad 145
broad beans
  Baked barley & broad bean
    casserole 256
  Broad bean, pea & goat's cheese
    salad 145
  Tomato & bean salad 100
broccoli
  Aromatic green casserole 240
  Broccoli & asparagus fusilli 488
  Broccoli salad 120
  Broccoli with feta & tomato sauce 543
  Chicken broccoli casserole 210
  Red curry with cashews 550
  Spiced noodle salad 140
  Spicy noodle salad 97
  Stir-fried broccoli pasta 141
  Tofu & broccoli stir-fry 486
  Vegetable fritters 59
  Vegetable soup 30
  Vegetable-stuffed conchiglioni 546
Broccoli & asparagus fusilli 488
Broccoli salad 120
Broccoli with feta & tomato sauce 543
Brown fish stew 236
brown rice
  Brown rice & chicken salad 110
  Brown rice stew 238
  Cheese & rice casserole 237
  Marinated tomato & rice salad 146
Brown rice & chicken salad 110
Brown rice stew 238
Bruschetta 54
  Stilton & pear bruschetta 66
Brussels sprouts

  Aromatic green casserole 240
  Autumn barley stew 240
  Baked lentil & vegetable stew 249
  Chestnut & sprout sauté 494
bulgur wheat
  Hot bulgur salad 119
  Tabbouleh & tofu 502
  Veggie burgers 528
Butter bean & chicken casserole 224
butter beans
  Butter bean & chicken casserole 224
  Quinoa & butter beans 498
  Tuscan bean & tuna salad 95
Butterfly cakes 675
Butterfly prawns 70
butternut squash
  Baked squash casserole 253

C
cabbage
  Beef & cabbage pie 170
  Cabbage soup 45
  Cabbage & tofu 489
  Duck with leek & cabbage 396
  Gado gado 513
Cabbage soup 45
Cabbage & tofu 489
Cajun chicken jambalaya 359
Cajun chicken pasta 158
Cajun lamb with rice 305
Calamari 65
Calamari stew 230
Californian baked pears 657
Californian prawn & scallop stir-fry 410
calves' kidney
  Calves' kidney stew 195
Calves' kidney stew 195
Camembert
  Camembert with garlic 124
  Cheese pie 162
Camembert with garlic 124
Cappuccino creams 606
cannellini beans
  French bean soup 18
  Tuna & bean salad 104
cantaloupe melon
  Grilled chicken with hot salsa 368

Melon medley 649
Mango & melon ginger salad 656
Persian melon cups 644
Spiced fruit platter 651
capers
Dover sole with capers 435
Feta cheese & capers 124
Caramelized apple tarts 669
caraway seeds
Seed cake 676
Carrot & coriander soup 13
carrots
Baked bean & vegetable
casserole 241
Carrot & coriander soup 13
Curried carrot & apple soup 38
Gado gado 513
Leek & carrot gratin 551
Minestrone soup 23
Mustard carrot salad 114
Spring vegetable stir-fry 532
Tomato & carrot soup 37
Vegetable soup 30
cashew nuts
Asparagus cashew stir-fry 481
Chinese chicken with cashew nuts 365
Lamb with cashew nut curry 303
Nut roast 507
Red curry with cashews 550
Casseroled beans & penne 501
Catalan soup 13
cauliflower
Cauliflower fritters 62
Cauliflower & walnut soup 14
Gado gado 513
Mixed bhajias 74
Oyster & cauliflower stew 226
Vegetable fritters 59
Cauliflower fritters 62
Cauliflower & walnut soup 14
caviar
Devilled eggs with caviar 70
Pasta with caviar 134
celery
Baked bean & vegetable
casserole 241
Bean & celery stew 237

Black bean & salsa salad 101
Celery & Stilton soup 14
Clam chowder 16
Minestrone soup 23
Stuffed celery 88
Swiss chicken casserole 211
Vegetable soup 30
Celery & Stilton soup 14
Ceviche 438
Champagne granita 631
Chargrilled kebabs 545
Chargrilled peppers & sweet
potatoes 509
Chargrilled pork fillet with apple
sauce 282
Cheddar cheese
Apple & cheddar pie 172
Cheese & crabmeat casserole 232
Ham & cheese casserole 191
Macaroni cheese 527
Olive cheese balls 56
One-pot macaroni & cheese 239
Cheese & courgette quiche 165
Cheese & crabmeat casserole 232
Cheese & rice casserole 237
Cheese & spinach puffs 83
Cheese pie 162
Cheese-stuffed rice balls 145
Cheesy garlic bread 80
Cheesy potato skins 80
Cheesy stuffed peppers 55
cherries see also black cherries and glacé
cherries and Morello cherries and sour
cherries
Cherry clafoutis 667
Cheery mousse 605
Red fruit salad 648
Cherry clafoutis 667
Cherry mousse 605
Cherry pie 592
cherry tomatoes
Beef, tomato & olive kebabs 276
Couscous vegetable loaf 511
Duck with tomatoes 389
Cherry turnover 660
chestnut mushrooms
Mixed mushroom ragout 544

index

Chestnut & sprout sauté 494
chestnuts
  Chestnut & sprout sauté 494
chicken *see also* poussins
  Almond chicken casserole 220
  Apple-stuffed chicken 343
  Brown rice & chicken salad 110
  Butter bean & chicken casserole 224
  Cajun chicken jambalaya 359
  Cajun chicken pasta 158
  Chicken & bacon kebabs 61
  Chicken & beef satay 350
  Chicken & chickpea stew 341
  Chicken & crackers casserole 215
  Chicken & leek casserole 205
  Chicken & pasta broth 216
  Chicken & potato bake 206
  Chicken & ricotta in wine 345
  Chicken & sausage pie 175
  Chicken & sweetcorn stew 216
  Chicken & vegetables 378
  Chicken & vegetable terrine 369
  Chicken breasts & balsamic
    vinegar 373
  Chicken broccoli casserole 210
  Chicken casserole with yogurt 211
  Chicken chop suey 355
  Chicken chow mein 353
  Chicken green masala 340
  Chicken in peanut sauce 346
  Chicken in spicy yogurt 367
  Chicken jalfrezi 381
  Chicken korma with green beans 356
  Chicken macaroni casserole 209
  Chicken macaroni stew 221
  Chicken noodle soup 15
  Chicken pasanda 208
  Chicken peperonata 374
  Chicken pie 168
  Chicken saltimbocca 75
  Chicken soup 15
  Chicken stock 730
  Chicken tikka 86
  Chicken with beansprouts 375
  Chicken with ciabatta & Parma
    ham 336
  Chicken with lime stuffing 342

  Chicken with sage & lemon 351
  Chilli chicken casserole 221
  Chinese chicken with cashew nuts 365
  Chinese-style chicken 358
  Cock-a-leekie 16
  Coq au vin 352
  Coronation chicken 349
  Fragrant saffron chicken 364
  Garlic & herb chicken 366
  Garlic & lime chicken 380
  Garlic & nut butter chicken 338
  Grilled chicken with hot salsa 368
  Indian charred chicken 371
  Indonesian-style satay chicken 339
  Jerk chicken 372
  Khara masala balti chicken 335
  Kung po chicken 354
  Medium balti chicken 337
  Mulligatawny 24
  Mustard chicken 363
  One-pot Cajun chicken gumbo 213
  One-pot chicken couscous 213
  Paella 157
  Pan-fried chicken with red wine
    sauce 361
  Parsley, walnut & orange chicken 332
  Pepper chicken with ginger and
    garlic 333
  Peppered chicken pasta 151
  Pesto chicken salad 135
  Sage chicken & rice 379
  Sautéed chicken with herbs 362
  Sherry chicken casserole 219
  Soy-braised chicken 344
  Special chow mein 153
  Spiced chicken casserole 205
  Spicy masala chicken 377
  Swiss chicken casserole 211
  Szechuan beaten chicken 92
  Tarragon chicken casserole 224
  Thai chicken green curry 347
  Tortilla chicken casserole 217
  Traditional fried chicken 348
  Tuscan chicken 360
  Vietnamese chicken & sweet potato
    curry 334
  Waldorf chicken salad 98

Warm chicken & feta salad 357
Winter chicken stew 217
Yellow bean chicken 376
chicken liver
Chicken liver pâté 76
Pâté en croûte 78
Chicken & bacon kebabs 61
Chicken & beef satay 350
Chicken & crackers casserole 215
Chicken & leek casserole 205
Chicken & pasta broth 216
Chicken & potato bake 206
Chicken & ricotta in wine 345
Chicken & sausage pie 175
Chicken & sweetcorn stew 216
Chicken & vegetables 378
Chicken & vegetable terrine 369
Chicken breasts & balsamic vinegar 373
Chicken broccoli casserole 210
Chicken casserole with yogurt 211
Chicken chop suey 355
Chicken chow mein 353
Chicken green masala 340
Chicken in peanut sauce 346
Chicken in spicy yogurt 367
Chicken jalfrezi 381
Chicken korma with green beans 356
Chicken liver pâté 76
Chicken macaroni casserole 209
Chicken macaroni stew 221
Chicken noodle soup 15
Chicken pasanda 208
Chicken peperonata 374
Chicken pie 168
Chicken saltimbocca 75
Chicken soup 15
Chicken stock 730
Chicken tikka 86
Chicken with beansprouts 375
Chicken with ciabatta & Parma ham 336
Chicken with lime stuffing 342
Chicken with sage & lemon 351
Chickpea & artichoke stew 248
Chickpea chole 490
Chickpea salad 138
chickpeas
Armenian stew 239

Chicken & chickpea stew 341
Chickpea & artichoke stew 248
Chickpea chole 490
Chickpea salad 138
Falafels 523
Greek-style chickpea casserole 247
Hummus 725
chicory
Banana & chicory salad 119
Orange & chicory salad 120
Child's birthday cake 671
Chilled avocado soup 11
Chilled cucumber soup 20
Chilled pea soup 26
Chilled noodles & peppers 547
Chilli beef in tortillas 267
Chilli tomato dip 724
Chilli-flavoured pork 299
Chilli-garlic crab sticks 69
Chillies stuffed with turkey 386
chillies
Chilli beef in tortillas 267
Chilli chicken casserole 221
Chilli-garlic crab sticks 69
Fig & chilli tagliatelle 151
Piperade 131
Chinese cabbage
Stewed cabbage hotpot 242
Chinese cabbage soup 35
Chinese chicken with cashew nuts 365
Chinese egg flower soup 43
Chinese lettuce wraps 146
Chinese mushrooms
Braised Chinese vegetables 487
Mushroom & ginger duck 390
Tofu with mushrooms 496
Tofu with mushrooms & peas 541
Chinese prawn salad 108
Chinese spare ribs 292
Chinese-style chicken 358
Chinese vegetable casserole 251
Chive omelette stir-fry 127
chives
Beetroot & chive salad 113
Chive omelette stir-fry 127
Chocolate & apricot squares 703
Chocolate & pear crumble 581

index

Chocolate banana sundae 633
Chocolate brandy cream 634
Chocolate cake 679
Chocolate charlotte 614
Chocolate chip muffins 680
Chocolate cream pudding 640
Chocolate crêpes 585
Chocolate crunch biscuits 708
Chocolate éclairs 662
Chocolate fluff 638
Chocolate fudge pudding 600
Chocolate ice-cream sandwiches 624
Chocolate meringue pie 665
Chocolate pecan pie 694
Chocolate roulade 681
Chocolate rum pots 623
Chorizo sausages
    Asparagus & chorizo salad 72
    Cajun chicken jambalaya 359
Christmas pudding 594
chuck steak
    Spiced beef & onions 261
    Chunky vegetable chilli 254
    Steak, kidney & mushroom
      pie 270
ciabatta
    Bruschetta 54
    Chicken with ciabatta & Parma
      ham 336
    Parma ham & pepper pizzas 89
    Roast garlic toast 50
cinnamon
    Cinnamon ice cream 627
    Cinnamon & nutmeg ice cream 620
Cinnamon & nutmeg ice cream 620
Cinnamon ice cream 627
Citrus jelly 622
Citrus tart 666
Clam & Prosecco spaghetti 149
Clam chowder 16
Clam stew 227
clams
    Baked stuffed lobster 445
    Clam & Prosecco spaghetti 149
    Clam chowder 16
    Clam stew 227
    Seafood spaghetti 144

    Spaghetti marinara with seafood 454
Classic Caesar salad 96
Classic custard 592
Cock-a-leekie 16
cocoa powder
    Chocolate & pear crumble 581
    Chocolate cake 679
    Chocolate cream pudding 640
    Chocolate crêpes 585
    Chocolate fudge pudding 600
    Chocolate pecan pie 694
    Chocolate roulade 681
    Mississippi mud pie 690
coconut
    Coconut cake 661
    Coconut ice 714
    Coconut sweet 699
Coconut cake 661
Coconut ice 714
coconut milk
    Baked coconut rice pudding 584
    Curried prawns in coconut milk 476
    Fish with coconut & basil 474
    Red curry with cashews 550
    Red mullet & coconut loaf 465
    Spicy coconut prawns 407
Coconut sweet 699
cod see also salt cod
    Baked cod with tomatoes 463
    Cod stew 230
    Crunchy-topped cod 464
    Cullen skink 45
    Deep-fried fish 64
    Fish chowder 18
    Fish loaf 414
    Fish pasties 467
    Fish with coconut & basil 474
    Hearty fish stew 226
    Layered fish & potato pie 457
    Noodles with cod & mango 478
    Ocean pie 440
    Paella 157
    Seafood balti 417
    Seafood medley 437
    Seafood pie 173
    Spaghetti marinara with seafood 454
    Taglierini & seafood sauce 450

Thai fish green curry 473
Thai-style fish cakes 67
Cod stew 230
Coeurs à la crème 611
Coffee almond ice-cream cake 689
Coffee & walnut cake 674
Coffee granita 630
conchiglie
    Spinach & ricotta shells 525
Consommé 32
Continental pie 170
Coq au vin 352
coriander
    Carrot & coriander soup 13
    Ginger & coriander noodles 156
Cornish game hens
    Autumn fruit game hens 403
    Baked Cornish game hens 402
Cornish pasties 167
Coronation chicken 349
cottage cheese
    Cheese & rice casserole 237
    Cheese & spinach puffs 83
    Coeurs à la crème 611
    Cottage cheese flan 166
    Devilled eggs 90
    Gooseberry cheese cooler 643
    Macaroni & four cheeses 540
    Peach & ginger pashka 620
    Pear & grape salad 109
    Pineapple boats 90
    Strawberry rose-petal pashka 602
    Stuffed celery 88
    Vegetable-stuffed conchiglioni 546
Cottage cheese flan 166
Cottage pie 180
Courgette & asparagus parcels 535
Courgette & corn casserole 24
Courgette flan 163
Courgette fritters 53
Courgette quiche 504
Courgette & spinach soup 17
courgettes
    Baked bean & vegetable
        casserole 241
    Cheese & courgette quiche 165
    Courgette & asparagus parcels 535

Courgette & corn casserole 24
Courgette & spinach soup 17
Courgette flan 163
Courgette fritters 53
Courgette quiche 504
Courgettes stuffed with mince 72
Ratatouille 529
Rice-stuffed courgettes 139
Ricotta cheese & courgette rolls 126
Spaghetti with courgettes 149
Courgettes stuffed with mince 72
couscous
    Apple couscous pudding 569
    Couscous & haddock salad 106
    Couscous salad 136
    Couscous vegetable loaf 511
    One-pot chicken couscous 213
    Spiced fruity couscous 521
Couscous & haddock salad 106
Couscous salad 136
Couscous vegetable loaf 511
crab
    Baked seafood salad 110
    Cheese & crabmeat casserole 232
    Chilli-garlic crab sticks 69
    Crab & crispy noodles 99
    Crab & cucumber savouries 89
    Crab & ginger soup 46
    Crab & seafood one-pot 225
    Crab, melon & cucumber 100
    Crab pâté 76
    Crab quiche 160
    Stuffed crabs 443
    Terrace crab pie 171
    Warm pasta & crab 103
Crab & crispy noodles 99
Crab & cucumber savouries 89
Crab & ginger soup 46
Crab & seafood one-pot 225
Crab, melon & cucumber 100
Crab pâté 76
Crab quiche 160
cranberries
    Apple cranberry casserole 250
    Apple strudel 591
    Cranberry biscotti 710
    Cranberry cream salad 115

index

Cranberry biscotti 710
Cranberry cream salad 115
cream cheese
    Anchovy & garlic dip 721
    Bermuda cheesecake 676
    Cucumber & herb dip 722
Cream of artichoke soup 42
creamed coconut
    Pineapple & coconut curry 497
Creamed tomato sauce 729
Creamy fish gratin 428
Creamy fruit baskets 607
Creamy puddings 584
Crème caramel 616
Crêpes Suzettes 587
Crispy seaweed 58
Crispy shredded beef 265
crown of lamb
    Crown roast of lamb 308
Crown roast of lamb 308
Crunchy-topped cod 464
cucumber
    Chilled cucumber soup 20
    Crab & cucumber savouries 89
    Crab, melon & cucumber 100
    Cucumber & herb dip 722
    Cucumber salad 118
    Cucumber yogurt dip 722
    Gazpacho 19
    Greek cucumber salad 104
    Green soup 38
    Smoked trout with cucumber &
      cumin 68
    Szechuan beaten chicken 92
Cucumber & herb dip 722
Cucumber salad 118
Cucumber yogurt dip 722
Cullen skink 45
Curly endive salad 107
currants
    Bread & butter pudding 590
    Christmas pudding 594
    Dundee cake 671
    Plum cake 685
Curried carrot & apple soup 38
Curried prawns in coconut milk 476
Curried rice salad 141

curry leaves
    Indian eggs & chillies 131
Curry & mayonnaise dip 723
Custard tart 566

D

dark chocolate *see also* plain chocolate
    Banana split 655
    Brandied chocolate cake 674
    Chocolate banana sundae 633
    Chocolate cake 679
    Chocolate charlotte 614
    Chocolate chip muffins 680
    Chocolate crêpes 585
    Chocolate éclairs 662
    Chocolate meringue pie 665
    Chocolate pecan pie 694
    Chocolate roulade 681
    Chocolate rum pots 623
    Dutch macaroons 709
    Marshmallow ice cream 619
    Marzipan cherries 713
    Mississippi mud pie 690
    Orange & ginger cream cheese
      fudge 702
    Pain au chocolat 663
    Queen of puddings 573
    Tollhouse cookies 715
    Truffles 706
    Viennese chocolate fingers 698
Date & apple muffins 678
Date flapjacks 707
dates
    Date & apple muffins 678
    Date flapjacks 707
    Orange & date salad 658
    Perfumed pineapple salad 603
    Spiced date & walnut cake 683
Deep-fried fish 64
dessert plums
    Plum & cardamom fool 630
Devilled eggs 90
Devilled eggs with caviar 70
Devilled prawns 64
Devils on horseback 74
dolcelatte
    Two-cheese dip 720

Dolmades 79
Dover sole
    Dover sole stew 231
    Dover sole with capers 435
Dover sole stew 231
Dover sole with capers 435
dried fruit
    Christmas pudding 594
    Dried fruit fool 604
    Rock cakes 684
    Sweet-stewed dried fruit 646
    Tuscan pudding 629
Dried fruit fool 604
dried fruit salad
    Fruited rice ring 612
duck
    Duck & pomegranate stew 218
    Duck breasts with orange 394
    Duck casserole 210
    Duck stew with turnips &
      onions 219
    Duck, tomato & pepper
      stew 209
    Duck vindaloo 393
    Duck with Cumberland sauce 392
    Duck with leek & cabbage 396
    Duck with pineapple 395
    Duck with tomatoes 389
    French-style stewed duck 223
    Mahogany duck 391
    Mushroom & ginger duck 390
    Sweet & spicy duck 397
Duck & pomegranate stew 218
Duck breasts with orange 394
Duck casserole 210
Duck stew with turnips & onions 219
Duck, tomato & pepper stew 209
Duck vindaloo 393
Duck with Cumberland sauce 392
Duck with leek & cabbage 396
Duck with pineapple 395
Duck with tomatoes 389
Dundee cake 671
Dutch macaroons 709

E

Easter biscuits 714

Easter nests 703
Egg curry 128
Egg salad 122
eggs
    Amaretti 610
    Baked Alaska 595
    Cheese-stuffed rice balls 145
    Chinese egg flower soup 43
    Chive omelette stir-fry 127
    Chocolate meringue pie 665
    Chocolate rum pots 623
    Classic custard 592
    Couscous salad 136
    Devilled eggs 90
    Devilled eggs with caviar 70
    Egg curry 128
    Egg salad 122
    Eggs with spinach 123
    French omelette 128
    Frozen egg nog 639
    Gentlemen's pudding 575
    Indian eggs & chillies 131
    Lemon curd ice cream 629
    Mayonnaise 725
    Minced beef with eggs 75
    Piperade 131
    Prawn omelette 460
    Salad niçoise 105
    Spanish omelette 132
    Stuffed eggs 122
    Vegetable omelette 130
    Zabaglione 588
Eggs with spinach 123
Emmenthaler cheese
    Chicken saltimbocca 75
    Mini mushroom quiches 56
    Swiss chicken casserole 211
endive
    Curly endive salad 107
Eton mess 654
Exotic fruit pancakes 559

F

Falafels 523
fennel
    Baked fennel 84
    Chilled pea soup 26

index

Guinea fowl with fennel 399
Roasted Mediterranean
  vegetables 537
Vegetable paella 531
feta cheese
  Broccoli with feta & tomato sauce 543
  Feta cheese & capers 124
  Feta cheese tartlets 63
  Greek salad 103
  Greek spinach & cheese pie 55
  Greek-style chickpea casserole 247
  Greek-style tomato platter 84
  Leek kuftadas 49
  Spinach, feta & pear salad 94
  Warm chicken & feta salad 357
Feta cheese & capers 124
Feta cheese tartlets 63
fettuccine
  Beetroot fettucine 518
  Smoked salmon pasta 154
Fig & chilli tagliatelle 151
figs
  Fig & chilli tagliatelle 151
  Fresh figs in wine 657
  Grilled fresh figs with crème fraîche
    650
Fillet of beef with porcini & sweet
  peppers 263
Filo mince pie 177
filo pastry
  Baklava 688
  Filo mince pie 177
  Filo rhubarb pie 689
  Greek spinach & cheese pie 55
  Plum filo pockets 554
  Redcurrant filo baskets 638
  Tomato & cheese tarts 91
Filo rhubarb pie 689
Fish chowder 18
Fish fillets in wine sauce 413
fish flakes
  Japanese tofu hotpot 241
Fish loaf 414
Fish pasties 467
Fish stock 732
ish Wellington 422
flageolet beans

Simple bean salad 99
flank steak
  Orange beef with green peppers 260
Floating islands in hot plum sauce 564
Fragrant saffron chicken 364
Frangipane tart 691
French bean soup 18
French beans
  Gado gado 513
  Hot potato & bean salad 112
  Red curry with cashews 550
  Tomato & bean salad 100
French braised lamb 317
French mussels 470
French omelette 128
French onion soup 19
French vinaigrette 727
French-style pot-roast poussin 212
French-style stewed duck 223
Fresh backed sardines 439
Fresh figs in wine 657
Fresh herb risotto 143
Fresh salad with raspberry vinaigrette 113
Fried bananas 560
Fried mozzarella 125
Fried squid curry 429
Fried venison steaks 329
fromage frais
  Cappuccino creams 606
  Fromage frais with hot plum
    sauce 554
  Frozen citrus soufflé 606
  Raspberry mousse 615
Fromage frais with hot plum sauce 554
Frozen citrus soufflé 606
Frozen egg nog 639
Fruit & nut torte 696
Fruit cocktail 85
Fruit fondue 642
Fruit salad cake 670
Fruited rice ring 612
Fruity bread pudding 582
Fruity pasta & prawn salad 118
fudge
  Highball cups 716
fusilli
  Broccoli & asparagus fusilli 488

Fusilli with tomato & mozzarella 519
Fusilli with tomato & mozzarella 519

G

Gado gado 513
galia melons
    Green fruit salad 605
game meat
    Game pie 171
    Mixed game pie 327
Game pie 171
gammon
    Ginger & honey-glazed gammon 281
garlic
    Camembert with garlic 124
    Cheesy garlic bread 80
    Garlic & herb chicken 366
    Garlic & herb mayonnaise 726
    Garlic & lime chicken 380
    Garlic & nut butter chicken 338
    Garlic breadsticks 57
    Garlic dip 723
    Garlic mayonnaise 726
    Lemon & garlic pasta 155
    Roast garlic toast 50
    Spaghetti with garlic & chilli oil 143
Garlic & herb chicken 366
Garlic & herb mayonnaise 726
Garlic & lime chicken 380
Garlic & nut butter chicken 338
Garlic dip 723
Garlic breadsticks 57
Garlic mayonnaise 726
Gazpacho 19
Gentlemen's pudding 575
gherkins
    Beetroot & yogurt salad 49
ginger
    Crab & ginger soup 46
    Ginger & coriander noodles 156
    Ginger & honey-glazed gammon 281
    Ginger upside-down pudding 577
    Peach & ginger pashka 620
    Poached peaches with ginger 643
Ginger & coriander noodles 156
Ginger & honey-glazed gammon 281
Ginger parfait 626

Ginger upside-down pudding 577
glacé cherries
    Marzipan cherries 713
    Rich fruit cake 677
Glazed berry pudding 574
Glazed nectarine tart 639
goatmeat
    Spicy goatmeat stew 195
goat's cheese
    Broad bean, pea & goat's cheese
      salad 145
golden syrup
    Rum & raisin ice cream 637
    Traditional oat flapjacks 704
    Treacle pudding 583
goose
    honey-glazed goose 404
gooseberries
    Gooseberry cheese cooler 643
    Yogurt ring with tropical fruit 611
Gooseberry cheese cooler 643
Gorgonzola
    Gorgonzola dip 720
Gorgonzola dip 720
grapefruit *see also* pink grapefruit
    Grapefruit in apricot brandy 647
    Melon & orange cups 650
    Mulled Florida cocktail 654
Grapefruit in apricot brandy 647
grapes
    Fruit cocktail 85
    Green fruit salad 605
    Pear & grape salad 109
Greek cucumber salad 104
Greek lemon soup 39
Greek salad 103
Greek spinach & cheese pie 55
Greek-style chickpea casserole 247
Greek-style tomato platter 84
Greek-style yogurt
    Brazilian coffee bananas 632
    Cucumber yogurt dip 722
    Eton mess 654
    Nectarines with marzipan &
      yogurt 644
    Strawberry frozen yogurt 625
green beans

index

Chicken korma with green beans 356
Satay noodles 516
Veggie burgers 528
green chillies
Beef & cabbage pie 170
Chillies stuffed with turkey 386
Chilli tomato dip 724
Green chilli & meat stew 183
Indian eggs & chillies 131
Tortilla chicken casserole 217
Green fruit salad 605
green lentils
Baked lentil & vegetable stew 249
Lentil & rice salad 140
Okra with mango & lentils 493
green olives
Beef, tomato & olive kebabs 276
Green soup 38
Griddled smoked salmon 85
Grilled apple stack 647
Grilled artichoke salad 94
Grilled asparagus & leeks 48
Grilled chicken with hot salsa 368
Grilled fresh figs with crème fraîche 650
Grilled pink grapefruit 642
Grilled sardines 66
Grilled stuffed sole 406
grouse
Grouse stew 197
Grouse stew 197
Gruyère
Cheese & courgette quiche 165
Guacamole 719
guinea fowl
Guinea fowl stew 200
Guinea fowl with fennel 399
Poached guinea fowl 400
Guinea fowl stew 200
Guinea fowl with fennel 399
haddock see also smoked haddock
Ceviche 438
Smoked fish with white sauce 442

H
hake
Seafood fajitas 432
halibut

Halibut casserole 233
Halibut stew 227
Mixed seafood chowder 423
Pan-seared halibut 415
Halibut casserole 233
Halibut stew 227
ham see also Parma ham and
smoked ham
Chicken saltimbocca 75
Ham & cheese casserole 191
Leek tart 164
Steak & onion pie 179
Tomato & ham pie 177
Turkey, pea & ham pot pie 214
Ham & cheese casserole 191
hare
Hare stew 203
Hare stew 203
haricot beans
Bean & celery stew 237
Blue cheese hotpot 534
Casseroled beans & penne 501
Hazelnut pavlova 608
Hazelnut pesto tagliatelle 150
hazelnuts
Hazelnut pavlova 608
Hazelnut pesto tagliatelle 150
Hearty fish stew 226
Herbed pork cutlets 294
Herb-scented lamb with balsamic
dressing 307
herring
Soused herrings 453
Highball cups 716
honey-glazed goose 404
honeydew melon
Melon medley 649
Melon & orange cups 650
Hot bulgur salad 119
Hot chocolate custard 568
Hot plum batter 590
Hot potato & bean salad 112
Hot prawn stew 236
Hot & sour soup 17
Hummus 725

I

Iced honey & lemon mousse 617
Indian bread pudding 581
Indian charred chicken 371
Indian eggs & chillies 131
Indian spicy lamb 306
Indonesian-style satay chicken 339
Irish hotpot 189
Irish lamb stew 188
Italian pork escalopes 290
Italian sausages
    One-pot sausage jambalaya 190

J

Japanese noodles
    Spicy Japanese noodles 505
Japanese tofu hotpot 241
jasmine rice
    Thai jasmine rice & prawn
        casserole 232
Jerk chicken 372
Jerusalem artichoke soup 10
Jerusalem artichokes 51
juniper berries
    Quails with bacon & juniper 398

K

Kettle-cooked sea bass 433
Key lime sorbet 623
Khara masala balti chicken 335
Kidney bean Kiev 524
kidney beans
    Bean & tofu enchiladas 542
    Bean croquettes 137
    Kidney bean Kiev 524
    Mixed bean salad 138
kidneys
    Rich kidney soup 40
king prawns
    Curried prawns in coconut milk 476
    King prawns in sherry 58
    Seafood kebabs 418
King prawns in sherry 58
kiwi fruits
    Green fruit salad 605
    Yogurt ring with tropical fruit 611
Kleftiko 315

Kung po chicken 354

L

lamb *see also* crown of lamb *and* minced
  lamb *and* rack of lamb
    Basil-stuffed lamb roast 313
    Cajun lamb with rice 305
    French braised lamb 317
    Herb-scented lamb with balsamic
      dressing 307
    Indian spicy lamb 306
    Irish lamb stew 188
    Lamb & anchovies with thyme 319
    Lamb & leek stew 186
    Lamb & mint stir-fry 309
    Lamb & tomato koftas 316
    Lamb & vegetable stew 187
    Lamb hotpot 186
    Lamb hotpot with dumplings 185
    Lamb with cashew nut curry 303
    Lamb with mint sauce 304
    Lamb with mushroom sauce 318
    Scotch broth 29
    Turkish lamb stew 310
    Ulster Irish stew 187
Lamb & anchovies with thyme 319
Lamb & leek stew 186
Lamb & tomato koftas 316
Lamb & vegetable stew 187
Lamb & mint stir-fry 309
lamb chops
    Persian lamb 314
Lamb hotpot 186
Lamb hotpot with dumplings 185
lamb shanks
    Kleftiko 315
Lamb with cashew nut curry 303
Lamb with mint sauce 304
Lamb with mushroom sauce 318
lamb's kidneys
    Lamb hotpot 186
    Steak, kidney & mushroom pie 270
lamb's liver
    Liver hotpot 194
    Peppered liver 322
Layered fish & potato pie 457
Leek & carrot gratin 551

index

Leek & herb soufflé 538
Leek & potato soup 20
Leek kuftadas 49
Leek pie 161
Leek tart 164
leeks
    Chicken & leek casserole 205
    Cock-a-leekie 16
    Duck with leek & cabbage 396
    Grilled asparagus & leeks 48
    Leek & carrot gratin 551
    Lamb & leek stew 186
    Leek & herb soufflé 538
    Leek & potato soup 20
    Leek kuftadas 49
    Leek pie 161
    Leek tart 164
    Mixed bhajias 74
    Potato & leek casserole 238
    Salmon yakitori 81
    Vichyssoise 31
Lemon & garlic pasta 155
Lemon chocolate cake 682
Lemon curd ice cream 629
Lemon mustard vinaigrette 727
Lemon syllabub 636
Lemon syrup pears with pancakes 558
lemons
    Citrus jelly 622
    Citrus tart 666
    Crêpes Suzettes 587
    Frozen citrus soufflé 606
    Greek lemon soup 39
    Iced honey & lemon mousse 617
    Lemon & garlic pasta 155
    Lemon chocolate cake 682
    Lemon curd ice cream 629
    Lemon mustard vinaigrette 727
    Lemon syllabub 636
    Lemon syrup pears with pancakes 558
Lentil & rice salad 140
Lentil hotpot 250
lentils
    Armenian stew 239
    Bacon & lentil stew 192
    Beef & lentil soup 21
Lentil & rice salad 140

    Lentil hotpot 250
lettuce
    Chinese lettuce wraps 146
    Lettuce soup 21
Lettuce soup 21
Lime meringue tarts 693
Lime sherbet 642
limes
    Citrus jelly 622
    Frozen citrus soufflé 606
    Garlic & lime chicken 380
    Key lime sorbet 623
    Lime meringue tarts 693
    Lime sherbet 642
    Mango & lime mousse 640
    Pineapple wedges with
      lime 603
linguine
    Cajun chicken pasta 158
    Salmon & asparagus linguine 447
    Smoked ham linguine 148
liver see also chicken liver and lamb's liver
    and pig's liver
    Liver, bacon & onions 321
Liver, bacon & onions 321
Liver hotpot 194
lobster
    Baked stuffed lobster 445
    Lobster bisque 22
    Lobster rolls 63
Lobster bisque 22
Lobster rolls 63
Loin of pork in wine sauce 297
long-grain rice
    Bean & tofu enchiladas 542
    Cheese-stuffed rice balls 145
    Nutty rice salad 111
    Rice salad 136
    Rice-stuffed courgettes 139
    Rice verde one-pot 244
    Spinach & rice salad 137
    Vegetable paella 531
lychees
    Exotic fruit pancakes 559

M
Macadamia blondies 706

macadamia nuts
Macadamia blondies 706
macaroni
Chicken macaroni casserole 209
Chicken macaroni stew 221
Liver & macaroni casserole 194
Macaroni cheese 527
Macaroni & four cheeses 540
One-pot macaroni & cheese 239
One-pot tuna pasta 228
Turkey & macaroni cheese 387
Macaroni & four cheeses 540
Macaroni cheese 527
Madeira cake 684
Madeira roast pheasant 328
Madeleines 686
Mahogany duck 391
mandarins
Mandarins in syrup 658
Mandarins in syrup 658
mangetout
Spiced noodle salad 140
Spicy noodle salad 97
Tofu salad 101
Vegetable fritters 59
Mango & lime mousse 640
Mango & melon ginger salad 656
Mango fool 627
Mango sorbet 618
mangoes
Exotic fruit pancakes 559
Mango & lime mousse 640
Mango & melon ginger salad 656
Mango fool 627
Mango sorbet 618
Noodles with cod & mango 478
Okra with mango & lentils 493
Yogurt ring with tropical fruit 611
Marinated tomato & rice salad 146
marmalade
Sticky marmalade pudding 578
marrow
Quorn-stuffed marrow 549
Marshmallow ice cream 619
marshmallows
Marshmallow ice cream 619
marzipan

Marzipan cherries 713
Nectarines with marzipan &
yogurt 644
Marzipan cherries 713
mascarpone cheese
Cinnamon & nutmeg ice cream 620
Creamy fruit baskets 607
Summer fruits with ricotta & vanilla
dip 653
Tiramisù 636
Two-cheese dip 720
Mayonnaise 725
Meatloaf 274
Mediterranean plaice rolls 419
Medium balti chicken 337
melon *see also* cantaloupe melon *and*
honeydew melon *and* watermelon
Crab, melon & cucumber 100
Fruit cocktail 85
Fruity pasta & prawn salad 118
Grilled chicken with hot
salsa 368
Melon in wine 61
Melon & strawberries 52
Melon with Parma ham 82
Melon & orange cups 650
Melon & strawberries 52
Melon in wine 61
Melon medley 649
Melon with Parma ham 82
Mexican nacho casserole 184
Mild prawn curry 411
milk chocolate
Chocolate crunch biscuits 708
Mince pies 593
minced beef
Beef & cabbage pie 170
Beef & mushroom burgers 277
Beef fajitas 259
Catalan soup 13
Chilli beef in tortillas 267
Chinese lettuce wraps 146
Courgettes stuffed with mince 72
Dolmades 79
Meatloaf 274
Mexican nacho casserole 184
Minced beef with eggs 75

index

One-pot beef dinner 183
One-pot spaghetti 184
Shepherd's pie 178
Spaghetti bolognese 147
Minced beef with eggs 75
minced lamb
   Cottage pie 180
   Filo mince pie 177
   Lamb & tomato koftas 316
   Leek tart 164
   Moroccan lamb koftas 73
   Moussaka 312
   Stir-fried lamb with orange 320
minced pork
   Aubergine with pork & prawns 284
   Pork & brown bean sauce 288
   Pork crumble 293
minced turkey
   Bacon-wrapped turkey burgers 385
   Turkey meatloaf 384
   Turkey & tomato hotpot 383
mincemeat
   Mince pies 593
   Spicy fruit biscuits 700
Minestrone 23
Mini mushroom quiches 56
mint
   Pea & mint soup 26
Mississippi mud pie 690
Mixed bean salad 138
Mixed berry sorbet 624
Mixed bhajias 74
Mixed game pie 327
Mixed mushroom ragout 544
Mixed seafood chowder 423
molasses
   Molasses cake 672
Molasses cake 672
monkfish
   Barbecued monkfish 458
   Creamy fish gratin 428
   Fish Wellington 422
   Monkfish & mussel skewers 461
   Seafood pilaki 455
Monkfish & mussel skewers 461
Morello cherries
   Cherry pie 592

Moroccan lamb koftas 73
Moules marinière 448
Moussaka 312
mozzarella cheese
   Baked mozzarella & tomatoes 83
   Cheese-stuffed rice balls 145
   Fried mozzarella 125
   Fusilli with tomato & mozzarella 519
   Macaroni & four cheeses 540
   Mozzarella sticks 53
   Pasta frittata 129
   Pasticcio 512
   Seafood lasagne 408
   Tomato & bean salad 100
   Turkey spinach lasagne 388
   Vegetable-stuffed conchiglioni 546
Mozzarella sticks 53
Mulled Florida cocktail 654
Mulligatawny 24
Muscat grape frappe 655
muscovado sugar
   Sticky toffee pudding 576
Mushroom & corn soup 37
Mushroom & veal pie 176
Mushroom pizza 517
Mushroom soup 23
Mushroom vol-au-vent 508
mushrooms *see also* chestnut mushrooms
   and Chinese mushrooms *and* oyster
   mushrooms and Portobello mushrooms
   Baked mushrooms 48
   Beef & mushroom burgers 277
   Breaded mushrooms 58
   Lamb with mushroom sauce 318
   Nut roast 507
   Salmon-filled mushroom caps 81
   Chicken & bacon kebabs 61
   Mini mushroom quiches 56
   Mixed mushroom ragout 544
   Mushroom & corn soup 37
   Mushroom & veal pie 176
   Mushroom pizza 517
   Mushroom soup 23
   Mushroom vol-au-vent 508
   Spinach & mushroom bhaji 485
   Stuffed mushrooms 62
   Veal chops & mushrooms 279

Mussel salad 97
mussels
    French mussels 470
    Mixed seafood chowder 423
    Monkfish & mussel skewers 461
    Moules marinière 448
    Mussel salad 97
    Paella 157
    Seafood pilaki 455
    Seafood spaghetti 144
    Spaghetti marinara with seafood 454
Mustard carrot salad 114
Mustard chicken 363

N

Naan bread 57
nectarines
    Glazed nectarine tart 639
    Nectarines with marzipan &
        yogurt?644
    Nectarines with spiced ricotta 569
Nectarines with marzipan & yogurt 644
Nectarines with spiced ricotta 569
new potatoes
    Chicken & potato bake 206
    Smoked mackerel salad 108
noodles *see also* Japanese noodles
    Chicken chow mein 353
    Chicken noodle soup 15
    Chilled noodles & peppers 547
    Ginger & coriander noodles 156
    Noodles with cod & mango 478
    Peppered chicken pasta 151
    Pork chow mein 298
    Satay noodles 516
    Singapore fried noodles 154
    Special chow mein 153
    Spiced noodle salad 140
    Spicy noodle salad 97
    Thai noodle salad 106
    Tuna & tomato noodles 150
Noodles with cod & mango 478
Nougat 714
Nut roast 507
nutmeg
    Cinnamon & nutmeg ice cream 620
Nutty rice salad 111

O

Oat & fruit puddings 582
oatmeal
    Oatmeal cookies 708
    Spicy oatmeal soup 44
Oatmeal cookies 708
Ocean pie 440
okra
    One-pot Cajun chicken gumbo 213
    Okra stew with prawns 235
    Okra with mango & lentils 493
    Prawn gumbo 446
    Spicy okra 492
    Turkey gumbo 382
Okra stew with prawns 235
Okra with mango & lentils 493
olives
    Greek-style tomato platter 84
    Olive cheese balls 56
    Tapenade 724
One-pot beef dinner 183
One-pot Cajun chicken gumbo 213
One-pot chicken couscous 213
One-pot macaroni & cheese 239
One-pot pork chop supper 190
One-pot sausage jambalaya 190
One-pot spaghetti 184
One-pot tuna pasta 228
Onion avgolemono soup 34
Onion rings 52
Onion tart 161
onions
    Duck stew with turnips & onions 219
    French onion soup 19
    Liver, bacon & onions 321
    Mixed bhajias 74
    Onion avgolemono soup 34
    Onion rings 52
    Onion tart 161
    Pepper & onion pizza 499
    Potato & onion pizza 484
    Red onion & beetroot soup 36
    Roasted Mediterranean
        vegetables 537
    Spanish omelette 132
    Spiced beef & onions 261
    Steak & onion pie 179

index

Sweet & sour baby onions 88
Orange & chicory salad 120
Orange & date salad 658
Orange freeze 618
Orange & ginger cream cheese
  fudge 702
Orange granita 621
Orange ice cream 608
Orange syllabub trifle 614
oranges
  Citrus jelly 622
  Citrus tart 666
  Creamy fruit baskets 607
  Crêpes Suzettes 587
  Duck breasts with orange 394
  Frozen citrus soufflé 606
  Melon & orange cups 650
  Mulled Florida cocktail 654
  Orange & chicory salad 120
  Orange & date salad 658
  Orange freeze 618
  Orange granita 621
  Orange ice cream 608
  Orange syllabub trifle 614
  Port & orange jellies 610
  Sticky marmalade pudding 578
  Stir-fried lamb with orange 320
Oriental noodle soup 39
Oxtail soup 25
oxtail
  Oxtail soup 25
Oyster & cauliflower stew 226
oyster mushrooms
  Mixed mushroom ragout 544
Oyster soup 25
oysters
  Oyster & cauliflower stew 226
  Oyster soup 25

P
Paella 157
Pain au chocolat 663
pak choi
  Chinese cabbage soup 35
  Crispy seaweed 58
  Tuna with pak choi 427
  White pork with pak choi 286

Pan-fried chicken with red wine
  sauce 361
Pan-fried crusted fish curry 425
Pan-fried scallops 456
Pan-seared halibut 415
pancetta
  Potato, pancetta & sage one-pot
    roast 242
Panna cotta 617
papaya
  Exotic fruit pancakes 559
  Spiced fruit platter 651
Parma ham
  Chicken with ciabatta & Parma
    ham 336
  Garlic & herb chicken 366
  Italian pork escalopes 290
  Melon with Parma ham 82
  Parma ham & pepper pizzas 89
Parmesan cheese
  Macaroni & four cheeses 540
  Parmesan balls 125
  Pasta frittata 129
Parmesan balls 125
Parsley, walnut & orange chicken 332
parsnips
  Rabbit hotpot 201
partridge
  Spanish partridge & chocolate
    stew 202
Passion fruit & apple foam 604
passion fruit
  Exotic fruit pancakes 559
  Passion fruit & apple foam 604
  Pineapple & passion fruit salsa 649
  Strawberries in raspberry & passion
    fruit sauce 607
Pasta frittata 129
Pasta salad 135
pasta shells
  Fruity pasta & prawn salad 118
  Spinach & ricotta conchiglioni 525
  Vegetable-stuffed conchiglioni 546
Pasta with caviar 134
Pasta with Sicilian sauce 533
Pasticcio 512
Pâté en croûte 78

patty-pan squash
   Spring vegetable stir-fry 532
Pea & mint soup 26
Peach cobbler 597
Peach & ginger pashka 620
Peach melba 645
peaches
   Peach cobbler 597
   Peach & ginger pashka 620
   Peach melba 645
   Persian melon cups 644
   Poached peaches with ginger 643
   Roast fillet of pork with peaches 289
peanut butter
   Baked peanut tofu 491
   Peanut butter cornets 712
   Peanut butter slices 702
   peanut-frosted brownies 712
   Satay noodles 516
Peanut butter cornets 712
Peanut butter slices 702
peanut-frosted brownies 712
peanuts
   Chicken in peanut sauce 346
Pear & blackberry crumble 572
Pear & ginger crumble 573
Pear & grape salad 109
Pear cream pie 668
pears
   Blushing pears 646
   Californian baked pears 657
   Chocolate & pear crumble 581
   Lemon syrup pears with pancakes 558
   Oat & fruit puddings 582
   Pear & blackberry crumble 572
   Pear & ginger crumble 573
   Pear & grape salad 109
   Pear cream pie 668
   Pears with strawberry sauce 561
   Poached allspice pears 651
   Spiced pear & blueberry parcels 567
   Spinach, feta & pear salad 94
   Stilton & pear bruschetta 66
Pears with strawberry sauce 561
peas
   Broad bean, pea & goat's cheese salad 145
   Chilled pea soup 26
   Couscous salad 136
   Pea & mint soup 26
   Peas pilaff one-pot 245
   Rice salad 136
   Tofu with mushrooms & peas 541
   Turkey, pea & ham pot pie 214
   Tuscan veal broth 193
Peas pilaff one-pot 245
pecan nuts
   Banana & pecan salad 114
   Chocolate pecan pie 694
   Pecan & raisin muffins 683
Pecan & raisin muffins 683
penne
   Casseroled beans & penne 501
   Pasta salad 135
   Pasta with Sicilian sauce 533
   Ratatouille penne bake 548
   Sausage & ricotta penne 158
Pepper & onion pizza 499
Pepper chicken with ginger and garlic 333
Peppered chicken pasta 151
Peppered liver 322
pepperoni sausages
   Sausage & bean casserole 291
   Sausage & ricotta penne 158
Perfumed pineapple salad 603
Persian lamb 314
Persian melon cups 644
Pesto chicken salad 135
pheasant
   Madeira roast pheasant 328
   Pheasant & wild rice casserole 199
   Pheasant breast with cinnamon marmalade 330
   Pheasant casserole 198
Pheasant & wild rice casserole 199
Pheasant breast with cinnamon marmalade 330
Pheasant casserole 198
pig's liver
   Liver & macaroni casserole 194
   Pork & liver pâté 77

index

pig's trotters
  Woodpigeon casserole 196
pine nuts
  Barley & pine nut casserole 243
  Dolmades 79
pineapple
  Duck with pineapple 395
  Fruit cocktail 85
  Perfumed pineapple salad 603
  Pineapple & passion fruit salsa 649
  Pineapple boats 90
  Pineapple & coconut curry 497
  Pineapple flambé 652
  Pineapple upside-down cake
  Pineapple wedges with lime 603
  Prawn salad 95
  Spiced fruit platter 651
Pineapple & coconut curry 497
Pineapple boats 90
Pineapple flambé 652
pineapple juice
  Pineapple sorbet 631
Pineapple & passion fruit salsa 649
Pineapple sorbet 631
Pineapple upside-down cake 673
Pineapple wedges with lime 603
pink grapefruit
  Grilled pink grapefruit 642
pinto beans
  Boston bean soup 12
Piri piri prawns 451
pistachio nuts
  Cranberry biscotti 710
plaice
  Mediterranean plaice rolls 419
plain chocolate see also dark chocolate
  Chocolate brandy cream 634
  Chocolate fluff 638
  Highball cups 716
  Spanish partridge & chocolate
    stew 202
Plum cake 685
Plum & cardamom fool 630
Plum Charlotte 571
Plum filo pockets 554
plums see also dessert plums
  Floating islands in hot plum sauce 564

  Fromage frais with hot plum
    sauce 554
  Hot plum batter 590
  Plum Charlotte 571
  Plum filo pockets 554
  Sticky plum tart 664
  Venison with plums 326
Poached allspice pears 651
Poached guinea fowl 400
Poached peaches with ginger 643
Poached red emperor 420
pomegranates
  Duck & pomegranate stew 218
Poppy seed custard with red fruit 556
poppy seeds
  Poppy seed custard with red fruit 556
porcini
  Fillet of beef with porcini & sweet
    peppers 263
pork see also minced pork
  Beef & pork ragù 272
  Braised pork slices 295
  Chargrilled pork fillet with apple
    sauce 282
  Chilli-flavoured pork 299
  Leek tart 164
  Pork chow mein 298
  Pork & liver pâté 77
  Pork with apples 296
  Pork with port & coffee sauce 280
  Pork with Stilton 287
  Potato & pork soup 33
  Roast fillet of pork with peaches 289
  Singapore fried noodles 154
  Tangy pork fillet 300
  White pork with pak choi 286
Pork & apricot casserole 191, 192
Pork & brown bean sauce 288
pork chops
  Baked cranberry pork chops 285
  Loin of pork in wine sauce 297
  One-pot pork chop supper 190
  Pork & apricot casserole 191, 192
Pork chow mein 298
Pork crumble 293
pork cutlets
  Herbed pork cutlets 294

pork escalopes 290
   Italian pork escalopes 290
Pork & liver pâté 77
pork sausages
   Irish hotpot 189
   Turkey one-pot 207
pork shoulder steaks
   Pork steaks with gremolata 302
pork spare ribs
   Chinese spare ribs 292
Pork steaks with gremolata 302
Pork stroganoff 301
pork tenderloin
   Pork tenderloin Diane 283
Pork tenderloin Diane 283
Pork with port & coffee sauce 280
Pork with Stilton 287
Port & orange jellies 610
portobello mushrooms
   Mushroom risotto 142
Pot roast of venison 204
Potato & leek casserole 238
Potato & onion pizza 484
Potato & pork soup 33
Potato apple cake 682
Potato curry 500
Potato, pancetta & sage one-pot
   roast 242
Potato soup 27
potatoes see also baking potatoes and
   new potatoes
   Asparagus & potato salad 98
   Basque tuna stew 409
   Green soup 38
   Hot potato & bean salad 112
   Irish hotpot 189
   Layered fish & potato pie 457
   Leek & potato soup 20
   Liver hotpot 194
   Potato & leek casserole 238
   Potato & onion pizza 484
   Potato & pork soup 33
   Potato apple cake 682
   Potato curry 500
   Potato, pancetta & sage one-pot
      roast 242
   Potato soup 27

Salmon & potato casserole 225
Salmon with lemon mash 416
Seafood pie 173
Spanish omelette 132
Ulster Irish stew 187
Vichyssoise 31
poussins
   French-style pot-roast poussin 212
   Poussins in vermouth 401
   Roast baby chickens 370
Poussins in vermouth 401
Prawn & paneer kebabs 424
Prawn & spinach lasagne 444
Prawn & spinach stew 231
Prawn cocktail 68
Prawn crackers 69
Prawn gumbo 446
Prawn jambalaya 449
Prawn kebabs 65
Prawn omelette 460
Prawn pies 169
Prawn salad 95
Prawn wonton soup 41
prawns see also king prawns and
   tiger prawns
   Artichoke & prawn cocktail 86
   Aubergine with pork &
      prawns 284
   Bacon-wrapped prawns 71
   Californian prawn & scallop
      stir-fry 410
   Chinese prawn salad 108
   Crab & seafood one-pot 225
   Creamy fish gratin 428
   Devilled prawns 64
   Fruity pasta & prawn salad 118
   Hot prawn stew 236
   Mixed seafood chowder 423
   Okra stew with prawns 235
   Paella 157
   Piri piri prawns 451
   Prawn & paneer kebabs 424
   Prawn & spinach lasagne 444
   Prawn & spinach stew 231
   Prawn cocktail 68
   Prawn crackers 69
   Prawn gumbo 446

index

Prawn jambalaya 449
Prawn kebabs 65
Prawn omelette 460
Prawn pies 169
Prawn salad 95
Prawn wonton soup 41
Red prawn curry 466
Seafood balti 417
Seafood chimichangas 452
Seafood fajitas 432
Seafood medley 437
Seafood pie 173
Singapore fried noodles 154
Spicy coconut prawns 407
Taglierini & seafood sauce 450
Thai noodle salad 106
pretzels
Soft pretzels 54
Prosecco
Clam & Prosecco spaghetti 149
prunes
Devils on horseback 74
Spiced fruity couscous 521
pudding rice
Rice pudding 596
pumpkin
Beef & pumpkin curry 268
Pumpkin pie 695
Pumpkin soup 27
Pumpkin turkey stew 222
Pumpkin pie 695
Pumpkin soup 27
Pumpkin turkey stew 222

Q

quail
Quail stew 200
Quails with bacon & juniper 398
Quail stew 200
Quail's egg & tomato salad 123
quail's eggs
Feta cheese tartlets 63
Quail's egg & tomato salad 123
Quails with bacon & juniper 398
Queen of puddings 573
Quick apricot whip 634
quinoa

Quinoa & butter beans 498
Quinoa & butter beans 498
Quorn
Quorn-stuffed marrow 549
Quorn-stuffed marrow 549

R

rabbit
Rabbit casserole 198
Rabbit hotpot 201
Rabbit with parsley sauce 324
Thai-style rabbit 323
Rabbit casserole 198
Rabbit hotpot 201
Rabbit with parsley sauce 324
rack of lamb
Roast rack of lamb 311
Raisin gingerbread 685
raisins
Apple strudel 591
Christmas pudding 594
Dundee cake 671
Pecan & raisin muffins 683
Plum cake 685
Raisin gingerbread 685
Rich fruit cake 677
Rum & raisin ice cream 637
Vegetable raisin curry 495
raspberries
Creamy puddings 584
Fresh salad with raspberry
vinaigrette 113
Peach melba 645
Poppy seed custard with red fruit 556
Raspberry buns 667
Raspberry fool 632
Raspberry mousse 615
Raspberry sorbet 635
Red fruit salad 648
Strawberries in raspberry & passion
fruit sauce 607
Strawberry & raspberry parfait 626
Tofu berry brûlée 615
Raspberry buns 667
Raspberry fool 632
Raspberry mousse 615
Raspberry sorbet 635

Ratatouille 529
Ratatouille penne bake 548
red chillies
    Duck vindaloo 393
    Spaghetti with garlic & chilli oil 143
    Spicy goatmeat stew 195
Red curry with cashews 550
red emperor
    Poached red emperor 420
Red fried rice 156
Red fruit salad 648
red lentils
    Armenian stew 239
    Beef & lentil soup 21
    Lentil hotpot 250
red mullet
    Red mullet & coconut loaf 465
    Sardinian red mullet 469
Red mullet & coconut loaf 465
Red onion & beetroot soup 36
red onions
    Red onion & beetroot soup 36
Red pepper soup 28
Red prawn curry 466
Red snapper casserole 229
red snappers
    Brown fish stew 236
    Red snapper casserole 229
Redcurrant filo baskets 638
redcurrants
    Mixed berry sorbet 624
    Redcurrant filo baskets 638
    Tofu berry brûlée 615
refried beans
    Mexican nacho casserole 184
rhubarb
    Filo rhubarb pie 689
    Rhubarb & apple cobbler 599
    Rhubarb cake 692
    Rhubarb crumble 570
Rhubarb & apple cobbler 599
Rhubarb cake 692
Rhubarb crumble 570
Rich kidney soup 40
rice see basmati rice and brown rice and
    jasmine rice and long-grain rice and
    pudding rice and short-grain rice and

    risotto rice and wild rice
Rice pudding 596
Rice salad 136
Rice-stuffed courgettes 139
Rice verde one-pot 244
Rich fruit cake 677
ricotta cheese
    Chicken & ricotta in wine 345
    Creamy puddings 584
    Nectarines with spiced ricotta 569
    Ricotta cheese & courgette rolls 126
    Sausage & ricotta penne 158
    Spinach & ricotta conchiglioni 525
    Spinach & ricotta pie 514
    Spinach & ricotta ravioli 522
    Summer fruits with ricotta & vanilla
        dip 653
    Tuscan pudding 629
Ricotta cheese & courgette rolls 126
risotto rice
    Fresh herb risotto 143
    Mushroom risotto 142
Roast baby chickens 370
Roast beef & Yorkshire pudding 273
Roast fillet of pork with peaches 289
Roast garlic toast 50
Roast rack of lamb 311
Roasted Mediterranean vegetables 537
Roasted vegetable pasta 152
Rock cakes 684
rocket
    Rocket salad 111
Rocket salad 111
rolled oats
    Oat & fruit puddings 582
    Traditional oat flapjacks 704
rosemary
    Rosemary biscuits 711
Rosemary biscuits 711
Romano cheese
    Macaroni & four cheeses 540
Rum & raisin ice cream 637
rump steak
    Beef hotpot 182
    Beef satay 73
    Beef, tomato & olive kebabs 276
    Cornish pasties 167

index

Crispy shredded beef 265
Thai beef salad 107
rutabaga
Baked lentil & vegetable stew 249

S

saffron
Fragrant saffron chicken 364
Saffron rice salad 102
Saffron rice salad 102
Sage chicken & rice 379
Salad niçoise 105
salmon *see also* Alaskan pink salmon *and*
smoked salmon
Creamy fish gratin 428
Ocean pie 440
Salmon & asparagus linguine 447
Salmon & potato casserole 225
Salmon burgers 471
Salmon casserole 233
Salmon-filled mushroom caps 81
Salmon in aspic 426
Salmon with lemon mash 416
Salmon yakitori 81
Salmon & asparagus linguine 447
Salmon & potato casserole 225
Salmon burgers 471
Salmon casserole 233
Salmon dip 720
Salmon in aspic 426
Salmon with lemon mash 416
Salmon yakitori 81
Salmon-filled mushroom caps 81
salt cod
Salt cod fritters 477
Salt cod fritters 477
Salt & pepper squid 431
sardines
Fresh baked sardines 439
Grilled sardines 66
Sardinian red mullet 469
Satay noodles 516
satsumas
Orange & ginger cream cheese
fudge 702
Sausage & bean casserole 291
Sausage & ricotta penne 158

Sausage & sweet pepper casserole 189
sausage meat
Chicken & sausage pie 175
Sautéed chicken with herbs 362
Scallop casserole 234
scallops
Baked seafood salad 110
Californian prawn & scallop
stir-fry 410
Creamy fish gratin 428
Mixed seafood chowder 423
Pan-fried scallops 456
Scallop casserole 234
Seafood fajitas 432
Seafood kebabs 418
Seafood lasagne 408
Scotch broth 29
sea bass
Kettle-cooked sea bass 433
Sea bass stew 229
Taglierini & seafood sauce 450
Sea bass stew 229
sea bream
Sea bream in a salt crust 462
Sea bream in a salt crust 462
Seafood balti 417
Seafood chimichangas 452
Seafood fajitas 432
Seafood kebabs 418
Seafood lasagne 408
Seafood medley 437
Seafood pie 173
Seafood pilaki 455
Seafood spaghetti 144
Seared squid 67
Seed cake 676
Semolina 598
Shepherd's pie 178
sherry
Sherry chicken casserole 219
Sherry trifle 613
Sherry chicken casserole 219
Sherry trifle 613
shiitake mushrooms
Hot & sour soup 17
short-grain rice
Baked coconut rice pudding 584

Fruited rice ring 612
Souffléed rice pudding 568
shrimps
Seafood spaghetti 144
Simple bean salad 99
Singapore fried noodles 154
sirloin steak
Beef daube 271
Beef & pumpkin curry 268
Beef, tomato & olive kebabs 276
skate
Skate with black butter 441
Skate with black butter 441
Sly cakes 660
smoked back bacon
Bacon & lentil stew 192
French-style pot-roast poussin 212
Hare stew 203
Smoked fish with white sauce 442
smoked haddock
Couscous & haddock salad 106
Cullen skink 45
Layered fish & potato pie 457
Smoked haddock quiche 421
Smoked haddock quiche 421
smoked ham
Smoked ham linguine 148
Smoked ham linguine 148
smoked mackerel
Smoked mackerel pâté 77
Smoked mackerel salad 108
Smoked mackerel pâté 77
Smoked mackerel salad 108
smoked salmon
Griddled smoked salmon 85
Salmon & asparagus linguine 447
Salmon dip 720
Salmon & potato casserole 225
Smoked salmon pasta 154
Smoked salmon rolls 71
Smoked salmon pasta 154
Smoked salmon rolls 71
smoked trout
Smoked trout with cucumber &
cumin 68
Smoked trout with cucumber & cumin 68
snapper

Pan-fried crusted fish curry 425
Snow-capped apples 648
soft cheese
Fruit fondue 642
Orange & ginger cream cheese
fudge 702
Tomato & cheese tarts 91
Soft pretzels 54
sole
Fish fillets in wine sauce 413
Grilled stuffed sole 406
Sole Véronique 436
Sole Véronique 436
sorrel leaves
Sorrel tart 165
Sorrel tart 165
Souffléed rice pudding 568
sour cherries
Cherry turnover 660
Soused herrings 453
Soy-braised chicken 344
spaghetti
Bottarga spaghetti 155
Clam & Prosecco spaghetti 149
One-pot spaghetti 184
Pasta frittata 129
Seafood spaghetti 144
Spaghetti bolognese 147
Spaghetti marinara with seafood 454
Spaghetti with courgettes 149
Spaghetti with garlic & chilli oil 143
Warm pasta & crab 103
Spaghetti bolognese 147
Spaghetti marinara with seafood 454
Spaghetti with courgettes 149
Spaghetti with garlic & chilli oil 143
Spanish omelette 132
Spanish partridge & chocolate stew 202
Special chow mein 153
Spiced beef & onions 261
Spiced chicken casserole 205
Spiced date & walnut cake 683
Spiced fruit platter 651
Spiced fruity couscous 521
Spiced noodle salad 140
Spiced pear & blueberry parcels 567
Spicy avocado dip 718

index

Spicy coconut prawns 407
Spicy fruit biscuits 700
Spicy goatmeat stew 195
Spicy Japanese noodles 505
Spicy masala chicken 377
Spicy noodle salad 97
Spicy oatmeal soup 44
Spicy okra 492
spicy sausages
    Prawn jambalaya 449
    Sausage & sweet pepper
      casserole 189
spinach
    Courgette & spinach soup 17
    Greek spinach & cheese pie 55
    Prawn & spinach lasagne 444
    Prawn & spinach stew 231
    Spinach & artichoke casserole 248
    Spinach & ricotta conchiglioni 525
    Spinach & ricotta pie 514
    Spinach & ricotta ravioli 522
    Spinach tagliatelle with veal 134
Spinach & artichoke casserole 248
Spinach & ricotta ravioli 522
Spinach tagliatelle with veal 134
spiral pasta
    Pesto chicken salad 135
split peas
    Bacon & split pea soup 11
spinach
    Cheese & spinach puffs 83
    Chunky vegetable chilli 254
    Eggs with spinach 123
    Greek-style chickpea casserole 247
    Rice verde one-pot 244
    Spinach & bacon salad 116
    Spinach & mushroom bhaji 485
    Spinach & rice salad 137
    Spinach & ricotta conchiglioni 525
    Spinach & ricotta pie 514
    Spinach, feta & pear salad 94
    Spinach tart 162
    Turkey spinach lasagne 388
    Veal & spinach stew 193
Spinach & bacon salad 116
Spinach & mushroom bhaji 485
Spinach & rice salad 137

Spinach & ricotta conchiglioni 525
Spinach & ricotta pie 514
Spinach, feta & pear salad 94
Spinach tart 162
spring onions
    Sweetcorn chowder 43
    Tomato & spring onion salad 109
Spring vegetable stir-fry 532
squid
    Calamari 65
    Calamari stew 230
    Fried squid curry 429
    Paella 157
    Salt & pepper squid 431
    Seafood medley 437
    Seafood pilaki 455
    Seafood spaghetti 144
    Seared squid 67
    Squid casserole 235
    Squid sambal 412
    Squid with wine & rosemary 459
Squid casserole 235
Squid sambal 412
Squid with wine & rosemary 459
Steak, kidney & mushroom pie 270
Steak & onion pie 179
Stewed cabbage hotpot 242
stewing beef
    Beef & lentil soup 21
    Beef goulash 258
    Beef paprikash 185
    Green chilli & meat stew 183
    Thai beef curry 262
Sticky marmalade pudding 578
Sticky plum tart 664
Sticky toffee pudding 576
Stilton & pear bruschetta 66
Stilton cheese
    Celery & Stilton soup 14
    Pork with Stilton 287
    Stilton & pear bruschetta 66
Stir-fried broccoli pasta 141
Stir-fried lamb with orange 320
stout
    Beef & stout casserole 182
strawberries
    Creamy fruit baskets 607

Creamy puddings 584
Eton mess 654
Melon & strawberries 52
Mixed berry sorbet 624
Pears with strawberry sauce 561
Perfumed pineapple salad 603
Persian melon cups 644
Poppy seed custard with red fruit 556
Red fruit salad 648
Strawberries in grape jelly 645
Strawberries in raspberry & passion
 fruit sauce 607
Strawberries Romanoff 653
Strawberry & apple crumble 575
Strawberry & raspberry parfait 626
Strawberry frozen yogurt 625
Strawberry mousse 616
Strawberry rose-petal pashka 602
Strawberry shortcake 635
Summer berries in Champagne
 jelly 656
Tofu berry brûlée 615
Strawberries in raspberry & passion fruit
 sauce 607
Strawberries in grape jelly 645
Strawberries Romanoff 653
Strawberry & apple crumble 575
Strawberry & raspberry parfait 626
Strawberry baked apples 567
Strawberry frozen yogurt 625
Strawberry mousse 616
Strawberry rose-petal pashka 602
Strawberry shortcake 635
Stuffed eggs 122
Stuffed mushrooms 62
Stuffed peppers 503
Succotash 91
Stuffed celery 88
Stuffed crabs 443
Stuffed peppers 55
sugarsnap peas
 Aromatic green casserole 240
 Spring vegetable stir-fry 532
sultanas
 Bread & butter pudding 590
 Christmas pudding 594
 Dundee cake 671

Pasta with Sicilian sauce 533
Plum cake 685
Rich fruit cake 677
Summer berries in Champagne jelly 656
Summer fruits with ricotta & vanilla
 dip 653
sun-dried tomatoes
 Baked Brie with sun-dried
  tomatoes 126
Sweet & sour baby onions 88
Sweet & sour tofu 515
Sweet & sour venison 325
Sweet & spicy duck 397
sweet peppers
 Bean & tofu enchiladas 542
 Beansprout & pepper salad 117
 Chargrilled kebabs 545
 Chargrilled peppers & sweet
  potatoes 509
 Cheesy stuffed peppers 55
 Chunky vegetable chilli 254
 Chilled noodles & peppers 547
 Chinese egg flower soup 43
 Duck, tomato & pepper stew 209
 Fillet of beef with porcini & sweet
  peppers 263
 Orange beef with green peppers 260
 Parma ham & pepper pizzas 89
 Pasticcio 512
 Pepper & onion pizza 499
 Red pepper soup 28
 Rice salad 136
 Roasted Mediterranean
  vegetables 537
 Roasted vegetable pasta 152
 Sausage & sweet pepper
  casserole 189
 Stuffed peppers 503
 Two-cheese dip 720
 Vegetable fritters 59
Sweet potato casserole 244
Sweet potato salad 51
sweet potatoes
 Chargrilled peppers & sweet
  potatoes 509
 Sweet potato casserole 244
 Sweet potato salad 51

index

Vietnamese chicken & sweet potato
  curry 334
Sweet-stewed dried fruit 646
sweetcorn
  Black bean & salsa salad 101
  Chicken & sweetcorn stew 216
  Courgette & corn casserole 249
  Couscous vegetable loaf 511
  Mushroom & corn soup 37
  Rice salad 136
  Sweetcorn chowder 43
  Sweetcorn pancakes 87
Sweetcorn chowder 43
Sweetcorn pancakes 87
Swiss biscuits 699
Swiss chicken casserole 211
Szechuan beaten chicken 92

T

Tabbouleh & tofu 502
tagliatelle
  Fig & chilli tagliatelle 151
  Hazelnut pesto tagliatelle 150
  Spinach tagliatelle with veal 134
Taglierini & seafood sauce 450
taglioni (taglierini)
  Tagliolini with herbs 152
Tagliolini with herbs 152
Tangy pork fillet 300
Tapenade 724
tapioca
  Tapioca pudding 612
tapioca flour
  Prawn crackers 69
Tapioca pudding 612
Taramasalata 719
Tarragon chicken casserole 224
Terrace crab pie 171
Thai beef curry 262
Thai beef salad 107
Thai chicken green curry 347
Thai fish green curry 473
Thai jasmine rice & prawn casserole 232
Thai noodle salad 106
Thai-style fish cakes 67
Thai-style rabbit 323
tiger prawns

Butterfly prawns 70
Mild prawn curry 411
Monkfish & mussel skewers 461
Special chow mein 153
Thai jasmine rice & prawn
  casserole 232
Tiramisù 636
tofu
  Baked peanut tofu 491
  Batter-dipped tofu 482
  Bean & tofu enchiladas 542
  Braised Chinese vegetables 487
  Cabbage & tofu 489
  Chinese vegetable casserole 251
  Japanese tofu hotpot 241
  Ratatouille penne bake 548
  Sweet & sour tofu 515
  Stewed cabbage hotpot 242
  Tabbouleh & tofu 502
  Tofu & broccoli stir-fry 486
  Tofu berry brûlée 615
  Tofu salad 101
  Tofu with mushrooms 496
  Tofu with mushrooms & peas 541
Tofu & broccoli stir-fry 486
Tofu berry brûlée 615
Tofu salad 101
Tofu with mushrooms 496
Tofu with mushrooms & peas 541
Tollhouse cookies 715
Tomato & bean salad 100
Tomato & carrot soup 37
Tomato & cheese tarts 91
Tomato & ham pie 177
Tomato & spring onion salad 109
Tomato rice 539
Tomato sauce 729
Tomato soup 29
tomatoes see also cherry tomatoes and
  sun-dried tomatoes
  Baked cod with tomatoes 463
  Baked mozzarella & tomatoes 83
  Basque tomatoes 116
  Bruschetta 54
  Chilli tomato dip 724
  Chunky vegetable chilli 254
  Creamed tomato sauce 729

Duck, tomato & pepper stew 209
Fusilli with tomato & mozzarella 519
Greek salad 103
Greek-style tomato platter 84
Lamb & tomato koftas 316
Marinated tomato & rice salad 146
Pasta salad 135
Quail's egg & tomato salad 123
Stuffed mushrooms 62
Tomato & bean salad 100
Tomato & carrot soup 37
Tomato & cheese tarts 91
Tomato & ham pie 177
Tomato & spring onion salad 109
Tomato rice 539
Tomato sauce 729
Tomato soup 29
Tomatoes au gratin 510
Tomatoes on toast 50
Tuna & tomato noodles 150
Turkey & tomato hotpot 383
Tomatoes au gratin 510
Tomatoes on toast 50
Tortilla chicken casserole 217
Traditional oat flapjacks 704
Traditional fried chicken 348
treacle
    Treacle tart 600
Treacle pudding 583
Treacle tart 600
trout
    Trout stew 228
    Trout with almonds 472
Trout stew 228
Trout with almonds 472
Truffles 706
tuna
    Basque tuna stew 409
    One-pot tuna pasta 228
    Tuna almondine 475
    Tuna & bean salad 104
    Tuna & tomato noodles 150
    Tuna fish casserole 234
    Tuna mornay 174
    Tuna with pak choi 427
    Tuscan bean & tuna salad 95
Tuna almondine 475

Tuna & bean salad 104
Tuna & tomato noodles 150
Tuna fish casserole 234
Tuna mornay 174
Tuna with pak choi 427
Tunisian vegetables 526
turkey *see also* minced turkey
    Chillies stuffed with turkey 386
    Pumpkin turkey stew 222
    Turkey & macaroni cheese 387
    Turkey casserole 215
    Turkey gumbo 382
    Turkey one-pot 207
    Turkey, pea & ham pot pie 214
    Turkey spinach lasagne 388
Turkey & macaroni cheese 387
Turkey & tomato hotpot 383
Turkey casserole 215
Turkey gumbo 382
Turkey meatloaf 384
Turkey one-pot 207
Turkey, pea & ham pot pie 214
Turkey spinach lasagne 388
Turkish delight 705
Turkish delight ice cream 621
Turkish lamb stew 310
Turnip salad 115
turnips
    Duck stew with turnips & onions 219
    Turnip salad 115
Tuscan bean & tuna salad 95
Tuscan chicken 360
Tuscan pudding 629
Tuscan veal broth 193
Two-cheese dip 720

U
Ulster Irish stew 187

V
Vanilla & caramel parfait 625
Vanilla ice cream 622
vanilla ice cream
    Baked Alaska 595
    Chocolate ice-cream sandwiches 624
    Orange freeze 618
    Peach melba 645

index

Strawberry & raspberry parfait 626
Vanilla & caramel parfait 625
vanilla yogurt
veal
    Mushroom & veal pie 176
    Spinach tagliatelle with veal 134
    Tuscan veal broth 193
    Veal & spinach stew 193
    Veal chops & mushrooms 279
    Veal Marsala 278
Veal & spinach stew 193
Veal chops & mushrooms 279
Veal Marsala 278
Vegetable biryani 530
Vegetable fritters 59
Vegetable jalousie 520
Vegetable minestrone 30
Vegetable omelette 130
Vegetable paella 531
Vegetable raisin curry 495
Vegetable soup 30
Vegetable stock 730
Vegetable-stuffed conchiglioni 546
Vegetarian pizza 506
Vegetarian spaghetti sauce 480
Veggie burgers 528
venison
    Fried venison steaks 329
    Pot roast of venison 204
    Sweet & sour venison 325
    Venison & wild rice casserole 197
    Venison with plums 326
vermicelli
    Oriental noodle soup 39
    Pasta with caviar 134
Vichyssoise 31
Viennese chocolate fingers 698
Vietnamese chicken & sweet potato curry
    334
vine leaves
    Dolmades 79

W

Waldorf chicken salad 98
walnuts
    Baklava 688
    Cauliflower & walnut soup 14
    Coffee & walnut cake 674
    Spiced date & walnut cake 683
Warm chicken & feta salad 357
Warm pasta & crab 103
water chestnuts
    Bacon-wrapped prawns 71
    Chinese lettuce wraps 146
    Chinese vegetable casserole 251
watercress
    Fresh salad with raspberry
      vinaigrette 113
    Watercress soup 31
Watercress soup 31
watermelon
    Melon medley 649
white chocolate
    Chocolate & apricot squares 703
    Macadamia blondies 706
    White pork with pak choi 286
wild rice
    Pheasant & wild rice casserole 199
    Sage chicken & rice 379
    Venison & wild rice casserole 197
Winter chicken stew 217
woodpigeon
    Woodpigeon casserole 196
Woodpigeon casserole 196

Y

Yellow bean chicken 376
Yellow split pea casserole 246
yellow split peas
    Yellow split pea casserole 246
yellow squash
    Vegetable soup 30
yogurt see also Greek yogurt
    Banana lassi 609
    Beetroot & yogurt salad 49
    Chicken casserole with yogurt 211
    Chicken in spicy yogurt 367
    Lemon curd ice cream 629
    Orange syllabub trifle 614
    Yogurt flapjacks 714
    Yogurt ring with tropical fruit 611
Yogurt flapjacks 714
Yogurt ring with tropical fruit 611

Z

Zabaglione 588